J. REUBEN CLARK

THE PUBLIC YEARS

J. REUBEN CLARK

THE PUBLIC YEARS

First of a multivolume set on the
life and work of J. Reuben Clark, Jr.

David H. Yarn, General Editor

J. REUBEN CLARK

THE PUBLIC YEARS

FRANK W. FOX

Brigham Young University Press
Deseret Book Company
1980

Library of Congress Cataloging in Publication Data

Fox, Frank W
  J. Reuben Clark, the public years.

  Bibliography: p.
  Includes index.
  1. Clark, Joshua Reuben, 1871–1961.
  2. United States—Foreign relations—20th century.
  3. Ambassadors—United States—Biography.
  4. Mormons and Mormonism in the United States—
  Biography. 5. Lawyers—United States—Biography.
  I. Title.
  E748.C55F69   327.73'0092'4 [B]   80-17903
  ISBN 0-8425-1832-0

Library of Congress Catalog Card Number: 80-17903
International Standard Book Number: 0-8425-1832-0 (Brigham
    Young University Press), 0-87747-834-1 (Deseret Book Company)

Brigham Young University Press, Provo, Utah 84602
Printed in the United States of America
80   47085

To my wife, Elaine

CONTENTS

Contents

FOREWORD

I am honored to have the invitation to write a foreword to these volumes about President J. Reuben Clark, Jr., my close friend and fellow servant in the work of the Lord. His kindness, thoughtfulness, and concern for others were always apparent to those who worked under his direction. I recall vividly one occasion when I drove through a raging snowstorm to return home from a welfare meeting in Burley, Idaho. President Clark knew that I was on this assignment, so he telephoned my home several times before I arrived. Soon after I finally reached home, the phone rang again. "Marion," he said, "where have you been?" I told him.

"Did you come through that storm?"

"Yes, sir."

"Alone?"

"Yes, sir."

He then proceeded to give me a scotch blessing. As soon as I could get him off the line, I began to tell my wife in vehement terms what I thought about his reprimand. In the midst of my fury the phone rang again. "Marion, this is President Clark. I'm just calling you up in the spirit of the 121st section of the Doctrine and Covenants"—referring, of course, to the statement: "Reproving betimes with sharpness, when moved upon by the Holy Ghost; and then showing forth afterwards an increase of love toward him whom thou hast reproved, lest he esteem thee to be his enemy." It was his bluntness, his humility, and his concern for my well-being and safety that made him the great and true friend that I grew to love, respect, and admire. Without this strength of character he would not have affected so many lives so deeply. Those who did not know him well may remember only his strong will and firm resolve. His undeviating loyalty to the truth and to the men who lead the cause of truth was a source of strength to all of us. When it was a question of integrity he would never betray a principle, nor renege on a promise, nor shirk a duty.

I have always hoped that those who would write about J. Reuben Clark, Jr., would remember this: to him it mattered little whether he was being praised or criticized; it mattered much, however, whether his course was right and true. Any biographer of President Clark must write the truth about him; to tell more than or less than the truth would violate a governing principle of his life. When I first met with those who are writing his biography, I explained that I did not want them to produce a mere collection of uplifting experiences about President Clark (although I knew that numerous such stories could be told), nor did I want a detailed defense of his beliefs. I wanted a biography of the man himself, as he was, written with the same kind of courage, honesty, and frankness that J. Reuben Clark himself would have shown. An account of his life should tell of his decisions and indecisions, sorrows and joys, regrets and aspirations, reverses and accomplishments, and, above all, his constant striving to overcome any and all obstacles. In reading over the materials included in this first volume, I have found what I had hoped to find.

This volume treats J. Reuben Clark's government experience prior to his church service. In it readers will meet a man who made a daily battle of overcoming. When he preached against internationalism, it was because he himself had been an internationalist and knew firsthand of its inherent dangers. When he condemned foreign interventionism, it was because he himself had been an interventionist and had witnessed the tragic consequences. If he warned repeatedly of too much governmental power, it was because he himself had been handed such power and knew how ill equipped he or any mere man was to wield such power.

In this volume, readers will find a man who was, at times, unsure of himself, a man who altered his decisions, a man who made mistakes and repented of them. They will find a soul who struggled harder than most and who faced numerous obstacles, trying temptations, and severe challenges that many of his friends never imagined. Still—and those who were close to him know this well—he never hesitated to say or do what he thought should be said or done. As I read back over his life, I am convinced that it was his repeated and continual striving to *overcome,* coupled with his constant willingness to be forthright and decisive even at great cost, that made J. Reuben Clark one of the great and noble men of our time.

Marion G. Romney

PREFACE

Members of the Mormon church—at least those who are over thirty—need no introduction to J. Reuben Clark, Jr. For almost thirty years—between 1933 and 1961—he was a highly visible and extremely influential member of the church's First Presidency in Salt Lake City. He was a kind of fixture in that august body: a face, a voice, a set of mannerisms, a constellation of ideas which were recognized so widely and so clearly that they became associated with the very substance of Mormonism.

An important dimension of the Clark persona was the knowledge that behind the religious leader there stretched an equally long and equally distinguished public career—a career founded in the law, matured in diplomacy, and capped by Clark's appointment as United States ambassador to Mexico. The exact course of that career tended to be somewhat murky in many minds, but this only made it seem the more glamorous. When President Clark rose to address the assembled body of the church at its general conference, parents were wont to urge a special attention from their children, for here was a man who had sat in the counsels of the nation.

Indeed he had. In 1906, when he had barely graduated from Columbia law school, Reuben Clark became assistant solicitor of the Department of State. In that capacity he virtually ran the State Department's legal operations for four years, until he was officially appointed solicitor in 1910. In the meantime he cemented personal ties with those who were formulating and implementing American foreign policy, especially Assistant Secretary of State F. M. Huntington Wilson and Secretary of State Philander Chase Knox. By means of such friendships, Clark came to exercise an influence in the State Department out of all proportion to his formal duties. Indeed, his was one of the hands on the helm during the troublous years of the Mexican Revolution.

In 1913, when Woodrow Wilson and the Democrats swept into power, Reuben Clark left the State Department to set up a private legal practice. Nevertheless, through his earlier contacts, his international clientele, and his continuing service with the American-British Pecuniary Claims Commission he remained securely tied to American diplomacy. Such was the power of these ties that in 1917, when the United States declared war on Germany, Clark was recruited simultaneously into the headquarters of the army's provost marshal general and the office of the United States attorney general. In the latter capacity especially he was instrumental in resisting what he considered to be the abuses of executive authority occasioned by the war.

This experience proved to be the beginning of a personal crusade against the League of Nations, bringing Clark together once again with Philander Knox, who was now in the Senate. The two of them, in fact, designed and battle-tested many of the political weapons used in the League fight and were credited—or blamed—for considerable responsibility in the League's defeat.

With the return of the Republicans to power in 1920, Reuben Clark went on to serve as special assistant to Secretary of State Charles Evans Hughes at the Washington arms conference, as a supporter—albeit one with mixed motives—of the Kellogg-Briand Pact, and as an energetic and resourceful opponent of the World Court. Although his international legal practice during these years for the most part dwindled into a local western practice, Clark continued to be consulted by public officials and former eastern clients. It was by means of these consultations, in fact, that the next major turning point in his career was effected.

In 1926 he was requested to assume charge of the American agency of the United States–Mexico Mixed Claims Commission, an international arbitration charged, among other things, with settling the horrendous legal problems created by the Mexican Revolution. Clark's work on the claims commission led to his appointment the following year as legal counsel to Dwight Morrow, the recently named U.S. ambassador to Mexico, with the responsibility of defusing a major diplomatic crisis over Mexican oil. The two men worked side by side in Mexico City for almost two years, interrupted only by Reuben Clark's temporary assignment as undersecretary of state in Washington. Soon after Clark rejoined Morrow in Mexico in 1929, it became evident that he would probably be named as Morrow's successor; in October of the following year that appointment became official.

Although his years as ambassador (1930–33) marked the high point of Clark's public career, there was a good deal more to follow. He attended the Seventh Pan-American Conference in Montevideo as a delegate in 1933, served on several blue-ribbon committees devoted to the codification of international law, and for several years effectively ran the Foreign Bondholders Protective Council—all of this in addition to his extensive church responsibilities. At no time, really, did he retire either from public life or from his ecclesiastical duties in Salt Lake City; he was still putting in his legendary fourteen-hour days when he died in 1961 at the age of 90.

Capturing this life and career in the confines of a conventional biographical format seemed inadvisable from the beginning. There were simply too many of those fourteen-hour days and too vast a number of undertakings to deal with manageably. It was for this reason that I decided instead to deal with five broad themes in characterizing my subject. Each theme is represented in a separate section of the book, and each is set off from the others by Roman numeral designations. Thus, the theme of Part I is Reuben Clark's education—his learning experience broadly conceived—while Part II deals with his role as a policymaker, and so on. These themes are arranged in the book in a roughly chronological way—but only roughly. Inevitably there is a certain amount of overlap between one theme and another, and the first or last chapter of each section may stray across the temporal boundaries marked out in the table of contents. Thus, the surest time-line indications are in the text itself.

This book would not have been possible without the efforts of a great number of people. The awesome task of research was greatly facilitated by the staff of the National Archives in Washington, D.C., and by E. Dennis Rowley and his capable assistants in the archives of Brigham Young University's Harold B. Lee Library. The path of research in the Clark papers was cut first by Rowena Miller, Reuben Clark's fine secretary, who through the years culled many important biographical items out of his files; and by David H. Yarn, Jr., who, together with his wife Marilyn, faithfully explored, digested, and analyzed the Clark papers long before the writing of this volume was begun. Steven Smith and Steven Guynn assisted in the process of background research. Stephen Jerry Sturgill patiently waded through the voluminous family correspondence and pieced together much of the material presented in Part IV. He also served as a first-rate editor and critic.

Special information was kindly supplied by John W. Clark, Belle S. Spafford, Gene A. Sessions, Ezra Taft Benson, Constance Morrow Morgan, and Anne Morrow Lindbergh. Rowena Miller was most helpful in supplying first-hand reminiscences as well as expert advice. Taped interviews were often and liberally granted to me by Louise Clark Bennion, Marianne Clark Sharp, Luacine Clark Fox, and J. Reuben Clark III. In addition, each of the Clark children read through several drafts of the manuscript and made helpful suggestions. Reuben III walked me over the ground of his father's Grantsville farm, not just once but several times, and rendered aid to the project in literally hundreds of ways. Technical information and advice were contributed by Professors George M. Addy and David L. Chandler in Latin American studies; Blair R. Holmes in European history; and Thomas G. Alexander, James B. Allen, Eugene E. Campbell, and Marvin S. Hill in Mormon history. Dean Martin B. Hickman at Brigham Young University and Professor Edwin B. Firmage at the University of Utah imparted valuable information on international law and diplomacy.

The manuscript was typed and retyped in the faculty support center of the Brigham Young University College of Family and Social Sciences, principally by Christine L. Minson and Alison Wooley. Sandra W. Longenecker and Marilyn Webb supervised these seemingly interminable operations with truly Christian patience. Other assistance was given by Mariel P. Budd and Kimberly James, the latter of whom prepared both the bibliographical essay and the index. Successive stages of the manuscript were read in entirety or in part by David Michael Quinn, Louis C. Midgley, Elizabeth D. Gee, Donlu Thayer, John N. Drayton, Robert J. Smith, Martin B. Hickman, Gordon Burt Affleck, Marion G. Romney, and all four of the

Clark children, and all made useful suggestions. Professor Neal E. Lambert provided special editorial consultation. At the BYU Press, Howard A. Christy and Elizabeth Wilkinson gave editorial service far beyond the call of duty.

Almost all of the photographic illustrations used herein were taken from the picture files of the Clarkana papers (see *Notes*) or from the private collection of the Clark family. Retouching, where called for, was done by Claudius E. Stevenson and Ralph Reynolds, the latter of whom was also responsible for the book's design.

Tracing the origins and authorship of these photographs proved to be no simple task. In some cases the most diligent efforts proved unrewarding. The fine portrait of Reuben Clark appearing as the frontispiece was taken by the Wilcox Studio of Salt Lake City in 1928 when Reuben became undersecretary of state. Reuben's father-in-law, C. R. Savage, took the graduation portrait appearing in chapter one and presumably the contemporary portrait of Luacine, but the origin of other early family photographs remains unknown. Harris & Ewing Studio of Washington, D.C., was responsible for both the portrait of Huntington Wilson and the group photograph of the American-British Claims Commission, while two other Washington studios, Edmonston and Paine, took the pictures of the three Reubens and the three soldiers respectively. The Moffett Studio of Chicago did the portrait of Philander Knox, and the New York Times Studio of New York did that of Dwight Morrow, gratefully reproduced here with permission.

Henry Miller of the News Picture Service is credited with the photograph of Reuben Clark and Calvin Coolidge opening telephone service to Spain. Both photographs of delegates to the Montevideo Conference were taken by the *Servicio Fotocinematografico Oficial* of the Pan American Union. Since neither of these photographic organizations has survived to the present day, it was impossible, after repeated attempts, to secure specific authorization to reproduce the pictures in question. Similarly frustrating was the attempt to locate Enrique Díaz, the Mexican photographer on Avenida Doncelos whom Reuben called in for state occasions. Díaz was responsible for virtually all of the photographs from the later Mexican years.

I am especially indebted to James T. White & Company, publishers of the *National Cyclopedia,* for permission to use the photograph of James Brown Scott appearing on page 33; to Mrs. Karl T. Frederick of Rye, New York, for permission to use the painting of her father, John Bassett Moore, on the same page; and to the United States Department of State for the photograph of Old State used in chapter two. This treasure was secured for me in Washington by Professor Neil L. York. The picture of the Knox Farm came from the private collection of Rebie Knox Tindle, and the reproduction of page sixteen from "Data on the German Peace Treaty" is from the Special Collections department of Brigham Young University's Harold B. Lee Library, directed by Chad J. Flake.

Both encouragement and financial support were supplied liberally by the trustees of the Clark estate, by Brigham Young University, and by President Marion G. Romney of The Church of Jesus Christ of Latter-day Saints. Ted J. Warner, chairman of the history department at Brigham Young University, intercepted many a distraction, in addition to reading the manuscript section dealing with Mexico. Robert K. Thomas and Robert J. Smith of the university administration saw to it that nothing needful to the project was ever lacking. President Dallin H. Oaks supplied an abundance of inspiration, enthusiasm, and tangible assistance.

David H. Yarn, Jr., deserves to be remembered as the pioneer of the Clark biography project. His almost limitless devotion to the study of J. Reuben Clark's life and work has been an awesome example to those of us who followed him. As editor of this multivolume series, Yarn has directly and indirectly shaped great portions of the final product, and his influence at every point has been one for restraint, moderation, and scholarly integrity.

Finally, Steven R. Faires merits a short paragraph of his own. He joined me as a fledgling graduate student assistant in the beginning of the project and remained staunch to the end. There was literally no aspect of the work with which he was not associated in some way, from research to interpretation to writing to criticism to editing to footnoting. He brought to these activities not only a keen mind and a willing heart but numberless applications of analysis, insight, and perspective—often, happily, different from my own. "He fought me every inch of the way," as Theodore Roosevelt recalled of Elihu Root, "and, together, we got somewhere."

PROLOGUE:
BETWEEN WEST AND EAST

They huddled in their goodbyes on the railroad platform—Reuben Clark, his wife Luacine, their two young daughters, and the group of friends and family that had accompanied them to the station. The waiting locomotive hissed steam; somewhere up the line of cars a bell clanged steadily. People bustled about all around them: passengers, porters, well-wishers, all of them awaiting the departure of the Union Pacific's *Los Angeles Limited.* It was September 19, 1903, a few minutes past seven o'clock in the evening.[1]

The man who stood at the center of attention appeared neither young nor old. At thirty-two Joshua Reuben Clark, Jr., still had the soft lines of what might have been a baby face, but the dark mustache that cut across it added years of maturity. Indeed, the soft lines might as plausibly have been those of middle age, of the chin beginning to double, the neck thickening, the contours of the face filling in and becoming less severe. Only the blue eyes sparkling fiercely in the excitement of the moment were decidedly those of youth. Reuben's life was still very much ahead of him.

His wife, Luacine Savage Clark, was a quietly attractive woman with hazel eyes, soft matronly features, and chestnut hair done up tidily in a bun. There was a certain shyness about her, an instinctive edging away from the focus of events, but this could transform into hawklike alertness where the children were concerned. Despite her six years of married life and the air of domesticity that had mellowed her still-girlish face, Luacine seemed to possess the radiance of a bride. She too was excited about the embarkation—excited and fearful.

The other couple to stand out among the throng was Joshua Reuben, Sr., and his wife Mary Louisa Woolley Clark. Joshua was easily identified as the patriarch of the family—a tall, spare man with

1

a leathery face, flowing white beard, and brilliant, piercing eyes. He was seeing his firstborn onto the train, and for him the occasion was heavy with solemnity. He stood outside the circle of attention, and yet there must have passed between him and his departing namesake glances that carried more meaning than either father or son could put into words. Mary Louisa, too, had little to say and even less to do. She was the epitome of the pioneer woman, shriveled from a life of toil and already beginning to bend into the crippling stoop that would mark her old age. Events were taking her son away—but events did things like that.

The two little girls were dodging in and out among the legs of the well-wishers. This was to be no ordinary trip, as well the toddlers might sense; and even though they were only two and four years old respectively, they seemed to catch the significance of it. Their eyes shone in the early evening light.

Then the conductor, watch in hand, began calling all aboard. Reuben Clark and his family were leaving everything that was familiar to take up the study of law at Columbia University in New York City, further away from Utah than any of them cared to contemplate. Luacine in particular was torn with uncertainty. All that she loved—her family, her church, her friends—was here. Her husband had managed to maintain a comfortable living for them as a schoolteacher and principal; it was not the prosperity that some people enjoyed, but it was steady and respectable. To be sure, New York City had a certain allure; but with only three hundred dollars in their pockets and promises from Reuben's friend Joseph Nelson for money on credit, life in the East could not be glamorous.[2]

After hugs and kisses and parting tears, the family climbed aboard the train to find their places among the wicker seats. Through the windows of the car the waving and advice-giving continued as coats and carryon luggage were stashed in racks and under seats. Then the cars creaked and a ripple of motion passed through the train. Up the line the locomotive hissed, puffed, gave a blast on the whistle, and belched clouds of dark smoke. The lighted station platform slipped back into the chill September twilight.

The *Los Angeles Limited* wound its way through the rail yards and along the western outskirts of the city. The mountains to the east towered above the Salt Lake Valley, red with the last light of

2

day. As the train accelerated, the city too slipped into the evening shadows—the spires of the temple, the Hotel Newhouse, the lights of the university up on the foothills. From the other side of the coach the passengers could see the Great Salt Lake reflecting the sunset, and beyond its southern rim the flatlands of Tooele and Grantsville. This, for the Clarks, was the last view of home. The train would stop again in Ogden and then steam up Echo Canyon toward Wyoming. Far beyond it in the East, under the skies of night, was New York City.[3]

ii

The young Clark family, responding to the American Dream, was traveling to the city to seek its fortune. The pioneer Saints had foreseen that the coming of the railroad would open the way back East for the youth of Zion. Not many had departed as of that moment, but they would soon begin to leave in ever-increasing numbers. In fact, in a symbolic way, this trip might have been considered the first. It would not be without its effect on Deseret.*

Some thirty-five years earlier Joshua Reuben, Sr., had come West in the same search for opportunity. He had been born December 11, 1840, near the little town of Navarre in Stark County, Ohio, the son of Hendricks Clark and his second wife, Esther.[4] Hendricks owned a small ranch and was a devout Dunkard, and he taught his son the virtues of hard work and middle-American Christianity. Joshua was a good-looking boy and he grew into a handsome man, over six feet tall and weighing one hundred eighty pounds, with a swarthy complexion and a shock of thick, black hair. But his eyes remained his most notable feature—flashing, searching, boring into the soul, they were not the eyes of an ordinary man.

Joshua rallied to the flag in 1861 and was assigned to Company B of the 48th Regiment of the Indiana Volunteers. After the Civil War—and desultory action—he got the itch to go West. He worked his way as trapper, hunter, freighter, and lumberman. Finding that

*The formal name of the Mormon church is The Church of Jesus Christ of Latter-day Saints. Mormons are often called Latter-day Saints, Saints, or simply LDS. Upon their arrival in what was to become the Utah Territory, the Mormon pioneers designated it the State of Deseret, a name taken from an allusion in the Book of Mormon to the industrious honeybee. A more loosely applied term, "Zion," was derived from biblical references.

his mail often became mixed with that of other "J. Clarks" in the lumber camps and freight stops, he added "Reuben" to it for distinctiveness. Eventually his work took him through Utah. He promised himself that he would come back.[5]

Leaving Montana in the spring of 1867, Joshua did return, traveling southward on horseback. But this was Brigham Young's Utah; and with its managed economy, its suspicion of "Gentiles,"* and, most of all, its institution of polygamy, it was a place that one either loved or left. Joshua did not yet love it, but he paused in Farmington on March 10 and attended his first Mormon church service. He was impressed so favorably that he radically revised some opinions. In little more than a month he was baptized in Brigham Young's millpond in Salt Lake City, on a Sunday morning so chill that it left frost on the ground and ice on the water. The next evening found Joshua at prayer when, according to his journal, a "bright light" shone around him and a "peaceful Holy influence" settled upon his soul. Now convinced of the truth of the gospel, he threw himself into its work.[6]

Joshua took up teaching, initially with a position in the Salt Lake Tenth Ward school.† Within a couple of years there was an opportunity to go to Grantsville; on Tuesday, November 3, 1868, he rode out to reconnoiter the ward school there.[7] The town he entered, there on the southern shore of the Great Salt Lake, was not impressive by most standards. Its roads were dusty and its houses seedy. The Lombardy poplars which lined the prosaically numbered streets were in various stages of decay, and their whitened skeletons cast a pall over the landscape. North of Main Street the farmland was marshy and alkaline, stretching but a mile or so to the sterile waters of the lake; south of Main Street the land was fertile enough but arid,

---

*The Book of Mormon recounts the history of Lehi and his family, who in 600 B.C. were led by God out of Israel to the shores of America. Here they established a biblical-like civilization, built cities, fought wars, were by turns faithful and unfaithful to God's teachings, and in the end perished in a series of apocalyptic conflicts. The scripture prophesied, however, that America would once again become a holy place, the site for the restoration of the Church of Jesus Christ, and the gathering place for one branch of the house of Israel in the last days. Because of this strongly biblical orientation, Mormons often referred to non-Mormons as "Gentiles," especially in pioneer Utah.

†A *ward* is the equivalent of a parish or congregation in the Mormon church, presided over by a bishop. A *stake* is the equivalent of a diocese and is presided over by a stake president. General officers of the church are referred to as *general authorities,* the highest of which are designated *apostles.* Presiding over the entire church is the First Presidency, consisting of a president and two counselors.

extending toward the parched Stansbury Mountains. In fact, bleakness confronted the viewer from almost any angle. But Grantsville, as Joshua discovered, was difficult to view objectively. There was a sort of magic in the crystalline air, in the afternoon light, in the gentle rise of the valley floor, and in the chiseled façade of the mountains. Grantsville would remain Joshua's home from that time on.[8]

After a few weeks of teaching, Joshua returned to Salt Lake City for the Christmas holidays. He was in the company of Samuel Woolley, a trustee of the school; and for the return trip Joshua was obliged to pay a call at Woolley's father's home in the city. There in the parlor, as he waited for his traveling companion, Joshua watched a pretty young lady busily ironing. She glanced up only once at the rumpled schoolteacher, but she noticed the bold features and the remarkable eyes. He smiled. It was not until Samuel was ready to leave that the two were introduced. At that moment, with something like precognition, Joshua knew that this young lady, Mary Louisa Woolley, was to be his wife.[9]

Mary Louisa was the daughter of Edwin D. and Mary Wickersham Woolley, who had been among the pioneers of 1848. Mary Louisa was born on the journey west, at Goose Creek on the North Platte on July 5.[10] From her birth onward there was something solid and self-reliant about this child of adversity, something suggested by her receipt at the age of eight of first prize in the Salt Lake Fair's "Homespun Girl" contest. Mary Louisa was indeed a homespun girl.

Their marriage at the Endowment House in the summer of 1870 joined more than man and woman; it joined Clark and Woolley, and the conjunction was significant. Joshua Clark, looking for all the world like an Old Testament prophet, spoke always of high-minded things, of love, of duty, of truth. The Woolleys, by contrast, were noted—indeed famous—for plain hardheadedness. If a Woolley ever drowned, Salt Lakers used to say, look for the body upstream, for it would never go along with the current.[11] When a grandson once asked Joshua why he had never taken up polygamy, the answer came from Mary Louisa, who was in another room and supposedly deaf: "He's still alive, isn't he?"[12]

Of their ten children, some were Clarks and some were Woolleys. Samuel, for example, was a Clark. He was unquestionably the spiritual member of the family, but earning a living came with difficulty for him. Frank, by contrast, was full of Woolley feistiness. His touch never failed him when it came to worldly affairs—only when it came to religion. As for Joshua Reuben, Jr., the firstborn of the family, his inheritance somehow derived from both Clark *and* Woolley—and that was significant too.

He was born in a small stone house on a quarter-section of Grantsville brushland. The newlyweds had first moved into a log cabin beside Samuel Woolley's home. A year later Joshua had acquired a small piece of homestead acreage on the outskirts of the town and started work on a family dwelling. The finished house had two rooms and a half-basement, and each stone in its rock walls had been hauled laboriously from the Stansbury Mountains. On September 1, 1871, while Samuel's wife, Maria Woolley, attended Mary Louisa, Joshua went for the midwife, "Mother" Orr. He returned breathless but late. Through blue eyes obviously inherited from his father, J. Reuben Clark, Jr., was already gazing at the world.[13]

Birthplace of J. Reuben Clark, Jr., west of Grantsville, Utah: Close to the primary facts of mortality.

6

iii

Joshua continued to teach school in Grantsville. Every Monday morning he trekked the three-and-a-half miles to town through the sagebrush and alkali. He spent the school week there and on Friday evening walked back out to the homestead with groceries and supplies. So the first few years of Reuben's life were spent mainly in the company of his mother, she usually pregnant with one of the ten children. Thus his childhood memories came to revolve around the difficulties of pioneer life. His earliest memory was of his mother beating a rattlesnake to death on the front doorstep.[14] Another was of her yanking a snake from the stone wall of the half-basement.[15] Still other recollections were of the Indians walking freely into the house and demanding sugar, flour, and salt.[16] Mary did not lock the doors, for Brother Brigham had instructed the Saints not to oppose the Lamanites* but to feed and comfort them.

As Reuben grew older, life resolved itself into work, religion, and learning, with precious little time left over for play. Work was the focal point of the family's attention, for no living was wrung easily from the Grantsville soil. By the time Reuben was nine, he regularly milked two cows. When he was eleven he helped brand cattle and drive them to range in the grazing lands south of town. At thirteen he was plowing with moline and sulky plows, jerked along by a double team of horses. As the family acreage expanded he helped plant, cultivate, and irrigate the crops of corn, wheat, barley, and oats. He helped cut, pitch, haul, and stack the sweet clover and lucerne. He dug and cleaned ditches, cared for and harvested the fruit from the orchard, and looked after the array of vegetables that grew in the backyard garden. At sixteen he hired out to his uncle Samuel to tend herd on the range north of Grantsville. But his father missed him terribly and rode out one dark night to bring him home again.[17]

Sometimes the boy went with his father to help shear sheep, one of a number of jobs that Joshua took to supplement the family in-

---

*Some of the peoples dealt with in the Book of Mormon were the descendants of Laman, son of Lehi, who took their ancestor's name. As Mormons believe the American Indian to have descended from the Lamanites, the term *Lamanite* is often used as a synonym for Indian.

Reuben as a boy: His mother's companion in a world of loneliness and hardship.

come. Soon Reuben could process with hand shears as many as eleven sheep in a day. He would also go with his father into the Stansbury Mountains to cut wood for burning and building. While high in the aspens they would gather chokecherries, currants, and wild gooseberries to be used for jams and jellies. In 1883, when Reuben was twelve, he helped haul rock, mix mortar, and split clapboards for the new family dwelling his father built.[18] The two of them were together constantly. Reuben was never certain exactly how he came by the ideas that the American nation was sacred, that selfish and corrupt Democracy—with a capital *D*—had once attempted to destroy it, and that Abraham Lincoln and the Republican Party had stepped boldly forward to save it; but somewhere amid the clapboards and the gooseberries he clearly acquired these ideas from his father.

Such a childhood confronted Reuben with relentless responsibility and incessant demands of work. And work, as he learned, was not only needed for the survival of the body but also for the salvation of the soul. Living amidst the unadorned facts of the land—the dust, the rain, the withering desert sun—and breathing in the smells of life—the blood and membrane of newborn calves, the warm acridity of fresh-laid eggs, the sweetness of newly cut hay—developed in the boy a homing sense for the farm and for Grantsville. Wherever he went, this would always be the spiritual center.

For the Clark household, work and religion were inseparable. The ground was plowed in reliance on the Lord's will and with an eye to the building of His kingdom. Each spring, after the sowing was finished, Joshua took his sons out into the fields where they had spent the day. There, as the sun was dropping behind Stansbury Island, they knelt among the furrows and dedicated the crop to the Lord.[19] After the harvest, there came the ritual trip to the tithing office to pay in kind the Lord's tenth. The wagon loaded with hay, barley, plums, potatoes, peaches, turkeys, or other products of their labors, Joshua and the boys always made the journey together so as to underscore the meaning of it all.[20] Later the boys would go by themselves to pay tithing on their own personal crops or livestock. And Joshua's observances were strict. Over the objections of his bishop, Joshua hauled in a tenth of his harvest and then *another* tenth of any subsequent improvements, so that there was one tithe on the grain and another on the milled flour.[21] Where the Lord was concerned, there were no compromises.

When the time arrived for each of the children to be baptized, the family climbed into the wagon and rode out to the warm springs, a cluster of brackish ponds in the alkali flats northwest of town. Though the water stung the eyes and was bitter to the taste, it was warm and preternaturally clear. The baptismal ordinance was performed on a ledge in one of the larger pools. Local lore had it that beyond this ledge the pool was bottomless, dropping away to unsounded depths. Reuben was baptized here the day after his eighth birthday—on September 2, 1879—and confirmed the following Sunday by his father.[22]* Soon he was participating in the church's activities. When he was nine he gave a short recitation before the assembled congregation. "He was frightened but did very well," his father recorded.[23] He went ward teaching with one of the elders and was soon officiating in the administration of the sacrament.[24]

Besides the observance of religion, there was strong emphasis in the Clark home on education. Joshua soon had to give up teaching, but he never abandoned his passion for knowledge. He maintained a small personal library to which the children, if respectful, had access. Among the volumes were *The Model Book of Natural History, The Model History of the United States, The Story of Man,* and *Young Folk's History of Rome.* There was a *Life of the Savior* in which young Reuben took a special interest. There were no novels; Joshua did not consider them to be among "the best books."[25]

On January 2, 1882, apparently for the benefit of his eldest son, Joshua returned to the lectern. He opened a private school in Anderson's Hall with thirty students. Among them were Reuben, ten years old, and brother Edwin, eight.[26] Joshua strove to suffuse his teaching with what he believed to be the three fundamentals of education: mental, physical, and moral stimulation. But Joshua's approach was already dated. Reuben spent only a year in his father's school before

---

Confirmation is a part of the baptismal service, usually performed the following day at formal church services. Since there is no professional clergy in the Mormon church, such ordinances as baptism, confirmation, and administration of the sacrament (or communion) are performed by lay members of the congregation who hold the priesthood. Among their other sacerdotal responsibilities is ward teaching, or visiting church members in behalf of ward authorities.

moving on to a new graded school under the direction of B. F. Kes-
ler. To Joshua, the opening of this facility marked the end of an era
in Grantsville education, and he questioned his own teaching qualifications for "such a progressive age."27

Reuben took readily to schoolwork. When he could not attend
class he grew restless and morose. More than once, when the temper-
ature dropped below zero and the Skull Valley wind howled across
the lake, Reuben left his younger brothers behind and struck out
alone for the schoolhouse—even against his father's admonitions.
"Reuben would rather miss his meals than miss a day from school,"
wrote Joshua.28 After finishing the eighth level, the highest grade offered in Grantsville, Reuben returned to repeat it twice. "I was not
quite that dull," he later explained, "but there was nothing to do, so
I went to school in the winter time and went over the same
ground."29

Sometimes, after the work, schooling, and church activity were
taken care of, there was time left over for recreation. There were traditional games of hide-and-seek, bucking bronco, and snap-the-whip.
Making molasses candy filled many an evening at home. Joshua
splurged on a magic lantern to cast pictures on the wall, at once entertaining the children and instructing them.30 There were holidays
and family outings too. At Christmas time the house was warm and
sweet with the smells of baking pastries. Two or three days before
Christmas each year, Joshua and his sons traveled to Salt Lake City
to sell an assortment of chickens and turkeys. There they drank in
the festive atmosphere of the city and shopped for Christmas gifts
with their profits.31 The Independence Day celebrations also took
them to the capital, where bands paraded through the streets and
speeches rang out across Liberty Park. The Clarks often stopped by
the temple block to walk reverently through the sacred building
which after forty years was now nearing completion. Back home in
Grantsville, they enjoyed the even headier celebrations of Pioneer
Day, the twenty-fourth of July. That event was filled with speeches,
songs, and band music at the town pavilion; picnics at the park; and
boat races on the Great Salt Lake.32 As Reuben and his brothers became older they took to riding off for camping, hunting, or fishing
expeditions in the nearby mountains. In the hot evenings of July
they frequently slipped over to the warm springs for a midnight

11

swim, then returned home to sleep on the haystack under summer stars.[33]

Because of the Mormon enthusiasm for such things, recreation included cultural events. Recitations, concerts, and literary get-togethers were sponsored by the local schoolteachers and held in any convenient location. Once the Clark family saw an art exhibit of sorts called "The Grand Mormon Panorama"—eleven large paintings depicting the rise of Mormonism.[34] Joshua bought Reuben a piccolo and, later, a flute; Reuben played them in the Grantsville Juvenile Band and then in the Town Band that accompanied public occasions.[35] And, like other Mormon settlements, Grantsville had an amateur dramatic troupe. Reuben played parts in several plays and displayed a certain flair for comedy.[36] Such cultural roots may have seemed shallow enough by some standards, but they grew into Reuben's consciousness and he soon developed a taste for full-blown music drama.

In some ways, Grantsville lacked nothing for a barefoot boy. But it was evident by the time Reuben had plowed through the eighth grade for the third time that he needed more schooling and greater opportunity. The most significant decision in his life, perhaps, was the one he made in September of 1890—to strike out for Salt Lake City.

iv

As in the lives of so many notables, the difference between plowboy and public figure was ultimately to turn on delicate pivots of fortune. Reuben encountered not one but two such pivots when he matriculated at the LDS College in Salt Lake City. The principal of the college was Dr. James E. Talmage, lion of the Mormon intelligentsia; and his second counselor was a restless but kindly entrepreneur named Joseph Nelson.[37] Without either of them—without both of them, in fact—Reuben Clark might have pursued a desultory career at middle education and then returned to his hometown. But after a few weeks of their company his life was transformed irrevocably.

To be sure, it was a none-too-self-certain Reuben Clark who climbed down from his father's buggy that September and swung his

12

baggage into Aunt Rachael Simmons's spare bedroom. After all, he had only gone through the eighth grade—and in a hit-or-miss fashion at that. But in his first semester Reuben did amazingly well, scoring in the nineties in every subject but penmanship.[38] This performance soon came to the notice of Dr. Talmage. In consideration of the boy's apparent abilities—and precarious finances—Talmage offered him a job at the new Deseret Museum, of which Talmage himself had just been appointed curator by the Mormon church.[39] The contents of the museum were not impressive: a pile of shells, assorted minerals, and a few relics from the collection of Brigham Young's son, John W. But they were deemed worthy of public display, and it was Reuben's job to display them. He was to take charge of the items, catalog and arrange them, see to custodial and secretarial services, and give museum tours at twenty-five cents a head. Acceptance of the position necessitated his leaving school, but he would receive fifty dollars a month and the labor would be counted as the equivalent of foreign mission service.[40]* It was such an important opportunity and such a high personal compliment that, upon hearing of the offer, Joshua rode all the way to Salt Lake City to urge Reuben's acceptance of it.[41]

The museum was initially located on the main floor and mezzanine of the Hotel Templeton. The room was filled with oak display cases with glass sliding doors, and its wooden floor creaked in agony as patrons wandered among them. Next door was a billiard hall, separated from the museum by curtained glass partitions. People would come to the glass and peer through into the museum; and sometimes when things were slow Reuben would stand on his own side and watch billiards.[42]

The Templeton room was cramped, so the museum was eventually attached to the new Church University and moved to more spacious quarters. Reuben continued as Talmage's assistant. He picked up some shorthand to aid in his secretarial duties; he learned to type on the machine Talmage had bought for the museum; and he aided his mentor in preparing experiments, setting up apparatus, and run-

---

*Missionary work in the Mormon church is performed by lay members who voluntarily spend a period of several years in intensive proselyting activities. As they receive neither compensation nor expenses for these efforts, the missionary experience can be an economically challenging one.

Graduation portrait, 1898: High ambition and driving intensity.

ning the hydro-oxygen lantern.[43] At the same time he enrolled in a year of courses at the new university, taking science, physics, and chemistry.[44] And he endured Talmage's meticulousness. Early in the experience an item was somehow misplaced. Dr. Talmage flew into a fury. His rage became so virulent that Reuben innocently suggested, "I'll buy you another if you feel that way about it." But Talmage stormed, "That is not the point. The point is that something could be misplaced or lost. Not that this could be lost, but that anything could be lost."[45]

Such experiences were instructive, but even more instructive was Talmage himself. He was a kind of intellectual whirlwind. Now in geology, now in chemistry, now in medicine, now in Biblical scholarship, he swept the horizon before him. Reuben found his own interests beginning to multiply.

In the late summer of 1894, the fledgling Church University was ceded to the University of Utah. As part of the transaction James Talmage went along as president. The facilities of the Church University (including the Deseret Museum) were made available to the University of Utah and so, as secretary and clerk to the president, was Reuben Clark. He suddenly found himself in a remarkably advantageous position.[46]

Yet the same question remained: how could Reuben convert his assets into a real education? He had hoped that by working for Dr. Talmage and laying aside most of his pay he could begin regular studies at the University of Utah. At a critical moment, however, the Clark family was shaken by the death of Reuben's younger brother Elmer; and then, just two days after the funeral, Joshua Clark was called away to two years of missionary service in the northern states.[47]

The added burden of supporting his father in the mission field almost finished Reuben off. Far from the respite he had anticipated, his education became a nightmare procession of deadlines and responsibilities. He plunged into his fourth year of service for James Talmage, working ten hours a day and six days a week for fifty dollars a month.[48] And he went to school. He earned his Bachelor of Science degree in four years, working for Talmage throughout and during the last year of school serving as editor of the *University Chronicle*. At the spring graduation of 1898 he delivered the valedictory address, fiery with the patriotism of the Spanish-American War, and graduated magna cum laude.[49] Ever afterward he was a workaholic.

v

With the flush of graduation behind him, Reuben had completed his education. Yet, as he was the first to admit, there remained something unfinished about him. As he trudged to and from Aunt Rachael's house on soft spring mornings or leafy autumn afternoons, he cut a noticeable figure. Though not tall, slender, or especially handsome, he presented a forthright manner and self-assured bearing that people found attractive. His eyes had narrowed a little, probably from overwork, and his jaw was set tight. The straight, firm mouth suggested toughness of spirit, and the chin could be thrust forward in a gesture of determination. Yet these Woolley features could dissolve in an instant into Clarkean mirth. Mischief could flash through the blue eyes and telegraph a pun or wisecrack. Indeed, for one so absorbed in workday cares, Reuben Clark incongruously acquired the reputation of a funnyman.[50] A sort of Grantsville boisterousness welled up in him from time to time, and its manifestations often seemed uncontainable. Nor was he exactly urbane in other ways: he could ride in from a hard day in the saddle and feast contentedly on congealed gravy, and his table manners were for the most part no more refined than his tastes.[51] The young ladies were not at all sure about this young man: if he was impressive, he was also a little unsettling.

One of the young ladies gradually became less disconcerted. Luacine Savage lived on these same avenues, at 80 D Street, and she had watched the Clark boy walk past her house for years. If his striding gait denoted earnestness and sobriety, his ways seemed frankly hickish. One evening, however, her sister Ida invited a group of college students to the house and the "Reube" from Grantsville appeared in their midst. It was not love at first sight, exactly, but at least the two of them were officially introduced and their mutual interest began to develop.[52] For his part, Reuben had long awaited the introduction. He had chanced to pass the Savage home one evening at dusk, when the lights of the city were winking on. Through

Luacine Savage at the time of her marriage: For the young man, at least, it was love at first sight.

the window he saw Luacine standing in the parlor, her arms reaching up to light the overhead chandelier. He had paused only long enough to take in the picture before marching off into the gathering dusk—but in that moment he had resolved to marry this girl.[53]

It was generally known that Reuben was Dr. Talmage's personal assistant; and in the course of affairs Luacine's father, C. R. Savage, a local photographer of considerable renown, had conceived a real admiration for the young man. Luacine was especially impressed with a eulogy Reuben delivered at a funeral one day.[54] "There's lots more to that Reube Clark than just noise," she announced to her friends. Events reached the pass where Reuben hired a hack to escort the young lady to the theater, where he purchased the best seats in the house. It was their only date together, but it was enough. "I soon discovered that I was falling in love with this indifferent, studious boy from Grantsville," Luacine later recorded.[55]

By 1894, when both Reuben and Luacine were twenty-three, she was ready to settle down. But marriage was out of the question until he had completed his education. First he must graduate from the university; next he must find a job; and only then might the two of them plan a wedding. In August of 1898, three months after Reuben's graduation, C. R. Savage received a visit from a Heber City photographer who had been recently elected trustee of the Heber School District. He was looking for a qualified teacher to open a new high school in his town. C. R. blithely recommended Reuben and rushed home with the news.[56]

Nuptial plans unfolded immediately. One of them, as it turned out, was for Luacine, a young lady of some account, to embark upon the western American equivalent of the grand tour—to California. This did not sit well with her betrothed. Apart from the absence of his bride-to-be, Reuben dimly sensed the social implications of her trip.[57] In the dusty world of Grantsville he had never concerned himself with questions of rank and station; now both were being thrust before him. As with the opera he was learning to enjoy, new worlds were opening to his sight.

On September 14, 1898, with one hundred dollars saved and the prospect of a walloping eighty-five dollars per month in Heber, Reuben and Luacine were married in the Salt Lake Temple. James Talmage performed the ceremony. Afterward there was a small reception where Reuben's family mixed rather stiffly with the visibly prosperous Savages.[58] Two days later Reuben set out for Heber City, tucked away high in a Wasatch mountain valley, to find a place to live. Luacine waited impatiently for ten days and then joined him in the search.[59] They finally located two upstairs rooms over a widow's parlor. There was little furniture, and water had to be carried up the back stairs from a well behind the house. Luacine Savage Clark was not used to such conditions.[60]

For all its alpine splendor, Heber City was evidently not home to the young couple. Whatever had been missing from Reuben's life at the time of graduation was still missing, and the schoolteaching experience did not seem to supply it. Although he threw himself into a whirl of activities—organizing a reading club for his students, teaching Sunday school, establishing himself as a fixture in the community—he still faced difficulties. Heber City was far from family and friends. The weather was forbidding. One of the schoolgirls swore, to Reuben's utter mortification, that he had kissed her in the hall, setting the town ablaze with gossip.[61] And the roads between Heber and Salt Lake City were so bad that Luacine had to leave three months early to prepare for the arrival of their first child.[62] So when the school year wound up on June 2, 1899, Reuben left Heber City for good, returning to Salt Lake to assist in the birth of their daughter Louise.[63]

vi

The essential failure of his teaching venture raised a pertinent question: what, exactly, *was* Reuben to do with his life? Of his gifts and abilities there was no question, but these must be applied resourcefully in order to have meaning. Reuben pondered the matter during many a long summer evening. The more he thought about it, the more convinced he became that he was somehow cut out for the law. He had taken some legal courses at the University of Utah, and now he took to reading law books in his spare time.[64] As he read, he began to wonder what possibilities might exist for him there.

It was of peculiar significance that at this juncture Reuben ran into his old friend Joseph Nelson from LDS College days. The college had had its ups and downs, and at one point had been merged into the short-lived Church University, but somehow Joseph Nelson had hung on. In fact, with some of his own money, Nelson had developed a business school as an adjunct to the college, and this had proven extremely promising.[65] During the summer Reuben signed a contract to teach business.[66]

Life was little less rocky in Salt Lake than it had been in Heber City. The Mormon church owned the business school, and it insisted on paying the teachers two-thirds in money and one-third in tithing orders redeemable in produce. When a fiscal crisis came along, the church retrenched by reversing the ratios: one-third in money and two-thirds in tithing scrip.[67] At this the faculty rebelled and a long season of bitterness ensued. Joseph Nelson, finally deciding on bold

19

action, sold out his own interest in the school and turned around to purchase a competing institution, the Salt Lake City Business College. The entire faculty, including Reuben, picked up and went with him. It was a remarkable demonstration of solidarity—and it cemented for life the friendship of Joseph Nelson and J. Reuben Clark.[68]

Reuben spent six months teaching at the Salt Lake City Business College before he was approached with a clearly preferable proposition. The University of Utah was seeking a new principal for the southern branch of the state normal school in Cedar City. In the spring of 1900 Reuben signed a contract for one year's work and prepared his family for a long remove southward.[69] If any experience might have inclined him toward a serious career in education, surely this was it.

Cedar City was a pleasant mining and ranching community in the southwest corner of the state. With three scenic wonderlands— Bryce, Zion, and Cedar Breaks—within hailing distance, and with much interest in the coal resources of the area, the town was brimming with people and opportunity. Reuben had two hundred earnest students and a competent teaching staff. Facilities were located in a three-story building, new and well equipped.[70] Though his contract was only for one year, Reuben would have accepted another and probably looked forward to it. Almost immediately, in fact, he made recommendations for the expansion of the school. He believed that a fourth year should be added to the curriculum in answer to the difficulties encountered by Cedar City students in attempting to complete their training at the University of Utah. Somewhat offhandedly perhaps, he incorporated this recommendation into his budget request for the succeeding school year—neatly quadrupling the existing budget.[71]

Reuben's progressivism won the hearts of students and citizenry alike, but it was the state legislature and university regents who needed to approve it. And they were outraged. In the spring of 1901 word trickled down to Cedar City that a new principal had been appointed.[72] Students at the school circulated a petition pleading for the retention of the forward-looking Mr. Clark, but it was unavailing.[73] With this second disappointment on his hands, Reuben was beginning to doubt that his future lay in education. While in Cedar City he had dabbled in coal-bearing properties and had gained a sense of the importance of minerals to the state. He was still reading law-books in the long evenings. He began to think of mining law.[74]

Reuben also began to see that lawyers were not made by hearth-side reading. The very progressivism that had mandated expansion of the normal school was then revolutionizing the study of law as well. Although a Harvard or Yale seemed increasingly beyond the reach of the struggling young family—the Clarks were now expecting their second child—Reuben nonetheless began dashing off inquiries.[75] In order to save money, the couple moved in with Luacine's father, C. R. Savage, and his new wife Annie. C. R. had plastered and other-wise renovated for them the old storeroom and workshop at 80 D.[76] Reuben took up his work again at Joseph Nelson's Salt Lake City Business College, teaching commercial law and shorthand.[77] He grew attentive to every possible opportunity to go East.

At length he thought he had it. In the fall of 1902, Reed Smoot, a prominent Mormon apostle, ran for the Senate with enough church backing to assure his election. Smoot was famous for crusti-ness and unapproachability, but Reuben decided to take a long shot with him. He wrote to the senator-to-be and offered his services as private secretary. Through Joseph Nelson he even persuaded the president of the church, Joseph F. Smith, to pen an endorsement at the bottom of the letter.[78] But, for reasons unexplained, Smoot gave the application exceedingly short shrift. Meanwhile the replies fil-tered back from Harvard and Yale, with their out-of-reach price tags. This only made the object more sublime.

Then, without warning, Joseph Nelson stepped into the breach. He was a strange little man, with elfin features and bushy dark brows; but his commercial pursuits were as bold and extravagant as Talmage's intellectual adventures. Nelson, moreover, had a habit of suddenly dropping considerable sums of money on some struggling young man or other, almost in fairy-godmother fashion. In the sum-mer of 1903 he singled out Reuben Clark and told him to get his affairs in order for law school. Nelson would pick up the bill by an arrangement described as a loan, but without interest, terms, or pen-alties. The dream was suddenly a reality.[79]

21

So with Nelson's letter of credit and the three hundred dollars Reuben had saved, the Clark family was on its way to law school. Harvard had been too "high-hat" in its response to Reuben's inquiry, so he had decided instead on Columbia.[80] At thirty-two years of age, the farmboy still lingered in him—a passion for land and for living things. That was the West in his make-up and it was indelible. But Reuben had acquired an equal passion for education and for the possibilities that knowledge and culture opened before him; and whether he realized it or not, it was this urge that was sending him toward the different world of the East.

vii

The coach in which the Clarks were riding rocked gently along the track as the *Los Angeles Limited* whistled on into the night; Reuben Clark, who had never been closer to New York than Heber City, Utah, contemplated his dozing wife and children, then turned his gaze to the window and the dark outlines of the passing landscape. He was the plowboy going to the city. He was the Mormon journeying among the Gentiles. He was the westerner traveling East. It would be remarkable if he did not wonder that night what the future held in store.

PART I

APPRENTICESHIP

1903–10

THE MAKING OF AN INTERNATIONAL LAWYER

When Reuben stepped from the train in New York, a new phase of his life began. Despite his college training, his experience as a teacher, and his years of dabbling in the law, the adventure that began for him on that September morning of 1903 was in a very real sense his education. It was to commence with law school at Columbia University, but it was certainly not to end there. Indeed, it was not to end until March of 1913, when he would resign from the Department of State to practice law on his own. In the course of that decade the character of Reuben Clark would be transformed from western to eastern, from rustic to urbane, from naive to world-wise. At the same time Reuben himself would mature from an essentially young man, unsure of himself and his direction in the world, to a man of middle age, settled and self-possessed. In the process he would learn both the feeling of power and the lessons of responsibility. In the course of this apprenticeship he would become an international lawyer—and he would sharpen tools for a dozen careers beyond.

Chapter 1

MORNINGSIDE

The world that opened before the Clarks as they crossed the Hudson was marvelous indeed. Even though the towers of the 1920s were not yet in place, the buildings of Manhattan already seemed to scrape the sky. Vessels of every description littered the waterways, hooting angrily at one another. The late summer air was dense with moisture and with the coal smoke that seemed to ooze from everywhere. The streets, some of them square and others shearing off inexplicably, were thronged with a dizzying array of vehicles: horse-carts and wagons, taxicabs and trolleys, even motorcars. The congestion was worst on the Lower East Side, where alleys like Hester Street fairly teemed with immigrant multitudes; but even beyond the ghettos the traffic buzzed fearfully. A city of light and shadow, this was the New York of both Edith Wharton and Jacob Riis. Nothing could have focused its various images better than Grand Central Station, rising cathedral-like above the skyline and aswarm with activity. Amid the shrieking of whistles and gasping of locomotives, the Clarks detrained along with thousands of others from the continental interior and walked through the cavernous lobby. To these people of rural Utah for whom Salt Lake had been the big city, this may as well have been Baghdad.

ii

Happily, life was more placid at Morningside Heights, where Columbia University was located. The apartment that Reuben and Luacine found was not far from the campus. It was long and narrow, with a hall running from front to back—the likeness, some said, of a railroad car. It was too spacious by half for the Clark family alone, so Luacine hired a cook and turned the spare rooms to profit. With

27

fellow Utahns numbered among her boarders, she felt tentatively at home. The neighborhood in 1903 was far removed from the blight that would subsequently creep over it. With a friendly drugstore on the corner, Morningside Park across the street, and Columbia students as its citizens, it was a reasonably pleasant place to live.

iii

The year 1903 was a fortunate time to begin. Theodore Roosevelt was in the White House and progressivism was in the air. Machinery was easing human drudgery, science was rationalizing behavior, and politics was coming to grips at last with the problems of the ages. The Republican Party, in power more or less continuously since the days of Abraham Lincoln, had refashioned the nation in its own image. The watchword of this new America was confidence, and it was written everywhere—in the smokestacks that blackened the sky, in the throbbing city streets, in the neo-Gothic mansions dotting Fifth Avenue, in the value of stocks on the New York Exchange, and most convincingly in the style of the man who headed the nation. Nicholas Murray Butler, president of Columbia University, captured the spirit of the time perfectly when at Reuben's commencement he predicted "a social, economic, and political reconstruction of American society."[1]

And Columbia was a fortunate place to begin. Recently moved to Morningside Heights from cramped downtown quarters, it sprawled luxuriously among the semirural surroundings. The site had previously been occupied by the Bloomingdale Insane Asylum and reminders of this ancestry persisted. Two buildings from the old facility now functioned as classrooms, and Mr. Spencer, the white-whiskered groundskeeper, still spoke of the undergraduates as "inmates."[2] But there were signs of better things to come. By the time of Reuben's arrival Columbia boasted six beautiful new buildings, including the magnificent Low Memorial Library, an adaptation of the Roman Pantheon in white marble. Its solid masonry dome, towering one hundred and fifty-two feet above street level, was an architectural wonder of the day.[3] Every view of its classical elegance bespoke confidence.

For the time being, Low Memorial was also the home of the law school. Founded after the Revolution by such luminaries as John Jay and Alexander Hamilton, Columbia School of Law had traditionally been a path-breaker. Its first professor had been James Kent of *Commentaries* fame; and from this beginning the school had gone on to expand the law curriculum, pioneer the case-study method, and develop the law review as a pedagogical tool.⁴ Now, under the leadership of Dean George W. Kirchwey, the school was in the forefront of several new movements which were shaping the course of American law. The first was the political science movement, expressing the idea that politics, the great game of power, could be subdued and made scientific. The second was the international law movement, expressing the hope that law might move beyond individual nations to become truly world-wide in scope and application. The third was the international peace movement, expressing the fear that science was leading man toward the Apocalypse with weapons of undreamed power.

All three movements had just begun to advance beyond the talking stage. Among the firstfruits of the political science movement was the work of Professor Charles A. Beard, whose *Economic Interpretation of the Constitution* (1913) would effect a profound upheaval in American constitutional thought.⁵ The international law movement was also coming into its own. In 1899, at the first of the Hague conferences, delegates from the world powers had undertaken to haul the law of nations into the twentieth century. They had managed to outlaw only a few of the dreadful new weapons of war, such as poison gas and dum-dum bullets, but they had succeeded in establishing a Permanent Court of Arbitration to resolve international disputes.⁶ Even the peace movement was fermenting with change. Nowhere was the new look better illustrated than at the Lake Mohonk Conferences on International Arbitration, held annually at a resort hotel in the Catskills and traditionally attended only by the sentimental pacifists of the American Peace Society. Now, rather suddenly, new faces were beginning to appear—faces of men like Robert Lansing, who would first come to Mohonk in 1904, and Chandler Anderson, who would appear the following year. Hardly sentimental, these were veterans of actual arbitrations. In such celebrated cases as the Bering Sea arbitration (1892), the Alaskan boundary settlement (1903), and the Venezuelan asphalt dispute (1905), they had taken part in the very process of laying wars to rest.

They were lawyers, of course, but until now they had not really described themselves any more precisely. Gradually the term "international lawyer" was gaining currency. In 1905 it acquired professional stature with the founding of the American Society of International Law.[7]

This is the world that would stamp its impress on J. Reuben Clark. In time he would become a Constitutional scholar, a diplomat, a negotiator, an arbitrator, an expert in arms control, a director of the American Peace Society, a participant at the Lake Mohonk conferences, a prospective delegate to the Third Hague Conference, and, above all else, a practitioner of international law. He came to this world through the State Department, through various claims commissions, through five Republican administrations, and through his own international legal practice. But he came to it first at Columbia.

iv

Just how the Columbia magic touched Reuben is, of course, an open question. His experience at the law school was much like that of any other student, and his class curriculum of "torts," "contracts," and "real property" was in the familiar mold. It was individual teachers who apparently made the difference. Through extensive contact or through the sheer force of personality, five different members of the law faculty seem to have exerted a commanding influence on the Utah Mormon.

The first was John W. Burgess. A fugitive from the Confederate draft, Burgess had splashed across the Ohio in 1861 to become a princely figure in academe. Almost single-handedly, he had authored Columbia's postwar greatness with his efforts to liberalize the legal curriculum. Economics, sociology, history, and philosophy became under his sponsorship a part of the study of law, or what he preferred to call "public law." As dean of the newly established School of Political Science and founder of the *Political Science Quarterly,* Burgess had also led out in the movement to find a rational basis for political behavior.[8] When he lectured, his students listened with rapt attention. "To hear these lectures," one of them reminisced, "was like setting out on a voyage for the discovery of new lands."[9] Reuben Clark must have agreed. He took more classes from Burgess than from anyone else, and he emerged from the experience to become a public lawyer himself.

In contrast, Reuben took only one class—criminal law—from Harlan Fiske Stone and acquired nothing but disdain for the business of defending criminals. But Stone too influenced the young man's development. Standing shyly before his class and twirling his glasses as he talked, Stone never glanced at a note and never opened a book, yet his lectures were so well knit that latecomers were hopelessly lost. Stone's enduring quality was kindness. His door was always open to his students, and he was never too busy to hear their troubles.[10] Later in life he wrote warm expressions of congratulation to Reuben for one advancement or another, and he must have done the same for countless others. In the early 1920s he was appointed to the Supreme Court, and in 1941 he became chief justice. To Reuben, however, Stone was best remembered as an embodiment of simple Christianity.

Dean Kirchwey was noted for his wit, as two students discovered one day upon attempting to leave class early. "Just a moment, gentlemen," he called out serenely, "I have a few more pearls to cast."[11] Beneath the merriment, though, Kirchwey was all business. He was a pioneer of the case-study method, a stalwart of the American Peace Society, and a founder of the American Society of International Law. Peace and international law occupied a good deal of his entire career, in fact, with the result that he catalyzed important developments in both fields. Indeed, it was under the broad influence of Kirchwey's tutelage that a generation of international lawyers came of age.[12]

If the influence of these professors was felt at some distance, that of both James Brown Scott and John Bassett Moore was direct and immediate. Taken together they were a curious pair. Both taught international law, both were known for extensive writings on the subject, and both were to become high-ranking officials in the United States Department of State. Yet the two could not have been more unalike. One was lean and the other corpulent. One was swarthy and the other fair. One was clean-shaven and bald in his youth; the other wore a broad mustache and beard and retained his silver-white hair lifelong.

31

More importantly, one of them typified the classical man of thought while the other typified the classical man of action. Scott represented thought. He had studied at the great European universities—Berlin, Paris, Heidelberg—and there had acquired the theoretical approach to the law.[13] Abstractions for him, as for Plato, seemed to be the ultimate realities—so much so that they often overshadowed mere facts. Though he worked in many capacities, none suited him quite as well as the editorship of the *American Journal of International Law,* a position he held for seventeen years. Here as nowhere else Scott could surround himself with ideas and move independently of some exceedingly difficult realities. Scott was the lean, swarthy, and bald one, with cleanly chiseled features and expressive dark eyes. His Latinesque air was appropriate; for Scott's training lay in the civil law, with its ancient Roman origins, and to Reuben he always symbolized its inner spirit. The civil law was the law of the grand design, the law of brilliantly crafted completeness. It was also, Reuben believed, the law of tyranny.

Moore represented action. While Scott was sitting at the feet of the German savants, Moore was clerking in the Department of State. Dealing with problems as he found them, he worked his way from clerk to assistant secretary before pursuing his academic career in earnest. By 1913 Moore was back at the State Department again, this time as counselor. Where Scott took to theories, ideas, and elaborations of thought, Moore preferred facts, results, and applications.[14] His contribution to international law was nothing so refined as the *Journal* but rather was a hefty compilation of actual cases, *A Digest of International Law.* As a practical diplomat Moore was widely respected, and his advice—which was always hardheaded and often hard-boiled—was sought by any number of presidents. Broad, affable, and forthright, Moore, like Scott, seemed to be historically symbolic, sounding a modern-day echo of King Henry II's tough and practical privy counselor-judges. Thus, where Scott evoked the civil law of Rome, Moore evoked the common law of England. Dressed in his dark suit and waistcoat with its expansive gold watch chain, he struck the very image of Anglo-Saxon conservatism.

Reuben Clark came to know both of these men well, and in the course of his career he came to draw upon each of their philosophical approaches. In the personal system by which Reuben would strive to equilibrate theory with practice, ideas with applications, and thought with action, Dr. Scott became one arm of the balance and Mr. Moore the other. To the extent that Reuben would involve himself with schemes of international justice, would preach diplomatic morality, would pursue serious attempts at abolishing war, and would seek to lift foreign policy above the level of brute conflict, he probably had James Brown Scott to thank as much as anyone. And to the extent that Reuben would distrust juridical solutions and turn his back on international institutions, would suspect human motives and fall back on self-interest and power politics, and would in all things respect the severe limitations of the possible, he owed much to the influence of John Bassett Moore. If there were two sides to Reuben Clark—the idealistic and the realistic—and if they occasionally got in one another's way, Reuben had Columbia law school to blame as much as the Clarks and the Woolleys.

v

Like any fledgling class of law students, Reuben's was told that they would learn to "think like lawyers." The phrase, a bit cryptic at

James Brown Scott and John Bassett Moore: The two sides of the law.

first, was one of the many riddles that law school promised to unfold. In time Reuben came to know what it meant. The law, he discovered, was not something mechanical that one could dismantle and observe like a clock; nor was it so much information that one could ingest and memorize. The law was a kind of mystery, an enigmatic process of growth and adaptation, an accretion of wisdom that was at once both trivial and beyond the wit of man. In the beginning, in medieval England, there was no law as such, but only the individual judgments of the king and his counselors written down and preserved as precedent. From decision to decision the common law thus developed and altered with changing circumstances—while at the same time remaining essentially conservative. (Even in the twentieth century, traces of the ancient writs and pleas survived like ancestral memories in legal discourse.) Because this blend of steadiness and flexibility was agreeable to the English jurists, they tried not to think of their work as complete or of the common law as a "corpus." They did not attempt to lay everything out, codify it, or render it wholly consistent; they were content to let the process remain as it had begun, with one decision resting upon another. Accordingly, the common law never became anyone's grand design. It was the work of no single Hammurabi or Justinian; and so, happily, it was the tool of none. It came to possess a life of its own, a life that coursed independently from—and sometimes in opposition to—the monarch on the throne, a life that was as strange and unique as the English spirit itself. One might easily conclude that it was the common law, as much as the nation's constitution, that made the people of England free. Reuben Clark so concluded, and the lesson was one he never forgot.[15]

In the meantime, as predicted, he did begin to think like a lawyer. He became intrigued by the concept of law as applied history. When given an assignment, he did far more than brief a case or two in the customary fashion; he hounded the errant problem back into its past, rooting through precedents, commentaries, ancillary discussions, and anything else he could find. Then, amid a chaos of notes, citations, and open books piled high, he observed step by step how the matter had come into being. It was a principle of life as well as a principle of law, he concluded, that one knew what to do next only when one knew what had gone before.

The law library became for Reuben a place of special enchantment. He learned to cherish its stately grace—the sixteen columns of polished serpentine, the dark-blue dome, the statues of ancient jurists gazing down from the balustrade upon those toiling to emulate them.[16] Cloistered away in the stacks, he felt as remote as a monk from the workaday world. He loved the smell and feel of the old calf-bound legal reporters, the quiet, dusty half-light, the sense of detachment that came from physical immersion in the past. "I acquired a familiarity with the Law Library that I thought was very good," Reuben later remembered fondly. "There were almost none of the reports I did not know and I could find my way about."[17]

This bibliomania was symptomatic of Reuben's inner drive. "I have learned," he later recalled, "that work, more work, and more work is the only way in which one may acquire knowledge."[18] Such a philosophy did not particularly endear him to classmates. Never had Reuben been thrown together with such bright, quick, and chillingly ambitious company. Part of his flight into "work and more work" may have been the simple fear of competition which gnawed at everyone. Flunking, of course, was the ultimate horror. The class of 1907 lost twenty-two of its one hundred and six members the year before graduation, and Reuben's class fared little better. But even more immediate than failure was the fear of public humiliation. The Socratic method of teaching was moving swiftly to the fore at Columbia, and the opportunities it presented for making a fool of oneself were abundant. Singling out one student, the professor would begin with an innocent, straightforward question on the case at hand and then steadily bore in, each interrogatory tightening the logical screws tighter:

Q. Was defendant liable?
A. Yes, sir.
Q. Why?
A. Because defendant was striking the door of the tavern and disturbing the peace.
Q. What if defendant had been striking at a poisonous snake over the door? Still liable?
A. Well, no, sir, not if he was striking at a snake.
Q. What if he only imagined the snake to be there?[19]

One professor, Charles Thaddeus Terry, was regarded as a "terrifying master" of the technique, grilling the same student every single class session for four months because of the liveliness of the response.[20] Reuben was happy enough to make it through Terry's contracts course in one piece; a classmate by the name of Franklin Roosevelt flunked it miserably.[21]

By degrees the fledgling lawyers did learn to think differently. They discarded the emotional response in favor of those more complex and subtle. They immersed themselves in the legal culture, absorbed its values and perceptions, and became familiar with its perspective of things. They grew accustomed to a universe of controlled, orderly change, and they came to agree with Mr. Justice Holmes that the pathway of change must be experience. On the other hand, they learned to live in an unfinished universe too, where problems rarely led to final solutions—where, indeed, solutions only created new problems. In the course of these developments they were tinged with a certain skepticism, to be sure, but they acquired little of that devil-may-care cynicism for which law schools would later be famous. If Reuben and his classmates were "scared to death" the first year and "worked to death" the second, they never quite made it to the third and final stage of the triad—"bored to death." The excitement of studying law in the era of progress kept their spirits alive.

vi

The communal life of the law school extended beyond the classroom. On autumn afternoons the students were regularly to be found kicking a football among the elms; and in the evenings they gathered convivially at Lion Cafe, Cafe LaFayette, or College Tavern—where Potters Field Club pursued its declared purpose of "ascertaining the presence of amoeba ... in New York beer."[22] However, for the beer, the pretzels, the famed sherry cobblers, and even the friendly conversation J. Reuben Clark had neither time nor appetite. He was the only Mormon in the law school, and at thirty-two he was one of the acknowledged "old men." Believing his place to be either behind the books or else at home with Luacine and the children, he stood apart—and perhaps aloof—from his fellows.

As it was, the Clark home life was none too idyllic. Luacine had been less than enthusiastic about the law school adventure in the first place. "I shrank from it under the circumstances," she reminisced.[23] But she was the faithful Mormon wife, and she had gone to New York without a whimper. Now she found herself confronting all of the old difficulties of Heber City and three or four new ones besides. She missed friends, she missed family, and she sorely missed the church. Her two young daughters were more than a handful. Her husband was scarcely ever home and even then scarcely ever available. Recreation was virtually nonexistent. Luacine kept a calendar and drew X's across it as the weeks passed by. She was like a prisoner awaiting parole.[24]

To make matters worse, Reuben had to work—or so he believed. Despite Joseph Nelson's regular support, Reuben took a job during the second year teaching English to foreign immigrants. He was assigned twenty or thirty pupils of several nationalities. He could not speak to them, nor they to him—nor, for that matter, any one of them to another. Throughout this pedagogical Babel a shadow moved back and forth across the frosted glass partition dividing an adjacent hallway—an eavesdropping supervisor, no doubt.[25] Trying though it was, Reuben was resolved to stick it out. But no sooner had he received the first month's check (to buy a coat for Luacine) than he was persuaded by events to abandon his efforts. He had been tapped for the *Columbia Law Review.*

vii

Law reviews were a new phenomenon in those days. Their distinctive feature was that students and students alone performed the entirety of the editorial work. Writing a note or comment on some landmark decision, the student editor was quite on his own. He could go to professors for lines of inquiry, perhaps; but when it came to putting everything together, he was of necessity his own legal scholar. And the scholarship was not insignificant. Lawyers, jurists, and the professors themselves came to read the law reviews as much for what students were saying in the case notes and commentaries as for the learned discussions in the lead articles. Law review staffers regularly went on to secure the plums of the job market, and with good cause.

The *Columbia Law Review* was barely an infant of three years in 1904, but under the influence of redheaded and amiable Francis M.

Burdick it was destined for the front ranks of legal periodicals. The editorial staff was selected on the basis of class performance during the freshman year. New staffers were given an assortment of menial tasks during the second year in order to allow each to show his mettle. The following autumn an election was held and editorial officers for the senior year were chosen. Reuben leaned into the work of the *Law Review* with accustomed energy. When handed his first case to evaluate for "Recent Decisions," he immediately determined that the opinion was interesting, significant, and deserving of better coverage in the more prestigious "Case Notes" department. With these conclusions he happily approached the editor, "Pop" Weathers. Weathers regarded the challenge to his own judgment frostily. He read the case over again, grumpily conceded that it was worth a "note," and saw to it that someone other than this uppity sophomore got the assignment of writing it up. But Reuben was undaunted, and by the end of the year he had distinguished himself. When the election was held in the fall of 1905, he was nominated for editor-in-chief along with a prominent classmate, Carr Morrow. Morrow won. As runner-up, Reuben became the "Recent Decisions" editor, and another classmate, Russell T. Mount, was made secretary. The three of them ran the *Law Review*.[26]

"Recent Decisions" proved to be, if not the most coveted position on the staff, at least the most rewarding. By their very definition, recent decisions were the cutting edge of the legal process, the advance guard of discovery. Reuben had to stay abreast of the entire appellate court system and one step ahead of a sizable staff. Each month thirty or forty recent decisions were reviewed. For each of them a short essay was submitted to the editor, along with scores of supporting citations. Already known as the glutton for labor, Reuben undertook to read, evaluate, and then reread—perhaps even rewrite—each of these essays. Then he fell upon the citations, looking up each one, reading it, assessing the decision, and weighing its relevance to the writer's argument. On top of his regular studies, such work was nothing short of gargantuan. At the same time it reflected that passion to know everything—all of the ins and outs, all of the details, all of the necessary history and background of the business at hand. It was Reuben's special way of finding truth.[27]

Then, too, the work of the *Law Review* afforded the Utah Mormon his first real opportunity to socialize with peers. He shared his reputation for aloofness with another staffer named Griffiths. Now the two of them were closeted daily with the rest of the staff, interminably talking over the cases under review. Unfortunately, this round-table discussion took place in a closed room, its air gummy and choking with tobacco smoke, while Clark and Griffiths, the two nonsmokers, exchanged doleful glances. But the talk was lively. There was a free-wheeling give-and-take of ideas, unencumbered by the presence of professors. One staffer, Allen Bradley, was free to work his own brand of deviltry, as Reuben conceived it, by asking the Mormon editor to rehearse the facts of any salacious divorce or adultery case. But achievement far outpaced deviltry and a touch of the latter was bracing.[28]

viii

His workhorse reputation, his stolid maturity, and his *Law Review* accomplishments inevitably brought Reuben to prominence in the law school. He became known, not just as "the Mormon" or "the old man," but as a truly remarkable student of the law. As Carr Morrow put it, he "more nearly than any other officer approached the ideal."[29] Reuben could not know it, of course, but this illumination was to effect the next turning point in his career. He was approached one day in the spring of 1905 by Professor Scott, who was looking for the most capable student he could find to work as a research assistant for the summer. Reuben took the job.[30] The work at hand was a casebook on quasi-contracts, those odd legal circumstances in which parties incur binding obligations without quite intending to do so. Reuben Clark himself entered into a sort of quasi-contract that summer—one that would tie him to James Brown Scott, for better or worse, throughout the next half decade and affect the course of his life ever afterward. The work itself was pedestrian enough. Scott outlined general ideas for the book and Reuben sifted through thousands of possible cases to come up with the right ones for illustration. In terms of the investment of toil and expertise, it was Reuben Clark's book far more than James Brown Scott's. Yet Scott chose to acknowledge Reuben's contribution only in a minor way. That too presaged the future.[31]

In January, James Brown Scott was made solicitor (legal officer) of the United States Department of State. Ten years earlier such an appointment would have been of no particular moment, but in the recent decade a great deal had transpired at the State Department. The United States had had a critical confrontation with Great Britain, had annexed the Hawaiian Islands, and had fought an imperial war with Spain. Then Secretary of State John Hay had sent out his famous Open Door notes on China, drawing America into the diplomatic duel of the century. Finally, Theodore Roosevelt had alighted resoundingly upon the world stage, securing the Canal Zone in Panama, embroiling the United States in the quarrels of the Powers, and building a navy of first-rank importance.[32] These seismic innovations, together with the redoubled interest in arbitration and legal settlement, had transformed the solicitor's office from a staid and folksy legal bureau—previously run by an Indiana judge—into something dramatically new. Indeed, the solicitor's chair promised to be both hotseat and throne.[33]

Throughout the spring, as Reuben finished up his law work and prepared for graduation, Scott was in Washington settling into his new responsibilities. The work on quasi-contracts had continued into the school year, and Reuben was still fussing with it—mostly in the evenings at home. Scott, busy in Washington, was falling behind on his end of the project, and Reuben had to gently chide him to keep up. Nevertheless, Scott was already blocking out another casebook and wondering out loud if Reuben might be in Washington during the summer to help out with it. Reuben said that he would ponder the matter.[34]

ix

At a swing of the baton, the Columbia Philharmonic Orchestra crashed into the famous prelude from *Lohengrin*. Reuben, who loved grand opera, drank the music in. It was a steaming summer day in June of 1906, and the graduates in their scholastic regalia were seated in the spacious gymnasium, most of them doubtless wishing to be outside. At ten o'clock they had lined up beside the Low Library and marched to the gymnasium with President Butler in the lead, his gray-and-red Oxford robes flashing in the sun. Now, with Wagner's heroic crescendo still trembling in the air, they rose, a row at a time, and began making their way toward the dais for the conferral of degrees. As with any commencement, it was a happy-solemn occasion, especially for those whose lives it punctuated. Butler spoke in his flat, matter-of-fact way of the rebirth of American society, urging the class of '06 to meet it sanely and tranquilly, following in the footsteps of Abraham Lincoln.[35] Luacine Clark—less eloquently, perhaps, but with far greater trenchancy—said: "As everything comes to an end, this three years did also."[36]

And so it had. Reuben had fulfilled his ambition and graduated with a Bachelor of Laws. But the rest of the old dream was beginning to fade. For a year now he had been a member of the New York Bar, and the prospect of a career in the East somehow loomed larger at the moment than the original idea of returning home.[37] Only a few days before the ceremony Reuben had decided to accept Scott's offer of summer employment.[38] Just what that decision might ultimately mean remained to be seen as the graduates filed out of the gymnasium and headed off toward their individual destinies, but the chances were increasingly slim that Reuben's own destiny lay in the West. Luacine, who had been counting the months and weeks and days until the family could return home to Salt Lake City, probably knew deep in her heart that it was not to be. However, she accepted it stoically. "Fate," she said simply, "willed otherwise."[39]

Chapter 2

ASSISTANT SOLICITOR

The old State Department building on Pennsylvania Avenue was not an especially attractive edifice. Its odd assortment of pediments and porticoes seemed to embody the late Victorian dictum that too much was not enough. Inside, however, the building possessed a mellow charm that old diplomats fondly recall. Corridors gleamed with white marble and burnished mahogany. Balustrades curved gracefully around majestic, sweeping staircases. The cool and airy rooms had about them a comfortable law-office atmosphere, complete with black leather rockers, polished brass cuspidors, and the aroma of Havana cigars.[1] Diplomacy at the turn of the century was still a gentleman's business, and Old State provided the perfect setting for it.

It was at this building, in the late summer of 1906, that J. Reuben Clark arrived to officially launch his professional career. He had been hired by Dr. James Brown Scott to be assistant solicitor of the Department of State. This appointment had grown out of the the casebook research which had brought Reuben to Washington after graduation. The details of that research—the cases, the notes, the endless parade of citations—had not at all been Scott's cup of tea. Reuben, by contrast, had managed them with ease. The lesson had not been lost on Scott when as solicitor he had suddenly been faced with even heavier work, stickier details, and more unremitting deadlines. He requested permission to add a second assistant to his staff and began sounding out Reuben Clark with the prospect of a job. Fresh from law school and under the onus of the Nelson debt, Reuben needed little time to ponder Scott's offer. A position of this stature, at an unbelievable $3,000 a year, exceeded his highest hopes.[2]

For her part, Luacine was more terrestrial about the appointment. Washington was and ever would be a compromise for her,

42

Old State: A mellowness that diplomats fondly recall.

and the oppressive heat of early September merely underscored that fact. The Clarks found a house on Calvert Street, three-storied and roomy but a little run-down, and rented a set of furnishings for it. Although it was not Luacine's dream house in Utah, it was solid and substantial. The tenuousness of these arrangements symbolized the ambiguity of the family's life in Washington.

ii

Within the space of Reuben Clark's lifetime, the State Department was to become a vast bureaucracy, employing uncounted functionaries and housed in sprawling facilities at Foggy Bottom. In the days of Secretary Elihu Root, however, life was much simpler and the department was a mere embryo of its later self. Washington in 1906 still had the serenity of a small town. Root himself was driven about the streets in a carriage, and diplomats were casually entertained in the homes of private citizens.[3] Such quaintness extended to the work of the department. Office hours were a leisurely nine to four. The hundred and fifty employees knew each other well, communicated informally, and felt more or less at ease in one another's company. Typewriters were still a novelty in the offices, and there were no telephones at the desks. When the secretary of state wished to communicate with the secretary of war a few doors down the hall, he usually did so by dictating a telegram, summoning a messenger, and waiting for the hand-delivered reply. The slow pace of life was measured by chimes from an ancient grandfather clock.[4]

Even so, times were beginning to change. As Theodore Roosevelt captured the attention of the world, life in the department quickened. Seventeen positions were added to the staff in 1906 and twice that number the following year. People began doubling up on offices and then moving out to rented quarters along Pennsylvania Avenue. The old family-like ties became formalized and rigid. Quitting time was nudged to 4:30.[5] Reuben Clark may not have felt the change in the air, but he himself was a part of it. His expert qualifications, like those of other recruits, stood in sharp contrast to those of immediate predecessors; and the work load escalated steadily. Far down the corridor of the south wing, the solicitor's office looked out from the third floor to the east, over the placid grounds of the White House. The rooms, although spacious and well proportioned, were unsuited to the recent expansion. Reuben Clark and William Dennis (the first assistant) were forced to share the office anterior to Scott's, while a sizable contingent of clerks and secretaries were jammed together elsewhere. In time they would have to leave the building altogether.

iii

Only gradually did Reuben learn how many and varied were the tasks before him. The solicitor was the chief legal officer of the department. (Technically he was an assistant attorney general in the Department of Justice who was specifically detailed to the State Department.) Wherever the activities of the State Department interfaced with the law, the solicitor or his deputies had to be on hand. Considering the hundreds of embassies, legations, and consulates maintained by the United States around the world and the overlay of municipal, constitutional, and international law that could bear on the diplomats' work, the solicitor's job was challenging indeed. When Reuben Clark would leave the State Department in 1933, there would be not two but twenty-three assistant solicitors, each one directing a corps of highly trained specialists.[6]

Basically the solicitor had four kinds of responsibility. He was first of all a legal advisor; any time a question of law was raised in the conduct of diplomacy, the solicitor was the first line of consultation. Since it might range from probate procedures in Morocco to the real estate laws of Poland, the question could be exceedingly esoteric; since it might involve the international debt of China or a bloody revolution in Chile, it could be exceedingly important. Either way, the advice had to be sound.[7]

Secondly, the solicitor was a legal apologist. Not only must he advise the policymakers, but he must on occasion convince others that the policymakers were "observing the law." This task could be rather delicate; for policymakers did not in fact always observe the law, just as they did not always act upon sound legal advice. Add to this the fact that policymakers often changed their minds and thus required, at different times, justification for opposing policies, and one can appreciate how the solicitor might find himself in tenuous situations.[8]

The solicitor's third responsibility was to be a policymaker himself. In the hierarchy of the department, he was roughly on a par with the three assistant secretaries of state and, like them, he could be called upon to draft diplomatic instructions, to pass upon the wisdom of a contemplated measure, or even to make high-level decisions on his own. This task by itself could give him sleepless nights.[9]

Still, it was the solicitor's fourth responsibility that was most important. Beyond the roles of advisor, apologist, and policymaker, he was first and foremost the department's advocate—its champion of justice. Just as any good attorney battles for his client's welfare, so too was the solicitor expected to take up the juridical sword, most often in the settlement of international lawsuits called *claims*. The plaintiff in these cases was usually a private individual or corporation and the defendant was usually a foreign government. The complaint could be anything from breach of contract to wrongful death. Since governments were not liable in the ordinary sense, claimholders were obliged to appeal to their own government for help. At this point, all manner of complications set in. Claimholders with political muscle began pressing their government to secure the speediest and most liberal of settlements, while the foreign government generally balked, stalled, or tried to duck the whole proceeding. Questions were raised as to how the parties should air their cases and as to the type of law that should be applied. The haggling could be interminable. And yet claims, if unresolved, could turn into disputes and disputes could—and did—turn into wars. In Reuben's own time, claims wound their tentacles through nearly every diplomatic crisis involving the United States—and with catastrophic results. On the win or loss of a big claim, moreover, a million dollars might change hands and the law of nations might progress or suffer accordingly. For these reasons alone, the office of solicitor became exceedingly important.[10]

So also did the personality of the solicitor. Given the demands of his job, he had to be something of a politician, something of a diplomat, and something of a barrister all rolled into one. He had to be both the lion and the fox, able to fight heroically for some crucial national interest while at the same moment assuring Mr. Citizen (and his congressman) that his claim, which may have little merit in law, was receiving fullest possible attention. The required combination of poise, resourcefulness, and motherwit was demanding.

And there was some doubt that James Brown Scott could altogether meet the demands. That he was a man of impressive qualifications was questioned by no one, but there was something missing from the total composition. His eyes, dark and intelligent, had the faintest touch of melancholy about them, as though in reflection of some remote sorrow. He and his wife Adele were childless, and it was whispered that she drove him relentlessly toward success as a compensation.[11] Whatever the explanation, Scott did occasionally seem a driven man. In sad, wistful glances, in sententious verbal expression, in woodenly artificial human relationships, he betrayed an inner turmoil of self-doubt. His personal flaw, whatever it was, was to cast a long shadow over the solicitor's office.

iv

Reuben's own misgivings began with his first assignment. In June of 1906 Congress asked Scott's office to study the interrelated legal problems of citizenship, expatriation, and the protection of citizens abroad. Interest in these matters was not academic. Only months before there had been a near showdown between Germany and France over the possession of Morocco. When word had it that American citizens were somehow involved, the United States participated in a saber-rattling conference on the Moroccan question. The "American citizens" later turned out to be native Moroccans who had acquired their citizenship fraudulently.[12] Accordingly, there was great pressure in the solicitor's office to accomplish the citizenship study with dispatch. Reuben found himself hard at work on it before he had had time to arrange his desk. He quickly determined that the project called for his own historical approach. With the zeal of an old law-review staffer, he unearthed some 472 cases dealing with judicial determinations of citizenship, and these he meticulously assembled according to the various facets of the question.[13] The results vindicated his effort. So clearly, in fact, did the lineaments of the citizenship problem emerge from this compendium that it remained only for Scott to recast Reuben's outline into the draft of a congressional bill.[14] Such was the story of the Citizenship Act of 1907. The way its architecture was managed by the solicitor's office became a source of considerable acclaim, but Reuben Clark soon learned that the acclaim—like the credit for their earlier casebook—was to go exclusively to James Brown Scott.[15]

v

But he was not discouraged. The citizenship study was a solid, if unacknowledged, success and opened the way to greater responsibility. Meanwhile, Reuben began to get his bearings about the solicitor's office. From the blur of new faces, first one and then another resolved itself into a distinct personality. William Cullen Dennis, the first assistant, was already an acquaintance from Columbia law school, where in Reuben's day he had been an adjunct professor.[16] Dennis had a smooth, narrow face, mild features, and a fair—almost delicate—complexion. On the bridge of his nose perched an under-sized pair of pince-nez glasses, the effect of which was to impart an expression of mild fright. Actually there was little of the timid about Dennis. The son of the distinguished Indiana Quaker family, he possessed a keen, straight mind and agreeable personality. He had taught law at Illinois, Stanford, and Columbia; and as secretary of the Lake Mohonk Conferences on International Arbitration he had become one of the pioneers of the judicial settlement movement.[17] Dennis and Clark, the Quaker and the Mormon, worked extremely well in tandem, and the mix of their capabilities proved more than fortuitous.

Below the assistant solicitors were the clerks. Most of them were trained in the law and several had earned degrees. They performed much of the leg- and shoulder-work that went into each undertaking. Some of them—like Clayton Carpenter, a New England Yankee with a Harvard twang, or Otis Cartwright, a reserved Kansan with a serious drinking problem—became personal friends of the new second assistant.[18] One of the clerks, Harry B. Armes, became Reuben's closest friend in the office. A Virginian with courtly bearing and Southern manners, Armes took to Reuben Clark with such fervor that he was soon nicknamed "The Shadow." Together the two of them swung off to work every morning (Armes lived next door to the Clarks) and returned side by side in the late afternoon. Eventually they even pushed their desks together so as to give Reuben handier access to Armes's resourcefulness.[19] In addition there were half a dozen temporary clerks and secretaries—and then there was old John Butler, who had been born a slave in Virginia and now spent his days sleeping peacefully in a corner while waiting to deliver messages.[20]

Dr. Scott showed little of the administrator's address and still less of his demand for order. As a result, patterns of work and lines of responsibility established themselves willy-nilly. Clark, not surprisingly, gravitated toward research and analysis. Dennis, on the other hand, was a natural administrator with a talent for mobilizing large numbers of people. Consequently, a division of labor evolved. Clark looked after a few big projects—those requiring continuous attention—while Dennis, supervising the clerks, kept track of everything else. As for Scott, he concentrated on his personal relations with the secretary of state. At the outset Scott had known Root only casually and had not quite known what the formidable secretary expected of him. Indeed, he had anxiously polished and repolished his first memorandum for Root and had then passed it to a member of Root's staff for evaluation before handing it to the secretary.[21] But relations gradually warmed, and soon Root, who had read the first memoranda with sharp attention, began passing on the solicitor's work as a matter of course. This was symbolic, Scott boasted, of the "confidential relations" he was coming to develop with the secretary.[22] And the secretary agreed. "I consider it one of the most fortunate events of my administration ... that I was able to secure him for Solicitor," he recalled. The two men went on to become lifelong friends.[23]

vi

In light of their rapport, it was only natural that Root should invite Scott to attend the Second Hague Conference in the summer of 1907. The conference was regarded as one of the great events of twentieth-century diplomacy, and Scott was properly honored to accompany the American delegation. This meant, of course, that for several months the solicitor's office would be entirely in the hands of Clark and Dennis; but Dr. Scott seemed confident that the two of them could manage. Indeed, they were already managing.

When the solicitor returned from the Hague in September, he was a person of consequence among international legal scholars. He had been to Mecca. Soon he was showered with invitations to speak and write of the doings of the Hague conference. For a man of his disposition, this all must have stood in glittering contrast to the routine of the State Department. Whatever the explanation, colleagues in the office began noticing changes in Scott. Never eagerly involved in his duties, he now seemed to have lost interest in them altogether. He wrote books, taught courses at local universities, delivered guest lectures, climbed aboard official junkets, looked after the affairs of the American Society of International Law, and dutifully continued to edit its journal. Collectively, these distractions added up to a full-time job—and they incidentally doubled his income.[24]

A second problem was simple vanity. Scott had always possessed an abundance of it, but now by degrees it seemed to possess him. He spoke without focus of returning to Europe, of attaching himself to some great international arbitration or other, of setting up a law partnership with Root. And he suddenly seemed eager for the downfall of rivals. Charles Henry Butler, from the office of the secretary, was an early casualty.[25] Francis Huntington Wilson, third assistant secretary of state, proved particularly vexatious to Scott, who schemed obsessively for his removal.[26] Even William Dennis was licked by the flame of this strange malice, and in time there were others.[27] It went without saying that Scott's presence soon created discomfort all around.

Finally Scott began to exploit people. Virtually all of his work had to be performed by someone else. Office stenographers composed his lectures; typists hammered out his private manuscripts; clerks edited entire issues of the *Journal*. As for the elegant memoranda which he carefully initialed and personally carried to the secretary of state—these were part and parcel the work of William C. Dennis and J. Reuben Clark. Scott even trained the assistant solicitors to counterfeit his "J.B.S." on the report covers during his frequent absences.[28]

For Clark and Dennis this situation became increasingly awkward. Neither of them had a disposition to expose the solicitor's misconduct, especially in view of his "confidential relations" with Secretary Root, yet both of them chafed under the knowledge that they were gaining no recognition for their own labors—indeed, that the secretary of state hardly knew of their existence. Each day, meanwhile, there were a hundred and fifty communications to read and answer; each week eight or nine memoranda had to be prepared; each year a million and more dollars in claims came up for adjudication.[29] And there were budgets to formulate, supplies to order, visitors to entertain, politicians to appease, and the problems of a dozen underpaid clerks and secretaries to solve. For the present the two assistants resolved to hold things together as best they could and keep their own counsel. But the strain began to wear on them.

Fortunately the staff closed ranks behind them. As Dr. Scott's behavior became increasingly difficult, an ever greater sense of office solidarity emerged. Acquaintances became friends. Friends became fast friends. Several of the clerks began addressing one another as "brother." And Scott was transformed in their conversation from an ineffectual administrator into an out-and-out villain. References to him varied from the contemptuously short "Doctor" to the pseudo-elegant "His High Serenity the Most Loquacious One."[30] A particular favorite was the undeciphered acronym of "MAH".[31] Jokes were endlessly told about his duplicity, his vanity, and his poetically high-flown speech. Clayton Carpenter wrote a farce about him, and the names of its characters were absorbed into the departmental argot as code names.[32] Cartwright, for example, became "Herk the Errand Boy." Any burst of laughter amid the office humdrum—usually triggered by Armes's dry cackle—was a good sign that "Doctor" had come in for more ridicule. The two assistants attempted to remain above all of this; but as outrage piled upon outrage they too joined the fun. When the sufferers, with mock solemnity, finally banded themselves into a formal brotherhood, both Clark and Dennis were charter members. The association was called the Society of the Mockahi and was replete with high signs and watchwords. Armes, Carpenter, Cartwright, and three recent arrivals—Stanley Udy, Ellery C. Stowell, and Hugh Gibson—were all enthusiastic members.[33] The oath of the Mockahi was to undo the tyranny of Scott and to support Dennis (code-named "In Loco Filii") in his efforts to keep the office running. But it was the seal of the Mockahi that most clearly embodied the society's program. Typed with studied care and affixed to all correspondence, this seal expressed the desire that all Mockahis found animating:

· · · · · · ·
· DARK HORSE ·
⟋ · · KICKING ·
· · · · · · ·

"Dark Horse" was the code name for J. Reuben Clark.[34]

vii

The defection of the solicitor could not have come about at a worse time. Every so often the State Department found itself in the middle of some exceedingly difficult contretemps, usually created by a foreign government, often fraught with domestic complications, and always, it seemed, turning delicately upon some point of law; and in the beginning of 1908 just such a predicament presented itself. It involved a question of extradition and, since Reuben had for some time been handling the department's extradition cases, he was stuck with it.[35]

The Pouren case began quietly enough on a frosty day in January. Secretary Root received a letter from Baron Rosen, the Russian ambassador, requesting the arrest and extradition of one Jan Pouren, said to be residing in New York. The charges in the complaint included arson, robbery, assault, and murder. Although extradition cases were not tried in the strict sense, the hearing upon the foreign request was often conducted like a trial; and this hearing, held in New York over the next eighteen months, proved to be an unusually spirited proceeding. For several weeks the United States commission of extradition heard evidence establishing Pouren's guilt. It was shown that he had broken into inns and farmhouses in Russia, stolen personal property, beaten or shot the owners in cold blood, and then applied the torch.[36] Pouren heard this testimony in grim silence. He was a small man with wispy blond hair and distinctively Slavic features. He seemed frail—almost fragile—sitting alone in the witness dock. He certainly did not look the brigand.[37]

When the defense had its turn, a completely different picture of Pouren's crimes emerged. He was not the Russian Jan Pouren at all, it was pointed out, but the Latvian Jānis Puren; and he was no more

The Mockahi, 1909: Brotherhood of common woe.
From left to right: W. Clayton Carpenter, Otis T. Cartwright, Ellery C. Stowell, Hugh Gibson, William C. Dennis, J. Reuben Clark, Harry B. Armes.

a criminal than Paul Revere. Indeed, he was a great patriot of the Latvian revolution.[38]

The Latvians, an ancient and proud people who had settled on the shores of the Baltic, had been oppressed for centuries. Their present overlord was the Czar of Russia, and he seemed determined that the oppression should continue. In a land of palatial hunting lodges and sumptuous estates, the native Latvian populace had little status, few rights, and no future. Then, in 1905, with the outbreak of revolution in St. Petersburg, the Latvians caught a brief glimpse of freedom. As with one will, they rose up against their Russian masters. It was a joyful, exhilarating time, blossoming with the hopes of a millennium; and the Latvians believed that they were on the threshold of victory. But ultimately things went against them. The Russian army descended in force, martial law was declared, and the revolution was crushed.[39]

A few of the revolutionaries—Puren among them—refused to lay down their arms. They proceeded instead to conduct their own guerrilla campaign, replete with robbery, arson, and murder—never being too careful, it seemed, about purely political objectives nor too choosy about targets. The details were ghastly, and in far-off New York the galleries of reporters heard them in horrified silence. Yet Puren was unapologetic. His band, adopting such picaresque names as "Forest Friars" and "Brothers of the Wood," became Latvian national heroes, he asserted, as fondly regarded as Francis Marion or Nathaniel Greene in America. Nevertheless, one by one they were hunted down and killed. Jānis Puren somehow escaped to America, the asylum of liberty, where he now stood on trial for his life.[40]

The Pouren story, despite its touches of the macabre, clearly appealed to the American popular imagination. There was enough of the underdog, the minuteman, and the Robin Hood about it to fetch almost everyone. A Pouren Defense Conference was formed and eventually claimed the support of over three hundred separate groups. Herbert Parsons, congressman from New York, served as a member of its executive committee, while such luminaries as the writer William English Walling and the feminist Alice Stone Blackwell energetically pled its cause. Contributions flooded into its New York office. There were mass meetings and public protests, too. One of them, held at Cooper's Union in September, threatened to become disorderly, with a surging throng of East Siders, themselves mainly political refugees from Russia, angrily demanding Puren's release. When Theodore Roosevelt sat down to consider the case in October, he was handed a "monster petition" in behalf of the accused with some eighty thousand signatures from forty-three states.[41]

On the other side, Russia seemed equally determined to get Puren back. This was a test case, it was said: if the Czar's government could win it, the asylum of some five thousand political refugees would be wiped out at a stroke. The issue turned upon the definition of *criminal acts*. *Political* acts, even violent revolutionary ones, were carefully excluded as a basis of extradition; but Puren's acts seemed to have amounted to pure mayhem, and no one outside of Latvia recognized the "Forest Friars" as a bona fide political organization. Questions of such moment were clearly not to be decided by the commissioner of extradition, but by the secretary of state himself. For his part, Root needed plenty of time to ponder the matter, and he needed someone to help sort it out. In terms of technical problems alone the case presented a juridical nightmare. Beyond the technical were the legal issues, and beyond these loomed the political and moral ones, chief among which was whether America was to remain a land of refuge for the oppressed.

So hot a potato was not easily handled. Elihu Root tossed it gingerly to his friend James Brown Scott, and he in turn dropped it squarely in the lap of Reuben Clark.[42] The latter, true to his style, immersed himself in the case completely, logging countless hours in the State Department law library and hauling home deskloads of papers in the evening. One piece at a time, he began to formulate replies to the secretary's questions. He made the decisions on granting bail (negative), extending continuances (affirmative), and cross-examining witnesses (negative or affirmative, depending on circumstances). He wrestled with such legal hydras as international double jeopardy. He outlined complex routes of appeal. By the time he had reconciled procedural due process with the requirements of the Russian-American extradition treaty, Reuben had pretty well run the gamut of constitutional guarantees.[43]

Root was apparently well satisfied with these results. Of course, as with the majority of Reuben's work, Dr. Scott passed it off as his own. Such deception was not without its dangers, however: more

54

than once, Secretary Root called Scott into his office for an impromptu conference on some obscure aspect of the case. The solicitor always had to plead a pressing urgency until he could get Reuben Clark to draw up a memo or brief him orally.[44] Reuben remained outwardly stoical about this exploitation, but a quiet resentment began to gnaw at him. He indeed felt like a dark horse in the solicitor's office or, more aptly, like a bureaucratic Cyrano de Bergerac. Unthinkingly, perhaps, he began recording Scott's misdeeds for future reference.

For the moment, the Pouren affair helped take Reuben's mind off departmental politics. He soon found himself grappling with the central issues of the case. As of February, 1909, he seemed to believe that Puren should be extradited. If Russia could make out a prima facie case against the Latvian, he explained apologetically to the defense counsel, "feelings of mere sympathy" would have to be subordinated to international obligations.[45] But by April he had changed his mind. "Political crime," he ventured, "may perhaps be considered as not in any real sense a crime, within the meaning of international agreements for extradition."[46] Reuben was personally appalled by Puren's atrocities, and he raised the question of "whether or not a political act may not be carried out with such barbarity or inhumanity as to deprive the offense of immunity under the treaty." Nevertheless, Reuben Clark eventually came down foursquare for the right of revolution abroad and the right of asylum at home.[47]

Elihu Root came down the same way, and on a gusty March day in 1909 Jānis Puren went free. Commissioner Samuel Hitchcock was instructed to rule that, since the Latvian peasants were still under martial law when Puren's offenses took place, the terms of the extradition treaty did not apply. "However revolting these acts may have been," he said, "we must still consider that they were committed while the country was in a revolutionary state, and were more or less justified."[48] A jubilant celebration at the Grand Central Palace was sponsored by the action groups that had seen the defense through. Puren himself was the guest of honor, but he left the speechmaking to others.

viii

One week later there was a celebration of a different sort in Washington. The occasion was the annual meeting of the American

Society of International Law. Elihu Root presided.[49] Among the papers delivered was one by a young and hitherto unknown functionary in the solicitor's office of the State Department: J. Reuben Clark, Jr. The presentation, titled "The Nature and Definition of Political Offense in International Extradition," was thoughtful, workmanlike, and, of course, timely. Moreover, it revealed the extent to which it had been J. Reuben Clark and not James Brown Scott who had worked through the complications of the Pouren case. And in the presentation, Reuben moved beyond the Pouren case proper and toward the larger issue of political crime. After identifying a number of issues, he went on to propose a new test by which the authentic political offense could be distinguished from common criminal behavior. The problem, he said, was that traditional tests had always depended on the recognized belligerency of the revolutionary group in question. The Social Democrats or Social Revolutionaries of Russia were recognized belligerents in the Revolution of 1905, and hence their partisans would have been immune from extradition. But such a tiny splinter as the "Forest Friars" went unnoticed. Reuben proposed to change the test. The "real question," he suggested, was whether or not there existed "a revolutionary movement in the general rather than in the technical meaning of that term." If so, and if the fugitive belonged to the movement generally, and if his crimes were carried out in the course of the political activities of his party, then he should be granted immunity.[50] This was obviously the linchpin by which the Pouren case had been decided.

At any rate, the ASIL address provided a certain amount of exposure to its author, as though Cyrano were being recognized in spite of himself. Dr. Scott, a little grudgingly perhaps but with ostensible heartiness, complimented Reuben on the quality of his presentation. After all, the solicitor may have told himself, an official is no better than the subordinates who stand behind him.

Chapter 3

FRIENDSHIP AND ALLIANCE

One result of the Pouren case was that it opened the world of diplomacy to Reuben Clark. Where before he had seen only law and legal problems, now he came to see that beyond the legal problems stretched the more difficult and ambiguous problems of policy-making. More and more Reuben began to view himself not simply as a researcher in the office of the solicitor, but as a resource in the broader economy of the State Department. Inevitably the quality of his work and the depth of his involvement brought him down the stairs of Old State to the second floor, where the life of the department pulsed more quickly and where it could be observed in greater detail.

And here as well Reuben met new people. Among the first of those he encountered were the bureau chiefs like Wilbur Carr and Sidney Smith. Carr, chief of the consular bureau, was sunny and unassuming, the departmental nice guy. With his bald head and walrus mustache he might have passed for a Keystone Cop, but beneath the amiable exterior Carr was a businesslike and resourceful public servant.[1] Sid Smith, chief of the diplomatic bureau, was less versatile than Carr but no less talented. With his feet on the desk and his mouth crammed with chewing tobacco, he could lift from a wire basket one prolix memorandum after another and, in a casual, rasping voice, render each into faultless English prose. Virtually every diplomatic dispatch from department headquarters came about in this way, taken down by a stenographer who sat well away from the spitoon.[2]

Then there were the arbitrators, like Chandler Anderson and Robert Lansing. Designated as "special counsel," these two were essentially private lawyers, high powered and high priced, who were in and out of department affairs on demand. Between them they had participated in every negotiated settlement involving the United States, from the Bering Sea Claims Commission to the Venezuelan asphalt dispute.³ At present they were sharpening their tools for the Atlantic fisheries controversy, soon to be settled at the Hague. Both reared in the Ivy League, both tinctured with Brahmin reserve, both fastidious in manners and dress, they differed only as to politics. Anderson, the Republican, parted his hair in the middle and looked out at the world through shrewd gray eyes. Lansing, the Democrat, was taller, more angular, and more consciously dignified. When his hair turned white in late middle age, he became a truly impressive figure.

Reuben also met the assistant secretaries, like Robert Bacon and Alvey Adee. Bacon, the first assistant, was a man of consummate style. Suave, gracious, and warm-handed, he numbered among his personal friends J. P. Morgan and Theodore Roosevelt. So utterly captivating was Bacon, in fact, that Secretary Root arranged to resign from office a month early so that "Bob" could have the honor of being secretary of state. Yet the qualities that spared Bacon from controversy seemed to deprive him of accomplishment as well; he lacked intellectual interests generally and diplomatic imagination altogether. He was what the reformers had in mind when they spoke of political appointments.⁴ Alvey Adee, on the other hand, was the epitome of conscientiousness. Small, stooped, and almost totally deaf, the second assistant secretary was both the department's steadiest hand and its most colorful eccentric. The steadiness was evident in his long years of service, his encyclopedic store of knowledge, and his passionate attention to detail. But the eccentricity was equally well marked. Adee annually toured Europe on a bicycle, carried a pocketful of silver spoons custom-contoured to his mouth, and purchased his garments three dozen at a time, numbering them sequentially in order to detect loss by theft. Where Bacon was an instant and overwhelming social success, Adee, trundling out his spoons, left something to be desired.⁵

Above the assistants was the secretary himself, Elihu Root, and his alter ego in foreign relations, Theodore Roosevelt. The two of them worked as a team. During the San Francisco schoolboard crisis, when Roosevelt fought to head off a confrontation with Japan, Root accompanied him to the bargaining table, where he sat on the president's left with a pencil in his hand. Whenever Roosevelt began to bluster and threaten, Root's pencil would click sharply on the edge of the table and the excitement would abate.[6] That symbolized their relationship. Where one was strenuous, the other was calm. Where one was emotional, the other was rational. Where one spoke of power and purpose, the other spoke of law and constraint.[7] "He fought me every inch of the way," said the president of an encounter with his secretary of state, "and, together, we got somewhere."[8]

Elihu Root had been a corporation lawyer in New York and in his years at the bar had represented, among others, Boss Tweed. He was known among friends for his warmheartedness and sense of humor. Once, when accommodations were tight for foreign dignitaries at a conference, a young functionary approached him, greatly perturbed. "Why, Mr. Secretary, the hotel is so small that I have got to put the Italian Ambassadress in the same room with the Italian Ambassador!"

"Of course you can't do that," replied Root with a look of horror. "Why not put her in the room with the French Ambassador?"[9]

But among lesser functionaries the secretary was regarded as unfeeling, unsmiling, and aloof—"the mind packed in ice."[10] His countenance nourished the myth: the lean, haggard face, sad gray eyes, and habitually dolorous expression were reminiscent of El Greco. Root joked about suffering from "too much Anno Domini," and indeed, bouts of exhaustion drove him to Muldoon's Sanitarium more than once.[11] Still, he attended to his duties with energy and meticulousness, seeming to be everywhere, working on everything, and somehow holding it all together. He arrived at the office early, stayed late, took work home, and slaved through the weekends to keep the State Department running. An aide observed that the secretary's idea of heaven was to be surrounded by angelic stenographers and attend to the world's business himself.[12]

ii

In time Reuben became acquainted with each of these people. Carr became a good friend; so did Adee, although he had the disconcerting habit of removing his ear trumpet in the middle of a conversation when he had heard enough. Bacon was cordial in his patrician way. Even Anderson and Lansing, both coolly austere, acknowledged Reuben as one of their own, if not much more than a journeyman. Only Root, with his "aura of awfulness," was rarely to be approached by the likes of an assistant solicitor, and he seemed scarcely aware that such creatures existed.[13] Reuben passed him in the corridors with a faint chill.

Yet it was in the office adjacent to the secretary's that Reuben Clark made the warmest, strongest, and most consequential friendship of his early career. There he met Francis M. Huntington Wilson, third assistant secretary of state.* Huntington Wilson, by five years Reuben's junior, was well featured, well dressed, and well-to-do. He had dark and slightly wavy hair, heavy eyebrows, and eyes that glittered sardonically. It is unclear how Clark and Huntington Wilson first became acquainted, but the former initially found the latter more than a little arrogant.[14] But, then, everyone found Huntington Wilson arrogant.

One did not need to seek far to find the reason. Huntington Wilson was tactless, stiff, egotistical, touchy, and high-strung. In society he bridled haughtily at the least imagined insult. In administration he alienated those he meant to inspire. In bargaining he could be mean, ungenerous, and hard as flint. His own definition of diplomacy—"knowing without showing, ascertaining without inquiring, hating with the appearance of loving"—seemed to say it all.[15] For a diplomat Huntington Wilson was remarkably undiplomatic.

But this was only one side of the man. If Huntington Wilson was pompous and haughty, he was also cultivated and articulate; if nearsighted as to human relations, he possessed other qualities of long-range vision. He was dedicated to excellence in himself and others, and his quarterdeck bluntness may have expressed only that. When he saw a wrong, or thought he did, there was neither shilly-shallying nor the consideration of fragile distinctions—he met it

---

*Huntington Wilson's name is a source of endless confusion. He was born Francis Mairs Huntington Wilson. "Huntington" was a family name, and its attachment to "Wilson" formed a sort of double surname. However, he never went by the name "Francis"; friends called him "Huntington," using it as a first name. Later in life he changed his name to Francis Mairs Huntington-Wilson, the double surname being made official with a hyphen. Historians have referred to him variously as "Wilson" or "Huntington-Wilson." I shall use the double surname—Huntington Wilson—but without the hyphen, as it was originally intended. But I shall refer to his wife as she referred to herself: Mrs. Wilson.

openly and head-on. Francis Huntington Wilson was no doubt erratic, but he was fired with his own kind of brilliance.[16]

His most notable trait was dissatisfaction: Huntington Wilson was dissatisfied with everything. He came from a wealthy Chicago family and had an independent income. He had traveled widely, learned several languages, gone to Yale, and grown bored. His actions became those of a man in search of himself. He first took to wearing fancy waistcoats and puff-ties with scarf pins; then he progressed to striped trousers, spats, brilliant yellow gloves, brown derbies worn at a rakish angle, and even a walking stick. One evening he appeared at a ball sporting a monocle. Later in life he changed his name.[17]

Nor did Huntington Wilson find repose in the foreign service. In the legation in Tokyo, his first assignment, he encountered disorder and inefficiency at every turn and applied his restless mind to the challenge of repairing it. Tokyo, however, offered no more than a taste of what Huntington Wilson found awaiting him in Washington. Here the situation verged on chaos. Memoranda circulated aimlessly about the department, picking up colored tabs and miscellaneous annotations but not much velocity or purpose. Clerks handled correspondence alphabetically by countries, so that China and Cuba would be given to the "C" group, while Korea would be given to the "K." Records were kept or lost according to the merest vagaries of circumstance; Huntington Wilson once had to rummage through the cellar of John Hay's house to find notes of important conversations. Such "antiquated organization," said he, "remained pitifully inadequate for the conduct of foreign relations."[18] Before long Huntington Wilson had embarked on nothing less than a plan to reorganize the department.

But obstacles to reform were many and formidable. The State Department fairly teemed with the sons of the wealthy and the well-connected. Huntington Wilson himself had come to Washington in the train of his dazzling wife and influential father, who between them had had to charm two senators, two presidents, and an icily forbidding secretary of state in order to secure his appointment.[19] The political coming and going of the diplomats had a touch of the comic about it, but there was nothing humorous about the apathy and incompetence of some appointees. Drinking, loafing, and other disgraceful behavior became all too characteristic of American diplomacy abroad.[20] In one notorious example, a man appointed to relieve an American consul purportedly found his predecessor tied to a chair in the consulate. "He's been crazy for three years," explained a clerk.[21]

It was little wonder, then, that things did not run smoothly at the State Department. That they ran at all was evidently due to the personal energy of Secretary Root. And yet here, asserted the third assistant, lay the greatest weakness of all. By refusing to delegate authority, by burdening himself with trivialities, and by attempting to tackle every problem personally, Root had succeeded only in creating a diplomacy after his own image. The result, concluded Huntington Wilson, was empty legalism, noble sentiments, and "an appalling lack of realism" in American foreign policy.[22]

iii

All of this was unfolded for Reuben Clark in the course of long evenings of conversation. As his initial aversion to Huntington Wilson softened, Reuben discovered that the two of them had important things in common. Each in his way felt oppressed. Each bridled at the domination of a superior. And each labored against the mindlessness of a bureaucratic system. Strengthened by this resonance, the friendship took hold and flourished. By the end of 1907, each man counted himself fortunate at having found a kindred spirit.[23]

It was probably not from Reuben Clark, however, that Huntington Wilson learned of the situation in the solicitor's office. The knowledge most likely came to him through Hugh Gibson, a clerk in the State Department and, incidentally, its resident madcap. Gibson's frail body, fine features, and limpid, dark eyes suggested a contemplative nature, but the sedate appearance only made his volcanic bursts of whimsy the more startling.[24] Once, during a lull, he stole into Secretary Root's office, pushed the bell buttons summoning all bureau chiefs, and then, according to witnesses, "[flew] down the corridor ... like an Apache on the war trail."[25] Gibson became a member of the Mockahi Society. He also became Huntington Wilson's private secretary. Undoubtedly it was this "wild Indian," as Joseph Grew called him, who spilled the beans.

F. M. Huntington Wilson: Fired with his own kind of brilliance.

By whatever means, the beans were spilled. Huntington Wilson became aware, as he said, that the smiling visage of the solicitor on his way to Root's office with another memorandum was not an honest representation of reality. Had it been any other assistant secretary who found out—an Adee or a Bacon—doubtless nothing would have come of the matter. But Huntington Wilson was neither discreet nor timid: he decided to take the situation in hand. Without warning, he collared Clark and Dennis one day and marched them into the secretary's office. There, while Elihu Root listened sternly and the two assistant solicitors (as one must imagine) fidgeted nervously, Huntington Wilson set forth the whole story of the absentee solicitor. "It was no concern of mine," he recorded, "if Dr. James Brown Scott should stand in high favor; but I did feel that the men under him who were doing such brilliant work should also receive some recognition."[26]

One could project any number of scenarios for the ensuing twenty-four hours. One could visualize an explosion of wrath, a general housecleaning, a Scott resignation. But in point of fact, nothing happened at all. Huntington Wilson, of course, gained Scott's undying hatred; but aside from that there was no result whatever. The solicitor continued to pursue his private interests and the assistants continued to do the work.

There was an explanation for this anticlimax. It seemed that Huntington Wilson, through just such gestures as this, had managed to become the State Department's *bête noir,* isolated and without influence. Arriving as he had with impeccable political credentials and even field experience, the Chicagoan had taken Root and the others completely by surprise. When they eventually recovered, they did everything possible to contain the man. Huntington Wilson was given few responsibilities. He was resolutely ignored. Of his many specific—and sound—proposals for improving departmental procedures, only a few were acted upon, and those only grudgingly. Root went so far as to encourage the abrasive third assistant to take a leave of absence to study law—anything at all to minimize his presence.[27]

So the *beau geste* in behalf of the two assistant solicitors remained empty and futile. It gave J. Reuben Clark a good deal to think about. If the once-awesome Elihu Root could be so blind in this, was he not likely to be blind in other matters as well? Moreover, the causes for which Root stood—peace, arbitration, international law—happened also to be the causes of James Brown Scott. Indeed, there was much to ponder.

iv

Forces other than personal contact were also beginning to pull Reuben away from the narrow concerns of the solicitor's office. Early in his career he became involved in Latin American diplomacy, something very much in vogue under Root. Latin America represented the wave of the future. There as nowhere else were to be found markets for the expanding commerce of the United States, and with the construction of the Panama Canal the Latin American crossroad assumed an unheard-of strategic importance.[28] Yet until the advent of Elihu Root there had been little appreciation of these facts. Roosevelt and Hay had smugly alluded to "dagoes" in their private conversation and had treated Latin American problems as minor irritations. Of the 3,479 vessels that had put into Rio de Janeiro in 1905, only seven had been under the flag of the United States and two of those were in distress.[29] Almost singlehandedly, Root turned the situation around. He worked to establish friendships among Latin American diplomats and entertained them lavishly. He made a tour of Latin America and poured forth *Yanqui* charm. He even persuaded his friend Andrew Carnegie to erect a new Pan American Union Building, beautifully sculptured in the style of the Spanish Renaissance, and supervised the dedication personally. When Root left office in 1909, there was a new application of the term *simpático*.[30]

Not all of the obstacles to diplomatic progress were in Washington, though; some lay south of the border. There was the proverbial instability of the Latin republics, for example, and their not-wholly-unreasonable mistrust of American motives. Both of these factors came into play in the famous Alsop claim—one of the worst and most abiding obstructions to inter-American understanding. The controversy had begun decades earlier in the Atacama Desert, a six-hundred-mile stretch of wasteland on the western coast of South America. The Atacama contained rich deposits of guano (bird droppings highly prized as fertilizer) and nitrates. This mineralogical treasure-trove nominally belonged to Bolivia; but, owing to uncertainties of the old colonial boundaries, no one knew for certain whether Bolivia or Peru had the better claim—and Chile, which was stronger than either of them, looked on with covetous eyes. The bickering was interminable.[31]

By the 1870s the dispute was being watched with special interest by John Wheelwright, a one-time partner and now liquidator of Alsop and Company. This American investment firm had been active in the Atacama Desert and had expired holding a million dollars' worth of Bolivian notes. In 1876 Wheelwright reached an agreement with the Bolivian government by which the proceeds of a customhouse and two silver mines were to be earmaked for repayment of the debt. But the old boundary squabble undid everything. In

February of 1879 Chile pounced on the Atacama and decisively settled the argument. When the War of the Pacific was over the entire
Atacama—including the Arica customhouse and the two silver
mines—was Chilean.[32]

Still hoping to regain his fortune, Wheelwright transferred his
claim from Bolivia to Chile on grounds that the wherewithal, and
hence the obligation, to repay the Alsop debt was now in Chilean
hands. The Chileans did not agree. That was the basis of the struggle
which was to roll thirty years into the future and wind up on Reuben Clark's desk.

Contests of this description were much like an international
game—with very high stakes. One side usually had a significantly
stronger case than the other. This side, whichever it happened to be,
always played so as to force the issue to a decision. The weak side, by
contrast, always played so as to elude a decision indefinitely. Accordingly, the challenge of the contest was not so much that of winning
a court battle as it was that of bringing a court battle into existence—or, on the other side, of quashing it. It was for just such a
contest that John Wheelwright and the Republic of Chile now
squared off.

The first recourse of the claimant was to the offending government itself. Wheelwright patiently exhausted that recourse. For
more than six years he lived in the Atacama while his representative
in Santiago bombarded the Chilean government with petitions. They
initiated more than two hundred lawsuits in the Chilean courts, all
of them unavailing. So Wheelwright turned to the U.S. State Department, his next recourse. The Chilean response to this move was
to contend that the Alsop dispute was a private affair—which indeed
it was—and thus that the American State Department had no right
to meddle with it. This tactic sufficed to prolong the struggle by
another full decade, while one claims commission after another
poked at the case uncertainly.[33]

Meanwhile, in May of 1895, a peace treaty was concluded between Chile and Bolivia containing an agreement, in principle, to
pay the debt. That left only the small matter of how much Chile
would pay—a question good for ten more years of wrangling.
Wheelwright's original agreement had recognized a debt of
$805,775, with 5 percent interest running from the date of the con-

tract (1876). As of 1903, when the subject of payment was broached again, the interest was accruing logarithmically; it had topped the three-million mark and was mounting faster than ever. So in December of that year, Chile made an offer to settle the entire question for $343,542, or about ten cents on the dollar. Secretary Hay rejected it. The Chileans regrouped and submitted a new offer—$190,647—and of course Hay rejected that too, indignantly. In June of 1907 the Chileans made their "final offer"—$200,000. "If the claimants are unwilling to accept it in full satisfaction," the diplomats said curtly, "they are invited to turn for payment to Bolivia."[34]

Interest on the principal and frustration at the bargaining table were not the only things piling up around the Alsop claim. So were the complications. John Wheelwright had died by this time, and the receivership had broken up into a maze of heirs, creditors, and other claimants, all of them clamoring for a share of the swelling prize. Yet even without this constant badgering, the Alsop case was an increasing embarrassment to the State Department. There could never be easy communication between North and South America as long as such an impediment persisted. It hung over Root's commercial dream like a death's-head.

By 1907 President Roosevelt had had enough. In August he went in person to the State Department and asked for a complete report on the progress of the claim.[35] As a result of this visit, the Alsop case, hex and all, was handed over to Reuben Clark.

The choice of Reuben could hardly have been more fortunate. What the case needed more than anything else was calm, thorough legal research. The pledges, the promises, the conditions, and the conventions were a confusing jumble, half-remembered and half-forgotten; only by piecing them back together could any progress be made. And this was what the assistant solicitor set about to do. With a patience as long as the Alsop history, he began picking determinedly at the mass of information before him. He worked his way through drawer after drawer of State Department files, sifting, ordering, and assimilating the materials. He then tackled the even larger accumulation of documents offered by the claimants themselves. Often working late into the evenings, he digested and organized the yellowing papers into a coherent picture of the Alsop controversy. Before long a report was ready for the secretary of state.[36]

Two consequences followed from this work. First, the Alsop claim, more or less dormant for years, once again began to show signs of life. On the strength of Reuben's evidence, in fact, Root decided to take over the claim on the government's behalf, converting it from a private suit into a public one.[37] Chile could no longer contend that the Alsop claim was nobody's business but its own.

Secondly, the American hand was visibly strengthened. The United States had always based its case on historical documents; but now, owing to the precision and completeness of Reuben's research, the State Department could venture a little further. It could insist that Chile submit documentation equal to its own to show why the claim should *not* be paid. The first such demand was made on August 29, 1908. When no reply was forthcoming, the request was repeated on November 26 and again on January 24, 1909. This new tactic, together with Chile's increasingly awkward silence, would prove to be decisive.[38]

So delighted was Secretary Root by the sudden progress that he gave Reuben even more responsibility in the case. Soon the assistant solicitor found himself dealing directly with the Chileans.[39] This was a lively development—but it came at its price, as Reuben soon discovered. It happened that a certain Madame Teresa de Prévost, the comely and high-spirited daughter-in-law of one of the original Alsop partners, had come to Washington from her native Peru in order to facilitate the settlement of the claim. Little precise information on the woman remains, but as Reuben later recalled, "So far as I know she never remained on good terms for any length of time with anybody, including her husband."[40] At the State Department she had made a special nuisance of herself, picking on Judge Walter Penfield who, as Scott's predecessor, had had responsibility for the case. And Madame de Prévost was apparently given to more than verbal modes of persuasion, for it was later whispered that she had "endeavored to compromise" Judge Penfield and that he had resolved to avoid the woman at all costs.[41]

The Peruvian seductress was nothing if not persistent; and soon after Reuben took over the Alsop negotiations, he too began receiving visits from her. "Being young—in experience—" he recalled, "I was rather frank with her in telling her about the negotiations."

I [soon] found that Mrs. Prevost was going to the Chilean Minister, one [Anibal] Cruz, and telling him all about what the next move was. As soon as I found this out, I of course became more reticent with her about our plans. She then began suspicioning that because I did not talk with her, I must be talking with Cruz.[42]

Madame de Prévost suggested more than once that Reuben come to her apartment to see some papers pertaining to the case. Even a Utah farm boy could see through that ruse, however, and Reuben made sure that discussions never proceeded beyond his office.[43] For the time being, he succeeded in avoiding Madame de Prévost's wiles; but it was not long before she would haunt him again.

By the spring of 1909, the Alsop negotiations had swung decidedly in favor of the United States. Following Reuben's advice, the department continued to press for evidence showing why the claim should be reduced, and on April 15 the Chilean minister in Washington privately admitted that no such evidence existed.[44] Indeed, Chile was running out of cards. Chilean diplomats found themselves looking at their last trump when a new administration took office in Washington in March of 1909, and the new secretary of state, Philander C. Knox, declaring himself unwilling to continue the game, presented Santiago with an ultimatum: either the claim must be settled in a reasonable amount (one million dollars was suggested) or it must be submitted to arbitration.[45] To show he meant business, Knox withdrew the American minister from Santiago and ordered that Reuben's case be telegraphed in its entirety to key Latin American legations.[46] The game was over. On December 1, 1909, the United States and Chile formally submitted the Alsop controversy to arbitration by Edward VII, King of England.

v

The election of William Howard Taft and the replacement at the State Department of Elihu Root by Philander Knox brought other matters to a head as well. Just as any new administration comes with its surprises, so too did this one—surprises and heavy ironies. The fortunes of Francis Huntington Wilson, for example, took a strange turn indeed. With the passage of time Root had come to admire his prickly third assistant less and less, and the business with the two assistant solicitors had very nearly been the last straw.

At the urging of his friend Scott, Secretary Root had decided to give Huntington Wilson's job to William Phillips, a Back Bay Bostonian who looked as though he had just stepped out of a clothing advertisement and whose charm and grace made a sorry contrast of Huntington Wilson's awkwardness.[47] So the hapless third assistant began putting his affairs in order. He was to be "promoted" to the position of minister to Argentina, where he could hardly do less damage.[48]

Suddenly, in the midst of the farewell dinners, Huntington Wilson was summoned for discussions with Knox, the new secretary designate. Knox had come upon the draft of a plan, he said, for reorganizing the State Department and was seeking all available advice on it. Huntington Wilson of course lit up like an aircraft beacon and acknowledged the reorganization scheme as his own. He knowledgeably flipped through the tables and charts, done in his own handwriting, and expounded at length on the virtues of geographical specialization, rotation of personnel, and the centralization of responsibility in the office of an "undersecretary." This meeting led to a second, and that to a third. "Then," Huntington Wilson recalled, "came the fateful Sunday at the Shoreham."

> The telephone rang and it was Senator Knox asking me to come over to his house. I supposed he had one more question to ask about my plan for reorganizing the Department. Eagerly I climbed the two long flights of stairs to the little library and sanctum where he worked. There he greeted me and introduced Judge Day, his old friend, and the three of us sat and conversed casually for a while. Then, to my utter amazement, Knox said: "Would you be willing to give up being Minister to the Argentine Republic and to stay in the Department as my second in command?"[49]

This odd quirk of fate turned the State Department upside down. Suddenly, all of the insiders were outsiders, and all of the outsiders were in. A few people resigned in dismay. One or two others were urged into early retirement. But the real upheaval occurred in the office of the solicitor. James Brown Scott, up to now the secretary's right-hand man, precipitately found himself seated far to the left. And just as precipitately, J. Reuben Clark found himself among the ruling elite of the State Department.

A new day was dawning.

Chapter 4

DARK HORSE KICKING

William Howard Taft did not really want to be president. He was a lawyer by training and by nature, and his judicial mind rebelled at the prospect of exerting bold leadership. To the joys (and hazards) of political combat, Taft preferred quiet chats with old cronies, an occasional game of bridge, or a warm evening spent sitting on the porch of the White House listening to the "music machine."[1] Accordingly, Taft saw the world through different eyes than had Roosevelt. Where Roosevelt had thought in terms of power, Taft thought in terms of wealth, and he consequently viewed foreign policy in the context of American business needs. Like many who had lived through the depression of the 1890s, he worried about finding markets for U.S. manufactured goods; and his interest quickly riveted on two overlooked areas of the commerical world: Latin America and the Far East.[2]

With remarkable fidelity, these attributes of Taft the president were reflected in the man he chose to be secretary of state, Philander Chase Knox. Knox too was a lawyer. Knox too harbored no great political ambition or talent. And Knox too regarded diplomacy as a useful tool of domestic purpose. Indeed, the president and the secretary agreed on virtually all fundamental questions and trusted one another implicitly.[3] One result was that Knox was left to run his department pretty much as he saw fit. Another was that Taft and Knox, with a minimum of discussion, were able to work out a new and, as they believed, promising foreign policy for the United States.

If the Columbia professors were the first influence in Reuben Clark's professional life, and if Francis Huntington Wilson was the second, Philander Knox was to become the third and most significant. Standing but five feet five inches tall and known variously as "Little Phil" or "the sawed-off cherub," Knox managed, with his

71

fashionable tailoring and his huge Partaga Invincible cigars, to look intimidatingly important. He had the face, some said, of an Italian churchman; his eyes, like Queen Victoria's, closed by the lower as well as the upper eyelid. He was a Pennsylvanian, a corporation lawyer, and a self-made man. Lacking social ambitions, he was also an intensely private person on whom the good life seemed to have first claim. He fished expertly, played golf, matched the professionals at poker, and kept a beautiful pair of trotters. Vacationing seemed a way of life for him, whether to his farm at Valley Forge, up to Maine fishing, down to Cape May, or yearly to Palm Beach, where he kept a room at the Royal Poinciana. One day, when he and the president were playing golf with China expert John Hays Hammond, the latter asked Knox to accompany him to the Far East and study the Chinese situation firsthand. Knox teed off, and while watching the ball in flight replied: "Hammond, I'm just learning this game, and I'm not going to let anything so unimportant as China interfere."[4]

Yet Knox was not a common playboy. He is better described as a holdover from the nineteenth century, when high government officials were expected to be leisured gentlemen. Details of administration bored him acutely, but he maintained an active interest in policy matters.[5] The greatest service he could do the State Department, Knox once told an aide, was never to darken its doors—and in truth he did not darken them often. He seldom arrived before ten-thirty in the morning; and except for Thursdays, his day of appointments, he seldom remained after lunch. Yet Knox habitually arose at five o'clock in the morning, shut himself away in his private study, and, with coffee in hand, thought long and hard about American foreign policy.[6]

The Knox style of administration came to depend upon Huntington Wilson, who in day-to-day matters wielded the authority of the department.[7] Still, the secretary audited his assistant regularly. The occasion might be a brisk morning trot through Rock Creek Park or a leisurely lunch at the Shoreham. At some point, Huntington Wilson drew from his pocket a list of items to clear, and in the course of the conversation these would be covered. Occasionally the problem would be a difficult one, and Knox would have to ponder it at length. He once returned from a weekend of golf to hand the first assistant a crumpled envelope on which he had scrawled three sentences—but these scrawls supplied the combination to a diplomatic puzzle of weeks' standing.[8]

Huntington Wilson, in his turn, reserved the right to do things his own way. He immediately began to shuffle the department around and to implement his reorganization plan. Ransford Miller was brought in from Tokyo to take over the division of Far Eastern affairs; and another battle-hardened veteran, Thomas C. Dawson, arrived from Colombia to set up a division of Latin American affairs. Other geographical divisions followed, along with a redistribution of basic responsibilities, new procedures for recruitment, a new system for rotation of posts, a pension plan, better financial remuneration, a building program—and the list of changes went on. Before the midpoint of Knox's tenure was reached, the State Department, as Huntington Wilson put it, "was leavened with a new spirit."[9]

The mixed metaphor was apt, for not all of the changes were salutary. For example, after telephoning the department on an urgent matter the U.S. ambassador to Italy still had to wait a week for a reply.[10] Moreover, Huntington Wilson proved to be surprisingly like Root in the way he conducted business. He supervised everything personally, from four-alarm diplomatic crises to the standardization of State Department soap.[11] And rather than putting the question of the moment through an orderly circuit of opinion gathering, Huntington Wilson pulled together a few trusted friends and simply kicked it around. Sometimes these brainstorming sessions occurred at the office during business hours, but more often they took place over highballs at the Metropolitan Club or at the secretary's house on K Street. Frequently the group gathered in Huntington Wilson's library, a long, comfortably appointed room ideal for loosened ties and unbuttoned waistcoats. Huntington Wilson, flourishing his Turkish cigarette, would pace back and forth in front of the fireplace while the others relaxed in wicker chairs and tossed out ideas. Membership in this "kitchen cabinet" informally conferred the status of policymaker, and it soon became evident that a select few were once again running the State Department. W. T. S. Doyle, sloe gin in hand, was a frequent guest, as were many other of the Latin American experts—Henry Janes, Seth Low Pierrepont, and Fred Morris Dearing. Ransford Miller and Willard Straight from the Far Eastern division were also often there. But the visitor most often mentioned was J. Reuben Clark.[12]

This fact symbolized Reuben's dramatically altered stature in the department. He too emerged as a kind of Cinderella. In the old Root regime, Reuben had scarcely been noticed. Once, when Wilbur Carr had been seated at a banquet table with him, the consular chief had fumed with outraged dignity.[13] Now suddenly Reuben Clark was the acknowledged confidant of the terrible new assistant secretary, and that fact stood him in different stead.

Scott, of course, saw this as an evil omen—but then, for him the new administration abounded with them. Knox, for example, had already brought his friend Henry Hoyt into the department and set him up with a high-flown title and high-paying job. As far as Scott was concerned, this new "counselor," who was supposed to work on "advanced legal questions," was nothing but a competing solicitor.[14] Disaffection fed upon itself. Soon Scott was referring to President Taft as "Tub of Guts" and to Knox in terms no more kindly. One evening, after a Knox speech, the solicitor wandered among the guests making invidious comparisons between the present secretary and the former one.[15] Not surprisingly, Scott spent even less time in the office than before. His exact whereabouts, in fact, became rather vague from August of 1909 on; much of the time he apparently spent in Europe. At any rate, by this point Scott and the assistant secretary had effectively parted ways. Huntington Wilson referred no longer to the solicitor but the solicitors, and the reference was clearly to Dennis and Clark.[16] Reuben, writing home, passingly mentioned "changes in the wind."[17]

ii

The Knox–Huntington Wilson style of diplomacy represented a distinct departure from the idealism of Root. Knox himself was not a professional diplomat. When he first made the rounds of the department in March of 1909, it was but the third time he had ever set foot in Old State.[18] Moreover, for special nuances of the diplomatic art, including relations with Congress and the press, he seemed to have no touch whatever.[19] But there were compensating strengths. Knox possessed an incisive mind untrammeled by constraints and

74

conventions, and he was adept at cutting through to what he termed "the bones of the matter." He rebelled against sterile theorizing and reached instead for hard, practical answers. Such action-oriented diplomacy was in tune with Huntington Wilson's own predilections; and the two of them carried it forward with gusto, if not always with success.[20]

After two years of Scott and Root, Reuben Clark was ready for the change. Huntington Wilson had convinced him that all of the talk about high principles had been so much hot air and that realism alone could underwrite a truly successful diplomacy. John Bassett Moore, Reuben's old mentor at Columbia, had more or less contended the same thing, and by the spring of 1909 the assistant solicitor was in full agreement. By degrees he became accustomed to the new rough-and-tumble foreign policy. Indeed, he became one of its architects.

To begin with, Reuben was now openly acknowledged as the hero of the Alsop controversy, and it was clear that the Knox State Department would back his case to the limit. Root, significantly, was furious about the power politics employed in bringing the Chileans to arbitration, and he lashed out heatedly from his Hudson River retreat.[21]

Nevertheless Knox and Clark pushed ahead. By the spring of 1909 Reuben had learned certain things about international legal procedure, and not all of them were comforting. Although the newspapers termed the Alsop proceeding an "arbitration," it was actually a genus of the arbitration species called "friendly composition." Unlike other genera, friendly composition did not necessarily depend on international law. The King of England as *amiable compositeur* could invoke legal principles if he chose to, or he could invoke anything else. There was a strong temptation for *amiable compositeurs* to decide cases by vague notions of equity—or worse, by compromise.[22] Compromise, of course, pleased the side with the weak case far more than the side with the strong. In this instance, the Chileans looked warmly upon King George V;* they still hoped to come away with half of the Alsop pie.

---

*Edward VII died on May 6, 1910, to be succeeded by his son George.

And Reuben Clark was determined that they should get no pie at all. According to the provisions of the arbitration agreement, each side had six months to prepare and present its written case to the king and another four months to present countercases. Due to the pressing business of the solicitor's office, work on the Alsop case had to be done after hours; but this was nothing new for Reuben.[23] He pushed forward with grim resolve. The issue now was the exact amount the United States should request as an award. Interest had presently compounded the original debt to a staggering $3,000,000 (closer to $30,000,000 in contemporary terms) and Reuben saw no reason why the claimants should get a penny less. In the spring and summer of 1910, he held informal talks on this subject with Manuel Foster, agent of the Chilean government. Foster pointed out that claims like the Alsop were never settled at face value, and that it would be more realistic for the United States to accept some sort of percentage. Reuben's own sense of justice was simpler. He himself was struggling at the time to pay back Joseph Nelson for his legal education, and he regarded any such obligation as unnegotiable. "If a debtor [owes] a debt," he told Foster with a shrug, "he should pay it."[24]

So it was that the United States, when its case was officially submitted in the summer of 1910, requested an award of $2,803,370.36 in gold.[25] "This gov.'t [has] no desire to humiliate Chile," Reuben explained, "nor to be arbitrary; nor force unjust settlement: [It] merely wishes [a] fair decision on merits as to amount equitably due."[26] He had gone to great lengths to assure such a decision—the official U.S. case, as prepared by him, ran to 352 pages, with 1,100 pages of appendices. Even from the Chilean perspective such material was impressive. The latter's own case filled only 54 pages—hardly a footnote, in Reuben's terms—and the *amiable compositeur* himself would comment on the paucity of the Chilean documents.[27] By the time Reuben had finished preparing the 600-page U.S. countercase in late 1910, he must have felt certain of the outcome.

The king reached his decision on July 5, 1911. He found for the United States. The award itself was a compromise—Reuben hardly expected anything else—and less than one-third of the amount requested; nevertheless there was ample cause for rejoicing. The $906,000 specified by the *amiable compositeur* amounted to the single largest international award up to that time.[28] Personal congratulations flooded in. Suddenly it was Reuben Clark, rather than Huntington Wilson, who was seated beside the secretary in an early-morning ride through the park, while Knox repeated over and over his delight with the outcome.[29]

Like Knox, Reuben understood that outcome in diplomatic rather than pecuniary terms. To John Bassett Moore he wrote: "If some of our weak sisters get the idea that they can promise in diplomatic correspondence in order to relieve a situation, and then not be obliged later to live up to such promises, I am apprehensive that our difficulties may be hereafter increased."[30] In fact, the Alsop case cleared the air of such misunderstandings. Chile went on to purchase naval craft from the United States, as did its friend and cohort in the Alsop difficulties, Argentina.[31] It was not Root's champagne diplomacy, to be sure, but it promoted its own kind of understanding.

iii

A second way in which Reuben came to the fore in the new administration was in promulgating Huntington Wilson's reforms. In 1906 Huntington Wilson, together with Wilbur Carr, had worked out a system of qualifying examinations for consular candidates in order to assure that recruits would have some verifiable capacity for their tasks.[32] Later on, in 1908, they set up a "consular school" to give appointees a full thirty days of orientation and general training.[33] Law being at the crux of the consular duty, Reuben was regularly called upon to lecture.

From Reuben's standpoint, the activity of the consular school was routine and the materials elementary. Even so, his lectures, which he typed out and delivered verbatim, were highly sophisticated in terms of the actual problems consuls might encounter. He pointed out that American ideals and values, however worthy in themselves, were not necessarily the ideals and values of the rest of the world, and that all presumptions of national superiority were only so many friction points in the workings of diplomacy. He attempted to untangle the popular confusion about international law and to delineate the frontiers between international law and the laws of the sovereign nations. And he hammered away at a theme that was to run through his entire career—that Americans abroad, far from Mark Twain's happy innocents, were potential sources of difficulty and embarrassment whose problems must be handled with care.[34]

More important still was Reuben's collaboration with the assistant secretary on a new qualifying examination for the diplomatic service. A board of examiners, with Huntington Wilson at its head and Reuben Clark as one of its five members, was established for the purpose of recruiting diplomatic personnel on the basis of merit. A written examination was designed to test the knowledge and general intelligence of the candidates, but the real examination was given orally. The object here was to identify a certain kind of personality, one that would be flexible and resourceful under pressure. The five examiners sat star-chamber style in a small room, each one with a printed list of qualities to be measured. Then, with the same impersonality that one might expect from live diplomacy, they hurled hypothetical situations at the candidates, grouped in twos and threes, and observed their responses under fire. Reuben's ready wit was often needed to relieve the tension. After the session, with tentative marks beside each name, the group would retire to more informal surroundings and chat amiably about casual matters. This too was a part of the examination, enabling the examiners to evaluate the candidates' behavior at ease.[35] Although politics continued to play its inevitable role in the making of diplomatic appointments, the Huntington Wilson reforms were a milestone in the development of true professionalism. During Reuben Clark's years on the board of examiners, some of the bright lights of modern American diplomacy found their way into the State Department.[36]

iv

A third way in which Reuben fitted into the Knox–Huntington Wilson State Department became apparent only in time. He was a member of what the assistant secretary called "the international law crowd," and in the beginning both Huntington Wilson and Knox had mixed feelings about international law. For example, one afternoon word arrived that an American-owned wharf in a Central American port was in danger of being seized. A debate burst forth, with Reuben in the middle of it, over whether and under what circumstances the nearby U.S.S. *Petrel* should be asked to intervene. In the midst of the discussion a telegram arrived reporting that Captain Dismukes of the *Petrel* had acted on his own authority and taken possession of the property. "The captain's initiative," Huntington Wilson reported, "enabled us happily to lay aside the subtleties of international law—and go home to late dinners."[37]

But experience began to show that most international problems were not to be solved by gunboat methods. For every happy accident there were a score of baffling diplomatic conundrums, and for these the "subtleties of international law" could sometimes work wonders. For instance, when Knox was negotiating a loan agreement with Honduras he came up against an unpleasant dilemma. He wanted to insert a clause allowing the United States forcibly to collect the debt in the event of default; but, like any man of affairs, he was hesitant to use the hard and possibly offensive language necessary. Reuben examined the contract carefully and showed the secretary how he could have his cake and eat it too. An obscure rule known as the Porter Convention enabled Reuben to invoke all the substance of a force clause merely by including an arbitration agreement in the contract.[38] Philander Knox was impressed.

He was even more impressed with the day-in, day-out work of the solicitor's office which, even in the absence of Scott, hummed along smoothly. Developing a nimble omnicompetence, Reuben handled questions that cut across every nationality and into a bewildering variety of activities. In Portugal it was the issue of recognizing the recent revolution and the legitimacy of the Portuguese republic. In France it was the importation of wines. In Belgium it was the "Congo matter," an unfathomable mess, and in Italy it was the Turko-Italian War. Vacuum Oil was in trouble in Austria-Hungary, Standard Oil was in trouble in Germany, and all of the oil companies were in trouble in Morocco, where the oil was. There were steamship and railway difficulties in Turkey and insurance difficulties in Italy. Elsewhere there were mining rules, tonnage dues, and questions of extraterritoriality; there were police regulations, damage claims for massacre victims, and foreign privileges for American colleges; there was the Monaco business, and the Maiorana case, and the Spitzbergen coal problem.[39] In Russia there erupted a crisis verging upon complete diplomatic estrangement. Huntington Wilson absented himself from his own birthday party, and together he and Reuben Clark decided to abrogate the Russian-American treaty in order to avert disaster.[40]

Any of these imbroglios might occupy weeks, even months, of Reuben's time. The Passamaquoddy Bay boundary dispute, as an example, is a mere footnote to the history of Canadian-American relations, but its resolution entailed years of diplomatic headache. Through the bay—an estuary of the St. Croix River opening into the Bay of Fundy—ran the dividing line between Maine and New Brunswick. As set forth in the original Treaty of Paris, the boundary line was reasonably well described; but a problem arose in the disposition of certain islands lying in its path. For example, between the fog-shrouded coast of Campobello and the Maine fishing village of Lubec was a tiny island inauspiciously named Pope's Folly. Encompassing a grand total of eight acres and producing no commodity save wild blueberries, Pope's Folly proved to be the sticking point in the international negotiations. It seemed that possession of the island conveyed title to five broken-down fishing weirs and a few square miles of shoal water. No one cared about any of this except the fishermen of Lubec and their anxious-to-please senator, Eugene Hale. But Hale also happened to be the Senate majority leader.[41]

The cumbersome job of ascertaining the nationality of Pope's Folly was passed down through the State Department to Reuben Clark. It was his kind of assignment. It took him through old files, parish records, land titles, probate reports, letters, diaries, maps, charts, sailing directions, even interviews with the old salts of the fishing town.[42] But even as the dossier of evidence grew larger by the month, it still stubbornly pointed both ways: Pope's Folly, for all its uselessness, might have been a Canadian island as easily as an American one. Happily, though, Knox finally woke up to the absurdity of it all, bought up the contested fishing weirs, and settled the matter amicably.[43] Still, questions of such maddening complexity continued to be Reuben's daily fare.

v

By the spring of 1910, Dr. Scott's disenchantment with the Knox State Department was a matter of record. He had spent a considerable part of the winter traveling in Europe, ostensibly to promote the International Prize Court; and Clark and Dennis, as ever, had been left in charge.[44] It had been a difficult winter, bleak and sullen, with Central American politics posing an ever-larger threat to the peace of the hemisphere and with Reuben Clark increasingly involved in the turmoil. His job seemed to demand more and more of his time.

For one thing, Reuben was engaged in an increasing amount of administrative work. Cullen Dennis had become involved in an arbitration proceeding with Venezuela, and the distraction tied him up for weeks on end. For another, the Alsop case, with its long evening drudgery, was now moving toward its own climax. The pace of the diplomatic grind seemed to run faster by the month, with more letters to write, more memoranda to research, and more decisions to weigh. At one juncture Reuben found himself facing a minor rebellion among the clerks, who objected to working on Saturdays. Wearily, he settled the matter by agreeing to work Saturdays himself.[45]

The timing of this new commitment could not have been worse. As the affairs of the solicitor's office mounted in difficulty, so did the affairs of Reuben's domestic life. Luacine had never reconciled herself to Washington. For her the capital was fraught with every sort of discomfort and inconvenience, and she fled from it with the children whenever an occasion presented itself. Significantly, the Clarks never quite found a permanent home, and they drifted from one rental to another. Reuben was still deeply in debt for his education and still committed to Scott for work on their second casebook. The children were ill much of the time—dangerously ill at one point—and Luacine was left to care for them as best she could. Things were piling up fast.

Several people picked up the distress signals. Joshua, Sr., for one, who had always written movingly of life back in Zion, put a new note of urgency in his letters and promised all sorts of rewards if Reuben would consent to return. Joseph Nelson went so far as to schedule a business trip to Washington, avowedly to bring the Clarks back to Salt Lake with him.[46] Reuben himself began to see the logic of their arguments. By midwinter he frankly spoke of coming home.[47]

81

vi

But with the bursting of the cherry blossoms on the Potomac, there were suddenly signs that Reuben's difficulties might be coming to an end. For one thing, two very old and troublesome cases had begun to move at last. The Atlantic fisheries dispute with Great Britain, stretching far back into the nineteenth century, was finally ready to go to arbitration. Chandler Anderson had been designated American agent—the person in charge of presenting the case—and Robert Lansing was numbered among the counsel. Traveling to the Hague as special counsel was none other than Elihu Root himself, and on the eve of departure the mood of the department was festive. The other case was also a quarrel of long standing. It had begun with the cancellation by Caracas of a trading concession to the Orinoco Shipping and Trading Company in 1900, but now was known simply as the Venezuela arbitration. Since no one knew the case better than assistant solicitor Cullen Dennis, he too was traveling to the Hague.[48]

Indeed, the two landmark arbitrations occasioned a general decampment from the State Department. Among those packing their bags, besides Dennis, Anderson, and Lansing, were Clayton Carpenter, Otis T. Cartwright, Stanley Udy, and W. T. S. Doyle. Even Scott was going. He had evidently become infected with the growing excitement. There was nothing so firing to the imagination, he had said, as watching a courtroom battle between nations. He had begun intruding himself upon the Venezuela arbitration first, with broad hints to the effect that Dennis, in view of his inability to speak French, might not be the right person to handle the case.[49] Then, when that tack failed, he had somehow attached himself to Anderson and Root as special counsel and had joyously begun preparing for a holiday.

Dr. Scott might have been advised not to travel to Europe in the company of the Mockahi, for they had been plotting his downfall for a year. And by May of 1910 Huntington Wilson was plotting right along with them. It was the assistant secretary, in fact, who had transformed the Mockahi Society from an after-hours frolic into a deadly earnest guerrilla campaign. Bursts of lighthearted laughter had long since given way to solemn intrigue. Even Joseph Grew, stopping by the department between assignments, had noticed the atmosphere of conspiracy. After a week, he said, he would have welcomed the Sphinx "with shouts of joy at finding something really human again."[50]

Scott's day of reckoning gradually drew near. As Cartwright whispered in a letter to Reuben, "a few more blows will undoubtedly kill father."[51] Finally, as the U.S. delegation sailed for the Hague, the Mockahi saw their chance. They decided that this latest truancy, on top of all the others, might be presented to the president and secretary as the intolerable last straw. As soon as Scott set sail, in fact, Huntington Wilson asked Reuben to draw up a bill of particulars that would convincingly indict the solicitor before his superiors. Reuben had plenty of material to draw upon, of course; the question was whether or not to do it. His own sense of estrangement from the solicitor was now nearly total. He was convinced that Scott was not just eccentric or arbitrary but a positive detriment to the welfare of the department—and the United States. "He would place private ambition before official duty if necessary," Reuben wrote, "and jeopardize or sacrifice American interests if necessary or expedient."[52] That was the deciding factor.

So Reuben set to work, in collaboration with Armes and Stowell. The document they produced ran to seven typewritten pages and it vividly rehearsed the apathy, the duplicity, the bad judgment, the petty graft, the intrigues, and, topping the list, the essential absence of Scott from the office of the solicitor for a period of two years. One copy of the memorandum, titled "Departmental Trickery," went to Huntington Wilson for the secretary's approval.[53] Another was sent to Dennis in the Netherlands, who made a few emendations of his own. Scott, he reported, was lolling about Europe, spending incredible sums for needless services and turning in ridiculous expense accounts. "Even E R is disappointed in him." Chandler Anderson, whose opinion would prove to be vital, was even more disappointed.[54]

Accordingly, between Anderson on one side of the Atlantic and Huntington Wilson on the other, the decision was made to give Scott the ax. He would be "promoted" from solicitor of the Department of State to, of all things, "solicitor of arbitrations."[55] Huntington Wilson must have gloated over the title, for it obviously had no meaning. In theory, the arbitrations solicitor would render legal advice to any American arbitrations in progress. But since these proceedings were already endowed with prodigious legal talent, there was absolutely nothing for the man to do. Dennis shrewdly summarized the former solicitor's plight in the words of Caesar: "[He is] fighting for life, not honor."[56] Cartwright put the matter more bluntly. "I think it [will] be about the end of Doctor unless he [makes] good."[57]

Scott had never cared for the solicitor's job, but now that it was stripped from him he mourned the loss bitterly. He made an initial attempt to put a happy face on the "promotion," but to no avail. In a hotel room with Cartwright—one of the Mockahi's own—the Scotts broke down and poured out a flood of vituperation and woe. Harry Armes came in for a major share of the blame, and then they started in on Clark and Dennis, whereupon Cartwright pulled himself up and made a speech.

> I told Doctor that I thought he should be congratulated on being relieved from his office without criticism, that it had been apparent to the whole office that ever since the Hague Conference he had had no interest in the work of the office and that it was better for him to be out, and that he should have gone out when the Administration changed.—I added that he ought easily to see that it was better for the Dep't, *under all the circumstances.* He *agreed.* [italics in original][58]

For her part, Mrs. Scott—whom Dennis dubbed "the dangerous guiding brain"[59]—took to bed for several days, fearful of what the papers would print.[60] But she soon recovered. Within a fortnight the Scotts were back to touring the Continent while the former solicitor searched for a convenient French professorship.[61] On July 13 he wrote to Reuben Clark a letter beginning with these words:

My Dear Reuben:
    Had I been in Washington I would have been the first to congratulate you upon your appointment as Solicitor of the Department.[62]

The Dark Horse had triumphed at last.

vii

If Cullen Dennis was displeased at the outcome, he performed a masterful act of dissembling.[63] Unlike Scott, whose rancor hissed through his saccharine words like a curse, Dennis seemed sincerely delighted. Reuben wrote a kind of farewell to his fellow assistant, one that illuminated the special bond between them.

For almost four years I have been happy in your friendship and closest companionship. During that time I have seen you daily, under varied and oftentimes trying circumstances and conditions, but I have yet to see you swerve, even ever so slightly, from the path of strictest truth, honesty, honor, and friendship. Guided always by a truly pure and lofty patriotism, and filled with a virile belief in the great destiny of this nation, and in the holiness of the principles upon which it is founded, your every official act has been timed and framed to hasten as much as might be the consummation of that for which you worked. May I express the prayerful hope and belief that the same high motives will ever guide you?[64]

Clark and Dennis would remain friends for life.

The Mockahi, of course, were jubilant. Cartwright proposed a lavish celebration at the Hague, with posters blocked out in "MAH" for the principal decorations.[65] Stowell, among others, wrote hearty congratulations to Reuben: "I am delighted that our worthy president has done himself and the society proud—Your fine honest steadfast work has been rewarded and against all obstacles you have forged ahead turning defeat into victory and confounding the heathen."[66] Mrs. Hugh Gibson, an honorary Mockahi, wrote: "I . . . am thoroughly glad that recognition has come to you after the strenuous and unpleasant time you have endured." She then asked, "Will you disband 'the society' or merely change the high sign?"[67] The society was not disbanded. Six years later, while the war was raging in Europe, the following letter issued from the law offices of William C. Dennis in Washington.

To the New York Members of the
    Ancient and Honorable Mockahi Society,
        To wit: President Clark and Bro. Stowell:

Greetings, Dear Brethren:

At a telephonic meeting of the Mockahi Society, called by me at my request in the City of Washington and attended by all the Brethren in good standing who were not absent, to wit: Bros. Carpenter, Armes and Dennis, it was unanimously voted that there should be sent to Bro. Hugh Gibson in partibus allyorum a cablegram in words and figures as follows, to wit:

"GIBSON AMEMBASSY LONDON
GREAT SCOTT! CONGRATULATIONS.
MOCKAHI SOCIETY."

It was at first thought to make the message read:

"CONGRATULATIONS, GREAT SCOTT!, MOCKAHI SOCIETY"

but on reflection it was seen that this might be read:

"CONGRATULATIONS, GREAT! SCOTT"

and it was therefore deemed inappropriate.

The letter was signed by the "President Pro Tem, Mockahi Society" and made official with the seal of the Dark Horse Kicking.[68]

viii

The final break with Scott involved more than a promotion for Reuben. It marked a clear turning point in the development of his thinking. He had grown up under Scott's tutelage and had absorbed in some measure Scott's view of the universe. Disaffection with James Brown Scott the man had necessarily entailed a disaffection with Scott's ideas. Arbitration, judicial settlement, international courts of law—these had been the watchwords of the Columbian scholar, and they had carried with them an overweening legalistic, moralistic, and formalistic conception of humankind. In this conception men did not make war out of greed or passion, but out of misunderstanding. International disputes were seen as the cause of this misunderstanding, and international law was seen as its cure. Reuben Clark would not entirely abandon this system of thought, but he would increasingly come to view it through a lens of experience different from James Brown Scott's. The new solicitor and the old were not finished with one another. Indeed, what they had experienced together in these early years was but a prelude. For better or worse, Scott left a mark on Reuben Clark that would be indelible to the last day of his life.

Chapter 5

DOLLAR DIPLOMAT

Some things changed in the solicitor's office; others did not. Reuben had been solicitor in fact if not in name for some time, so the general style of operations did not alter dramatically. On the other hand, he had been imprisoned by Scott's organization and structure, and these he began to modify at once. Then too, the work of the office was still expanding. Where there had been one assistant in the days of Scott's predecessor, now there were three; where there had been two clerks, now there were nine; where the office had fit comfortably into a small suite on the third floor of Old State, now it literally overflowed the building. By 1911 the entire operation had to be relocated in a lovely old Victorian house across the street.[1]

Of the old office force, only a few remained. Dennis, Carpenter, and Harry Armes all found opportunities in private practice. Cartwright and Udy eventually returned from The Hague, and Stowell had never gone; but Reuben resisted the urge to promote any of these old friends to assistant. Instead he began canvassing the law schools for promising graduates and sending inquiries throughout the profession.[2] At length he made three appointments. Edward Henry Hart, who, despite his Brooklyn upbringing and Yale education, had the features of a western farm boy, was the first. The second was Frederick Van Dyne, another New Yorker and a recognized expert on naturalization and citizenship. Van Dyne took over as Reuben's second-in-command.[3]

But it was with the third of his appointments that Reuben really struck gold. In response to one of his inquiries, there arrived from the University of Chicago a letter recommending Preston D. Richards, touted as the top of his class and a likely candidate for the job.[4] Reuben must have blinked at Richards's vita. He was a Utahn, a Mormon, a farmer's son, a one-time high school principal, and one who comparatively late in life had embarked for the East to study law. It was with some trepidation that Reuben asked Secretary Knox to hire this doppelgänger. He wanted to make it clear, he said, that Richards was a coreligionist and member of an unpopular sect. However, the secretary gave his approval. "I do not care how many Mormons I appoint," he said, "provided they can do the work."[5] And so Richards came aboard. He had a kindly and genteel face, thin sandy hair, and a long, straight nose. There was an aura of bonhomie about him that drew people. He and Reuben became fast friends in a matter of weeks; and as colleagues, law partners, and boon companions, they were to remain close for the rest of their lives. Preston Richards comfortably filled the shoes of Cullen Dennis.

There were a number of clerks to hire as well. Some of them, like Henry Crocker and Donald DeLashmutt, Reuben lured away from the State Department proper or from sister agencies. Others, like C. R. Whitney, Bertin Toulotte, and John Prince, he hunted up elsewhere. With one exception they comprised an effective team. The exception, unhappily, was a man of considerable promise but also of brittle temperament and inflated self-importance. Fred Kenelm Nielsen's career was one of those destined to crisscross Reuben Clark's for the next twenty years, and not to the particular felicity of either.[6]

With personnel in place and procedures streamlined, Reuben was ready for his tour of duty. He made it clear at the outset that he intended to be his own man and no solicitor in absentia. All authority and responsibility he centralized in himself, and he oversaw the work of subordinates with a fussiness reminiscent of the *Law Review.* At no time did he fail to keep abreast of the most minute of developments; and for all that he trusted his lieutenants, he never gave them the freedom of action that he and Dennis had known. Reuben Clark still worked Saturdays himself.

All of this made for a sense of continuity in the solicitor's office. Indeed, Reuben himself continued to work on the same kinds of problems and in much the same manner as before, and the problems continued to pose their same challenge. The simplest of them could be bewildering, and the more ominous ones could come hurtling out of nowhere like cyclones. Reuben literally never knew from one day to the next what a morning might bring: a crisis in China perhaps,

The solicitor, watching a ball game on the lot south of the White House: In the company of four future ambassadors and three assistant secretaries of state.
From left to right: John Van Antwerp MacMurray, acting chief of the division of Near Eastern affairs; J. Reuben Clark; Percival Heinzleman, assistant chief of the division of Far Eastern affairs; Fred Morris Dearing, assistant chief of the division of Latin American affairs; Joshua Butler Wright, on special duty in the State Department; Henry L. Janes, assistant chief of the division of Latin American affairs; Evan E. Young, foreign trade advisor; Richard W. Flournoy, Jr., chief of the bureau of citizenship.

or a knotty little contretemps in Honduras, or a clash between Turkish soldiers and the Greek captain of an American ship.[7] Increasingly, such problems drew him closer to the inner circles of power in the department. Reuben perfected his friendship with Huntington Wilson and at the same time his rapport with Secretary Knox. As a lawyer he found that he had ever more to say in a lawyer's administration, and he found that what he said was received with ever greater respect.[8] Reuben, in fact, had not been solicitor for many months before it could be said that he qualified as a bona fide "dollar diplomat."

It was for "dollar diplomacy" that Philander Chase Knox would be remembered as secretary of state. In 1913 the term was not yet pejorative—Knox had coined it himself. Still, it was easily misunderstood. Dollar diplomacy was not simply commercial diplomacy—the use of diplomatic muscle to secure commercial advantages—even though Knox and Huntington Wilson, like any foreign ministry of the time, practiced commercial diplomacy too. Dollar diplomacy was genuine foreign policy. It was a program for exercising American influence in the world without resorting to force.

In two areas of the world the United States had substantial and growing interests; and since both areas tended to be unstable, American policymakers had their hands full. One area was the Far East. Ever since the Spanish-American War with its devolution of the Philippine Islands, the United States had been a Pacific power. The Philippines, however, happened to be situated on the doorstep of mighty Japan, and Japan was moving toward confrontation with several powers (including the U.S.) over the question of China. The other area was Latin America. Here too the United States had crucial interests—the more crucial with the soon-to-be-completed Panama Canal—and here too the wolves were prowling. Germany and Japan, both regarded as hostile to the United States, were intriguing constantly in Latin America, and the hair-trigger politics of the region made a perfect setting for intrigue. President Roosevelt had had sleepless nights about both areas, and he had learned a few lessons. One was that the United States did not easily stabilize a troubled situation without committing its own armed forces. The president had indeed committed them several times in Latin America and had wound up, in the so-called Roosevelt Corollary to the Monroe Doctrine, pledging to commit them whenever and wherever necessary in order to hold the other powers off.* The question for President Taft was whether to honor those commitments.[9]

He would, of course, honor them if he had to. But Secretary of State Knox thought that there was a better solution than sending in the marines every few months, and that was where dollar diplomacy came in. Knox believed that political instability grew out of economic weakness. Accordingly, he proposed to strengthen the economies of China and certain Latin American governments with American financing. The recipients, thus rehabilitated, would presumably be in a position to look out for themselves, and at a cost far below that of policing them militarily.[10] This substitution of "dollars for bullets," as Knox put the case, was a reasonably sound approach to the problem—certainly no worse than the Truman Doctrine or Marshall Plan of later years—but it had a fatal flaw. Knox, unlike his cold war successors, could not use public dollars for dollar diplo-

---

*See note on p. 514.

macy; he had to go begging for them on Wall Street—with all of the unpleasantness that name evoked.[11]

Whatever Reuben Clark thought of dollar diplomacy in the beginning, he became a warm advocate of it later on. For the election of 1912 he drew up an elaborate white paper in which he knowledgeably defended both the theory and practice of the new diplomacy.[12] It was an illuminating document. It spoke powerfully of ending America's "hermit kingdom" isolationism, of winning the "bloodless war" of commercial rivalry, and, most importantly, of protecting American sovereignty. The "fundamental principle," Reuben said,

is that no nation must under any pretext whatsoever be permitted to occupy, or acquire the right to occupy or establish on American republican territory, or acquire any interests or privileges which would ripen into any such right, any naval base or naval coaling station or any other foothold of any kind or description within striking distance of either end of the Panama Canal.

But Reuben did not stop with a casual gloss of Knox's ideas; he followed the ideas further than had Knox himself. Those nations which most needed steadying, he went on to note, happened to be the very ones in which there was the least regard for law and the most regard for coercion. "Force only," he said, "commands respect." From this circumstance there resulted a disquieting chain of cause and effect: capital investment brought development; developers sustained injury; injury justified protection; and protection, in a country where force alone commanded respect, drove Reuben to the final "ergo" of the syllogism. "It may be necessary at any moment," he wrote, "to exercise a compelling physical force."[13] Thus would occur exactly the sort of intervention that Knox meant to avoid—not a happy prediction.

ii

The dollar diplomats had their first tilt at the Far East. Here they had to pursue two delicately contradictory objectives: to shore up the sagging fortunes of China, and to maintain friendly relations with Japan. Reuben was involved with both. Initially, Japan seemed to be the more difficult challenge, and the State Department had to

91

proceed with extreme caution. The Japanese, fiercely proud and easily offended, had been angered for years by the tinkering of western states like California with schemes of Oriental exclusion. One such law, segregating Japanese school children, had been passed by the San Francisco School Board in 1906, almost resulting in head-to-head confrontation between the two nations.[14]

In the fall of 1910 the Japanese government requested an early abrogation of the Japanese-American treaty and the negotiation of a new and better treaty—one that would forbid discrimination against Japanese citizens.[15] This request put Secretary Knox on the spot. Treaties of commerce and navigation were not ordinarily subject to early termination—and besides, what the Japanese were asking for might be politically impossible to deliver. Reuben Clark had been studying the problem of discriminatory legislation for some time and, on the basis of his findings, Knox knew that there were many state laws of an anti-Oriental character. Nevertheless, Knox asked his solicitor to find out whether the treaty could be legally abrogated; and, on the strength of the one serviceable precedent Reuben turned up, the Japanese were granted their wish.[16] Now came the real problem: phrasing the new treaty in such a way that the Japanese could keep their pride intact and the Americans their freedom to regulate immigration.

On a chill Sunday morning in January of 1911, the secretary met with a handful of advisors in his K Street library to work through the treaty puzzle.[17] The problem was that Japan, in the so-called gentlemen's agreement of 1906, had promised to restrict emigration voluntarily. If the State Department relied upon the gentlemen's agreement and inserted no clause in the new treaty preserving the right to restrict immigration, western senators would probably kill the treaty; if, on the other hand, the troublesome clause *was* inserted, the Japanese would probably kill it. This was a lawyer's dilemma, and Solicitor Clark made a number of suggestions for resolving it—most of them tight, subtle, and, for someone of Reuben's inexperience, extremely clever.[18] But Secretary Knox on this occasion was more clever still. (In his day he had assembled the legal behemoth known as Carnegie Steel Corporation, and as Roosevelt's attorney general he had cleared title to the Panama Canal.) "We won't mention immigration at all," he said in a burst of triumph. "We'll just put in a clause saying 'All existing understandings and agreements between the two governments are hereby made part of this Treaty.' "[19] Everyone was happy. The Japanese diplomats did not have to initial a document restricting immigration, and the American Congress had a promise in writing that the Japanese would continue to honor the gentlemen's agreement. For the time being, at least, the threat of a face-off with Japan was averted.

iii

China, meanwhile, was drifting ever closer to the rocks. Social and political disintegration was eating rapidly into the imperial government, and collapse seemed only a matter of time. Here was a situation made to order for dollar diplomacy, and Knox was not laggard in applying it. Between 1909 and 1911, in fact, the secretary of state negotiated no fewer than six major financial projects with the Manchu rulers, each of them designed in some way to halt the deterioration. Some of the projects contemplated overhauling the Chinese currency or modernizing the Mandarin bureaucracy. Others underwrote capital improvements, such as the Hu-Kwang and Chinchow-Aigun railroads, aimed at consolidating Western influence. All were fraught with political and financial perils, and not infrequently they came to bad ends.[20]

The business of hauling reluctant partners into complex financial consortiums had its legal challenges too, and most of them crossed Reuben Clark's desk.[21] This was his introduction to the world of international finance, and it could not have been bumpier. Arrangements would be made, technicalities worked out, legal barriers chipped away—and then suddenly a snag would appear and the process would have to begin anew. In cycles of hope and frustration a project would thus be born and reborn a dozen times until it either careened forth alive or uttered its last gasp. And all the while the China of the empress dowager was approaching inevitable doom.[22]

The shooting started in Wuchang on October 10, 1911. By the end of the year the Chinese revolution was in full course and the situation was giving special alarm to the country's foreign residents— for whom the Boxer Rebellion and the siege of Peking had left unpleasant memories. In early January, while Yuan Shi-kai and Sun

Yat-sen were bargaining over China's fate, a mutiny broke out east of Peking, imperiling the rail exit from the capital. Persuaded that the situation was genuinely dangerous, Knox agreed to cooperate with the other powers in guarding the track and dispatched five hundred troops accordingly.[23]

Reuben was assigned to devise a legal justification for this use of military force. In accomplishing it, the solicitor drew upon what he called "the well-established right" of a government to protect the lives and property of its citizens, even in a foreign country. Such limited, pointed, and small-scale interventions had taken place before, Reuben pointed out, "perhaps as many as half a hundred [times]."[24] In any event, the danger quickly passed, and the Chinese revolution began sorting itself out. At the time, only an especially acute observer might have noted that what had begun as dollar diplomacy—affirmative and nonviolent—had ended up as military intervention; and only a clairvoyant might have seen that this would become a pattern.

iv

And in Latin America it became a regular blueprint. Reuben soon learned that Caribbean diplomacy, like Caribbean politics, was a game with no holds barred. In Venezuela, for example, there was a blue-ribbon tyrant by the name of Cipriano Castro whose chief diversion seemed to be the concocting of international turmoil.[25] In his headlong career Castro had nullified some concessions granted to a Venezuelan subsidiary of Kunhardt and Company of New York. Reuben Clark, while still an assistant solicitor, had been asked to evaluate the legal merits of the resulting claim.[26] It was a tiresome, bootless business, full of broken faith and cynical promises, and it opened the young lawyer's eyes to a world of nefarious dealing. Soon, because of this experience, Reuben was assigned to keep a running dossier on the Venezuelan dictator—which he did with mounting revulsion. Eventually, when things became intolerable, Elihu Root broke diplomatic relations with Venezuela and set Castro up for a swift demise. By that time Reuben was convinced of the necessity of dollar diplomacy or something very like it for Latin America.

V

If Venezuela guarded the southern approach to the Panama Canal, Cuba guarded the northern; and Cuba also provoked waves of alarm. The United States, in its war with Spain, had secured Cuban freedom in 1898, but there was a string attached. The so-called Platt Amendment was inserted into the new Cuban constitution, Article III of which gave the United States the right to intervene at will for the preservation of Cuban "independence."[27] Secretary Root had invoked the Platt Amendment and dispatched American troops to the island in 1906 when irregularities had reduced Cuban elections to a shambles, and Knox was aware that he might have to follow suit.[28]

One of Reuben's responsibilities was to keep an eye on Cuba, and in January of 1911 he decided that something was definitely amiss.[29] A Cuban Ports Company had been organized for the purpose of improving existing port facilities. There was a sizable issue of bonds involved and an equally sizable chunk of port revenues to cover them. The solicitor smelled a rat. By setting the cost of the proposed improvements against the sum of the projected revenues, he discovered a discrepancy of some fifty million dollars. He then noticed that most of the company stockholders happened to be the very politicians who had pushed the scheme through. At this point Reuben himself was ready to send in the marines.[30]

There was a spirited debate in the State Department over just how to handle the situation. Some took the position that the ports company swindle was an internal matter of the Gómez government and not at all the business of the United States.[31] Reuben disagreed. He could see another intervention coming, as he wrote to William Doyle, and he did not want to find the island's finances tied into knots when the day of reckoning arrived.[32] Knox agreed. In a significant restatement of Cuban policy, he instructed the American minister in Havana "to deter the Cuban Government from enacting legislation which appears to you of an undesirable or improvident character, even though it seem improvident or ill-advised purely from the Cuban standpoint."[33]

There were other schemes like the ports company, and Reuben grew adept at detecting them.[34] And there were worse difficulties. In the spring of 1912 Cuban blacks touched off sporadic revolts and finally open rebellion against the government.[35] Knox began gearing up for the intervention Reuben had predicted, and he wondered about possible legal grounds for it. It was six-thirty on a bright June morning when the secretary called his solicitor. As the two of them cruised through the park an hour later, Knox shared his concern about the Cuban situation and asked if Reuben would take another look at the Platt Amendment. He wanted to know, he said, just what he could and could not do in the next few days.[36]

A preliminary answer was ready for the secretary by ten o'clock, in time for cabinet meeting. Knox read the memorandum carefully, idly chewing his cigar, and looked up at Reuben. "Then you say Cuba is not free?" he asked. Reuben nodded. In that moment the Cuban policy of the United States was altered dramatically.[37]

Reuben's next job was to make the alterations clear to Havana. This he did in a long and heavily documented follow-up memorandum. Here he frankly argued that the Platt Amendment had few, if any, limitations to its scope and that the kinds of intervention it authorized were broad and open-ended. So long as the intervention was undertaken for a legitimate purpose, he concluded, "Cuba has absolutely nothing to say."[38] This document was then transcribed by the solicitor into a draft note, and a month later the note was approved by the president for delivery to Cuba.[39] It forcefully asserted the right of the United States to give Cuba advice and warned that measures "peaceful and otherwise" would be taken if the advice went unheeded.

Fortunately for the Cubans, the island's chaos never quite reached critical mass; but had it done so there is little doubt that Knox would have acted. J. Reuben Clark had come very close to converting dollar diplomacy into *realpolitik.*

vi

So it was with nearly every episode of Latin American diplomacy. The solicitor did not make foreign policy per se, but he ranged himself with the hard-liners of the State Department and gave legal sanction to aggressive measures. Huntington Wilson, another hard-liner, found Reuben's support entirely consonant with his own spread-eagle ideas; and the secretary himself, whose instincts were more moderate, was often carried along. If a given course of action was "legal," Knox seemed to believe, it must also be "right"—and that, frequently, was the long and short of the policy debate.

Yet none of these measures was undertaken in a cynical spirit. Knox, Wilson, Dawson, Doyle, and Clark himself all sincerely believed that the interests of the United States mandated a supervisory activism in the Caribbean and that any show of force short of actual combat was to be read as a gain, not a loss, for diplomatic morality. Reuben especially was strongly moralistic. In 1910, in fact, he became involved in a series of negotiations with Haiti in which his moralism almost undid him. Haiti, scarred by genocide and haunted by voodoo, had lain beyond the pale of America's Caribbean interests until that year, when a consortium of European bankers suddenly began discussing a Haitian loan.[40] Immediately Washington became alarmed, and Reuben found himself dickering with the Europeans for American participation. The incident was remarkable not so much for its application of Knoxian principles as for Reuben Clark's behavior as the arrangement began to take shape. With a solicitude rare among dollar diplomats, Reuben became suspicious of both European *and* American motives and ended up coming to the Haitians' defense. The bankers, he charged, were going to reap unearned and unfair benefits, and the Haitians stood to be victimized by alleged corruptions. The solicitor wound up opposing the whole scheme as stoutly as he had opposed the Cuban Ports Company.[41]

And with Colombia too, Reuben's influence was felt on the side of fair-mindedness. Colombia had been roughly treated by the United States. In 1902, when Bogotá had dragged its feet in negotiations over the Panama Canal right-of-way, a revolution had suddenly broken out in the Panama district—some said with American connivance—and in the ensuing melee the United States proved anything but helpful to the Colombian government. As a result Panama successfully broke away and became an independent republic.[42] This "rape of Colombia," as it was called, was still unrecompensed when Knox assumed office. Root had negotiated a series of treaties which would have settled up with the Colombians and even granted them an interest in the canal itself, but Bogotá had angrily refused to ratify them.[43]

Early in 1912 Reuben became involved with the effort to indemnify Colombia, and soon he was actively shaping the negotiations. The task was concluded at one of those day-long sessions in Huntington Wilson's library.[44] As Clark, Huntington Wilson, and the Latin American experts stitched their proposals together, they decided to offer $10,000,000 for Colombia's ratification of the earlier Root treaties, the lease of two offshore islands, and an option to build a second isthmian canal across Colombia's Atrato district.[45] (Reuben was concerned that Germany or Japan might build a competing canal.) Although the Colombians ultimately rejected this offer too, it was by no means an ungenerous one. It seemed that even the staunchest of dollar diplomats could feel pangs of remorse.

vii

Nonetheless, they essentially held to their course, and American diplomacy remained rugged, individualistic, and not infrequently self-serving. Reuben oversaw the finances of Panama with the same fussy paternalism he had shown to the Cubans, and he freely disallowed measures that struck him as reckless or improvident. In a score of other matters the solicitor vigorously asserted himself. There was the Tacna-Arica dispute in Peru, the Galápagos Islands affair in Ecuador, and brushfire revolts in half a dozen places. There were difficulties with iron mines in Venezuela, with railways in Uruguay, with wireless telegraph in Brazil, with cacao in Panama, with naval armament in Argentina, and in Mexico with the mammoth Tlahualilo cotton plantation. There were loans, claims, bankruptcies, seizures, mediations, and the murder of at least one American entrepreneur. There was the development of water resources, the exploration of oil lands, the drainage of swamps, the sanitation of cities, and in El Salvador the elimination of bandits.[46] As each of these matters crossed the solicitor's desk, he exercised a strong influence in behalf of American interests. For Reuben Clark there was little difference between diplomacy and courtroom combat: the law in either case was not so much a balance for achieving abstract justice as a sword for vindicating one's client. This bias was not Reuben's alone. It was written into the very grammar of dollar diplomacy, and sooner or later it was bound to lead the dollar diplomats into making a fatal misstep. As it turned out, the misstep came sooner—in the spring of 1910—and it occurred in the very center of the Caribbean danger zone.

viii

The five republics of Central America stretched through the tropics from Mexico to Panama. In background, language, and culture, the five—Guatemala, El Salvador, Honduras, Nicaragua, and Costa Rica—were virtually interchangeable, as they were in political style. And the style was familiar. Insurrections, palace coups, and other forms of political roughhouse were its distinguishing characteristics, and their appearance in any one of the five republics usually proved contagious to the others. Central America was also a hothouse for dictatorship, and its history rang with the names of Barrios, Carrera, and Estrada-Cabrera. Politics, while laced with ideological terms like "liberal" and "conservative," was actually more a business of "ins" versus "outs," with the "ins" being the party in control of the customhouse. A particularly rich customhouse could even become the target of foreign filibustering, substantially multiplying the intrigue. Amid revolutions, invasions, and desperate calls for help, Central America was a land of high adventure.

In Reuben's time, the chief instigator of the Central American tumult was José Santos Zelaya of Nicaragua. Ruthless, devious, and remarkably agile, Zelaya had managed to ride the crest of Nicaraguan politics for sixteen years, during which he had jailed opponents, suppressed dissent, rigged elections, harassed foreigners, and put down six insurrections against himself. He had also managed to get mixed up in the domestic politics of all four of his neighbors. He had threatened Costa Rica, invaded El Salvador, and maintained a running vendetta with Guatemala; and he found the customhouse of banana-rich Honduras as beckoning as Solomon's mines.[47]

No one had quite hit upon the right cure for Zelayism. Secretary Root had called a regional peace conference and pledged the five republics to good behavior. He had even set up a Central American court of justice to hear their incessant quarrels. But in the end all of these attempts had failed, and life in the region continued to careen uncertainly.[48]

And to make matters worse, American capital absolutely pervaded the area.[49] Gold mines, coffee plantations, timber operations, fruit groves, and the ubiquitous railroad and steamship lines all attested the Yankee presence. Trouble attested it too. In Zelaya's own Nicaragua there were several nettlesome disputes in progress, for Zelaya had a habit of granting monopolistic concessions and then wrangling with the concessionaires. By 1909 giant American corporations like the United Fruit Company and the United States–Nicaragua Concession dominated vast segments of Nicaraguan life. Many of these companies based their operations not in the populous lake district, where Zelaya could keep an eye on them, but in the wild and desolate reaches of the Atlantic seaboard, where they were impossible to control. Secure in this isolation, they tended to behave like private governments and to treat Zelaya as a rival sovereign. One of them, the George D. Emery Company, had been given a concession to exploit the rich hardwood forests of the interior. At a dollar a log for mahogany, cedar, ebony, and rosewood, the terms of the contract were generous; and Emery showed profits of $180,000 annually. But Zelaya suddenly claimed that the company was not meeting its end of the bargain. Charges and countercharges flew back and forth, and in May of 1909 there appeared at the State Department a Mr. Charles Wood Noyes representing the Emery Company and presenting a claim against Nicaragua for $750,000.[50]

This visit marked Reuben's entrance into the Central American miasma. At the initial meeting with the Emery representatives, Huntington Wilson performed the necessary introductions, placed Mr. Clark in charge, and walked out of the room. Thereafter Reuben was on his own. He kept a leather-bound notebook on the progress of the negotiations, in which he recorded the various conferences, the legal developments, the involute maneuvering of the settlement process.[51] Nicaragua did not want the matter to go to arbitration, and in September of 1909 it agreed to settle out of court for $600,000.[52] Reuben was pleased with this outcome, but he could not quite rest easy with it. For one thing, he knew that a claim "settled" was not necessarily a claim "paid." And for another, he sensed that disaster was impending.

ix

Secretary Knox sensed it too. He fretted over Central America as no other place on earth, and he was not long in concluding that dollar diplomacy alone could meet the crisis. Thomas Dawson was dispatched to negotiate a customs-secured loan with Honduras, and Reuben Clark was asked to draw up the necessary treaties and contracts. Even this did not stabilize Central America, however—and now that American private capital was committed, Knox was in deeper than ever.[53]

In February of 1909 Zelaya launched an attack upon El Salvador. The following month he massed troops on the Honduran border. Reuben Clark found himself being consulted almost daily about possible legal bases for an American military intervention. Even though Dawson, Doyle, and the other Latin Americanists kept a close watch on the unfolding events, it was the solicitor who was requested to keep a daily account of them—and it was he, ultimately, who determined their outcome.

x

No one was really surprised when in October another revolt broke out against Zelaya. The surprise, rather, was that the revolt did not erupt in León, the stronghold of Zelaya's conservative foes, but in Bluefields, the stronghold of the American corporations. Indeed, the tie between the corporations and the insurrection seemed more than coincidental: second in command of the rebel forces was Adolfo Díaz, who was also secretary and treasurer of the American-owned La Luz and Los Angeles Mining Company. The mine operators faithfully anteed up into the revolutionary coffers, as did most of the other Yankee enterprises in Bluefields. It was reminiscent of Reuben's equation regarding developers and trouble: the American entrepreneurs had apparently decided to deal with Zelaya themselves.[54]

The question for the State Department was whether to let them do it. Thomas Moffat, the American consul at Bluefields, voted yes. He enthusiastically cabled the early progress of the revolt and reassured Washington that Juan José Estrada, the nominal leader, would be an excellent replacement for Zelaya.[55] Moffat's exuberance was easily transmitted to Huntington Wilson, who saw the Estrada uprising as a godsend. If the Bluefielders could rid Central America of Zelaya, reasoned the assistant secretary, by all means let them do it. But Knox was not so sure. He respected the law of nations and had strong doubts about mixing in foreign revolutions. Accordingly, he declined to recognize Estrada and held nearby U.S. cruisers on a tight leash.[56]

The secretary of state did nothing, however, to discourage the involvement in Nicaraguan affairs of private individuals. One collection of mercenaries from New Orleans consisted of "beachcombers and bums" rounded up at so much per head and given high-flown military titles. Bluefields's El Tropicale Hotel, where these recruits were sumptuously quartered, was wryly rechristened the "War College."[57] More serious contributions were made by two soldiers of fortune named Leonard Groce and Lee Roy Cannon. Dynamiters by trade, the pair was captured while laying mines in the San Juan River, their intended targets being heavily laden government troop transports. Zelaya wrathfully condemned Cannon and Groce to death and made swift preparations to carry out the sentence.[58]

This incident presented Reuben Clark with the first of several critical decisions he would have to make about the Estrada revolt. What, if anything, should the State Department do about the arrest of the two Americans? Reuben looked up the law and found it to be reasonably clear. Cannon was a professional revolutionary. Groce had all but discarded his American identity. "It seems to be a well established rule of international law," wrote the solicitor* to Thomas Dawson, "that where American citizens take up arms against a Government with which the United States is at peace, such person forfeits his rights for protection as an American citizen."[59]

Zelaya obviously agreed: Cannon and Groce were shot. New York papers carried the news on November 19; and the following afternoon, in Knox's library, principals of the State and Navy departments met to determine the reaction of the United States.[60] At this meeting it was again pointed out that Zelaya, in applying the death

---

*Reuben was technically not solicitor at this time; he became acting solicitor on May 15, 1910, and solicitor on July 1 of that year. However, since Scott was out of the country throughout most of the winter of 1910, Reuben was solicitor for all intents and purposes.

penalty for rebellion, was only following the Nicaraguan constitution, and that firebrands of the Cannon-Groce description were usually disavowed by their own governments. Nevertheless the secretary of state, for reasons of his own, decided to make a stand, and his legal officer had little choice but to stand beside him. In a complete reversal of his earlier opinion, Reuben labeled the saboteurs bona fide American citizens and officers of the Estrada military, entitled to be treated as prisoners of war.[61] Huntington Wilson was delighted with this interpretation. He said that it would justify the American occupation of Corinto, and perhaps even Managua itself, in what he oddly termed a "pacific demonstration in force."[62] Philander Knox would not go so far by half; but after thinking matters over, he decided that the Cannon-Groce affair did justify the elimination of Zelaya. On December 1 he officially broke diplomatic relations with Nicaragua. Then, in a tough note, he indicted Zelaya for destroying republican government, violating international agreements, and fomenting turmoil in Central America. For the "murder" of Cannon and Groce, Knox demanded a heavy indemnity—but this he offered to reconsider in the event of a change in government.[63] The note accomplished its purpose: Zelaya stepped down.

xi

That should have ended the revolution and cleared up the Central American malaise. But it did neither. In place of the deposed caudillo, the Zelayist-controlled *congreso* installed José Madriz, a politician who himself bore all the earmarks of Zelayism.[64] So the Estrada revolt thrummed along unabated and politics continued to boil. Secretary Knox decided to recognize neither Estrada nor Madriz and see what happened.[65]

In early February 1910, Madriz parried a thrust at the capital by the Estrada forces, and two weeks later he all but crushed the revolt. Estrada fell back on Bluefields with the shattered remnants of his army, while Madriz perfected plans for the coup de grace. Consul Moffat watched with alarm as the Estradists filed wearily back into town. He cabled Washington that the revolution had "practically collapsed" and that its leaders were fighting among themselves. Madriz, too, believed that the end was near. He sent three liberal armies to converge upon Bluefields from the interior, while from the sea approached his secret weapon: the *Máximo Jérez*.[66]

But Bluefielders had seen revolutions before. They traced their ancestry back to the seventeenth-century Dutch freebooter, Abraham Blauvelt (anglicized to "Bluefields"), and in a rough-and-ready way they had remained true to it. In a setting out of W. Somerset Maugham, the town—with its clapboard buildings, grass-bound streets, and littered landscape of oil drums and mining machinery—seemed yet to challenge the world. As a weather-beaten sign over the post office put it, *"El rifle y el libro cimenta la paz."*[67]* In that spirit the three hundred fifty followers of Estrada dug in for a last stand.

Estrada held three cards. In order to reach Bluefields on the jungle-bound Atlantic coast, his enemies would have to stretch their overland supply lines dangerously thin. Then too, his own partisans were fighting for home and patria. But Estrada's ace lay in the fact that here, in what one American called "the jumping-off place of the world," was to be found a veritable treasure-trove of Yankee enterprise—and the Yankees might not want to see it disturbed. If Madrizist forces entered Bluefields, Moffat cabled nervously on April 12, U.S. lives and interest would be "severely endangered."[68]

Yet Madriz held the trump, and when the *Máximo Jérez* hove to off Schooner Key on May 16 the revolutionists were stunned. This "man-of-war," as the Nicaraguans described it (it was named for the George Washington of their history) amounted to the entire Madriz navy. It was a converted British merchantman, rusty and barnacled, but it mounted three-inch guns; and against the tin roofs and tarpaper walls of Bluefields it promised to be devastating. The ship was under the command of tough and resourceful Julián Iriás, a one-time Zelayist minister who now stood as heir apparent to Madriz. He must have relished the anticipation.

xii

In Washington, Reuben Clark was also digging in. The Estrada revolt—and for that matter Nicaraguan history—would turn on the decisions he made in the next few days. Bluefields was defenseless

---

*"The rifle and the book establish peace."

against the *Máximo*. Whatever Iriás was or was not permitted to do with the warship would therefore decide the issue.

One decision was made on the spot by Captain William Gilmer of the U.S.S. *Paducah*. He informed Iriás that he would permit no naval bombardment of the city, for American life and property were at stake. Gilmer then landed marines to enforce the interdiction.[69] The following day Major Smedley Butler, in charge of the landing party, told Madrizist Generals Lara and Godoy that he had "no objection" to their taking Bluefields by storm "if it could be managed without shooting." The generals were dumbfounded. Would the *insurrectos* also be forbidden to shoot? they asked. "There is no danger of the defenders killing American citizens, because they will be shooting outwards," Butler replied suavely, "but your soldiers would be firing toward us."[70]

Reuben Clark was expected to reason the same way. Given the assumptions of the State Department, Zelayism in whatever form had to be arrested at all costs. Iriás had several uses to which he could still put the *Máximo Jérez*—he could starve the Bluefielders out with a blockade or capture their customhouse and bankrupt them— and Captain Gilmer was at the end of his authority. Whatever Washington did now would have to be bold if it was to be effective—but it would also have to be "legal." That depended upon Reuben. At this point, he was virtually alone in the solicitor's office, arranging his things in Scott's old desk and feeling for the levers of his own power. He would never make a decision of greater consequence.

His decision was to intervene. On the morning of May 18, in a conference between Reuben Clark and Thomas Dawson, it was agreed that the *Máximo Jérez* would be prohibited from blockading, as well as bombarding, Bluefields.[71] This was an exceptionally delicate judgment. Reuben Clark himself had often and insistently rendered judgments to the contrary. Indeed, it was only on the slenderest of legal pivots that he believed he could reverse himself now. The *Máximo*, it seemed, had originally been purchased as the *Venus* in New Orleans, loaded with arms and ammunition, and then sailed under the British flag to Greytown where its Nicaraguan identity had begun.[72] The State Department had known about the sale of the vessel and had regarded itself as powerless to prevent it. The American neutrality statutes did not forbid selling ships or guns or ammunition to anyone—only "arming" a ship or "launching" a military expedition. [73] No one had "armed" the *Venus* in New Orleans; and so, while Reuben's office was still muttering about the ambiguities of the case, the *Venus* had cleared port for Central America.

Reuben now claimed that the ship had cleared unlawfully. Ironically, he himself had tried to hold the *Venus* in New Orleans by various legal maneuvers and had been forced to admit that none of these would suffice.[74] Nevertheless he now put his foot down: no blockade by the *Venus*. Julián Iriás was thunderstruck. Only months before his adversary, Estrada, had blockaded Greytown under nearly identical circumstances—and with the full approval of Washington.[75] Somehow the justice of the situation escaped him.[76]

xiii

Iriás had one card left to play. On May 27 he attacked and captured the rebel customhouse across Bluefields Bay. If he could not starve Estrada out, he would bankrupt him. No sooner had the smoke cleared, however, than Iriás received word that the State Department would not recognize the conquest as valid. On top of everything else, Solicitor Clark had decreed that the rebels might lawfully collect customs anywhere they pleased, and thus that their hastily established emergency customhouse on Schooner Key was a legitimate facility.[77] Iriás was clearly stymied. "The Estrada Revolution exists today," exulted Moffat, "only because a strong hand saves it from annihilation."[78]

Like a long balance arm poised in equilibrium, Nicaraguan politics needed only this tiny shove to swing it ponderously in the opposite direction. Madriz's landward generals were finished off piecemeal by Estrada's rejuvenated forces, and the government commenced a dolorous retreat. Defeat buckled in upon defeat, and on August 28 the jubilant *insurrectos* thronged the streets of the capital. It was just as well. The State Department, having committed itself irrevocably in the Bluefields intervention, was now readying even stronger measures.[79] Reuben Clark, in fact, had gone on to submit a policy memorandum calling for a complete military takeover of Nicaragua and had drawn up a congressional resolution granting the necessary authority.[80] Only the fall of José Madriz spared the United States this adventure.

All seemed well that ended well. The United States government duly recognized the new regime, insisting only that Estrada dignify the presidential office by marrying his mistress. The ceremony took place at an army barracks across Bluefields Bay, the guests shuttling to and fro on banana barges and numbers of them, in alcoholic revelry, tumbling overboard.[81] Thomas Dawson traveled to Managua and completed a series of agreements with Estrada and Díaz. These "Dawson Pacts," as they were called, provided for a customs-secured loan together with American supervision of Nicaraguan finance, a new national constitution abolishing the troublesome monopolies, and an avowal to punish the murderers of Cannon and Groce. As with the earlier Honduran agreement, Reuben Clark drafted and executed the legal instruments.[82] As a final gesture of good will, Major Butler, in a midnight raid, rounded up the American "bums and beachcombers" at the El Tropicale Hotel and dropped them out on a sandbar, where they caught a ride back to the States on a passing freighter.[83]

But the Hollywood ending obscured a pair of exceedingly obdurate facts. The first was that Estrada's was a minority government and hopelessly incapable of ruling the Zelayist majority without American help. Estrada himself did not last long: he soon quarreled with his congress, handed the presidency over to Díaz, and fled the country. Díaz, in turn, weathered a relay of comic-opera misfortunes that demolished the tranquility of his own party. The conservatives, it seemed, could not even govern themselves, much less the country.[84]

The second fact was that dollar diplomacy had failed. The U.S. Senate killed the loan treaty and the bankers hastily withdrew their money.[85] This "treachery," as the Nicaraguans conceived it, made a bad situation far worse. Where once they had regarded the American presence as benign and even beneficient, Nicaraguans now came to see it as unbearably oppressive. No longer a magic word in the banana republics, *Yanqui* was increasingly conjoined with *imperialismo*.

Mercifully, no one at the State Department could peer into the future. Neither Knox nor Huntington Wilson nor Dawson nor Clark could see the trail of grief that wound ahead of them—the lies, the broken faith, the double-dealing, and the inevitable resurgence of violence. None could see the Mena revolt, the bombardment of Managua, the Sandino movement—and the thousands of American soldiers who would eventually be required to maintain order. But these things were in store. Nicaragua was to become America's first Vietnam.

xiv

This episode marked the end of Reuben Clark's apprenticeship. He had learned many lessons in the course of this larger education but none more important or far-reaching than the lesson that was to emerge from Nicaragua. No matter how well intentioned, the intervention at Bluefields proved to be ill considered—and worse. In time, Reuben would learn that power and responsibility went hand in hand and that governments did not exercise the former or assume the latter without serious and long-lasting consequences. The lesson may not have seemed particularly significant in August of 1910, while the hand-shaking and back-slapping over Nicaragua were still going on. But in two short months the tidy western world that Reuben Clark had grown up in would come to an abrupt and shattering end—and Reuben would have cause to consider the lesson again and again.

PART II

WHIRLWIND
1910–13

THE LAWYER AS
DECISION-MAKER

Shortly after the Taft administration left office, George D. Parkinson of the University of Chicago began working on an article about J. Reuben Clark, eventually to be published in *The Improvement Era*. Huntington Wilson got wind of the project and asked if he might lend a hand in its preparation. Just what the former assistant secretary would have come up with was anyone's guess, of course; but the uncertainty seemed disconcerting to Reuben, who feared nothing so much as the specter of vanity. He wrote to Preston Richards and asked him to take the article in tow after Huntington Wilson had finished with it, seeing to any little extravagances that might have crept in. In particular, Richards was supposed to watch out for references to Mexico. It would not do, Reuben explained, "to assert in any unmodified way that I had charge of and directed the policy in the Mexican matter." He then made a truly cryptic allusion.

You may recall that Admiral Togo, after his victory in the battle of the Sea of Japan, telegraphed the Emperor congratulating the Emperor upon his the Emperor's victory in that battle. That is the attitude which must be carefully observed throughout the article.*

Accordingly, whatever else the Parkinson article did or did not discuss, there was no mention whatever of "the Mexican matter." So, while readers learned of the summer storms of claims and controversies, they did not hear about the whirlwind, the killer tornado that sucked up the lives of a million people and scattered them over the Mexican desert—nor did they learn of the crucial decision-making role played by J. Reuben Clark.

---

*JRC to Preston D. Richards, 30 November 1913. Box 345. (See *Notes*.) *The Improvement Era* was at that time the official magazine publication of the Mormon church.

Chapter 6

DARKENING SKIES

Mexico in 1910 was a striking mixture of old-world charm and new-world affluence. Nowhere else, it seemed to visitors, was there a land so perfectly balanced between the picturesque and the prosperous. On the one hand was the romantic Mexico of the travel brochures—the Mexico of fiestas and guitars, of cultured aristocrats and quiet peasant folk dozing in the sun. This Mexico survived in lonely rural villages and on the opulent *haciendas* that still sprawled across the countryside. On the other hand, science and technology were creating a new Mexico on the foundations of the old—a Mexico of mines and railroads and factories, all drawing their strength from an immense natural bounty. If Mexicans treasured the old ways, they placed their hopes for the future on the industrial giant now beginning to bestir itself. Mexico City perhaps best exemplified the convergence of old and new. With its wide streets, ornate buildings, and lavish monuments, this ancient capital was unblushingly called "the Paris of the Americas." It bustled with busy and purposeful people who fairly exuded confidence in the future.[1]

The architect of this grand society was President Porfirio Díaz. He had come to power in 1876 in the midst of political chaos and, unlike a score of predecessors, he had stayed. By 1910 Díaz was serving his eighth term as president. Riding in his carriage through the streets of the capital, the old soldier, now eighty, cut a truly impressive figure. Every strand of his snow white hair was still in place. The eyes, flickering with occasional shrewdness, were outwardly calm and benevolent. The flowing walrus mustache, the dazzling panoply of decorations, the erect military bearing all marked Díaz as a ruler among rulers. As for the nation he ruled, who could deny that it had come far during his thirty years in office?[2]

Unfortunately for the average Mexican, the golden age of Díaz was not all it seemed at first glance. Behind the graceful Victorian facade lay several awkward realities. Mexico City's expansive boulevards ran past some of the worst slums on the continent. In the villages, where wages had not risen in a century, peasants subsisted on a diet of beans and tortillas washed down with cactus juice. As for the great *haciendas,* these were but monuments to feudalism, built upon land stolen from the Indians and manned by peons who hopelessly toiled and slowly starved to sustain their owners' luxury. As late as 1910, eighty percent of all Mexicans were illiterate and their average life expectancy was but twenty-seven years. And as time passed, the gap between splendor and squalor widened steadily.[3]

The cement binding this society together was fear. Despite his kindly, patriarchal manner, Porfirio Díaz was a ruthless dictator who had brought order to Mexico at the point of a gun. Soon after taking office he had organized the *rurales,* a special police force of licensed killers, and had given them orders to maintain discipline at whatever cost. Their acts of terrorism soon became legendary. In Hidalgo a group of Indians who had refused to surrender their ancestral lands were buried up to their necks and galloped over by the *rurales.* Other opponents were bought. An elaborate network of graft eventually placed even the lowliest provincial *jefe* under the control of Mexico City. And atop the whole pyramid sat Don Porfirio himself. Assured of perpetual reelection, confident of his control of the courts and the press, Díaz was master of all he surveyed. His was, noted one observer, "the most perfect one-man system on earth."[4]

That the democratic United States should come to be associated with such despotism was one of the great ironies of the age. Shortly after assuming power, Díaz had recognized the necessity of luring foreign capital to the service of Mexico's economic development. In order to secure it he offered entrepreneurs from abroad many special privileges in the form of favorable laws, tax advantages, broad concessions, and even monopolies. Before long the money was pouring in, most of it from the United States. The result was predictable. By 1917 the Mexican oil industry ranked third in the world, but almost all of the profits were flowing into American hands. U.S. firms owned three-quarters of all Mexican mines as well as many of the great sugar, coffee, and maguey plantations. The same went for the great cattle ranches. In a nation where seventeen families owned one-fifth of the arable land, one family alone (the Hearsts of California) boasted a spread the size of Maryland and Delaware combined. By the time William Howard Taft entered the White House, forty percent of all U.S. foreign investments—some two billion dollars' worth—were lodged in Mexico; that was more capital than the Mexicans owned themselves. "Poor Mexico," ran one lament, "so far from God and so near the United States."[5]

Thus intertwined, the relations of these North American neighbors were of two contrary descriptions. Official relations were sunnily positive. To dollar diplomats like William Howard Taft and Philander Knox, Díaz was the perfect Latin American ruler. His regime, with all its faults, was both a model of stability and a willing economic partner. No less a statesman than Elihu Root called Díaz "one of the great men to be held up for the hero-worship of mankind."[6] A widely circulated photograph of Taft and Díaz standing side by side on the international bridge near El Paso somehow said it all. "Two great Presidents of two great Republics," the caption read.[7]

Unofficial relations were something else. It seemed that few Mexicans-on-the-street could share the enthusiasm of their government for *americanos del norte.* To village peasants and urban workers alike, the fifty thousand Americans living south of the border were constant reminders of the regime which had beggared them in their own land. While Mexican peons starved, the foreigners grabbed the choicest jobs, the best houses, and the finest food, and returned to the United States laden with Mexican wealth. Small wonder that *gringos* were hated almost everywhere. The result was that at the very moment when Mexican-American diplomacy was achieving new levels of cordiality, relations between the private citizens of these nations were strained almost to the breaking point.[8]

And there were other signs of impending trouble. Here and there charismatic leaders began giving more definite shape to the popular dissatisfaction with Díaz. In 1900 two brothers by the name of Ricardo and Enrique Flores Magón began publishing a newspaper in opposition to the dictatorship. Imprisoned and later chased from Mexico by Díaz, the would-be revolutionaries moved their headquarters to Los Angeles. From this sanctuary they proceeded to launch a series of ill-planned and poorly executed raids against Mexican border settlements, raising much dust but little revolutionary consciousness.[9] Meanwhile, in the southern state of Morelos, Emiliano

Zapata was organizing a revolt of a different sort. Handsome, dapper, and a dashing ladies' man, Zapata was also deeply committed to agrarian reform. His peasant followers, among the most sorely oppressed in all of Mexico, carried out a brutal guerrilla campaign against the wealthy *haciendados* of the region, one in which such barbarisms as crucifixion and staking victims to anthills were common. Before long Zapata would make his presence felt in Mexico City.[10]

By far the least likely of these nascent revolutionaries was Francisco I. Madero. He stood but five feet two inches tall, appeared frail, and possessed decidedly weak features. His mannerisms were generally nervous and his thin voice often spiraled into falsetto. Teetotaler, vegetarian, spiritualist, maverick, Madero inspired anything but confidence; but he had the one thing which the Flores Magón brothers and Zapata all lacked: a comprehensive national program. Somehow this son of one of the great families of Mexico had become obsessed with the idea of democracy. In 1910 he published a book entitled *The Presidential Succession of 1910* in which he argued passionately for freedom of suffrage and an end to reelection. Showing the strength of his convictions, Madero declared himself a candidate for the presidency, to run against Don Porfirio himself. Predictably, this indiscretion landed him in jail, where he reposed until the election was safely past. But this was only the beginning of Madero's revolutionary career. When he escaped from prison in October and fled to the United States, it was with the promise of a speedy and triumphal return.[11]

To Porfirio Díaz, watching over his domain in the fall of 1910, there seemed little cause to take any of these *insurrectos* seriously. On the surface at least, his control of Mexico was more secure than ever. In September dignitaries from the nations of the world gathered in Mexico City to commemorate the centenary of Mexican independence. The climax of the celebration came on September 15 – the president's birthday – with a parade worthy of Cecil B. DeMille. Ten thousand participants, including fifty pure-blooded Aztecs, depicted the history of Mexico from Montezuma to independence. That night a gala ball and fireworks display were held at the National Palace.[12]

And yet there were strangely discordant notes amidst the rejoicing. Only five days earlier a mob had stoned the president's home, and there had been ominous threats against his life. Madero and the

Flores Magóns might have fled Mexico, but the unrest they had kindled was still flickering. In truth, although none of the revelers knew it at the time, the Díaz regime was in its final year. "I often think back to that night," one American later wrote of the party at the palace. "It celebrated so gorgeously the beginning of the end."[13]

ii

Officials in the U.S. State Department apprehended none of the warning signs from Mexico in the fall of 1910; other problems held their attention. In the Far East Secretary Knox was engaged in a frantic effort to keep his diplomatic foot in the Open Door. At the Hague the arbitrations with England and Venezuela were nearing their climaxes. And the Caribbean cauldron, never far below the boiling point, was bubbling up once again.[14] Mexico alone appeared serene. Looking southward, administration leaders noted with relief that here at least was a bastion of tranquility.

Reuben Clark was no more prescient than his colleagues, despite the fact that his duties as solicitor afforded a particularly clear view of the Mexican scene. One of his principal responsibilities was the protection of Americans abroad. Another was keeping track of political exiles and their activities in the United States.[15] Either of these concerns might have led Reuben to the trouble festering in Mexico.

The safety of U.S. citizens in Latin America had historically been a ticklish problem even in the best of times. The frequent bursts of internecine fighting always seemed to catch an American or two in the line of fire. Such isolated incidents, however, were of minor importance compared to the virulent anti-Americanism which began to grip Mexico in 1910. Suddenly the Americans were no longer mere innocent bystanders but actual targets of domestic violence.

A particularly dramatic example of such violence occurred soon after Reuben became solicitor. On the night of November 4, 1910, a young Mexican accused of murder was lynched by a mob near Rock Springs, Texas. As word spread across the border pandemonium broke loose. Crowds gathered in Mexico City crying "Down with the *gringos!*" and "Death to the Yankees!" Soon they had attacked the offices of the American-owned *Mexican Herald* and gone on to destroy several other properties. In the days following, American homes, hotels, and restaurants came under assault while dozens of American citizens, including the son of the ambassador, were numbered among the casualties. By the week's end the riots had spread to other Mexican cities and appeared to be quite out of control.[16]

Despite the intensity of these outbursts, Reuben and his colleagues in Washington took them in stride. This was, after all, no backwater banana republic with which they were dealing, but the Mexico of Porfirio Díaz. The standard diplomatic protests were filed, but there seemed no special cause for alarm. Díaz solemnly promised "to ascertain who are the persons guilty . . . so that they may be duly punished," and there the matter rested.[17]

Another sign of the coming storm was the continuing exodus of political refugees from Mexico. By the fall of 1910 scores of actual or potential revolutionaries had crossed the northern border. Ricardo Flores Magón in Los Angeles and Francisco Madero in San Antonio were only the best known of the expatriates. American newspapers carried almost daily accounts of other Mexicans who were forced to flee their homeland for conscience' sake. So acute did the problem become that the Political Refugee Defense League, which had once come to the aid of a young Latvian named Jānis Puren, now began turning its attention to the Mexican exiles. In Congress there was introduced a resolution calling for a joint committee to investigate the "persecution of Mexican citizens."[18]

Unlike the anti-American riots, the refugee problems proved to be a serious bone of contention between the two countries. Understandably, Díaz resented the fact that his friend and neighbor was giving asylum to avowed enemies. In November he instructed the Mexican ambassador in Washington to request Madero's arrest on grounds that he had slandered the Mexican government. But officials at the State Department displayed scruples against that kind of summary action. "It should be recalled," Secretary Knox explained after consulting Reuben Clark, "that since under the American Constitution liberty of speech and of the press is guaranteed, mere propaganda in and of itself would probably . . . not be punishable [under U.S. law]."[19]

That considerations of law might hamstring a counter-revolutionary effort had never entered Don Porfirio's head. In Mexico the laws did not protect revolutionaries—they protected power and property. The mere suspicion that someone like Madero was up to no good would have sufficed under the Díaz version of "due process" to land him in jail. But the Díaz version stopped at the Rio Grande. The U.S. State Department had decided some time ago in the Pouren case that political dissidents were not to be handed over on demand. "I venture to remind your excellency," Knox explained, "that the mere fact that a man is engaged in revolutionary activities in another country does not render his presence in the United States illegal."[20]

Eventually this difficulty also passed and the skies over Mexico cleared once again. Still, an uneasy quality remained in the political air. Like a sudden storm, events were about to overtake the placid Mexico of Porfirio Díaz. The exiles fleeing northward were but harbingers of that storm. Americans in Mexico had already felt its warning blasts and had begun to seek out shelter. Before long the horizon would be black with clouds of revolution.

iii

On November 19, 1910, Francisco Madero and a handful of followers crossed the Rio Grande to commence their war against Díazpotism. The event was anything but auspicious. The army which Madero had expected to find waiting for him in Mexico turned out to be twenty-five dusty recruits from the surrounding countryside. A shipment of arms and ammunition (for which he had already paid) failed to materialize. And the general uprising which his return was supposed to have triggered had apparently misfired. Disconsolate, Madero headed back to San Antonio.[21]

He should have waited. Despite its comic-opera touches, the Madero "invasion" indeed proved to be the spark in the tinderbox. Within a matter of hours anti-Díaz riots had erupted in several Mexican cities. Groups of armed riders continued to gather in the northern chaparral, and with loud *vivas* and much *aguardiente* they began doing battle. By November 22, Gómez Palacio was reported to be in rebel hands; and similar victories were rumored to be pending in Durango, Torreón, Parral, and Zacatecas. From Chihuahua in the north to Puebla in the south, federal troops and Maderist *insurrectos* were reportedly locked in bloody combat.[22] The years of hatred and suffering could be contained no longer.

High in his fortress palace in Mexico City, Porfirio Díaz reacted with characteristic disdain. "The political situation in Mexico does not present any danger," he proclaimed on November 24, "and the lives and interests of all foreigners are absolutely secure." He conceded that there had, in fact, been "a few mutinies of small importance" but that these were now under control and order had returned to the republic.[23] Henry Lane Wilson, the American ambassador in Mexico City, informed Washington that the Madero revolt—"unorganized and without responsible leadership"—posed no significant threat to Díaz.[24] Two weeks later he reported the collapse of all organized resistance to the government.[25]

Nevertheless, hints of another version gradually began to filter in. Americans fleeing northward across the border brought with them horror stories of attacks on their countrymen in Mexico. At Pachuca there were said to be placards all over town reading "Death to the Yankees," "Down with *gringos,*" and "Kill Díaz and his Yankee friends." Some Mexicans, it was rumored, had taken it upon themselves to translate these slogans into action. At Torreón unconfirmed reports had it that at least two Americans and possibly more had already been killed. No one knew for sure how many Americans might be in danger—or already dead.[26]

Even the actions of the Mexican government seemed to belie the official optimism. In a conversation with U.S. ambassador Henry Lane Wilson on November 16, the supposedly invincible ruler expressed his concern over arms and ammunition being purchased by the rebels in the United States. This, he urged, was a breach of the U.S. neutrality law and a boon to the revolutionaries.[27] Another of Díaz's concerns was the use of American sanctuary as a base of operations for the *insurrectos.* On November 18, the Mexican president passed along a plea that "the Mexican Government would greatly appreciate it if these men could be prosecuted for attempts to subvert the Government of a friendly power from American soil."[28] The next day the Mexican ambassador in Washington sent a letter to Secretary Knox in which he expressed the urgent hope that

the American Government, acting in its habitual spirit of justice, may be pleased to order the guarding of its frontier by mobilizing the necessary forces, in order to prevent the gathering of rebels and the importation of arms into Mexico, the passing of armed bands or suspected persons in either direction across the boundary, or commission of other acts that might disturb the domestic peace of Mexico.[29]

iv

By the year's end the State Department realized that the old man was in real trouble. But how much trouble? It was the oldest of diplomatic questions. Any foreign ministry would want to remain loyal to a friend like Porfirio Díaz—especially when it must look to him for the continued protection of its own nationals under his jurisdiction. On the other hand, no foreign ministry would want to overcommit itself either—especially in the event that Díaz lost and the protection of the foreign nationals fell to his victorious enemies. It was a little like betting on a horse race, except that there was nothing to win and absolutely everything to lose.

With terrifying possibilities before them, Taft and Knox groped for a policy. Their instincts were conservative. They knew that in practical terms there might be precious little they could actually do to help Díaz, even if they wanted to. Could they, for example, really police the border? The U.S.-Mexican border was a wide-open frontier where empty horizons shimmered in the noonday sun. Army patrols might range over the dry chaparral in search of suspicious activities, but there could be no real scrutiny of that thousand-mile wasteland.

There were other problems. Despite the talk of "our partner in Mexico," few American politicians genuinely sympathized with Porfirio Díaz and virtually no one favored his methods. How far, asked some, must a democracy go to bail out a despotism? And Madero had widespread sympathy in the United States. Four hundred eighty-eight El Pasoans affixed their names to a forthright plea for neutrality, "believing with all that is in us that this is a struggle for . . . life and for liberty on the part of the *insurrectos*."[30] As the policy choices took shape, more and more of them appeared to be losing ones. It seemed to be one of those situations where, no matter what the United States did, it would be wrong.

This, in the final analysis, was why President Taft and Secretary of State Knox cautiously backed into legalism. Not only were the two of them lawyers, but they headed a cabinet of lawyers and a government of lawyers; and they took unusual comfort in the clean abstractions of the law. In their hearts they seemed to sense that the wisest policy for U.S.-Mexican relations, at least for the time being, was no policy—certainly no *new* policy. Thus they decided not to close the border, not to embargo the guns, and ultimately not to help Porfirio Díaz at all. Here, to be sure, they were taking some calculated risks; that was where legalism came in. The law must be called upon to provide justifications—any number of them—for this sudden indifference to a longtime ally; it must be used to convince Díaz that the U.S. State Department, in doing nothing, was doing all that it lawfully could.

So it was that all eyes turned toward J. Reuben Clark. As solicitor of the State Department and resident expert in the law of nations, Reuben was called upon to paste together—and as new situations arose, keep on pasting—an elaborate rationale for nonaction.[31] Reuben accepted the assignment. Soon he was communicating with the Mexican ambassador in homilies like this: "It would be most unwise and unsafe, as well as immoral for this Government or its agents to attempt to take any action which was not warranted by law."[32] The solicitor may or may not have guessed that these disclaimers were drawing him into the very vortex of the Mexican situation.

v

Reuben soon learned that there were two separate bodies of law bearing upon the matters before him, and that either of them could be counted on to sustain the administration's position. First of all there was international law, which governed the acts of neutral nations in case of a war between their sisters. International law, however, only applied where the belligerents were recognized as sovereign nations; it had no relevance to domestic insurrections involving "unrecognized" rebels. Thus, while a neutral was obliged to aid *neither* side in a war between sovereigns, it was free to aid *either* or *both* sides in a civil war or revolution. As Reuben put it, "Since there is no recognized state of belligerency in Mexico at the present time, the rules and laws governing warfare and the conduct of neutrals are not involved."[33]

Second, there were the domestic neutrality statutes of the United States. These laws, which aimed at preventing private citizens from dragging the nation into war, prohibited such unneutral acts as fitting out ships for use against another state and launching military expeditions from American soil.[34] As Reuben was quick to point out, however, these laws imposed no *international* obligations on the U.S.

They are mere private laws. The neutrality of the United States is governed solely by the rules of international law, and the Mexican Government may expect our observance of the international rules of neutrality only. It has no further rights under the neutrality statutes than for example a statute regulating the right of aliens to hold property. Where the so-called neutrality statutes, and the international rule coincide, the Mexican Government may of course expect the observance of such statute; not, however, because it is a statutory enactment, but because it is an international rule.[35]

Reuben, of course, had already demonstrated that international law did not apply. Thus, as Taft and Knox were relieved to learn, no proscription anywhere required a change in the hands-off policy they had adopted. The United States could go on selling guns to both Madero and Díaz and hoping for the best. And as long as American policymakers were merely applying the law, neither side would have reason to find fault with them.[36]

The State Department lost no time in passing the word to the Mexican dictator. On December 14, Knox replied to Díaz's request to cut off arms shipments to the rebels. Unfortunately, the secretary said, there was no legal justification for such action. "Even in a state of war," he had learned from Reuben Clark, "mere trade in arms, ammunition, and other articles of contraband is considered legal and subject to no penalty save the loss of the goods if captured in trade."[37] And this was not even a state of war, only an "insurrection" of unknown proportions. Díaz's own rhetoric was returning to haunt him.

Don Porfirio drew an equally unsympathetic response to his request for patrolling the border. "The policing of the Mexican border," ran the official U.S. policy, "is a matter for the Mexican Government, and not for this Government, and while this Government will continue to use every legitimate endeavor to prevent illegal and hostile expeditions, it can not be charged with ... the exclusion from Mexico of bands of unorganized Mexicans who are returning to their native land."[38] If Mexico desired stricter enforcement of U.S. neutrality laws, said Knox, Mexico would have to provide hard evidence of violations.[39] The ball was back in Díaz's court.

vi

By the beginning of 1911 the policy to which Knox and Taft had given birth and which Reuben Clark had given form was being circulated to State Department personnel in Mexico. On January 25, Wilbur Carr sent the following instructions to U.S. consuls below the border:

> You will, therefore, while continuing to be most vigilant in preventing violations of the neutrality of the United States, which this Government has the strongest desire to observe, be certain to keep strictly within the law, and have special care that you take no action which will, under the circumstances given above, appear to shift the responsibility of maintaining peace on the Mexican side of the border from the Mexican Government, where it belongs, to this Government, where it does not belong.[40]

Not all members of the Taft administration could agree with this policy of restraint, and some of the opponents were in high places. One such was George W. Wickersham, U.S. attorney general. Wickersham, with his white hair and rimless glasses, had the benign, kindly face of an old family doctor. His background, however, included high-powered corporate law and extensive dealings with monopoly. He had a no-nonsense attitude about American enterprise, especially on foreign soil, and he backed the Díaz regime to the limit.[41]

Needless to say, Wickersham's view of the neutrality question was at some variance with Reuben Clark's. For him "neutrality" meant the systematic strangulation of the Madero revolt by the United States government. Even before the Mexican crisis, Wickersham had clashed personally with Philander Knox. As Reuben later recalled,

> On one occasion something had come up and it looked as if he [Knox] might get into trouble with Wickersham who was the Attorney General. He did not like Wickersham any better than Wickersham liked him, and so I finally said to him, "Mr. Secretary, if you get in jail I will get the Attorney General to get you out." And he said, "No, not the Attorney General. Get me a lawyer."[42]

Since Wickersham was ultimately charged with the enforcement of the neutrality laws, a collision between himself and the State Department was not long in coming. When consular chief Wilbur Carr offered his instructions to the border consuls in January, the attorney general fired an angry letter of protest back at the State Department. There followed a quick-moving exchange of memos between the Departments of State and Justice, climaxed by a face-off between Knox and Wickersham at a meeting of the cabinet. Wickersham came away convinced that he had carried the day and that the border traffic would now be monitored closely. But Knox was not to be put down so easily, and another volley of notes ensued. By this time aides were whispering about the affair in the corridors of the State Building, and the Knox-Wickersham correspondence, which Huntington Wilson described as "extremely outrageous," was finding its way to the president.[43]

Clearly Taft had to do something. At stake was not only the harmony of his cabinet but his entire policy toward the Mexican Revolution. Instinctively he fell back upon legalism once again, asking in effect which side had the better case. Upon receiving a general report from Solicitor Clark on the legal ramifications of the Mexican situation, the president made his decision.[44] The Knox-Clark view, he said, was the correct one. His ensuing letter to the Treasury Department, in fact, drew upon Reuben's own language.

> The mere sale of supplies in El Paso to Mexicans, whether *insurrectos* or supporters of the Government, and their delivery across the border ... is not a violation of international law or of the neutrality statute.... But international law favors the continuance of commercial transactions and holds them innocent in a neutral country until those transactions become really a part of the military operation against a friendly government.[45]

From that moment on, the Mexican policy of the Taft administration was in the hands of J. Reuben Clark.

vii

And what sort of policy was it? First of all, it was a policy of self-restraint. Despite the fact that the United States had an enormous stake in Mexico, the decision had been made to hold back from any active interference in the revolution and to allow the Mexicans to settle matters for themselves. Secondly, it was a policy of de facto neutrality. Official, or de jure, neutrality was diplomatically out of the question, but Reuben and many of the others still sincerely felt neutral: they did not want to make a choice between Díaz (and order) and Madero (and freedom).[46] Finally, it was a policy of rigorous legalism. In part, this resort to the law was but a means of disguising more realistic considerations—the dilemma of backing the losing side—but apart from that President Taft, Secretary Knox, and Solicitor Clark (all devoted lawyers) were entirely honest in their belief that the law, if devoutly respected, would bring its own kind of healing. All in all, idealism and self-interest were mixed about equally.

It was not to have been a permanent policy—only a temporary expedient. But the situation itself was not as temporary as the policymakers supposed. Indeed, it turned out to be an endless wrenching turbulence, winding serpentine into the future. So, aware or not, the president, the secretary, and the solicitor were not merely devising a stopgap; they were laying the cornerstone of a new American foreign policy toward Mexico, toward Latin America, and toward revolution itself. Like any new policy, this one would bring in its train unforeseen consequences, both for good and for ill. Many issues would still have to be resolved. For the present, what mattered most was that American policymakers—rightly or wrongly, by design or by accident—had at a critical juncture seen fit to place their faith in the rule of law. Whether that faith would be sufficient to deliver them from the tempests ahead remained to be seen.

Chapter 7

HAWKS AND DOVES

The decisions made in Washington during the early days of the Mexican Revolution had two far-reaching consequences. The first was that the United States surprisingly refused to assist a friendly government in the suppression of revolutionary activities. The second was that the solicitor of the State Department, a staff officer of strictly technical qualifications, was thrust into a pivotal policy-making role. What followed next was even more surprising. Instead of the solicitor returning to his desk and resuming the mundane business of the department's law office, he gravitated steadily closer to the center of Mexican affairs, participating in decisions ever more distant from the law and ever more proximate to diplomacy.

The reason for this was to be found in the State Department's working dynamics. The president himself was not an active policy-maker. He was ready to go to war, if need be, to support a position in which he truly believed; but the process of formulating and defining positions he left up to others. The principal other, of course, was his secretary of state. Philander Knox, for all his leisurely repasts and afternoons of golf, *was* an active policymaker; but Knox had his areas of interest—Manchuria, for one—and none of them happened to be Mexico. The same could be said for his alter ego, Huntington Wilson, who, while absorbed in virtually every detail of State Department operations, found some operations more satisfying than others. Mexico, with its painful dilemmas, was one of the least satis-fying of all.[1] That brought up the Latin American division, headed by H. Percival Dodge. Where the first division chief, Thomas Dawson, had been a remarkably effective diplomat, Dodge was not cut from the same bolt of cloth, and his duties as resident diplomatic officer kept him busy elsewhere.[2] His assistant and eventual succes-sor, W. T. S. Doyle, was a more fortunate choice, perhaps, and it was observed that he "seemed to thrive on trouble";[3] but Doyle, like some others, was too often the fireman answering three different alarms and too seldom able to concentrate on any of them.

Apart from the individual failings of State Department officers, the Mexican matter suffered another sort of handicap. The fighting in Mexico was clearly not in the usual tradition of brushfire revolts. In fact, it seemed to be in no tradition whatsoever. In reality, this was the first of the twentieth century's great social upheavals, with recognizable likeness to the Russian and Chinese revolutions later on. Not yet having experienced those cataclysms, State Department officials could be forgiven for the disquiet and unease which events in Mexico tended to evoke. They were used to questions of the "ins" versus the "outs," not questions of the "haves" versus the "have-nots." In a word, the Mexican Revolution was a diplomatic pariah—no one wanted to deal with it.

When vacuums form at the top of an administrative structure, someone down below is usually drawn in to fill them. This was essentially what happened with Mexico. The revolution and its problems were kicked around for several months between the assistant secretaries and the Latin Americanists; then gradually they came to settle on the desk of the solicitor. J. Reuben Clark had most of the necessary qualifications for handling such problems. He was a good lawyer. He was trained specifically in the law of nations. He was a tireless, methodical worker who could be trusted to read every wire, oversee every dispatch, and keep abreast of every new development. By February of 1911, Reuben had more or less assumed responsibility for Mexico. A policy of de facto neutrality had been enunciated by Knox and given the blessing of President Taft. Henceforth it would be up to Reuben Clark to see that this policy was kept on track.

Reuben's first step was to assemble copies of all correspondence pertaining to the neutrality problem since the outbreak of the revolution.[4] Thereafter he made sure that important dispatches from Mexico came to his immediate attention. He also began keeping a rough-and-ready historical narrative of the Madero revolt, as he had done earlier with Venezuela and Nicaragua.[5] He wanted to know step-by-step what was happening and in what sequence, the better to decide what step to take next. Reuben's office also became the clearinghouse for the revolution's associated complications. As solicitor he naturally handled the claims for damage, the allegations of injury or injustice, the violations of neutrality, the questions of legal status, and the whole apparatus for determining the rights and duties of the respective sovereignties. In addition, there were the routine reports and requests for legal advice from Ambassador Wilson and the U.S. consuls in Mexico. By the end of March, the volume of daily correspondence had reached such a level that Reuben was unable to deal with it all before quitting time. "Quite often," recorded his father, who was visiting in Washington, "he has to go back to his office after dinner and work awhile. . . . There is a great amount of foreign matter to attend to."[6]

In an effort to sharpen himself on the particular questions of the revolution, Reuben also undertook an intensive study of the subject of neutrality. Systematically he collected all past presidential proclamations, special messages, and other pronouncements on neutrality. His personal copy of John Bassett Moore's *Digest of International Law* grew dog-eared from repeated readings and its margins were soon filled with notes on such topics as belligerency and the recognition of revolutionary governments.[7] The firstfruits of this study were a series of memoranda for department superiors, including one on "the use by the President, without special authorization of Congress, of the military forces of the United States for the purpose of preventing violations of neutrality laws."[8] This was the first hint of possible military action.

ii

As it became increasingly clear that Madero was not going to blow away, Reuben's custody of the Mexican matter became increasingly perilous. By February of 1911 even Ambassador Wilson was forced to concede that "the revolutionary situation in a general way is becoming worse."[9] Time was at last revealing the Díaz regime for what it was—the rotten husk of a once-powerful government. The dictator himself had grown old and his grip on the country had weakened. Not a single member of his cabinet—once called "a group of doddering mummies"—was under sixty. His toothless congress provided no help whatever. More dangerous still, the army, on paper some thirty thousand strong, actually numbered only eighteen thousand; was honeycombed with graft; and, like the government, was paralyzed by senility. Morale among the soldiers was abysmally low: before the Battle of Juárez it was necessary to post officers with loaded revolvers at the carriage gates to see that the soldiers stayed aboard the troop trains. And beyond morale there were mountainous other difficulties, from poor planning to incompetent leadership to faulty ammunition. Díaz himself seemed to know deep down that he would not win.[10]

Madero, by contrast, grew stronger with each passing day. When on St. Valentine's Day he was driven back across the Rio Grande by U.S. marshals, he was greeted in Mexico by women bearing armfuls of flowers and, more importantly, by several hundred eager volunteers. They had been rounded up by the likes of Pascual Orozco—a tall, gaunt muleteer of flamboyant mien—and Doroteo Arango—a bowlegged and barrel-chested mestizo who at the age of sixteen had killed a *hacendado*'s son, taken up the life of a bandit, and changed his name to Pancho Villa. Both of these men understood the life and psychology of the disadvantaged and knew how to translate that understanding into action. Soon they were actually winning battles—at San Andrés, at Guerrero, at Parral—and making life miserable for Díaz. All they lacked to make their victories stick was military hardware.[11]

Hardware, in fact, was emerging as the decisive factor of the war. With the balance of morale tilted in favor of Madero, Díaz could measure his advantage in weapons alone. And he had the best: Maxim guns, heavy mortars, Mauser rifles, carbines. If he could maintain this superiority in firepower, Díaz still had a fighting chance.

The trouble was that he could not maintain it. Thanks to Reuben Clark's interpretation of the neutrality statutes, the rebels could get guns too. In Douglas, Nogales, Laredo, El Paso, and a dozen other border towns the contraband could be purchased openly on the street, to be smuggled across the river in the dark of the moon. Quickly, the possession of these guns began to make a difference. For example, the capture of Galeana, Chihuahua, in January, 1911 (the first solid Maderist victory), was attributable in large measure to the added firepower of the American arms.[12] The Díaz government could throttle this trade as it might from the Mexican side, but from the American side it was helpless. The Mexican ambassador, Don

Francisco de la Barra, continued to protest shrilly. From the frequency and duration of their exchanges, Reuben Clark and Don Francisco came to know one another well.

iii

An equally important breakthrough for the rebels came with American public opinion. Like his Mexican counterpart, the average American citizen had little love for Porfirio Díaz. The outbreak of violence in Mexico brought secret loathing to the surface—not only in the borderlands, where the populace was to a large extent Mexican-American, but throughout the entire country. Suddenly the revolution and its outcome were exciting public issues.

In truth, it was not hard to identify with the *insurrectos*. Dressed in the ragged overalls they had worn as section hands, or in faded dungarees, or in dilapidated dress suits with the coats carefully buttoned for photographers; wearing an assortment of Stetsons and bowlers and twenty-gallon *sombreros* festooned with stolen jewelry and flapping in the wind; armed with Winchesters, Brownings, flintlocks, and zip-guns; sporting beer-bottle hand grenades and the obligatory crossed bandoliers; grimy, sweat-stained, travel-worn, unshaven, redolent of *tequila*; laughing, singing, cleaving the air with ear-splitting *vivas*, and happily shooting at anything that moved, they comprised as ragtag and swashbuckling an army as ever went to war. Since battles were fought along the railroads, the *insurrectos* traveled from one to the next aboard the trains, usually atop the cattle cars. There, in fact, they lived. The señora could be seen in the noonday sun, sheltered by a tattered parasol, cooking tortillas over a fire as a dog yapped at the children about her and the señor sharpened his bayonet—while the train clattered on toward their fate. This was all indescribably picturesque and exciting for jaded Americans. "Never," said newspaperman Timothy Turner, "was there such a colorful, romantic, noble, and foolish period as the first Revolution in Northern Mexico."[13] It was like Lexington and Concord all over again.

This fact possibly explained the fatal attraction that the revolution seemed to exert on Americans. They found innumerable ways to help out. They would flock to the river and throw apples and oranges—even silver dollars—across to the *insurrectos*. After a bloody battle in some border town, they would cross over in their automobiles and attend to the wounded, nursing some back to health in their own homes. The involvement of many Americans went deeper still. There were those like Dr. Ira Bush who crossed the border to patch up the wounded and stayed on as battlefield medics. Oscar Creighton gave up Wall Street stockbrokerage and became so adept at blowing up trains that they called him "The Dynamite Devil." One young El Pasoan survived the revolution to make a Hollywood career for himself as Tom Mix. By the year's end there were so many Yankees in Madero's ranks that they organized themselves into a separate unit called "The Foreign Legion."[14] "If it had not been for American filibusters and adventurers," remarked a Díaz minister sourly, "the revolt in Mexico would have been put down in two weeks."[15]

iv

The enlistment of these volunteers created unnumbered difficulties for the State Department. It meant that American citizens in Mexico were constantly being killed and wounded—which possibly served them right. But it also meant that they were being captured, which was a different matter. Participants in an "unrecognized insurrection" were traitors, technically speaking, subject to summary execution; and captured foreigners were no exception. While it was one thing for an American soldier of fortune to die in battle, it was quite another to have him hanged ignominiously from an oak tree in the plaza. On Reuben Clark's registry of casualties there soon began to appear entries like the following:

Elbert Pope, who had served with revolutionary troops and had been captured by the federal forces, was shot and killed in the vicinity of Altar on or about June 7, 1911.[16]

For most of these unfortunates there was no hope, and the only question left for Reuben to settle was that of compensation for their families. Not so, however, in the case of Converse and Blatt, an incident that kept the solicitor's office buzzing for weeks. When these two American boys, who had packed off to Mexico to take part in the great adventure, learned that it included mud, flies, and live ammunition, they went AWOL together and headed for home. Before they recrossed the border, however, they were arrested by the Mexican authorities and consigned to an uncertain fate. The fact that the young men were actually captured in an area between El Paso and Ciudad Juárez which had been in dispute between the two countries for years made this an especially nettlesome problem for Reuben.* Perhaps it was this circumstance that saved them. After the father of Converse had personally appealed on his son's behalf, Díaz, himself desperate for American support, decided to let the boys off with a stern lecture.[17]

Unfortunately, few incidents involving Americans ended so happily. As the death toll mounted, Reuben even toyed with the idea of extending recognition to the rebels in order to protect the U.S. citizens in their ranks. "Should belligerency be recognized," he wrote in a memorandum for the president,

we might of right demand treatment of American citizens as prisoners of war. If belligerency is not recognized, our rights are by no means so clear, though perhaps we might on general grounds of humanity, insist that the insurrection has now reached such proportions as to entitle the insurrecto prisoners to be treated in some way other than as traitors.[18]

But the problem was not as simple as that. Any recognition of belligerency by the United States government would violate its own policy of neutrality. It would dramatically strengthen Madero at the expense of Díaz—on whom Washington must continue to rely for the protection of American lives.

That was the other half of the problem, the worst half. As the revolution blazed on, American citizens in Mexico became ever less secure. In fact, suspicion and contempt for *gringos* were soon open and commonplace. "The great masses of the population hate Americans with an intensity that is awful to contemplate," exclaimed a mine operator upon his return to the United States.[19] Illustrations of the hatred were easy enough to produce. There was, for example, the case of the American mechanic, J. A. Farrell, who was sentenced to ten years in prison for lending a pistol which later became a murder weapon.[20] Or there was the American farmer, Robert Swazey, who

---

*This dispute is discussed on pp. 552–54.

was surprised by bandits, tied up, and burned to death in his own house.²¹ The most unfortunate incident occurred at El Alamo in Baja California. In May of 1911, Governor Celso Vega, believing the Americans in town to be somehow in league with the insurrectionary forces, hired a gang of cutthroats to work a little frontier justice. Fifty of them rode into town on a beautiful Sunday morning, rounded up four of the suspected collaborators, and marched them to the outskirts of the village, where they gunned them down in cold blood and threw their bodies into placer holes.²²

v

As incidents like these became known in the United States, critics began to toll against Taft's policy of noninvolvement. One especially vocal dissenter was Senator William J. Stone of Missouri. Stone argued on the floor of the Senate that it was wrong to "remain passive and inactive and permit disorder to run riot to the peril of the lives, liberty, and property of American citizens lawfully resident in [Mexico]." And the senator knew what to do about it.

The Congress should at once and without delay authorize the President to employ whatever force may be necessary ... in whatever way he may deem expedient and necessary to accomplish the desired end, even though it should lead to intrusion upon Mexican territory. Moreover, if any act done under this authority by the President for the proper protection of our own people ... should lead to hostile demonstrations against American citizens resident in the interior of Mexico, the President should be authorized ... to use the military forces of the United States, if that is found to be necessary, to protect the lives and liberty of peaceable American citizens, wherever domiciled in any quarter of Mexico.²³

When he spoke Stone was still a lone voice in the congressional wilderness, and his speech drew fire from colleagues.²⁴ All the same, by the spring of 1911 increasing numbers of Americans were coming to think in terms of intervention in Mexico. How easy it would be, they supposed, to send in the troops, forcibly call a halt to the slaughter, and then revitalize Mexico with an application of Yankee know-how. In February U.S. ambassador Henry Lane Wilson traveled to Washington to personally deliver a request from the American colony in Mexico City for intervention.[25] And no less a jingo than Theodore Roosevelt could smell a fight coming on. "I would not wish to take part in a mere war with Mexico," he proclaimed in a letter to President Taft.

But if by any remote chance ... there should be a serious war, a war in which Mexico was backed by Japan or some other big power, then I would wish immediately to apply for permission to raise a division of cavalry, such as the regiment I commanded in Cuba.[26]

Some Americans were ready for direct action even without Washington. When Texas rancher Paul Clarkson was kidnapped by rebels and held for ransom in Mexico, some of his cowhands let it be known that they were prepared to carry the fight below the border. "Unless word is received from Paul Clarkson that he has been released from his captors in Mexico," warned one source, "nothing will keep the half hundred cowboys from invading Mexico and taking him."[27]

No one was more painfully aware than J. Reuben Clark of the Mexican atrocities and of the necessity of shaping a policy to deal with them. As the official charged with protecting the legal rights and bodily safety of Americans abroad, he appreciated the colossal irony of the situation: that, at a time when no American living in Mexico could rest easy at night, his own countrymen back home were working to undermine the very government that had once kept him secure. Moreover, as an old dollar diplomat whose campaign ribbons bespoke a half-dozen interventions, Reuben fully appreciated the seductive simplicity of military solutions. Nevertheless, as the man responsible for day-to-day supervision of the Mexican matter, he had come to recognize the one critical element of the diplomatic equation that had been overlooked by the advocates of armed force. Reuben Clark knew that intervention in Mexico would mean an American bloodbath.

The Mexicans had heard about intervention before—and it happened to be the thing they feared most of all. Partisans on both sides of the barricades feared it morbidly, almost hysterically. Even the humblest of peasants shared the phobia. One of them, encountered by John Reed in the isolated reaches of the north, lamented that Yankee soldiers would come in the end and take away his goats.[28] Rather than submit to occupation, the Mexicans were prepared to resist at all costs. Mrs. Anna Sherwood, the American proprietress of a hotel in Manzanillo, was told by her boarders that at the first sign of intervention they would shoot her and drown the American consul.[29] Such sentiments were echoed in hundreds of newspaper editorials.

Mexico does not need piles of gold, nor millions of soldiers to defend her spoil from profanation. We, her sons, would fight like lions in the unequal contest of one against a hundred. But our inflamed patriotism would not count the number, and who knows if the Yankee conqueror might be left bleeding and overcome.[30]

It was this attitude that Reuben had to bear in mind when weighing the alternatives before him. And it was precisely for this reason that he never indulged in the moral outrage of a William Stone. He understood, as the critics apparently did not, that Mexico was different from Cuba, Haiti, or Santo Domingo—it was different because of the far greater numbers of American citizens involved and because of their dispersion over a vast terrain. They were absolute hostages. To be sure, Teddy Roosevelt might take his Rough Riders and storm Chapultepec as he had stormed San Juan Hill, but who, Reuben asked himself, would be left to cheer when the shooting stopped? Certainly no *gringos.*

vi

So began Reuben Clark's own quiet war of the revolution—a war to defend the policy that he himself had helped devise, a war to forestall intervention. It was a contest in which the relative strengths of the adversaries never seemed quite equal. The lone dove imagined himself surrounded by hawks. Of course, the case was not really that extreme: William Howard Taft had little inclination to send the U.S. Army into Mexico, and Philander Knox had not much more. But the difficult truth of the matter was that neither of these officers had taken firm hold of the Mexican matter, and the vacuum of leadership that had sucked Reuben into a decision-making role had tempted others as well. In Congress, in the press, in the administration, and in the State Department itself were any number of Clarkson's cowboys who saw in the policy of self-restraint not strength and wisdom but weakness and folly. Ambassador Henry Lane Wilson posed a particular problem, for he was situated in Mexico City and his reporting of events seemed always to point toward intervention.[31] Where Ambassador Wilson was an avowed interventionist, Assistant Secretary of State Huntington Wilson was a crypto-interventionist who fairly resonated with the ambassador's reports. Indeed, no State Department official save the solicitor himself seemed entirely set against military solutions. And they were tough opponents for Reuben to meet. In every case they either outranked him, outshouted him, or had conspicuously heavier throw weight. Reuben's only real weapon was the law, and he could not afford to be chary in the use of it. He knew that where decision-makers were indecisive they frequently looked to the law as a substitute for policy. President Taft and Secretary of State Knox, for example, often asked what was legal before asking what was right—and the solicitor had to be ever ready with the answers.

Reuben's first confrontation with the interventionist mentality came at the end of February, 1911. Several factors conspired at that moment to produce a serious situation for the State Department. On top of the constant pleas from the Mexican ambassador for stricter enforcement of the neutrality laws and demands for protection from Americans in Mexico, reports began arriving that a major battle was brewing on the border. The Maderist general Pascual Orozco was rumored to be closing in on the federal stronghold of Ciudad Juárez.[32] Juárez was separated from El Paso, Texas, by nothing more than the width of the Rio Grande, and the effect of a Mexican battle on the Americans across the river was not hard to foresee. Helpless, State Department officials watched the developments with dread.

At precisely the same time another crisis was building in the desert of Baja California. The Flores Magón brothers, having repeatedly wasted their ammunition on such trivial objectives as Mexicali, suddenly discovered where the big prize lay. It was not in an urban center or military fortification but in a harmless earth-moving project along the lower Colorado River. The project meant little or nothing to Porfirio Díaz, but it meant life itself to the residents of California's Imperial Valley. The lush valley had been reclaimed from the desert a bare decade earlier by a series of levees and diversion channels that brought Colorado River water down to the valley floor. But in 1904 and again in 1906 heavy rains had washed out the levees and come very near to converting the Imperial Valley, with its elevation of minus 287 feet, into an inland sea. What the Flores Magóns saw as a new target for their anarchism was a project to construct new and better levees on the Mexican side of the border.[33]

No subject between the United States and Mexico had been more sensitive than this one. The construction work was undertaken by American engineers on lands owned by an American corporation and with funds supplied by the American Congress. The only obstacle had been the Mexican recollection—stretching back to 1848—that economic arrangements had a way of prefiguring political arrangements; and no Mexican wanted to see the lower Colorado become another Gadsden Purchase—or worse. So Mexico had demanded an ironclad agreement to the effect that the levees would not be used as a legal pretext for more Yankee expansionism.[34]

Here, then, was the strongest possible case for intervention—for American lives and property stood in peril—and at the same time the most explicit possible violation of international law. As the *Magónistas* began breathing threats, making nuisance visits, and stealing equipment and explosives from the construction site, Mexicans and Americans alike dug in for the worst. The American consul at Ensenada, who at that moment suffered a complete mental collapse, issued hysterical reports that were picked up by the press. The California legislature asked President Taft to take special measures. There was even a debate in the United States Senate as to what, if anything, should be done.[35] The first impulse was to ask Díaz to send some troops. Don Porfirio, however, already had his hands full; and anyhow there was no practical way of reaching the levees without crossing American soil. Solicitor Clark had received earlier requests from the Díaz government to ferry troops across the Gadsden corridor, and he had routinely denied them.

The remaining alternative was to send American troops. The plan to do so coincided with a visit of Henry Lane Wilson to Washington, and Secretary Knox was clearly tempted by it.[36] He suggested that the Mexican government might "request" the troops; when that was rejected by the Mexicans, he asked Reuben about the possibility of sending the troops anyway.[37] After all, the *Magónistas* were Marxist Jacobins, not "responsible" revolutionaries like Madero; and wasn't there something in the law of nations about protecting one's own property?

Reuben Clark had heard of such a law; he had invoked it himself in the Bluefields intervention. But now he hauled it out and used it like a bludgeon on the advocates of the Colorado adventure. He dismissed the distinction between *Magónistas* and *Maderistas* as irrelevant. What was relevant, he said, was not any aspect of Mexico's domestic travail but, rather, the willingness of the United States to honor its solemn agreements. Item by item, he sorted through the arguments for intervention and held them up to Moore, Vattel, and Fish, offering the same conclusion to all.

It would appear therefore from the above that there is no generally recognized rule of international law, nor is there any recognized custom which could be invoked to justify the throwing of American troops across the Mexican border for the protection of the construction works of the Colorado River levee. It would, moreover, appear that such action upon the part of this Government, if taken without the consent of Mexico, might be regarded by the Government of Mexico as such a hostile act as would justify it in considering it to be an act of war, particularly, in view of the care taken by Mexico to exclude this Government from any rights in this work of permission to enter upon Mexican territory in connection therewith.[38]

The troops were not sent into Baja California. Decision-makers at the State Department thought better of the whole idea. Mexico, recognizing the danger, made sure that the levees received protection at the earliest moment; and Magónism eventually gusted itself out in the Baja desert.[39] Orozco, meanwhile, was turned back by federal forces before he could mount an attack on Juárez and the Texas border returned to its uneasy peace.

vii

If the doves won the first round, however, the hawks won the second. In March of 1911 Henry Lane Wilson succeeded in touching off the most serious crisis in North American relations since the Mexican War; and when the dust cleared, one-quarter of the United States Army was poised on the Rio Grande. It happened while Secretary Knox was vacationing in Palm Beach and Huntington Wilson was on an extended visit to South Carolina.[40] The ambassador had returned to the United States on some private business. He telephoned the president on March 6 and asked if he could stop by for a talk. Taft agreed. "His view of the situation in Mexico was very pessimistic," the president later recalled. "He said that all of Mexico was boiling; that disturbances in the north and south were merely symptomatic of a condition in the body politic which made him afraid of an outburst at any moment; that all that was necessary was a successful leader and the explosion would come."[41] Wilson went on to paint a lurid picture of the wrath awaiting the American community in Mexico, a picture more or less confirmed by recent events. After the interview the president, badly shaken and without benefit of his secretary of state, contacted the Navy and War departments to see what might be done. They were all too ready with ideas. By the following day orders were being delivered for a general military mobilization, to take place immediately. Some twenty thousand soldiers and at least two battle cruisers were put on the alert, with the troops to collect at Galveston, San Antonio, and Los Angeles and the ships to converge on Mexican ports. The reasons for this thunderbolt were unclear, even to the president, but afterward he spoke vaguely of strengthening the forces of law and order in Mexico and of better policing the border against filibusters. To General Wood, however, he confided the real reason.

It seems my duty as Commander-in-Chief to place troops in sufficient number where if Congress shall direct that they enter Mexico to save American lives and property, an effective movement may be promptly made.[42]

Mexico, of course, quite correctly interpreted the mobilization as the first step of an armed intervention by the United States. "The newspapers here boil with conjecture," reported Fred Dearing from Mexico City. "The Mexicans are in a ferment."[43] The president, stunned by the Mexican reaction, then began to backpedal, ordering the warships back out to sea and explaining to the press that his intentions had been misunderstood. But his alibis only worsened the situation.

This blow weakened Díaz as much as had the combined military operations of the *insurrectos*. So paralyzed was the government, in fact, that it missed an opportunity to bag Madero and end the revolution. The rebel chief had been routed and seriously wounded in the March 3 battle of Casas Grandes, and sustained pressure on his dispirited forces might well have turned the tide at that point; but the federal army had been seized by immobility. Taft never understood this little moment of history.[44]

The president did understand that he had made a serious mistake, however. Knox explained it to him. Washington gossip had it, in fact, that the secretary of state was incensed to the point of resignation at his boss's hasty turn at diplomacy.[45] On hotel stationery of the Royal Poinciana, he scrawled a scathing memorandum on the rudiments of international law.

The President cannot undertake to supersede and discharge the functions of the Mexican Government by invading her territory to furnish police protection to Americans without by so doing declaring the inadequacy of the Mexican government or its intentional refusal to protect Americans. This would be cause for war.[46]

Here, of course, the secretary was simply reciting J. Reuben Clark. There had evidently been some more bludgeoning behind the scenes, with Knox very likely being treated to the same lecture that he now passed along to the president. "Our obligation to our citizens," Knox concluded in the oft-spoken words of his solicitor, "is to insist upon Mexico extending to them the full protection of her laws under which our citizens have elected to live and which protection is secured to them by treaty guarantees."

In the end, the mobilization fiasco redounded to Reuben's credit. Having burned his fingers once, President Taft was not likely to toy with intervention again in the near future. Thinking to take advantage of this penitence, Reuben went so far as to propose that the president issue a proclamation irrevocably committing the United States to the policy of noninvolvement and warning all Americans in Mexico to remain aloof from the revolutionary struggle. On March 15 he submitted a draft of the proclamation to Taft for his signature, and the president gave it his approval.[47] At the last minute, however, after the proclamation had returned from the printer, Taft changed his mind; and the document was consigned to the solicitor's files.[48] There it would repose until a new Mexican crisis, as yet unforeseen, would call it forth.

Chapter 8

BLOOD ON THE BORDER

Among his souvenirs Reuben Clark saved an odd postcard. The black-and-white photograph on its face showed a rough-looking *hombre* of the Pancho Villa ilk surveying a file of human corpses. The caption read: "After the Battle of April 13, Agua Prieta, Mexico."[1]

Agua Prieta—"Black Water"—was fittingly named. A desolate little border town across the tracks from Douglas, Arizona, this cluster of adobe hovels seemed anything but a prestigious military target. Agua Prieta was characteristically taking its afternoon *siesta,* in fact, when Red Lopez—the man on the postcard—first came to town. The only notice given of his arrival was a laconic "Rebels coming in on train" flashed by the telegraph agent at Cabullona. There was just enough time to scatter Mexican federal soldiers along the track—not enough to warn the Americans nearby.[2]

It was Robert Harrington's first taste of revolution. He was a switchman for the Southern Pacific, and at one o'clock in the afternoon of April 13 he was standing atop a boxcar in the American sector of the international rail yards. The train that Red Lopez had commandeered at Cabullona steamed in at full throttle, *insurrectos* hanging from every window. In the next moment the rebels were boiling from the coach exits and all hell was breaking loose. Robert Harrington was too dumbfounded to duck as bullets whined through the air. Whether the one that struck him in the head was fired by a *federal* or an *insurrecto* did not matter: he stumbled blindly and toppled from the car. The Mexican Revolution had claimed its first victim on American soil.[3]

ii

One might argue that Harrington's death was brought about by Reuben Clark's policy. For in a situation where any course of action

142

AFTER THE BATTLE OF APR. 13, AGUA PRIETA, MEXICO.

Red Lopez and trophies: Among the casualties was Mexico's feudal past.

was bound to be wrong, the State Department had indeed made a serious mistake. By refusing to embargo the sale of guns to the *insurrectos,* the Taft administration had made guns the magical touchstone of the revolution—and at the same time had made Mexican ports of entry the prime targets. In a revolution where generals like Orozco were expending a million rounds of ammunition in a single engagement, guns and ever more guns were necessary to sustain the momentum.[4] Gunrunners could not supply them fast enough; they had to be secured wholesale. Somnolent little Agua Prieta had been picked for the Lopez assault because of its direct access to Douglas.

Douglas, Arizona, was still a frontier town in the spring of 1911, albeit a prosperous and well-ordered one. Founded at the turn of the century as a center for copper smelting, the hamlet passed quickly through the saloon and gambling-hall stage to acquire sturdy limestone edifices, sixty-five hundred inhabitants, and an aura of staid respectability. Among its bankers and businessmen not much notice was taken of the Mexican slum town across the tracks.[5]

Like Robert Harrington, the shoppers on Third Street were quietly going about their business when the shooting began. Three blocks away, in the American customhouse, goods were being routinely inspected for delivery across the border. A block further, at the

143

Mexican depot, several American passengers were disembarking from a Sonoran train. All of them were taken unawares by the commando raid.

Everything, of course, happened fast. Guns were firing, and people were screaming, and Maderists were sounding forth with the rebel yell. The Americans in the railroad depot suddenly found themselves engulfed in pandemonium. They tried to take refuge in a corner of the lobby. They even threw up a white flag. But the federals closed in on the station with a withering fusillade, and it was not long before someone was hit.[6]

Meanwhile, the Mexican citizens of Agua Prieta made straight for the international boundary. Bullets from the railway station snapped through the air as they ran, dropping an occasional civilian in his tracks. In the American rail yards a second switchman was hit as he turned to gape at the lifeless body of Robert Harrington. The customhouse became a refuge for the panic-stricken, but not for long. Soon the federals' steel-jacketed bullets were crashing through the windows and zipping through the adobe walls with puffs of white dust. The casualty list grew longer.

The battle raged on through the afternoon. Both sides made use of American sanctuary. By the time the sun was low, one group of *insurrectos* was strung out along the railroad embankment a bare ten yards from the customhouse doorstep, their rifles propped on the shimmering steel rails, daring the federals to return their fire. The switching yard was strewn with bodies now, some of them motioning feebly for help. At five o'clock Troop K of the U.S. First Cavalry galloped across the international line and, seeing that the Mexican federals were about done for, ordered them to give up and accept asylum in the United States. As the dispirited government troops filed into Douglas, the Americans were already driving across the border to attend the Mexican wounded. Among the *insurrecto* dead they found the body of a handsome young Virginian of 25 who had made the ultimate sacrifice.

But it was the civilian casualties that counted politically. Some of them were people who had been minding their own business in Douglas—a few inside their own homes. Still, the majority were curiosity-seekers who had pressed close to the international line with ghoulish enthusiasm—like Carlos Lennon, a baker from nearby Bisbee who had been standing by the customhouse when he was wounded, not once but twice, and then carted off to the hospital.[7]

iii

It was a grim and agitated William Howard Taft who picked up the telephone the next morning and put in a call to the State Department. As luck would have it, Knox was out of town again. This time, however, the president was not going to be his own secretary of state for anything in the world, so he told Huntington Wilson to get to the White House on the double. The acting secretary buzzed Reuben Clark, and the two of them went immediately to see the president.[8] Taft explained briefly what he knew about the fighting in Agua Prieta: two Americans dead, perhaps eleven or twelve others wounded, some of them gravely. Nor was the news from Mexico City much brighter. Instead of apology, vituperation seemed to be the fare from the Díaz government. Foreign minister Enrique Creel charged that this was just the pretext the United States had been looking for in order to launch its projected "invasion" of Mexico. (Taft's mobilization was barely a month old.)[9] Besides, Creel claimed that he had verified reports of shooting *from* Douglas as well as into it—a likely possibility under the circumstances.[10] Ambassador Wilson was already at work on a scorching note demanding apologies, indemnities, and a heavy dose of punishment for those responsible. But with the fall of Agua Prieta, Díaz was against the wall; he was in no mood for notes demanding this or that.[11]

Reuben may well have considered himself on the spot at the president's meeting. The open sale of arms had boomeranged dramatically and cost more American lives. Yet if Taft was having doubts about the continued wisdom of his Mexican policy, either he chose not to voice them or else Reuben persuaded him to the contrary. In any event, the president decided to hold to his course. A telegram was sent to the mayor of Douglas, urging that citizens be kept away from the border district in the event of further hostilities. Then a note was dispatched to the Mexican government, warning it not to fire on American soil in the future. The same warning was sent unofficially to the rebels in Agua Prieta.[12] The outrage would be treated as an incident, the acting secretary explained, but any similar

145

occurrence might "compel action by this country." As for the existing damage, claims would duly be submitted through regular diplomatic channels. There was even a possibility, Reuben intimated to the press, that Mexico might file counterclaims based upon the contributory negligence of the Americans. The Taft administration had chosen to turn the other cheek.[13]

Evenhandedness, however, was no guarantee of the peace. The mayor of Douglas was still up in arms and the interventionists still hopping mad. Ambassador Wilson wanted to "fire a hot telegram" to the State Department and demand an immediate showdown.[14] There was talk in the Senate Foreign Relations Committee of a resolution to intervene.[15] And most discouragingly, Mexico, far from being mollified, now began imagining that the order not to shoot into Douglas was itself designed to boost the revolution. How could Agua Prieta be recaptured, the Mexican ambassador asked testily, if government troops could not fire northward?[16]

iv

And recapture Agua Prieta the Mexican federal government must. Everything depended on it. Not only was Red Lopez enjoying open access to American armaments, but he was also collecting Mexican customs. By a series of rulings after the battle, Solicitor Clark had decreed that the *insurrectos* could collect the duties as a bona fide government and that the established, recognized, and for three decades friendly government of Porfirio Díaz could not collect them a second time.[17] Later he declared that Mexico City could not close ports of entry in the hands of the rebels other than by effective military blockade.[18] There was a certain legal consistency in these pronouncements; they were the same ones that Reuben had rendered a year earlier for Nicaragua. All the same, they made a military counteroffensive at Agua Prieta obligatory–together with all of the probable consequences.

On April 17 Díaz made his move. Beginning at dawn federal forces some sixteen hundred strong arrayed themselves in a fan-shaped formation and began to move against the rebel positions. Within minutes every citizen of Douglas had heard the news, and by breakfast time a crowd had jammed itself along Third Street. This time, however, the army was ready. Soldiers drove the crowds up to Sixth Street and then posted themselves in a picket line along the border. As the day-long battle progressed, one soldier lost his hat and several others their horses; but there was no point-blank shooting into hordes of spectators.[19]

Still, several people were hit. It seemed that, danger or no, Douglasites could not resist the temptation of watching a war from their own doorsteps. Hostesses of the town actually invited friends to "battle teas," where a group would assemble on some handy flat roof, enjoy light refreshments, and then take turns watching the action through field glasses.[20] What they saw did not disappoint them. The federals, with two machine guns and a three-pound cannon, worked slowly and patiently against the *insurrecto* fortifications. And the *insurrectos* blazed back with deadly accuracy, their bullets turning the sun-baked earth into what one witness described as "smoking ground." The ground was smoking on one knoll in the cemetery, too. Federal machine gunners, aiming at an *insurrecto* redoubt there, were heedlessly skipping their thirty-millimeter bursts off the brow of the hill and into the American streets beyond. Several battle teas were abruptly dispersed by this fusillade, and some of the guests were hauled off on stretchers. Other of the casualties were less culpable. A Mr. John Keith was crossing Eighth Street when he was struck in the leg. Seventeen employees of the Copper Queen were at work in the company's main office when a bullet buzzed through the room. And a blacksmith's helper named Frank Williams was standing with his family in the center of the business district when he suddenly winced and fell to the pavement, a Mauser bullet lodged beside his heart.[21]

v

It was the hardest fought and most significant battle of the revolution yet. Casualties on both sides ran into the hundreds. More important to the U.S. State Department, however, seven Americans were injured on their own soil.[22] The political damage, however, far surpassed the physical. It was a crisis of the first order for Taft's non-interventionism in general and Reuben Clark's legalism in particular. Diplomatic notes, appeals to reason, considerations of humanity, tenets of international law—all of these had proven ineffective. Now, with the administration poised on the brink of humiliation, the only questions remaining seemed to be those of naked power. Could the troops go in? Should they go in? What recourse, if any, remained open if they did not go in?

One at a time, these queries were tossed out onto the State Department's conference table by Philander Knox. It was April 17, Easter Sunday, bright and balmy, and the second battle of Agua Prieta was still sputtering furiously on the Arizona border. The secretary was not interested in abstractions or theoretics, as one participant observed—only in concrete results. As Knox posed his questions, the answers took a symptomatic turn. Wilbur Carr gave a laconic summary of the discussion.

Question as to how to protect Douglas from fire on Mexican side. Agreed that would be justified in crossing line with troops, but not desirable in interest of preventing injury to Americans in interior. John Hay said to have held that troops could be landed anywhere to protect American interests. Knox said he did not believe Hay had so held without qualifications in his mind.[23]

Once again, the secretary was using Reuben Clark's arguments and even echoing the solicitor's exact words. He was, as Carr concluded, "very much against sending troops into Mexico because 'if you do you will never come out.'" Knox had been brought squarely to terms with the two central problems, as Reuben saw them, of armed intervention in Mexico: controlling the intervention once it began, and accepting all of the consequences the intervention might bring. Few department officials had given much thought to such problems. Rather, they had conceived the matter in *code duello* terms of national honor and national satisfaction, as though the American hostages in Mexico did not exist.

Reuben left the conference victorious once again, but his margins were steadily growing slimmer. For what appeared to be the last time politically feasible, the Taft administration swallowed its pride and declined to take action. Agua Prieta was recaptured by the federals. But for Red Lopez—who had been in Douglas sleeping off a hangover during the battle and awakened to find it lost—there would soon come another opportunity.[24] The dynamics of the Mexican Revolution had settled into a pattern: it was only a matter of time before Madero would try again.

vi

In fact, it was only a matter of two weeks. In a kind of nightmare revisitation, the Agua Prieta story unfolded all over again, this time at El Paso–Juárez. There, of course, the same essential geography existed: the American city and the Mexican city separated only by the Rio Grande. Ciudad Juárez, however, was a bigger prize than sleepy little Agua Prieta—a much bigger prize. For El Paso, with its vast rail connections and sprawling commercial network, was nothing less than the gateway to Mexico. Opening this port of entry to the revolution would be opening the entire United States. "If Juárez falls," predicted Francisco Madero's brother Gustavo, "the Mexican administration will fall. Give us Juárez, and we shall have the country in sixty days."[25]

The rebels massed for an attack in late April. Madero himself was on hand to lead it, for his whole cause hung in the balance. Both Orozco and Villa were on hand too, spoiling for a showdown with Díaz. Spared the surprise that had thrown Douglas into confusion, American residents of El Paso were implored to keep away from the combat zone. Even a *few* more deaths like the ones at Douglas might destroy the president's Mexican policy once and for all. This time there was no trusting to self-interest: a troop of mounted cavalry was on hand to shoo the American spectators out of harm's way. But it was all to no avail. When Colonel Steever's troopers drove El Pasoans from the river banks, they jammed the roofs of buildings, jostled for place on the Franklin and Krazy Kat mountains, and even aligned themselves atop boxcars in the railroad yards.[26] The more committed were not content merely to watch the battle; instead, they crossed over to render military service. One imaginative group made off with the muzzle-loading Civil War cannon that guarded the city hall and trundled it across a shallow spot in the river. It doubled the *insurrecto* artillery.[27]

In Washington the air was charged with expectancy. At the State Department there was an around-the-clock telegraph vigil, with a handful of officers joining Assistant Secretary Huntington Wilson at the watch. J. Reuben Clark took his place with the others. They were already discussing what options they might play if forbearance should fail this final test.

And fail it did. The three-day battle of Ciudad Juárez exceeded anything that had gone before in the Mexican Revolution. Madero and the *insurrectos* shot, smashed, and in the end literally blasted their way through the city, street by street, until only an exhausted remnant of the federal defenders cowered in the bull ring. Amid such fireworks, more American casualties were foreordained. Five noncombatants died and another two dozen were wounded as bullets by the thousands ricocheted through the streets of El Paso.[28]

vii

For a Roosevelt or a Wilson, this indignity would have marked patience's end. But the stolid William Howard Taft was still impressed by those long-range questions about intervention: How to control it? How to end it? How to deal with its consequences? He was at dinner with Mrs. Taft and military aide Archie Butt when the dispatch from El Paso was delivered to him. He read the telegram in silence and handed it to Colonel Butt. "I suppose, Mr. President, you hate to contemplate what may be the outcome of this Mexican business," ventured the latter. But the president had already resolved to go on keeping the faith. Said he,

"I'll tell you what I am going to do, Archie. I am going to sit tight on the lid, and it will take a good deal to pry me off."

"Do you think we are going to have war with Mexico, Will?" asked Mrs. Taft.

"I don't know, Nellie. I only know that I am going to do everything in my power to prevent one."[29]

viii

There was at least one member of Congress who thought that "sitting on the lid" was not enough. He was the tireless Senator William J. Stone, Democrat, from Missouri. "Gum-shoe Bill," as his constituents knew him back in Columbia, was a good mixer, an ardent Bryanite, and a practical politician second to none. As governor of the state and three-term member of the House of Representatives, he had ridden out a quarter-century of Missouri politics with the Democratic machine still intact.[30] Stone was not much given to diplomatic idealism, especially in dealing with Mexicans, and by May of 1911 he had had quite enough of Christian meekness. In the aftermath of the bloodshed on the border he arose and addressed the Senate. He began with a vivid description of the casualties in El Paso and then passed on to analyze the government's inability to respond.

The newspapers report the President as saying that he will take no affirmative action until he is authorized to do so by the Congress, and Senators say that Congress can not, without violating some red-tape precedent, take any action until the President first calls upon the Congress for its advice and direction. And so, between the upper and nether millstones of this disgraceful governmental inaction, peaceable American citizens residing on the border are being ground to ashes.

With this nicely mixed metaphor, the senator hit his stride. He depicted the folly of those who banked foreign policy on international law; he berated a president and congress who "stand with bowed heads and folded arms"; he inveighed against governmental inaction so pronounced "that it smacks ... of something I do not like to name." And his cadenza was rousing and patriotic.

Mr. President, there was a time in the history of this country when Americans were made of more rugged stuff. There was a time when they would take the hazard of war if it were necessary to protect the life or liberty of a single citizen whose life or liberty was in peril. Then the American flag was indeed an emblem of protection and a symbol of safety. Are we of this generation made of such soft material that we dare not lift our hands to protect our people, fearing, forsooth, that it might involve us in war? If that be true, then we are indeed degenerate sons of noble sires! If that be true, we no longer have the spirit of our fathers![31]

Stone was not without his detractors. Stately Elihu Root, for example, accused him of "[taking] a step backward in the pathway of civilization."[32] But Gum-shoe Bill had been too long in politics to be put down easily. He was the ranking Democrat on the Senate Foreign Relations Committee and was in a position to do a great deal of harm. Moreover, he was soon to acquire a powerful ally from the border state of New Mexico, and the two of them would proceed to wreak vengeance upon Taft's Mexican policy. So while the speech of May 9 was but one straw in the wind, it marked a turn of the wind that was ominous. Solicitor Clark, who had not found much to say since El Paso, was soberly impressed—a fact which was to have significance for the Mexican Revolution later on.

ix

Meanwhile, it turned out that Gustavo Madero had been right: the fall of Juárez changed everything. With the rebels now installed on the border and in command of the customhouse, even Díaz could see the writing on the wall. Fortunately the surrender and abdication of his government were arranged in such a way as to encourage constitutional process and discourage reprisals against Americans. None other than Francisco de la Barra, the recent ambassador, was named to head an interim government to conduct a free election for the presidency. Madero of course won. On November 6 the *insurrecto* chief, looking more like an undersized vaudeville comic than a dignified statesman, took the oath as president of the Republic of Mexico.[33]

x

As for Reuben Clark, traveling home to Grantsville for the Christmas holidays, there seemed to be hope in the Mexican situation. Mexico had made a stride toward democracy. The government had changed hands—not peacefully, to be sure, but at least constitutionally. Madero showed no ill disposition toward the Americans living in his country and gave every indication of being willing to cooperate with Washington. Most importantly, the United States Army had not crossed the border. True, Robert Harrington was dead and there was not much consolation for his widow—but how many Robert Harringtons would have died in Chihuahua and Sonora and Durango and Coahuila if the soldiers had gone in?

Most of these results could be attributed in one way or another to the Mexican policy of William Howard Taft and many of them to the direct influence of J. Reuben Clark. Working behind the scenes in his unassuming way, Reuben had managed both to make capital decisions and to guide the thrust of policy. In the process he had run up against an ambassador, an attorney general, a ranking member of the Senate Foreign Relations Committee, and the combined influence of the Mexican federal government. In the end he appeared to have won the day, and his point of view seemed dramatically vindicated.

Except that this was not the end.

Chapter 9

JUÁREZ

Both elation and unease marked Washington's attitude at the passing of *Porfirismo*. On the one hand, there was a profound sense of release, as if the nightmare were over at last. On the other hand, whereas Díaz, with all his faults, had been a known quantity to the State Department for thirty years, Madero was only a question mark. Had he not, for example, campaigned against "imperialism" as well as "despotism"? Were not his principal supporters essentially anti-American, the same people who threw bricks at the Yankees in Guadalajara and assaulted schoolchildren in Mexico City? And what did he propose to reform in the first place if not the entire structure of investment and politics of which American interests were so much a part? Ambassador Henry Lane Wilson, for one, saw nothing but trouble ahead.

There exists a very powerful and numerous opposition to Madero throughout the country among people who believe his policies to be impracticable, his intelligence dubious and his character lacking in firmness, vigor and consistency, but a large proportion of these elements believe that the sooner Madero has had his fling and is placed in power the sooner he will demonstrate his incompetence and lack of the qualities so essential at this moment, and that his loss of popular favor and prestige will eventually result in loss of power, leadership, and perhaps the loss of the Presidency in the new revolution which it is thought the anticipated misgovernment will bring about.[1]

Despite the ambassador's gloominess, the department as a whole was essentially accepting of the new president. There was a general sigh of relief when it became evident, in Madero's first months of office, that he was not the radical demagogue some had feared. Before long, in fact, he and Washington were well on the way toward accommodation.

ii

Such difficulties as remained had mostly to do with the claims. Solicitor Clark's casualty list had grown to lengthy proportions by this time, and each name represented (in addition to humanitarian concern) a certain amount of domestic pressure on the administration. Settling the claims became a matter of the highest priority, for until settled they would provide a rallying point for any and all dissatisfaction with Taft's Mexican policy. But Madero was under pressure as well. His entrance into Mexican politics had been effected largely in the name of anti-Americanism, and if he now handed over large indemnities to the Yankees it might look like a payoff. Moreover, Madero could ill afford to lay out millions for foreign claims while his own people verged upon starvation.

President Taft's critics did not understand these points, and they did not want to. They understood only that enormous wrongs had been heaped upon American citizens and that apparently nothing was being done about it. Before long the complaints set off rumblings in Congress and the press. Reuben's first job was to turn that situation around. As the remembered virtuoso of the Alsop settlement, he was supposed to work whatever magic the circumstances called for—and quickly.

Unfortunately, though, complications were already setting in. The claims were large in number, astronomical in amount, and possessed of fatal attraction for dilettantes, sharpies, and plain humbugs. Worst of all, they were inseparable from domestic politics. Every claim, it seemed, had circling around it at least one inside dopester, one friend of somebody's, and one prominent congressman. By the time all three had stopped by to see the solicitor, the claim itself was in tatters and Mexican-American relations had taken another step backward.

A case in point was that of Judge Wilfley. Lebbeus Redman Wilfley owned a prosperous mine in Chihuahua and was connected to some of the most consequential investors in northern Mexico. He was also a personal friend of President Taft, an international lawyer of modest reputation, and a gadfly second to none. Eventually he came to represent all sorts of claimholders against the Mexican government, himself among them. Judge Wilfley knew Reuben Clark, too, and had no compunctions about using the friendship to speed up the wheels of justice. Reuben, however, did not agree as to how the wheels should be accelerated. Undaunted, Wilfley turned to another friend, Senator William Stone, and asked him to twist Reuben's arm. Gum-shoe Bill was well situated to do just that, and he made a couple of heavy-handed attempts at it. But Reuben held firm. In fact, all Wilfley got for his pains was a sharp reproof for supposing that such tactics would succeed. Yet still the judge did not go away. He continued to buzz around Mexican-American relations like a fly at a picnic—until he discovered that the way to settle claims aginst Mexico was to depose Mexican presidents.[2]

For his part, Reuben was making some limited headway. Soon after Madero's inauguration, the American solicitor persuaded the new president to set up a consultative claims commission to hear the American grievances.[3] Next he devised a system for separating the truly meritorious claims from the undeserving. When approached about the latter, Reuben gave out the stock reply that

a claimants [*sic*] against a foreign government is usually not regarded ... as entitled to diplomatic intervention by his own government until he has exhausted his legal remedies in the appropriate tribunals in the country against which he makes his claim; and that a sovereign government is not ordinarily responsible to alien residents for injuries they receive within its territories from insurgents whose conduct it cannot control.[4]

Finally, Reuben mounted a public relations campaign to reassure critics that the claims situation was well in hand. The campaign was carried out in private with such congressmen as Garner and Sharp of the House Foreign Relations Committee as well as through memoranda for wider circulation.[5] By January, 1912, the solicitor was able to publish a booklet describing the work of his office on behalf of American claimants.[6]

iii

But neither Reuben Clark nor anyone else at the State Department was able to deal with both these niggling details of the Mexican situation and the great imponderables too. Clearly the solicitor needed some help. It arrived in December of 1911, in the person of

156

Fred Morris Dearing. Vigilant, bright, quick to catch on, and one of those Missourians who had to be shown, Dearing was pulled into department headquarters from the American embassy in Mexico City to be assistant chief of the Latin American division and unofficial head of the Mexico desk. Dearing knew all about Mexico. He had observed the tumult at close range and had arrived at essentially the same conclusions about it as had the solicitor. Together they doubled the anchorage for Taft's policy of nonintervention.

Dearing was put in charge of the bulky correspondence with Mexico and made a sort of all-purpose watchdog and troubleshooter. He set up a communications center for receiving and digesting consular reports. From these reports he daily prepared two maps, one for the department and one for the White House, showing the numbers and concentration of Americans in Mexico and the movements of potentially troublesome armed forces.[7] It was very likely Fred Dearing who spotted the sudden reappearance of the whirlwind.

iv

Contrary to the assessment of Ambassador Wilson, Francisco Madero was neither weak nor foolish. During his tenure of office he proved to be a forthright, courageous, and devoted patriot who strove to make the revolution a living reality. But he strove against overpowering odds. The Mexican people were still poor and uneducated. Contention and dissatisfaction were still rife among them, and their taste for power at the dethroning of Díaz merely encouraged the delusion that they could handle matters for themselves. Some of them, of course, like the businessmen and industrialists, had been relatively satisfied with the *ancien régime* and regarded any change as being for the worse; the rest wanted changes so sweeping that nothing could have satisfied them. Once, in a personal confrontation, Díaz had said to Madero: "Señor, a man must be more than honest to govern Mexico." The new president now came to know what that meant.[8]

Weakened by disaffection, Madero quickly ran into difficulties. The first was Zapata. Still aflame with revolutionary passions, the *Zapatistas* of Morelos were far too radical to come to terms with a moderate like Madero. Ultimately he had to do battle with them as had Díaz before him.⁹ Next, Madero had to deal with Bernardo Reyes. Reyes was an old Díaz affiliate who had harbored designs of his own for the presidency. With Porfirio out of the way, Reyes saw his chance. He rose in rebellion in December—only a month after Madero took office—and, in the best tradition of Mexican revolutionaries, headed north for San Antonio.¹⁰

These outbreaks were bad enough for the government, but the next one spelled disaster. Malcontents in the north began rallying behind Dr. Francisco Vázquez Gómez, once a high-ranking *insurrecto* but lately on the outs with Madero. By January of 1912 the *Vázquistas* were loudly claiming that Madero had betrayed the revolution. Far more than Zapata's or Reyes's followers, this group had to be taken seriously. The *Vázquistas* hailed from Madero's own Progressive Constitutional party and from revolutionary Chihuahua as well. They were in a position to move against the American border as Madero himself had done, and they had a chance of appealing to the convictions of fellow Chihuahuans Pancho Villa and Pascual Orozco—the two most dangerous men in Mexico.

With Villa they got nowhere. He had conceived a doglike devotion to Madero. Besides, he had returned to Chihuahua City, married his childhood sweetheart, taken up the life of a butcher—fittingly, some said—and was resting content with the revolution. But Orozco was another matter. He had been, as friends constantly reminded him, the best general of the war, gathering troops where no one else could find them; sniffing out the enemy's weaknesses at Parral, Torreón, and Hermosillo; and, finally, engineering the fall of Ciudad Juárez. And how had Madero repaid him? Not with a cabinet post, not with an appointment as military chief of staff, not even with a field-grade command in the regular army. Orozco had been relegated to the Department of Chihuahua as commandant—an embarrassingly paltry recompense.

The *Vázquistas,* many of them prominent politicos of the state, went to work on Orozco at once, playing to his pride and his disenchantment. So did cattle baron Luis Terrazas, who lived in palatial splendor in the northern desert and who wanted to have Madero's head on his gatepost. Winning over Orozco would very nearly amount to granting Terrazas his wish.

But for the time being, Orozco would not take the bait. He was of two minds about his pride and disenchantment, about the revolution he had fought so well, and about the unfathomable man who was now president of Mexico. He would bide his time. Meanwhile, just what sort of mettle, he wondered, did these so-called *Vázquistas* really possess? Were they just political blowhards gusting up a passing storm, or were they genuine revolutionaries capable of real success? As if in response to Orozco's challenge, four hundred *Vázquistas* saddled their horses in February and, under the fiery leadership of Emilio Campa, started northward. How better to convince the old mule skinner, Orozco, than by duplicating his conquest of Juárez?[11]

As Fred Dearing watched the colored pins move steadily northward on his map, it became evident to him that *Vázquismo* was a different sort of movement than Madero's had been. For one thing, the violence of the *Vázquistas,* or *colorados* as they were coming to call themselves (Americans anglicized the name to "Red Flaggers"), was far uglier, more sadistic, and less rational than had been the case with the Maderists. They destroyed life and property with abandon, scorching the earth in their passing. Anyone who opposed them was dealt with summarily; they cut the soles from the feet of one poor devil and drove him over the desert for a mile before he died. Moreover, while Madero's concern had been for the plight of the masses, these new revolutionaries had no qualms about exploiting the civilian populace.[12] The civilian populace, of course, included thousands of Americans.

v

The appearance of *Vázquismo* in northern Mexico shattered both the calm and the optimism in Washington. Things were back to the beginning again. Madero had been lawfully elected and duly recognized by the United States; thus he now stood exactly where Díaz had stood before him, charged with protecting the lives and property of foreigners in Mexico. And like Díaz, Madero was preoccupied with a domestic insurrection that endangered himself as much as the resident foreigners. Now, incredibly, here was another pack of rebels homing in on the border and threatening to repeat the tragedies of

Douglas and El Paso. The pressures on the administration began mounting: from Americans in Mexico crying for protection, from Henry Lane Wilson urging a hard line toward Madero, from Democrats in Congress demanding firmness all around, from the Mexican Foreign Office pleading for assistance. Over the whole confusion hovered the old specter of intervention.

Even before the advent of the *colorados,* President Taft, now in an election year and fighting for his political life, had been growing restless. Staying clear and remaining neutral had not, apparently, calmed the turbulence of the revolution or ameliorated the situation of resident Americans. Now, with the appearance of more violence, it became evident that the forces unleashed by Madero might have no foreseeable end. Taft suddenly wanted some new—and different—answers.

The president's dissatisfaction worked as a mandate for more aggressive measures. Appropriately, Assistant Secretary Huntington Wilson took personal charge of the ensuing discussions, soliciting suggestions from all quarters. Over the course of several weeks, three different positions gradually emerged. The first was that of Ambassador Wilson in Mexico. He believed that the entire dilemma could be resolved by ordering the evacuation of all U.S. citizens south of the border.[13] Indeed, on his own authority Wilson had been privately urging Americans to withdraw for some time.[14] Once the hostages were out of the way, he argued, the United States could do what it well pleased about the border fighting. But the assistant secretary saw certain dangers in that course of action. The withdrawal of nationals, as he explained to the president, "is an act so often associated in the mind as a precursor of war" that the Mexicans could not help but see it as a first step toward invasion. Huntington Wilson himself had another policy in mind.

If an overwhelming force, including plenty of artillery, were massed on the line at El Paso, from all I have heard I cannot but still believe that it would speedily end any shooting into El Paso without crossing into Mexican territory.

I still feel most strongly that rather than send troops across we should warn Mexico publicly that the first bullet fired into American territory will be regarded as an invasion and that such invasion will be forthwith repelled, if possible by firing from the American side, but if that be ineffective, by such temporary crossing of the line as may be necessary as a police measure to meet the emergency.[15]

The third position was Solicitor Clark's. He waited until the others had made their cases before submitting his own, which took the form of a carefully reasoned memorandum submitted in late February.[16] Like the assistant secretary, Reuben rejected out of hand the ambassador's evacuation plan. How would the Americans be evacuated? he asked pointedly. Who would alert them? What would convince them to abandon the work of a lifetime? How would the Mexican government ever raise the staggering sum necessary to compensate their losses? The questions answered themselves.

Reuben next turned his attention to Huntington Wilson's scheme for a show of force on the border, which he liked no better. It was one thing to talk about the "technical invasion" of returning Mexican fire, he said, but it was an altogether different matter to talk about an actual invasion by American troops. International law could hardly condone such a response to a few stray bullets. And then there were the practical issues to consider.

Once in Mexico, it is impossible to tell when we should be able to return. If the Mexican contestants refused to observe our warning not to fire into American territory and desist from their intention only when actually driven from their position by an armed force, it is probable we would have to maintain such armed force in Mexico until a central Mexican Government had again gained control.

And when, asked Reuben, might that be? The central government was virtually powerless in large sections of Mexico. In those same sections anti-Americanism was rife. What would happen if crossing the border proved, as it might, to be the match in the tinder box? Obviously, more troops would be necessary to protect the resident Americans—meaning that intervention would feed upon itself again and again. "This," concluded the solicitor,

obviously would mean the over-running of Mexico by a large force, how large it is impossible to determine, but certainly a force numbering far more than our regular army and perhaps even the regular army plus the existing state militia. In other words, this Government would have on its hands what in reality would be a war of conquest of a people animated by the most intense hatred for the conquering race. History has a sufficient number of instances of this kind of conflict to demonstrate that such work is not child's play. . . . It would seem most unwise, if not indeed much worse, to open fire upon Juárez or to invade Mexico unless this Government is adequately prepared for war.

161

What was left after Reuben's process of reduction was a narrow course, to be sure, but he saw it as the only one feasible. Americans would have to stay in Mexico and the troops would have to stay out—and the citizens of El Paso would have to shut up their homes and move beyond the shower of death. Such dislocation would undoubtedly work a hardship on individuals, and it would be viewed by the hawks as a dishonorable retreat. But any other action was simply unthinkable.

The solicitor's memorandum was an effective piece of persuasion. Looking over it, Huntington Wilson came to see the flaws in his own position. In late February the assistant secretary approved Reuben's document for the president as the official recommendation of policy.[17]

And yet, what seemed most striking about the Clark memorandum was not the power of its arguments so much as their strange sense of abstraction. For all its concern with practical consequences, the report was curiously dissociated from the realities of life at El Paso. Evacuating Americans in Mexico was dismissed as unworkable—but removing thousands of El Pasoans from the danger zone was proposed as a defensible alternative. Reuben might have applied his own hard questioning. How was this logistical nightmare to be undertaken? Who would accomplish it? And who would accept the responsibility for its unforeseen consequences? The same sorts of queries might have been leveled at the idea of firing back across the border, which Reuben seriously discussed. How were American officers to know who had fired which bullets where? And how were they to return the fire without killing scores of innocent civilians?

Nothing better illustrated the dreamlike quality which the Mexican Revolution had taken on for American policymakers. In near-academic isolation, they were earnestly debating neutrality, intervention, and a dozen other abstractions; while in Mexico human beings were perishing daily in the revolutionary holocaust. The two worlds moved steadily farther apart. When in early February the commander of the American troops in El Paso requested instructions on what to do if, despite all warnings, bullets were actually fired into U.S. territory, his inquiry went unanswered.[18] Few at the State Department were thinking about actualities.

To complicate the situation, events on the border were themselves slipping out of control. In mid-February a detachment of U.S. soldiers boarded a streetcar in El Paso for a short trip across town. Unbeknown to the young lieutenant in charge, the streetcar line crossed the international bridge into Juárez; and before the officer woke up to his mistake, the State Department had a de facto intervention on its hands.[19] A hasty note of apology defused the incident, but a heavy sense of impotence lingered. Who could tell when some other anonymous lieutenant might bring the whole structure of American neutrality crashing down around his ears—especially when cannons were being primed for firing into Mexico and troops were being held at ready? As Campa and his *colorados* closed in on Juárez, a distinct paralysis began to grip Washington.

vi

In fact, when matters came to a head on February 26, the State Department was caught napping—and this in spite of numerous warnings. As early as February 14, Consul Luther T. Ellsworth at El Paso reported that Mexican authorities expected an attack on the city "some time in the near future."[20] Nine days later there were "persistent rumors of [an] impending sack [of] Juárez and even [an] attempt on El Paso."[21] The following day Consul Alonzo B. Garrett at Nueva León wrote that "the situation is very serious."[22] But the State Department had heard cries of wolf before, and on February 23 Secretary Knox departed for Palm Beach to prepare for his goodwill tour of Latin America.[23] Division Chief W. T. S. Doyle accompanied him.[24] Even Huntington Wilson was in a holiday mood, and on February 24 he too left Washington for a long weekend.[25] The expected battle at Juárez, as these officers doubtless consoled themselves, was still many days away. And in any event, Reuben Clark and Fred Dearing were there to mind the store.

Unfortunately Clark and Dearing were little better prepared than the others. When Reuben arrived for work on Monday the 26th, he was handed a dispatch from Consul Ellsworth. "About seven hundred *insurrectos* are closing in on Juárez," it ran. "An attack expected within the next twenty-four hours."[26] To his alarm, Reuben noted that the telegram had arrived at nine o'clock Sunday evening, nearly twelve hours earlier. Immediately he summoned Fred Dearing and the two of them took charge.

One thing was clear at the outset: there was no time for the much-discussed evacuation of El Paso. Reuben's plan had seemed practical enough when a battle at Juárez was only a tactical possibility, but now that it was a cold reality the whole scheme appeared remarkably quixotic. The question was, what to substitute in its place? One by one options were tossed onto the table, and one by one they were discarded. In the end, Huntington Wilson's plan was the only one remaining. Thus, Clark and Dearing decided to warn both armies that firing into El Paso would be regarded as an invasion and that the invasion would be repelled by force.

The two of them were committing the Taft administration to a gigantic bluff. As they well knew, a threat to meet force with force was empty unless the United States was in fact ready to intervene. Huntington Wilson himself had warned that no such threat should be made "until both the army and the navy were prepared for the worst conceivable eventuality; namely, war."[27] War was the very last thing for which Clark and Dearing were prepared. Even the president, for all his saber-rattling, still recoiled at the thought of intervention. Hopefully, however, the Mexicans would be intimidated enough to back down. In the spirit of gamblers placing a very large bet, Clark and Dearing set the new policy in motion.[28]

The first step was to inform the president of the contemplated action. Just after dinner that evening Reuben found himself sitting in the hallway of the White House, solemnly explaining the situation to Taft. He had met the president on his way up from work, and the latter appeared none too alert. As Reuben carefully rehearsed the events transpiring at El Paso and the plans he and Dearing had devised to deal with them, the president's head nodded forward and his eyelids closed. "He sat there sleeping," Reuben later recalled, "but when I got through, he roused himself immediately and he had heard everything I said, and he rendered his decision." He gave Reuben the go-ahead.[29] Telegrams should be readied at once for the Mexican government and for the rebels, warning both against firing into El Paso and threatening intervention if the warning went unheeded. After depositing his own policy memorandum with the president for future reference, Reuben left the White House to draft the telegrams.[30]

Hardly had he entered the door at the State Department when he was handed a fresh dispatch from Consul Thomas P. Edwards at Juárez. A communication had been received from General Campa, stating that he intended to attack Juárez at once and warning all foreigners to withdraw from the city.[31] Hurriedly, Reuben dictated two telegrams. One was addressed to General Campa, admonishing him to avoid any firing across the border and ominously suggesting that "any violation of this warning will almost certainly lead to consequences which it is in the interest of all true Mexican patriots to avoid."[32] The second telegram was directed to Ambassador Wilson in Mexico City.

Immediately bring this matter to attention of both President Madero and Foreign Office. Refer to the matter in Department's February 26, 6 p.m., and say, with all possible seriousness and earnestness, as under express directions from the President, that it is absolutely necessary to prevent firing into American territory at El Paso; otherwise consequences which it is to the best interest of both countries to avoid will almost surely follow. Urge immediately telegraphic action by the Mexican Government.

If this warning was fairly routine, the next sentence of the telegram was to make history. "If Juárez is inadequately defended by Federal troops," Reuben said,

the Mexican Government may, in view of the peculiar situation existing and the possible eventualities, deem it best either that such troops shall make such defense as they contemplate outside of Juárez, and in a place that would not threaten the lives and property of American citizens on American territory, or possibly withdraw without making defense in the immediate neighborhood.[33]

Reuben Clark knew what he was saying. He was saying: "Surrender the city—or else." The solicitor had decided to push his bluff to the limit.

Within the hour, Reuben had returned to the White House to seek approval for the draft telegrams, and this time he took Fred Dearing with him. The president read the drafts through carefully. When he had finished, he looked up and gave a wistful smile. "You know I am not going to cross that line," he said. "That is something for which Congress will have to take the responsibility." The United States, vowed the chief executive loftily, would never embark on a war of conquest while he was in the White House. Then, almost as an afterthought, he added: "But I suppose it will do no harm to threaten them a little."[34]

On the contrary, it did a great deal of harm and might have done far more. As soon as the communications were sent, the fate of the American people rested in the hands of the Mexicans. If Madero had chosen to ignore the ultimatum and El Pasoans were killed in the ensuing battle, Taft might have been very hard put to avoid war. At the very least, his presidency would have been put on the line. The telegram to the Mexican government left the Taft administration no room whatsoever for maneuver.

Fortunately for Taft, Madero had even fewer real choices than he. With legion concerns weighing upon him, with his people hungry and restless, with one rebellion boiling away in Morelos and another brewing in the north, Madero could ill afford an American intervention. Accordingly, after pacing the floor of the National Palace in anger and frustration, he gave in and ordered Ciudad Juárez to be abandoned. The following morning, without firing a shot, Emilio Campa rode triumphantly into the city for which Madero had paid four hundred lives.[35]

vii

Seldom in the annals of American foreign policy had so great an apparent victory been won at so little apparent cost. No guns were fired. No lives were forfeited. No soldiers crossed the line. Without speeches in Congress, angry editorials in the newspapers, or internecine strife in the State Department, the United States emerged unscathed and with enhanced international prestige. Two small telegrams in the tradition of the Big Stick had accomplished in a stroke what doubt, vacillation, and humanitarian supplication had repeatedly failed to achieve.

So much for appearances. As for realities, the tally for the El Paso affair was not quite so encouraging. In the first place, the surrender of Juárez transformed a sandlot revolt into a full-blown rebellion. Now safely installed on the American border and with access to unlimited quantities of arms, the Red Flaggers had a virtually secure base of operations. And in the second place, *Vázquismo,* in this moment of triumph, was magically transmogrified into *Orozquismo,* for the old bandit Orozco could hold out no longer against its seductions. His enlistment meant more than the accession of a winning general and his six-thousand-man garrison in Chihuahua City; it meant charisma. Suddenly Madero was no longer seen as the dashing young Galahad but as the tired conservative on the ropes.

The sea change was dramatically illustrated by what happened next. Madero's government found itself imploring the United States to cut off arms shipments to the rebels, eerily echoing the entreaties of its predecessor. The Orozco revolt, wrote the Mexican ambassador, Manuel Calero, owed its existence "solely to the ease with which arms, munitions, and war material can be obtained from private persons in this country."[36] How was the Madero government supposed to protect resident Americans, he asked tartly, if the United States continued to place weapons in the hands of its enemies? And like de la Barra before him, Calero had his point. Orozco was not content with buying mere pistols and carbines: he wanted the latest and best of everything—including an "aeroplane" equipped to drop explosives![37] If he secured this wherewithal, what was to prevent history from repeating itself? The ambassador quoted no less an authority than John Bassett Moore's *Digest* to the effect that a government might not "plead the defects of its own domestic penal statutes as justification or extenuation of an international wrong to another sovereign power."[38]

He was, however, quoting Moore to the wrong person. Reuben Clark had heard it all before, and he found Madero's latest argument unconvincing. He believed that if the United States really wanted to keep its nose out of Mexican affairs it must be absolutely impartial in applying the law. "It seems to me," he wrote in exasperation to Dearing,

that we might as well, once for all, get before the representatives of the established government in this revolution the various fundamental principles of our duty as "neutrals", both under the principles of international law and the rules of our so-called neutrality statutes.[39]

Finding other means unavailing, the solicitor once again took it upon himself to lay out the law. It all sounded familiar.

Two Classes, —

I Pro-administration
~~For~~ if nothing foolish is
done.

II Contra- administration

Democrats {
Regular = { For – probably
if plan is
worse

(Radical)
Insurgent Repub's {
anti administra-
tion – Probably
against no
matter what is
done.

Whether Regular Contras are
for or against probably be
influenced, —
A. Sympathy { For or against } Revolution
B. Wisdom of course adapted
from standpoint of U.S.

Outline and justification of the policy of neutrality: A situation in which any move was the wrong one.

— 2 —

DEPARTMENT OF STATE,
OFFICE OF THE SOLICITOR.

Federals Secure,—

Formal declaration that neutrality
laws are obeyed and will
be enforced.

That persons serving with insurrectos must take consequences

They get what they have requested

Insurrectos Secure:

Recognition of armed disorder

That citizens serving with Federals
in same position as citizens serving
with them.

First step towards belligerency.

It is in effect a declaration of
neutrality so far as the executive
action is concerned.

Us Secure:—

Warning that will relieve pressure
in case of calamity.

Clear definition of neutral attitude

A statement of position that is due to
our citizens

Under the principles of international law, as well as under the so-called neutrality statutes of this country, the mere commercial sale of supplies in El Paso to Mexicans, whether insurrectos or supporters of the Government, and their simple delivery across the border can not be looked upon as a violation of international law or of the so-called neutrality statutes. This Government can not but admit that the possession of a border port like Ciudad Juárez by insurrecto forces gives the insurrectos a great advantage; but however that may be, it is not an advantage for which this Government is in any way responsible, and grows, rather, out of the misfortune of the Mexican Government or its ineffectiveness at the place, (for which also this Government is not responsible) and the duties and rights of this Government and of persons within its jurisdiction to carry on legitimate business are in nowise changed.[40]

Hard as this was on the Madero government, an even harder blow fell at the same time, and it too was the work of Reuben Clark. On March 2 the solicitor finally persuaded President Taft to issue a proclamation of neutrality.[41] The document, prepared by Reuben a year earlier, was a study in diplomatic subtlety. While calling for complete impartiality on the part of all Americans in Mexico, it conferred no formal recognition of the rebels. Huntington Wilson, who delivered the document to the Mexicans, was carefully coached to explain that it was merely "the usual form and had nothing to do with proclamations of neutrality which carried with them recognition of belligerency."[42] On its face at least, the proclamation did not alter relations between the United States and Mexico by a single jot.

But Reuben Clark knew that the face of the proclamation did not tell the whole story. The document was actually designed to curry favor with Orozco in hopes that he might leave the Americans in Chihuahua alone. To accomplish this end, Reuben had gone as far as possible toward recognizing the *Orozquistas* without actually mentioning the word. To Knox and Huntington Wilson, he confided that the proclamation was the "first step toward belligerency."[43] Surely Orozco, hard though he might be, would not overlook such a gesture as this.

viii

Or would he? To Orozco-watchers like Fred Dearing, opposite answers to the question seemed to run nip and tuck. This was because Orozco was under pressure both to patronize the Americans and to punish them. Like Madero before him, he needed American guns and a certain amount of American moral support. However, he

170

needed a righteous cause too—and what cause could be more righteous than getting rid of the *gringos*? Orozco continued to walk the
line between these conflicting interests as long as it paid him to do
so. Outwardly he seemed willing to live in peace with Mexico's
Yankees.

Until disaster struck. Unfortunately, President Taft chose this of
all moments to make another foray into Mexican-American relations;
when he was through Reuben's diplomacy was in a shambles,
Orozco was an avowed enemy, and the Red Flaggers had declared
open season on Americans. The president had apparently decided
that the time had come to move beyond grand gestures and do
something forceful. And the particular forcefulness, he supposed,
ought to take the form of a total embargo of arms across the border.
He was right. Nothing could have possibly hit Orozco harder than
this, and he reeled and staggered with the blow. Then he set about
to get even.

The decision was made in spite of the solicitor, and State Department officials—including Fred Dearing—handled it as gingerly as possible with him. Even so, they ran afoul of legal justification and
wound up having to come to him anyway. (Someone had dug up an
1898 resolution authorizing the president to cut off arms shipments
to Cuba, but no one was certain whether it would stretch thinly
enough to cover Mexico.) So Reuben got his views on the record.
Yes, he told Dearing, the president probably did have the authority
to shut off the El Paso arms traffic, but to do so would be the
gravest folly. "If we stop such traffic in the case of one revolution,"
he argued earnestly, "we will be faced with difficulty if we decline to
stop it in other revolutions."[44] Prophetic words.

To keep things impeccably legal, the administration went back
to Congress for a new grant of authority; and on March 14 the resolution passed both houses. Henceforth it would be unlawful to export, without the president's approval, arms and ammunition to any
American nation experiencing rebellion.[45]

ix

In time all of this would sort itelf out, and J. Reuben Clark
would have the satisfaction of seeing himself vindicated. For the

present, only one fact seemed important: Pascual Orozco, with the worst possible gang of cutthroats, was loose in the worst possible place—northern Mexico. It was here that the great American mines and cattle ranches were located, that the largest number of American citizens resided, and that the protection afforded by the Mexican federal government was weakest. Orozco would assuredly be a fox in the hencoop—and he would have none of Madero's compunctions about killing chickens.

For Reuben Clark there was one additional concern. Strung across northern Chihuahua, squarely in the path of danger, were eight of the prettiest, tidiest, and most successful settlements on the North American continent. And all of them were Mormon.

Chapter 10

THE MORMON TRAVAIL

When Emilio Campa had cantered into Ciudad Juárez after the evacuation of the federal garrison, his second-in-command had been José Ynez Salazar. Salazar did not much look the brigand. He wore rumpled Panama suits and possessed the mild features of an insurance agent. Nevertheless, José Salazar—like any of Orozco's lieutenants—was not to be taken lightly. With the Panama suits he wore jackboots, and he carried a gun. There was, claimed some, a sinister flicker of malevolence in his slate-gray eyes. And any American he happened to find among captured government forces he summarily ordered shot.[1] Unhappily, it was Salazar who was assigned to work the "Mormon district."

ii

The American Mormons who arrived in northern Mexico in the mid-1880s were a singularly unfortunate people. In their quarrel with the United States over polygamy they had faced an array of civil punishments and the final indignity of exile. But with their unquenchable spirit they had begun anew. By the eve of the revolution they had regained lost affluence and even increased it. For the most part their *colonias* were located in north-central Chihuahua where the Río Casas Grandes cut across a grassy plain below the glistening Sierra Madres. The soil was rich and wildlife abounded. By the time the new settlers had dotted the landscape with churches and schools and sturdy brick farmhouses, there were those who proclaimed that life here was better than back home in Utah. A few even renounced their American citizenship.

Nor was the idyll much disturbed by Mexican politics. The Mormons had a tacit understanding with Porfirio Díaz that as long as they were good citizens they should be left alone. Still, inhabitants of the seedy Mexican towns of the valley did not always want to honor that understanding. They looked to Colonia Díaz and saw sleek horses and fat cattle, to Colonia Dublán and saw opulent mercantile establishments like Farnsworth & Romney, to Colonia Juárez and saw the stately Juárez Academy on its well-manicured campus. It was hard to escape the conclusion that these Americans had made a good thing out of life in their land. There was always a temptation–out of curiosity or out of envy–to poke around the Mormon settlements; and, when the Madero revolt had swept northward toward the border, the poking around had drastically increased. Yet, the *colonos* did not worry much. They would keep out of Mexican affairs and the Mexicans would keep out of theirs.[2]

iii

But Orozco's rabble-rousers found the Mormons too useful to ignore. For one thing, they symbolized the hateful Yankee-in-our-midst. "See how these Americans prosper in your land!" cried one recruiter vengefully. "How they build colleges! and look at your little hovels that you and your fathers have lived in for ages! We want to get rid of these Americans."[3] For another thing, the Mormon lands and improvements would be up for the taking if the proprietors should be put to flight–an enticing possibility. Finally, the Mormons were good for the considerable quantities of food and fodder necessary to a horseback campaign.

As long as Orozco had to pose as a friend of the Yankees, he could use the Mexican Mormons for only the latter of the three purposes, and he gave Salazar strict orders to be polite. Thus, when flour or hay were requisitioned for "the army," foragers were careful to give the *colonos* written receipts which might be presented to the Mexican government for reimbursement–as soon as Orozco won. Not every good businessman, of course, would want to trade in this particular currency, and there were a few ugly incidents associated with those who refused; but by and large the Mormon settlers knew that they had no choice in the matter and they submitted peaceably.[4]

Even so, the ugly incidents multiplied. Salazar's men were undisciplined at the very best, and he could not begin to control them all. And what could one say to a band of four or five armed rebels who, reeking of *aguardiente* and smug with political rectitude, strode through the door of one's co-op and began gathering up merchandise?

In mid-February one group of Mormons approached General Salazar himself about such problems, and the general responded by reading an ostentatious proclamation of protection in the Dublán public square. Yet the looting persisted. Within a week's time Dublán's Union Mercantile Store had lost an additional $2,500 worth of merchandise.[5]

In such circumstances it was only a matter of time before someone took the law into his own hands. Soon groups of Mormon vigilantes were having run-ins, and then shoot-outs, with the looters, while the looting itself degenerated into out-and-out assault: a rape, a knifing, several cases of missing persons, and in Colonia Díaz a Mexican with a chip on his shoulder who simply gunned down the first Mormon he saw.[6] The inhabitants of the *colonias* were happy enough when in early March Orozco assembled his legions and rode off to hang Madero from the tallest tree in the Zócalo.[7]

iv

President Madero, who did not want to be hanged, dispatched no mere general to meet the *Orozquista* advance; he sent none less than his minister of war, José Gonzáles Salas. Gonzáles Salas was a capable commander, but he was ill prepared for the hardball tactics Orozco employed. At Rellano his army was speeding northward in three separate trains when suddenly a locomotive was seen hurling toward them at full steam, its throttle jammed open and its whistle shrieking like a bomb. It *was* a bomb, stuffed with high explosives and aimed with fail-safe accuracy at Gonzáles Salas's vanguard train. The resulting explosion so scattered and demoralized the federal troops that they were decimated within a few hours, while Gonzáles Salas committed suicide.[8]

Madero did not know where to turn next. Finally, and with greatest reluctance, he turned to Victoriano Huerta, a talented but insubordinate officer he had been obliged to cashier during the Zapata campaign. Bald, bullet-headed, and suffering from poor eyesight which caused him to squint sourly much of the time, Huerta was acknowledged to be the measure of Orozco. But he was a constant and heavy drinker who had to be led off to bed every night; he was consumed with insatiable ambition; and, most significantly, he was a man utterly devoid of honor. When relieved of his command in Morelos, Huerta had sworn to get even with Madero. He had then brooded remorsefully in alcoholic semiretirement. Yet the bitterness seemed forgotten when he was recalled to active service against Orozco. "I will whip him. I guarantee it," he told Madero.[9]

Thanks to some timely help from the U.S. government, Huerta proved as good as his word. Orozco's munitions were already becoming depleted before he finished off Gonzáles Salas, and it was only days after that when President Taft's arms embargo was announced. Orozco felt the effects immediately. On May 10, when Huerta massed his forces and struck at the rebels near Bermejillo, some of his adversaries were armed only with homemade weapons. The result was a resounding federal victory. A fortnight later at Rellano, the scene of the Gonzáles Salas debacle, Huerta triumphed once again.[10]

Soon Orozco's retreat northward became a full-scale rout. As June wore into July, the Red Flaggers lost at Bachimba and again at Chihuahua City, their headquarters. Left in the ranks now were only the true believers; Orozco himself had all but given up. But the *colorados* had one last option still open to them: they could dissolve into guerrilla bands and continue the war indefinitely. After all, there were plenty of *gringos* in northern Chihuahua, and *gringos* had both guns and supplies for the taking. Besides, it was the Yankee arms embargo that had ruined their hopes in the first place. And suppose they provoked an American intervention; who would be hurt the most by that—themselves or Madero?[11]

v

The new state of affairs was painfully evident as soon as the Red Flaggers returned to the Casas Grandes in July. If there had been tension before, what followed now was chaos. Soon the battle-weary soldiers were wandering the streets of Colonias Juárez and Dublán, begging food, stealing fruit, accosting any and all *colonos*. The random looting of the stores gave way to brusque and systematic confiscation: a hundred sacks of flour here, a dozen head of cattle there, while horses and saddles simply vanished. Then the real blow fell. General Salazar addressed an order to Junius Romney, president of the Juárez Stake and leader of the Latter-day Saint colonies, to furnish a list of all arms and ammunition in the possession of the colonists. That, as Romney knew, was the beginning of the end.[12]

Junius Romney was a good example of the courage and industry which had transformed northern Chihuahua into a yeoman's arcadia. He was thirty-four years old in 1912, and even then his calm countenance could have been that of a bank president. As the spiritual anchor of his people, President Romney was not one to excite easily or behave rashly. Even better than the men in Washington, he appreciated the danger of precipitant action. A wrong word or gesture could set into motion a sequence of events which might draw the United States into the Mexican conflict; and Romney, expatriate that he was, was determined that no action of his would have that result. Yet neither was Romney a man to be cowed. If Salazar really meant to disarm the Mormons, they had no choice but to fight back or flee.

vi

The Mexican Mormons were not without their friends in the United States, and at least one of them was a person of consequence. Reed Smoot, senior senator from Utah and member of the Mormon church's Council of the Twelve Apostles, had long been recognized as the Latter-day Saints' man in Washington. As soon as reports from the Mexican colonies began arriving at church headquarters, they were rushed on to Smoot for action. Smoot began paying visits to anyone in a position to help his people: the secretary of state, the secretary of the treasury, even the president himself. Finally, as an afterthought, he put in a call to J. Reuben Clark.[13]

In spite of his well-publicized success in Washington, Reuben was not one to command the attention of the church in an international crisis. Few Utahns realized that Reuben had moved into a position of real authority in the State Department. Smoot himself knew Clark only as an occasional participant in the religious services held at the senator's home. Even after the two of them began work-

ing together Smoot persisted in referring to Reuben, somewhat ob-
tusely, as "R. G. Clark."[14] Little did the senator dream of the influence this anonymous Utahn was then exerting on Mexican policy.

Senator Smoot's first contact signaled a crisis of conscience for
Reuben. On one hand, he was acutely sensitive to the suffering of
the Saints below the border. In his mind's eye it was easy enough to
substitute Grantsville, Utah, for Dublán, Chihuahua. On the other
hand, Reuben had his own career to think about. In the Washington of 1912, "Mormon" was still a badge of opprobrium. Senator
Smoot had worn the badge himself; but nobody could fire Smoot
except the sovereign people of Utah, and eventually he had won his
battle with the East. Reuben's situation was different. He knew all
too well that he had been appointed solicitor in spite of his religion
and not because of it. If a Huntington Wilson or an Adee asked him
with a roguish wink why the Mormons of Mexico had so many women and children to worry about, he could smile stoically and swallow his embarrassment—but he could ill afford to abuse his authority
in behalf of the polygamous expatriates. Indeed, so scrupulous was
the Utah lawyer that in all references to his coreligionists the word
"Mormon" was carefully set in quotation marks.

So Smoot and Clark worked out a little modus operandi. The
senator would continue to coordinate communications from the
Mormon world, and Reuben would render whatever unofficial,
behind-the-scenes counsel he could. Then, after the two of them had
decided upon a plan of action, Smoot alone would take the responsibility for putting it into effect. In July, for example, Smoot received
a letter from church president Joseph F. Smith regarding a critical
situation at Colonia Morelos. After consultation with the solicitor,
Smoot directed the letter to Secretary Knox, asking that "the Department of State take immediate and appropriate action in the matter." As expected, Knox forwarded the request to Reuben Clark, and
soon a telegram was on its way to the consul at Nogales.[15] All the
while, Clark's alliance with Smoot remained a secret.

But the question remained, just what could the State Department do to help? One angle of advice was instantly available from
the interventionist hawks: send in the troops and clean the mess up.
Even as the first reports of Mormon harassment filtered across the
border, this solution was put forth urgently.[16] Senator Stone was still

active in Mexican affairs and ever more insistent with the military point of view. It was partly on account of his pressure, in fact, that President Taft had decided upon the arms embargo in the first place. And that fact aptly illustrated the main problem: the loudest defenders of the Mexican Mormons instinctively wanted to do the wrong thing.

Clark and Smoot had to come up with a better way. What if, they asked, the Mormon *colonos* could be armed to the teeth? If, as reports had it, Orozco's Red Flaggers were really perishing for want of firepower, heavily armed colonists might be able to hold them off indefinitely. Of course, the idea worked the other way too. The *colorados* might know exactly where to come for needed military hardware. Yet it seemed worth a try.

The problem now was to circumvent the arms embargo. Smoot toyed with several devices to that end, not all of them legal. In April a Mormon named O. P. Brown was apprehended at the border while attempting to smuggle a large quantity of munitions across to the colonies. His case necessitated appeals by Smoot to four separate cabinet departments before the confiscated arms were finally released.[17]

Reuben Clark preferred a less questionable approach. In conference with Smoot on April 14, he suggested seeking a special exception to the arms embargo on behalf of the Mormons in Mexico.[18] Such exceptions, as he knew, had already been granted in order to reinforce the American embassy in Mexico City.[19] It was agreed that Senator Smoot would approach the secretary of state on the matter. Within forty-eight hours Smoot was able to notify President Smith in Salt Lake City that Taft had granted permission for fifty rifles and twenty thousand rounds of ammunition to be sent to the Mormon colonists at Casas Grandes. President Madero was not enthused by the plan, knowing, as he said, where the fifty rifles would eventually wind up. But in the end he acquiesced rather than alienate President Taft, and the guns were shipped quietly into Mexico.[20]

vii

Meanwhile, life for the Mormon *colonos* had gone from bad to worse. Late in the evening of July 12, Junius Romney and his first counselor, Hyrum S. Harris, found themselves standing in the darkened hallway of a house in Casas Grandes, waiting for aides to awaken General Salazar upstairs. They had arrived with a disturbing report. That morning, a certain Colonel Arriola, while making the usual "requisition" of supplies in Colonia Díaz, had casually added that he expected all of the arms and ammunition belonging to the colonists to be delivered to him at ten o'clock the next morning. Was disarmament of the Mormons now to be Salazar's policy—in spite of repeated assurances? they asked. The general blinked twice and flew into a tirade against the offending officer. No such demands were to be made against the Mormon colonists, he declared with an oath, no such demands whatever. But then, absently—and possibly because he was still half-asleep—Salazar added, "not yet." Romney looked at Harris. The game was up.[21]

The only decision remaining was whether to fight or flee. They had the fifty new rifles from the United States, but there were some four thousand colonists to defend and a disproportionate number of them were women and children. Romney passed the word to hide the best guns—and he prayed as never before in his life.[22]

The blow fell on July 26. Salazar summoned President Romney back to Casas Grandes, and this time there was no trace of his former unctuousness. He announced point-blank that General Orozco had decided to gather up the colonists' arms and ammunition. This was to be done immediately. Any delay would prompt him to take out his wrath upon the women and children, removing all restraint from the soldiers and turning them loose. President Romney had been braced for this news, and he took it without flinching. He was not, however, braced for what came next. Salazar said that he had determined not only to disarm the colonists, but to withdraw all protection from them as well. From now on they were on their own and at the mercy of their Mexican neighbors. Romney was stunned. He could think of nothing to say but a confused and barely audible reference to the general's promises of the past. To be sure, Salazar replied, he had given the Mormons guarantees of protection from time to time. Those were "mere words," he said with an ominous smile, adding: "The wind blows words away."[23]

The decision to leave Mexico was made on the day of Salazar's ultimatum. Meanwhile the Mormons, their settlements encircled by rebel cannon, had no choice but to comply, or at least to make a show of compliance while they stalled for time. By the 28th a solemn procession was wending its way toward the public park of Dublán, carrying guns to lay at the feet of the enemy. The arsenal taking shape there was an interesting one, comprised of assorted antiques and conversation pieces, some with hammers missing and others with rusty barrels. One citizen turned up with a weapon of such vintage that a crowd gathered to admire it. Concurrently, and with far greater dispatch, preparations were being made to send the women and children out first. It was a pitiful scene: packing a few scant belongings onto an old mule, burying an heirloom or two beneath the back porch, stashing the strawberry preserves in the attic, bidding farewell—perhaps forever—to family members, leaving behind the work of a lifetime. And all the while the looting continued apace and confrontations with the Red Flaggers multiplied.[24]

Once the Mormons were visibly on the run, the sense of order, such as it was, disappeared altogether and tensions on both sides uncoiled like wire springs. The lightly escorted convoys of women and children were easy marks for rebels and bandits alike. Thirst, crowding, primitive modes of travel, and plain combat fatigue worked unspeakable hardship. Nor were things much better for those who remained behind. The semideserted *colonias* became battlegrounds through which vigilante and terrorist gangs prowled in near anarchy. Within a week the situation had become impossible, and men of the once-proud "Zion of Mexico" followed their wives into exile. In El Paso they were welcomed into an abandoned lumberyard and supplied with government rations.[25]

viii

The fate of the Mormon *colonos* dramatically focused opposition to Taft's Mexican policy. And by now there was a good deal of opposition to focus. The whole business of Douglas and El Paso still rankled on unsatisfactorily. Members of the House Foreign Affairs Committee, such as Congressman John Nance Garner of Texas, were wondering publicly why the State Department had not interceded diplomatically on behalf of the American claimants.[26] And here, suddenly, was a spate of new outrages, as evidenced by the refugees flocking to the border. Moreover, the sight of these people was more than a little unnerving. It was one thing to read accounts of atrocities in the newspapers; it was quite another to visit the camps in El Paso and see "the strained, frightened look in the eyes of the children, the haggard faces of the women and the gaunt-silent men."[27] Unlike the victims at Douglas and El Paso, these Mormon settlers had contributed no negligence of their own to the tragedy that befell them. The question of what to do about Mexico once again came surging to the fore, and with a new pitch of intensity.

A new spokesman of the criticism emerged in the person of Senator Albert B. Fall of New Mexico. Fall, fifty-one years of age, had been in the United States Senate a bare three months when he arose to attack the administration frontally. What he lacked in experience, however, the freshman senator more than made up in flair. With his long hair, his bronzed complexion, and his soft, indolent drawl, he seemed to be the archetypal man of the West. Indeed, Fall had roughed it in the badlands, labored in the mines of Kingston, and taken part in a bloody range war. Once, during a bitter debate in the New Mexico territorial legislature, he had stridden across the aisle to slap the face of a recalcitrant colleague.[28] It was in just such a spirit that he now addressed the Senate on July 22, 1912, speaking, as he said, for all the Americans in Mexico.

I do not believe that the people of the United States have realized that within the last 12 or 14 months Americans in Mexico have not only had property destroyed to the amount of, possibly, I should estimate at a low figure, $500,000,000, but that American citizens have been killed. American women have been outraged within 50 miles of our borders, and not one word of protest has been uttered to the Mexican government diplomatically, so far as I am able to ascertain, against such conditions and against such outrages and against such murders.[29]

Fall then gave examples. The Douglas and El Paso incidents were easily enough called back to mind, but his most dramatic examples were drawn from the recent experience of the Mormons. Brown, Taylor, Combs, and others shanghaied; Goldner and Hollingsworth falsely imprisoned; flour seized at Colonia Juárez; attempted outrage of Mabel Richardson; murder in cold blood of Mrs. James Mortensen, of James D. Harvey, of William Adams, and who knew how many others. Fall did not always have his facts straight, but what he said had a ring of authenticity and much of it was true.

182

The senator was not long in coming to his point, which was to propose scuttling the administration's Mexican policy. At the very least, he avowed, "an ultimatum should be sent to the so-called Mexican government that within a given length of time killing and destruction of property must cease."[30] But even ultimata were not enough: Fall wanted intervention.

As I said, I am not going to dwell upon the horrors of this revolution ... in Mexico, but I want to say that the indignation of the American people would be aroused to such a degree that all the American troops in this service could not keep the people of the United States from going across the Mexican border if they knew the conditions of affairs and what some of our American citizens have had to suffer.[31]

Geared as it was to the presidential campaign, the Fall speech was potentially lethal. Theodore Roosevelt was already denouncing the president as a sissy and a do-nothing, and here was a two-fisted western senator with supporting evidence. Administration allies on the Foreign Relations Committee urged that a strong rebuttal be made. The assignment was given to Reuben Clark, who, it was believed, could defend the president's Mexican policy as if it were his very own. Reuben set to work at once on a white paper which would reply to Fall point by point and hopefully vindicate the administration. The first draft was written in a cold fury and punctuated by bitter sarcasm.[32] Gradually, however, as time passed and further events transpired, drafts of the memorandum began to take on new shape and meaning. The anger mellowed. The *ad hominum* potshots at Fall were excised. The scope and subject matter were steadily broadened. The essay matured into the serious attempt of a Mormon man of conscience to explain—perhaps to himself—why Mormonism in Mexico should not be rescued at gunpoint.[33] Reuben, for the first time, was taking a long, hard, thoughtful look at the meaning of events in which he had been so long embroiled.

ix

In the meantime the solicitor's hands were more than full. He and Senator Smoot continued their confidential alliance in behalf of the Mormon colonists. In August, following the exodus from Chihuahua, Smoot secured passage of a resolution appropriating $100,000 to help relocate the refugees in Utah and Arizona.[34] But plans to mitigate the suffering hardly alleviated its cause, and by late summer it became evident that neither the cause nor the suffering were yet at an end. "Your American newspapers have called us robbers, looters and bandits, and have a lot to say about intervention," Orozco sneered to a Mormon official. "We are now going to live up to our record ... and we want intervention more than anything else."[35] It was true that the Mormons of Chihuahua had slipped from Orozco's grasp; but as his ragged bands retreated northwestward, it became apparent that the Sonora Mormons of Colonia Morelos would be right in his path and the fun would all begin anew.

Awaiting this fate, Morelos Bishop Charles W. Lillywhite had other difficulties as well. His colony was presently under the "protection" of Mexican federal forces, and it was hard to see how Salazar's invaders could be much worse. Morelos was a different sort of place from the Casas Grandes settlements of Chihuahua. Life was less urbane and more primitive. The Mormon *colonos,* dressed in their faded dungarees and broad-brimmed *sombreros,* were involved in a daily battle against the encroaching mesquite and catclaw; they had no time for the intricacies of Mexican politics. Thus they were utterly bewildered when the federal soldiers descended upon them in July. The troops arrived without warning. They camped any place that seemed convenient, and of course the church house was the most convenient place of all. Lacking provisions of their own, they appropriated the colonists', remarking that the victuals had never been better. As supplies dwindled, the number of soldiers increased; they soon outnumbered the civilian populace. By the end of the month Bishop Lillywhite had a thousand of them on his hands.

And it did not take long for a thousand soldiers to turn staid Morelos into an Alsatian den. They spent their nights drinking, shooting, and riding wildly through the streets. They spent their days bathing nude in the city canal, frolicking with camp followers, and generally making a mess. Beef were slaughtered in any handy doorway and the offal left to putrify in the sun; horses were rounded up and hitched to federal wagons; women were routinely insulted and girls learned to watch out.[36]

184

The colonists made humble application to General Sanjinez, the officer in charge, but with no effect. He was too busy, he said, to worry about civilian molestation in the face of Salazar's threatened approach. In fact, when that approach was confirmed Sanjinez added his own injury upon the Mormons by commandeering virtually all of their remaining teams and wagons for the battle. This development made the situation critical. The time of harvest was almost upon them, and these animals were crucial for gathering the crops. Moreover, without horses and wagons (there was no railroad) the colonists could not hope to escape from Salazar themselves.[37]

Bishop Lillywhite headed for Douglas, Arizona, and cabled church authorities in Salt Lake City. They apprised Senator Smoot of the situation and he alerted the State Department. A series of dispatches flashed along the Smoot-Clark network for Mormon affairs, but the replies from Mexico were filled with foreboding.[38] Sanjinez's troops were out of control, as far as Mexico City could ascertain, and they were not seriously planning to intercept Salazar at all.

So the anxious officials turned to General Huerta, who was still pursuing Salazar from the south. When informed that the *Orozquistas* would probably destroy Colonia Morelos, Huerta volunteered to try to head them off. But this was simply not possible. The Red Flaggers had systematically demolished all rail lines as they moved westward, and beyond the Sierra Madres no lines had ever been built. The only chance—and it was a slim one—of beating Salazar to Morelos was for Huerta to ferry his troops around the rebels' flank and cut them off from the rear. This could be accomplished only by utilizing the rail lines between Douglas and El Paso—by moving the federal troops, in other words, through the territory of the United States.[39] At every turn, it seemed, the Taft administration was back on the spot. Now the choice lay between violating its own laws or seeing another Mormon colony torn to shreds.

And once more, the dilemma was Reuben Clark's intensely personal one. Time and again, the government of Porfirio Díaz had made this selfsame request in order to steal a march on the Maderist *insurrectos,* and time and again the solicitor had rejected it. His practiced response had been that American neutrality statutes prohibited the launching of military expeditions from U.S. soil, regardless of how noble the end to be served. Now here was the request staring up from Reuben's desk once again—and this time it was American lives, not Mexican, that hung in the balance. Reuben could help fellow Mormons, perhaps, but only at the expense of the law, of neutrality, and of the integrity of his own Mexican policy. He must have gritted his teeth at the choice.

On September 10 the Mexican government was notified that permission would be granted for the troop haul, and after awaiting special action of the Mexican senate the operation was put into effect.[40] Ingeniously, Reuben avoided any technical violation of the neutrality laws by instructing the federal officers to transport their weapons in different railroad cars from those which held the troops. (The law prohibited only "armed" expeditions.) The decision to circumvent the neutrality statutes in this manner was both difficult and statesmanlike. In reaching it, Reuben had to acknowledge a kind of higher truth. There were times in the course of human affairs when even the law was not enough, when considerations of justice and humanity must overturn the dictates of the statute books, and when it was given to a single individual to make some exceedingly difficult choices. Unfortunately, Huerta's forces did not arrive in time to save Colonia Morelos from Salazar, and so the episode was soon forgotten.[41] J. Reuben Clark, the devout legalist, would not have called this his finest hour, yet it was a fine hour nonetheless.

x

Back in Colonia Morelos, the Mormon colonists, who knew nothing of the feverish activity in Washington, decided that they must help themselves. Salazar's troops were closing in and every minute counted. They rounded up sixty heavy lumber wagons spared them by Sanjinez and began the heartrending process of loading up their movable belongings. By August 30 a vanguard of women and children was ready to pull out. "As the company left the colony," recalled one church elder, "sobs were heard on every hand." Then it started to rain, drenching everyone and completing the scene of misfortune. Even some of the men wept as the wagons slogged off into the downpour—and well they might. They would never see Morelos again.[42]

As this second glut of Mormon refugees neared the border, Senator Fall renewed his attack. "Where," he asked in anguish,

has the voice been lifted in behalf of the common, every day, homemaking, honest, industrious American with his family, teaching the Mexican modern methods of agriculture and handicraft, who has, while tied to a tree, seen his daughter raped and his wife disemboweled in his presence?[43]

And amid the passions sweeping over the country, such demagoguery was not without its reward. Fall was promptly installed on the Senate Revolutionary Claims Committee and then, as a tribute to his forensic abilities, on the all-powerful Committee on Foreign Relations. Soon his was the dominant voice in special hearings on Mexico.

By early October Solicitor Clark was ready with his reply to the New Mexico senator. The document was not intended as a memorial to the Mormon experience, but that experience certainly illustrated some of Reuben's points. Reuben believed that in the Mexican matter policymakers had to make choices not among the theoretical, the desirable, or the ideal, but among the possible. In making such choices a person admittedly made mistakes—but then in the world of the possible things never came out perfect. The best one could do, Reuben seemed to affirm, was distinguish between mistakes of the head and mistakes of the heart and try to refrain from the latter.

By contrast, Senator Fall's proposals paid scant heed to the world of the possible; they seemed to spin out of a theoretician's neverland. Fall would either invade Mexico or else evacuate it. These were the alternatives of an all-or-nothing mentality—so typical of American diplomacy—which by turns wanted to make the world over in its own image or else wanted to cut and run. Reuben held each alternative up to the test of experience. Intervention, he said, could not seriously be contemplated by anyone who understood Mexico.

It has been already pointed out how there were thousands of American citizens living as isolated families or as isolated groups of families all over Mexico and particularly in that northern zone which, it must be added, was at this time and has ever since been literally infested with roving bands of insurrectionists proper (poorly disciplined but fully armed) and an equal number of bands of highway robbers wholly without discipline, but equally well armed, all willing and eager to loot, to rape, and to murder; it has been already shown how these isolated American families, deprived of all their arms and ammunition, were absolutely and hopelessly defenseless; and one must add to these conditions that for one cause or another there is and has been smoldering in Mexico a deep feeling among the lower classes closely akin to race hatred against the Americans in Mexico; finally, one must mix with these ingredients of the situation a more or less well defined purpose upon the part of all such persons to visit vengeance upon all Americans within reach upon the slightest provocation and excuse. Under these circumstances can there be any doubt what would have happened if we had undertaken to protect our own citizens with our own forces? Has anyone any doubt but that the slaughter would have commenced at the moment when our first soldier crossed the border and that before the nearest ranch, the nearest settlement, could have been reached by the foremost invading column thousands of unarmed and defenseless American men, women, and children at these places and beyond, would have been murdered in cold blood with such accompanying atrocities as the mind refuses to contemplate?[44]

"Intervention would not have been war," Reuben concluded, "it would have been murder."

How about evacuation then? Again Reuben answered with the voice of experience.

Everyone conversant with facts knows that there are thousands of American citizens in Mexico who could not on a moment's, or a week's, notice raise money enough to get out of Mexico; that at the very first symptom of such movement such Americans could not if they wished sell the little they had which could not be taken with them, for the prospective purchaser would at once ask, why buy what we may in a few days take for nothing? Moreover, anyone familiar with the covered wagon, the slow plodding team, the dry dusty road, and the burning sun of the arid west, knows of the hardship and the sufferings incident to the long weary journey which thousands of Americans must take; of the days and nights of wholly unprotected wagon travel through a country infested with robbers and murderers which these same Americans must make in order to reach a place of safety. Everyone knows how it is all but certain that these Americans would never be permitted to get to a rendezvous or to the border, and that even if they had reached either the rendezvous or the border, they would have found themselves in the position of having left every worldly thing they possessed save the little they stood in and carried with them, at the time they had deserted; that they would have found themselves penniless and helpless not only as to their future, but as to their present needs; and that they would have abandoned the work of a lifetime which would have been thus irretrievably lost.[45]

188

No invasion and no evacuation. What was left? A course, Reuben urged, which the hawks would doubtless regard as bloodless and uninteresting: "The ordinary, well established and clearly recognized methods of diplomacy." Granted, he said, these methods had their defects. Americans in Mexico had suffered loss, hardship, and atrocities. But all of these—including atrocities—accompanied war and would escalate manyfold if it came to that. As matters now stood, few Americans had died. Property loss was substantial, admittedly, but it in no way approached the wild figures used by Senator Fall. Reuben closed the memorandum with a day-by-day exposition of what he meant by "methods of diplomacy," demonstrating with the case of the Mormons that the slow, steady, patient application of reasonable pressure could and would produce results.

> The constant problem which has confronted the President has been to secure the maximum amount of protection for American life and property with the minimum amount of danger thereto. So far no one with any adequate understanding of the situation believes that we should have intervened in Mexico or that we should intervene now. There will probably never come a time to intervene if we exercise the forbearance with (Mexico) that we should desire for ourselves. But, however that may be, it is clear that the time to intervene will be when we can save more American lives by going into Mexico than by staying out of Mexico. At present we seem to be a long distance from that contingency.[46]

Within the limits of the possible, said Reuben Clark, the president's had been the only course imaginable.

xii

The solicitor knew whereof he spoke. While he was energetically staving off one intervention in Mexico, he happened to be busily directing another one in Nicaragua; and he could have hardly missed the applicability of the lessons.

One lesson, surely, was that intervention begets more intervention. At Bluefields in 1910 Reuben himself had intervened in a Nicaraguan revolution in his capacity as solicitor. Now the chickens had come home to roost. The minority government installed by the earlier American intermeddling had proven incapable of governing, and its own officers had revolted anew.[47] Led by war minister Luis Mena, these new rebels quickly demonstrated that they meant business. Between August 11 and 14 they poured some six hundred rounds of artillery into Managua, forty or fifty of them within "dangerous proximity" of the American legation. There appeared to be plenty of cause for concern.[48]

But what was the cure, other than more intervention? Secretary Knox was out of the country, attending the funeral of the Japanese emperor, and Huntington Wilson had been left in charge.[49] Together he and Reuben Clark did what the circumstances seemed to require: they sent in the troops.[50] Soon a battleship and two cruisers were racing toward Nicaraguan ports, while the acting secretary and the solicitor puzzled out some way of making a military adventure appear to be only the defense of American property.[51] Reuben's notes of their conversation, which were translated into the necessary military orders, told the whole story. American troops were directed to secure all important towns, "[leaving] the regular troops generally free to follow the insurgents." Arms and ammunition of the rebels were to be confiscated and quietly turned over to the regular government. Rebels taken prisoner were also to be handed over. Reuben even noted that American officers might have to "handle Nic. troops" themselves.[52]

Admiral Southerland followed the hidden agenda to the letter. Under the guise of protecting American property, his men pushed along the rail lines from Corinto to the interior. Wherever they went, government control was quickly reestablished. Central American leaders—notably President Araujo of El Salvador—bitterly complained that the American forces had "entered into warlike action against the revolutionists," but without effect.[53] Such forces were only "protecting property," replied the State Department.[54] As time went by, this fiction became more and more difficult to sustain, and finally it collapsed altogether. On the morning of October 4, a battalion of Southerland's bluejackets stormed Barranca and Coyotpe Hills outside of Masaya. In the battle four Americans were killed and six more wounded—but no one could quarrel with the final result.[55] General Mena surrendered to the same Major Butler who had taken charge at Bluefields and was taken "quasi prisoner of war" to the American Canal Zone in Panama.[56]

None of this pleased Reuben Clark, despite his own hand in it. It seemed uncomfortably like Brer Rabbit flailing away at the tar baby and getting stuck worse with each blow. Indeed, with this open invasion by American military forces there was now no prospect whatever of pulling out of Nicaragua. Reuben's dark prophecies were coming to pass before his eyes, and he himself was powerless to forestall them.

xiii

The end of the Mormon travail in Mexico coincided with the denouement in Nicaragua, and the two were by no means unrelated. The plight of the Mormons was the other horn of the intervention dilemma and it was sorry to behold. By September of 1912 there were some two thousand refugees quartered in sheds and stables in the United States. A dozen or more had been killed outright. Another dozen were still missing.[57] But the uprooting was the worst part—the physical and emotional havoc of lives torn up, hopes ruined, and years wasted. After the remnants of Orozco's army were mopped up by General Huerta, the Mormon settlers were naturally eager to return to their homes. Even if there were still guerrillas and bandits infesting northern Mexico, the thought of being victimized by desperados was hardly less appealing than living out one's life in an abandoned warehouse. Soon spirits rallied to the idea of going home. Reuben Clark facilitated the trek back to Mexico by waiving some rules and bending others in order that the colonists could take weapons with them, and he saw to it that they received plenty of advice on how to conduct themselves.[58]

The *colonos* made the journey with a hopefulness almost festive— but bitter disappointment awaited them in Mexico. Colonia Díaz was gone entirely, burned to the ground: nothing but charred ruins and blackened chimneys greeted the arrival of the scout parties. Colonia Morelos fared little better. Houses and stores had been looted and ripped apart. Furniture was smashed. Musical instruments had been used for kindling. Carcasses of animals were strewn about the streets. A few drunken Mexicans lounged in the shade here and there, keeping watch on the scene of destruction. On one broken organ was written the epitaph of Mormon colonization in the state of Sonora: "Long live the Liberals and death to the Mormons."[59]

Colonias Juárez and Dublán too were desolate. Houses stood empty and silent, stripped bare of movables. The bloated bodies of animals dotted the landscape. Crops rotted in the fields. Local Mexicans had already appropriated the best dwellings for themselves and by all appearances were there to stay.[60] The Casas Grandes settlements would eventually be reoccupied, at least in part; but life for the Mormons in Mexico would never regain the promise or prosperity of 1910. An era had come to an end.

xiv

What the colonists beheld was the price of nonintervention. It was a stiff price, to be sure; but it had been paid almost wholly in property, not in lives. Of course, people who are not killed do not make headlines. Walking around alive and well, they did little to rescue the Taft Mexican policy from popular opprobrium. For this, among other reasons, President Taft and the Republicans were in serious trouble as the November election drew near. Yet occasionally there was someone who saw and understood what had been at stake and knew that, all things considered, the story had ended remarkably well. Reuben Clark must have had real satisfaction in reading these words of President Joseph F. Smith, delivered at the Mormon church's October conference: "I feel so thankful in my heart that wisdom, a higher wisdom, has dictated the course of the executive authorities of our nation, by which they have kept their hands free from the shedding of blood."[61]

Chapter 11

AN END AND A BEGINNING

The presidential campaign of 1912 provoked an all-out assault by the opponents of William Howard Taft's foreign policy. As early as 1910 doubts were being expressed about the president, and the Mexican crisis helped bring them to the surface. Theodore Roosevelt himself took alarm at the course pursued by his hand-picked successor. "I am absolutely unable to understand what the administration means by permitting the killing of Americans on American soil to go on," he wrote to a friend, adding: "Personally I would have handled the whole thing differently from the way it has been handled."[1] By the early months of 1912 Roosevelt had decided that Taft must go. On February 24, just as the Juárez crisis was coming to a head, the former president made his move. "My hat is in the ring," he announced to a throng of enthusiastic followers. "I will accept the nomination of President if it is tendered to me."[2]

After a fitful start, the Roosevelt campaign began to pick up momentum; and upon winning a crucial victory in the Pennsylvania primary in April, he captured one delegation after another. Had not President Taft commanded the prestige of his office and the machinery of his party, it would have been all over at the Republican convention in June. As it was, Taft was renominated by a bare twenty-one votes. The rest was history—the old Bull Moose stormed out of the Chicago convention, and only hours later the Progressive party was organized to return him to the White House.[3]

ii

The three-cornered campaign that followed was one of the oddest in American history. With incumbent Republicans split down

193

the middle, Woodrow Wilson, the Democratic nominee, was any betting man's favorite; but the real battle was between Roosevelt and Taft. As president, Roosevelt had scored his greatest triumphs in foreign affairs—where Taft had suffered his worst defeats. And as the campaign took shape, Taft's defeats continued. The Mormon refugees could not have struggled to the border at a worse time for the beleaguered president. "I wouldn't have got [the Nobel Peace Prize]," Roosevelt told an audience in Manchester, New Hampshire, "if I had wanted peace because I was afraid of war."[4]

So it was that U.S. Mexican policy came in for a change of direction. Heretofore that policy, right or wrong, had at least been steady. Now Taft opted for a change. He wanted what a later generation would call a new image, one of firmness and command, and the pussyfooting alleged by critics was obviously not going to call it forth. Instinctively almost, the president began relying less and less on his secretary of state and considerably more on himself.

Huntington Wilson was glad to bear a hand too. He was not a hawk of the ordinary beak-and-talon variety, but his inclinations were far more aggressive than Philander Knox's, and he had proposed some fairly drastic remedies to Mexican problems. In the wake of the Mormon debacle, the president was ready to listen.

The first flex of the new toughness took the form of a diplomatic offensive launched by the State Department in late summer.[5] For two years the department had been prodding first Díaz and then Madero to take action. Suddenly the dispatches increased dramatically, both in volume and in vigor. Between July 10 and September 19 the solicitor turned out no fewer than eleven major communications.[6] This correspondence kept reminding the Mexican government that it was not meeting its international obligations, that American lives and property were in grave danger, and that forces of law and order must bestir themselves.

Still, the message did not seem to be getting through. On August 28 an agitated Philander Knox approached the president about the Mormon situation in Sonora. Continual pressure on Madero had done little to ameliorate American suffering, he explained; perhaps the president might prevail personally upon the Mexican foreign office. The new Taft was only too obliging. On September 4 he summoned the ambassador, Manuel Calero, to the Oval Office. Huntington Wilson was present. The United States government, the president began, had been both patient and helpful with regard to the situation in Mexico. In return it expected more consideration than it had thus far received. He, the president, could not and would not tolerate Mexican indifference much longer. If conditions did not improve, he would have no recourse but to call a special session of Congress to consider official action.[7]

Calero went away shaken. If he had not received an ultimatum in precise terms—there had been no time limit set—he had received the nearest thing to it that William Howard Taft would ever pronounce. Nor was the president bluffing. He had already ordered the army and navy to draw up contingency plans for the invasion of Mexico.[8] Immediately after the interview with Calero, Taft contacted General Leonard Wood and learned that the plans had been perfected.[9] Given the signs of increasing impotence in Mexico City, there would most likely be a need for them soon. Henceforth, in fact, the Taft administration would discuss intervention not in terms of "whether" but "when."

iii

Reuben Clark viewed these developments with alarm. A number of items relative to the invasion plans had already crossed his desk, so he knew that the president was serious.[10] The disaster he had seen coming from afar was well nigh upon him, and there was nothing, apparently, that could stay its arrival. Worst of all, in a strange twist of fate Reuben himself was suddenly called upon as solicitor to build a legal foundation for the projected invasion. The formal justification for one national state's attack upon another was obviously an important document. It stood to have enormous significance for the larger community of nations, for the future of Latin American relations, and for the very course of American diplomacy. Needless to say, it had to be good.

Ever the stoic, Reuben set aside his personal misgivings and went to work. His aim was to devise a document that would fulfill all of the necessary political, legal, and diplomatic requirements, while at the same time salvaging as much as possible of his own doc-

195

trine of noninvolvement. The result was the *Right to Protect Citizens in Foreign Countries by Landing Forces,* one of the ablest and most influential papers of his entire career.[11]

Considering Reuben's own experience with Mexico, the *Right to Protect Citizens* memorandum could only be called an exercise in benevolent cunning. It began by addressing extant legal opinion on the subject of intervention and identifying two separate species of the genus. The first of these Reuben called "political intervention," which he defined as the attempt by one nation to interfere in the domestic affairs of another for the purpose of achieving a political result. Reuben noted that almost all the authorities had unkind things to say about political intervention and justly so. There was, however, a second species of the genus which Reuben called "nonpolitical intervention" or, a bit euphemistically, "interposition." Interposition, he said, might have the same look about it as intervention, but the purpose behind it was markedly different. With interposition there was no political motive. The only desire, as the title of the memorandum suggested, was to protect foreign citizens and their property in a situation where the host government was unable or unwilling to do so. Culling through the precedents, Reuben could find plenty of examples of interposition. Unfortunately, these had never been adequately distinguished from their look-alike cousins and had come under the same blanket of condemnation. But Reuben Clark could draw a clear distinction between them. Surely it was one thing to go thundering pell-mell into someone else's domestic quarrel and quite another to stand guard over one's own helpless citizens.

Reuben went on to dress up the memorandum with suitable frills. He tacked on the suggestion that interposition was perhaps an innocuous little matter that the president could handle by himself without bothering Congress. There was also the familiar Clarkean appendix of twenty-eight pages, listing out instances of interposition in American history. So well crafted was the document and so directly did it respond to the need at hand that it was published and republished by the Government Printing Office on three separate occasions. It was often cited in learned discussions and consulted by decision-makers. And decades later, when President Kennedy faced down the Russians in the Cuban missile crisis, he was said to have read it over carefully. It stands today beside the Clark *Memorandum on the Monroe Doctrine* as a monument to the career of its author.

Even so, *Right to Protect Citizens* incorporated some visceral flaws. Its distinction between political and nonpolitical intervention was often misleading and occasionally false. Historically, almost every instance of real intervention had been dressed up as some sort of interposition. One never sent in the marines avowedly to fix up a foreign government; one sent them in only to secure justice, honor, and human decency—fixing up the government was incidental. In the case of the United States and Mexico, of course, the desire to protect citizens was indeed genuine; but how was the Mexican government to know that, or to distinguish the real from the rhetorical? Then, too, Reuben's memorandum seemed to ignore the fact that a military operation on foreign soil would have devastating repercussions regardless of the intention behind it. Reuben might have recalled that fact from Bluefields, where the simplest exercise of power—in behalf of foreign nationals and their property—turned the tide of a revolution.

But these sophisms were gentle enough in view of the larger circumstances. If the soldiers *had* to go into Mexico, it was better to put sound, unselfish, and humanitarian reasons on the record.

iv

That Taft's invasion of Mexico never came to pass was paradoxically due to the voters, who on November 5 rejected the incumbent as feckless. Had he faced four more years of the Mexican Revolution, the president doubtless would have had to get as tough as he sounded. As it was, any further pugnacity could not but ill serve his purposes. He was a lame duck now, and his interest lay in keeping the Mexican matter as calm as possible until handing it over to Woodrow Wilson. The safest course, then, was to resume "sitting on the lid." Reuben Clark received this newest turnabout happily enough; others received it less well. And one key figure in the policy establishment did not receive it at all—and went on to bring about exactly the sort of interventionist fiasco that Reuben had dreaded all along.

v

Few men in the history of American diplomacy have been at once so enigmatic and controversial as Ambassador Henry Lane Wilson. All attempts to explain him have fallen short. Daniel James wrote that "a worse representative of the United States could not have been picked at a worse moment by its worst enemy, and his tour of duty in Mexico should stand as an example to all American diplomats of how they should not act."[12] Reuben Clark was more charitable. "Henry Lane Wilson," he wrote, "has been much misrepresented, though doubtless very unwise and deserving of criticism."[13] But then, Reuben Clark never knew the whole story.

Henry Lane Wilson grew up in a distinguished Indiana family. He worked for the election of his father to Congress, his brother to the Senate, and Benjamin Harrison and William McKinley, both family friends, to the presidency. As a reward he was launched upon his diplomatic career with so much thrust that by 1910, when he might otherwise have expected a first secretaryship, he sailed into the most prestigious post in the American foreign service: Mexico City. Despite these successes, Wilson seemed to lack confidence. Physically, he was spare and rangy with sunken eyes, high cheekbones, and a perpetual scowl. He also had a number of physical ailments, recurrent bouts of moodiness, and a rumored drinking problem.[14]

Still, Wilson was an achiever, and the goals he set for his mission in Mexico were ambitious. What he wanted above all else was to reestablish order and stability, conditions which would permit the United States to resume exploiting Mexico's immense resources. Wilson was an unabashed imperialist. "My experience has taught me," he wrote, "that these Latin-American countries should be dealt with justly and calmly but severely and undeviatingly. Any other course will forfeit to us the respect with which they have been taught to regard us."[15] Predictably, Wilson had special affection for strongmen like Porfirio Díaz. As for the brave new Mexico of Francisco Madero, the ambassador shook his head in dismay.

Even more dangerous than the open acts of violence to which I have referred, is the spirit of disregard for law and authority, of contempt for the ordinary conventions and restraints of society, of insolence in the public highways, of industrial strikes based upon impossible demands, which are all indications of a changed spirit among the people, the tendencies and fruits of which cannot be clearly estimated.[16]

Not surprisingly, Reuben Clark and Henry Lane Wilson did not quite get along. More than once the solicitor voiced exasperation with the ambassador, and for his part Wilson dismissed Clark as "a badly educated lawyer."[17] The bone of contention between them was the question of intervention. Where Reuben Clark believed that the Mexicans should be left to work things out for themselves, Henry Lane Wilson believed that things must be worked out for them. And if legal precedents stood in the way of such intrusion, then, as the ambassador explained to the solicitor, there would just have to be "new precedents."

We cannot go on indefinitely giving this Government and people the same consideration and deference we show to a highly organized state in the face of the fact that in some ways it is a practical anarchy.[18]

From the first, Wilson employed every means at his disposal to undermine Reuben's policy of neutrality. He possessed an arsenal of weapons for such work, but three proved particularly useful. The first was his diplomatic rank. The only full-fledged ambassador in Mexico, Wilson was ex officio head of the Mexico City diplomatic corps—which meant that, in addition to his enormous influence with envoys of the other powers, he had direct access to the Mexican head of state.[19] The second weapon was his boldness. Wilson enjoyed the advantage of serving a government increasingly paralyzed at the top. The essential dereliction of decision-making responsibility on the part of the president and the secretary of state meant that in difficult situations the decisions would have to be made by someone else. Reuben Clark had made many such decisions himself. Henry Lane Wilson would now prove that he could make them too.

Finally, the department was almost totally dependent upon Wilson for first-hand information. The ambassador soon learned that this dependence was his most powerful weapon. If he did not like President Madero, it was the simplest thing in the world to embellish his Cassandra-like reports with belittling anecdotes; and if he wanted to create the impression of anarchy, all he had to do was pick up some folklore from the street and send it to Washington as data. A typical dispatch reported that

entire villages have been burned, their inhabitants—men, women and children— slaughtered and mutilated indiscriminately; plantations have been ravaged and burned, trains have been blown up and derailed, and passengers slaughtered like cattle; women have been ravaged and men mutilated with accompaniments of horror and barbarity which find no place in the chronicles of Christian warfare.... With this situation, as far as my observation goes, the Government is either wholly incompetent or wholly impotent to deal.[20]

Reports like this had a remarkable effect on William Howard Taft. One of them had triggered the ill-fated mobilization of 1911. For that matter, every single time the administration's mood turned hawkish, Henry Lane Wilson could be found not far away.

vi

Unsurprisingly, the State Department eventually grew suspicious of Ambassador Wilson's behavior. By the end of 1912, the reliability of his reports was a matter of open concern. It was Fred Dearing who made the startling discovery that Wilson's horror stories compared almost verbatim with newspaper clippings from the anti-government press in Mexico City.[21] Meanwhile, Reuben Clark made a discovery of his own. The solicitor had often been called upon to draft communications to the Mexican government, and Wilson, as he learned, was blithely taking it upon himself to alter the text of these before officially presenting them. "Isn't it about time," Reuben asked with exasperation, "to suggest that the Ambassador is not our instructor in English Grammar and Rhetoric—and that 'we want what we want when we want it?' "[22]

Wilson had always been outspoken and headstrong, but with the approach of the election he became downright insubordinate. Sensing that the time was ripe to put pressure on the weakened Madero government, he decided to bring the claims controversy to a head. The pile of claims was indeed high at this point, and claimholders like Judge Wilfley could congratulate themselves at having found at last an official who was willing to act. Wilson certainly was that. His method of advancing a claim against Mexico was not to send it through the mills of bureaucracy, but to lay it personally on President Madero's desk—and then pound the desk with both fists. "In dealing with Mexico," he said, "halfway measures are of little value."[23] Now the ambassador decided to reject the solicitor's "halfway measures" and pursue his own course—hoping in the process to force the issue.

Secretary Knox became alarmed immediately. Since early January the department had left the claims imbroglio up to Reuben Clark, and it was finally showing signs of progress. Taft and Knox had been holding daily talks with Pedro Lascuráin, the Mexican foreign minister, and the snarls were slowly being untangled.[24] But Wilson's latest tangent threatened everything. Reading the recent dispatches with care, Knox could see with a start what the ambassador's true purpose must be. "We must take some vigorous and drastic action with the purpose of securing redress for our wrongs," Wilson had written, adding, "and perhaps, incidentally, the downfall of a Government which is hateful to a vast majority of the people."[25]

The secretary gathered up the dispatches and sent them to the president, explaining that he detected

an intention on the part of the Ambassador to force this Government's hand in its dealings with the Mexican situation as a whole, the apparent disagreement between the Ambassador and the Department being so fundamental and so serious that the Department feels it would err if it did not bring the matter pointedly to your attention.[26]

For the moment, the president decided against taking action. It was harder to ignore the ambassador's next transgression. On December 19 Henry Lane Wilson spent an entire day in Washington conferring with the president and the secretary of state on the Mexican situation. That evening the discussions continued at a dinner hosted by Knox. The main topic of conversation was a note to the Mexican government which had recently been drafted by Clark and Doyle. Among other things, the note threatened repeal of the arms embargo unless Madero took immediate steps to protect American nationals. This was the sharpest message to Madero since Taft's ultimatum of September 4, and it represented a desperate final effort at a diplomatic solution. As the party broke up, the note was approved for transmission to Mexico.[27]

President Taft, having reverted to his lid-sitting, was equally desirous that the note accomplish its work quietly: there must be no appearance of bluster. State Department officials were thus mortified the following morning to see the headline "Note of Warning to Mexico" blazoned across the *New York Times*.[28] Reuben in particular was livid. He summoned Donald A. DeLashmutt, his most trusted clerk, and ordered an immediate investigation of the leak. One by one, DeLashmutt interviewed each of the clerks and secretaries in the office who had seen the dispatch. In the end he was able to account for every single copy and to clear all persons of suspicion—except one. Henry Lane Wilson, of course, had every reason to publish the message to Madero, for it advertised his own hard line toward the Mexicans. Reuben informed the secretary—who had to cancel the note to Madero—and carefully saved all the incriminating evidence. To DeLashmutt's report he appended a handwritten note. "Here is an important historical document," it announced. "This has to do with a 'leak' from the Dept. of State—the leak being by Ambassador Wilson."[29]

Again Wilson had been implicated and again the president took no action. Despite clear evidence that the ambassador had plotted his own course in Mexico, despite his efforts to embarrass the department in the press, despite an unprecedented request from Madero that Wilson be removed from his post at once,[30] the president stood pat. After all, to publicly sack Henry Lane Wilson at this point would be to confess the failure of his entire Mexican policy. What Taft did not know, sadly, was that this was the last chance an American president would have to stem the tide of events in Mexico and bring the tragic slaughter to an end. By letting that chance slip away, he had put the fate of the Mexicans in the hands of Henry Lane Wilson.

vii

The misdeeds of Wilson would have made life difficult enough for a thoroughly sound Mexican government; Madero's by this time was not sound at all. Resistance to the government had not died with Huerta's victory over Orozco, and resistance was not something the Mexican president knew how to handle. "He does not shoot, sir!" one observer complained to a friend.

An End and a Beginning

Do you believe that a president who does not shoot, who does not punish, who does not make himself feared, who always invokes laws and principles, can preside? If within the Apostle there was a Don Porfirio, hidden and silent, Mexico would be happy. . . . Madero is good. But it is not a good man that is needed.[31]

Assorted plotters against Madero well knew that he did not shoot. They owed their lives to the fact. The first to learn the secret was Félix Díaz, nephew of the deposed dictator, who revolted in Veracruz in October of 1912. The uprising was quickly suppressed, and Díaz, who might ordinarily have expected the firing squad, was packed off to prison instead. Immediately he began to plot anew, gathering about him some of the most consequential men in the country. By the first of the year, Díaz had formed an alliance with Bernardo Reyes, also jailed for mutiny—and with General Huerta himself.[32]

Patiently, the Díaz-Reyes-Huerta triumvirate plotted Madero's downfall. By February of 1913 they were ready to strike. The coup almost came off as planned, the only hitch developing at the last minute when the president's brother Gustavo got wind of the plot and managed to shore up the defenses of the National Palace. But the hitch proved to be costly. Reyes and Díaz arrived at the palace on the morning of February 9, having been released from prison by their followers—but instead of encountering only token resistance, as planned, they were met by a hail of machine gun bullets. Reyes was killed in the first volley, and Díaz and his troops were sent scurrying to a nearby barracks for cover. To all appearances the rebellion had been crushed.

But the fates were not to have it so. In order to mop up the remnants of resistance, Madero was forced to bring in a new general. Reluctantly, and with almost premonitory misgivings, he selected Huerta, one of the conspirators' own. What followed has come to be known in Mexican history as the Ten Tragic Days. Instead of aiming his artillery at the rebels' barracks, Huerta engaged in a random and leisurely shelling of the entire city, the purpose of which, as one observer said, was "to destroy the appetite of the people for a voice in their government." Díaz cannonaded back with similar aimlessness. Systematically, the two of them began reducing the once-proud city of the Aztecs to rubble.[33]

As death rained from the skies, Henry Lane Wilson became the man of the hour. Emerging like a knight from the fortresslike American embassy, he rode everywhere and saw everything, a huge U.S. flag fluttering behind his black Packard. He received a flood of foreign refugees seeking protection, organized a medical corps, set up a telegraph office, and even established a temporary bank.[34] But most of the ambassador's activity was political. He made his way through the bullet-riddled streets to demand of a bewildered Madero that the fighting be stopped.[35] He cabled Washington and advised "prompt and effective action," which he later clarified to mean sending warships and marines to Mexican ports.[36] He then requested "firm, drastic instructions, perhaps of a menacing character" to be sent to both sides. "If I were in possession of instructions of this character or clothed with general powers in the name of the President," he said, "I might possibly be able to induce a cessation of hostilities."[37]

The State Department was not so sure about that. The warships and marines were speeded southward as requested, but after much discussion, the decision was made to deny the ambassador's appeal for special authority. If the United States was going to intervene now, Henry Lane Wilson seemed to be the last person who should be given control of the troops. Wilson was unflustered. He simply acted as though the request had been granted, and proceeded to warn Madero that the forces would be landed, if necessary, to maintain order.[38]

By February 15 the streets of Mexico City were littered with corpses. A shell had demolished the American Club, and the YMCA had become a battleground. Wilson's embassy was now crowded to capacity with foreign residents and dignitaries. Water and lights had been cut off and sanitary conditions were approaching the intolerable. Moreover, the embassy stood directly in the line of fire.[39] Wilson understood this fact—the shells were screaming past like express trains—yet, in what seemed to be the death-wish extraordinary of the interventionist mind, he refused to evacuate the building. Upon learning of the situation through the Associated Press, Reuben Clark all but ordered him out.

Almost intolerable as is the situation, it should be remembered that fighting within cities is by no means without precedent and that the convenience of foreigners and the dignity of diplomatic establishments can not in all cases be interposed in a manner to affect the issue of such fighting where the danger to foreigners and diplomatic representatives is incidental and where they may escape such danger by removal.[40]

But the ambassador was now busy elsewhere. In fact, he was trying to force Madero to resign. He need not have bothered, however; for by the ninth day of the bombardment Mexicans were ready for peace at any price, and Huerta made his move. Of course, he checked with the American ambassador first; and Wilson, naive to the last, calmly informed Washington that a coup d'état was nigh.[41] Before anyone at the department could catch his breath from the shock Huerta had struck, placing President Madero and Vice-president Pino Suárez under arrest and ordering a general cease-fire.[42] The Mexican Revolution, so Wilson thought, had finally come to an end.

Actually it had just begun.

viii

Henry Lane Wilson had not planned the coup against Madero, but in the instant he knew of it he became responsible. And the ambassador found that he could cover the responsibility only by involving himself the more. Thus, obligingly, he brought Huerta and Díaz together and made them work out their differences. The resulting agreement, contemptuously known in Mexican history as the Pact of the Embassy, stipulated that Huerta would become provisional president and then support Díaz in a general election.[43] Later that evening the ambassador hosted the two conspirators at a reception in the embassy. Huerta, glassy-eyed and stuttering, was too drunk to appreciate the event; but Díaz beamed with pleasure when Wilson toasted: "Long live General Díaz, the savior of Mexico."[44]

As for Madero, Huerta asked Wilson whether it was better to send the deposed president out of the country or to lock him up in an asylum. "I replied," said Wilson, "that he ought to do that which was best for the peace of the country."[45] Obviously, what was "best for the peace of the country" would be Madero's death, since alive he would surely challenge the government again. Wilson denied having intended to incite murder, but it would have been an obtuse revolutionary who failed to read it that way. Reuben Clark read it that way immediately and saw to the cabling of another warning to Wilson: "Huerta's consulting you as to the treatment of Madero tends to give you a certain responsibility in the matter."[46] But the ambassador, for once, was not up to taking responsibility. When asked by Señora Madero to insure the safety of her husband, Wilson coolly replied that he wished not to intervene in Mexican domestic affairs.[47]

Late in the evening of February 22, Madero and Pino Suárez were told that they were to be transferred from the National Palace to the city penitentiary for greater safety. En route, so the story went, the automobiles carrying the two men were ambushed by partisans seeking to liberate them. In the ensuing gun battle, both were killed—shot neatly in the head at point-blank range. This account proved convincing to very few people.* Wilson, however, accepted it in toto and for good reason. At that moment he was frantically negotiating for the immediate recognition and support of the Huerta government, both by Washington and the European powers, and the going was proving to be difficult. As word of Madero's death hit the headlines, Wilson's task became more difficult still; but in the crucial days following, he kept at it. Somehow the Mexican Revolution had wound up in his lap. He could only clear himself, it seemed, by seeing to it that the poisonous Victoriano Huerta succeeded.[48]

ix

And Huerta would succeed only if the United States recognized his regime. It was as simple as that. European recognition, which came haltingly in dribs and drabs, made no real difference. There were, of course, solid reasons for recognizing Huerta, and most of them came to the surface in the State Department debates that followed. He was a strongman like Porfirio. He might bring an end to the killing. He was avidly pro-American, pro-business, pro-foreign investment. As for his complicity in the murder of Madero, it was not—and still is not—definitely established. In any event, the moral character of rulers had rarely, if ever, been a criterion of diplomatic action; what counted was not whether they were good men or bad

---

*This sort of summary execution was a very old custom in Mexican politics known as the *ley fuga* or "law of escape." Shooting prisoners who were "attempting to escape" spared all the time and expense of a trial. Díaz was said to have dispatched thousands of political adversaries in this way.

men but whether they were actually in power. And Huerta certainly was.

This was a fairly strong case. But there was a case on the other side, too. Recognizing Huerta seemed uncomfortably like condoning murder. True, Huerta himself may not have pulled the trigger, and conceivably he may have had no foreknowledge of the deed. Nevertheless, Huerta could have and should have prevented the death of Madero, just as Henry Lane Wilson could have and should have prevented it. And Madero's death represented far more than a simple assassination—it amounted to nothing less than the murder of the revolution itself. Madero had become a great symbol of hope to millions of Mexicans who deserved far better than they received. To betray Madero was to betray them, and to install Huerta in the National Palace was to hold for naught everything for which they had fought. Did the United States of America want to do that?

Finally, there was Huerta himself to think about. As his regime took shape in the following weeks, everyone's worst fears were confirmed. He quickly rid Mexico of all obstacles to his rule, including his recent cohort, Félix Díaz. Political foes were jailed, shot, or packed out of the country. Cronies milked the national treasury. Cabinet members became, as one Mexican put it, "accomplices," and the congress proved only that it could be crushed like an insect if it objected. Huerta had one legislator assassinated and one hundred ten others put under arrest in order to make the point. As for the new president himself, he was rarely to be found at the National Palace. Three sheets to the wind, he conducted the nation's business from an assortment of bars and brothels about the capital city. Often as not, ministers tracked him down at the fashionable El Globo tea room, where he would pass the time sipping brandy from a teacup and matching coins with the cashier.[49]

x

All told, the considerations both for and against recognition were exceedingly troublesome. They bothered everyone. And on top of them was the conduct of Henry Lane Wilson, which, even when its full dimensions were unknown, amounted to impropriety of Miltonic proportions. Reuben Clark spent a long time weighing the pros and cons. He had no particular sense that his opinion one way or the other would be decisive, but it was the most experienced and informed opinion available. In fact, it would determine the outgoing president's final policy.

There was a colossal irony involved in this climax of a situation fraught with ironies. Henry Lane Wilson, by personally intervening in the Mexican situation, had placed the United States government in a position where it might only escape further intervention by ratifying his work. Solicitor Clark grasped this fact immediately. He could condone absolutely nothing that Ambassador Wilson had done—but unless he did condone it, the United States would become the custodian of the Mexican Revolution, passing on the fitness of every presidential aspirant from this time forward. It was checkmate either way.

xi

Reuben had recently written a memorandum defending armed invasion. He now wrote one defending Huerta. Like *Right to Protect Citizens,* this document, titled "Suggestive Points on the Mexican Situation," close-hauled many of his own cherished ideals. Debauchery, treason, and regicide were only a few of the charges that Reuben had to justify in behalf of the new regime. "Why visit the sins of this one man upon practically a whole nation?" he asked gamely. But through his prose there glowered his own distaste for Huerta.[50]

More important than taste, however, were the fundamental principles at stake. One of them was the right of revolution.[51] Reuben had not much liked any of the revolutionaries—nor, for that matter, Díaz before them—but that was not the point. "Refusal to recognize a republican government because you do not like or approve the manner in which the head of the government attained his position is novel in American diplomacy and wholly unsound," he declared.

> Mr. Huerta obtained his position as the outcome of a successful revolution. Is this nation in a position to say that successful revolutionary governments shall never hereafter be recognized? What becomes of the principle upon which our own Government was built? What becomes of Washington?[52]

"What becomes of Washington?" was a vexing question. It would still bother Reuben twenty years later, when the Mexican Revolution would yet be churning along and when J. Reuben Clark, as U.S. ambassador to Mexico, would again find himself in the middle of it. Reuben took no pleasure in social upheaval, nor in the bolshevism he detected in *insurrecto* rhetoric. But what indeed became of Washington?

Another principle to defend was the one Reuben had championed from the beginning. "This situation," he said with bridled vehemence,

is more than a failure to recognize; it is positive intervention to control another nation in the matter of its local government; it is intervention by dictating who cannot be the head of that government, and by compelling the establishment of a new government under our censorship. This is political intervention and is our maiden effort which, perhaps may account for its lack of skill and art.[53]

Consider, he said, how it felt to be on the other side. In America's own Civil War, for example, there had been lawlessness, brigandage, and property loss to foreigners. "Did any one talk of intervening here and stopping the war, and if they had what could have been the answer?"

Reuben drove deeper still. "Suppose," he posited,

a new government is set up in Mexico by our effort and intervention. It is a moral certainty that it will not have peace until it has demonstrated its ability to maintain itself by force. . . . What under these circumstances will be our legal and moral responsibility?[54]

The question was unanswerable. Those who took it upon themselves to oversee the affairs of their neighbors—what did become their responsibility? Where did it end? How did it end? Was it not conceivable that once the die was cast there were—quite literally—no limits whatever to the ensuing political liability, and that the only end in sight was the one achieved by the ancient Romans when they too began to intervene beyond their borders? The ethic of the busybody, said Reuben, too easily swelled into the ethic of the imperialist.

There was one final principle to stand up for, and now that the solicitor had pulled out all the stops he might as well say what it was. If there had been muddle-headedness and vacillation in the American response to the whirlwind, there was, he believed, a significant reason for it. It derived from the unfortunate historical accident by which one nation had effectively come to own another. As Reuben ranged back over the months and years of turmoil, he concluded that it was the proprietary interest more than any other which had promoted the cause of intervention. The Albert Falls, Judge Wilfleys, and Henry Lane Wilsons would not be happy, apparently, until their Mexican property was absolutely and unquestionably safe; and that state of affairs would not be achieved until the ruler of Mexico became someone of their own personal choosing. For Reuben Clark, on the other hand, property interest had always taken a back seat to considerations of human life and dignity. "International law," he said,

knows no principle authorizing intervention in a civil war merely because of property loss. International law recognizes the inherent fundamental right of every people to determine for themselves the kind of government they will have and the methods, in case of opposition, they will take to secure it. They do not lose that right merely because foreigners see fit to come and reside among them.[55]

The tug-of-war between hawk and dove, then, really came down to a simple question of priorities. "American blood," Reuben affirmed bluntly, "is worth more than American dollars." And just as the orientation toward dollars had consistently pointed toward intervention, the orientation toward blood had consistently pointed against it. J. Reuben Clark, at least, had never found it difficult to choose between them.

xii

As the solicitor's last word on the Mexican matter, "Suggestive Points" marked a fitting close to his career as decision-maker. And the Knox State Department was convinced. Huntington Wilson, who stayed on for a few weeks under the new administration, personally sat down with President Wilson and tried to convince him too. "There was no doubt of the cleverness and agility of his intellect," reported the assistant secretary, "[but] it was the habit of his remarkable mind to ponder principles and general ideas and then to apply these to the facts of a situation, whether they fitted or not. I wondered later whether he had even listened that evening."[56] Woodrow Wilson had not wrestled with the Mexican Revolution and he was not interested in the experience of those who had. Nor was Secretary of State William Jennings Bryan. Where the president was untaught in diplomacy, Bryan was unteachable. Huntington Wilson stood with him for an hour on a windy Washington street corner and tried to explain the intricacies of Mexican banditry. Orozco had done this and Orozco had done that, he outlined patiently. "Yes, yes," Bryan replied vacantly, "Orinoco."[57]

Reuben, of course, had sought by that last memorandum to avoid handing Mexico over to the Democrats at all. He had tried to push Taft into acting on his own. But Taft, as usual, had preferred sitting on the lid. This was the final irony and tragedy of the Mexican matter. The genius of America's Mexican policy, in the last analysis, was that William Howard Taft had done nothing. By refusing to act, month in and month out, he had been unaccountably wise, and the results had borne him out consistently. But the Huerta question was the one issue that demanded action, as Reuben had so urgently tried to explain, and yet Taft had still been unable to act. So the Huerta question changed hands with the administration and was settled, decisively, by the new president.

As history would record, it was a hard settlement.

Chapter 12

TO REAP THE WHIRLWIND

"I think often and regretfully of the interesting and hard working days at the Department with the splendid men all about us and the great enthusiasm and desire to do something for one's country."[1] So reminisced Fred Morris Dearing from Brussels, where the fateful year of 1914 found him biding his time dispiritedly. He brought up the subject again fifteen years later. "Remember the afternoon when we requested the combatants to retire south of the city and have their battle there ... and saved ourselves from intervention in Mexico? Hm!"[2] Dearing was still writing about it fifteen years after that, in his memoirs. "You figure in Number II," he explained to Reuben, "which is about the Mexican Revolution and you too possibly may find it not too hard to keep on reading."[3] For Fred Dearing Mexico had become the golden age, and he could never quite escape its memory.

What had cast such a glow over it all was certainly not the dilemmas and frustrations of the time but rather the jarring events that followed. For it was only in the light of these events that the Mexican policy of the Taft years stood forth as wise, farsighted, and statesmanlike. The first shock was the resumption of the Mexican Revolution, which now became a true holocaust. This, as Reuben Clark had predicted, was the direct result of President Wilson's refusal to recognize Huerta. Huerta was a usurper, proclaimed Wilson, and a murderer to boot; the United States would have nothing to do with him. Around those charges Mexican opposition to the new strongman galvanized quickly, and soon the country was back at war. Ultimately Wilson succeeded in forcing Huerta out of office, but there was no end to the bloodshed. Huerta was replaced by Carranza, who was himself forced from office and then murdered; and Carranza was accompanied by a three-cornered donnybrook among

Villa, Zapata, and Obregón. Eventually they too were all murdered. In the meantime, rebel armies were crisscrossing Mexico with swaths of destruction. Villa and Obregón, in one engagement alone, ran up a numbing nine thousand casualties. Salazar died in the revolution. So did Rojas, who had helped him destroy Colonia Morelos. Pascual Orozco was hunted down and killed by a Texas posse while attempting to ignite another round of *Orozquismo*. In the end the whirlwind claimed them all.[4]

And of course the United States finally intervened, precisely as Reuben had said it would. Once Wilson had set himself against Huerta, the intervention was inevitable. It was touched off by a trifling incident in Tampico, in April of 1914. The Mexicans profusely apologized for the incident; but President Wilson, seeking to force the Huerta issue, demanded a twenty-one-gun salute to the American flag. When no salute was forthcoming, he sent in the marines and occupied Veracruz. This exhibition brought none of the desired consequences and several distinctly undesired ones. The landing party sustained nineteen dead and seventy wounded. Mexican casualties ran into the hundreds, many of them women and children caught in the line of fire. Far from forcing Huerta from power, the action caused dissidents to rally around him to repel the hated *gringos.* Then there followed a week-long rampage against Americans and their property all over Mexico. Stores, shops, and hotels were looted, smashed, and burned, while snipers, shooting across the international line, felled three Americans in the streets of Laredo. Only the timely interposition of British officials allowed the Americans to be evacuated from Mexico City in some degree of safety, leaving their belongings behind. The American flag, although trampled, spit upon, and burned in the streets, was never saluted.[5]

Nor did this disaster mark the end. In January of 1916 it happened all over again. The U.S. president had openly backed one rebel faction in preference to another, and the latter decided to retaliate. The border town of Columbus, New Mexico, was invaded and nineteen Americans were killed. Once again the troops were sent into Mexico, this time under the command of "Black Jack" Pershing, with orders to bring back the scalp of one Pancho Villa. The wily bandit eluded them, of course, and they wound up clashing instead with units of the Mexican army—that is, the side Wilson thought he was supporting—and ultimately with the government itself. Pershing's expedition straggled home $130,000,000 the poorer and with forty fewer soldiers.⁶ Meanwhile the United States and Mexico, in the words of Reuben Clark, "had drawn perilously near the brink of war, indeed ... so near that the loose stones at the top of the precipice began to fall into the abyss."⁷

American citizens in Mexico profited from none of this activity. Where the casualty list had lengthened one name at a time in Reuben Clark's day, now it proceeded to mount in double digits. Villa's men once gunned down seventeen Americans in a single afternoon;⁸ another bandit killed fourteen.⁹ And it was only by the slenderest turns of fate that the reoccupied Mormon *colonia* at Dublán was not wiped out entirely. Early in 1916, a *Villista* raid there was thwarted at the last moment by the fortuitous arrival of Pershing's troops.¹⁰ Most Americans simply gave up and got out of Mexico—they had no other choice.

It was only in reflection of all this that Reuben Clark's Mexican policy really came into focus. Interventionist hawks were never so quiet as when the Pershing forces limped back home empty-handed. Reuben himself rarely missed a chance to draw out the lesson. "While ... the revolutions with which we had to contend were of comparativity [*sic*] short duration," he wrote to Knox,

there has been in Mexico practically ever since Wilson came in and refused to recognize Huerta, one long continuous orgy of murder, robbery, rape and general and indiscriminate bloodletting. By this I mean that there never was a time during your administration of the Department of State when there was not in Mexico City a Government recognized in a large part of Mexico, and conducting its foreign relations with the world. Huerta, who came in so shortly before we went out, was recognized by some twenty odd countries, as I recall it, including practically all if not all of the great powers of Europe, so that we left the Mexican situation with Mexico pacified and holding the power in Mexico the strongest man who has appeared since the palmy days of Díaz.¹¹

Reuben had a right to his I-told-you-sos; he had literally foretold the disasters that followed. "Their controversy is no more our business, than our controversy in the '60's was the business of England and France," he had asserted in his final memorandum. "Let them work it out for themselves as we did."¹² Had that advice prevailed with the Wilson administration, the course of Mexican-American relations

214

after 1913 might have been substantially different. But history books do not concern themselves with what might have been. They are concerned with what in fact was, and for that reason they are biased toward those who *did* something, even if it was wrong, and against those who *refrained* from doing something, even if that proved to be right. Because Reuben Clark the lawyer was deeply imbued with precepts of legal restraint, he was much more the refrainer than the doer. His Mexican memoranda comprised a sort of textbook on what *not* to do about a revolution on one's doorstep. In retrospect, the soundness of this wisdom was hardly open to doubt. Yet American history pays but scant honor to William Howard Taft, the man of restraint, in whose policy the wisdom was expressed. Rather, it remembers Woodrow Wilson, the man of action, of whom it could be said that he did something—even when it was wrong.

And that was the crowning irony of all.

PART III

ARMAGEDDON AND AFTER

1905–26

THE LAWYER AS CRUSADER

The First World War sired a generation of crusaders. It was one of those epochal experiences that divide past from future and galvanize permanent change. Different individuals came through the war in different ways, of course; but everyone came through it profoundly shaken, and those who were concerned with America's relationship to the world were shaken most of all. The crusading spirit was a general result. There were crusaders for peace and crusaders for war. There were zealous advocates of a League of Nations and bitterest opponents of the same. There were champions of international law, of a supernational judiciary, and of multinational moral pacts. There were antimilitarists vowing to dismantle armies and navies and Cassandras pleading to fortify them. There were ardent internationalists and fervent isolationists and believers in a score of private "-isms." The welter of discordant voices rose to a veritable crescendo as each new question came to the fore. J. Reuben Clark was a part of all this—indeed, he was very close to its center. As international lawyer, as diplomat, as believer in world peace, as one of those concerned with America's relationship to the world, he had much at stake—emotionally and intellectually—in the final outcome. For him, Armageddon and its aftermath became the single most pressing question of his life.

Chapter 13

THE NEW LAWYERS

On a cold Saturday evening in December, 1905, while Reuben Clark was reading for midterm exams at Columbia law school, a dinner party was being held a few blocks away at the home of Oscar Straus. Present were Nicholas Murray Butler, George Kirchwey, John Bassett Moore, James Brown Scott, and Chandler Anderson. Among the remainder of the twenty guests were diplomats, jurists, educators, and politicians; and rounding them out, smiling and beneficent, was Andrew Carnegie. They were gathered for the purpose of founding the American Society of International Law.[1] It was an auspicious occasion, one upon which American international lawyers would look back as marking the birth of their profession. For J. Reuben Clark, Jr., it was a beginning as well.

There had always been "international lawyers" in the sense that some law practices had been international in scope or that someone with legal training had been required to interpret international law. But the sense here was different. It grew out of an activity of comparatively recent origin called "judicial settlement"; and so pungent was this activity with meaning, so bright was it with hope, that new definitions seemed in order. Where once there had been only lawyers international, now there were genuine international lawyers. And exactly like their domestic counterparts, they were engaged in the pursuit of justice.[2]

Judicial settlement was a process designed to settle, or "arbitrate," diplomatic controversies through specially constituted tribunals. Historically, a nation had few means short of war by which to resolve disputes with its neighbors. Beginning around 1800, however, the idea gained currency that international courts of law might be developed to handle these disputes in a manner similar to domestic litigation. The usual procedure was for the contending parties to

221

sign a special treaty setting up a tribunal. Then, as in domestic law, each side would engage attorneys to prepare and argue its case, and the final decision of the court would be considered binding. In this way, hopefully, peaceful solutions could be found.

The first instance of an arbitration agreement in American history was found in Jay's Treaty of 1795, but it was not until after the Civil War that the practice really took hold. The turning point came in 1872 with the successful arbitration of the *Alabama* claims against Great Britain. Because this proceeding involved major powers, concerned national honor, and, most importantly, presented the stronger of the litigants (Great Britain) with an adverse decision, the *Alabama* arbitration came to symbolize soaring expectations.* Yet, no less significant were the more than twenty-five international adjudications involving the United States over the next two decades. In 1898, when John Bassett Moore published his *History and Digest of the International Arbitrations to Which the United States Has Been a Party,* he was already drawing upon a tradition.[3]

At the First Hague Conference in 1898, judicial settlement got another hefty boost when, almost as an afterthought, the delegates suddenly adopted a convention setting up the world's first Permanent Court of Arbitration. Actually the permanent court was neither truly permanent nor truly a court; it was simply a panel of judges from which any two nations could assemble their own tribunal in reaching an agreement to arbitrate. Still, the establishment of the Hague court seemed to give physical shape at last to an extremely important principle.[4]

Once again, many who rejoiced were Americans. From the very beginning, Americans had felt a sense of evangelism—of mission, as Jefferson put it—toward the rest of the world. The missionary spirit was nicely captured by the American Peace Society, which was organized during the early flush of Jacksonian reform and which carried on an active and determined campaign to eliminate war. The

---

*The *Alabama* and two companion ships, the *Florida* and *Shenandoah,* were commerce destroyers built in Liverpool for the Confederate States of America. After the Civil War, Secretary of State Seward pressed claims against the British government for $15 million in direct damages caused by the raiders and $2 million in indirect damages for prolonging the war. Owing to the patient diplomacy of Canadian Finance Minister Sir John Rose and Secretary of State Hamilton Fish, an agreement to arbitrate the claims was signed in May of 1871. The tribunal met in Geneva in December of that year and in September of 1872 awarded the United States $15.5 million in gold. The award was promptly paid.

campaign was not always successful, and the moralists of the APS had a good deal to learn about raw power and tangible programs before they could hope to become effective; but by the end of the century the search for peaceful alternatives was beginning to settle down to earth. In 1895, for example, Quaker philanthropists Albert and Daniel Smiley began holding their annual Conferences on International Arbitration at Lake Mohonk in the Catskills. Despite the romantic setting, the Mohonk conferences became ever more mindful of man's belligerent nature and ever more practical in their efforts to deal with it.[5]

And none too soon. With the development of the telephone, the electric light, and the horseless carriage had come also the dreadnought, the submarine, and the machine gun. Progress, it seemed, was a two-edged sword, and at least one of the edges was made for cutting off heads. Only in America, really, did the hope for peace continue to outpace despair, for here Jefferson's dream still survived. As Philander Knox proclaimed in a speech that he and Reuben Clark wrote together:

> From the ages when barbarism and cruelty dominated the world, through the intervening eras when advancing civilization slowly extended to states the forces of enlightened and beneficient private conduct, we have reached a point when it is evident that the future holds in store a time when wars shall cease, ... when in deliberate international conjunction the strong shall universally help the weak, and when the corporate righteousness of the world shall compel unrighteousness to disappear and shall destroy the habitations of cruelty still lingering in the dark places of the earth.[6]

So it was with considerable excitement that the American Society of International Law came into being on that December night. The task of the international lawyers was clearly cut out. They must first convince a skeptical world that judicial settlement could work – and then they must indeed make it work. Individuals suited to one or the other of these objectives had been attending the Lake Mohonk conferences regularly, and they came together in critical mass at Straus's dinner party. The first group included academicians such as George Kirchwey, John Bassett Moore, and James Brown Scott, whose concern with international law was primarily scholarly. The second group included veterans of actual arbitrations – men like Robert Lansing, Chandler Anderson, William Renfield, and John W.

Foster. Better organized and more businesslike than the old-line pacifists, the international lawyers had soon wanted an organization of their own. With the founding of the ASIL, the time had come, as Kirchwey said, to move beyond mere "treading the wine press of ancient wars" and take "some definite step" toward the goal.[7]

The new lawyers were not simply respected men – they were men of authority. By organizing themselves they transformed judicial settlement from an amateur crusade into a professional campaign and carried it to the highest realms of government. John W. Foster, Elihu Root, Philander Knox, and Robert Lansing each served as secretary of state between 1890 and 1920. All were active in the ASIL. Another stronghold was the office of solicitor, which under James Brown Scott became a veritable pulpit for judicial settlement. A third post of importance was that of counselor, occupied consecutively from 1910 to 1915 by Chandler Anderson, John Bassett Moore, and Robert Lansing, all members of the ASIL's original executive committee. The trend was clear.[8]

ii

How the lawyers used their public influence was illustrated by the career of Elihu Root. Although trained in corporate rather than international law, Root had developed an interest in world peace while serving as President McKinley's secretary of war. By the time he reached the State Department in 1905 he was wedded to the cause of judicial settlement. But Root was never blind to the difficulties. He knew, for example, that the court of arbitration set up by the Hague conference had serious shortcomings. As an open-ended panel of judges rather than a court of fixed membership, the Hague tribunal left itself open to abuse. Selecting the judges to hear a case often ended in rough-and-tumble court-packing by the litigants. Then, once the judges were chosen, they seemed rarely to behave judicially. They were more often trained as diplomats than jurists, and their inclination was for "negotiating a settlement" rather than "deciding an issue" – often simply splitting the difference between the parties. Finally, the Hague court had no settled jurisdiction. Litigants might make use of it or they might not, depending on their own self-interest; and, given the court's weaknesses, a nation could be pardoned for choosing the latter alternative.[9] Such, concluded Root, were not the makings of true justice. Only by having a real court with real judges applying real law was judicial settlement ever to become a working reality.

Root worked tirelessly to achieve these modifications, but it was all uphill. He instructed delegates to the Second Hague Conference (convening in the summer of 1907) to push ahead energetically. He established the Central American court of justice as a sort of mockup of the ideal court he had in mind. He negotiated bilateral arbitration treaties with each of the major powers, and in the famous Atlantic fisheries arbitration with Great Britain—which he argued personally—he proved that the United States could accept an adverse decision itself.* For this work Root was awarded the Nobel Peace Prize in 1912—yet every one of his projects ended in disappointment.[10]

Philander Knox carried the torch ignited by Root, but with little more success. He too tried to perfect a prototype of the world court, using the International Prize Court as his model, and ran up against British opposition.† He too tried his hand at negotiating arbitration treaties and ran afoul of the Senate. He too laid plans for an ambitious assault at the Third Hague Conference, scheduled for 1915, and ran headlong into the world war.[11] But then, advocates of peace were always being stymied by war.

iii

Impressive as were the efforts of Root and Knox, it was another founder of the ASIL who was destined to become the apostle of judicial settlement. James Brown Scott was well versed in international law—as neither Root nor Knox had been—and his credentials were impeccable. Upon graduating from Harvard in 1890 he had traveled to Europe to pursue graduate studies. After returning to the United States, he had organized one law school (Southern California) and

---

*See pp. 229-30.

†Unlike the amorphous Permanent Court of Arbitration, the International Prize Court was a genuine tribunal with fixed personnel, settled procedures, and a definite (though limited) jurisdiction. Knox hoped to expand this jurisdiction from the hearing of wartime prize cases to the hearing of general international disputes.

presided over another (Illinois) before coming to Columbia. Eventually he taught at George Washington, Georgetown, and Johns Hopkins as well. His academic background was equaled by few.[12]

It was, however, exclusively academic. At the time he reached the State Department, Scott had never argued a case at law and he had never so much as witnessed an arbitration. Curiously, he was a leader of the international law movement before he was really converted to judicial settlement. This happened at the Second Hague Conference. Suddenly Scott was swept up in the excitement over the new permanent court as never before in his life. He plunged into the study of international arbitration and emerged devoted to the cause of world judiciary. Even more clearly than Root and Knox, Scott apprehended the flaws of the existing court; and his zeal to eradicate them bordered upon the religious. He returned from the Hague, as the Mockahis noted, a changed man.[13]

Much of Scott's subsequent career derived from his Hague vision. In 1909 he published his monumental *Hague Conferences of 1899 and 1907*. The same year he traveled to Europe as Knox's personal representative in the prize court negotiations. The following year he was back at the Hague again, this time as U.S. counsel in the Atlantic fisheries arbitration, where the actual experience of judicial settlement confirmed his enthusiasm. Upon his return to the United States, Scott joined with Theodore Marburg to organize the American Society for Judicial Settlement of International Disputes (ASJSID), whose announced purpose was "the creation of a permanent tribunal for the judicial settlement of international controversies."[14] As organizer and propagandist, Scott carried the work forward determinedly, founding or affiliating himself with several more action groups and delivering any number of spirited calls to the colors. By 1910 he was the unchallenged leader of the movement.[15]

Ever the man of theory, Scott chose ambitious models to explicate his dream. For example, he likened the proposed world court to the development of the English common law and Roman civil law systems, pointing out how each had progressed through stages of anarchy and arbitration to true judicial settlement.[16] But Scott's favorite analogy was based upon American history. Under the Articles of Confederation, he explained, the only way to settle disputes between the states was by voluntary arbitration, and the result had been legal chaos. With the establishment under the Constitution of a unified judiciary, order was miraculously achieved. In the same way, Scott argued, international peace and stability were bound to result from the improved judicial system he had in mind—a system more and more resembling the United States judiciary at every turn. "[It] would," he said, "bind the states as a whole as well as the individual litigants, just as the Supreme Court of the United States binds the forty-six states of the union as well as the individual litigants."[17] This extra dividend of binding the states largely escaped notice in the analogy; nonetheless, many lawyers—even dedicated adherents of the movement—thought that Scott might be going a bit far. The most thoughtful of them could see that what James Brown Scott was advocating was a new world order.

iv

J. Reuben Clark came of age professionally with the new lawyers. In 1898, when the proposal for the original Hague conference was made, Reuben was beginning his first job at Heber City High. By the time the Second Hague Conference convened nine years later, he was a graduate of Columbia law school, an assistant solicitor of the Department of State, and a respected member of the international law fraternity. With every new advance of judicial settlement Reuben had some connection. He belonged to all of the organizations.[18] He subscribed to all of the journals. When approached by the Lake Mohonk organization for a speech on unlimited compulsory arbitration, he sailed into the assignment zestfully.[19] As for the world court, Reuben, like Scott, spent long hours pondering the matter, and in 1910 he even sketched out a model system of his own.[20] He appeared well qualified for membership in the movement.

But the appearance was deceiving. If Reuben shared a measure of James Brown Scott's enthusiasm for judicial settlement, it was only a measure. He had little of Scott's passion for theory. Indeed, *his* connection to the international law movement had been overwhelmingly practical. While Scott had been all but incapacitated by his devotion to arbitration, it was Reuben who had had to prepare the actual arbitration of Alsop. He had helped set up the American-British Claims Commission in 1910 as well as the Nicaraguan-

American Claims Commission in 1912, and he exhaustively analyzed the Prize Court negotiations.[21] When President Taft began preparing for the Third Hague Conference, Solicitor Clark was the person he put in charge.[22]

And where the "Scott side" of Reuben seemed to respond to the call for judicial settlement, the "Moore side" had some rather serious doubts. From his own hard experience Reuben had observed three recurrent difficulties in the arbitration process, any one of which might eviscerate it. The first was jurisdiction. In the Alsop arbitration the great problem had not been in arguing the merits of the case but in forcing the Chileans to arbitrate at all. Thus, Reuben came to see that the real roadblock for judicial settlement was not an incompetent court—the Alsop court had been competent enough—but the lack of compulsory jurisdiction.[23] The second difficulty was international law itself. Unlike the English common law, international law had not evolved through the centuries to adapt to the complexities of modern life. On crucial questions, in fact, there was no international law whatever.

I gave a hypothetical case of Great Britain trading British Honduras for Lower California, which I stated was entirely proper under international law; that thereafter Great Britain should begin to fortify Magdalena Bay, also an operation entirely within her rights. I stated that when the matter had progressed far enough, our country would probably be at fever heat, that thereafter Great Britain would propose arbitration since she had committed no offense under international law, [and] we probably, quite properly, would refuse to go to arbitration and then become the aggressor under these pacts, etc.[24]

The only answer was either to codify international law, so that all nations would know precisely what to expect of it, or else to confine arbitration to those issues for which the law was well settled. Reuben's third difficulty was even more realistic. There were have and have-not nations in the world, he observed, and international judges from either class would carry a bias hostile to the other. In 1910 he warned that Scott's court in particular "will be composed in its majority of European and Latin American powers who do not love us, and who, unless human nature changes, will not forget it when we are involved either with Europe or Latin America."[25] For this reason, Reuben said, Scott's favorite analogies broke down. When Scott spoke of the common law uniting England, he missed a crucial point: "The English courts ... were acting upon a homogeneity of people, custom, ideal, interest, and economic condition"—radically different from contemporary international society.[26]

v

All three were cogent indictments. International lawyers had no real answers to them. Reuben Clark, however, began to suppose that he did have some answers, based once again on his own experience. While still an assistant solicitor in the State Department, Reuben had assisted in the preparation of the Atlantic fisheries arbitration; and here, as he believed, he had found an important clue. The history of the case ran far back. From the earliest voyages to the New World, it was known that the Grand Banks off Newfoundland provided some of the richest fishing grounds on earth. Access to them had occasioned endless bickering between the United States and Great Britain. The interests of the sea-based fishermen from Gloucester were at odds with those of the shore-based fishermen from Newfoundland, and the chowder was further thickened by the interests of the big canning companies. The Canadians, it seemed, wished to regulate the taking and processing of fish in such a way as to put everyone else at a disadvantage. It all added up to a century and more of conflict and acrimony—with many a royal cruiser pursuing many a nimble seiner down the Acadian coast.[27]

After attempts to deal with the problem had repeatedly failed, diplomats ceased to believe that it was resolvable. Then in 1907 James Lord Bryce, British ambassador to the United States, suddenly proposed that the entire matter be submitted to arbitration before the Hague court. This was a crucial test: if the United States and Britain could pass it, they would do more for the cause of judicial settlement than all of the boosting combined. The experience indeed proved to be a grueling one. Root, Anderson, Lansing, and the others held onto their tempers through three months of hard verbal slugging. The judges seemed biased against them. British counsel resorted to cheap tricks. Airtight arguments fell on deaf ears. And in the end the whole thing ground down to a simple compromise. But smooth-running or not, the Hague arbitration did lay the fisheries question to its final rest.[28]

Knox, Clark, and Huntington Wilson all shared the same retrospective opinion of the Atlantic fisheries proceeding: that no other two nations in the world could have brought it off. Acting on that belief, Secretary of State Knox sat down with Britain's Lord Bryce and drafted a new type of arbitration agreement. The Knox-Bryce treaty, unlike all others before, provided for compulsory arbitration of all justiciable disputes that might arise between the two countries. "Justiciable disputes" exempted questions of vital interest, independence, or national honor, and, more importantly, questions for which there was no law controlling.[29] Reuben came to believe in the Knox-Bryce approach to arbitration as sincerely as Scott believed in the world court approach. It alone provided for compulsory jurisdiction; it alone acknowledged the actual gaps in international law; and it alone surmounted the barriers of class, race, and culture.[30] As solicitor, Reuben consulted with Knox on details of the proposed treaty, and as State Department advocate, he helped stump the country in support of it.[31] Rejection of the treaty by the Senate in 1911 was a crushing blow to him.

vi

So it was that Reuben came to question the object sublime of the new lawyers—the world court. "I do not believe," he confided to Huntington Wilson in 1910, "that arbitration is such an unmixed and undiluted blessing as it is by many considered."[32] The solution, at any rate, was not to be found in Scott's simplistic appeals for improved arbitral machinery. In fact, the more Reuben thought about the matter, the more convinced he became that Scott was dead wrong; and by 1913, when Reuben was chairman of the American preparatory committee for the Third Hague Conference, he was in a position to say so forcefully. As he explained in his report to the president, the problem with judicial settlement was not that the existing Hague court failed to do justice but that it did justice all too well and hence alienated wrong-doing nations. Crisply he concluded: "The perfection of court machinery would, therefore, not meet this situation."[33]

That these ideas were now appearing in state papers did not augur well for Scott's program. The preparatory committee, not Scott, was making American policy toward judicial settlement, for the Third Hague Conference was supposed to be the one finally charmed with success. James Brown Scott was now associated with the Carnegie Endowment for International Peace, and his efforts in behalf of the revitalized court were undiminished. Indeed, the dream seemed more real than ever now, approaching like a great ship on the horizon. Little did Scott know that his own protegé had set about to scuttle it.

vii

By the time Reuben left the State Department in 1913, an open break with the judicial settlement movement was near. To John Bassett Moore he wrote that "the ignorance, hysteria and impracticality which lies behind much of the present propaganda passeth human understanding." Without men of Moore's steadiness, he added, "I fear that we shall run amuck in this matter of arbitration."[34] When the world war burst upon Europe in the summer of 1914, the worst of Reuben's fears were confirmed. When Theodore Marburg, president of the ASJSID, wrote to him afterward and requested an article for the society's quarterly, the reply was icy. "I am sure," said Reuben, "that I shall not be able to produce anything you will deem it wise to print."[35] Marburg persisted. What Reuben eventually sent him was not the requested article exactly, but a lengthy broadside against judicial settlement. "Man is what he is," began the author, "not necessarily what he ought to be. Every peaceful settlement movement must reckon with the facts as they are." From this opening, Reuben fired salvo after salvo at the ascendant wisdom of the movement.

So far behind us as we can reach with history, tradition, or myth, there are in man the same selfishness, envy, avarice, cruelty, ambition, domination, love, and hate, that exists in him today, no other or different.... It is true [*that man*] has in his normal state somewhat softened his manner, he has restrained somewhat his animal instincts, but in times of great stress, when he thinks his existence threatened, man is again the primal brute. The elemental still wells up in him and bursts out from him, and when it comes it is naked, with all its primitive ferocity and attended by all its accompanying virtues and vices.[36]

The root problem was man himself. As long as man was what he was, no judicial system reaching across the nations could bring him peace. Arbitration had its possibilities, perhaps, but the possibilities were meaningless unless jurisdiction was compulsory, unless the law itself was brought down to earth, unless the parties to the proceeding possessed some store of shared understanding. "The cause of arbitration," he stated bluntly, "does not presently require a new court."

Reuben's apostasy was strange indeed. The new lawyers had grown out of the old Jeffersonian tradition that envisioned America as moral leader of the world. J. Reuben Clark shared their romantic idealism. A divinely appointed destiny for the United States was a fundamental tenet of Mormon theology, and he subscribed to it ardently. What, then, had divided Reuben from his fellows? The practical objections about jurisdiction and codification were important. Equally important was Reuben's growing pessimism about humankind and his sense that no judicial system could constrain man's seemingly inborn nature to contend. But there was a third issue as well, and in time this became the central one. The Scott conception of the world court with its all-pervading legal hegemony frankly contemplated active American direction. The court would run the world, so to speak, and America would run the court. Scott believed in the moral leadership of the United States, but he would italicize the word "leadership." This was not Reuben's idea at all. America to him meant an experience separate and apart from the rest of mankind—a green vision of renewal that must ever be isolated from Old World decay. Reuben also believed in moral leadership, but he would italicize "moral."

The outbreak of the world war made each man cling the more tightly to his vision. Scott's vision dovetailed with the ancient dream of Camelot, and against the nightmare of modern warfare it now stood forth in bold relief. A court was suddenly not enough; there must be a congress as well, a magnificent roundtable of the nations—and all under the aegis of the United States. And Reuben's vision ironically dovetailed with that of the "Hermit Kingdom isolationists" he had so recently debunked. "This nation," he said with sudden rapture,

[must] cooperate in no way and participate in no measures which shall not leave it completely free and independent, wholly sovereign. For it is my abiding faith that

232

this nation has performed and will yet perform a mighty work for human government among the nations of the world.[37]

viii

By 1915 the battle lines were drawn and Reuben was openly in the opposition. Root, Scott, Anderson, Lansing—all of them were stronger than ever for a world court at the Hague. Root was a towering figure in the Senate; Scott was with the Carnegie Endowment; Anderson was a justice on the American-British Claims Commission; and Lansing was secretary of state. "The international law trust," Reuben dubbed them disdainfully—but in terms of what they had come to represent, he may as well have called them "the four horsemen of the Apocalypse."[38] Reuben Clark, just now achieving consequence in the international legal profession, had suddenly become its arch renegade.

But by 1915 events were rushing too swiftly for all of them. Something about the pleas for a supernational judiciary had come to seem unreal against the actualities of the holocaust in Europe. Certainly the optimism of Oscar Straus's dinner party had been blasted. Judicial settlement had not solved the problems of man's political state, and pessimists doubted that it ever could. Several of the action groups, notably the ASJSID, would not survive the world war. Others, if they did survive, would emerge wholly transformed.[39] At any rate, the relevant problem was increasingly the political rather than legal one, and the world congress was moving past the world court to center stage. Reuben had not thought much about the congress— the League of Nations, as they were coming to call it. It was clear, however, that his opinion of it had already been determined.

Chapter 14

CLAIMS AND CONTROVERSIES

Before the world war broke upon them, however, Reuben had an excellent opportunity to assess judicial settlement firsthand. Between April of 1913 and July of the following year he served as general counsel to the American-British Claims Commission, whose job it was to conduct judicial settlement on a daily basis. The experience confirmed some of his fears and denied others. It also forced him to explore more deeply the concept of peace through law and to think more specifically about alternatives to the world court.

ii

But judicial settlement was not on Reuben's mind on March 4, 1913, when he witnessed the inauguration of Thomas Woodrow Wilson as twenty-eighth president of the United States. A dignitary of the outgoing Taft administration, Reuben had been accorded a place of honor on the inaugural platform, from which every detail of the ceremony could be observed closely. It was a somber, overcast day, the weather quite matching his own joyless mood.[1] As the new president took the oath of office an era of American foreign policy decisively came to an end. Reuben would look back upon it as a time of honesty and dignity. By constrast the future seemed bleak indeed, for the new secretary of state was to be none other than William Jennings Bryan himself. Bryan, the "boy wonder of the prairie," the "silver-tongued orator of the Platte," the author of that historic "cross-of-gold" speech that turned American politics inside out in 1896 and won him the Democratic nomination, the man who denounced empire in cathedral tones and then slyly voted for the empire in order to provide himself with a campaign issue, the candidate who wanted to nationalize the banks and socialize the railroads and idealize everything under the sun, the political maelstrom who, like the Platte (as Republicans said), was an inch deep and a mile wide at the mouth—this was the one who would take the place of Philander Knox. American foreign policy, so it now seemed to Reuben, was to be entrusted to a double-barreled James Brown Scott.

With others of the old guard, Reuben had tendered his resignation from the State Department a few days earlier. Some of his colleagues were now at loose ends, but the former solicitor was looking forward to the prospect of the claims arbitration. Even though he had settled a number of claims in his day, Reuben would find this to be a new experience. Dealing with Great Britain had a significance all its own; for if the United States was one leader in the judicial pursuit of peace, Great Britain was the other one. Together they had worked out Jay's treaty, the *Alabama* claims, the fur seal arbitration, the Alaskan and Venezuelan boundary settlements, and, most recently, the Atlantic fisheries arbitration. Now, as the centenary of Anglo-American peace approached, it was only fitting that the two of them should post another milestone in their epic march.[2]

Then, too, the commission itself had been something of Reuben's own brainchild. At the conclusion of the fisheries arbitration, the two governments had raised the question of settling outstanding claims between them. Many of these claims had grown directly out of the turmoil around Newfoundland, but others had rankled through history from the War of 1812.[3] Early in 1910 Assistant Solicitor Clark had been asked to prepare an opinion on the question of whether a special claims agreement (involving only the fishing claims) or a general claims agreement (involving all claims) ought to be negotiated with Great Britain. Reuben had voted to clear the slate, and so it was the general agreement that was adopted.[4]

There were important reasons for clearing the slate. Pioneers in the peace movement or not, the United States and Great Britain had had a history of contention dating from the Stamp Act. True, American policymakers had traditionally been pro-British in their sympathies; but rank-and-file politicians—especially Irish-American politicians—had always been able to wring out a few more votes by twisting the British Lion's tail, and incidents like the *Caroline*, *Trent*, and *Alabama* affairs had enabled them to do so.* But by 1910 England was becoming increasingly isolated in the European rush of alliance and counteralliance and was turning to her once-faithless American child with new gestures of reconciliation. J. Reuben Clark, for one, felt fully reciprocal.

iii

On August 18, 1910, a general pecuniary claims convention between the two countries had been signed. By its terms a tribunal was established to rule on all outstanding grievances. Each party was to present its claims to the other within four months, with the understanding that no claim would be included in the schedule without the consent of both. In this way all the hoary misunderstandings of the decades would hopefully be laid to rest.[5] After many months of negotiation (a good many more than planned), the first inventory of cases was agreed upon. It included fifty-eight American and eighty-six British claims divided into various categories of complaint.[6] It was a diverse and, as Reuben would discover, highly challenging docket.

Then had come the selection of the tribunal. By common agreement this was to be done in accordance with the Hague convention of 1907, which called for each side to appoint one associate commissioner (judge) and for those two to select the third. The latter, presumably a neutral, would act as presiding commissioner and was sometimes referred to as the umpire. It was anticipated that in the difficult cases the two associate commissioners would vote in favor of their respective governments, leaving the real decision to the presiding commissioner; the selection of this officer was therefore all-important. The person chosen to be the American commissioner was Chandler Anderson, veteran of numerous arbitrations and, since 1910, counselor of the State Department. The British commissioner,

---

*The *Caroline* was an American steamboat being used to shuttle supplies across the Niagara River to Canadian insurrectionists. It was sunk by Canadian authorities in December of 1837. The *Trent* was a British packet carrying, among other things, two diplomatic representatives from the Confederate States of America to England in November of 1861. It was stopped on the high seas by a headstrong Northern captain, and the would-be diplomats were carted off to a Boston jail. Both incidents raised a storm of war talk.

Sir Charles Fitzpatrick, was equally distinguished. Besides serving as chief justice of Canada, he too had participated in international arbitrations, most recently as a member of the north Atlantic fisheries tribunal.[7]

Together Anderson and Fitzpatrick set about to find a presiding commissioner. Since each of them would have to angle for the support of this man, they had to come up with a veritable Janus. And that proved difficult. Anyone too friendly to the United States was immediately vetoed by Fitzpatrick and anyone too anglophilic got the same treatment from Anderson—month in and month out. Solicitor Clark, at one point, had stepped in with a suggestion of his own. He believed that, rather than trying to find a neutral for the role of presiding commissioner, the commission ought to remain "entirely Anglo-Saxon" in composition, with an American or Briton assuming the umpire's chair by the simple toss of a coin.[8] If this betrayed a little too much of the gambling spirit for most diplomats, it also showed a hearty faith in Anglo-American goodwill. It placed the understanding of English-speaking peoples on a far higher than rhetorical level.

In the meantime other staff positions were filled. After a bit of shuffling Robert Lansing was designated American agent—in charge of the collective legal effort of the United States—while the position of general counsel was offered to Reuben Clark.[9]* Since Reuben would be leaving the solicitor's office in a few months, he accepted the appointment willingly. He had already determined to set up a legal practice of his own along the lines of Anderson's and Lansing's, and what better way to do so than this? Then too, the claims com-

---

*Each claims commission maintained three separate bureaucracies, so as to protect the integrity of the judicial process. The commissioners themselves had their own staff of clerks, typists, secretaries, and translators, organized into a secretariat and placed under the supervision of an administrative officer. In addition, each of the two litigants maintained its own agency, consisting of a separate corps of secretarial and clerical personnel as well as legal counsel of various descriptions. The general counsel was usually the senior and highest paid of the attorneys, while counsel was the title applied to the others. Special counsel might designate an expert in some technical area who was retained for specific consultations. Supervising the entire agency was the agent, whose chief responsibilities were administrative but who was also trained in the law. It was through the agent that each government maintained its contact with the claims commission, so he exercised joint supervision over the commissioners' secretariat as well as his own agency. In the American-British Claims Commission, which was quite small, several of these positions were consolidated.

mission job gave him a measure of security. "As you may be able to appreciate," he wrote to John Bassett Moore, "a man with a family is not in a position to take too many chances."[10] The general counsel's $7,500 annual salary compared favorably with the $5,000 he had earned as solicitor, and the work was only part-time.[11] This point Reuben established with great emphasis in his correspondence with Knox. "My employment as General Counsel," he stipulated,

should not mean that I would be expected to give all of my time to the work of the commission, and further that I would be entirely at liberty to open a private office, and engage in private practice at the same time I held this Government employment.[12]

In the Washington of 1913 such arrangements were commonplace. Talented lawyers moved back and forth between government service and private practice, often engaging in both at once, and rarely were their ethics called into question. Reuben only wanted to make his intentions plain in advance.

iv

With the work of the claims commission before him and the prospect of a flourishing law practice, Reuben could afford to sit back and watch the new administration with interest. Viewed strictly as entertainment, Bryan was no disappointment; and Reuben reported on him with droll scorn. The new secretary, he said, was hamming it up for the movie cameras, insulting foreign dignitaries left and right, and reducing the once-proud State Department to a shambles. Believing that "any American citizen of average intelligence can do any of the work," Bryan hired and fired with abandon, replacing experts like Evan Young of the bureau of trade advisers with common stenographers. His only useful appointment was that of John Bassett Moore as counselor, but even Moore was helpless in such a bear garden. One anecdote told all.

The Japanese Ambassador is telling the story, so it is said, that on one occasion he called to see the Secretary of State and was shown into the diplomatic waiting room where, after remaining for some time, as he thought, forgotten, he was suddenly brought to his senses by Wyvell (the Secretary to the Secretary) shouting in the corridor "where is that little Jap."[13]

Reuben looked at the solicitor's office with special sadness. Capable clerks had been pirated away, the best officers had been asked to resign, and the worst ones had been promoted to their places. "I am told that [it] is but a shadow of its former self," he lamented.[14]

Yet Reuben himself was an employee of the Bryan State Department, and he did not need to reflect long on the "perfectly brutal" conduct of the secretary before recognizing his own vulnerability. The Democrats were nothing if not hungry, he reasoned. "Whether or not the hunger ... will require for its appeasement this job also remains to be seen."[15] He had expressed similar misgivings about his future with the Hague preparatory committee, writing a friend that "changes impending on March 4th may forestall my ever reaching the Hague."[16] He had no choice, though, but to carry on with both assignments—and to whistle bravely through the political darkness.

v

The first session of the American-British Pecuniary Claims Arbitration convened at the Commerce Court in Washington on May 13.[17] Among the notables in attendance were the British ambassador to the United States, James Lord Bryce, and John Bassett Moore, acting secretary of state.[18] In charge of the proceedings was Henri Fromageat of France, recently named as presiding commissioner of the tribunal. His selection—at the eleventh hour—may have reflected des-

The American-British Claims Commission: Parable of entente.
From left to right: Sir Charles Fitzpatrick, Henri Fromageat, Chandler Anderson.

peration at finding the perfect Janus, but it seemed to augur well for the commission's ultimate success. Himself a participant of many arbitrations, Fromageat was primarily known for his scholarship, which included wide publication in international maritime law.[19] In brief opening remarks he praised the United States and Great Britain for giving the world "another example of . . . confidence in the law."[20]

All in all it was an impressive scene, with the three judges seated upon high-backed chairs behind an ornately carved bench. Yet there was something curious to be noted in their individual appearances. The American and the Briton, flanking either side of the Frenchman, might easily have passed for father and son. Differing only as to age, they possessed the same square face and the same gray eyes. Their collars, their neckties, their evenly brushed mustaches, even their businesslike facial expressions were nearly identical. Fromageat, on the other hand, was clearly the odd man out. He had a narrow Gallic face, no mustache, and an expression that reflected nothing so much as puzzled benevolence. It was like a family portrait into which an intruder had suddenly stepped—and it foretold much of the commission's subsequent history.[21]

Most of the work of the first session dealt with procedural matters, but three claims were presented as well. These cases seemed small compared to mammoths like the Alsop claim, yet small cases could turn on large principles; and in any event, the opening cases in any arbitration had a heavy impact on what came afterward. So in the case of the Yukon Lumber Company, Reuben Clark, victor of Alsop, found himself earnestly pleading a cause valued at $200.[22] (A private firm had cut timber on Canadian territory without paying the timber dues required by law. The United States, as ultimate purchaser of the timber, was now charged with payment.)[23] The Yukon Lumber case touched upon vital issues, however; and in the following case, equally small and equally vital, the American-British Claims Commission confronted its first major difficulty.

William Hardman, a British subject living in Cuba, had suffered damage to his property during the Spanish-American War.[24] The facts of the case were simple enough and neither side cared to dispute them. The problem was that just such a fact situation had never

240

yet come before an international tribunal. According to its convention, the claims commission was to render its decisions in conformity with "the principles of international law and equity." The first of these—international law—having failed them in the Hardman case, the commissioners now turned to the second—equity. But the word had two possible meanings. "Equity" could be anything at all that was equitable or fair—such as a compromise—or it could refer to that curious auxiliary legal code which had evolved in fifteenth-century England as a companion to the common law. M. Fromageat believed—and with considerable justification—that the first alternative was correct, while the English-speaking commissioners tended to opt for the second. It was not the first disagreement along linguistic lines. In the Yukon Lumber case Fromageat had inquired as to the existence in English law of a certain French legal principle, to which the assistant agent for Great Britain had testily replied that French law ought not enter into their discussions and that only "Anglo-American law" should be permitted.[25]

On May 16, following the discussion of the Hardman case, Robert Lansing requested permission for Reuben Clark to address the tribunal on the meaning of the phrase in question. The following afternoon Reuben presented the American position. He dealt first with the suggestion that "equity" as set forth in the American-British claims convention referred only to fairness. This, he said, was unthinkable if the commission was supposed to behave like a real court. Since courts operated according to law, mere fairness would not suffice. The claims, in other words, were not to be settled by simple negotiation or compromise, and the word "equity" could not be used to alter that fact. But what of those cases not covered by law? Reuben's answer was surprising. When two English-speaking nations were attempting to settle their differences lawfully and when the established international law failed to cover a point at issue, they had no choice, he argued, but to turn to the principles of their own legal systems. "Equity" in this light obviously meant "the same thing . . . that it would mean in the equitable jurisprudence of the two countries." Only a layman could have missed the revolutionary implications: Reuben Clark wanted to use international law and Anglo-American law interchangeably as a way of bringing judicial settlement down to earth.[26]

The address was received enthusiastically. Sir Charles Fitzpatrick called it "one of the ablest legal arguments" he had ever heard.[27] Great Britain and the United States were supposed to be the adversaries of this proceeding, yet from the beginning the two of them had displayed an astonishing consonance of opinion. Paradoxically, it was Henri Fromageat whom they apparently regarded as the outsider and whom they now joined hands to convince. As one member of the British agency confided to Reuben, "I will be glad when we can settle our difficulties between us without calling in these damn foreigners."[28]

vi

The second session of the commission was held in Ottawa in June. The pattern of cases was becoming familiar now: two of them arose from ship collisions, a third from unpaid mining dues, and a fourth, the most interesting, from the loss of a steel suspension bridge in transit from the United States to South Africa where, amid the confusions of the Boer War, it was actually misplaced.[29] As general counsel, Reuben bore the major burden of conducting these multiple arguments, handling the most difficult of them, like the Union Bridge Company case, entirely by himself.[30] Accordingly, he was especially gratified when the first decisions were handed down on June 18; for with a tally of three cases won by the Americans, three cases disallowed for the British, and only one case—for a paltry thirty-two pounds—going against them, the Yankees were clearly ahead in the game.[31] Robert Lansing was jubilant. "The success is chiefly due," he declared, "to the counsel who so faithfully studied and presented the cases to the Tribunal." To Reuben Clark he offered special congratulations.[32]

Up to this point the pace of the commission's work had been nothing less than breathless, and Reuben, who had talked so freely of a private law practice, had in fact found little time for it. There was a respite of sorts between June of 1913 and March of the following year, during which Reuben was able to attend to the preparatory committee for the Third Hague Conference and ultimately to the law practice itself. By the end of the year his Washington office was bowling along prosperously and Reuben was discussing with Preston Richards the possibility of opening a second office in the West.

But the respite was brief. Long before the third session of the claims tribunal was scheduled to begin, Reuben found himself shackled once again by its demands. The number of cases on the docket was four times that of the previous sessions, and Reuben Clark was to argue half of them personally.[33] To Richards, inquiring about certain of their private legal affairs, Reuben confessed, "I haven't been able to do anything with them because of the great pressure of work on the British claims."[34] It was good to have a big client, as any lawyer knew, but for Reuben Clark the United States Government tended to become the only client.

This was indeed heavy irony. For no sooner had he laid aside the other work of his law office than Reuben heard the first distant rumblings of Secretary Bryan's displeasure with him. With dry sarcasm he told the story to Preston Richards.

The greatest Secretary of State that we have *ever* had (not excepting Tom Jefferson) is much disturbed over the fact that I should be spending part of my time on private practice. He asserts, with all the sanctified earnestness of which his Apollo-like figure will permit; with all the resonant sonority of which his magnificent voice will compass; with all the facial holliness [*sic*], which long practice enables him to put on, that every man in the service of the government, should spend all and every whit of his time in the government service. He seems particularly disturbed over the fact that I do not measure up to these requirements, and this disturbance is recurring at such close intervals, that I do not see how it will be possible for him to control them much longer; so I wish you would be getting ready for me, a soft, downy pile of feathers, upon which I may dissend [*sic*] after the kick. I have, however, made up [my] mind on this point—subject to change—that I am as much entitled to the job as is he, and so I propose to remain until I am kicked off, unless, in the meanwhile, my own convenience enables me to kick him first.[35]

The secretary of state, as Reuben well knew, was himself a frequent and well-paid lecturer on the Chautauqua circuit and one who had no compunctions about dual affiliation.[36] So Bryan's quarrel with the general counsel was strictly partisan. He wanted Reuben's job for one of the deserving Democrats in his retinue and was fishing for a pretext to get it. Reuben would have been, as he said, all too happy to oblige, except that the matter—and Bryan's handling of it—had now become one of personal honor. "I am wondering," he wrote to Knox, if you would be willing to write me a letter, stating the facts in order that, should necessity arise, I may make it clear to Mr. Bryan that my employment upon the Commission was with the express understanding that I should be permitted to engage in private practice, and that my doing so is therefore no breach of my duty as a public servant. In this matter, I am infinitely less concerned in holding my employment, than in having my record accord with the facts.[37]

There was more to come, however. At the pitch of Bryan's disapproval, word was brought to Reuben one evening that other Democrats were out gunning for him as well. (It was even alleged that they had put the Secret Service on his trail.[38]) Judge William H. King of Utah had reportedly assembled several of these luminaries in a Washington hotel room and, in the presence of reporters, "broke forth in a bitter denunciation" of the claims commission's general counsel.

He ... said that the position I held was one of purest "graft"; that I did not do one hour's work a week in exchange for my salary; that I was given the position solely from a desire to take care of me; that it was an outrage that I, a Republican, should be permitted to hold such a job; that I should soon lose the job.[39]

Judge King denied the story. According to his version, the attempt to oust Reuben had been abandoned as soon as King had learned that the claims commission position was only temporary, and the alleged accusations had simply not been made.[40]

Whatever the truth of the matter, Reuben could not but see it as part of a Bryanesque conspiracy to steal his job and ruin his name. The job he might forfeit—but for his name Reuben was ready to fight in the trenches if need be. Accordingly, on February 19 he fired off a telegram to Joseph Nelson in Salt Lake City, denying any wrongdoing and pointing up the cheap politics of the case.[41] He also wrote to Dr. Talmage. He explained that the Taft administration, in the interest of securing an effective arbitration, had taken care to appoint equal numbers of Republicans and Democrats to the claims commission. Under Wilson, by contrast, every vacancy had been filled by a party regular. It was the Democrats, not the Republicans, he concluded, who must bear the charge of graft.[42]

The counteroffensive was not without its effect. By the end of February Reuben could write that "the enemy appears to be clearly in retreat" and "I think we shall wholly defeat him."[43] "The fact is,"

Preston Richards replied, "that so much pressure was brought to bear on the Judge that he was glad to get out of it any way he could, gracefully or ungracefully."[44] Even so, the Judge King affair, timed as it was with Secretary Bryan's own little blitz, would leave scars. "I thoroughly understand," Reuben wrote to Dr. Talmage, "[that] war and politics are synonymous."[45]

vii

With the approach of its third session in March of 1914, the American-British Claims Commission swung into high gear. The ground rules were now laid, the processes established, and the questions of theory laid to rest. To be resolved now were some two dozen cases involving upwards of six million dollars—and both sides trundled out the heavy artillery.[46] Once again Reuben Clark was in the middle of the firing. For example, during the first two weeks of the session he was involved with no fewer than six concurrent cases dealing with maritime revenue disputes.[47] "This American-British Claims Commission work," he wrote plaintively to a friend,

has made it impossible for me to do anything else but labor and try to sleep each night from 12 A.M. or 12:30 A.M. Were I not good-natured, fat, and generally easy-going, I should have been down by this time with nervous prostration. I have already argued the sealing cases (the Kate, the Wanderer, and the Favorite), and the sea otter cases (the Jessie, the Thomas F. Bayard, and the Pescawha). I am now preparing to begin the argument of the Argonaut, French and Tattler claims, and myself argue the David J. Adams; all of this is to be done next week. You will, therefore, perceive something of the maelstrom in which I now live, move, and have a being.[48]

As for his "graft," he told another correspondent, "it requires the expenditure of much more time, and much more energy to do my work for the government, than to do private work bringing me in the same returns."[49] The irony deepened further when at the end of March Robert Lansing was appointed counselor in the State Department—Moore could abide Bryan no longer—giving Reuben the responsibilities of agent as well as general counsel. He accepted the new burden stoically—but his private practice went entirely by the board.[50]

The third session was one of high accomplishment. Indeed, virtually all of the claims were settled to the satisfaction of both governments. To be sure, most of them were scaled down considerably in the process, so that claims advanced in five and six figures were awarded in three or four. The largest settlement of the commission to date, in fact, was nine thousand dollars won by Reuben in the Frederick Gerring, Jr., case.[51] (Reuben could thank his law review experience for the favorable decision; the principles he incorporated into his brief came to him from that first case he had reviewed for "Pop" Weathers at Columbia.)[52] But the broader achievement was gained not in terms of monetary awards but of Anglo-American friendship. Every case seemed to enhance the understanding of the supposed adversaries—and to underscore the dysfunction of the umpire. Reuben Clark and his British counterpart, C. J. B. Hurst, agreed most cordially that the presence of the Frenchman created "all but insuperable" problems of language and legal training. The two of them decided, in fact, to suggest to their respective governments that future arbitrations be entirely Anglo-American in composition— a strange sort of comment on judicial settlement.[53]

viii

The claims commission adjourned in mid-May with the intention of reconvening in London in July. To that prospect Reuben looked forward with anticipation.[54] (The trip to Ottawa had been his first outside of the United States and with boyish enthusiasm he had taken Luacine along.) As he was readying affairs for the departure, however, partisan politics reared its head again, this time in Congress. A budgetary committee reviewing the commission's appropriations for the forthcoming year decided that certain minor modifications might be in order. Instead of granting a lump sum for the work of the commission and allowing the secretary of state to apportion it at his pleasure, the committee decided to specify certain salaries for certain job descriptions. Thus there would be an agent at $7,500 and a counsel at $5,000, and that would be all. Anyone who happened to hold either title was welcome to remain on the commission staff—but only one individual, Robert Lansing, seemed to qualify ("agent"), and he was in the process of resigning. Reuben Clark, who was listed as general counsel; Arthur P. McKinstry, listed as associate counsel; and William Snowden, listed as clerk, accordingly found their jobs legislated out of existence. How unfortunate that all three were Republicans.[55]

The author of this happy little measure was an obscure senator from Tennessee by the name of Luke Lea, and he had friends in mind for the resulting vacancies.[56] Not all of his Senate colleagues had the stomach for such political hatchet work—especially on the one diplomatic agency that was doing its job—but enough went along to carry the measure out of committee. On the floor of the Senate, however, the going got rough. Both Elihu Root and George Sutherland flailed mercilessly at the Lea Bill as a blatant piece of spoilsmanship, obliging supporters to claim in deadpan innocence that their only thought had been to spare public expense. Neither side could overcome the other. Finally Robert Lansing proposed a compromise. Passage of the bill might go forward, he suggested, as long as Reuben Clark and Arthur McKinstry could be retained in some private capacity to assist with the more difficult and technical cases. Bryan seized upon the proposal as a way out.[57]

So it was that on June 24, 1914, Reuben was reappointed as special counsel to the American-British Claims Commission.[58] He now had a contractual guarantee against Bryan and the patronage artists, at least for a few more cases; but he had lost his chance to go to Europe and he had effectively been fired at last. He would remember that fact to his dying day.[59]

Yet, if he thought that the Lea affair had finally placed him beyond the reach of public spectacle, Reuben was in for one last surprise. The final installment of trouble grew, oddly enough, out of his greatest professional triumph, the Alsop case, and it centered in none other than Madame Teresa de Prévost. Under the award distribution that Reuben had worked out in 1912, Madame de Prévost had received only a paltry $6,250. Hardly was the ink dry before she had begun filing suit against other Alsop claimants to recover her "rightful" share of the bounty, estimated by her at $100,000.[60]

Knowing of the Peruvian seductress, Reuben would have done well to keep clear. However, soon after leaving the solicitor's office in 1913 he was retained by the estate of George G. Hobson to defend against Madame de Prévost's claim. Reuben succeeded in having her case thrown out of court—but Teresa de Prévost was assuredly not to be reckoned with so lightly. As far as she was concerned, a cabal was afoot to defraud her of the Alsop prize, and J. Reuben Clark was obviously at the center of it. In court she attempted to introduce allegations of wrongdoing against the former solicitor and his assistant on the Alsop case, Robert A. Young. She pointed out that the latter had ultimately received more than thirty thousand dollars from the award, and with Clark in the employment of Hobson, what further proof was needed?[61]

The court rejected these charges out of hand, but Madame de Prévost, undaunted, recast them in a petition to the secretary of state. Unlike the trial judge, Bryan found the allegations entirely plausible; after all, hadn't he himself presciently called attention to irregularities in the conduct of Mr. Clark? This was the cruelest blow of all. "When I think," Reuben wrote to Knox,

of the many weary hours, days, weeks and months I spent in preparing the Alsop case, and later in studying out how to distribute it justly and equitably, and then realize my humiliation over the charges that are preferred against me, and seemingly are seriously considered by those before whom they are placed, I cannot avoid a feeling of heartsickness. However, the thing will not kill, and I suppose eventually all will be well.[62]

Eventually all *was* well. State Department officials, even partisan ones, could not long take Madame de Prévost's accusations seriously. Whatever Reuben's "shortcomings" as a Republican, he was known throughout Washington as an honest man.[63] The affair quietly subsided.

ix

His days on the claims commission now numbered, Reuben was confronted with the larger meanings of the experience. One meaning, surely, derived from the political fuss and bother which had dogged the commission's efforts. Under Taft and the Republicans the commission had been kept rigorously nonpartisan—an honest and sober endeavor to field-test an instrument of peace.[64] Under Wilson and the Democrats, by contrast, the claims commission, like the State Department itself, had simply been hitched up to party wheel-horses and trundled away. To some this turn of affairs might not have been surprising, much less reprehensible, but to Reuben Clark it was totally beyond forgiveness. After all, the Wilsonian Democrats

248

were supposed to be *idealists*. Had they not, amid a fanfare of trumpets, rejected dollar diplomacy as ruthless and cynical? Had they not ostentatiously negotiated "cooling-off treaties" with every government between Iceland and Monaco?* Had they not fired the rhetoric of diplomacy with born-again evangelism? If the Democrats really wanted peace so ardently, Reuben asked, how could they repeatedly jeopardize the work of the claims commission for trivial political advantage? It gave him much to ponder.[65]

A second meaning had to do with Anglo-American entente. Fraternal bonds between the two countries had never been stronger or more clearly in evidence than during the early work of the claims commission. M. Fromageat was the unlucky foil for this display of affection, but he was in no wise its cause. War clouds were darkening over Europe, and England must soon make the decision of her life. Indeed, Great Britain needed the United States in 1914 as never before in history. The American-British Claims Commission helped solidify bonds that would enable the British to redefine their place in the world. It convincingly demonstrated intangible ideals and gave substance to inarticulate sentiments.

Finally, the commission and its work said something about judicial settlement itself. But the message was unconventional. Judicial settlement was supposed to work anywhere, at any time, and among any people, grounded in a fundamental respect for law. Perhaps it did. Reuben, however, was now less certain than ever that the right-mindedness of man or the universality of his nature would ultimately suffice. Whenever the British and Americans had tried to reach across the chasm of legal culture to Henri Fromageat they had failed to make contact. And if a jurist of Fromageat's stature had his limitations, what hope had the average lawyer of escaping language, culture, and nationality? Increasingly, it seemed to Reuben Clark, the success of judicial settlement lay in individual examples rather than universal systems. And what example could be more persuasive than that of the great English-speaking peoples?

---

*These treaties supplemented the usual bilateral arbitaration treaty by requiring that disputes first be submitted to an international commission for investigation. Neither side could commence hostilities until the investigation was complete. The basic idea was to provide a space of time during which passions would presumably subside.

But there was little time left for examples. The old century, beginning at Waterloo and unfolding as an epoch of peace, was nigh coming to an end. Just as Reuben was putting his final affairs in order with the claims commission, news of the assassination of the Austrian archduke at Sarajevo reached the press. That this news vanished so quickly from the front page attested the continuing American optimism. One by one, however, the European powers began girding up for war. On July 23 Austria delivered its historic ultimatum to Serbia, and within the fortnight Germany, Russia, and France each hurried to its own station in the denouement. As nation after nation slipped into the abyss, Americans themselves awoke to the fact that Armageddon was upon them.[66]

It was an Englishman who best captured the spirit of the hour. Standing at his Whitehall window with a friend as the street lamps were being lit below, Sir Edward Grey, British foreign secretary, seemed to sense the passing of the world he had known and loved–a world whose finest aspiration had been for universal peace. "The lamps are going out all over Europe," he remarked solemnly. "We shall not see them lit again in our lifetime."[67]

Chapter 15

THE HORDES OF SATAN

Reuben Clark could not have encountered Enoch Crowder under more ironic circumstances. They had served together on the preparatory committee for the Third Hague Conference, the conference that was to have solved the riddle of war for good.[1] Now, on a sultry morning in June of 1917, as they regarded one another across Crowder's desk, they were standing together at Armageddon. Of the two men, Reuben Clark easily looked the more out of place in uniform. General Crowder, by contrast, was a soldier's soldier. He had fought Geronimo in New Mexico, Sitting Bull in South Dakota, and Aguinaldo in the Philippines. In posture he seemed always to be at attention and when talking always to be giving orders. "The general [used] tones that you could hear all over the house," Reuben later recalled, "no matter how big the house was."[2]

Enoch Crowder was a lawyer too, and since 1911 he had been judge-advocate general of the army. It was in that connection that he had sought Reuben out in the autumn of 1916. Would he, Reuben, be interested in joining the judge-advocate's division of the Officer's Reserve Corps? This could be accomplished, the general said, without undue incommodity—even without boot-camp training.[3] There was a special reason for the urgency. For some years General Crowder had been giving his attention to problems of recruiting and enlistment. He had come to the conclusion that the volunteer system was inadequate, impractical, and unfair, since it drew recruits from industrial and professional life indiscriminately and permitted shirkers to remain at home. In response to the problem he had evolved a new idea called selective service which would enable the military to draw upon those elements needed most while passing over the rest. So it was that Enoch Crowder had become responsible for the draft.[4]

ii

That Reuben Clark had accepted the general's offer attested the wrenchings and twistings of the world war. Three years earlier, in the summer of 1914, military thoughts would have been farthest from his mind. After all, human progress had supposedly outmoded war, judicial settlement was underwriting peace, and the worst problem in the world had seemed to be William Jennings Bryan. Now here Reuben stood—overage, overweight, stuffily uncomfortable in his major's uniform, but ready to join battle with the minions of the kaiser. Needless to say, it had been a difficult three years.

The first casualty had been international law. The Germans had come roaring through neutral Belgium in their haste to knock out Paris and, when asked about the treaty to which they themselves were signatory, had replied that it was a "worthless scrap of paper." The Belgians, unfortunately, had chosen to resist the German invasion and in the end had paid dearly. Entire cities had been wiped out—all, oddly enough, in the name of international law, which the Germans claimed had been violated not by themselves, but by the Belgian snipers. A witness described the devastation graphically.

A lot of the houses were still burning, but most of them were nothing but blackened walls with smouldering timbers inside. . . . Then we began to see more ghastly sights—poor civilians lying where they had been shot down as they ran—men and women—one old patriarch lying on his back in the sun, his great white beard nearly hiding his swollen face, all sorts of wreckage scattered over the street, hats and wooden shoes, German helmets, swords and saddles, bottles and all sorts of bundles which had been dropped and abandoned when the trouble began. For three-quarters of a mile the boulevard looked as though it had been swept by a cyclone.[5]

So wrote Hugh Gibson, onetime madcap of the Mockahis and now first secretary of the American embassy in Brussels, over the smoldering ruins of Louvain. His account made the point convincingly.

Perhaps friends gave their condolences to Reuben, as they did to international law professor George Grafton Wilson, on the sudden demise of his profession.[6] If so, Reuben's answer was unequivocal. "To base our security," he said, "upon . . . international law will prove absolutely fatal to us."[7] It may not have been a deliberate gesture, but he allowed his membership in the American Society of International Law to lapse.[8]

The second casualty had been pacifism. Soon after his election to the American Society for Judicial Settlement of International Disputes, Reuben had found himself appointed as that organization's representative to the American Peace Society. With the opening of the artillery in Belgium, Reuben suddenly understood that guns and guns alone would decide the fate of western civilization. "You will see that entertaining these feelings, it is quite obvious that I should be entirely out of place in associating with my peace-at-any-price colleagues on the Peace Society directorate," he explained with his resignation, adding, "To me ... there is nothing in the situation that can be compromised."⁹

Two years later Reuben was in the forefront of the military preparedness campaign of 1916. "The immutable laws of nature," he declared, "have decreed that every organism, be it animal, plant, or social, which is not prepared to defend its existence by opposing when necessary force [with] force, must perish from the earth."¹⁰ For his old pacifism Reuben now had nothing but contempt. To Theodore Marburg, a fellow expatriate from the APS, he wrote: "If we get into war, as now seems all but inevitable, we shall have to put some of [these pacifists] in jail."¹¹

The third casualty had been faith in progress. When the Belgians took to their "impregnable" fortresses at Liège and Namur, the Germans, as out of some science-fiction nightmare, trundled up a pair of titanic siege mortars and blasted the forts to rubble.¹² Thus was unveiled the true nature of progress. The new "Big Berthas," the new rapid-fire Maxims, the new fast dreadnoughts, the new gun-mounted Halberstadts, the new armor-plated "tanks"—these had not outmoded war at all. They had only multiplied its horrors.

Reuben Clark was deeply shocked by it all. He had watched the Hague conferences pridefully and had taken heart from their timid outlawry of dum-dum bullets. When the zeppelins began sowing death over London, when mustard gas engulfed the Meuse-Argonne trenches, when German submarines unleashed their undersea terror, he was appalled beyond expression. "I confess that modern war does not have for me any of the glamour that hangs around the conflicts of ye olden times," he wrote to a friend. "The present war too much resembles butchery and the field of battle an open slaughter

253

house."[13] So much for progress. "Untold centuries have made man," Reuben observed ruefully. "A day cannot unmake him."[14]

iii

The other two changes that the war brought about for Reuben Clark were ordained by the experience of the claims commission. First of all, he took sides. He had not wanted to. The international lawyer in him had responded eagerly to President Wilson's call for absolute neutrality and had criticized American actions that seemed to favor the allies. But for Reuben there seemed to be no denying ancestry and heritage, and the achievements of the American-British Claims Commission were still fresh in his mind. In fact, it was to his British counterpart on the commission, C. J. B. Hurst, that Reuben committed his first expression of partiality.

I hope it may not be either unwelcome or ungratifying to you to know that in this hour of trial England has the sympathy and the well-wishes of practically the whole American people.[15]

As for Germany, what was there to say? "I am at a loss to understand how the Germans justify their indiscriminant bomb dropping," Reuben wrote to Hurst in 1915; then he added, "Perhaps they do not try to justify it."[16]

Accordingly, Reuben moved solidly behind the Allied cause. When asked to give an opinion on the legality of the British blockade, he severely strained conventional usage to call it "extralegal."[17] (He then wrote to Hurst and advised him, as one friend to another, to stop exercising the blockade in such a "harsh and rigorous way."[18]) And when J. P. Morgan & Co., which had become sole purchasing agent for the Allies in the United States, sought a legal opinion as to whether the sale of munitions to England and France violated American neutrality, Reuben's eighty-page memorandum minced few words in its pronouncement of legality.[19] The Germans, by contrast, came off as congenital lawbreakers—partly because Reuben held them to a different standard of judgment. For example, when it came to submarine warfare (as opposed to the British blockade), the American lawyer could be punctilious as a pharisee. That the submarine was new and untried, that its periscope fogged up easily, that it was pathetically vulnerable on the surface of the water did not alter for Reuben a single jot of the international law of visit and search. If submariners could not board and inspect cargoes or provide for the safety of noncombatants, then they should cease operations, he said. "Let them stop whimpering and face the situation with courage like men."[20] The Germans ignored this advice, of course, and one after another they sent their mistakes to the bottom along with their legitimate targets. No innocent neutral, no passenger liner, no unarmed merchantman was safe, as attested by the *Fabala,* the *Gulflight,* the *Arabic,* the *Sussex,* and, most tragic of them all, the *Lusitania.* "It is utterly indefensible," Reuben fumed of the depredations. "The fiendishness of the thing has not only shocked the civilized world but has made modern warfare butchery."[21] More and more the Germans became barbarians in his eyes. "The ambition and arrogance of the German warlord," he wrote to a friend in Canada, "will probably stop at nothing short of the achievements of a second Alexander the Great."[22]

Secondly, Reuben came to a new understanding of domestic politics. He had always mistrusted the Democrats, of course, but when it came to issues of peace and war he had at least accorded them a basic humanity. "I . . . absolutely believe that they are doing their best to keep out of any difficulty," he wrote to his brother John, "and as it is an old saying that the Lord looks after the United States and fools, I suppose they will be able to do so."[23] But that was early in the war; later on Reuben began to have his doubts. He came to regard President Wilson as being extremely fuzzy on the subject of war, as though the man did not quite comprehend it. Reuben noted that after sending American soldiers to fight and die in Veracruz the president had spoken dreamily about vacant abstractions. "When [men] shoot at you they can only take your natural life," Wilson had said. "When they sneer at you they can wound your heart."[24]

Reuben began to entertain even darker suspicions. He observed that any response the Wilson administration made to the European situation had the effect of expanding executive authority. For example, the president seized two German wireless stations on Long Island without bothering to check the legality of the action. He then proposed building a fleet of government-operated merchant ships to run the British blockade.²⁵ Finally, he gave permission for a German U-boat to pay a courtesy call at Newport—after which the guest sank nine Allied merchantmen.²⁶ At this last Reuben, livid with rage, told Lucy James that the government needed to be rescued from the "Bolsheviks."²⁷

iv

That was the point at which Knox had found him. The former secretary of state had not been idle since his sojourn in office. He had been sent back to the Senate from Pennsylvania, and word had it that he was eyeing the election of 1916 with presidential hopes. At any rate, he contacted Reuben in the summer of 1915 and asked if the latter would write some political speeches for him.²⁸ The two of them had collaborated on a number of such endeavors while at the State Department, and Knox knew a good campaign style when he saw one. In the summer of 1914, while working for the reelection of Boise Penrose to the Senate, Knox had commissioned a Clark speech that won lavish praise.²⁹ Now he wanted another one, he said, full of patriotic fireworks for the Fourth of July. Reuben obliged, and in the oratory that followed he set forth his perceived connection between the world war abroad and the Democratic administration at home.

We are accustomed, when we speak of an enemy, to think of a man decked in the full panoply of war, and such a one being arrayed against us is indeed an enemy. . . . But, there are other enemies, without ensignia [*sic*] who are just as dangerous as the man of war against which I take it, you have sworn to defend our constitution. A man who would undertake to underride or overthrow any of the fundamental principles of the constitution, is just as truly an enemy of the constitution as the man who would undertake to overthrow it by force. That man who would seek to destroy the rights of the individual by subjecting them to unauthorized governmental authority is an enemy of the constitution against whom you must protect that document. A man, or body of men, who would unduly and oppressively enlarge the powers bestowed upon him by the constitution, is an enemy within the meaning of your oath, and the constitution must be protected against him.³⁰

The speech was prepared for a military audience, but its logic worked equally well upon Reuben Clark the civilian. The more he thought about the matter, in fact, the more convinced he became that America faced a potential enemy within who was every bit as powerful and sinister as the kaiser. This may not have been a reasonable view of American politics. For that matter, it was not reasonable for J. Reuben Clark, father of four, to give up a prosperous law practice and join the army, nor was it reasonable for imperial Germany, in January of 1917, to face war with the United States in an all-out gamble to crush the Allies. But then, these were not reasonable times.

v

If Reuben could take the war seriously, he could not, so it seemed, the military. He joked endlessly about its quirks and folkways, its pretensions and presumptions. He poked fun at the "swivelchair heroes" who thronged wartime Washington, including himself in their number.[31] "You know well the dangers I passed through," he later quipped of his own military service, "—the hair breadth escapes I had, the exploits I performed, and the bravery manifested in the face of the enemy, with the enemy several thousand miles away."[32] Nor was he above seeing to it that his brothers remained far from the front and that Preston Richards, who toyed with the notion of joining the infantry, was told, "Now, don't be a damn fool!"[33]

Nevertheless, in the broader sense of the metaphor, Reuben was a good soldier. He was prepared to work as long, as hard, and as indefatigably for military patrons as he had for civilians, arising at 6:00 A.M. to beat Crowder, a bachelor who slept in the office, to work at his desk.[34] The first item of business was the selective service regulations. Reuben fell to work on them while still a reservist. The draft system operated through some four thousand local boards and a hundred and fifty district boards, ultimately touching the lives of 24 million Americans. Its elaborate scheme of ratings enabled selection to be made at once upon rational priorities and sheer chance. Through its mechanisms 2.8 million men were inducted into the armed forces of the United States—the greatest mobilization of manpower in the world's history.[35] At the end of June 1917, when the last of the regulations was tucked into place, Reuben, near exhaustion from the pace, composed a cover memorandum that attempted to set the entire undertaking in perspective. "Heretofore, save in rare cases," he wrote, "war has been a fight between armies."

But this war is a contest between peoples themselves. It is correspondingly determined, bitter, relentless. It is a war of systems; kings against the people. If our enemy wins, kings will dominate the world. That domination continued means the death of democracy. This issue must be fought out now. In this sense, this is truly a war of absolute and complete extermination, not of peoples, but of systems, and so far as the vision can pierce the future, the life of the one system or the other waits on its outcome.[36]

vi

Reuben's own personal war was considerably less exalted. One enemy was bureaucracy. For example, there was a delay in his orders to active duty. Investigating, he learned that not one but two agencies were attempting to secure his services. Attorney General Thomas W. Gregory was vying with General Crowder for the Mormon lawyer and he meant to have him.[37] Rather than being flattered at this, Reuben was annoyed; for he and Crowder had worked out a tentative agreement by which he could retain at least part of his private practice while performing work for the army. (His law practice by this time was not only lucrative but was built around a few clients—like the government of Cuba—who had to have continuing access to him.[38]) Somehow, in the bureaucratic ping-pong that followed, this agreement went by the board. After considerable vacillation, Crowder decided that the private practice, Cuba and all, would have to go.[39] With heavy heart Reuben told his family to brace for hard times. Soon his income had dwindled to exactly one-tenth that of the flush prewar years. Reuben lamented the situation in a plaintive letter to Preston Richards. "This damned war does come at a most inconvenient time for me," he said.[40]

And ultimately Gregory bested Crowder at the tugging match. Thus Reuben, having barely ordered his desk in the War Department wing of Old State, wearily packed up again and trooped off to the Justice Department building on Fourteenth Street, there to assume the title of special assistant to the attorney general. In the Justice Department he encountered not less bureaucratic folderol but more. He seemed to have no fixed duties or responsibilities, and lines of authority were tangled; in one moment he would be assigned to undertake important war-related research, and in the next he would be, as he grumbled, "a law clerk."[41]

The fault did not seem to lie with the attorney general, who soon made his way into Reuben's pantheon of heroes. Reared on the Mississippi plantation of his grandfather after losing his father in the Civil War, Thomas W. Gregory had the white hair and easy manners of the legendary southern cavalier. Yet he was an astute and incisive lawyer, and as administrator of a burgeoning wartime agency he proved to be remarkably effective. Under his proximate charge were all of the difficulties of espionage, sabotage, control of enemy aliens, sedition, sequestration, jurisdictional disputes, war legislation, enforcement of the draft, and constitutional guarantees of protection.[42] Reuben came to agree that, however much Enoch Crowder needed his services, Thomas Gregory needed them more. Still, he was appalled by the confusion, the overlap, the wasted motion, the hazy focus of responsibility, and the pandemic tendency to pass the buck. It was but a microcosm of wartime Washington, with its boards and agencies and committees and bureaus, all of them under the direction of "dollar-a-year men" and all of them moving in different directions. As an international lawyer bereft of his practice, stuck in the military, detailed to the judge-advocate general who was also the provost-marshal general, and on special assignment to the Department of Justice where his international expertise was sorely needed but where most of his assignments were domestic and virtually none of them military, and where he could have served equally well as a civilian and thereby retained his practice, Reuben Clark himself perfectly symbolized the mess.

vii

In time Reuben came to discern two additional enemies more dangerous than bureaucracy. The first of them was demagoguery. He was wholly unprepared for the virulent Germanophobia that overtook the American people in the spring of 1917, when hamburger became "swiss steak," frankfurters "hot dogs," and dachshunds nothing less than "liberty pups." Among the less humorous examples of this mindlessness, Fritz Kreisler was not allowed to perform in New

Jersey and the renowned Bruno Walter was dismissed from the Chicago Symphony. In Minnesota a German pastor was forbidden by a vigilante group to speak his native tongue; when caught praying at the bedside of a woman who spoke only German he was tarred, feathered, and ridden out of town on a rail. Like wildfire, the hysteria swept to other victims. Socialists, pacifists, and dissenters of odd sorts were soon engulfed in the flames. Those who refused to buy liberty bonds found their houses painted yellow. A South Dakota farmer who advised a young man not to enlist was sent to jail for five years. Eugene Debs, the socialist, received a ten-year sentence for denouncing the war, and Mrs. Rose Stokes merited the same punishment for saying, "I am for the people and the government is for the profiteers."[43]

Reuben himself had scored the Germans a time or two. In writing copy for a liberty bond campaign, he had spontaneously branded them "the hordes of Satan."[44] But there was nothing spontaneous about the hysteria he saw around him now—and he frankly smelled a rat. It was one thing, he supposed, to make a rational decision to fight Germany; it was something else to excite the populace to the frenzy of a lynch mob. Such madness could serve but one purpose: to render the people pliant to someone's will.

With these reflections in mind, Reuben Clark began to notice a kind of basso-continuo theme running through American war propaganda. Behind the parades, the films, the posters, the speeches, and the songs he detected a message of unquestioning obedience. "Support the President," it said. "Be a red-blooded American." The advice was summarized in a single memorable image of Liberty wielding her sword wrathfully, and in the caption: "In the Cause We Are One."[45] Material of this sort was being turned out wholesale by the Committee on Public Information, headed by one-time newspaper editor George Creel. The Creel committee was nothing if not effective. By any of the Madison Avenue standards of measurement, Americans were hearing and responding to the overt message of the campaign. Reuben Clark wondered whether they were also responding to the covert message, the one suggesting that support of Democratic policies be uncritical, nonpartisan, and automatic.

The other enemy was one that Reuben had glimpsed before—executive usurpation. With the entrance of the United States into the world war, presidential authority no longer grew by incremental inches but mushroomed forth by the square mile. In June of 1917 the Lever Food Control Bill was passed, enabling the federal government to oversee the production and marketing of foodstuffs. In July the War Industries Board was set up and eventually given sweeping powers. Similar organizations seemed to pop out of nowhere and pounce on surviving remnants of free enterprise: the Fuel Administration in August, the National War Labor Board the following April, the War Labor Policies Board in May. But the most frightening was the United States Railway Administration under the president's son-in-law, William G. McAdoo, which nationalized the entire network of rail transportation. By the war's end there was censorship of the mails, control of cable and radio communications, regulation of exports, fixing of wages and hours for labor, and a blanket prohibition of alcoholic liquors. The authority for this revolution was claimed to be found in the so-called war powers of the Constitution. Administration supporters argued that such powers must be broadly construed and that the national government could, in the words of Minnesota's Frank Kellogg, "in fact do anything necessary." The opposition was equally adamant; their word for it all was "Prussianization."[46]

The personal impact of these developments was substantial. Far more than the kaiser Reuben now came to fear Woodrow Wilson. The fear had been some time in the building, growing through stages of uneasiness and dismay into a full-blown dread. To Henry Clay Frick, in May of 1918, he wrote that Americans were faced with "one of the most critical periods in all our history," and then darkly explained his meaning.

There has been since the outbreak of the war in Europe, but more particularly since our entry therein, a gang of revolutionists lodged in high places in this country whose primary purpose has been to conduct our activities in and during the war, so that at its close the world in general shall be thoroughly "Bolsheviked" and that the people of the United States shall have been robbed of the free institutions which our fathers bought with their blood and gave us.[47]

He went on to describe "these robbers" and their works, noting that "no one can now be chosen for the most responsible positions of government unless he is tainted with the destructive heresies they preach." He discussed their methods of infiltration and control, their links to the Creel committee, their "reign of terror over the press," leaving open the question of precisely who "they" were.

We, thus, have not only a war of arms abroad, but also, and of more far-reaching importance as affecting the destinies of us and our children, a war of principles at home. And I confess to a grave apprehension that unless every available effort is made we shall lose the war at home and with it the priceless freedom we have heretofore enjoyed with all its attendant blessings.[48]

viii

J. Reuben Clark's war, then, was to be fought in Washington, D.C., and it was to be fought rearguard. Enemies so insidious, so entrenched, and so implacable were not to be easily overcome, especially with war hysteria on their side; yet Reuben believed that he had no alternative but to try. His powers of persuasion were not inconsiderable. His connections to influential dissidents would be helpful. But far and away the most important weapon in his arsenal was the fact that he, through some quirk of fate, happened to be on the staff of the United States attorney general—and that the daily grist of his work happened to be war powers.

The war powers named in the Constitution were purposely left vague. Accordingly, a complex three-way struggle between the legislative and executive branches of the federal government and between the federal government and the states was always possible, with the Bill of Rights adding further confusion. The Supreme Court might have had a field day with the constitutional questions involved, except that there was not time enough to embody them in cases and send them up the ladder of appeals. In consequence, the attorney general's office in the executive branch and individual congressmen in the legislative had to thresh out the issues as best they could. Reuben Clark worked both sides of the street.

His first set of problems had to do with the treatment of enemy aliens. The public, spurred on by Creel's propaganda, was recklessly calling for their blood—and indeed, individuals among them had proven to be dangerous. (The contents of a stolen briefcase had recently implicated the Austrian ambassador in a network of munitions sabotage.) Attempting to balance human rights against the need for security, the attorney general's office drafted the Alien Enemy Act, registered some four million enemy aliens, and wound up interning twenty-three hundred of them for the duration of the war.[49] Reuben himself drew up some of the restrictions and approved virtually all of them. When asked whether the laws monitoring the movements of enemy males could legally be applied to females, he responded in the affirmative and personally urged the president to press forward.[50]

But he would go no further. To move beyond constitutional processes, even against spies and saboteurs, was not only to violate principles of Anglo-Saxon Law, he said, but it was to play into the hands of the agitators. Because it supported this position the Justice Department was arraigned in the press for gross laxness. Reuben answered the charges. In a public letter prepared for the attorney general's signature, he lashed back at what he called "lynch-law."

[The] occasional wild, nondiscriminating cry for the death of some "spy" no matter which one, is too close kin to the mob cry for blood to be heeded by those whose sworn duty it is to see that the laws are properly enforced, and the individual as well as the people protected. I shall do my utmost, use all the powers at my command, to bring to speedy and full justice all malefactors, but I shall be no party to hounding any man or woman to jail or to the gallows, merely because some one whispers a criminal accusation or levels against him an irresponsible finger of unsupported suspicion.[51]

Enemy aliens were not the only victims. Americans too were arrested on ridiculous charges and subjected to arbitrary punishment. Congress, with the Espionage and Sedition acts, contributed substantially to this terror; and the Supreme Court, in the Pierce and Abrams cases, came close to pronouncing it constitutional. But even with the loose wording of the wartime laws and loose construction of the "bad tendency" doctrine, there were those who imagined dangerous elements to be still at large. Public pressure was applied to the Justice Department to revise the old common law criteria for treason so as to include such things as expressing dissatisfaction with the government. J. Reuben Clark, himself often dissatisfied with the government, found this development especially alarming. When the attorney general asked him to comment, he pulled no punches.

[There] can, in my opinion, be no reasonable question but that an attempt at the present time to embrace within the term treason and to begin prosecutions therefore of many of the acts loosely declared by judges in the past acts of treason, would be most odious to the people of the country and could hardly fail to re-act upon the administration in a way that would be seriously detrimental to the interest of the Nation itself.[52]

Happily, the redefinition of treason was shelved.

Then came the issue of expropriating enemy property. Initially it seemed cut and dried: enemy property was regularly confiscated in wartime, international law recognized the practice, and Congress had given the president authority to carry it out. So Reuben reasoned, at least, in an early memorandum.[53] Gradually, however, the confiscation business began to trouble him. Property held by the alien property custodian soon soared to a disconcerting $800 million and, contrary to Reuben's recommendation, apparently none of it was being paid for.[54] He began backpedaling. When asked in February of 1918 about legal title to the docks of two German steamship companies at Hoboken, Major Clark concluded that executive fiat was insufficient; Congress would have to enact special legislation.[55] But that tactic got him nowhere. Congress proved only too obliging.

By war's end the alien property custodian was sitting on a fortune to rival Croesus'—and there was little disposition to give it back. This, for Reuben Clark, represented arrogation run amuck. If the president or anyone else could sequester and dispose of alien property, the same could be done with domestic property, precisely as Lenin was demonstrating in Russia. "These are dangerous ideas," said Reuben nervously, "in the present state of world thought."[56] As the government prepared to liquidate its accumulated German assets, Reuben took it upon himself to resist. He wrote two long memoranda seeking to enjoin the sale of the property and to mandate its return to the original owners. "Many supported the [confiscation]," he explained, "not because they believed in its wisdom or its efficacy but because they were unwilling to deny to those responsible for the conduct of the war any power such persons deemed necessary to win the war."[57]

ix

Such, for Reuben Clark, was the substance of the First World War. It was a fight, as he said, against "the hordes of Satan," but there was a certain ambiguity as to whether he meant the helmeted hordes along the western front or the "domineering and autocratic official clique" in Washington. He often confused the two, as when to Lucy James he confided: "The power of our national executive might raise the envy even of the Kaiser."[58] In the battle against this domestic despotism Reuben sought allies wherever he could. But Philander Knox, who might have been invaluable, was not with him—at least not at first. Knox was persuaded that the war emergency justified extreme measures. "If we are giving legislative sanction to startling innovations," he said in an early Senate debate, "we are compelled by a novelty of horror and of menace hitherto undreamed of."[59]

So, for the time being, Reuben fought alone. The battle was joined in earnest for him when the Justice Department faced the plethora of new wartime agencies with their unheard-of powers and tried to determine how far those powers extended. Memoranda littered the field like broken swords. July 20, 1917: May the president compel steel and cement manufacturers to furnish products to the state of Louisiana at the same prices as to the United States? October 1, 1917: May the president promise to reappoint employees of the government who are inducted into the armed services? October 30, 1917: May the president regulate the sale of radio apparatus? November 2, 1917: May the president declare a "dry zone" within a five-mile radius of every coal mine? January 31, 1918: May the president compel employers to grant an eight-hour day to their workers? Major Clark's reply to each of these queries was the same resounding negative. Only in those few cases where the constitutional authority was absolutely clear did the special assistant allow federal power to be exercised. If there was a doubt at all, the benefit of it went to private enterprise.[60]

x

As a one-man holding action Reuben's effort may have been notable, but he was the first to recognize its limitations. Far more effective would he be if the special assistant could somehow enlist the aid of Congress. Here, though, the signs were not encouraging. When the Lever Food Control Bill with its price-fixing clause passed the

Senate in July of 1917, only seven votes were cast in opposition.[61] Later on the so-called Weeks Amendment, which would have somewhat diluted the president's war-making authority, was killed by the House.[62] Congressional opposition was clearly not in season. It was not until the spring of 1918 that a mood of restiveness could be detected at all on Capitol Hill and then only among a minority of legislators—but by this time Philander Knox had swung around and was spearheading it.

The question of regulation, it seemed, had evolved into the question of nationalization. What the president had once only wanted to control, he now apparently wanted to possess. The nation's railroads, in truth, were not succeeding in the war effort. A combination of hard weather, obsolete equipment, and selfish competitive practices had by midwinter virtually tied American rail transportation into a knot. There was nothing else to do, sighed the Wilson administration, but step in and take over. Reuben could see what was coming, and with his guerrilla-style legalism he fought desperately against the nationalizers. In August the Georgia, Florida and Alabama Railway, suffering a rash of labor difficulties, came close to provoking nationalization single-handedly. Reuben's vigorous memorandum with its customary finding of no authority possibly served to delay the inevitable, but only for a short while.[63] Then in November the question came up again, this time in connection with Pacific Telephone and Telegraph, and once more Reuben energetically dissented.[64] But the writing was on the wall. In December the railroads were nationalized, placed in the hands of a director general, and operated as a single system.[65] Although the resulting efficiency was impressive, for Reuben Clark it was but the efficiency of the damned.

So bold an assertion of executive authority finally shook Knox awake. Suddenly he was ready to fight. Early in 1918 Reuben prepared a speech for him in which nationalization of the railroads was condemned out of hand. The railroads, he argued, amounted to an economic and social liability which the big interests were attempting to unload on the government.[66] More to the point was a draft article written by Reuben at the same time. In this manuscript, titled "Government Control of Railroads," he articulated the real substance of his fears.

All thoughtful men will, I am sure, agree that the assumption of possession and control of the railways is not only the most far-reaching and potentially disastrous purely national development of the war, but further that it is freighted with graver possibilities of calamity for the nation than any happening since the beginning of the Civil War. It is not that the principle involved, the taking of private property for public use in time of war is new, nor that this is an isolated example of its exercise, but we have during the present war, taken for the public use or welfare almost every sort of private property, even including, indeed, systems for water transportation and the terminal facilities therefor. The poison of this action is to be found in the circumstances attending its inception and in the practical effects flowing from it. For conceived in a gross usurpation of powers, it threatens for the promised saving of a little money the subjection of the nation to the domination of a microscopic minority.[67]

However, all of this came too late. The railroads were already nationalized and for once they were running on time.

xi

While Knox and a handful of senators vowed to challenge the executive juggernaut in open combat, Reuben returned to his boring from within. He availed himself of every opportunity to state his case, and by oddly recurring coincidences (which may have had to do with the southern upbringing and conservative principles of Attorney General Gregory), the opportunities were not infrequent. For example, while the railroad question was under discussion Reuben was assigned to compile, annotate, and index the sum total of emergency legislation to date.[68] For him, collecting together all of the foolish laws, gifts of power, and thrusts at despotism was not unlike gathering a basket of snakes, yet he accomplished it with dispatch. (He was assisted by Stanley Udy, his old Mockahi confederate from the State Department, who was now a clerk in the attorney general's office.[69]) Then, in a seemingly colorless little prefatory note, Major Clark was allowed to deliver a disquisition on the subject of usurpation. Here he argued that the war powers of the Constitution did not belong exclusively to the president and that they, like any other powers, must be separated among the various branches of government. "To change this," he said, "is to change the very form of our Government, and to make it something it now is not, whether aristocracy, oligarchy, or monarchy or"—he saved the loaded term until last—"despotism."[70]

267

General Crowder allowed Reuben to fire a few rounds too. Reuben was still officially under his command and occasionally found time for the affairs of judge-advocacy. Crowder, like Clark, was alarmed at the scale and intensity of the wartime hysteria. When invited to speak to the American Bar Association in June of 1918, he asked Reuben to prepare a speech asking, "Is the Law Silent amidst Arms?" Although nominally a Republican, Crowder was not a political man, and he may not have been ready for the particular address Major Clark wrote for him. It began in a dry, professional tone. Law, Reuben explained, was an abiding condition of modern society, as necessary for wartime efficiency as for the peacetime protection of rights. But the text was not long in coming to the real point.

[Seemingly] we have been so long freed from the dangers and evils of despotism and have been so far removed from those that are despotically oppressed that we now fail to appreciate, because we have not experienced, the truly terrible ills which oppression brings or to detect the signs by which despotism is established. For I think I observe that a not inconsiderable body of our citizenry are already so favorably disposed to what they euphoniously term responsible government, or centralized government and its efficiency as opposed to human rights and the freedom of man, which makes government an end not a means,—that I have grave apprehensions lest we be not now some distance on the road toward a vicious autocracy.[71]

And how was the United States to turn back from that road? Reuben's answer was constitutional. He believed that the Founding Fathers had apportioned the war powers as they had for a wise purpose, but he felt that in practice the apportionment and separation of these powers had not been respected: the executive had steadily encroached upon the legislative domain. The answer, simply enough, was to induce Congress to stand up to the president and recapture the ground it had forsaken.

An opportunity to do this presented itself in the late winter of 1918, with the introduction of the Overman Bill. This proposal, drafted by the administration, sought to grant the president unheard-of powers of reorganization. If passed, it would enable Wilson to shift about executive functions at will, transferring all of the duties of the State Department to, say, the Secretary of War, if he wished. The ostensible idea was to promote consolidation and streamlining, but the unprecedented nature of the measure immediately aroused congressional suspicions. The president was perhaps going too far.[72]

At this arousal Reuben Clark was initially hopeful. He and Knox collaborated in formulating an opposition stand,[73] and from the spiritedness of the ensuing debates it appeared that their optimism might have been well founded. Opponents of the measure pointed out that the president, armed with such powers, could undo the entire structure of executive government which Congress had laid in place; while administration supporters contended that the bill merely gave congressional approval to what the chief executive could probably do anyway. A few of the old stalwarts like Brandegee, Cummins, and Lodge made impassioned speeches against the Overman Bill. Brandegee went so far as to offer as an ironic amendment: "If any power, constitutional or not, has been inadvertently omitted from this bill, it is hereby granted in full." But when it came down to voting, the results were a washout. The bill passed the Senate by a vote of 63 to 13.[74]

xii

All the while there was a war going on. Germany had gambled that the United States would not be able to get into action fast enough to affect the outcome. Partly on account of Wilson's aggressive leadership and partly on account of American resourcefulness, the gamble did not pay off. American doughboys began reaching the western front in the early spring of 1918, just in time to meet the go-for-broke assault of the German army that was supposed to end the war. The Germans pushed the battle-weary French and British troops back to the Marne, only fifty miles from Paris. Between May and July it was touch and go. Gradually, though, the weight of the new forces began to be felt. American troops stalled a ferocious offensive at Château Thierry in May and broke through the German line at Belleau Wood in June. In the center of the line between Rheims and Soissons eighty-five thousand Americans participated in the seesaw battles that ended in an Allied victory in August. Thereafter, under Black Jack Pershing, they took over the southern front near St. Mihiel and defeated the Germans in an independent offensive. As the kaiser's army staggered backward toward the Rhine, the tempo of the fighting increased. It transpired in a netherworld of shell craters, shattered trees, rats, lice, and cordite, to the incessant scream of the German 80s. No doughboy who witnessed it was ever quite the same.[75]

Reuben lost no sons or brothers. There was the inevitable second cousin, Joe Wilkes, who was killed in action at Belleau Wood, and Reuben made a solemn visit to the War Department to learn the details. "I find I cannot sense the war at all, in the matter of life taken," he reported to his daughter Marianne.

I can't comprehend how men—God made beings—could deluge the world with the blood of their fellow men and send hundreds of thousands to eternity, just to gratify their own selfishness. We must surely try to the utmost to make them give place to better men and a higher order of people.[76]

This was as near as he came to Wilsonian idealism. Otherwise the war to him was only filth, hardship, and butchery. Only at one point, when his brother John was about to embark for France, did he seem to see a kind of purpose in it all. "You men who go out now are doing a great and noble work for your country and for the cause of human liberty," he said.

If this war lasts long enough to get us really into it, the men who return from France will be men indeed. They will be men of courage, stamina, and sterling character; men who have been literally tried in a fiery furnace. It is my faith that they will shape the policies and destinies of this nation, that they will strike down whatever we have amongst us that makes against liberty. The glimpse they will get of autocracy, what they will suffer as a result of this, will make them lovers of real freedom.[77]

Reuben Clark was a crusader to the end.

xiii

In the summer of 1918, the last of the war, Reuben requested a transfer back to General Crowder's office. In July the attorney general had announced a departmental reorganization that would have placed Reuben under assistant attorney general H. La Rue Brown, whom he did not admire. To make matters worse, the activities of the Justice Department seemed to be trailing off into boondoggling.

If he and his family must continue to starve, Reuben said, he wanted some "real war work" as a compensation. Military life had failed to win him over. "I am awfully sick of it," he said.[78]

But in the office of the provost-marshal general again he was back among friends. He and Crowder got along famously; they even talked about setting up a law practice together after the war.[79] As executive officer, moreover, Reuben was now Crowder's second-in-command, with far-reaching responsibilities. He got out a second edition of the selective service regulations in "pretty short time," and the day-and-night work had its usual therapeutic effect on him.[80] Soon he was shopping for a lieutenant colonel's insignia and looking forward to the prospect of promotion.[81] He was ready to finish out the war in uniform.

The end came in November of 1918, when Germany asked for an armistice. The end for Reuben followed by only a month. On a bright morning in December he was hard at work dismantling the selective service machinery when the general stolled in. "Beautiful day," Reuben greeted him.

"Not as beautiful as outside," Crowder replied, with an almost visible wink.

Reuben picked up the gambit. "Maybe you want to discharge me from the army," he suggested.

"Well," replied the general, "you might draw up the papers."

Major Clark, reaching into his desk, then spoke his last official words in the United States Army: "Here they are."[82]

xiv

To the end, Reuben had remained the reluctant soldier. For him the war experience had never seemed quite real. Still, although he had not manned the trenches, he had stayed with the army voluntarily and at great personal cost and had seen the war through to the finish. Enoch Crowder was favorably impressed with the quality of his service, and Thomas Gregory even more so. The latter, in fact, nominated Reuben for the Distinguished Service Medal; and on November 17, 1922, the medal was presented in formal ceremony at Governor's Island.[83] Reuben was sincerely bewildered. He combed through his record, not once but twice, to discover, as he said, "anything which even remotely approached ... the necessary achievement."[84] It was an Alice-in-Wonderland ending.

xv

The hordes of Satan had been beaten. Or had they? For J. Reuben Clark the more dangerous enemy was the enemy within, the enemy who arrogated to himself powers undreamed by the Founding Fathers and now proposed to use them in ways yet unknown. This enemy was not exactly a corporeal person, although he bore a certain resemblance to the austere, angular man who was president. Rather, he was a spirit, the spirit of despotism; and he exhibited, in addition to the caesarism of a Woodrow Wilson, the political avarice of a Boss Pendergast, the gift for mismanagement of a William Jennings Bryan, the demagogic energy of an Albert Fall, and the abstract, unfocused, and potentially lethal idealism of a James Brown Scott. Indeed, Scott and the "international law trust" were written all over that fourteenth and most conspicuously alarming of Wilson's Fourteen Points—the one calling for a League of Nations—and as the president boarded the U.S.S. *Cleveland* for the Versailles peace conference with a smiling Dr. Scott at the rail beside him, foreboding seemed to hang in the air. Reuben Clark's personal demobilization was, under these circumstances, decidedly anticlimactic. He may have been out of the army, but he was not yet out of the war.

Chapter 16

BITTER-ENDER

The history books refer to them with a mixture of awe and disdain. Borah, Reed, Brandegee, Moses, Johnson, Poindexter, LaFollette, Fall, Norris, Knox—"the Battalion of Death," "the irreconcilables," "the bitter-enders"—they fought the League of Nations at any and all costs, and in the end they defeated it. There was one of their number who was neither a United States senator nor a seeker of the political limelight. J. Reuben Clark, working quietly but very close to the battlefront, also fought the League of Nations. He fought it through the decision time of 1919 and the election of 1920. He fought it throughout the ensuing decade when most Americans had forgotten its existence. He continued to fight it in one way or another for the rest of his life, carrying his opposition to the heights of a crusade. His was not one of the names included in the roll call of irreconcilables, but none of them—including crusty old William E. Borah himself—battled with greater energy, more tenacity, or higher singleness of purpose than Reuben Clark. He was a bitter-ender to the bitter end.

It was the world war that made him into a crusader. The elements had been there beforehand—his doubts about global law, his skepticism of the court, his mistrust of moralistic diplomacy—but it took the heat of the war to fuse the elements together. For Reuben there had been two separate wars and two separate enemies. In 1917 the more immediate and threatening of them had been imperial Germany. By 1918, however, the real enemy seemed to be the enemy within. This enemy, as Reuben Clark came to believe, could only be vanquished by destroying the League of Nations.

ii

That Woodrow Wilson and others who supported the League entertained no such sinister design goes without saying. In fact,

273

proponents of the League had much in common with their adversaries. Both groups had grown up in the confident world of Queen Victoria, both had seen that world shattered by the war, and both were attempting to reorder the pieces. Their real disagreement was whether the best hope for the United States lay ahead in the future or behind in the past. Believing, as all of them did, in the paradox that America had been conceived in perfection and yet aspired to progress, some of them looked back to the truths of the Founding Fathers, while others looked ahead to a utopian destiny—and they came up with different answers.

President Wilson looked ahead. In the Fourteen Points he enunciated in January of 1918, there seemed to shimmer that final golden dream of abolishing human conflict. There would be no more secret diplomacy, no more economic barriers, no more oppressed national minorities. And there would be that magnificent world congress in which all maladjustments would be patiently worked out.[1] In comparison to the dream, the actual world of 1918 was a sorry contrast. European society had been shaken to its foundations. Confusion reigned. Half of the continent seemed threatened by upheaval while the other half faced starvation. Even in the United States there were strikes and bomb threats and eventually a full-blown "red scare." The president's all but insuperable task was to bring the ideal and real worlds together.[2]

He relied upon the League of Nations idea because it envisioned a process of ongoing adjustment rather than a fixed and permanent formula. The concept was an old one. It had achieved modern vogue with the rise of the legal settlement movement and startling relevance with the world war. On June 17, 1915, several hundred distinguished Americans gathered in Philadelphia to organize an association for bringing the concept to life. This League to Enforce Peace, as they called it, recognized the limits of voluntary measures (like arbitration) and proposed instead a world organization whose members would deploy "both their economic and military forces" against acts of hostility. The League to Enforce Peace was extremely popular and self-consciously bipartisan. William Howard Taft was elected its first president and Woodrow Wilson was its warmest public advocate. Both parties endorsed its platform in the 1916 campaign.[3]

There were opponents, as well as proponents, of the world organization idea, and as soon as the military crisis had slackened they too began to assert themselves. Some were opposed on principle. Others were partisan foes of Woodrow Wilson, biding their time for the resumption of politics. Both the ideologues and the politicos cheered happily when the opening salvo went off on October 24, 1918, for the hand at the lanyard belonged to none other than Theodore Roosevelt. He himself had once espoused the notion of a "league of peace" in his Nobel Prize speech of 1910, but the years of hatred for Wilson had quite erased it from his mind. Now, in the progress of the off-year elections, the old Bull Moose appealed to Senate Republicans to reject the Fourteen Points and Wilson's leadership. President Wilson responded the following day by asking voters to elect a Democratic Congress as a token of confidence in his policies. The battle was on.[4]

The next to speak out was Philander Knox. The senator from Pennsylvania had come to perceive Woodrow Wilson as headstrong and highhanded, a man against whom Congress must reassert itself. On October 28, in a speech before the Senate, Knox asked: Why all the rush? Ought not the war be ended and peace with Germany concluded before the League of Nations question should be considered?[5] In this, of course, he was striking at the very heart of the president's program which emphatically placed the League first. More dangerously still, Knox was seeking to provide a rallying point for moderate congressional opinion. Soon that opinion began to unravel. There were not a few, as it turned out, who had been quietly nursing doubts of their own about world organization, and they began looking to Senator Knox for leadership.[6]

The electorate as well may have been wondering about world organization, for in response to the president's plea for a Democratic Congress they elected an overwhelmingly Republican one.[7] That widened the rift between the White House and Capitol Hill. It also brought Henry Cabot Lodge, the new majority leader, to the chair of the Senate Committee on Foreign Affairs. Aristocratic in appearance and tastes, Lodge liked to style himself a scholar among statesmen. His mind, as one of his colleagues quipped, was like the soil of his native Massachusetts: "naturally barren but highly cultivated." He had impeccable credentials for the new post. He was a master parlia-

275

mentarian, he had literally written the handbook on senatorial treaty-making, and he had made a distinguished career of opposing presidential prerogative.[8] More than anything else, though, Henry Cabot Lodge was a man of the party who unabashedly put Republican loyalty first. Whether he was for the League (as he once maintained) or against the League was less a question of principle than of political advantage. He was for the League if the Republicans could somehow take credit for it. Otherwise he was against it.[9]

While President Wilson was in Paris negotiating the Treaty of Versailles, Lodge and Roosevelt held a council of war. Since there was much popular support for the League, no direct assault was advisable. As for an indirect assault, nothing could have been more cunning than the one they devised. When the peace treaty with its provision for a League of Nations came before the Senate, no open challenge to it would be undertaken—but there would be so many amendments and reservations tacked on that one of two outcomes would result. Either the treaty would become a Republican document for which the party might justly take credit, or else the president would look upon its disfigured remains and kill it himself. Either way Woodrow Wilson stood to lose.[10]

iii

Certain of Lodge's Senate colleagues were far more ideological in their opposition to the League. Politics aside, they said, the League had dreadful shortcomings. It proposed political rather than legal solutions to legal problems. It gave equal voice to the weak and the strong. It legitimized busybodyness on a global scale and allowed—indeed, pledged—members to mix into each other's affairs continually. But the worst flaw of the League, as these doubters believed, was what it portended for the United States. They saw America as standing proudly above ordinary politics. By virtue of republican institutions, democratic processes, written constitutionalism, and individual liberty, this nation was sui generis in human history. In order to maintain such purity, so the argument continued, two bastions of special protection had become necessary: Washington's farewell address (warning Americans against foreign entanglement), and the Monroe Doctrine (warning Europeans against American adventures).

The League threatened to undermine both of them. It might allow foreigners to compromise American freedom of action, and it might ensnare the United States in the cyclical calamities that Europe had known since the Romans. What better way to destroy youthful America, they asked, than by shackling it to a corpse?[11]

As early as the armistice, Senator James A. Reed, Democrat of Missouri, had delivered a stinging rebuke to the proponents of the League and had prominently cited the Farewell Address. Senator William E. Borah, Republican of Idaho, had followed suit on December 5 with the same appeal to the Founding Fathers and their time-honored principles. Senator Hiram W. Johnson, Republican of California, was the next to speak out, in January. "It is time for an American policy," he declared. "Rescue our own democracy. Restore its free competition. . . . Let American life, social and economic, be American again." Where President Wilson looked forward to Utopia, these opponents looked backward at Eden.[12]

The three of them—Reed, Borah, and Johnson—formed the nucleus of the irreconcilables and began reaching out toward like-minded colleagues. Eventually they enlisted Frank Brandegee of Connecticut, Miles Poindexter of Washington, George Moses of New Hampshire, Albert Fall of New Mexico, Lawrence Sherman of Illinois, George Norris of Nebraska, and Robert LaFollette of Wisconsin. They did not comprise a majority of the Senate, nor even a minority sizable enough to block the treaty; yet because they were eloquent, bullheaded, and extremely aggressive politically, this cadre of conservatives came to wield an influence all out of proportion to their numbers. In their strategy the irreconcilables were strangely assisted by President Wilson. He, like they, was quite unwilling to compromise principles deemed fundamental, and he would as readily destroy the League as hobble it with limitations.[13]

Somewhere between the purists like Borah and the pragmatists like Lodge stood Philander Knox, and his role became pivotal. Like the irreconcilables, Knox was motivated by principle; yet like Lodge and the moderates, he appreciated the necessity of compromise. No more than Majority Leader Lodge did Knox want to see the party shattered, something the irreconcilables were fully capable of doing. He believed, in fact, that there might be a ground on which both moderates and irreconcilables could stand together, and that if this

Senator Philander Chase Knox: Friendship based on the lost art of listening.

ground could be located the Republican party might come forth with its own alternative to Wilson's League. In a speech in December Knox put forth what he called the "American doctrine," a policy by which the United States would "consult with other powers with a view to concerted action" if some new kaiser should threaten the world. "[The American doctrine] entangles us in no way," he promised, "but it makes us the potential ally of the defenders of liberty whenever a great menace shall arise."[14] The Knox idea proved a shade too internationalistic for the isolationists and a shade too isolationistic for the internationalists. If it fell between stools, though, it also inspired both sides to contend for Philander Knox's soul, for he became the means by which each might win over the other.

iv

This was the situation Reuben encountered—full of delicate pivots and balances. He came into it as Senator Knox's speech-writer, legal counsel, and boon companion. Their friendship had both broadened and deepened since their State Department experience together.[15] Reuben had discovered that Knox, behind his mask of austerity, was gracious, witty, and personable. Together they had spent many a cool morning driving through Rock Creek Park and many a long evening in the Knox library.[16] It was there especially that Knox was in his element. Surrounded by the rows of legal tomes, the homey overstuffed furniture, and the warmth of a crackling fire, he put aside his icy dignity and came down to earth. Chewing pensively on his cigar, occasionally waving it around for emphasis, he could be a veritable cornucopia of aphorisms, homilies, and anecdotes, with a good scripture thrown in for spice. In the partnership that evolved between them, Knox was generally the dominant member. Reuben, by contrast, was often the sounding board, the "Dr. Watson." Having returned from the army and resumed his legal practice, he had been given important work by the Pennsylvania senator and his nominal deference was that of the astute counselor. But when the subject turned political, Reuben put aside his humble demeanor and spoke his mind.

And the League question was definitely political. Reuben thus found himself engaged in a selling job of no small proportions. It happened that back in 1910 he and Knox had once collaborated on a speech that strongly advocated internationalism.[17] What Reuben had to explain now was why he had changed his mind. The explanation might well have begun with James Brown Scott and the world court, and it might have wound through Reuben's encounters with the Democratic spoilsmen. But it was really the war itself that had altered his thinking. For him, the one-world concept of the internationalists had become as much a casualty of the European conflict as had Belgium. By June of 1915, when the League to Enforce Peace was organized, Reuben had begun to express his doubts openly. At the initial gathering of LEP dignitaries in New York, he had been asked to comment on the proposal for a world parliament. He had turned to former president William H. Taft and asked him if he was willing to send his son, say, to Bulgaria to intervene in one of the endless Balkan wars. Taft conceded that he was willing. Reuben, pausing, replied that he was not—and that he could not ask another man's son to go in place of his own.[18]

There were other mileposts in Reuben's march toward irreconcilability. By August of 1916, he had suggested to the League of Women Voters that "so long as there are worse things than death, there will be worse things than war." If laws against murder could not prevent its commission, how, he asked, could the world legislate an end to war, and how could the legislation be enforced? What besides war itself would conceivably be the penalty? "Must we not make up our minds that human agency at least is not able by mere fiat to usher in a millennium?"[19]

Soon his thinking had taken another step. By February of 1917, with American entry into the war imminent, he was writing to his father that it would be a mistake to participate in a European peace conference. "European local interests are not our interests and we have no business mixing therein," he said.

Moreover, if we get into the European situation, Europe will get into the American situation. Our Monroe Doctrine will disappear. We shall have strong European governments pushed under our noses. We shall have all of the rivalries incident to such a situation and those rivalries will certainly and inevitably lead to armed conflicts. One cannot but pray that we shall miss this cup. In this connection, the words of Washington, in his farewell address delivered 120 years ago, are just as apt as they were the day he delivered them.[20]

With the evocation of the Monroe Doctrine and the Farewell Address, Reuben had arrived at the irreconcilable position. He summarized that position for the League of Women Voters.

[It] is my abiding faith that this nation has performed and will yet perform a mighty work for human government among the nations of the world. I am not willing to do anything that will lessen its influence or power among the peoples of the world for there is immeasurably much to do to accomplish the political salvation of the world. It is not to be assumed that we should be more able to exercise our power for good—the moral influence of which so much is said—if we had been during the hundred and forty years of our national existence, a party to every European war, every diplomatic European squabble, every world difficulty that has arisen during that period.[21]

"Abiding faith" was the right way to put it, for Reuben's patriotism was in essence a kind of religious conviction. Philander Knox, himself a religious man, had on several occasions discussed with Reuben the spiritual implications of American history, and the two were in fundamental agreement. Now, in the early weeks of the League fight, while both sides hauled out their heaviest weapons, Reuben drove home the point to Knox that what was at stake here was far more than party, far more than foreign policy, far more even than questions of peace or war. It was the very meaning of America.

v

If Woodrow Wilson really meant to have his League, he did not pursue it wisely. He pushed on toward Versailles with political abandon. He left the country at a difficult time to attend to the peace negotiations personally. He took no senators or prominent Republicans with him. He failed to keep the Senate informed. He made disparaging remarks about the small-mindedness of those who would oppose him. Then in Europe, amid the tumultuous crowds and hailing banners, Wilson became convinced that the common people of the world were solidly behind him—and he resolved to push small-mindedness aside.[22]

The actual pushing was another matter. Although the Allies in Europe spoke passionately of peace, what they seemed to want most was revenge. France's indomitable Georges Clemenceau was particularly truculent. He wished to see Germany permanently crippled as a guarantee to French security. He also wanted his share of the spoils of war in the form of monetary reparations, and in this he was joined by the other Allies. In addition, all sorts of land grabs were under discussion, with France demanding the return of the Alsace-Lorraine region, Italy demanding Fiume, and several other powers demanding the former German colonies. "God gave us the ten commandments and we broke them," said Clemenceau. "Wilson has given us fourteen points—we shall see."[23]

Work on the League at least went well. Wilson himself headed the committee to write the League covenant, and his people patched together a draft in just ten days. Of the twenty-six articles, the essence of the covenant lay in Article X, which pledged signatories "to respect and preserve as against external aggression the territorial integrity and existing political independence of all states members of the League."[24] Here at long last was the object sublime, and Wilson could not doubt that Providence willed its attainment. As if in confirmation, word arrived on January 6 that Theodore Roosevelt had passed away in New York.[25]

Now that there was a specific document to attack, the irreconcilables lost no time in doing so. They found a great many weaknesses in the League covenant; James Reed drew five minutes of applause from a packed Senate gallery when he ripped through every one of them. But the jugular of the document was Article X, which the senators knowingly characterized as an "entangling alliance." For his part, the president rose to meet their opposition. "Any man who resists the present tides that run in the world," he said, "will find himself thrown upon a shore so high and barren that it will seem as if he had been separated from his human kind wherever." During a visit back home in late February, Wilson took the offensive. He hosted thirty-four congressmen for dinner at the White House and entertained questions on the League covenant until well after midnight. Detractors were unmoved, though. Said Brandegee afterward: "I feel as if I have been wandering with Alice in Wonderland and have had tea with the mad hatter." The president was not amused. "These men," he warned, "are going to have the most conspicuously contemptible names in history."[26]

Meanwhile, Senator Lodge had been quietly polishing his own speech, and on February 28 he delivered it. True to his strategy, Lodge offered no open assault, as had the irreconcilables, but only a polite list of doubts and questions. There were unclear passages in the document, he said, and some bothersome ambiguities. In order to clear them up he suggested four possible amendments. These would protect the Monroe Doctrine, exclude from League jurisdiction such domestic questions as immigration, provide for peaceful withdrawal from the League, and clarify how the League was to apply sanctions in the event that sanctions might be required. The speech was well received and widely quoted. It seemed to stand in judicious contrast to the verbal fireworks of the irreconcilables.[27] But it was overshadowed, on March 1, by an even better received and more widely quoted address, one that literally altered the course of the debate. This speech was delivered by Philander Knox—but it was written by J. Reuben Clark.

Reuben had never slackened in his drive to win Knox over.[28] For example, in February, when the president had sent around his invitations for the White House dinner, Reuben, hearing of the move, had mailed to Knox a draft letter declining the president's hospitality. "Not only the . . . Congress but the whole people of the United States must be full participants," he said, "in [discussing] this most remarkable and revolutionary document."[29] But Knox went to the dinner.[30] He was still trying to hold to the middle. "To dogmatize against any possible entente under any possible circumstances," he had said to the Senate in late December, "would be almost as unreasonable as to wish to rush headlong into some utopian world league."[31] Yet by February it was clear that the president's continued intransigence was beginning to have its own effect on Senator Knox. Wilson would not back up on the League covenant, he would not postpone its discussion, and he would not soften Article X. And all the while Reuben Clark was urging a frontal assault against the League. The March 1 speech was the first signal of Knox's new alignment.

They had begun planning it on February 17, two days after the League covenant was published, at a late evening session in the Knox library.[32] Reuben explained that he had read the document over carefully and had found it every bit the bombshell he feared. "Anyone can dream dreams or see visions," he had scrawled to himself. "We must have concrete ideas."[33] He now proposed to make the ideas of the League covenant concrete by subjecting them to closest possible scrutiny. Knox agreed.

The lawyer had set to work the following day.[34] He began dismantling the League covenant a piece at a time and holding each piece to the light of the American experience. From his notes and jottings a classification in four parts began to emerge, and by the end of the week he was putting the finishing touches on a full-scale indictment of the covenant.[35] The speech that Reuben then sketched out advanced far toward the position of the irreconcilables, but Senator Knox delivered it with only token changes. In his pin-striped suit and paisley tie, Knox was acknowledged to be the dapperest man in the Senate.[36] There was a commanding authority in his presence, and when he rose to speak on March 1 it was with the full attention of floor and gallery alike.[37]

What proceeded from the address was a step-by-step vivisection of the League covenant, replete with flourishes of the scalpel. Then Knox proposed four "simple and reasonable" tests. Did the League abolish war? Quite the contrary. "The scheme provided therein holds out a higher promise—nay, assurance—of a future worldwide war greater than any which has gone before, than any other document in the history of recorded time." Was the League constitutional? Not unless congressional powers to raise and support armies and navies and to declare war were deleted from the Constitution. Did the League compromise American sovereignty? "Pause ... and consider what it is proposed to do—to take from the social organism, not alone the right, but the power of self-defense. We shall stand not only naked, but bound and helpless." And, finally, did the League threaten national independence and life? "Judged by all the standards of the past ... we must answer that it does."

Knox then returned to an earlier theme, that of concluding peace with Germany *before* giving consideration to the League. But in Reuben Clark's campaign-trail rhetoric the plea took on a new iridescence.

Why, then, and I ask it in all sincerity, this feverish anxiety for the adoption of this plan? Why is there this racing up and down over the face of the whole land by propagandists urging its adoption? What benefit is to come from such a sale of country as is urged upon us? Who are the beneficiaries of this betrayal of our people? No nation threatens us; no group of nations seeks our destruction; never before were we relatively so strong. War itself, the great curse of mankind, is further away today than it has been in centuries. Have we shown ourselves recreant when the world labors big with potential disaster? Let our billions of treasure poured out as from perpetual fountains, our tens of thousands of young lives nobly sacrificed in a great cause, answer. Has famine failed to appeal to us? Count the millions of tons of food we send to feed the starving. Have we been deaf to the cry of the oppressed? Count our young men and friends. Have we failed to love liberty and humanity better than life itself? Ask the mothers whose sons lie on the battlefields of Europe.[38]

The climax was even more rhapsodic, playing on the theme of an American army stranded in Europe by cynical politicians. "How much longer," asked Knox, "shall their return wait on academic discussion of unattainable dreams?"

Observers on both sides agreed that it was the heaviest blow yet. Commented the pro-League *New York Sun:* "The voice of Senator Knox carried conviction which even the graceful elegance of Senator Lodge, the rounded phrases and sublime periods of Senator Borah, the smashing condemnation of Senator Reed, and the rugged oratory of Senator Poindexter cannot attain."[39] And on the other side William Howard Taft was moved to take public issue with the speech, point by point.[40] More importantly, the address once again provided a rallying point between the extremes. Knox, while damning this particular League covenant, had refrained from damning the League idea itself. There was a renewed appreciation in the Senate that Philander Knox might be the linchpin of the whole affair.

vii

This fact was dramatically borne out in the next round of maneuvering. Republican leaders mounted a filibuster in the closing days of the Sixty-fifth Congress (scheduled to adjourn on March 4), thereby forcing the president to call a special session of the Sixty-sixth, which they controlled. Thus the League debates could keep pace with the continuing peace negotiations.[41] Then Senator Brandegee, on the day after the Knox speech, visited Senator Lodge, and the two of them hit upon the idea of circulating a kind of senatorial petition against the League. They invited Knox to draft it. The following day, March 3, was spent in a furious effort to gather the necessary signatures. This "round robin," as it came to be called, had no standing in law, but thirty-seven senators pledged in it that they would not approve the League covenant in its present form. It represented a new high in the escalation of defiance, and the president replied in kind. On the eve of his departure to rejoin the peace conference he vowed: "The structure of peace will not be vital without the League of Nations, and no man is going to bring back a cadaver with him."[42]

Then Wilson, for the first and last time, tried compromise. When he arrived in Paris he began work on four amendments to the League covenant which, as advisors promised, ought to cut most of the ground from under his opponents. Three of the amendments straightforwardly exempted domestic issues like immigration and the tariff from the League jurisdiction, recognized the right to withdraw from the League, and provided for the refusal to accept a League mandate. On the fourth, dealing with the Monroe Doctrine, it was necessary to accept compromise language. "Nothing in this covenant," it said, "shall be deemed to affect the validity of international engagements, such as treaties of arbitration or regional understandings like the Monroe Doctrine, for securing the peace of the world."[43] The president had to make other compromises too. On the question of war reparations, he simply had to back down and go along with Clemenceau, fastening upon Germany a staggering debt in the process. On the question of French demands for security, Wilson assented to a fifteen-year occupation of the Rhineland by French troops and a similar occupation of the coal-rich Saar Valley by the League itself. He also agreed to a defense treaty with France in the event of another German attack. And he gave in to both the Italians in their desire for Fiume and the Japanese in their desire for Shantung. To the Japanese, under a League mandate, Wilson even ceded the German Pacific islands. No price was too high, it seemed, for securing general accord on the League of Nations.[44]

All of this was being watched with interest in the United States. And to heighten the interest, irreconcilable senators maintained a steady barrage of speech making and article writing. They even fanned out to stump the country in what was becoming the political contest of the century. These men, fired by their own energy, soon moved far beyond the pale of ordinary compromise, and in April they rejected Wilson's amended covenant out of hand. After all, they pointed out, the offensive Article X was still intact, and the "clarification" on the Monroe Doctrine was ambiguity itself. For his part, the president deepened in his conviction that no matter what he did the irreconcilables would oppose him. He duly called the special session of Congress on May 19 and made ready to meet the opposition. But the opposition was stiffening by the day. Senator Lodge, for example, packed the Foreign Relations Committee with irreconcilables, affording places of honor to Borah, Brandegee, Johnson, and Fall. With special care he included Philander Knox.[45]

Knox had still not abandoned hope in finding a middle way. He believed that his own American doctrine might yet provide some formula short of the League on which moderate internationalists like himself could unite. By the first week of June he and Reuben had completed work on a resolution incorporating the essence of the American doctrine. It stated that America's declared policy would be to regard any threat to Europe as a threat to itself and to act accordingly. This, as Knox tirelessly pointed out, was internationalism without obligation or prior commitment. Many moderates were in fact drawn to the Knox resolution, but the irreconcilables who sat on the Foreign Relations Committee would have none of it. After an acrimonious session in committee, the American doctrine was tabled for the second time and Senator Knox left the room in a huff. It was beginning to occur to him that the limits of conciliation had been reached.[46]

Accordingly, Knox found himself fighting more than ever beside the irreconcilables, and as he did so his rapport with Reuben Clark intensified. In early June the two of them collaborated on another speech. The target this time was Article XXI, dealing with the Monroe Doctrine. Rather than exempting the doctrine from League jurisdiction as intended, Article XXI had unfortunately resorted to murky language. Reuben blazed away at this indiscretion and claimed that any mention whatever in the League of Nations covenant would effectively make the Monroe Doctrine a part of the League. The thirty-five-page draft was also charged with references to the Founding Fathers and the Farewell Address.[47] Six months earlier Knox had characterized the Farewell Address as outdated ideology.[48] Now, however, he delivered the Clark speech exactly as Reuben wrote it.[49]

The final straw for Knox was the Versailles treaty itself, which arrived in early July. Perhaps he had held out hope that the completed document would somehow compensate for the deficiencies of the League covenant. If so he was disappointed. "It is indeed a hard and cruel peace," he wrote.[50] President Wilson had spoken much about "peace without victory," but such an ideal did not seem to be evident in the terms offered here. Reuben Clark was vacationing at the time in Grantsville. One of his daughters was at the Clark home in Salt Lake City when the wire arrived from Senator Knox. Recognizing it as something important, she hastened out across the salt flats to deliver it personally to her father. He read the dispatch with enormous pleasure. Philander Knox had joined the Battalion of Death.[51]

viii

A week later Reuben was back in Washington, and he and Knox were plotting strategy as full-blooded confederates.[52] It was clear that President Wilson did not have votes enough to ratify the treaty in the Senate without substantial compromise. It was also clear that most senators favored some sort of participation in some sort of League and thus that the elements of compromise were present.[53] But since Knox no longer wanted compromise, the object now was to find means of forestalling it. The tactic they adopted came to them by happenstance. Reuben was in his New York offices a few days later "gossiping" about the treaty. Harold Streeter, an associate, suggested that Reuben familiarize himself with the document "inasmuch as somebody connected up there ought to do so." Reuben took the advice seriously. Soon he was studying the Treaty of Versailles day and night, literally. "Mr. Tinsley observed that he supposed that I was sleeping with it," he noted in his diary. "I told him yes."[54]

Several things began to emerge from the study. The first was that Woodrow Wilson had indeed imposed a great deal of himself onto the peace-making process. This intelligence cut against the American grain: most countrymen would probably have agreed with Reuben that America's interest in the European negotiations was limited to insuring that they "sow the fewest possible seeds of future discord."[55] A second item to come forth was the conviction that Wilson's intermeddling, far from minimizing the seeds of future discord, possibly maximized them. In other words, the treaty was indeed the very death's-head some had feared. It amounted to what Reuben called a "neo–Holy Alliance" in which England, France, and the United States would conspire to keep Germany subject and the rest of the world disadvantaged—while new causes for war bristled like detonators on a mine. "The Treaty," said Reuben, "makes us co-participants and co-responsibles in matters which are none of our business."[56]

Reuben next asked himself how many specific little detonators there were in the Treaty of Versailles. The answer could only be learned by exhaustive research. As with the League covenant earlier, Reuben once again found himself dissecting the document a sen-

16   DATA ON GERMAN PEACE TREATY.

X. GERMAN PROPERTY TURNED OVER, SURRENDERED, ETC.

1. German national property, imperial and state, and the *private property* of the Ex-Emperor and other royal personages. (Compensation, where made, is turned over to Reparation Commission.)

Property and rights given up and duties and obligations undertaken by Germany.	Credit allowed for same.
To Belgium: Moresnet neutre and Prussian Moresnet, such property in.	No credit or compensation. (Art. 39, p. 59; *p. 23;* Art. 256, p. 313; *p. 114.*)
To France: Alsace-Lorraine, such property in.	No credit or compensation. (Art. 56, p. 95; *p. 36;* Art. 256, p. 313; *p. 114.*)
To Czecho-Slovak State: Silesia, such property in small area in southeastern part of.	Credit on reparation account. (Art. 256, p. 311; *p. 114.*)
To Poland: Eastern Germany, such property in ceded portions of.	Credit on reparation account, *minus* valuation of buildings, forests, and other state property belonging to the former Kingdom of Poland. (Art. 256, p. 313; *p. 114;* Art. 92, p. 139; *p. 51.*)
To Principal Allied and Associated Powers: Memel, such property in.	Credit on reparation account. (Art. 256, p. 311; *p. 114.*)
To Principal Allied and Associated Powers: Free City of Danzig, such property in.	Credit on reparation account. (Art. 256, p. 311; *p. 114.*) But property shall be given to Free City of Danzig or to Poland as the owning Powers may determine. (Art. 107, p. 155; *p. 58.*)
To Principal Allied and Associated Powers: German Colonies, all such property in.	No credit on reparation account. (Art. 257, p. 313; *p. 114.*)
To Belgium: Kreise of Eupen and Malmedy, such property in, if area ceded to Belgium after plebiscite.	No credit on reparation account. (Art. 39, p. 59; *p. 23;* Art. 256, p. 313; *p. 114.*)
To League of Nations as Trustee with possibility i France: Saar Basin, such property in, if area ceded to France after plebiscite.	No credit(?) (See Art. 257, p. 313; *p. 114.*)
To Poland: Upper Silesia, such property in portions of, if area goes to Poland after plebiscite.	Credit if to Poland. (Art. 256, p. 311; *p. 114.*)
To Poland or somebody else: East Prussia, such property in portions of, if area goes to Poland after plebiscite.	
To Poland or East Prussia: Kreise of Stuhm and Rosenberg, and a portion of the Kreise of Marienburg, such property in, if area goes to Poland after plebiscite.	
To Czecho-Slovak State: *Kreis* of Leobschutz, such property in a portion of, if area goes finally to Czecho-Slovak State.	Credit on reparation account. (Art. 256, p. 311; *p. 114.*)

A page from Data on German Peace Treaty: *A ledger that called Versailles to account.*

tence at a time and cross-referencing each clause on a given subject to every other.[57] Suddenly he had an idea. Suppose he were to pick out all the provisions of the treaty dealing with Germany alone and group them together—what would be the result? Startling! It seemed that Germany's liabilities in the treaty had somehow been sprinkled throughout the text in such a way as to soften their impact. It was only by drawing them back together that one could discern the real Treaty of Versailles, and this Reuben now set about to do. He took a piece of paper and drew a line down the middle. At the top, to the left of the line, he wrote, "Property and rights given up and duties and obligations undertaken by Germany." To the right he wrote, "Credit allowed for same." He then began arranging his notes to the left or the right under various headings. On the left there crowded all the cessions of territory, renunciations of rights, recognitions of new boundaries, consents before the fact to new treaties, abrogations of existing treaties, properties turned over, securities transferred, conditions and restrictions imposed, concessions relinquished, and, topping off everything, reparations exacted in the tens of billions of dollars. On the credit side of the ledger there could be found only a few desultory phrases. As the pages piled up, the Treaty of Versailles seemed to stand forth in new light. It little resembled Wilson's Fourteen Points, Reuben thought. Far more it resembled the peace of Carthage.[58]

The work was tedious and time-consuming. Fortunately for Reuben, the irreconcilables had agreed among themselves to stall the ratification proceedings, and Senator Lodge, the master parliamentarian, proved only too obliging. When his committee formally received the peace treaty on July 10, Lodge seized upon the document with pleasure. Even though every member of the committee had a copy of his own, the senator treated them all to a personal reading of the entire 264 pages, replete with long respites and trips to the water cooler. One by one, members of the committee slipped out to attend to their regular business, until Lodge was reading only to Charles Redmond, the clerk. Finally even Redmond deserted him—but the chairman droned on. The process took two weeks.[59]

The reading completed, even more time was burned up in hearings. All told, there were more than sixty witnesses, ranging from the president himself down to representatives of the oppressed European minorities. Six more weeks passed in this manner.[60] All the while Reuben was pushing forward with his labors, pausing only for hurried meals and short nights of rest. He was uncertain what role his work would play in the larger irreconcilable campaign, but he knew that arguments against the treaty were beginning to play out and that his was the only effort beyond conventional rhetoric. As July turned into August the project assumed encyclopedic proportions. Work papers now numbered into the hundreds, each with its familiar division of liability and credit, and the impact of leafing through them was impressive. The two columns marching side by side for page after page inexorably drew their picture of Germany being bled white.

On August 9 Reuben mailed the completed work, titled "Data on the German Peace Treaty," off to Knox, together with a thirty-eight-page speech draft to be used in conjunction with it.[61] Knox was delighted. He boiled the speech down somewhat and on August 29 rose to address the Senate. He began by introducing Major Clark's analysis of the peace treaty, a copy of which he promised to make available to everyone. It was a handy reference, he stated dryly, "[enabling] one to get at particular subjects that are dealt with in half a dozen places in the Treaty." He then went on to the body of his address.

Imperial Germany, he said, was unquestionably the villain of the world war. But the Treaty of Versailles was neither an appropriate punishment for villainy nor a likely formula for peace. "The instrument before us is not the Treaty but the Truce of Versailles," asserted Knox, and like any truce it offered nothing more than a breathing space in the battle.

Think you Germany—smarting and staggering under the terms of this the hardest treaty of modern times—will, even if we work to set up the League and she should join it, supinely rest content with the dole of grace and sufferance we are vouchsafing her, the crumbs from her victors' table? It is beside the point to say that such is but her just deserts and the full measure thereof. Lacking the wisdom to go forward and inflict a military punishment that would have uprooted their philosophy of force and taught them the lesson of live and let live, we have left them beaten but proud and arrogant, with their mighty spirit bent for the time but unbroken, with their damning philosophy unchanged, and with a will, fired by hate, to mete out revenge. That people will no more cease to plot and plan to recover their former higher estate than did Satan, plunged into the abysmal depths of Hell.[62]

The realities of the case were clear enough, Knox explained, but they had somehow been buried under Mr. Wilson's prodigious rhetoric.

"The people will judge this matter rightly," he promised, "if they but know and understand the facts." The facts, as it happened, were all neatly ordered in Reuben Clark's little "index" of the Germany treaty, and from that document Knox now proceeded to haul them out. Working his way through heading after heading, Knox essayed to show how the vindictiveness of the peace could not but breed further German hostility. By the time he reached the reparations clauses his point was made. "I have not sought to propound . . . any thesis beyond this," the senator concluded before the hushed chamber, "the treaty as it stands cannot be enforced. This is admitted by its proponents. The treaty as it stands is but a harbinger of other greater wars."[63]

The Knox speech and the treaty index, both of them the work of Reuben Clark, were widely reprinted and commented upon. For all the irreconcilables' denunciations of the League, they had never scored against the peace treaty itself. In fact, much of the pro-League sentiment in the United States was rooted in a belief that the League was part of a treaty which was otherwise highly desirable. Even President Wilson was unaware until the Knox address of August 29 just what he had initialed in the Hall of Mirrors and brought home for ratification. The following day he labeled the senator a Hun-lover and saw to it that the pro-administration press took up the cry.[64] But epithets or no, there was something hard and unanswerable about Reuben Clark's rearrangement of the facts. Indeed, history would demonstrate that "seeds of war" were scattered through the Treaty of Versailles in abundance.

ix

Nevertheless, irreconcilable councils were growing increasingly desperate. On August 21, the week before his speech, Knox called his confederates together for lunch and proposed that they mount a new speaking campaign. He envisioned mass meetings, parades, and a broad use of the publicity media. All of those present endorsed the plan, and Borah, Johnson, Reed, and Poindexter agreed to fan out across the West.[65] Reuben Clark, of course, had no part in this end of the campaign—or at least no intentional part. In mid-August he traveled home to Grantsville for his annual summer vacation.[66]

There, amid the quiet of the poplar-shaded streets, he could turn attention away from geopolitics and toward his old dream of cattle ranching.

But there was no peace in Utah. The entire state, as the lawyer could almost feel, was in favor of the Treaty of Versailles *and* the League of Nations. Former President Taft had spoken in the Tabernacle six months earlier, and "his advocacy of the plan to end war," according to one account, "bowled an already enthusiastic public completely over."[67] President Heber J. Grant and most general authorities of the LDS church supported the League, as did former governor William Spry; and both the *Deseret News* and *Salt Lake Tribune* were strongly pro-League.[68] Such being the atmosphere, it was not long before Reuben found himself heatedly engaging neighbors in back-fence debates. The effect was surprising. Here, it seemed, was a man in the know who openly doubted the sanctity of the League. His example gave heart to other Republicans, and almost overnight the League question was transformed from one of consensus to one of controversy. Then some Salt Lake Republicans, hearing of Reuben's spirited attack in Grantsville, arranged to have him duplicate it in the Tabernacle on September 2.[69]

Somehow the specter of the favorite son taking a defiant stand against the East became big news in a hurry. The newspapers began carrying articles about Major Clark, and they made journalistic hay when Senator Knox praised him on the floor of the Senate.[70] A few days before the scheduled address, the senator even wired Bishop Charles W. Nibley.

I congratulate you and all the true friends of Americanism in Utah that you have succeeded in getting Major J. Reuben Clark, Jr. to address the people of Salt Lake next Tuesday evening. By virtue of his long experience in diplomatic and international affairs, his splendid legal ability and fearless patriotism, I regard his views and opinions on the vital questions involved equal to those of any man in America.[71]

By the evening of the speech, the stage was set for *coup de théâtre.*

Accompanied by family and well-wishers, Reuben arrived at Temple Square in the early evening. He was unprepared for the reception awaiting him. All eight thousand seats of the Tabernacle were filled, and an additional two thousand spectators jammed the aisles. Even the choir loft was crowded to capacity.[72] Several hundred people had come by special train from Ogden, and there were parties from Provo, Logan, Nephi, and points further distant.[73] Reuben looked at the throng in wonder. He had a better audience at the moment than William E. Borah.

After band music, vocal solos, and a rousing chorus of "The Star-Spangled Banner," Reuben stepped to the podium.[74] He was no longer speaking through Philander Knox, and he relished the freedom. He addressed the sea of faces with an earnestness of deep conviction, his features animated, his mouth carefully forming the words. "I belong," he began,

to that great class of American citizens who see in the present situation such a departure from the traditional attitude of our government toward other nations and toward world politics as to constitute this one of the most critical moments in our history. Taught from my infancy that this constitution of ours was inspired and that the free institutions which it creates and perpetuates are God-given, I am one of those who scan every proposal to change or alter either with a critical eye. I am a member of that class which has a firm and unshakable determination to guard our institutions and our constitution at all cost; that believes that ours is the greatest and best government upon the face of the earth; that believes that it is worth all it cost the fathers of the Revolution to establish it, and all it cost our own fathers to preserve and perpetuate it in the great Civil War; that believes it has performed a mission and has still other missions to perform for the political salvation of the world; and that believes, if you will, that we the American people are the chosen of God for the perpetuation of a government which holds sacred those great fundamental inalienable rights of life, liberty, and the pursuit of happiness. It is with this spirit and with these feelings that I have studied the treaty, whose obligations it is proposed to place upon the American people, and out of such study followed in such spirit, there has come to me the conclusion that nothing looms before us that could be equally disastrous with its ratification by us.[75]

It was a Mormon message delivered in Mormon terms, and yet nothing could have better reflected the man's true feelings. The mission of America stood in peril. The very meaning of America hung in doubt. At this critical hour it was essential that God's people understand God's purposes and that the ultimate significance of politics and religion become manifest.

For the next two hours Reuben led his listeners through the intricacies of the Treaty of Versailles and the League of Nations covenant. Often he was interrupted by applause and just as often by loud disapproval, but the audience never once flagged in its interest. The arguments were the standard fare of the irreconcilables—the loss of sovereignty, the invitation to European meddling, the holocaust to come—and Reuben delivered them with irreconcilable panache. "Are we to lose our freedom?" he asked in closing.

Are we to cease to be the beacon light of liberty for the world? We entered the war free and independent. Let us not leave it in shackles. Let us preserve ourselves as we are. Let us maintain our freedom and our independence, that in the future, as in the past, we may act the knight errant succoring the oppressed of all nations. Let us not barter away our right to look every quarrel squarely in the face and espouse the just course as it shall be made known to us. Let us not waste the strength God has given us to establish an asylum for the heart-weary of all nations, in petty squabbles over a few rods of miserable European blood-sodden soil. Then guided over by the light of disinterested and impartial justice, we shall see the truth, uphold it and save the world.[76]

Reuben took his seat amid tumultuous applause. Yet no sooner had it died down than one of the audience, taking advantage of the eerie acoustics of the egg-shaped Tabernacle, sprang to his feet with his own message for the listeners. He was Brigham Henry Roberts, general authority of the Mormon church and captain of the pro-League forces in Utah. He pledged that he would answer each and every one of the charges made by Mr. Clark and answer them well. He then bid the multitude return to the Tabernacle the following week for the promised rebuttal.[77] If this was anticlimax, Reuben Clark was in for a good deal more of it. He suddenly found himself with invitations to speak on the League all over the state, but everywhere he went—Tooele on September 8, Logan on September 9, Ogden on the eleventh—B. H. Roberts dogged his heels with a counterblast.[78] It was rather like an election campaign, except that no one was running for office. But when Reuben finished his work, the League issue, at one time given up for dead, was alive and crackling in the Beehive State.

x

Back in Washington, events were marching toward their own denouement. President Wilson, convinced that Senate Republicans

295

would never yield, decided to make a speaking trip of his own and appeal his case to the people. The itinerary for this swing around the circle was an ambitious one, covering eight thousand miles by train, passing through twenty-three states, and calling upon Wilson to deliver forty speeches. For a healthy man it would have been a strenuous undertaking. For Woodrow Wilson, sixty-three years of age, frail by nature, and weakened by the ordeal of the war, it was a frightful gamble.[79]

And he lost. On September 25, after covering the western leg of the tour, the president had just addressed a cheering crowd in Pueblo, Colorado, when his health suddenly collapsed. A few days later he suffered a stroke which paralyzed the left side of his body. At the climax of the battle, the leader of American internationalism was confined to a sickbed and forced into seclusion.[80]

On September 10, while Reuben Clark was traveling to Ogden and Woodrow Wilson across the Midwest, the Treaty of Versailles was finally reported out of committee to the full Senate. It was a vastly altered document from that which the president had brought home from Paris. Under Lodge's supervision, some forty-five amendments and four reservations had been added to the text. Most dangerous were the reservations. Lodge knew that many senators would not vote outright against the treaty, nor would they vote outright for amendments since these would force the treaty's renegotiation. But reservations required no renegotiation and stood simply as declarations by the United States that certain portions of the treaty did not apply to itself. By attaching reservations, Lodge, according to his strategy, was making exactly the sort of alterations which would either convert the treaty into a Republican document or invite the president to kill it.[81]

The question was now up to the moderates, Republicans and Democrats alike. Moderate Republicans would probably vote for the treaty if it could be revised enough to quiet their misgivings; moderate Democrats would probably allow some changes in the treaty rather than see it defeated altogether. If the two joined hands, ratification was likely. One reason for not joining hands was President Wilson himself, who was still holding out for an uncompromised treaty. The other reason was the irreconcilables, who were still battling for outright rejection. By the strangest irony these bitterest of enemies were allies.

As the day of the voting approached, Reuben increased the tempo of his advice to Knox like a worried coach on the sidelines. So great was his mistrust of Wilson that he refused to believe that the president's collapse was real and darkly suspected malingering.[82] If this was Wilson's game, he said, the Senate should turn the tables and use the "illness" to justify more stalling.[83] Reuben was also suspicious of Senator Lodge, who seemed to be balancing on a tightrope between moderates and irreconcilables. "I am sure," he wrote to Knox on October 10, "that he is accessible to Root, Wickersham, Taft, etc. and they undoubtedly will seek to bring him to some kind of a selling out."[84]

Of this, however, Lodge gave no sign. He continued to steer the treaty with confidence. As he had predicted, the forty-five amendments were quickly defeated on the Senate floor, but the four reservations were voted on one by one and permanently attached to the treaty. By mid-November, in fact, moderate Republicans had assisted Senator Lodge in increasing the number of reservations from four to fourteen—an intentional parody of Wilson's Fourteen Points.[85] Few of the fourteen had real substance. But the crucial question now was of form, not substance: it was whether the president would tolerate any breach whatever of the Wilsonian faith. Reuben sensed that he would not. "If you recalcitrant ones insist on cutting out [the treaty's] heart, to wit, Article 10, and making other changes," he wrote to Knox on November 17, "I hope [Wilson] stands by his determination and that you stand by yours."[86]

Both did. As the final showdown appeared, President Wilson, to the delight of the irreconcilables, ordered administration supporters to vote against the treaty with reservations and then for the treaty without reservations. The following day, November 19, at 5:30 P.M., after frantic last-minute appeals by both sides, the voting commenced. The first motion was for ratification of the treaty with the Lodge reservations. Owing to the president's appeal of the day before, the motion failed, thirty-nine to fifty-five, with irreconcilables joining Democrats to seal the treaty's doom. Then came the motion for ratification without reservations. Now the irreconcilables recrossed the aisle and voted with fellow Republicans. When the tally was announced, the proportion of yeas and nays stood almost exactly the same: thirty-eight to fifty-three. Shortly thereafter Vice-president Marshall banged down his gavel and the first session of the Sixty-sixth Congress was adjourned. The Treaty of Versailles had been defeated.[87]

xi

In New York J. Reuben Clark received the news warily. It was almost too good to be true. It was also reversible. But for the time being he could rejoice in what seemed a stroke of the impossible. Four months earlier the League of Nations, by every reading of public opinion, was an accomplished fate for the United States. Now, in the space of an intensely political summer, that fate had been frustrated and the all-but-invincible combination of Democrats, Wilsonians, internationalists, and progressives had gone down to defeat. Reuben reached for his writing pad and began a letter to Philander Knox.

Armageddon was won.

Chapter 17

THE WASHINGTON
CONFERENCE

If the League of Nations question had really been dead in November of 1919, Reuben Clark might have returned to the "normalcy" of which President Harding spoke in his famous inaugural. But it was not dead. Like a phoenix, it kept rising from its own ashes. There were two reasons for this, the first being that most Americans continued to hope and believe in the League. They were so shocked by the world war and appalled by its tragedies that they would not bring themselves to believe that "something couldn't be done." The second reason was that history was on their side. Reuben himself recognized that the world was becoming ever more complex and interdependent and that the concept of sovereignty as Grotius had known it must steadily give way to internationalism. As a result, the irreconcilable cause was doomed to be an increasingly losing one. Even as the bitter-enders braced the door, the question of the League crept through the window, and when they raced to the window it started down the chimney. As their battle became ever more desperate, their voices grew ever more shrill. They began to lose touch with the world of political realities and to assume the role of the extremist. J. Reuben Clark had never been an extremist before, and he was not yet certain how well the role suited him.

ii

"The treaty outcome was certainly bully," Reuben wrote to Preston Richards after the Senate vote. "My anxiety now is to see it stick."[1] Less than a week passed before Reuben took the occasion of a luncheon address to blast the League again, for good measure.[2] His apprehensions, so it seemed, would not be quieted—and for good reason. Despite his own explanation of the voting, the League of Nations had not been defeated by a mandate of the people but by one of the strangest anomalies in American political history—an alliance of the extremes against the middle. Thus it was always possible, and in fact rather likely, that the middle would rise up and assert itself and that voices of moderation in both parties would yet reach an accommodation. Senator Lodge openly spoke of such a likelihood. He even held a series of conferences with Senate moderates for the purpose of drafting some compromise reservations, and by the end of January they were rumored to be close to agreement.[3]

Yet still the extremes held firm. The irreconcilables ambushed Lodge one day and put him on notice for his waywardness. And for his part, the president doughtily proclaimed that the upcoming campaign would be a "solemn referendum" on the League question. When a Senate vote was retaken in March, the score moved to forty-nine for the treaty and thirty-five against, but this was still seven votes short of the necessary two-thirds. And it was the last time the Senate would consider the League of Nations.[4]

In the meantime, the Republicans were beginning to reap what they had sown. The peace to end all war seemed somehow to have been sabotaged, and it was difficult to put blame on the Democrats. Not only had the League of Nations been defeated, but the United States had been cast into the grotesque situation of remaining at war with Germany. Even though the continued belligerency was only technical, it made the United States appear to be something less than peacemaker of the world—while the party opposed to Wilson now seemed to be the party opposed to everything. If this continued, there was apprehension that the solemn referendum might go against the Republicans in November and that the triumphant Democrats would have their League after all.

Accordingly, the fight against the League now became a fight to end the war, and Senator Knox was chosen to lead it. Together he and Reuben Clark attempted repeatedly to engineer a conclusion to the European hostilities. They tried sponsoring a partial ratification of the Treaty of Versailles "insofar as it provides for the creation of a status of peace between the United States and Germany."[5] They tried a congressional resolution to the effect "that peace exists between the United States and Germany."[6] They tried repealing the original declaration of war.[7] Nothing worked. Woodrow Wilson had the Republicans over a barrel: he alone could negotiate and submit a treaty to the Senate, and if he chose to submit no treaty at all the Senate could do nothing, so it seemed, but sit back and take the blame. It was a highly effective stratagem.

By the spring of 1920 the situation was growing desperate. The United States manifestly appeared to have lost its bearings, and the Republican party appeared to be responsible. With the election only months away, there was a clear mandate for action. In April Congressman Steven G. Porter submitted the most recent Knox resolution (in slightly altered form) to the House of Representatives and on the ninth it passed.[8] When the resolution also cleared the Senate Foreign Relations Committee the following week, there was an imperative sense of now or never among the Republicans in the upper house. Senator Knox announced that on the following Wednesday, May 5, he would deliver a major address on the resolution.[9] At this point he was already in possession of a draft speech that Reuben Clark had been working on for several weeks, and he thought it deserved a little fanfare.[10]

In a way the speech of May 5, 1920, was Knox's most dramatic in the entire League of Nations campaign. The senator walked alone to the Capitol in the morning.[11] By the time he arrived the visitors' gallery was packed to overflowing and there was a charge of anticipation in the air. Immediately before he rose to speak Knox was handed a telegram from Reuben Clark. "Best of luck, strength and spirit," it read. "Whole country watches expectant with hope."[12] A hush fell over the Senate chamber as the former secretary of state began speaking, and several Democrats—with unconscious symbolism—moved over to the Republican side in order to hear more clearly. The speech lasted an hour and twenty-five minutes.[13]

It began with a sharp attack on the president.

More than seventeen months ago the last shot of the great war was fired. . . . The whole world seethes with revolution. Our own nation is in ferment and turmoil. Force and strife are rampant and threaten the destruction not only of our property but of our free institutions and even of our very lives. And yet we stand and have stood for months, as a rudderless ship foundering in the trough of tremendous seas. We must not dare longer to delay a return to the ordered government of peace; we must not hazard a further postponement in turning our undivided deliberations to our home problems. They are great enough, sir, to tax the utmost wisdom which we possess.[14]

Citing legal authorities, State Department records, the writings of prominent historians, the works of the Founding Fathers, and—with conscious irony—the addresses of President Wilson himself, Reuben had set about in the speech to establish a two-part thesis: first, that by every standard of law and diplomacy the United States was actually at peace with Germany; and second, that the reason for President Wilson's refusal to recognize that fact was not because he wanted to force ratification of the Treaty of Versailles (which was exactly the case) but because he wanted to prolong the duration of his own war powers.

Our national executive with a stubborn irresponsibility continues to declare we are at war. But as a practical matter the only war which he wages is against American citizens and American industry. With Germany, he wages no war.... The situation is so anomalous and so iniquitous, it is so fraught with injustice and with possibility of disaster, that one cannot reconcile it with the operations of sane statesmanship.[15]

Once the premises were in place, the conclusion loomed inescapably that Woodrow Wilson was playing fast and loose with the United States Constitution.

The speech was a stunning success. Said one friendly editor: "It has patriotic sentiment, a fine wrath against the Constitutional abuse, legal and historical learning, eloquence of expression."[16] Unfriendly editors took exception, of course; but all of them took the speech for an "exposition of constitutional principles" rather than for the political sleight-of-hand that it was.[17] They missed the tactical point of transferring blame for the stalemate from the Republican Congress to the Democratic president—a transfer so deftly accomplished that the Democrats themselves failed to take note of it. For the Senate duly passed the Porter resolution and the president duly vetoed it; and before the air had cleared, the question of who stood for peace and who stood against it had been turned inside out.[18]

iii

There were still dangers to be found in the approaching election, however, and the principal one was that the wrong Republican might be nominated. Heretofore the question of the League had been a party question, with Republican standing against Democrat. Reuben now had to face the possibility of a fight within his own party or, worse, of his party siding with the dreaded League. It was a complex and confusing situation, he complained. "Taking a position on anything is like shooting in the dark—you are as likely to hit your friends as your enemies."[19]

On April 29 he wrote a long letter to Senator Knox and proposed a line of strategy. Everything must be done to thwart the designs of the pro-Leaguers. If necessary, a bargain must be made with Lodge whereby his chairmanship of the Republican national convention would be guaranteed in exchange for his support of the irreconcilables. A plank must be drafted broadly enough to unite the party behind some vague principle like "concerted action" without mentioning the League. And then, of course, there was the question of the candidate. One by one, Reuben considered the possibilities and discarded them. Herbert Hoover was too friendly to the League. Hiram Johnson was too radical. Leonard Wood was "by nature an autocrat" and a tool of the interests to boot. None of them had the acuteness, sagacity, and breadth of vision necessary for the job—nor courage enough to resist the League. "To my mind," concluded Reuben,

our next president should be a man who understands the viewpoint of both capital and of labor, but who in feeling and in spirit belongs to neither group and I can say to you for I know you will understand I am sincere that I think the only man of all, who completely fills out this requirement, is yourself.[20]

To underscore his seriousness, Reuben then vowed himself willing to bolt the party if necessary and to help found another one based upon "Americanism."

These hopes were too fond by half. Philander Knox was not presidential timber, and he had little ambition for the White House. As for deserting the party, he was too much the political man to dream of it. In small ways, in fact, Knox joined his voice to the chorus of Reuben's friends and associates who had begun suggesting that his opposition to the League was going too far. William Dennis, for example, gently reminded Reuben that disrupting the Republican party at this juncture would play directly into the hands of the other side. "Putting it another way," he said, "Henry of Navarre was not entirely cynical or entirely wrong when he said 'Paris is worthy a mass.' "[21] Reuben accepted these homilies in good spirit. The tides were running toward compromise, and he was swimming against them; what else did he expect?

As it turned out, Reuben did not have to make good on his threats, for the Republican plank on the League was wonderfully nebulous and the presidential candidate was Warren G. Harding. Harding was a political dark horse, the product of a deadlocked convention and a smoke-filled room, but as senator from Ohio he had strongly opposed the League and even flirted with the irreconcilables. To the extent that he was flexible on foreign policy, he might be urged even further toward League opposition. And flexibility was definitely one of Harding's traits.[22]

Reuben consoled himself with the thought that Knox would doubtless be made secretary of state and threw himself into the campaign.[23] His Utah speaking tour of the previous year had finally brought him to the attention of Reed Smoot. Now, at Smoot's request, Reuben traveled back home to participate in what he called "a campaign [of] red-blooded Americanism."[24] The tour marked out for him was an ambitious one, calling for eight speeches in two weeks.[25] Reuben did not consider himself a man of the hustings, nor was he in any personal way a supporter of Smoot; but he felt obliged to do what he could, and he took to the stump with fervor.

In town after town he blasted the League of Nations and all its works. Now the League was wrongheaded, now it was immoral, now it was impotent. Much of the diatribe was merely rhetorical and full of campaign hyperbole, but in Provo on October 18 Reuben went some distance toward presenting the irreconcilable position meaningfully. The question of the American Revolution, he said, was whether or not this land should remain subject to European domination, and the Founding Fathers had unanimously agreed it should not. While subject to that domination, America had been drawn willy-nilly into European squabbles and intrigues, the resolution of which was totally beyond American control. The struggle, then, had not been for independence alone; it had also been for sovereignty, for the exclusive right of Americans to govern their own destiny. Having established this premise, Reuben went on to suggest that the whole of subsequent history had consisted of "crises" in which the principles of the Founding Fathers must either be renounced or reaffirmed. In this, "the fourth and greatest crisis," the choice was particularly clear.

America ... must retain her independence, her sovereignty, her civilization, and her free institutions, and she cannot and will not do anything whatever to place these in jeopardy. To do so would be, both for herself and for mankind, not a blessing but a curse, and the ages that are to come would never forgive us. ... We shall not undo the work of the fathers, and once more place ourselves under the dominion of monarchic Europe.[26]

To fellow Utahns, it seemed, this made particularly cogent sense, for on election day they decisively forsook Wilsonianism and returned to the Republican fold. In celebration of the victory there was a torchlight parade in Grantsville to the family home on Clark Street, followed by a convocation at the opera house. Amid hurrahs and hymns and selections by the band, Reuben Clark was feted regally.[27] The mighty Goliath was slain at last.

iv

Or was he? No sooner had the congratulations been passed around than President-elect Harding suddenly seemed to falter. During the campaign he had been elusiveness itself on the question of the League, appearing to be for it or against it as the particular audience seemed to warrant. Now, but a month after the election, he announced his intention to send a seven-man commission to arrange a peace settlement with Germany, and in the vanguard he placed the father of Republican internationalism. "I confess the possibility of [Elihu] Root controlling our peace adjustment appalls me," Reuben wrote to Knox. "It would mean that the fight already made on this thing has been all but in vain, which is just what they intend it should mean."[28] What followed was a long winter of apprehension while pro- and anti-League forces within the party battled for the soul of the new incumbent. From Reuben Clark's point of view, the signs seemed increasingly ominous. Both Herbert Hoover and Charles Evans Hughes, energetic supporters of the League, were given significant cabinet posts, the latter as secretary of state. For Reuben this was nothing less than "the biggest bunko game in all our history." "I think I can promise you this," he wrote to John Bassett Moore, "—that any attempt to put life into the Treaty of Versailles by anybody will bring the biggest fight in the Republican Party in all its existence."[29]

In order to head off such a cataclysm, Clark and Knox put their heads together again. They revived the expedient of a legislative end-run which would bring peace with Germany on their own terms—before it could be brought on some other. After an exchange of letters in early April, Knox reintroduced his peace resolution in the Foreign Relations Committee. A week later it was favorably reported onto the Senate floor and, as in the old days of 1919, battle lines began forming.[30] Present were many of the familiar faces—Lodge, Reed, Borah, Hitchcock—lining up on their accustomed sides of the issue. But the enemy now was Charles Evans Hughes. "I spent two hours yesterday with [him]," Knox reported to Reuben on the seventh.

[He] insists that the proper policy is to excise the League of Nations and then ratify the treaty. We had it hammer and tongs and in very plain language during the whole period, Lodge and Colonel Harvey being present and playing the role of spectators, and I am sure I did not make a dent on Hughes and you may be equally sure he made none on me.[31]

It was, then, in defense of Republican policy, not Democratic, that Senator Nelson of Minnesota took to the floor on April 28 and implored his colleagues not to forsake "devastated and bleeding France," that Senator Underwood pleaded not to "abandon the fight and withdraw from the field," and that Senator Hitchcock argued that only the president could make peace.[32] And by the same token, it was against Republican policy, not Democratic, that Senator Reed rose on the following day and made one of the most impassioned and hard-hitting speeches of his career, in support of the Knox resolution.[33] Knox himself took no part in the formal debate, but his Mormon counselor kept up a running file of memoranda from which a speech, if needed, could be quickly assembled. These documents were increasingly marked by foreboding, mistrust, and a populistic fear of conspiracy. The question of the League, like the plague of frogs in ancient Egypt, was becoming persistent and ubiquitous—and Reuben Clark was darkly beginning to wonder why.

306

As it turned out, the debate over the Knox resolution effected another turning point in the crusade. On April 30 the resolution passed the Senate by a vote of forty-nine to twenty-three.[34] Two weeks later the House of Representatives passed its own version, and by July 1 a conference committee had hammered out the differences. On July 2 President Harding affixed his signature to the resolution, thus repealing the original declaration of war against Germany and ending four years of American belligerency.[35] Like the Congress and the presidency, the Republican party had been snatched away from the League of Nations.

v

The letter from Fred Dearing should not have come as a surprise. He had been made assistant secretary of state under the new Republican administration, and he was writing to make a request both orderly and reasonable. He simply wanted to know what the foreign policy of the United States ought to be.

Since you have so little to do, and are a true patriot and authority besides ..., I thought I would ask you to give me a concrete memo, as full as you care to make it, setting out your conception of what this country should do when the Knox Resolution is finally passed, *a* Treaty with Germany, *b* relationship with the League and its members, *c* American soldiers in Germany, *d* Guarranteeing [*sic*] the interest on indemnity and other foreign bonds, *e* State Department to pass on all Foreign Government or large Foreign bond flotations from point of view of seeing whether we ought not to secure certain things before allowing the flotations in this market, *f* observers in Europe, *g* codification of internation[al] law to exclude barbaric scientific warfare, *h* world court, *i* disarmament conference, *j* mandate policy. And anything else you can think of as flowing out of the general clearing up of the war.[36]

The letter amounted to a blueprint of the Republican dilemma. Ever since the battle of the League had begun, Republicans had been cast in the role of obstructionists. Now back in power, they must face all of the problems that had bedeviled the Democrats and find solutions for them. Creating workable policies would be altogether different from creating obstructions.

Thus, it was doubly significant that J. Reuben Clark was among the first to be asked for ideas. In a nice way, Dearing was telling

Reuben to put up his money. Reuben understood this; he recognized that it was time to switch from negative rhetoric to positive action—but he balked all the same at the prospect of cooperating with Charles Evans Hughes. "I sometimes wonder," he later wrote, "whether my own ideas and views are not so 'sot' as to make me of doubtful value."[37] Still, it was his only opportunity to do something affirmative. He had cut himself away from the Democratic policymakers early in the war, he had cut himself away from the Republican mainstream upon joining the irreconcilables, he had put a considerable strain on personal and political friendships, and he had even talked of abandoning the party altogether. Here was the chance to turn around.

Reuben seemed almost visibly on his guard when he visited the assistant secretary's office on July 1 and hastily dictated a memo to Dearing's secretary.[38] In this he made a number of recommendations. Aggregations of power such as the League, he said, were inherently dangerous and ought not to be recognized. Nations must be dealt with individually and held responsible for individual acts. There was some hope in arms limitation, perhaps, but a far greater chance that specific kinds of arms, such as the nightmare weapons, might be banned entirely by some Hague-like conference. To this end international law needed to move forward and its codification be taken seriously. "No more noble, nor far-reaching task . . . could be undertaken by the President and Secretary of State," he concluded, "than this work to place the world . . . back where it was when the last war began."[39]

Reuben soon realized that different consequences flowed from positive suggestions than from negative obstructions. A bare ten days after the visit, Secretary of State Hughes announced a formal proposal for precisely the sort of conference Reuben's memorandum had envisioned. It was to convene in Washington, probably in the fall, and was to consider among the principal powers of the world the interrelated problems of arms limitation and the Far East.[40] Although the idea for the conference had antedated Reuben's memorandum, that document seems to have had a catalytic effect; and J. Reuben Clark was the first person invited to help put the conference together. There could be little doubt that he had dramatically returned to power—and to all of the responsibilities that accompanied it.

vi

The Washington conference grew out of that universal longing for peace which followed the Great War. There was an understanding that the race for naval armaments had figured prominently in bringing on the world conflict, and yet still the arms race continued. The United States had pledged itself to build a navy second to none and was well on its way to that goal; Great Britain vowed that no one would overtake its navy; and Japan, spending half of its tax revenues for armaments, was rapidly moving up from behind. All three powers had solid economic (as well as humanitarian) motives for wishing to cut the race back, and yet none of them felt it could act unilaterally. To make matters worse, the United States was deeply suspicious of Japan. Without really participating in the war against Germany, the Japanese seemed neatly to have turned it to their own profit by pressing outrageous demands against China, intervening in eastern Siberia, and taking over Shantung and the German Pacific islands. As a further complication, Japan had a military alliance with Great Britain, and the sheer muscle of it allowed the Japanese to remain more or less insolent. American military planners had reacted strongly to these developments. They had transferred the bulk of United States naval power to the Pacific and were now shaping their thinking to the possibility of a Far Eastern war. The upshot was boggling. Britain and Japan could not reduce naval armaments until the United States did; the United States would not reduce naval armaments as long as the Anglo-Japanese alliance remained in force; and Britain could not sever the alliance without isolating and offending the Japanese. A conference was clearly in order.[41]

vii

With the war over and the question of the League laid to rest, Reuben Clark had at last closed his eastern law offices and was in the process of moving back to Utah. No sooner had he arrived, though, than he was met by the inevitable telegram from Fred Dearing.

Am authorized to ask whether you would consider assisting department in preparing for Disarmament and Far Eastern Conference. Reply by telegraph.[42]

A follow-up letter clarified the request. Reuben would work with John MacMurray, chief of the division of Far Eastern affairs, and the two of them would plan the conference agenda, formulate recommendations, and prepare the American case, employing specialists where appropriate. As an inducement, Dearing thought to offer Reuben a constructively blank check. "You will be wholly independent in working out your ideas," he promised, "except for the normal cooperation needed by Mac and the Secretary."[43] Cooperation with the secretary, however, meant cooperation with Charles Evans Hughes, and probably for that reason Reuben hung back. He had the choice once again of being on the outside and free or on the inside and compromised. Senator Knox liked the first alternative best. He was developing into one of the lone wolves of the Senate, and he thought Reuben ought to enjoy the same "liberty of action" that he did. But while Reuben was pondering this advice the secretary himself stepped in. "Very desirable you come at once for a few days," he cabled Reuben on July 20.[44] Two days later Reuben left for the East once more.

viii

Charles Evans Hughes was a statesman of the old school. With his buttoned waistcoat, his gold watch chain, and his trimmed white beard he looked a bit anachronistic in the jazz age, but there was nothing geriatric about his capabilities. A child prodigy, he had amazed parents and teachers alike, graduated fourth in his class from Brown at the age of nineteen, acquired two advanced degrees (one of them from Columbia law school) served as governor of New York, sat on the Supreme Court, and run for president against Woodrow Wilson. His restless mind cut to the bone and marrow of whatever was before him, and his forceful personality swept all opposition. As President Harding's secretary of state, Hughes was his own man. Not infrequently he would emerge from a briefing with the president leaving the latter bewildered. "Hughes," Harding would say sadly, "this is the damnedest job!"[45]

Hughes and Clark had never quite gotten on. Although both were Republicans schooled in international law and steeped in the ethic of work and more work, they seemed as unmixable as oil and water. Clark was the conservative and ever more the isolationist; Hughes was the progressive and ever more the internationalist. Reuben had supported Hughes's presidential candidacy in 1916 with greatest personal reluctance.[46] Then they had served together as special assistants to the attorney general, and it was Reuben's opinion that Hughes fit into the Democratic administration entirely too well. "I never saw a man who had more assurance and who apparently had less regard for the opinion of others," Reuben reported to Knox.

He has a disposition to rush matters and seems to feel there is nothing so complicated or far reaching in effect that it may not be handled within the space of a few hours. . . . This, of course, means that he has no adequate understanding of problems involved in his work.[47]

Accordingly, their first meeting was not particularly felicitous. Reuben Clark, in the company of Undersecretary Henry P. Fletcher, Assistant Secretary Dearing, and Far Eastern chief John MacMurray, paid Hughes a visit in late July. The secretary seemed as breezy as ever. He had had little time to think about the conference, he explained, and had no definite ideas about it. "He then proceeded," reported Reuben tartly, "to talk twenty-five minutes concerning it, during which time he completely demonstrated that his opening observations were quite accurate."[48] For his part, Reuben *had* thought about the conference, and he proceeded to lay out his ideas forcefully. There had been much talk about limiting armaments by imposing ceilings on their size and number. Reuben was not at all certain that this was a good idea. It raised a constitutional question about the congressional power to raise and equip armies and navies, and it pointed toward military impotence. To his mind the question of the hour was not whether there would be armaments, or indeed even wars, for he believed that both were unavoidable, but *what kind* of armaments and *what kind* of wars. Would there be good wars like the Spanish-American, limited, conventional, and just; or would there be bad wars like the world war, unlimited, unconventional, and satanically unjust? What seemed intolerable to him was not war itself but war in which civilian noncombatants were drowned by submarines, or bombed from dirigibles, or gassed in their own homes; and thus what was to be hoped for was not so much arms *limitation* as arms *control*. It was less important, Reuben believed, to regulate

311

the size and number of weapons than it was to forbid certain weapons outright. What he envisioned was nothing less than a complete rewriting of the rules of war.

Hughes was taken aback. Apparently the distance between himself and Clark was wider than he had thought. Although ostensibly devoted to peace, Hughes was every bit as hardheaded as Reuben Clark, and he regarded as absurd the notion that a nation at war would not make use of whatever weapons it could. A little tactlessly, perhaps, the secretary made his position known and dismissed Reuben's as impractical. It was useless to form rules, he said flatly, because the rules would be broken. Perhaps so, Reuben conceded.

It may well be that after we go into such a war, we shall do just what you apprehend, but the damage will not be nearly so great and the effect on humanity and civilization will be infinitely less, if we have to prepare for such measures after such a war begins, instead of planning and preparing it all beforehand.[49]

While the two Columbia lawyers slugged it out, Fletcher, Dearing, and MacMurray maintained a respectful silence. The Washington conference was getting off to a lively start.

Nothing was resolved. Reuben left the meeting as wary as ever, hedging his own participation with conditions. He would not take on the general supervision of preparations, he said, unless the conference were moved back to the following spring; if the State Department insisted upon a November target, he would "undertake any specific job that I felt I could satisfactorily accomplish."[50] But after strolling out of the secretary's office, Reuben's three friends resumed their arm-twisting. That they had an arms conference on their hands and did not know what to do with it was plain enough, and Reuben had every wish to help them out. Still, facts were facts. "I am not sure how anxious—if indeed he is anxious at all—Hughes is to have me undertake the work," Reuben reported to Knox.[51] And Reuben's feeling was mutual.

ix

So it may have been at something like the toss of a coin that Reuben finally elected to throw in with Hughes and the arms conference. Before leaving Washington for a return back to Utah, he

312

prepared a fifteen-page memorandum for Dearing in which he outlined general modes of attack. He included a sketch of the conference organization, the duties of the various officers, and a description
of their powers and functions. Reuben also paid heed to political
considerations. In order to place the right people on the right committees with the right results in view, he said, the permanent chairman (Hughes) would have to command inside knowledge of the
views and biases of all the delegates. Thus, there would have to be a
meticulous agenda of subjects, a definite roster of participants, and
time enough for exhaustive research. If this was going to be a Reuben Clark job, it would have to be accomplished in the Reuben
Clark way.[52]

Reuben also began to formulate substantive proposals, deciding
what the conference should and should not attempt to consider. On
the question of armaments he was still polemical. Problems dealing
with the size of armaments—Hughes's concern—were inevitable, he
allowed, and he listed out nine factors for tentative deliberation. But
when he came to the character of armaments—his own concern—
Reuben came alight with missionary purpose. "There is nothing that
can justify this government in a failure to exercise every power and
influence at its command to curtail the use of all these in-
strumentalities insofar as they affect non-combatants," he said. "No
effort must be spared to regain for the world the ground lost during
the last war in this connection."[53]

Persuasive though this may have been, it failed to persuade the
secretary of state. After all, if rules were made to be broken, as
Hughes believed, there was no point in laboriously refining them.
On the other hand, anyone could count battleships; and for that reason an agreement based upon sheer numbers must necessarily be
honored. But Hughes did not want to forfeit Reuben's services any
more than Dearing and the others did, so he told the press that the
conference would have to revise the rules of war.[54] This was mostly a
sham. Soon Dearing was delicately apprising Reuben of an adverse
decision. "My hunch is," he said, "that you will not be asked to do
much on the Limitation of Armament side."[55]

x

On the Far Eastern side, though, Reuben was to be kept more
than busy. For all his experience in hemispheric relations, he was also

regarded as an expert in East Asian affairs. He had worked on the Chinese financial consortia back in the Taft administration, had advised the Japanese legation on matters of American policy, and was repeatedly mentioned as a possible minister to the Orient.[56] More importantly, he had maintained an active and abiding interest in the relations between China and Japan—relations that added up to the "Far Eastern problem."

Soon after the war had broken out in August of 1914, Reuben, with clear prescience, had drafted a resolution to Congress reaffirming the territorial integrity of China, the principle of the Open Door, and the status quo in the western Pacific. Japan, as he knew, would take over the German concessions in China and use them as a bar against western influence; it would then seize the German Pacific islands and probably fortify them. By war's end the western Pacific would be a Japanese lake—which is exactly what it became.[57]

This resolution had died in committee, but Reuben had taken another tack. In November of 1914 he had proposed a draft treaty between the United States, England, and Japan, the purpose of which was to secure the same ends as the resolution. In Article I each of the three signatories was to recognize all titles and possessions of the others and agree not to interfere in the same. In Article II they were to agree, in the event of an external threat, "to consider together" the steps which should be taken for common defense. The proposed treaty had been no more fortunate politically than the proposed resolution, but it was to become vastly more important later on. It was the first blueprint of the Washington conference, and it fixed the design of the final settlement with mathematical precision.[58]

Shades of the earlier resolution and treaty were to be found in the proposals that Reuben now submitted to Dearing. The integrity of China must be respected and the Open Door kept open, he affirmed. There must be some sort of a status quo in the Pacific and the status quo must be formally recognized. Finally, there must be an agreement among the signatories "to concert measures" against hostile third parties. Reuben, of course, did not know what the British might propose at the conference or what the Japanese might demand. The whole business of the Anglo-Japanese alliance was yet to be worked through. He was reasonably certain, however, that if agreement could be reached on these broad principles the rest would somehow fall into place.[59]

Dearing and MacMurray were pleased: this was exactly the sort of groundwork they had hoped to lay. They urged the Mormon lawyer to return to Washington posthaste and fill in the details. But Reuben, back in the clear air of the West, was rapidly regaining his old mistrust.[60] Associate legal advisors to the conference were now being considered, and he was hardly encouraged by the tentative appointments. Fred K. Nielsen, Chandler Anderson, and, alas, James Brown Scott were among them.[61] Two of them—Nielsen and Scott—had helped draft the Treaty of Versailles, and all three had actively promoted it. "I think it would be well in case I am asked to come," Reuben said coyly, "to see that the Secretary really senses that I am coming and the purpose thereof, so that, arriving there, I shall not be as Othello—without an occupation."[62] Dearing carried this missive to his boss, and Hughes obligingly telegraphed another personal request for Reuben's appearance.[63]

xi

Reuben Clark left for Washington and the arms conference in early September, this time with his family.[64] On the fifteenth he was officially appointed special counsel for the Department of State at $7,500 per annum and told to go to work.[65] Even though he had earlier renounced the role of general supervisor (when the conference was moved up to November) he wound up stuck with it anyway. "It may be necessary," said Dearing adroitly, "to make just exactly the same preparation that should have been made in an ideal situation beforehand, during the process of the negotiations themselves."[66] Fortunately Reuben Clark and John MacMurray struck it off from the beginning. MacMurray was a career diplomat with broad experience in Far Eastern affairs, and the two of them generally spoke the same language. Nonetheless MacMurray deferred to Clark in substantive matters—as though he had been given custody of a precious bird that might fly away at any moment.

The first item of business was to pull together assorted work papers and begin firming up plans. On the Far Eastern problem there was little of substance to add to the structure Reuben had already

315

blocked out, although numberless details needed tucking into place. Surveying them, the Utah lawyer was struck by the awesome responsibility before him. "To the utmost possible extent," he penned on one heading, "causes of war with the Orient must be eliminated."[67] Reuben well knew how deep those causes ran. His friend Huntington Wilson had once nearly been run down in the streets of Tokyo by a trio of mounted samurai, and Reuben had come to share his Nipponophobia.[68] Yet Reuben had worked for the Japanese too, and he believed that he could see the world as they did. He would meet them halfway. He would acknowledge, for example, their claim to a special relationship with China, if such a relationship could be defined and agreed upon. He would not waste time punishing "individual wrongs of the past" but would concentrate on existing and future evils. He would carefully distinguish between the necessary and the desirable, remembering that the only real necessity was the security of the United States.[69]

On the side of arms limitation, Reuben was far from ready to throw in the towel. He proposed four fundamental elements to the arms problem and produced a draft article for each. The first sought to "outlaw" offensive war entirely.* The second and third dealt respectively with Charles Evans Hughes's and his own approaches to arms limitation. With the Hughes approach—the limitation of size—Reuben proposed a budgetary limitation in place of a direct quota on armaments, cutting the dollar volume of the arms race roughly in half. With his own approach—the limitation of weapon types—Reuben proceeded to write submarines, aircraft, and poison gases out of the military lexicon. "The future war must be fought by army against army," he wrote vehemently, "not army against people."[70] But Secretary Hughes paid scant attention. He was, as Dearing gingerly put it, "[doing] some and possibly a good deal of the necessary preparation himself."[71]

The fourth of Reuben's draft articles was to come in handy, but not for the cause of arms limitation. It dealt with what he called the sanction, the means of enforcing a collective agreement.[72] Considering such a problem five years earlier would have posed no particu-

---

*See pp. 326–28.

lar difficulty for the special counsel, but in the aftermath of the League controversy everything was changed. Any sanction that was effective would have to involve some form of military alliance, and any alliance would smack of the League. Yet on the other hand, Japan was not about to give up her naval program, much less the British alliance, for nothing; she had to have some guarantees. So it was a question of how far one dared venture toward the odious methods of the League in order to win an agreement. This was precisely the sort of dilemma Reuben had hoped to avoid.

In the end, as with countless statesmen before him, Reuben Clark laid aside his ideological purity and compromised. As sanction for the arms limitation treaty, he proposed "that in case of the violation thereof by any power, signatory or non-signatory hereof, [the signatories] will communicate with one another fully and frankly, and will consult and consider in common as to the means to be taken."[73] While falling short of the letter, this language was eerily suggestive of the spirit of alliance. It was not the League of Nations, to be sure; but neither was it isolationism.

Beyond the preparation on substantive issues, Clark and Mac-Murray undertook to plan out the entire conference. They had to set up an organization, describe titles, apportion powers, staff committees, schedule meetings, map out agenda, arrange for minutes, provide translations, prescribe rules, detail procedures, supervise voting, spell out protocol, and see to it that everything was graced with pomp and circumstance.[74] With such intricacies Reuben was fully at home. He even found time to lecture the American delegation on the imponderables of its task.[75] Since that delegation included such Democrats as Oscar Underwood, such internationalists as Elihu Root, and such chameleons as Henry Cabot Lodge, Reuben doubtless believed the briefing to be requisite.

xii

The Washington Conference on Arms Limitation and the Far East got underway on November 12. Nine nations were represented in the deliberations, but the real agreement was to be hammered out among the Big Four. Foreign ministers of the four cut impressive figures in their diplomatic attire: Prince Tokugawa of Japan, squat and bespectacled; Astride Briand of France, stoop-shouldered and smiling; Arthur James Balfour of Great Britain, affable and debonaire; and, towering over them all in both stature and influence, Charles Evans Hughes of the United States. This was his show and he intended to make the most of it.[76]

The secretary lost no time in getting started. Before a plenary session he began making what seemed like the usual introductory remarks. Delegates were still shuffling into their places and nodding to acquaintances. Before they realized what was happening, Hughes had calmly offered to destroy thirty battleships in the American navy and was proceeding to dismantle the British and Japanese. The diplomats sat in stunned silence while he ticked off names and classes of ships as casually as the inventory of a pantry, some sixty-six in all. In thirty-five minutes, as one British observer put it, Hughes did more naval damage "than all the admirals of the world."[77]

While the delegates cheered and threw their hats into the air, Reuben Clark managed only polite applause. This, after all, signaled his own personal defeat on arms limitation. He believed that the time had been ripe for bridling the horrors of scientific destruction, and with Hughes's brilliant performance it slipped by unnoticed. When next the world would turn attention to the outright curtailment of weaponry, mustard gas and dirigibles would seem quaint—and the issue would be one of human survival.

Yet this was unquestionably arms limitation, and the Americans were obviously serious about it. Whether or not it could be made to stick was another matter, however—one that had to be settled in committee. The difficulty was the Anglo-Japanese alliance. Balfour soon made it known that the alliance was expendable if a workable substitute could be found to mollify the Japanese.[78] Both he and Tokugawa looked to the American secretary of state for concrete proposals—and as it happened, Hughes had some proposals to make. Reuben Clark sat quietly beside the secretary all the while. As special assistant he attended dozens of sessions of the conference—including the secret ones where he and Hughes alone represented the United States[79]—but as he reported to friends, there was nothing to do but shuffle papers and look important.[80] However, the papers he shuffled and occasionally passed to the secretary of state were no mere parcels of red tape. They represented the hard-wrought product of Reuben's

Far Eastern experience—and one at a time they provided the keys to the conference.

xiii

The Washington treaties of 1921 ended the arms race, stabilized the western Pacific, and brought hope to a devastated world. A five-power treaty, after reducing the size of naval armaments, established a 5-5-3 ratio of capital ship tonnage among the United States, Great Britain, and Japan; set a holiday of ten years on the construction of capital ships; and froze the status quo in Pacific fortifications. Accompanying this was a nine-power treaty binding all signatories to respect the integrity of China and to uphold the Open Door. And making these achievements possible was the four-power treaty. This was the document that officially abrogated the Anglo-Japanese Treaty of Alliance. In place of the alliance the new treaty substituted an arrangement whereby all four powers, in the case of a dispute among themselves, would agree to refer it to a conference, and in the case of an outside attack would "consult together" to determine the appropriate response.[81] In the collective bargain everyone gave up something: Great Britain its historic naval supremacy, Japan the Anglo-Japanese alliance, and the United States the right to fortify Pacific possessions. There were those who later maintained that the United States gave up too much, especially after Japan surreptitiously fortified her own islands, slammed shut the Open Door, and then wiped out the American fleet at Pearl Harbor. In each instance the Japanese played falsely, as doubtless they would have done without the Washington agreements—such were the hazards of history. In debating with Reuben, Hughes had said that laws were made to be broken; he eventually learned that treaties were made to be broken as well.

Reuben Clark made some discoveries of his own. An especially painful one was the difference between being the critic on the outside, who is true only to abstract principle, and the policymaker on the inside, who must weigh hard realities as well. His consulting arrangement with the Japanese did not win favor with Senator Borah and the irreconcilables, who straightaway denounced it as an "entangling alliance" and threatened to call up the Battalion of Death.[82]

Henry Cabot Lodge—who in Reuben's presence had harrumphed loudly about "some legal experts [who] were shouldering their way in" on the substantive discussions—found himself with the unhappy task of steering the four-power treaty through the Senate.[83] He wound up doing graceful acrobatics on the subject of commitments to use force, and he narrowly missed having the treaty blocked. "Who would have thought it," remarked one bitter-ender. "Senator Lodge is the father of a baby League of Nations."[84] The same might have been said of J. Reuben Clark.

Conversely, Reuben came to have a considerably higher degree of respect for those on the inside who must make the hard choices. With Charles Evans Hughes in particular he parted friends. "My dear Mr. Secretary," he wrote,

> Allow me a personal word to express my congratulations to you personally for the great achievements of the Conference. For more than 300 years, men of authority in and among the nations have unavailingly sought to secure an agreement to limit the armament of great nations. It has been vouchsafed to you to negotiate and conclude such an arrangement. Rarely does it come to any nation to lead the way in so great a movement, and fortunate is he who is so placed as to lead his nation in such a work.[85]

And the congratulation was returned. "You brought to the task," Hughes replied,

> not only the great advantage of your ability and aptitude and your experience as a former Solicitor of the Department, but an energy and sympathy with the objects we were trying to attain which made your association with our work a matter of the utmost personal satisfaction on my part.[86]

Such remarks grew naturally out of the conference's euphoric conclusion. The Washington conference and its treaties were acclaimed as the diplomatic achievement of the century. Japan, suddenly a nation of light, retracted the most onerous of its twenty-one demands, returned Shantung to the Chinese, and withdrew from Siberia. The United States and Great Britain gratefully shelved their programs for naval expansion and scrapped dozens of their existing heavy ships. One of them, the *Baltimore,* was towed out into the Atlantic and sunk by Captain Billy Mitchell, who wished to demonstrate what an enemy could do to the American navy with aerial bombing. The enemy he had in mind was Japan.[87]

320

Only with time and perspective did it become apparent that military might had *not* been transformed by the Washington conference. Deep in their hearts, both Charles Evans Hughes and J. Reuben Clark, Jr., knew it would not be. Still, there was something that kept bidding them to try. When Hughes had told his special counsel that rules were made to be broken, the latter had given the only response that modern man, ever on the edge of the abyss, could give.

I replied that the fact that ordinary treaties were broken did not and could not keep us from making other treaties on the same matters; and that the mere fact that the rules of war were broken ought not and must not keep us from making new rules.[88]

That was the essence of J. Reuben Clark.

Chapter 18

THE COURT FIGHT

There was something neatly symmetrical in the fact that Reuben Clark's career as crusader ended as it began, on the subject of world judiciary. For no sooner had the League of Nations been defeated in the United States than internationalists took up the cry for affiliation with the World Court. This was the same court that Scott and Root had envisioned two decades earlier, but it had come into being under the auspices of the League of Nations.[1] It sat at the Hague but was distinguished from the old Hague court, still in existence, as a court of law rather than a court of arbitration. Reuben, of course, had long ago formed his opinion about world courts in general; and this court was a child of the League. His course was set.

The participants were familiar. Root, more gaunt and gray than ever, was the acknowledged leader of the pro-court forces, and James Brown Scott was still his redoubtable lieutenant. Their support was broadly based. In one way or another, the entire founding generation of Republican internationalists took part in the court fight, attempting, as they said, to get the foreign policy of their party back on the rails. But the old irreconcilables were still around too. Their acknowledged leader was still Senator Borah, now something of a legend.[2] When it was remarked one day that Borah had been seen cantering through the park, President Coolidge had unsmilingly replied, "I'm surprised he was willing to go along with the horse."[3]

The one face that was missing was Philander Knox's. On the night of October 12, 1921, the Clarks, in Washington for the arms conference, were awakened by the ringing of the telephone. Seconds later Reuben was rushing about, throwing on his clothes.

"Daddy," cried Marianne, "it isn't a matter of life and death."

"That's exactly what it may be," he replied, and hurried off into the night. Senator Knox had collapsed at his home and now lay at the point of death. As Reuben drove through the misty darkness, he could think of nothing but how well his friend had appeared a few days before.[4]

Earlier that afternoon, however, when Fred Dearing had visited Knox's office, the senator had seemed drawn and pale. They had discussed business for a few minutes and then drifted onto the subject of Reuben Clark. In an uncharacteristic burst of emotion, Knox had declared the warmest regard for Reuben, vowing that the Utah Mormon should have been chief justice—and would have been if Knox had been president—and ended by expressing the hope that Reuben would soon join him in the Senate. As Dearing turned to leave, the senator, ashen-faced, asked him to convey his "affection and admiration" to Reuben personally.[5] A few hours later he lay dead.

As Reuben helped bear the casket to its resting place, the day was solemn indeed. Philander Knox had been more than a friend—he had been Reuben's access to power. By means of that access, Reuben's ideas had a way of turning up in the halls of Congress or in the Oval Office itself. Clark and Knox had made a curious pair—the workhorse and the bon vivant—but precisely for that reason they had been effective. At times they had functioned as a political party of two, yet in carrying forward their ideas they had compared favorably to the national organizations. Knox was gone now, and the national organizations were trending ominously toward accommodation with the League. In a few months, for example, the Harding administration, under the leadership of the forceful Hughes, had steadily improved its relations with the League: sending observers to Geneva, participating in the League's humanitarian causes, and finally preparing to join the League-sponsored World Court.[6] Reuben departed from the cemetery in the blackest of despair: the party of two had been cut in half—and just when a new fight was brewing.

ii

To the mind of Charles Evans Hughes, membership in the World Court was a natural outgrowth of the old Republican peace program. After all, no less a grand old man than Elihu Root had traveled personally to the Hague to organize the court, and no less a legal stalwart than John Bassett Moore had been elected among its first judges. Moreover, the American people appeared to support the court almost overwhelmingly. They seemed convinced that it was truly a *world* court with its own separate identity, and not merely the *League* court detractors labeled it. The very mention of its name evoked the days of Hague conferences and arbitration treaties.[7]

Hughes was also a political man and one possessed of common sense. So in February of 1923, when he made his recommendations public, he carefully hedged his advocacy for the World Court with four reservations—a magic term, as he had learned—designed to certify that the court and the League of Nations would continue to remain separate. Armed with the Hughes reservations, President Harding decided to take the plunge. On February 24, in a message to the Senate, he formally proposed U.S. adherence to the World Court.[8]

The reaction was instantaneous. Borah, Brandegee, Johnson, and Moses were all still sitting on the Foreign Relations Committee; Lodge had now swung over to full irreconcilability; and two recent arrivals, Harry S. New (Republican, Indiana) and John K. Shields (Democrat, Tennessee), had joined irreconcilable ranks. As with a single voice they charged that the World Court was a "League court" and a "back door" to the League itself. In their long war with Wilson these critics had perfected weapons to the caliber of their accusations, and in the spring of 1923 these were swung into position like naval cannon.

Reuben Clark accepted the back-door thesis of the irreconcilables. He saw the World Court as a harbinger of the League. Beyond this he retained all of his old doubts about international judiciary per se. Without compulsory jurisdiction, without a settled body of law, and without enforceable judgments, any tribunal would operate in a hit-or-miss fashion—the new World Court quite as much as the old Hague court. Reuben thought the whole idea was wrongheaded.

Reuben was not content, however, to say so in the same old prosaic way. He had learned a good deal from the irreconcilables in the matter of battle tactics. One of their favorite ploys was the so-called red herring technique, whereby a cause would be defeated by drawing away its support in favor of an attractive but insubstantial competitor—the same way in which hounds may be drawn away from a fox's trail by the strong smell of a red herring. In the ensuing battle over the World Court, Reuben was to propose or endorse a number of alternative court schemes, some of which went further than the World Court itself (and even further than the League of Nations) toward compromising American sovereignty. These were the red herrings. If taken seriously they hopelessly confuse the question of what Reuben actually believed. In truth, he never wavered in his original conviction that the cause of judicial settlement was best served by compulsory arbitration treaties, the codification of international law, and the existing court at the Hague.

iii

As the irreconcilable senators readied their guns, so too did Reuben. There was scarcely time to pause over the fact that he was once more abandoning the Harding administration and the Republican mainstream, but he had come to agree with Knox that "liberty of action" was a "much more interesting and valuable asset."[10] Reuben rummaged through his files and turned up an old draft article he had written back in 1920. At that time Chandler Anderson had published an enthusiastic essay on the world-court movement in the *North American Review,* and Reuben had been so incensed by it that he had zipped off one of his own.[11] Now, as he blew the dust from the folder, he must have been struck anew by the loss of Senator Knox. In the old days the article would have been handily trimmed and presented through Knox to the Senate. The crusader must now find a new mouthpiece. He sat down at the typewriter and pounded out a cover letter. Then, inserting letter and manuscript into a manila envelope, he addressed it to Senator William E. Borah and sent it off.[12]

The article contained Reuben's own philosophy of judicial settlement. It described the operation of compulsory jurisdiction and enforceable sanctions and pointed out that even lacking these the existing Hague court had "never yet failed fully."[13] Borah was pleased. He had remembered Reuben's name from conversations with Knox and therefore, as he said, had "double confidence" in the material received.[14] A short time later, in a speech in New York, Borah touched upon several of Reuben's ideas.[15]

Yet an association with Senator Borah would never replace the old Knox-Clark alliance. Impatiently, Reuben cast about for a new lever. Soon he was writing to the president himself. "I think it will prove unfortunate," he said of the Root-Scott campaign, "if the devouring ambition for fame of an old man (already richly honored by his country) and of his subservient satellite, has brought about so hazardous a thing as a desire for, or belief in the wisdom of, any sort of affiliation with the League of Nations."[16] Harding, like Borah, wrote back politely but he could do little more than defend his own policy.[17]

iv

It was at this point, and with no substantial success yet, that Reuben came into contact with Salmon O. Levinson. Levinson was a wealthy Chicago businessman, a lawyer, and a public-spirited citizen. Short and stocky, with a freckled face and vigorous growth of hair, he had the visual aspect of a human dynamo and the energy to go along with it. His amazing and entirely improbable career in American diplomacy mushroomed out of a single compelling, and yet not really persuasive, idea: that war, like robbery or murder, could be brought under control by the simple expedient of making it illegal. On December 9, 1921, Levinson gave a dinner party in his Chicago home, and before the night was over the American Committee for the Outlawry of War had come into being.[18]

Levinson made converts. John Dewey began grinding out murky essays on outlawry for the *New Republic*. Colonel Raymond Robbins, a powerhouse in his own right, began spreading the Levinson gospel among women's groups and civic organizations. And a host of other figures in business and politics took up the cry. One early proselyte had been Philander Knox, who had helped Levinson draft up a formal "Plan to Outlaw War." The plan included a declaration "that aggressive war is an international crime," an explicit code of international law, a court capable of enforcing the code, and a promise by the nations to mend their ways. The only sanction was to be moral force.[19]

Reuben had known about outlawry and had paid occasional lip service to it himself.[20] Nevertheless, he did not take it seriously. He doubted the deterrent value of moral force, especially with the "criminal nations," and placed his own faith in good old-fashioned guns and bullets. "If war is to be abolished," he said dryly, "it must be by virtue of . . . an overwhelming military force."[21] Still, in the spring of 1923 J. Reuben Clark took up with Salmon O. Levinson and the outlawry movement, and by May 3 he had become chairman of the executive committee of the New York Committee for the Outlawry of War.[22] Consciously or otherwise he was following the lead of Senator Borah—a consummate red-herringist—who himself had suddenly embraced the Levinson plan and proposed its adoption to Congress.[23]

The New York committee was delighted to come by someone of Reuben Clark's stature. He was only to be in the East temporarily, as he explained, but the outlawry people would take him on any terms. Indeed, less than a week after his appointment Reuben received a letter from Levinson himself, pleased and flattered about the new recruit. "You see," he bubbled, "our connecting link, Knox, gave me a super-abundance of confidence in you."[24] Levinson wanted a personal encounter with Reuben Clark, and one was arranged for late May at the home of Mrs. Willard Straight. It turned out to be something of a social event (Reuben was in danger of becoming the newest darling of the tea circuit) and might have been a delightful experience for everyone had the Utah lawyer not hauled out a typewritten manifesto and thrust it unceremoniously into Levinson's hands. Taken aback, the father of outlawry sat down and plowed through the document. If he expected a denunciation of war, he must have been surprised, for the subject under review seemed rather to be the League of Nations.

In essence, the League of Nations is, by intention and by actual operation, a military alliance among the Great Powers of Western Europe which, with their possessions and dominions and the flattered weak and small powers of the world, have regrouped themselves in a new "balance of power" arrangement. The real purpose of this alliance is to make secure to themselves the world-wide territorial, strategic, political, economic, and financial gains with which, through the intervention of the United States, they were able to enrich themselves at the end of the Great War.[25]

Five more paragraphs of this fusillade continued before Levinson discovered the real point. "Let proponents of this plan," said Reuben to the outlawryists, "frankly announce this as a plan for the whole world, not for a part of the world, and let them announce it as a substitute plan for the present League of Nations."

Salmon O. Levinson, who knew little about red herrings, was puzzled. After all, his business was outlawry, not irreconcilability. Yet Clark had gone on to discuss codification and compulsory jurisdiction with such self-assurance that Levinson was carried along. "Omitting details of possible differences," he wrote after a few days of reflection, "I am so impressed with your extraordinary ability in international affairs that I am all for you for Secretary of State."[26]

v

Reuben did not tarry long with the outlawry movement; he was anxious to mount an attack of his own. After more rummaging through his files he came up with another old memorandum, this one dated in 1910 and devoted, almost idly, to the conception of a worldwide system of international courts.[27] A product of the halcyon days before the world war, this system, with its various modes of jurisdiction and tiers of appellate review, seemed antediluvian in 1923. But like outlawry, it was a positive alternative to the present World Court and hence a possible diversion. Reuben tinkered with the plan and, as he may have thought, brought it up to date. His final design included three classes of courts. The first was the Hague court, which would continue to arbitrate cases as it had. The second was "courts of first instance," which would be constituted each time a dispute arose, would consist of three judges (representing the two litigants and a neutral), and would sit at the capital of the defendant nation. And finally there would be a supreme court composed of eleven judges sitting at the Hague.[28]

Except in complexity, this court plan did not differ materially from the World Court. It still depended on existing international law, and it still committed decisions into the hands of foreigners. Judged by the standards that Reuben himself had laid down, his own scheme would have been a failure all around. But it had the advantage of being highly discussable. As long as people were discussing it, they might not be discussing something else.

Reuben could have sent the court plan to Senator Borah or even one of the journals of opinion. Instead he mailed it off to the president.[29] In his two years in office Harding had shown himself abundantly open to persuasion; if he now so much as bowed toward the

Clark court plan, his commitment to the existing World Court might collapse in confusion. The manuscript reached the White House at an inopportune moment, just as the president was preparing to leave for Alaska and the West Coast. "I am taking it with me in my travels," he wrote in reply, "for a more leisurely study than I can give amid the rush of preparation."[30] Harding never returned. He suffered an undiagnosed illness in Seattle and died a few days later in San Francisco.

vi

Calvin Coolidge was now president, but Charles Evans Hughes was still secretary of state and American foreign policy remained unchanged. The court fight lurched on. Americans wanted more than ever to be affiliated with the World Court and fairly smothered Congress with petitions. The Edward W. Bok National Peace Contest, offering $100,000 to the person submitting the best proposal for peace, was won by an elderly New Yorker who urged immediate entry into the World Court.[31] Both political parties nailed pro-court planks onto their 1924 platforms, making the issue wholly bipartisan. Yet the irreconcilables too were still full of fight. They knew all the legislative passageways and managed to block off the crucial ones. Borah, having succeeded Lodge as chairman of the Foreign Relations Committee, systematically balked and stalled month in and month out while confederates on the Senate floor depicted scenarios of judicial tyranny and called out the tongue-twisting names of World Court judges.[32]

Reuben himself was far from ready to quit. Although he read portents of the court situation with alarm, he was more convinced than ever that his stand was the right one. As if in confirmation, Fred Dearing, now minister to Belgium, wrote from Brussels and took back everything he had said about Reuben's opposition to the League. "Indeed," he said,

it seems to me almost like clairvoyancy or something superhuman that you should have seen and have gauged so clearly what the effects of the damn foolishness at Paris would be. The thing comes back to me again and again, and every time with fresh force, and in your own case, it seems to me all the more remarkable, on account of the fact that you have never been in this part of the world.[33]

Of course Reuben, who had never been deterred by the doubts of his friends, could gain little satisfaction from their recantations. He filed the letter and determinedly pushed on.

He went back to the court scheme he had sent to President Harding and gussied it up still more. Now, on top of the Hague court, courts of first instance, and a supreme court, he added nothing less than a "world congress." The powers of the congress would be strictly recommendatory, he ventured, but it would have special charge of administering a global treaty to outlaw war. Signatories who subsequently waged aggressive war would be accountable to the congress. They might have to give up all conquests of the war, pay its costs, reimburse victims for its damages, and deliver to the world congress for trial and punishment those of its authorities who were responsible. Reuben even allowed the offending nation

to have applied against it, in cases of great gravity where the laws of war had been broken, the doctrines of retortion and reprisal, the World Congress determining the extent to which these doctrines should be applied.[34]

At this point, of course, the world congress of J. Reuben Clark was indistinguishable from the League of Nations.

Nevertheless, it offered attractions for everyone. There was something for the outlawryists, something for the court people, and something for the Leaguers—a whole catch of red herrings. Reuben polished off the presentation with smooth phrases about crystallizing public sentiment against war and giving form to the moral forces of the world—ideas he had pointedly rejected in a memorandum for Senator New—and sent it off to the religious journal *Unity*.[35] So alluring a piece could hardly have escaped publication; the October 4 issue of *Unity* presented "The Pacific Settlement of International Disputes" with considerable fanfare.

The response was explosively enthusiastic. "The October 4th issue," reported the editors, "was given a circulation unprecedented in the history of our paper."

Several thousands of special copies were printed, and distributed to Senators, representatives, distinguished public men, clergymen, professors, churches, peace societies, newspapers and magazines in this country and abroad. Widely varying comments are now coming in, most of them of a decisively encouraging character.[36]

Among these missives was one from Levinson, who praised the proposal as "superb."

I had a long conference with Senator Borah in Washington recently [Levinson continued]. He told me in confidence that the President had asked him about your qualifications as Ambassador to Mexico and that he had praised them most highly. I trust this will not mean that you will be lost to our cause as a valuable actor in this most important international drama. However, as I told you before, I am for you for everything.[37]

Soon other editors began cashing in on the new peace bonanza. The *Christian Science Monitor* called it a "rational and constructive" program and urged all factions of the peace movement to unite behind it.[38] In December, both the *Advocate of Peace* of the APS and the *Deseret News* in Salt Lake City reprinted the article in full.[39] That same month *Unity* published a symposium of pro and con responses to it.[40] Reuben found the congratulatories amusing in view of his own insincere purpose. But when John A. Widtsoe of the LDS Council of the Twelve congratulated him, the amusement faded.

I *did* enjoy the article, very, very much. At last I am satisfied. Occasionally when I have talked with you I have felt that you saw the flaws and impossibilities of world relations until I wondered if you thot [*sic*] reconstruction impossible—and civilization doomed! Now I can see that you are a Builder as well as an analyst, and I am glad.[41]

vii

So passed the weeks and months and finally the years, and still there was no decision on the World Court. Senator Borah and the irreconcilables carried on their relay of obstruction and oratory in Congress while pro- and anti-court forces skirmished indecisively in the press. Reuben Clark slogged ahead with his own guerrilla war. "I sometimes have the feeling that it is the old story of Canute bidding the waves to keep back," he wrote to Dearing wearily. "However," he added, "I am out in front of the waves."[42] Every speaking opportunity offered a fresh chance to pepper away at the court. To a gathering of Republicans, in February of 1925, he called the court "a mere creature of the League, subject not only to its control, but to its actual direction."[43] To the Star Legion, a week later, he pointed out that "America's love for the peaceful adjustment of international disputes needs no vindication."

Our first treaty with the mother country after the treaty of peace, provided for the arbitration of outstanding disputes between the two countries,—for boundary disputes and mutual claims of citizens. From that time until the present, America has always stood for this great principle. The actual arbitration by the United States and Great Britain of the latter's neutrality during the Civil War—the Geneva Arbitration—and the negotiation and signature of the Olney-Pauncefote treaty, and the Knox-Bryce treaty, are achievements unequalled by any other two powers in all recorded time.[44]

Yet Reuben knew he was marking time. National discourse on the subject of the World Court had plainly reached a deadlock, and neither side could seem to budge the other. Something had to be done to break out of the stalemate and it had to be done soon, for time was on the side of the court. Salmon Levinson and the outlawryists were still active and badgering Reuben to bear a hand in their cause. By the spring of 1925 he had decided that, however futile their ultimate goal, the outlawryists alone stood a chance of pushing the Coolidge administration off dead center and away from the World Court. "Not that I think that an International Convention declaring aggressive war to be a crime would actually do away with war," he confided to Dearing in February, but it might lead toward "an actual World Court" and a codification of international law. "In addition to these proposals having real merit," he said, "they are perhaps the only effective foil to our participation in the League World Court."[45]

Accordingly, the next time Levinson came around Reuben agreed to participate. He drew up a long memorandum, the purpose of which was to help the outlawryists square their obsession with diplomatic realities. "I am aware that the material which I am sending is not so wholly and completely altruistic as you might like it," he admitted in a cover letter, "but altruism like charity begins at home."[46] Patronizingly, the memorandum paused over such questions as whether in the post-outlawry millennium the United States ought to divest itself of its insular possessions, alter its Constitution, or settle back into economic lethargy. (Reuben's advice was negative on all three.) Despite its tongue-in-cheek tone, the document pursued a serious purpose and may well have achieved it. Reuben

332

wanted the outlawryists to speak credibly and responsibly when they laid their proposals before the president. And the president, who eventually saw the memorandum in some form, was apparently impressed. With increasing seriousness he began taking up the cause of outlawry himself.

viii

And in the final analysis, Levinson and the outlawryists may have had much to do with defeating the court. They provided an alternative form of Republican peace activity when movement toward the court suddenly became untenable. But the more immediate cause of the court's defeat was John Bassett Moore. He had been among the first of the new tribunal's judges, elected in 1921. The solid Anglo-Saxon name and the reputation behind it were good seasoning in a roster that included Didrik Galtrup, Gjedde Nayholm, Dionisco Anzilotti, Yorozu Oda, and Wang Ch'ung-hui; and the purpose of his election was frankly propagandistic. For that reason Reuben had been doubly shattered by it. Not only had Moore gone over to the court, he had gone over specifically as a Judas goat to lead the country behind him.

But once in the court, Moore was precisely the person to apprehend its shortcomings. He was particularly disconcerted by the court's practice of issuing advisory opinions on international legal questions. Since advisory opinions were not addressed to specific controversies, they were not bitterly contested and could be rendered almost painlessly; yet on the strength of such dicta foreign ministries might base far-reaching decisions of policy. John Bassett Moore, the lawyer's lawyer, became uneasy about advisory opinions—especially as they might affect the United States. In the fall of 1925 he assisted senators in drafting a fifth reservation to accompany the four Hughes had proposed; this would prohibit the court from issuing advisory opinions on any matter affecting U.S. interests without explicit American approval. It was the adoption of the Moore reservation at the end of December that finally triggered a showdown on the Hughes plan to join the World Court.[47]

The ensuing discussion approached in tone and ferocity the earlier debates on the League. The irreconcilables, cornered at last, fought like lions. William Borah warned that the League of Nations was becoming "a gigantic world military machine." "We are going into the Court," cried Hiram Johnson, "because we are going to be taken into the League of Nations." James Reed took the Senate floor and read off the names of the World Court justices again. How would the United States, he asked, like to have its fate decided by Antonio Sanchez de Bustamente?[48]

Reuben Clark plunged into the fray. At the height of the Senate debate, he gave an interview to the *Washington Post* which opened up new avenues of discussion. In order to make matters fair in appointing court justices, he suggested, the United States ought to be allowed fifty-four votes, since its constituent states and territories were as autonomous locally as the seven voting members of the British Empire. The interview was a study in sophistry, but it pointed up a fundamental weakness of international organization: the distribution of power.[49]

Not all the sophistry in the world could save them, though. The bitter-enders were outnumbered and they knew it. When the vote finally came on January 7, the Hughes plan for joining the World Court roared through the Senate by a vote of seventy-six to seventeen, and American internationalists could rejoice at last. Before the United States officially became a member of the World Court, however, it was necessary for the other League members to accept the American reservations. This problem was assumed to be minor and technical, but a League conference called the following September decided otherwise. With the original Hughes reservations there was little difficulty, and even with the Moore reservation there was acceptance in principle. All the conference asked for was an assurance that the Moore reservation would not jeopardize the interests of the other signatories. But that was too much.[50]

The Coolidge administration, it seemed, was prepared for anything but a conditional response to its conditional offer—only Americans were supposed to make conditions. Moreover, the long years of the court fight had left the administration with no room for maneuver. Even though few concessions had actually been made by the Americans, irreconcilable rhetoric had created the impression that the United States had gone right to the brink and hence that no further concessions were possible. On November 11, 1926, eight years to the day after the European armistice, President Coolidge issued a statement. "I do not intend to ask the Senate to modify its position," he said. "I do not believe the Senate would take favorable action on any such proposal, and unless the requirements of the Senate resolution are met by the other interested nations I can see no prospect of this country adhering to the Court."[51]

ix

Incredible fortune! For Reuben Clark it was literally a divine intervention. Twenty years had passed since his own involvement with the world court had begun. He was unaware, perhaps, how much the battle of internationalism had altered his conception of things, how it had deepened the religious dimension of his life. Armageddon was not too strong a metaphor for what had transpired. As far as Reuben was concerned, the forces of good and evil had squared off and the former had emerged victorious. What had seemed to hang in the balance was nothing less than America itself. "I am so convinced," he had written,

that the world without the steadying physical, moral, and spiritual influence of America would stand in grave danger of reverting to a second Dark Ages, that I am perfectly sure in my own mind that the first duty of any foreign policy upon which we enter is the preservation of the United States and its form of Government with its free institutions. This to the end that this steadying influence to which I have referred shall be indefinitely perpetuated for the world's good. I do not believe this estimate is inspired either by national egotism, jingoism, or ignorance, but that it is a fair appraisal of the world's condition.[52]

Armageddon, of course, was to have been the final battle before the Millennium, and it was to have ushered in peace at last. On that much Reuben Clark and the internationalists agreed. They believed that if the question before them could be satisfactorily resolved there would never be another of comparable weight. They were both wrong. There would be more world war on the one hand and more world organization on the other, and both would eventually be transcended by the chilling discoveries of science. That, perhaps, was to be the real meaning of the term "Armageddon"—the battle of the future of which there would be neither winners nor survivors. Possibly, in some dim way, this was what Reuben Clark had feared all along. His vision for the future was dark—even awful—and his heart and mind lay in the old century of law and order and peace. The crusade would continue and the crusader would come to seem more and more out of his time. But his wish for the nobility and integrity of things past would never be outmoded.

PART IV

INTERLUDE
1913–26

THE LAWYER AS PRIVATE CITIZEN

Reuben Clark was torn between public and private life. He originally went to the East not to enter politics or government service, but to train as a mining lawyer, one who would settle comfortably in a small town like Grantsville, open a one-clerk law office, and devote much of his time to farming. Events seemed to conspire against that goal but they did not obliterate it. Reuben continued to aspire toward private pursuits as he continued to be drawn into public ones. His problem was that there was no achieving the private aspirations without a large outlay of capital, and capital was always a little beyond his reach. Government service, then, was a stopgap for Reuben, a means to an end. It was a way of marking time until the right tumblers fell into place and unlocked the future of his dreams. Time and again he promised self and family that he would give up the government work as soon as he hit upon the magic combination, but the right numbers never quite came around. And so, oddly, J. Reuben Clark went from one public responsibility to another because, in effect, he could not make it as a one-clerk lawyer in Grantsville.

Not understanding the ambition, friends could not appreciate Reuben's frustration. It was utterly baffling to them that a man of power and influence would lay such heavy stress on domestic fulfillment, on brother-sister relationships, on simple friendships, on political causes of the unremunerative sort, and ultimately on religion. Given the opportunities he had had and the things he had done, it seemed unbelievable that this man would shy away from the limelight. Yet shy away he did. In the thirteen years between 1913 and 1926 he made a concerted effort to abandon public service and expand the private dimension of his career instead. For admirers of J. Reuben Clark the attempt represented but an interlude. For the man himself it represented his nearest reach to success.

but the right number never quite came around. And so, oddly, J. Reuben Clark went from one public responsibility to another because, in effect, he could not make it as a one-clerk lawyer in Grantsville.

Not understanding the ambition, friends could not appreciate Reuben's frustration. It was utterly baffling to them that a man of power and influence would lay such heavy stress on domestic fulfillment, on brother-sister relationships, on simple friendships, on political causes of the unremunerative sort, and ultimately on religion. Given the opportunities he had had and the things he had done, it seemed unbelievable that this man would shy away from the limelight. Yet shy away he did. In the thirteen years between 1913 and 1926 he made a concerted effort to abandon public service and expand the private dimension of his career instead. For admirers of J. Reuben Clark the attempt represented but an interlude. For the man himself it represented his nearest reach to success.

Chapter 19

THE BEST BOLTS

When Reuben Clark resigned from the State Department in 1913, he did so to make money. "The next four or five years of my life must be made to yield the maximum possible return," he wrote to Luacine, "for by that time I shall have shot my best and strongest bolts."[1] The idea was not altogether mercenary. For years in the State Department the men who had surrounded Reuben—Joseph Grew, Robert Bacon, William Phillips, Huntington Wilson, Elihu Root, Philander Knox—had exemplified the man of independent means who, comfortably established on his own broad acres, could pursue at his leisure the important things of life. *Noblesse oblige,* the ideal was called, and it ran back a long way; but it harked most vividly to the old English gentry. No less an English gentleman than George Washington had been able to turn attention to public concerns be-

The Knox farm at Valley Forge: Among the mementos, an old dream.

cause opulent Mount Vernon saved him from the cares of money grubbing. Washington's portrait still looked down from the wall of Philander Knox's estate at Valley Forge. In a setting of Georgian architecture and rolling green fields Knox raised his prize trotters, tied fishing flies, immersed himself in literature, and guided the American State Department. What life could have been more gratifying?

Reuben Clark was dazzled. The Knox "farm" gave shape to his own ancestral ambitions. It also confirmed his departure from the solicitor's office, for government service offered no route to the big money. Indeed, while Reuben had slaved away for his meager forty-five hundred a year, Robert Lansing and Chandler Anderson had been making twice that amount as part-time consultants, and Elihu Root had left a law practice worth two hundred thousand dollars a year![2] And in Reuben's own experience had there not been the Alsop claim with its million-dollar prize? If only he had been a private lawyer at the time and working on the customary thirty percent contingency, he would have come by his El Dorado in a single stroke. This, then, was the direction to which Reuben's best bolts must now be aimed. He must establish a law practice of his own. He must find himself one more Alsop case—just one. And then he could return in triumph to the West, lay out his own "Knox farm," and address himself unhurriedly to the issues of his day. In 1913 Reuben was forty-two years old. He was racing against time.

ii

On April 3, 1913, a month after resigning as solicitor, Reuben announced the opening of his office. A broad desk, mahogany bookcases, a few hundred law books, and engraved cards that bore in swirling script the notice of his "general practice of law, municipal and international," planted him in the world of individual enterprise. "I am certainly delighted to be out of the Department and the stipendiary governmental service," he wrote to Mockahi brother Hugh Gibson. "I am happy, however," he added, "in drawing a salary from the government as Senior Counsel in the American-British Claims Commission."[3] Public service was already pulling him back.

Still, there was every reason to be hopeful. The American economy was growing rapidly and mobilizing to capture foreign markets.

The young lawyer with his own practice, 1913: A few hundred law books and some good connections.

Exports had virtually doubled since the turn of the century, and manufactured goods represented a growing fraction of the total.[4] The prospects here for a seasoned international lawyer were intoxicating indeed, and there was the added exhilaration of standing on one's own legs. "It is a marvelous thing how differently a man feels about the business that is *his own*," wrote Carr Morrow. "A fellow can work twice as hard and enjoy every hour of it when he knows that the business came to *him* because of his personality, and that its successful conclusion is going to redound to his own personal advantage and prestige."[5]

The office was on the seventh floor of the Hibbs Building at the corner of 15th and H Streets. Here, in the suite of Frederick E. Chapin's law firm, Reuben rented two and a half rooms for $72.92 a month plus telephone and towel service. The location was only three blocks from Old State and the proximity was not accidental; Reuben frankly aimed to draw business from his government connections in the manner of Lansing and Anderson. It was a good strategy: Philander Knox would direct a number of cases his way and his ties to the State Department and the American-British Claims Commission would also prove helpful.

As the practice took shape it turned out to be—like the solicitor experience—a kaleidoscope of disparate images tumbling over one an-

other. Reuben cleared away the diplomatic barriers for a photographic expedition to Asia. He helped organize a syndicate to finance public works projects in Cuba. He investigated a proposed new tariff on
creosote. He was retained by the Italian community in Nicaragua to
advance a claim for damages growing out of the Mena revolt. For a
large manufacturer of cotton spindles he engineered a merger, floated
a bond issue, and applied for patents in eighteen countries. He negotiated the sale of a cattle ranch in Colombia. He was hired by an
octogenarian soldier of fortune—who in his day had annexed Uganda
to Egypt and discovered the ultimate source of the Nile—to secure a
comfortable diplomatic sinecure for his old age. He checked to see if
the word "ELITE" had ever been trademarked for hair tonic. (It
had.) He investigated a claim by Prince Kamaludin of Brunei to
three islands off the coast of Borneo which, as the prince alleged,
had been wrongfully transferred to the United States as part of the
Philippines. He defended two Chicano gunrunners who had helped
to bring down the Madero government in Mexico. He drew up a
will for a Kansas City heiress who bequeathed one dollar to each of
her natural children and the rest of her fortune to a dissolute
adopted son. He detained a notorious Swiss flim-flam man until extradition authorities could put together a case on him. He worked to
indemnify the victims of the *Lusitania*. He assisted Philander Knox
in arguing before the Supreme Court the *cause célèbre* of Harry Kend-
all Thaw, whose escape from the Matteawan Asylum in New York
raised the question of whether it was a criminal act to break out of a
madhouse.[6]

   Reuben's cases ranged all the way from local to international and
from the mundane to the sublime. Of the local and mundane cases
there was occasionally a surfeit, and they seldom paid high dividends.
Ruben supervised the sale of a mamma-and-pappa grocery store for
ten dollars. From another client, who suffered a prolapsed uterus in a
D.C. trolley accident, he received as payment a copy of Nicolay and
Hay's *Life of Lincoln*. When he assisted an orphaned half-wit child to
secure a modest pension, he charged no fee at all, and a good number of cases brought in the same return.[7] In time Reuben took to
farming out the local business to his secretary, Donald DeLashmutt,
who had been one of his clerks in the solicitor's office. The cases
Reuben handled himself were the weighty international ones where

the law was fuzzy, the courts unpredictable, and the methods of procedure wide open. Yet even these millionaire clients could be difficult to corner for payment. A typical case was the Caligaris claim in Nicaragua, where clients accepted the settlement that Reuben worked out for them and then refused to pay him a nickel. This was certainly no way to achieve financial independence, and Reuben began to see the necessity for being tough. To Angel Caligaris he wrote,

> I have no doubt that sometime an opportunity will present itself for me to collect this fee from you and I assure you that when the opportunity comes I shall collect it with interest.[8]

Even with friends, it seemed, Reuben was forced to put aside his amiability and become the two-fisted lawyer. When Judge Thompson of Titusville, Pennsylvania, thought to fudge a little on a fee arrangement, Reuben affably took him to task.

> This kind of proposition may look perpendicular in Titusville but it seems a wee bit out of plumb to us unsophisticated people here in Washington. I am sure that you will agree with me that inasmuch as you have had the only money that has been realized out of this whole transaction, namely, $1,500.00 that the least you could expect to do would be to pay half of the cost of collecting the balance fee whatever that may be. I would not care to go forward on any other basis.[9]

"It is a good thing I know dear old Reuben so well," replied the judge, "and that genial clasp of the hand, slap on the back, kick in the tail, all so well synchronized as to make the recipient uncertain whether he shall laugh or cry."[10] But this was as much flintiness as Reuben Clark could muster; and when it came to dealing with the big clients—the ones who followed him from the solicitor's office with business that glinted of gold—it was often not enough.

iii

The first of these big clients was the Japanese embassy. It seemed that the Japanese in California had not had an easy time of it since their run-in with segregation; in fact, they had barely managed to fend off mortal shame. The hostility of the Californians had heated up again in the campaign of 1912, which moved from school segregation to land ownership. As a result of the election, a California alien land law had been passed in May of 1913, prohibiting the purchase of real estate to persons "ineligible for citizenship."[11]

In building their case against the alien land law, the Japanese came to Reuben. Back when he was solicitor, Reuben had become well versed on the subject of discriminatory land legislation, and he was now convinced that the California statute went too far. He had also drafted the Japanese-American Treaty of Commerce and Navigation. On the basis both of that treaty and the Fourteenth Amendment, Reuben concluded that "the State of California may not . . . pass a law which shall provide as against the present owners of property held in fee any other or different treatment of such property than the treatment which it accords to the same kind of property owned by American citizens."[12]

The Californians would not budge, however, and Reuben could secure no help from Washington. In fact, three battleships were transferred from Hawaii to the Philippines, and there was another season of war talk in the papers. Yet despite the unsatisfactory outcome, the Japanese seemed satisfied with Reuben's efforts in their behalf. They came back to him with more legal work and eventually wanted to cart him off to Tokyo as permanent counsel.[13] Unlike some other clients, the Japanese faithfully paid their bills—but these fell short of the gold strike Reuben was seeking. He continued his search for El Dorado.

iv

Several more big clients came from the zone of the Caribbean. One of them, improbably enough, was Julián Iriás. Reuben had last heard of Iriás at Bluefields where, as commander of the *Máximo Jérez,* he had been systematically stymied by Reuben Clark's own version of neutrality. Now, five years later, Iriás appeared in Washington, attempting to press claim to the presidency of Nicaragua. (As Madriz's political successor, Iriás had become the most popular man in the country.) Much water had gone over the dam since the Estrada revolt of 1909–10, and very little of it reflected well on American diplomacy. Presently the regime of Estrada's old cohort, Adolfo Díaz, was being maintained literally at gunpoint, and U.S. Marines were holding the guns.

Iriás was a member of Zelaya's old Liberal party; but he swore himself to be no *Zelayista.* His only objective, he said, was popular government. For the upcoming election (scheduled for 1916) Iriás and the Liberals claimed to have the support of the vast majority of Nicaraguans, and events seemed to bear them out.[14] Still, no one at the State Department wanted to return to the days of Zelaya and the civil war. Given what he took to be this choice, Secretary of State Lansing had decided to keep things as they were.[15]

Just why Reuben agreed to take the case is uncertain. Perhaps he simply told himself that clients were clients, but perhaps there was more to it than that. As one who had involved himself in Central American politics and had braved five years of revolution in Mexico, Reuben had modified several of his ideas about intervention. He had come to doubt whether any American could know what was right for Nicaragua, and government by bayonet badly ruffled his conscience.

Yet if the former solicitor could change his mind, the State Department apparently could not. J. Butler Wright, now chief of the Latin American division, calmly listened to Reuben's presentation of the Iriás case and promised to think about it. When Wright confided his own opinion to Secretary Lansing, however, it was that Iriás was deep down both a Zelayist and an enemy of the United States.[16]

The bureaucratic mill ground slowly. Almost a year passed without State Department action, and as the election in Nicaragua approached the air seemed charged with violence. "If something is not done soon along the lines discussed with the Latin American Division," Reuben wrote to Robert Lansing in June of 1916, "I feel it to be inevitable that sooner or later another fratricidal war will break out in Nicaragua."[17] Lansing saw the point, but there were other considerations to bear in mind. With an intervention presently on his hands in Mexico and an ultimatum being readied for Germany, the secretary could ill afford to be found talking to "a Nicaraguan Revolutionist," as one newspaper alleged. When it came to making a decision, he sent J. Butler Wright's memorandum, rather than J. Reuben Clark's, up to the president.

Reuben decided on a showdown. In a face-to-face confrontation he forced Lansing to admit that U.S.-Nicaraguan policy was indeed lopsided. "Of course, you know the character of Iriás," the secretary put in weakly. "Yes!" replied Reuben. "I think I do know his character and I am convinced that it does not coincide with the reputation which has been brought to the Department by his enemies."[18]

But it was all to no avail. Iriás went back to Nicaragua for the election and was at first forbidden to go ashore. Then, under a promise of amnesty, he was traveling toward Léon when police suddenly fired on his train. As if the hint were not yet sufficiently clear, American minister Benjamin Jefferson informed him that any Liberal candidate who could not furnish satisfactory proof of his dissociation from Zelaya would not be recognized by the United States.[19] In desperation Iriás wired Reuben Clark and offered to withdraw from the election, "if we are permitted to choose freely another."[20] There was no need to withdraw, however. The way the election was managed, the Conservative candidate, Emiliano Chamorro, won handily.

v

As in Nicaragua, so too in Haiti did Reuben have a chance to witness the aftermath of dollar diplomacy. While solicitor, he had intervened in Haitian financial affairs in order to secure the participation of American bankers in a European-sponsored loan. Reuben had wondered at that time about the morality of the loan and its effect on Haitian stability.[21] Now, three years later, Haitian stability had dissolved into chaos and all foreign loans stood in default. It was, then, with some sense of irony that Reuben agreed to take up the claim of Kunhardt & Company against Port au Prince.

Bill collecting is never the easiest work for lawyers, and international bill collecting is more difficult still. Even with a thousand-dollar advance, fifteen percent of the total loan, a five-hundred-dollar bonus, and an additional five percent of the gross amount of recovery, inducements hardly matched the size of the task—because nothing less than peace in Haiti was likely to permit repayment of the Kunhardt loan, and nothing less than an American intervention was likely to restore peace. One possible approach would have been to lobby for just such an intervention, and there were not a few bill collectors who would do exactly that. Reuben Clark, however, was not one of them. He sat back and let events in Haiti run their course. In 1915, when the United States did finally intervene, he enjoyed a brief season of hope for recovery of the Kunhardt debt; but the American presence was intensely unpopular with the Haitians, and the chances of a settlement slowly dwindled. When Kunhardt & Company got around to inquiring about Reuben's progress, the world war had intruded and Reuben had closed down his Washington office. "I regret that all of my papers are in Utah and are still in boxes," he wrote back to the company.[22] It was not the reply of a zealous collection agent.

vi

The Cuban legation retained Reuben permanently as a result of his State Department work on Cuban affairs. What he had to deal with here was not a single large problem but a long parade of small ones. There were claims dating from a recent political disturbance, aliens sailing back and forth across the Straits of Florida, gunrunners, bootleggers, criminals fighting extradition, emigrés plotting against the government of the moment, taxes, trade regulations, damage suits, racial and ethnic animosities, and, for good measure, an international murder case.[23]

None of these cases turned out to be a big money-maker, but they did open the way to one opportunity that came close. The Kate Soler affair presented a legal and moral tangle as engrossing as any soap opera. Back in 1888 pretty Kathryn Howard of New York had become the bride of Cuban sugar heir Antonio Arturo Soler and mistress of his sprawling plantation, Santa Filomena. A life of affluence in the tropics should have fulfilled her fondest dreams, but what it actually brought were nightmares. The National Bank of Cuba conspired with the Sobrinos de Bea Company to wrongfully foreclose a mortgage on the plantation. Then bonds were illegally converted, machinery expropriated, books juggled, crops stolen, capital embezzled, and stockholders defrauded. To top it all off, Kate Soler found herself facing these difficulties alone: her father-in-law died suddenly and her husband abandoned her. Yet face them she did. She squared off against Sobrinos de Bea and the National Bank of Cuba with a fury that would have done Scarlett O'Hara proud. At one point she spiritedly reoccupied the mansion house and dared the Cubans to evict her.[24]

Through his connection with the Cuban legation, Reuben Clark became Kate Soler's lawyer. One at a time she mailed him installments of her difficulties and he fit them into the expanding outline of the case. For example, in May of 1923 Kate and her daughter were out for a stroll in the park when they witnessed a murder. They recognized the assailant as none other than their old nemesis, the chief counsel for the National Bank of Cuba. A week after so testifying in court, the Soler women were themselves the near victims in a murder attempt.[25] Reuben struggled to keep up with it all. So intricate did the plot become that he had to draw up a flowchart of principal events. His legal brief chronicled no fewer than thirty-four separate twists and turns in an amazingly complex design. But Reuben stayed with the case. Kate Soler's stake in the outcome approached two million dollars, and Reuben's contingency agreement was for eight percent of the recovery. But saving Santa Filomena from the Havana loan sharks was a losing proposition, and Reuben did not have the U.S. government to back him up. In the end, the Soler case was a dead loss.[26]

vii

Until he could find and win The Big Case, Reuben was essentially marking time. Of course, The Big Case, as he knew, might well take the form of a terrible long shot, a bleak and dismal proposition that could be turned to profit only by legal alchemy. Perhaps this was why he threw himself into chancy situations—like Tlahualilo.

The Tlahualilo Company, Inc., a British-American corporation, owned a mammoth cotton plantation on the Nazas River in Mexico. Like any *gringo* operation, Tlahualilo suffered the depredations of Mexican revolutionaries. For example, when Pancho Villa occupied Torreón in 1914 he stole a car and—in the best Villa style—a chauffeur from the estate. This and other damage became the subject of endless claims litigation, for which Tlahualilo needed a good lawyer.

But Tlahualilo had needed a good lawyer even before the revolution. The difficulty was water. In the days of *Porfirismo* the company had been granted water rights on the Nazas which virtually emptied the river into Tlahualilo's irrigation system. So parched became the farmers and ranchers downstream that Díaz himself thought better of the arrangement and rescinded it. From that day forward Tlahualilo was a multimillion-dollar proposition left literally high and dry.

A feisty young Englishman by the name of James Brown Potter took over management of the corporation at a time when organization, finances, and company morale were in a shambles, and he miraculously improved all three. He believed that he could solve the water problem too. For this, however, Potter knew he needed not merely a good lawyer but a legal alchemist indeed. And he thought he was getting one in the person of Severo Mallet-Prevost, who hailed from a distinguished New York family and maintained an even more distinguished law practice. The price alone must have convinced Potter: Mallet-Prevost's was astronomical.

There were a dozen convolutions in the story before it finally led to Reuben Clark. Reuben was still in the solicitor's office at the time, and he had come to know Tlahualilo's difficulties well. Born and raised in the arid West where water law principles were a little different than elsewhere, Reuben was the only legal authority in or out of the State Department who happened to agree with Mallet-Prevost's assessment of the Tlahualilo situation. (Western law treated water as a commodity amenable to private purchase; eastern law treated it as a resource of the entire community.) As solicitor, in fact, he provided several memoranda for the company's lawyers that helped get their case moving. So when Reuben hung out his own shingle in 1913, Severo Mallet-Prevost was not long in procuring his services for Tlahualilo.[27]

Meanwhile, the revolution had broken over Mexico and the company's problems had proliferated. Reuben was asked not only to interpret water law but to tackle political problems (like dealing with the Huerta government) and even to represent the company before the U.S. State Department. In all of these matters he reported directly to Mallet-Prevost, and in some of them he scored triumphantly for the beleaguered cotton corporation. Reuben began to believe, in fact, that Tlahualilo might be the El Dorado he was looking for. Timidly he suggested to Mallet-Prevost that the services he had rendered might be worth more than the twenty-five-hundred-dollar annual retainer they had agreed upon—perhaps as much as five thousand dollars. "Indeed," he added in a letter to the Tlahualilo general counsel, "had the Company's finances not been in the deplorable state which you report, I should feel that double this sum was not at all exorbitant."[28]

Reuben still had much to learn about big-time law. He learned some of it in the following months when he discovered that Mallet-Prevost had charged the Tlahualilo Company a staggering seventy-five thousand dollars for his own services and that most of the services described were those Reuben had performed himself. Nor was that the worst of it. The bill landed Mallet-Prevost in a furious row with James Brown Potter, and company officialdom was soon split down the middle. Reuben wound up in the grotesque position of trying to convince Tlahualilo trustees that seventy-five thousand dollars was an extortionate price for work that he himself had done.

With that sort of an overture, Reuben would have done well to skip the rest of the performance. Mallet-Prevost resigned in disgust at the paltry twenty-five thousand dollars Potter finally offered him, whereupon Reuben succeeded him as general counsel. He was still naive. "In my letter to Mr. Potter," he reported to Mallet-Prevost, "I expressed my sincere regret over the action you have taken, and told him that I was sure no other American lawyer could fill your place."[29] For the next decade Reuben filled it himself—always in the hope, sometimes in the expectation, yet never quite in the assurance that the gamble would pay.

It did not pay. With inevitable certainty Reuben was drawn into Tlahualilo's predicaments and squabbles and finally into its actual management. Throughout the remainder of the decade Reuben himself, James Brown Potter, and an accountant named E. T. Craig effectively ran the company, facing themselves off against both the trustees in England and the authorities in Mexico City. But the revolution went from bad to worse, and with it the fortunes of foreign businesses in Mexico. Although one regime after another shot its way into the National Palace, all agreed that the *gringo* cotton plantation should have no increase in water from the Nazas. By 1922 Tlahualilo was against the wall and there was nothing left but bankruptcy. Exhausted and broken, James Brown Potter turned from the battle and died.

The receivership went to H. A. Vernet of A. M. Kidder & Co. in New York, who had close ties with the deposed Mallet-Prevost. Vernet moved through Tlahualilo's management structure like an avenging angel, rooting out the Potter men and replacing them with his own. (Craig, for example, was succeeded by Mallet-Prevost's brother-in-law.) When he came to Reuben Clark, Vernet shrugged politely and fired him along with the others. Their final accounting wrote a fitting last chapter to the Tlahualilo saga. Reuben had represented the company since 1913 and in ten years had received but three months' worth of his yearly retainer; now, with the enterprise in ashes, it was too late to recoup the loss. He asked for a grand settlement of $1,250. "Unfortunately," replied Vernet to this audacious request, "in making our budget of expenditures we have to consider the precarious financial position of the company."[30] A check for $625 eventually made its way to Salt Lake City.

viii

Among other things, the Tlahualilo story revealed that Reuben Clark was probably not destined to become rich. One reason was that he possessed neither the talent nor the brass for playing against men like Severo Mallet-Prevost. There was another reason, too: almost without exception, Reuben had affiliated himself with losing causes. The Japanese in California, Iriás in Nicaragua, Kate Soler in Cuba, the Anglo-Americans in northern Mexico—all of them were foredoomed. Many others of Reuben's clients exhibited the same doubtful quality. If he meant to find his El Dorado, he did not seem to have the gold-seeker's eye.

Except on one occasion—and this was indeed the main chance he had been seeking. One day in the fall of 1915 Reuben happened to be in New York City when he ran into Willard Straight. He had known Straight from the State Department. Straight, in fact, had been the godfather of dollar diplomacy, bursting into Huntington Wilson's house one rain-blackened night and pulling from beneath his shirt an American loan contract signed by Tang-Shao-Yi. He had been consul-general in Mukden at the time, and from that remote outpost he had engineered greater towers of finance and diplomacy than the fathers of the Bourse.[31] Pale, thin, nearly bald, but with an expressive mouth and piercingly intelligent eyes, Straight—as diplomat, financier, artist, poet, prophet, and international gadfly—seemed less like a man than a movement. Now, as he and Reuben Clark lunched together amid the Elizabethan decor of the India House, he told Reuben that he wanted to study law as well. And he wanted to set up an international legal practice with J. Reuben Clark.[32]

Proposed by anyone else, the idea would have been ridiculous. But things that Willard Straight proposed—marrying a fortune, joining the House of Morgan, refinancing the Manchus—had a way of coming to pass. Still, the scheme he sketched out for Reuben beneath the glowering portraits of Hawkins and Drake seemed to top them all. Straight was willing to concede that dollar diplomacy had failed. It had been a mistake, he said, to suppose that government and private enterprise could join hands for the outreach of American influence; the task would have to be undertaken by private enterprise alone. Straight believed that the United States could successfully compete with the British and Germans, whose great corporations had laced together empires. In fact, what Willard Straight envisioned in 1915 was nothing less than the world of the 1950s, when American power, American products, and American ideas would straddle the earth. Straight believed that he and Reuben Clark could help bring that world into being.

Reuben had heard big talk before. Yet, with an intuition lacking in his other ventures, he sensed that Willard Straight was really on to something. Philander Knox confirmed the hunch. Straight was a brilliant man, he assured Reuben, and one who seemed charmed with good fortune: it was a rare opportunity.[33] Convinced at last, Reuben decided to plunge once again. He armed himself with a sizable loan from Senator Knox and prepared to open a second law office in New York. Clark & Straight would specialize in international finance and would lay the groundwork for Americanizing the world. The only conceivable cloud on the horizon was the fact that Reuben Clark would now be surrounded by Mallet-Prevosts—hundreds of them.

With his amazing luck Willard Straight had indeed caught the wave. As soon as the great powers had jumped at each other's throats in 1914, the resources and markets they had so carefully cultivated around the world suddenly lay fallow. Sensing opportunity, the United States government swept away the legal barriers to overseas corporate expansion, and the race for empire was on.[34] In November of 1915 Frank A. Vanderlip of the National City Bank of New York announced the organization of America's first multinational conglomerate. Capitalized at the heart-stopping figure of $50 million the new supercorporation would, in Vanderlip's words, "grasp the new opportunities that the tremendous events of the war have laid before us." "It is evident," he added, "that we must, as a nation, begin to think internationally."[35] So began the American International Corporation.

And who but Willard Straight should be made vice-president? The announcement came within two months of the plan for a Clark-Straight law partnership. The AIC, of course, was precisely what Straight had had in mind in the first place, and he could ill afford to turn Vanderlip's offer down. Reuben understood. He would return to his Washington practice, he said, and make the best of it. But Straight suddenly dug in his heels and declared that he would not go through with the AIC unless Reuben went through with the New York law office. Moreover—Straight's eyes came alight—the law office ought to be situated so that the officers of the AIC could have easy access to Reuben's services. After all, an international corporation must certainly need an international lawyer. Straight even promised to share expenses as they had originally agreed. "I told him that I could not accede to that sort of a plan," Reuben reported to Preston Richards, "[but] after some discussion, it was agreed that he should practically 'grubstake' me and this is the plan on which I am going forward."[36]

On New Year's Day of 1916, Reuben Clark announced the opening of his New York office.[37] It was located on the twenty-sixth floor of the recently completed Equitable Building on Broadway, and pyramiding high above it were the offices of the AIC. In this single client was represented the industrial might of America. Charles A. Stone of the Stone & Webster Engineering Company was president. On the board sat J. Ogden Armor of Armor & Company, Percy Rockefeller of Standard Oil, Charles A. Coffin of General Electric, James J. Hill of the Great Northern Railway, Otto H. Kahn of Kuhn, Loeb & Company, Robert S. Lovell of the Union Pacific, John D. Ryan of Anaconda Copper, Albert H. Wiggin of the Chase National Bank, and Guy Tripp of Westinghouse.[38] Reuben Clark was in the presence of wealth and power at last.

Looking down on Broadway from Reuben's Equitable Building office: View from the top.

And Willard Straight proved to be as good as his word. He not only financed the opening of the law practice, but he saw to it that Reuben was inundated with AIC business. Within the first year the AIC received 1,230 investment proposals from five continents, winnowed them down to 313, and then proceeded to consider each one carefully.[39] Not only did the financial and technological aspects of each proposition need to be scrutinized, but its political and legal background had to be investigated as well—and this was where Reuben came in. Commuting to New York on Monday evenings and checking into the Hotel Majestic, he would spend a succession of sixteen-hour days at his Equitable Building office grinding out file after file of memoranda before returning to his Washington practice on the weekends. It was a heroic schedule, but with El Dorado clearly in view it was worth it.

The first year's transactions of the AIC read like an evening's game of Monopoly, except that it was all real. First to be purchased was the Pacific Mail Steamship Company, with enough extra ships to fill out its trans-Pacific service. Then came the Allied Machinery Company of America, a leading exporter of machine tools. Next, the

Latin-American Corporation was organized to undertake heavy construction in South America. Similarly the AIC moved into Russia, specializing in steel and railroad equipment. The next move was to buy up large blocks of the United Fruit Company, establishing the AIC in Central America. Then it was more shipping, with the International Mercantile Marine Company and the American International Terminals Corporation. Not to be excluded from the Orient, the AIC organized the China Corporation and the Siems-Carey Railway and Canal Company. It rounded out its Asian holdings with the firm of Carter, Macy, & Company, a prominent exporter of tea. In celebration of its first anniversary, the AIC bought the New York Shipbuilding Company at Camden, New Jersey. It was now the largest private shipping enterprise in the world—and it was only getting started.[40]

Himself an old dollar diplomat, Reuben was very much in tune with the AIC. At the outset he had written to Straight,

I am very gratified to see such an organization made, for the reason that ... the United States must, if it is to live, not only maintain itself and what it has, but also grow in power and influence. There is no apparent effective way in which this can be done without form of government except through financial expansion, and such expansion can come only as the result of private initiative, because the people at large have not yet grasped the intimate relation which exists now and will increase hereafter between our foreign trade and domestic prosperity.[41]

Accordingly, Reuben found himself becoming ever more intimately concerned with AIC operations. From background research he moved into procedural regulations and finally into representation of the AIC before the State Department. The various officers of the corporation received him differently: Charles Stone, the president, largely ignored him; but Vice-president A. P. Tinsley, who probably held more real power, relied upon him heavily; and Willard Straight remained ever staunch. Soon Reuben, in his low-keyed way, was participating in upper-level management decisions, just as he had done at the State Department. The future looked bright.

There came, however, the matter of the first bill. Unlike Tlahua-lilo, there was no question here of the client's ability to pay; so when, after six months and fifteen carefully researched memoranda, Reuben presented the AIC executive committee with an itemized statement for $9,200, he was all but flabbergasted to have it rejected as too high. "The poor people don't know whether I am handing them wise advice or idiotic drivel," Reuben reported to his wife, "so I have at last persuaded them to write to Knox, Moore, Root and Chandler Anderson for their judgment as to what I am probably doing."[42] The bill was still too high. After a series of negotiations, Reuben settled for $8,500—not for the past six months of work, but as a permanent annual retainer. "I should have had $10,000," he grumbled to Luacine, "but concluded I would better take $8,500 and go on."[43] This was no more an example of successful hard-bargaining than were Reuben's dealings with Mallet-Prevost.

ix

There was no telling how things might have turned out had the war not intervened. But intervene it did, and it ruined any hope of large financial benefit. Desperate to maintain his foothold with the AIC, Reuben earnestly negotiated with General Crowder and Attorney General Gregory for a portion of his time, "to attend to private matters."[44] In neither case did he succeed. Of course, Reuben was under no obligation to be in the military in the first place. Moreover, the AIC offered him an "enormous sum" to quit the army and supervise its wartime legal work.[45] American International Shipbuilding, an AIC subsidiary, was engaged in a $200 million government contract to crash-build fifty ships at Hog Island.[46] Such undertakings could have kept Reuben just as busy and several times as comfortable as the army did. But he was a patriot to the end and, although he wrote long letters of frustration to his wife, he never so much as nibbled at the bait. There were some things more important than the dream of *noblesse oblige*.

At the close of hostilities Reuben returned to New York and the AIC, but it was a vastly different place. Bigger and stronger than ever, the company seemed even more brash and less restrained; and a slippery new managerial type had eclipsed the generation of Willard Straight. Straight himself had gone with the army to France and died tragically of influenza.[47] His death seemed to leave a wound in the AIC's moral sinews.

Nevertheless, Reuben Clark was determined to make a go of his AIC affiliation. Wartime changes had brought A. P. Tinsley into greater prominence, and the loss of Willard Straight elevated Reuben to ranking Far Eastern expert. If he was ever to break into that charmed circle at the top, the time was now. There was a postwar boom in full swing by 1920, and the AIC had resumed gobbling up investments. Recent acquisitions included the Symington Forge Corporation; the Rosin and Turpentine Export Company; the Horne Company, Ltd., an exporter from the Orient; and G. Amsinck & Company, an exporter from South America. The AIC now controlled the Allied Machinery Companies of France and Italy and had organized the Hispano-American International Corporation for penetration into Spain.[48] By April of 1920, the AIC and its affiliates employed over twenty-five thousand people. "We maintain offices in nearly all the principal countries of the world," Stone boasted.[49]

Ubiquity, however, was not particularly advantageous when the boom suddenly turned to bust during the late summer. In fact, the AIC had been a little too voracious and now it was bloated. Where other corporations could retrench and ride out the recession, the AIC was stuck fast. For the next four years its losses averaged between three and six million dollars annually.[50]

Financial derring-do had been bad enough in the AIC while prosperity lasted, but with the collapse it worsened appreciably. Reuben Clark was not among the reckless, however. He had constantly urged restraint and moderation, and as the economy plummeted he continued to do so. Indeed, he became a leading voice in the company for fiscal responsibility, a counterweight to the speculators. Stone thanked him in a perfunctory way for helping keep the AIC's neck off the block, but there was little real appreciation of his influence.[51] Quite to the contrary, Reuben began to find himself in predicaments with corporate officers over matters of ethics. Faced with millions of dollars in bad investments, the new breed would apparently stop at nothing to recoup losses. "Had a sort of knock down and drag out talk with the [AIC] people both yesterday and today," Reuben wrote to Luacine in January of 1921, "which more or less restored my own self-respect vis-a-vis them, and which I think did not hurt me but probably helped me with them."[52] But there was no permanent help. The decision-makers of the AIC would continue to look out for themselves and play fast and loose with others.

The inevitable moment of truth arrived in 1923. In February, Frank Vanderlip resigned as chairman of the board and Charles Stone resigned as president.[53] Stone was replaced by Matthew C. Brush, a ruthless manipulator and bachelor playboy who had begun as a hotel clerk and clawed his way to the top.[54] The questionable practices of the AIC now flourished more than ever. And to make matters worse, Brush took a shine to Reuben, seeking and following his advice in a way that Stone had never done. He even asked the lawyer to put aside all other practice and come aboard as a full-time corporate officer.[55] Reuben's dilemma was complete. He had at his fingertips the power and influence he had sought for a decade. All he had to do, as Brush liked to put it, was "play the game."[56]

At first it seemed worth a try. After all, Reuben had invested a great deal of himself in the AIC; and, besides, as Brush's confidant he was in a position to throw on the brakes occasionally. But it would not work, and the two men were soon on a collision course. Reuben faced a clear choice: he could bury his scruples and eventually realize his dream of financial independence, or he could persist in opposing Matt Brush and see the dream go glimmering. He chose the latter. Brush continued to abide the nuisance of a refractory counselor until midsummer, and then, without warning—indeed, without explanation—he gave Reuben the ax. "Naturally, I miss the gold," Reuben reported to Dearing, unconsciously alluding to El Dorado, "but confidentially, I cannot tell you how relieved I was, and am, to be rid of an association which became increasingly burdensome and distasteful to the point of nausea."[57] For a man of high ambition, Reuben Clark could be remarkably self-denying.

x

If his fortune was not in the East, then it must, as Reuben Clark now decided, be in the West. By the time he and Brush parted company, he had long been preparing for his return home. First, he had taken steps to insure that a law practice would be waiting for him. Preston Richards had departed from the solicitor's office in 1913, only a few months after Reuben, and had gone back home to Salt Lake City. There he had set up the law office of Clark & Richards. In correspondence Reuben had patronizingly referred to this as the "home office" while enthusiastically planning the move to New York;[58] but as fortunes with the AIC had begun to slump, the Salt

Lake office came to seem like home indeed. Once in a while Reuben had been able to throw some business out to Richards, like the so-called Mormon claims against Mexico, and in the meantime there were enough local matters—wills, trusts, property transactions—to keep the latter busy. In 1921, in fact, they took on a third partner, Albert E. Bowen, a well-known and highly respected attorney from Logan, Utah.[59]

Secondly, Reuben had moved to secure a house for his family. At the death of C. R. Savage, the family residence at 80 D Street had passed jointly to Luacine and her sister Ida. From his modest accumulation of State Department savings Reuben had drawn $2,250 in 1913 and bought Ida out, presenting the canceled documents to Luacine for Christmas.[60] The house was spacious and sturdy, with two stories and a broad veranda, and it was located in a pleasant, mellow neighborhood.

Finally, and most importantly, Reuben had begun buying land. With a parcel here and a parcel there he had moved into Grantsville real estate with quiet resolve. The first major purchase had been the old Anderson farm adjacent to the home of his parents.[61] Through

Number 80 D Street: Not the Knox farm, perhaps, but in its own way pleasant and mellow.

his brother Edwin, Reuben also purchased a few head of cattle, the beginnings of a respectable herd. On the marshy lowland stretches of the farm Edwin, under Reuben's direction, was raising hay and feed grains. On the upland stretches the Clark brothers began dry-farming operations. By the outbreak of the war they were in a position to capitalize on the bounteous trade with the Allies, and as the wartime prices soared Reuben added bits and pieces to his holdings almost monthly. With wheat going at $2.50 a bushel, it was not long before he was in possession of some sixteen hundred acres. The manor of his dreams had already begun to take shape.[62]

Still, it was no return of the conqueror that Reuben Clark made in the early twenties. He could not, as he had hoped, liquidate vast blocks of AIC holdings or cash in some gigantic Alsop award. On the contrary, his affairs in the East had steadily deteriorated. He had made very good money with the AIC, but with secretaries left manning his Washington and New York law offices the result in both places had been less than Prussian efficiency. He might have brought home a small fortune if he could have collected his accounts receivable—but he had simply not been hard-edged enough. By 1921 he had decided to return to Utah and commute back to the East periodically.[63] For two years and more he did just that, shuttling back and forth across the United States with his open briefcase on the train seat beside him, doing bit work for the AIC, dunning deadbeat clients, and filling in with such government assignments as the Washington arms conference.

Meanwhile, El Dorado now shimmered on western horizons. Reuben Clark was not above speculating—as long as it involved substantial things like land or minerals and not insubstantial things like stocks or commodity futures—and when he first adjourned to Utah it was with the avowed purpose of cashing in. Matt Brush agreed to put up the capital. The two of them would buy farm and ranch lands at the bargain-basement prices of 1921 and wait for the economy to bounce back.[64] But somehow nothing worked out.

Reuben undertook other ventures with his brothers, especially Frank. The two of them attempted to expand the coal-bearing properties Reuben had once purchased in Cedar City. They also considered building a glass plant there and exploiting the high-grade silicone sands of the area. They even jumped into the oil business to-gether, leasing drilling sites at Crown Butte, Montana, with the hope of subleasing them to the oil companies.[65] Some of these ad-ventures were small-time and halfhearted but others reflected the spirit of the East. At one point, for example, Reuben and his broth-ers launched a sophisticated attempt to corner the water rights to some important industrial properties. This project, shrouded in great secrecy, must have recalled the methods of the AIC too vividly, for upon reflection Reuben abandoned it. In truth, he lacked the touch of the successful entrepreneur. When his brother Frank suggested selling clean-burning oil furnaces to Salt Lakers—the valley fairly choked in coal smoke every winter—and then establishing a heating-oil distributorship to supply them, Reuben rejected the idea out of hand. People, he said, would just not go for that kind of thing.[66]

As a consequence, none of Reuben Clark's enterprises hit the big money; on the contrary, he almost went under. He bought too many properties too soon and too much on credit. Then, banking on the postwar agricultural boom, he laid too much into cash crops of the moment and too little into long-term staples. Ironically, when the AIC was caught short in the collapse of 1920–21, so was Reuben for essentially the same reasons. Once his fortunes started to slide, they slid rapidly. The house on the Anderson farm burned to the ground in 1920 and was a dead loss. Then the loans started coming due. Reuben was still in debt to the estates of Philander Knox and Will-ard Straight, and as market values capsized he had crops on his hands that could not be given away. The house on D Street languished in need of repair; the family took to flushing the toilet with a water pail. When Luacine made reference to "the usual Clark luck," every-one seemed to understand.[67]

Under such dismal circumstances Reuben became an active part-ner of Clark & Richards. Far from making a triumphal entrance, he barely beat the wolf to the door. Surveying the miscellany of traffic, divorce, and personal injury cases, he smiled at his partner of ten years and said, "It's a long way from Tipperary."[68] Yet he threw him-self into the practice with customary energy. Soon the office, with its habitual atmosphere of loosened ties and feet up on the desk, was a busy place. Reuben had to dig out from the wreckage of a lifetime of dreams. He was fifty-two years old.

Some of the dreams were still intact and others could be salvaged. Reuben owned the Salt Lake house outright and still clung, however tenuously, to his Grantsville real estate. There was hope of collecting from a few of his erstwhile clients and of realizing long-term gains on the farm acreage. Reuben unabashedly sought help from moneyed friends in the East and it was they, in the end, who bailed him out. He was able also to negotiate a settlement with the Knox estate in which he exchanged twenty-five thousand dollars in unpaid legal fees for the twenty-five-thousand-dollar note outstanding.[69] When in March of 1925 the AIC telegraphed him to say that U.S. Trade Commissioner Arthur Evans had urged Reuben's appointment as minister to China, Reuben, visualizing the endless round of champagne parties at his personal expense, had the good sense to refuse. "Not yet qualified in millionaire class," he cabled back.[70] By then he was beginning to feel solid earth beneath his feet once more.

More important, he was home. "The mountains," as he said, "belong to me and I to the mountains."[71] With that fundamental consonance, other things came into harmony as well. Clark & Richards did unexpectedly well. To be sure, the firm never moved into big-time international law; but it worked into mining, water, and land law and connected itself with prosperous western sugar interests. One hefty, though problematic, surge of business derived from the Mormon claims against Mexico, which totaled well into the millions. Reuben himself dealt with an insurance proposition for the LDS church, did patent work for several engineering firms, and represented his uncle Ernest Woolley—who had had a colorful financial career of his own—before various creditors. "It is a far cry, in every way, from Broadway to Salt Lake," Reuben wrote wistfully to Fred Dearing.[72] But the distance was not all downhill.

With increasing frequency, Reuben found himself back in public service. Within a few months of his return he was appointed to the Utah Water Storage Commission. The post took up a considerable part of his time, "with great detriment to my own work."[73] He had spoken those words before—in connection with the American-British Claims Commission, in connection with his wartime work for Gen-

eral Crowder, and in connection with the Washington arms conference. In fact, a transcendent theme of his private practice had been
the recurrent summons of the government. Reuben groused a good
deal about this sort of activity, but he could not seem to avoid it.
When in 1926 a situation developed which imperiled Clark & Richards's Mormon claims unless Reuben bailed the United States–
Mexico Mixed Claims Commission out of trouble, it seemed all too
familiar.[74] Nevertheless, Reuben grudgingly prepared to take the *Los
Angeles Limited* to Washington once again. Though he did not know
it, his private practice had come to an end.[75]

As for the dream that inspired the private practice, that too had
essentially played out. Back in Utah and among friends, Reuben's vision of the Knox estate, with its rolling fields and Pennsylvania-
Dutch barn, somehow seemed less seductive. He did continue to
hold on to his Grantsville acreage and he became increasingly proud
of the prize Herefords he raised. He built onto his home at 80 D
Street a startling replica of the Knox library, with two stories of
books looking down on a cozy assortment of furnishings. But he
gave up, decisively, on the idea of being rich.

xii

To the day he died, Reuben Clark may have supposed that his
best bolts had all gone wide of the mark. Yet that question depended on how one defined the mark. Reuben had never sought
wealth for its own sake, had never coveted objects for show, had never cared about badges or emblems. Rather, he had sought *noblesse oblige*–the disinterested service that wealth alone made possible. He
may or may not have realized that his own frequent bouts of government business amounted to a sort of *noblesse* and that his present return to Washington would entail more of the same. At any rate,
when the *Los Angeles Limited* pulled out of Union Station in July of
1926, Reuben, knowingly or otherwise, turned an important corner
in life. And who knew but that life's final meaning and destiny were
not still somewhere before him?

Chapter 20

FAMILY LIFE

On a cold and colorful Sunday morning in the autumn of 1923, Luacine Savage Clark left the house at 80 D Street with her husband Reuben and three of their four children. They turned north up the walk, then around the corner and along Second Avenue toward the red-brick Twentieth Ward meetinghouse. It was twenty years ago this month that the family had departed for Columbia and the East, but now they were back home and "permanently" established in Salt Lake City. Luacine was triumphant and happy on that crisp fall morning. It had been a very long twenty years.

ii

Originally, of course, the misery was to have been only temporary. Reuben was to go to law school while the family got along as best it could. Accordingly, on that first October morning in 1903, as Luacine stood in the doorway of their 124th Street apartment and watched Reuben swing off to class, she was braced for hard times. And they were indeed soon upon her. Columbia law school swallowed up her husband like Jonah's whale; he was in class all morning, in the library all afternoon, and often at work in the evening. Then he was tapped for the *Law Review* and, on top of that, asked to work for Professor Scott. Every endeavor, it seemed, brought its own kind of reward for him, and every reward called forth some new endeavor. For Reuben it was a remarkable story of success. For Luacine it was a chronicle of disappointment.

With pluck she began sandbagging for the worst. She worked magic with the apartment they had found. The outside was cold and drab, but with three hundred dollars' worth of relics from a second-hand store, Luacine turned it into a home. In fact, she turned it into a boardinghouse and home-away-from-home for other Utah students, and their company helped ease the strain. Yet Luacine was not hardy enough to withstand long hours of drudgery. Heat and moisture quickly enervated her, and too much effort with a broom or mop left bruises on her delicate hands. She hired a cook and was still able to run her pension in the black. Keeping up with two small children, however, was another matter.

Reuben could see that it was a sweatshop life she was leading, and he made efforts to ease her burden. While other students frolicked in the evenings, he spent them dutifully at home. Or he taught night school and used the proceeds to buy Luacine a coat. Or he helped out with the children whenever he could, sometimes walking the floor with a child in one arm and an opened casebook in the other. Still, he was fired with his personal quest and attacked his work with intensity. He worked days, nights, weekends, and holidays, retiring at one or two o'clock in the morning and then arising at seven and skipping breakfast. "I was a long time getting started," he explained to Scott, who told him to slow down, "and my present activities are merely the necessary concomitant of my early inactivities. When, if ever, I shall have caught up to where I ought to have been, I shall have time to pause and think about the rule you invoke."[1]

Then too, much of the time the Clarks were totally separated. Luacine took the girls back to Utah for the summers—the better to trim expenses—while Reuben slogged away at Dr. Scott's research. Life at the Savage home on D Street was revitalizing for her, and her sister Ida could bear a hand with the little ones; but she missed her husband dreadfully. By July her letters would unfailingly take on a note of melancholy and by August a note of desperation. Luacine was obviously not cut out for this sort of existence.

Graduation ought to have brought release. Instead it brought the question of working for Scott at the State Department—with all of its attendant ambiguities. The offer did not materialize immediately; it came forth in fits and starts that dragged on through the entire summer of 1906. As in the two summers previous, Reuben and Luacine were separated by the continent, and each of them struggled with an individual conception of their identity. Were they people of the West still, or had they become people of the East?

Should the marvelous law school connections be permitted to lead them toward an unknown, and perhaps unkind, destiny in Washington—or should the call of home, church, and community be heeded instead? The letters back and forth were filled with tentativeness and rationalization. Reuben instinctively pulled one way and Luacine the other. But Luacine was the Mormon wife and she was ready to follow her husband. If to him the State Department sounded better than his father's offer of a fat pig and a year's supply of flour, she would go with him to the State Department. "I do hope for your sake you get [the position]," she wrote. "It would certainly be very pleasant for you, if you are not worked to death and could spend a little time with your family."[2]

iii

As it turned out, he *was* worked to death and could not spend much time with his family. In the solicitor's office Reuben carried all of his own responsibilities and most of Scott's. Then in the evenings he continued to slave away on Scott's book. On top of everything else they were hopelessly in debt. For three years and more they had drawn one hundred dollars a month from the account of the faithful Joseph Nelson. The cumulative total by now seemed ruinous, and strive as he might Reuben could not seem to retire it. Accordingly, he conceived an idea. Rather than having Luacine and the children rejoin him in Washington in the fall, they could stay on in Salt Lake for the rest of the year. Reuben would remain in Washington, live in a boardinghouse, eat sandwiches, and work around the clock, piling all earnings on the debt. This all made fine sense to Reuben, for whom work and more work had become a way of life. He was obviously not thinking about Luacine.

"Nonsense!" exclaimed Aunt Annie. "No man would want to be away from his wife so long." Luacine wondered if the point was not well taken, but she wondered even more about Aunt Annie herself. Annie Smith Clowes had married C. R. Savage upon the death of Luacine's mother and even now had begun displaying jealousy toward her stepchildren. Elderly and frail and apprehensive about her own future, Aunt Annie had gone to the very limits of hospitality to accept Luacine and her lively daughters for the summer. When the

368

telegram came from Reuben, a look of despair visibly swept across her face. The message for Luacine was clear enough: she was apparently welcome nowhere.[3]

Even after the family was reunited and settled in Washington the following year, the Nelson debt continued to hang like a pall over their lives. Reuben could think of little else but its burden, and he continually came up with dubious strategems for paying it off. For Luacine the phrase "that hideous debt" became a single word. "When I think of this separation all because we must pay off that thing," she was writing two years later, "I feel desperate enough to do something rash."[4] And oddly, Joseph Nelson himself appeared neither to need nor especially want the money. In a hundred nice ways he told Reuben to forget about it. He took pleasure in helping aspiring young men—he had helped others—and he seemed repaid by their very success. He even felt guilty that Reuben had exiled himself in Washington in order to repay him, and he made it up to Luacine and the children as best he could. When they arrived in town for a visit, Nelson would greet them at the train station, his pockets bulging with tickets for plays and concerts, and during the warm summer evenings he would drop by 80 D Street to take everyone out for a cooling automobile ride. He became a substitute father.

Beyond "that hideous debt" Luacine had to contend with "that hideous book" and the man whose name was to go on the cover. She had a clearer perception than her husband that Reuben was being exploited by James Brown Scott, and she was outraged by the very thought of it. The customary tag line to each of her letters was an inquiry about Scott's latest indignity—more a reprimand to the slave than the slave-master. Nevertheless Reuben continued to toil away on *Equity Jurisdiction.* He had, as he said, dotted every *i* and crossed every *t* of *Quasi-Contracts* and was prepared to repeat the performance as long as the debt remained unpaid. He came home in the evenings too tired to focus his eyes, but still he hauled out Scott's research after dinner and ran down at least one more case for the compendium.

Then there was the weather. Luacine suffered a physiological defect which prevented her from perspiring adequately. Where the muggy heat of Washington drove others to the northern lakes or the Florida Keys, it drove Luacine Clark to the wall. She literally could not bear it. Salt Lake City was no highland resort in the summer months, but at least it was endurable. The Nelson debt and the Scott book were difficulties of duration that must eventually come to an end, but of Luacine's personal physical problem with the East there would never be a letup. With each of her husband's promotions, she had fresh cause to wonder about her ultimate fate.

Separation, loneliness, penury, servility, and prostration—these were the *extraordinary* discomforts of the situation; there were a host of ordinary ones. For example, Luacine was a hometown girl, simple and genuine. The terrifying obligations of State Department society utterly bewildered her. When to accept? When to decline? How to call? How to receive? Which fork, which gown, which smile? The solemnly engraved invitations began coming in like death notices—from the minister, from the ambassador, from the assistant secretary, from the secretary, from the vice-president, and ultimately:

> The President and Mrs. Roosevelt
> request the pleasure of the company of
> Mr. and Mrs. Clark
> at a reception to be held at
> The White House
> Thursday evening, January the ninth
> nineteen hundred and eight
> from nine to half after ten o'clock[5]

She could have picked up the requisite social skills quickly enough from an indulgent mentor, but her only contact was Adele Scott. "I hardly think Mrs. Scott will care to be sociable," Luacine accurately predicted, adding: "I hope there will be some Utah students who will be congenial to me."[6]

Reuben—still young, zestful, impatient for success, and tasting the first sweetness of it—did not really comprehend his wife's predicament. He made friends quickly and easily and took naturally to the Washington milieu. He gained admittance to the professional societies, attended regal luncheons at the Shoreham, joined the Chevy Chase and Metropolitan clubs, and then, after his work on the Citizenship Act, was inducted into that holy of holies, the Cosmos Club. If a hunger remained in his life, it was only for more work, wider recognition, and greater success. Sometimes he wondered idly if Luacine's inexperience was impeding the progress of his career, and he took to correcting her in manner and speech. It was plain to see that she was no Lucy James Wilson.

iv

And all the while the darkness of Luacine's life deepened. Her first winter in Washington was a disaster. Because of the Nelson debt the family attempted to make do in a tiny hotel room where the damp and stale surroundings were hardly salutary for the children. Within two weeks six-year-old Marianne had contracted acute nephritis, or Bright's disease, as well as abscesses in her throat. As the infection raged in her kidneys she grew pale and listless. Her eyes began to swell, and then her hands and feet; finally her whole body became painfully bloated. The rest of the winter was spent in a battle for the child's life. Luacine, over the telephone, rented more adequate lodging and the furnishings to go into it. Then followed an endless procession of doctors and medicines, none of them much availing. Doctors lanced the abscesses in Marianne's throat, administered cathartics of calomel and ipecac of soda. Luacine nursed her day and night in an endless vigil of cool hands, soothing words, and small sips of water. Reuben anointed her head each evening and prayed mightily for her recovery. But the child's condition went from bad to worse. Fluid gathered in her chest cavity and her breathing became more and more labored. Finally, in February, Reuben trudged down to the telegraph office to send word to Utah that the situation was hopeless. Luacine, standing over the bed and staring vacantly from the second-story window, saw dark forms materialize through the cold Washington mist. It was a funeral cortege and a certain omen of the future. As it plodded past the window she wept bitterly.

In March, however, Marianne suddenly began to rally—whereupon her sister Louise contracted bronchial pneumonia. The rest of the spring was spent curing Louise of her cough and teaching Marianne to walk again. Reuben, sick with worry, bore a hand where he could. He assisted with the nursing at night and bathed Louise's throat with salt water every morning. But with Dr. Scott out of the office and himself the actual solicitor, he had to give first attention to the State Department. The brunt of the siege was met by Luacine.

v

Another winter and another spring passed, and the Clark family settled into a semblance of order. Yet, just as they seemed to gain a grip on their lives there would come the annual springtime exodus to Utah. When Luacine left for the summer of 1908 she felt the old panic overwhelm her. She was pregnant with her third child, and establishing the family at home seemed all the more imperative. "Richard Young asked about you," she wrote hopefully, "and said he hoped you would come home. There is a good place for you here. He hoped you might be at the head of the law school."[7] But she was grasping for straws. Four days later she read Reuben's reply in the *Deseret News,* the announcement of his appointment to the law faculty of George Washington University. Her congratulation was barely civil.[8]

Luacine's crisis seemed to resolve itself into the single question of whether her husband would be on hand for the birth of the baby. (She remained in Salt Lake during the autumn where her sister could attend her.) The expected date of delivery was late November. In October Reuben wrote to say that affairs in Washington might detain him. Besides, he asked, of what use was a man at such times? Luacine lashed back in anger. "If you were to go through it," she fumed, "nothing could prevent my being with you. . . . Other men take a vacation and perhaps the Government won't fall to pieces if you are here long enough to see your wife delivered."[9] Humbled, Reuben poured on the steam to reach Salt Lake in time, arriving travel-worn by Thanksgiving. But to his dismay, J. Reuben Clark III had beaten him by twenty-four hours. It was the story of their life.

Reuben stayed on for Christmas—he had not been home for five years—but by New Year's Day he was off once more. "I have shed enough tears to float you home again," Luacine wrote after his departure, "and I found the more I cried the worse I felt."[10] In truth, she was losing her grip. The tension reached a climax in February, when it became evident late one night that her father, who had been ailing for several weeks, was suddenly nearing the point of death. All three children had come down with colds and there was no one to look after them. Fighting back her own panic, Luacine struggled frantically to make them comfortable enough to sleep. Finally, at

The three Reubens, 1911: There was more to the legacy than a name.

two in the morning, with Marianne still coughing and the baby wailing to the heavens, she rushed upstairs to her father's bedside, arriving only at the final moment. As she stood at the deathbed, bereft of her husband and now also of her father, Luacine Clark felt herself to be in the very depths.

Her home in Salt Lake was now more uncertain than ever. Aunt Annie evicted Luacine's sister Ida from her half of the house, moved furniture and books into her own room, and declared possessory rights unmentioned in the will. News from Reuben was equally cheerless. Scott had really abdicated, he said, and there was a definite promotion in the works. Dejectedly she answered the letter.

I was just thinking today that when June comes it will be a year since we were together barring the six weeks you were home. This of course has been a very unhappy one for me, owing to circumstances over which we had no control. It seems a pity for you to be alone when you have a family who should be with you. From what you said I supposed you intended to come home by fall unless some job extra good came along. You said it may be Christmas time but this would be the latest time. You know we have the house at home on our hands which if you came home would lessen our rent considerably. Now from your tone in the last letter I infer you intend staying on and on. It is needless for me to say how I dislike living in Washington ... but if you intend to live on there, I will go just as soon as the weather will permit.[11]

This may well have been the crucial decision of her life. Although neither of them realized it, Luacine and her husband were approaching disaster. True, they loved one another and wanted the very best for their marriage. But life had placed them in a difficult situation: if they were to survive, either the one or the other must essentially give up everything. Reuben, though he talked of it, was not ready to make such a surrender; Luacine must make it or it would not be made. Beneath her frailties she was a strong woman and preternaturally wise. She sensed that a moment of truth had arrived. She also sensed that her husband, if pressed to the ultimate decision, would make it for her rather than for his profession—but that the decision itself might destroy him. He had always said that he wanted to return home and settle down with his own people, and someday— though not now—he just might do it. Luacine decided to give him rein and trust to the future.

vi

This sacrifice became the bedrock of their marriage. From the spring of 1909, when Luacine mailed her letter, things gradually began to improve. The break with Scott put *Equity Jurisdiction* on the shelf for good. Reuben's promotion to solicitor, which was not long in the offing, came with a significant increase in salary (half again as much), and the Nelson debt was soon being retired rapidly. The separations of the summer continued to pose a problem, but this was minimized by making the process routine. Once Luacine had resolved in her own heart not to force the issue, she could return to Utah in the summers and to Washington in the fall not exactly with serenity, but at least with a sense of resignation. This would be her life—maybe forever.

A change occurred in Reuben, too. In October of 1909, after returning to Washington with the children, Luacine had a sudden bilious attack, and the doctors dosed her with morphine to kill the pain. She suffered an allergic reaction and for two hours hovered between life and death. "I almost felt cold to think what a narrow escape Lute had," wrote Reuben's mother, "and to imagine what your feelings must have been those two hours."[12] The feelings went unrecorded but they must indeed have been profound. Reuben told his parents that he was giving up the East and coming home; it was perhaps only Luacine herself who stayed him. At any rate, he seemed to see life through new eyes. His days at the office grew perceptibly shorter, while evenings at home lengthened. He learned, in fact, to do much of his work in a private study upstairs, his books and notes piled around him and his infant son propped on the desk beyond the lamplight. And when the children came down with chicken pox in December, he let his work go entirely and became a full-time nurse.

In time the Clarks began to prosper. Indeed, with the final installment of the Nelson debt paid, they suddenly seemed rich. Reuben quickly retired his wife from household drudgery by hiring a cook, then a maid, and finally a second maid who doubled as a nurse for the fourth child, Luacine, born in 1914. The following year Reuben bought an Oakland and hired a chauffeur who served as butler when they entertained. Once relieved of her daily chores, Luacine was able to turn full attention to mastering the social graces. Soon she was hiring a carriage—a common motorcar would never do—and going through the genteel ritual of "calling." She learned when and how to leave cards, carefully crimping the corner so as to indicate that a personal call was being made, and sending it to the door via the footman. In turn she arranged to have her own at-home days when she received the calls of others. Eventually she became quite adept at it all, even though privately she found it ridiculous. Once, in later years, when her husband was undersecretary of state, she shattered the sangfroid of one august—but crowded—gathering by giving her chair to an especially corpulent social inferior and seating herself demurely on the floor. And Luacine never abandoned the Utah crowd of students, minor clerks, and nobodies. In fact, her home became a mecca for them and her western dinners absolutely famous.

As for lodging, the Clarks continued their peregrinations for some time. They moved from one house or apartment to another, appointing each in turn with rented furniture, until moving into the house owned by the Armes family on Irving Street, where they remained throughout Reuben's solicitorship. The endless uprootings attested their impermanence in Washington, and even Reuben grew tired of them. When he launched his own practice in 1913, he decided it was time to settle down. "No first class man lives in a second class place and way," he declared, "and no man trying as I am to be first class can afford to."[13] So they went first class. The new house was on the corner of Irving Street and Sixteenth—"The Street of the Presidents"—and was only two blocks from Embassy Row. The neighborhood was one of pleasant parks and stylish homes, and every Sunday President Wilson's black limousine would pull up to the Methodist church across the street. In the evenings, through lighted windows, one could catch glimpses of the opalescent world to which J. Reuben Clark aspired.

And the world inside 3100 Sixteenth was not so bad either. Servants bustled around and saw to the perfection of home life. Evelyn, the cook, was a character out of popular folklore: busy, bossy, flirtatious with the porters and busboys, crafty in harmless ways, and absolutely devoted to the family. The kitchen was her acknowledged domain and into it the children dared not venture. She and young Reuben became good friends, however; and, if he chanced to be sent to his room for punishment, a shoebox lowered down the stairwell by a string would always come up with the forfeited meal. Evelyn's special anathema was recipe poachers. They always came away with the recipe, to be sure, but neatly sabotaged by the omission of one crucial ingredient. Emma, the maid-nurse, was much older than Eve-lyn, a wizened little woman with fundamentalist faith and an abundance of superstition. She had been engaged to marry a young black who had gone off to fight in the Civil War and never returned. One morning Emma told the other servants that he had come for her in a dream the night before, still clad in the knickers and tunic he had worn to battle. That night she died.

The house itself was three stories high and built sturdily of red brick. It had a full-sized yard and garden, enclosed by a wrought-iron fence. In the front hall stood implements of hospitality: mirrors, a coat stand, a hat rack and umbrella holder. The parlor sparkled with a crystal chandelier, and a pearl-grey carpet lay on the parquet floor. The four large windows, two of them opening on Sixteenth and the other two on Irving, were hung in lace glass and rose-colored silk. The sofa and chairs were of substantial mahogany and upholstered with rose-colored tapestry. Beyond the parlor was the library, lined with Warneke bookcases, furnished with an overstuffed sofa and two comfortable armchairs, and decorated with photographs of dignitaries. In the dining room was a large oval table surrounded by high-backed, leather-covered chairs and a long mahogany sideboard filled with china, silver, and linen. It was an impressive house and thoroughly eastern. Somewhere in its recesses, though, was the old guitar Luacine used to play under the western stars, along with photographs of the Wasatch Mountains and Temple Square. In a moment of nostalgia, Reuben had requested these items to be sent from Utah. He had even asked for pictures of Indians.

vii

The good life came not without its own challenges, however. Chief among them was the fact that the children were growing up. If Reuben and his wife wrestled with their own sense of identity, they fairly battled with the children's. For in good measure they were becoming eastern children, despite the summers in Utah, the bi-monthly sacrament meetings, and the four-color pictures of Indians. The girls were soon attending Western High School in Washington and steeping themselves in the classics. When they visited Grants-ville in the summers they were appalled by the dust and flies and

377

Roughing it in Grantsville: "A long way from Tipperary."

uncouth farmhands. They watched with morbid fascination as Aunt Lucille, readying herself for the Saturday-night hoedown, pressed her pinafore with stove-heated irons and colored her eyebrows with burnt matchsticks. And if a cow so much as looked at them, they screamed and ran. Soon the word went out on the Clark sisters, and at the hand-clapping, foot-stamping barn dances they remained wallflowers. Even cosmopolitan Wilbur Carr referred to them as "modern flappers with New York ideas."[14]

378

For Reuben III there was some hope. He too steeped himself in the classics, but there was something decidedly western in his ways. He took to Grantsville with abandon and even as a toddler loved the soil. "Sanpoon" (sand spoon) became the code word for his propensity to dig in ditch banks, and his sisters stood guard by the hour while he did it. By the time he was twelve years old he was a regular summer farmhand, assisting uncles with the herding and learning the ways of cowboyhood. "He seems to be perfectly satisfied out here and had a dandy time," reported Uncle John to Reuben. "It sure is surprising how quick he would catch on to doing things."[15] The picture of the boy after a hearty lunch napping in the warm dust at the side of the house somehow said it all.

But even Reuben III posed his problems; and the fourth child, Luacine—delicate, sensitive, marvelously gifted—promised to be the most trying of the lot. These were not rebellious children, but they were capable of becoming alien. When the older girls began encountering the polished sons of diplomats and congressmen, they saw the farm boys of Grantsville through a narrower focus still. The threat of an "outside" marriage clearly began to assert itself. In rural Utah, of course, every institution—home, school, church, and community—multiplied the leverage of the others in molding the shape of the young. Reuben and Luacine had but one of these institutions at their command, and they realized that they must use it to the full. Accordingly, the Clarks came to develop a remarkably strong home.

It was strong, first of all, in leadership. Reuben himself, thoroughly chastened by the dark years, became the measure of all things. When he was at home his presence was felt in the smallest details of family life, and when he was away he could actually intensify it. He and Luacine would exchange letters almost daily during an absence, and he would telephone every weekend. Before the annual pilgrimage to Utah, Reuben carefully took each child aside for a private talk. In these conversations he would prescribe modes of behavior and give fatherly counsel. The girls were instructed in their dealings with the opposite sex and were warned, among other things, of strange diseases that could be caught from handrails. Additional directives came by mail, covering such topics as how Louise might avoid colds, how Marianne could stay clear of a certain young man, and how Reuben III ought to moderate his use of farm language. The advice was always tendered gently, with respect for the child's integrity, and with good humor. But it was comprehensive.

Perhaps it was too comprehensive. Far from rejecting the ideas of their father, the Clark children verged upon accepting them uncritically. Thus all of them grew up Republicans, conservatives, isolationists. When a history professor at the University of Utah once thought to put in a good word for the League of Nations, reserved Marianne Clark suddenly came up scrapping from the back row.[16] And Reuben III could think of no profession save the law, nor was any other planned for him. Still, there were instances when Reuben's extraordinary solicitude for his children, confining though it was, paid off handsomely. On the evening of January 28, 1922, Marianne, a cousin, and Reuben III insisted on going to the movies. *Get Rich Quick Wallingford* with Doris Kenyon was playing at the Knickerbocker Theater three blocks away. Ordinarily Reuben would have consented, but a freak storm had dropped three feet of snow on the city and was dropping more at that moment. He refused permission. The disappointed children were making fudge and lemonade when they heard the first sirens. The roof of the Knickerbocker had collapsed, bringing tons of concrete and steel down on the heads of the audience. One hundred and seven people were killed and another hundred and seventeen injured.[17] As the Clark children stared at the red lights flashing in the winter night, their father's wisdom was invested with myth.

The family became strong, secondly, in its routines and traditions. The odyssey back and forth across the continent became as predictable as the calendar. So did the course of an average day. Rather late in the morning—perhaps around eight-thirty—Reuben marched off to the office, walking the twenty blocks to Old State or the Hibbs Building in preference to riding the trolley. Often one of the children would accompany him several blocks and then return; in the evening as well they might trek down the street to intercept him. Dinner was the parliament of family events. Reuben would listen intently as the children recited the day's happenings. His expression of interest never wavered, not even as his son launched into a detailed reprise of the latest movie. After dinner the family adjourned to the parlor, where Reuben would sink into his easy chair to doze. Almost at his feet the children would talk and play. If a comment or correction was in order, Reuben would duly pronounce it, his eyes still closed and his face immobile. That made his interest in them seem literally sleepless. After a few minutes of napping, there would be an hour of music or other diversion with the children. Reuben had bought a gramophone, a Columbia table model, and almost nightly he cranked it up and played opera, symphony, or any other music he thought the children should hear. Later, with the improvement of audio technology, he bought an Edison and flooded the house with Wagner. He also monitored the children's reading. On his regular audits of the subject matter, he would peruse the first few pages, the last few pages, and take assorted glimpses through the middle. With unfailing intuition he could turn right to the risqué part, cocking an eyebrow in dismay. After the family hour Reuben would retire to the library for work or study, remaining there until the early hours of the morning. Even here, however, he was careful to leave the door open and to receive the children individually if they had matters to discuss. Thus, while Reuben's work days were long and full, they were also addressed to family needs. To the children his presence and attention seemed pervasive.

Sundays, too, were family days. They would invariably begin with hearty laughter rolling up from the kitchen as Reuben had his weekly encounter with "The Katzenjammer Kids." What was so funny about these two Nordic hellions the children could never understand, but daddy would laugh so hard that tears ran down his face. Then there would be a family breakfast of hotcakes or waffles, followed by a day of conversation, reading, and, when they were available, worship services. Often there would be an outing as well— a family picnic, perhaps, or a trip to the museum or zoo. Sunday evenings were often a time for visitors, but here as well Reuben allowed and even invited the participation of the family. Regardless of the stature of the visitor—it might be the secretary of state himself— the Clark children knew they were welcome to remain in the room during the conversation and often did so. "But you sat quietly on the floor," Reuben III reminisced. "You didn't ham it up."

The third way in which Reuben and Luacine Clark maintained family solidarity was through discipline. It was Reuben once again who bore the heft of this responsibility and he discharged it with great effectiveness. Seldom one to preach or scold, his silence could devastate and his eyes provide a worse punishment than tongue or hand. Reuben III wished that daddy would use a switch and get it over with rather than torturing him with clipped sentences and disapproving glare.

Having applied authority at the early stages, Reuben found little need for it later on. Instead, he relied on the power of example. Reading of him in the newspapers, judging him by his company, hearing frequent reference to his exploits, the children held him in absolute awe. Accordingly, what he said became less important than what he did—and in his actions he never let them down. Once, while Reuben III was working as an office boy at the American International Corporation, he overheard his father talking with Matthew Brush in another room. "It's legally correct," his father was saying, "but it's morally wrong and I'll have nothing to do with it." Brush, upon seeing young Reuben through the doorway, smiled a little sheepishly. "Boy," he said, "if you will do as your father has just done, you will do all right."[18]

Reuben also softened his didactics with humor. "Do you see any green in my eyes?" was his oft-repeated reminder of the Clark standards and, delivered with mock consternation, the question usually drew a laughing response. Always witty, always smiling, his eyes ever twinkling with some gentle mischief, Reuben was rarely misunderstood. At home he would gather the children around him and entertain them with reminiscences of his childhood. They screamed with delight at his anecdotes and mimicry. Dinner, too, was always attended with snorts and sniggers at his recitation of the day's events. His humor became a symbol of his love and affection for the children. Years after his death it was the thing about him that they recalled most vividly.

Nevertheless, in his own kindly way Reuben cracked the whip. Realizing that the critical test of his eastern sojourn would come in the matter of dating and marriage, he simply forbade either one outside the pale of the Mormon church. That was a small pale in Washington, D.C., so Reuben himself had to take a hand in the courtship process. He and Luacine welcomed into their home LDS boys of whatever rank and station. There were students, of course, and a few minor clerks and functionaries of the government. A larger contingent descended upon them from the tidewater military camps when the war broke out. Luacine shuddered when they tracked mud onto the pearl-grey carpet, but she would not have shown it for the world. Instead she hung out decorations, loaded the table with delicacies, and flooded the windows with welcoming light. Young Reuben played the butler and took the coats. The standard greeting, as enunciated by regular guest Hyde Cowley, was, "Angry mob, Lamanites—Ugh-h!" When the girls complained of a certain hickishness to such home festivities, Reuben hired an orchestra and spangled the house with potted palms. He would beat the East single-handedly if he had to.

viii

The only weak spot in the entire idyll was the one that had existed from the beginning—the question of who they really were and where they really belonged. All of their harmony and bliss could not efface it. Reuben himself had his moments of doubt about whether they should remain in the East. A time or two he teetered on the verge of giving up and coming home. Yet just when his fortunes seemed bleakest, a ray of sunlight would burst through the clouds and he would take a new lease on international law. Besides, until his million was made what could he really hope to do back home? For her part Luacine, though she tried, could never quite reconcile herself to the East. Her disappointment was hardly ever vocal, but it was continuous nonetheless. At one point, with special frustration, she wrote: "I am afraid it is the money that is keeping you there"— and she was absolutely right.

Doggedly Reuben hung on. He hung on through the flush years of Wilsonian prosperity, through the crisis of the submarines, through the uncertainties of the war. The war almost ruined him; when it ended, his Washington practice was in a shambles and the AIC alone held out hope. It seemed pointless to remain in Washington, so the family vacated the house on Sixteenth Street and moved to New York. The tall brownstone townhouse they located there stood at 21 West 73rd Street, near fashionable Central Park West. Around the corner was the chateaulike Dakota, the city's first luxury apartment building, surrounded by a moat and guarded by a sentry box. In the neighborhood too were the Hotel Majestic, the American Museum of Natural History, and, of course, Broadway. The

383

house was large and its appointments sumptuous. It offered an appropriate setting for an eastern-style wedding, and in February of 1920 the Clark family had one.

Mervyn Sharpe Bennion had been one of the "angry mob of Lamanites" lured to the Clark home. Hailing from Benmore, Utah, just over the rise from Grantsville, this brilliant young man had cut a swath through Annapolis and then distinguished himself in the world war. He became known to Luacine as the "peppermint candy man," for he brought it to her by the armload. But it was lovely Louise that Mervyn really came to see. The match was a natural, and no one was surprised when they announced their engagement. At the wedding ceremony Lieutenant Commander Bennion stood at attention in his glittering navy regalia. The bride herself was something to behold, arrayed in a white satin gown and radiant with happiness. It seemed particularly appropriate that Louise should use her husband's saber to cut the wedding cake.[19]

In an important sense Reuben Clark, standing proudly beside his daughter, had won his first major battle with the East. Louise had married a Mormon boy—a gentle, devoted, and worthy one. But she had also married a professional military man, one whose life and career would be over the seven seas. As if through some strange calculus, Louise was being consigned to the same life as her mother, a life of separation and uncertainty—and a life away from Utah. Reuben Clark once again began to plan the exodus of his family from the Atlantic seaboard, and this time he was determined to carry it out.

He was almost too late. The children were already far gone in their cosmopolitanism. Louise would travel the earth with her husband and would love every minute of it. Her younger sister Marianne would attend the university and eventually teach classics there; she would go on to become an executive in the women's organization of the church. Young Luacine would also inherit an eastern legacy. Romantic of temperament and high-strung like her mother, Luacine would make a life of writing poetry, composing music, painting pictures, and directing plays, the most effortlessly creative of all the Clark children. In 1921, when the family departed for Salt Lake, she was still only a child of seven; yet the world of her father's dreams had undoubtedly left its mark on her.

Reuben III was in the most difficult position of all. The only boy of the family, he was the clearly designated heir. But what he seemed to inherit was the futility and frustration of it all. On the one hand, he was expected to fill his father's shoes, to become a successful eastern lawyer, and perhaps to enter the citadel of the State Department. And on the other hand, it was he, of all the children, who had the born love for Grantsville and the farming life. He was exactly in the quandary of his father. There was much else of his father in evidence in him: the merry twinkle of the eyes, the unconquerable sense of humor, the simple Christianity. But the pressure of his dilemma began to wear on him. He cut classes, played hookey, found ways to divest himself of responsibility. He fooled around with alcohol and tobacco, too, and squandered his money lavishly.* He was a good boy and at the same time something of a problem child, evoking more worry in his parents' correspondence than the three girls combined. While a young man, he got hold of a novel called *Sorrel and Son* that seemed to give definition to his plight. It was the story of a father and son who braved the world together and licked it. "It has brought keenly to me the fact that perhaps you and I have missed something in life by our separation," he wrote while his father was in Mexico, adding, "But what is done can't be helped."[20] Actually, it could be helped, as the boy himself lived to demonstrate. In 1937, at the age of twenty-nine, he suddenly raised himself to a pitch of decisiveness and cut the knot that had ever bound him to his father. With the simple announcement that he wanted neither to live in the East nor starve in the West, he abandoned his legal studies, took up the classics, and became a college professor. Later on he bought the Grantsville farm from his sisters and continued to raise whiteface Herefords.

ix

Owing to their singular financial luck, the Clarks returned to the West no better off than they had left it. "Our long expected move didn't prove to be so satisfactory after all," recorded Luacine, and for good reason.[21] No sooner had they unpacked their bags than Reuben, at the beck and call of the AIC, had to return to New

---

*Faithful Mormons do not use alcohol or tobacco. Coffee and tea are not used either, although the prohibition on these was observed rather loosely in the early part of the century.

Luacine and the children, circa 1920: No mere happenstance that daddy was missing from the picture.

York, where he was unaccountably stranded over Christmas. "May this never happen again," he vowed wearily.[22] But it did happen again and would continue to happen as long as the debts remained unpaid and the dreams unfulfilled. Indeed, where hitherto Reuben had remained in the East and the family had come out West, now the family remained in the West and Reuben commuted to the East. The distinction seemed unimportant to Luacine. One day, while surveying the financial wreckage of the Grantsville farm with Uncle Ted, she asked his advice. Edwin Clark was no international lawyer, but he possessed a store of common sense. Why, he asked, didn't Reuben "concentrate on one thing at a time"—which Luacine interpreted to mean "come home." "Please take Ted's advice," she implored her husband, "let go before your health gives out. Come on home. We won't starve, and if we do we will all go together. Let's live normally just a little while before we die." But it was her last line that carried the punch. "Forget your dreams," Luacine said. "What's the difference anyway."[23]

What, indeed? Reuben came home that fall and stayed. In essence, he made the decision that Luacine had envisioned fifteen years earlier when she had resigned herself to the East. "I thoroughly enjoy living out here in the desert wilderness," he wrote to Fred Dearing, "and while I miss the fleshpots of Egypt and sometimes I am in sad need of a helping from them, I am still quite willing to forgo [sic] the mere lucre for the sake of the real life which I am able to live."[24] His wife could not have put it better. She was home and he was home; and on that crisp autumn morning, as they walked from their own house to their own church, she had never felt better in her life.

x

Financially, the net gain of their twenty-year errand in Babylon was zero, or close to it. For two long decades of unremitting toil Reuben could show but a little farmland and a lot of image. When the local stake president learned that the repatriated lawyer was actually deeply in debt, he was shocked. "Why, I thought he was a wealthy man," he said.[25] So did everyone else.

One other way to evaluate the eastern experience was in experience's own terms. For Reuben, of course, the experience had been marvelous. Yet it had been equally salutary for the rest of the family. While they did not return wealthy, they returned in one piece and unshakably committed to their Mormon way of life. Moreover, they had grown in breadth and understanding. Luacine, once shy and uncertain, had matured into a fine, gracious lady. During the long separations she had studied French, read the classics, done church work, taken up the piano, and even tried her hand at serious fiction. And the Clarks derived something, too, from their trials and dislocations and from their constant search for place. In being off balance for so long a time they were obliged to find their own sense of balance — their own center of gravity. They learned to carry their way of life with them, like the Bedouin his tent, and to place it down in whatever landscape. Conversely, they learned the art of drawing upon that which was of value around them, without drawing indiscriminately. As their guide, J. Reuben Clark had become wise to the world without becoming part of the world. In the first dismal years he had learned a lifetime's worth of lessons, and when his wife asked him to abandon his dreams he did in fact abandon them. Behind the twinkle in his eye, the funny story, and the witty epigram — trademarks of his later life — there lay a cognizance of things that ran to the depths of human understanding.

Chapter 21

SON, BROTHER, AND FRIEND

Not an avid reader of fiction, J. Reuben Clark might not have recognized himself as a character out of Horatio Alger. Nonetheless he was. He was as poor and honest as "Ragged Dick" and in the end as satisfyingly successful. Reuben was not an avid reader of sociology either, and he was unfamiliar with the pitfalls awaiting real-life Alger figures. He did not know that the poor boy who made good might turn his back on the family of his birth; that siblings might feel compelled to duplicate his success; that jealous acrimony might break out if they failed to do so; or that he himself might assume the role of the "big brother" and proceed to tyrannize their lives. It was just as well that Reuben remained ignorant of the pitfalls—for in his ignorance he managed to avoid them.

ii

One reason for this deliverance was that he was Joshua Clark's son and never forgot it. When he was in the East he did occasionally assume a paternalistic stance toward brothers and sisters; but whenever he set foot in Utah, things came quickly back into focus. Joshua, Senior, and not Reuben, Junior, remained the patriarch of the Clark family. It was Joshua who baptized the grandchildren as they came of age, who advanced them in the priesthood, who presided at family gatherings, who dispensed paternal wisdom, who anchored the sense of Clark solidarity. Nor were the parents unduly impressed by Reuben's success. When visitors sang their eldest son's praises, Mary Louisa was apt to snap back, "We've got nine more just as good."[1]

For Joshua, his namesake stood as much in need of guidance as any other child, and perhaps more so. Thus, his correspondence to Reuben was studded with minute sermons.

The human family [is] rushing along at breakneck speed to happiness or misery, money and pleasure are fast becoming the ends of many of the inhabitants of the earth. It is perfectly right and proper to get money in any legitimate way. It is also proper to have pleasure and enjoy life, but when obtained in an improper way then someone suffers.[2]

Joshua could never reconcile himself to Reuben's sojourn in the East. "I think you had better come back to Utah and get hold of a good piece of land," he wrote. "Nothing better for the growth and development of children than plenty of fresh air and sunshine, which they don't get in smoky cities."[3]

For his part, Reuben ever held his parents in the highest esteem. Whenever he took a strong position on some public matter, he justified it first to his father. And to his mother Reuben's devotion was limitless; his first expenditure upon paying off the Nelson debt was a motorized washing machine to ease the burden of her drudgery, along with regular checks to pay for running it.[4] Later, Reuben had a bathroom installed in the Clarks' Grantsville home, complete with tub and toilet.[5] Later still, after his parents' death, Reuben, upon buying an automatic washer for his ailing wife, carried a chair to the basement of his Salt Lake City home and watched the new marvel run through its cycles. "Oh!" he exclaimed, slapping his knee, "if only my mother could have had this."[6]

Upon two occasions—once in 1911 and again in 1918—Reuben brought his parents back to the East for extended visits. Remarkably, the son was not abashed to parade his pioneer parents among the Washington elite, nor were the parents much awed by it all. "Many of the ladies were not fully dressed," recorded Joshua after nothing less than a presidential reception.[7] As for the wonders of eastern life, Joshua best remembered the toilet, which happened to be flushing one day when his false teeth fell in. Such down-to-earthness all around went far toward keeping the Clark family operational.

iii

And operation meant everything for a family on the western frontier, where all they had was the land and one another. So it had been in the Joshua Clark household when Reuben was a boy. As they all crowded around the table at mealtime, there was the strongest possible sense that the family functioned as a single unit, not as an aggregation of individuals, and that "all for one and one for all" was not an empty shibboleth but a way of life. As Reuben made his way in the world, his problem was in balancing his own uniqueness against the identity they shared in common. It became a question of reconciling individual success, on the one hand, with "all for one" on the other.

iv

Reconciling identities with his brother Edwin was easy. "Ted," as the family knew him, was but two years younger than Reuben, and the two of them were always close. Of medium height and very lean, his face leathery from the desert sun and his hands rough with toil, Ted was both the natural heir of his father's earthiness and the incarnation of his brother's western self. He had business sense as well, and he capitalized on it by operating a successful stage line between Grantsville and the railroad pushing westward from Salt Lake. By 1913 Ted was free from debt and ready to join with Reuben in buying agricultural land. The following year they made a down payment on the old C. L. Anderson farm located next door to Joshua's.[8] As other properties became available Ted would scout them out, make arrangements, and write to Reuben for financing. Reuben placed unqualified trust in Ted's judgment. It was a family joke that Ted never smiled for fear that he would not be recognized; and if a real estate prospect could overcome his natural pessimism, that was good enough for his brother.

Ted and his wife, Tilly, moved onto the Anderson place and began farming operations. The first year's crop was a failure and the second not much better. But with the war in Europe the Clark brothers entered upon a season of expansive prosperity, and their holdings soon ranked among the largest in the valley. There were reversals, of course. In the summer of 1915 Ted's daughter Lou fell from a second-story window while sleepwalking and shattered her skull. Though she recovered, the expense was enormous.[9] Two years later the house burned to the ground—a five-thousand-dollar loss. Two years after that the wartime prices broke and plummeted, leaving Ted with crops that were worthless. Through these lean years

Reuben remained faithful. He made his own summer cottage available to the homeless family and found a spare two hundred dollars to help Ted pay his taxes. "I suggest you keep this matter to yourself," he advised.[10]

v

With Frank, too, the fraternal rapport came naturally. Although ten years younger than Reuben, Frank was even closer to his eldest brother than Ted. As youngsters they had spent a good deal of time together, usually on horseback and often in the canyons of the Stansbury Mountains. Frank, square and muscular, with a heavy shock of chestnut hair and the face of an Ivy-League football hero, was by all odds the best looking of the Clark boys. And, like Reuben, he was determined to be a success.

Reuben was in Washington when Frank left Grantsville for the University of Utah. Since Luacine was then spending most of her time at the D Street house, Reuben arranged for her to take Frank in as a boarder. Frank managed the house and did odd jobs, earning enough in the process to stay in school. He became interested in geology and soon was spending his summer vacations in the Colorado Rockies on survey expeditions. Frank felt a strong sense of kinship to Reuben and nurtured it through constant correspondence. "Talk about your man [Scott]," he once wrote of a preemptory field supervisor, "why so far as little petty tricks and fool ideas our [man] has yours beaten by a mile."[11] There was a parallel, as Frank believed, to their fortunes.

In time the parallel became evident: Frank also had his season of wandering and doubt. Geology took him to the jungles of Chiapas, to the flatlands of Tabasco, to the coal mines of Tennessee, to the gold fields of South Africa. Here, without question, was the adventurous life of his longings—and yet it never quite seemed to satisfy him.[12] Finally, in 1923, Frank saw his chance to settle down when Standard Oil offered him a job in the burgeoning new field of petroleum geology. Although this seemed like the right opportunity, the romantic youth in him wanted one last fling—with an expedition to Jack London's Alaska. "If you talk adventure here it is in all its allurements," Frank wrote to Reuben.[13] Reuben happened to be cashing in his own dreams at the moment and moving back to Salt Lake. "I agree with you that it looks strong on adventure," he replied, "but I am wondering whether it is quite so strong on work. . . . If you didn't have a wife and three children it would look very attractive."[14] This was one of the few times when the big brother spoke out.

Frank took Reuben's advice and settled down in Tulsa, and the two of them remained close. Ultimately they became investment partners, speculating in oil and gas, developing coal properties, and toying with a miscellany of other schemes. They never hit the jackpot but they enjoyed themselves enormously. In 1928 each of the brothers was at the pitch of his career, Reuben having become undersecretary of state and Frank having achieved a similar pinnacle in petroleum geology. Finding themselves in Salt Lake City that summer, they left wives and families in town and drove out to Grantsville. There they rode horseback up into the aspens of South Willow Canyon as in the old days. After spending the day with stories and childhood reminiscences, they rode back across the flatlands and joined their aging parents for what was to be the last family reunion.[15] It was truly a moment of poignancy.

vi

As farmers the three older brothers—Reuben, Ted, and Frank—formed a natural triumvirate: Reuben put up the money, Frank located the water, and Ted worked the land. The three younger brothers, on the other hand, sometimes felt left out. Samuel, born in 1886; John, born in 1890; and Gordon, born in 1893, were almost a generation removed from Reuben, and the relationship was often more paternal than fraternal. When Reuben and Ted were pushing outward with their farm properties, the young trio worked as their hired hands and did not much like it. "He always expects more of us than his other help," John complained to Reuben of Ted, "then he [tells] you he can get us to do anything when he [wants] it done."[16]

Samuel was the tallest, sparest, and rangiest of the Clark children, with a thin, Lincolnesque face and slightly stooped posture. He seemed to lack the dynamism that drove Frank toward worldly success, and Reuben decided to take a hand with him. It was at

Reuben's instigation, in fact, that Sam returned from his mission in the Hawaiian Islands to pursue an education.[17] As with Frank, Reuben made the D Street house available to Samuel while he attended the University of Utah. Higher education, however, was not quite the thing for Samuel, and he dropped out with the explanation that the university did not offer exactly what he was seeking. Reuben persisted. He even offered to bring Samuel back to Washington and send him to school there. (Frank was staying with Reuben at the time and Sam was invited to join them.) The younger Clark sought to decline this hospitality, but Reuben would not be deterred. Almost by the heels he hauled Samuel to the East and enrolled him in school. Then Reuben and Frank tutored the boy every evening, Reuben in Latin and Frank in math. Still it was no use. Samuel returned to the West, married, and took up farming.

Even here Reuben continued to look after his brother. Things did not go well for Sam, domestically or financially, and the elder brother took to including small checks with his letters of encouragement. "This won't pay any grocer's bill," he appended to one, "but I hope it will give you some satisfaction."[18] Samuel responded gratefully. "It rather makes me feel small to accept so much from you," he wrote, adding, "I feel that you have already done more for me than I can ever return."[19] Reuben was not interested in returns at that point; he was interested in putting Sam on his feet. Soon a plan presented itself. Samuel, as spokesman for the younger brothers, wrote and asked Reuben to put up the capital for a joint dry-farming venture. Despite the war, which was then about to engulf the United States, and despite the precarious nature of Reuben's own finances, he decided to plunge. "I . . . am willing to go in on any plan that promises to assist you boys," he said. In the late summer he sent Samuel a down payment for the old Woolley dry farm on the Stansbury highlands. Thereafter Reuben was in business with his younger brothers as well as the older ones.[20]

vii

John was four years younger and several inches shorter than Samuel. He had Frank's athletic frame and an exceptionally vigorous growth of sandy hair. Although Reuben extended the customary invitation for John to study in the East, he, like Samuel, was still uncertain about education. And so John also decided on a mission.

Returning from the Southern States Mission in 1916, John had a more mature appreciation of schooling and decided to give it a try. He and the youngest brother, Gordon, matriculated together at the University of Utah that fall, and Reuben made the house on D Street available to them. Before completing his first year of studies, however, John was tapped for military service. Somehow Reuben, at the apex of the draft system, had never thought of his own brothers being hauled off to fight in France, and the sudden specter of it jolted him hard. By telegraph he pursued John to American Lake, Washington, and then across the country to Camp Mills, New Jersey, trying to learn the details. But there were no details to learn. John was going off to fight the Huns and he was thrilled about it.[21]

Reuben was not thrilled; in fact, he was exceedingly upset. It was one thing to volunteer oneself to the war effort; volunteering one's brother was something else again, and Reuben feared that by failing to keep John out of the trenches he might personally be signing the boy's death warrant. Pulling every string at his disposal, he managed to have John assigned to the War Risk Bureau of the American Expeditionary Forces, where he served under Reuben's old friend Willard Straight. John was built like a bull, and he had the pugnacious good looks of a war-poster veteran. "I shall never be satisfied entirely with myself if I do not get up there to the front," he wrote to Reuben. "It's true I am doing my bit and trying to do it well. But my physical make up seems to demand more of me."[22]

John distinguished himself behind his desk and left the service as a noncommissioned officer. But the nearest he came to battle was a midnight air raid that ripped through his Paris neighborhood. To Reuben he described the event with adolescent wonder: the bright flashes of the anti-aircraft shells, the shriek of the bombs, the enemy plane bursting into flames and plummeting to earth.[23] For John it was a narrative of personal despair—the war he was missing. For his once pacifistic elder brother it was a recounting of pure horror.

viii

Gordon too was served with a draft notice, and he too was kept away from the fighting. For Gordon, though, the disappointment

Reuben, Gordon, and John Clark in uniform: More to the war than battle.

was less acute. Unlike John, Gordon was not healthy; indeed, though their features were similar, Gordon had the sunken eyes and perpetual squint of one who lives with pain. His dream was to study medicine and become a doctor, but migraine headaches took an early toll on him and reading became increasingly difficult. To Reuben he wrote: "I guess I will have to give up my life long and greatest ambition of getting an education and being someone, and try some other way of making a livelihood."[24]

Reuben did not agree. He encouraged Gordon to stay with his classes—at least one or two of them—until a treatment could be found. Then, in the summer of 1917, Reuben brought Gordon to Washington and had the troublesome eyes examined by a specialist. The ensuing treatment lasted a month and Reuben happily picked up the tab for it.[25] But no more than the western could the eastern physicians cure Gordon Clark. Eventually the young man was obliged to give over the battle, abandon his dreams, and settle for a blue-collar life.

ix

Of Reuben's three sisters, two—Alice and Lucille—died tragically within weeks of one another. They were attended in childbirth by a nurse who communicated the same deadly infection to both.[26] The deaths were a terrible blow to the Clark family, one from which Ma Clark never fully recovered. Reuben himself was a long time recovering. One of the girls, Lucille, had asked him for the same financial help he had given the brothers in order that she too might receive an education; and Reuben, believing that college was no place for a woman, had refused.[27]

He tried to make it up to the surviving sister, Esther. This girl, seven years younger than himself, had inherited her mother's face and a certain amount of her Woolley toughness. With the right man, Esther might have looked forward to a long and happy life— but her husband Arthur was not the right man. Both of them became victims of their marriage.

Arthur lost his fortune in a southern Utah potash operation and the shock of it drove him to drink. From that point his domestic life deteriorated rapidly, one misadventure leading to another. One night in 1920 he pulled his clothes from the closet and departed for good. Then followed the allegations, recriminations, and slanders. Arthur leveled them freely enough at Esther, and Esther had reason to reciprocate. Inevitably the children were dragged into it as pawns and go-betweens. By the time Esther had turned to Reuben for help it was an exceptionally sticky mess.[28]

Reuben was contemplating a political career at the time, and he knew that scandal tarred with a broad brush. Yet there could be no turning his back on Esther as he feared he had on Lucille. He rolled up his sleeves and came in swinging. In order to engineer an equitable divorce it was necessary, first, to disprove the imputations being made about Esther and, second, to verify those being made about Arthur. This Reuben accomplished with lawyerly precision. Infuriated, Arthur struck back with a vengeance, transferring his defamation from Esther to her brother—and soon it was Reuben who was being carved up by the town gossips. For a year and more Grantsville was not a pleasant abode for the Clark family.[29]

Reuben also helped cushion the aftershocks for Esther. With his influence she was able to obtain employment at the state capitol. Also with his help she was able to retain her house and some of the property that would have otherwise been forfeited. And when Christmas of 1921 threatened to be a lean one for Esther's broken family, Reuben, himself verging on ruin, sent her a gift of money. "I think you are the most wonderful man," Esther wrote, "one of the best of brothers, and a real Santa Claus."[30]

x

Reuben played Santa Claus to Luacine's family as well. Her brother Tim, for example, grew up under Reuben's watchfulness. Having lost his mother as a child, Tim adopted Reuben and Luacine as his "Pa" and "Ma." Tim's visible weakness was the quick buck, and he leaped from one exploit to another in pursuit of it. And if he occasionally slipped and fell, "Pa" was always around to pick him up. Reuben signed notes for the young man and floated personal "loans" to keep him solvent. "I am glad to help Tim when I can," he explained to Luacine, "though I have the feeling that possibly he may not be able to pay back."[31]

When he began courting beautiful—and wealthy—Veda Eccles, Tim wanted to make a good showing, so he approached "Pa" for another loan. Reuben obliged again but this time with some fatherly counsel. "Resolve now, and live up to the resolution," he cautioned Tim, when the marriage seemed certain, "to earn the family a living, to pay your own debts, and never under any circumstances to use any of Veda's money for your own business matters and inventions."[32] But Tim was all right. In fact, he and Veda ended up with a marriage of storybook happiness.

Reuben never regarded his largess to Tim or any other relative as almsgiving; rather, it was an application of what he might have called the family covenant, the notion that all fortunes and sorrows were to be shared as common property. It is less easy to understand Reuben's extraordinary devotion to his friends. Indeed, since he was neither the glad-hander moving through social gatherings like a honeybee nor the crony ever out with the boys, Reuben did not seem to mold friendship into the usual patterns. Nor did he make the customary choice between having a few close friends and large number of superficial ones. Reuben Clark wanted a large number of close friends.

And he had them. There was something tropistic in the way people gravitated toward him. Harry Armes trailed Reuben around the solicitor's office like a puppy, and Donald DeLashmutt took a cut in pay in order to follow him into private practice. "Why aren't you near enough to talk to?" asked Fred Dearing in one letter, adding, "I hope to be up next weekend. You must save me an hour at least."[33] From Europe, Huntington Wilson wrote, "When I get back . . . I shall be ravenously hungry for a talk."[34] And when the Senate seemed "somewhat puzzling" to Dwight Morrow, he sent out the same appeal. "I wish I might have someone like yourself here with whom to counsel," he said. "I am not enjoying it very much."[35]

One explanation, certainly, is that Reuben was deeply and sincerely interested in people. He listened to them with unflagging attention. When he spoke, his face, which could be forbiddingly taciturn, became mobilized with expressiveness and he pounded on the arm of his chair for emphasis. And when the visitor of the moment had departed Reuben might sit morosely for hours, fingertips together, thumbs cradling his jaw, eyes staring into space at the difficulty with which he had been made acquainted. On a friend's behalf he was capable of noble—and reckless—deeds. Once, while he was still in law school, a lady friend of the family suddenly found herself penniless and at the mercy of her landlord, who proposed taking out his rent in sexual favors; Reuben marched off to a bank and arranged a loan in order to rescue her. And later in life he paid from his own

399

pocket the extensive personal debts of another close friend—for which, alas, the friend never forgave him.[36]

Reuben's charisma, however, was more than a mere willingness to be involved. He found answers. When Otis Cartwright and his wife began having marital problems, they came to Reuben as to a marriage counselor.[37] Clement Bouvé, agent for the U.S.-Mexico Claims Commission, became so dependent on Reuben's counsel that he could not discharge his responsibilities without it. "I cannot tell you how much I miss you and how lonely it seems without you," wrote Matt Brush after Reuben had moved back to Utah. "It is going to be a terrible handicap not to have you where I can reach out to get your advice."[38] Of course, friendship was more than advice-giving, too. Reuben corresponded lifelong with James Talmage, John Bassett Moore, William Dennis, Fred Dearing, Enoch Crowder, Dwight Morrow, Philander Knox, and many others on any subject from politics to diplomacy to public morals.

His long evening conversations were equally wide open. They usually took place in Reuben's parlor or study, where the host would sink into one of the sturdy matching armchairs and seat his visitor in the other one. There would be glasses of lemonade and perhaps a tray of cookies brought in by Luacine. The talk might begin early and carry on indefinitely. By midnight coats would be off, sleeves rolled up, and ties loosened. If the visitor was a smoker, the air might grow heavy and stale; and still the conversation would continue. It could last until the small hours of the morning while the rest of the household slept. It was in these marathon sessions that Reuben Clark cemented the friendships of a lifetime.

xii

The most colorful—and perhaps the most illuminating—friendship was with Francis M. Huntington Wilson. Huntington Wilson was something of an enigma. By turns alienating and terrorizing his silken-mannered colleagues, he became the *enfant terrible* of the State Department. Yet, early in their acquaintance, he and Reuben Clark struck up a bonhomie that ran deep and lived long. In a way it came to symbolize all of Reuben's friendships.

In the darkest hour of Scott's tyranny the brash young assistant secretary, at considerable risk to himself, had done Reuben Clark an enormous favor; Reuben never forgot it. Because getting rid of Scott was no ordinary good turn, repayment as such was quite unthinkable. Nevertheless, Reuben was to have an opportunity to repay—beginning on the day in 1913 when Huntington Wilson's glamorous marriage suddenly shivered into atoms.

To understand why this event so shattered the once-confident diplomat, one had to know Lucy James Wilson. That she was attractive was a significant understatement. With her classic features, flashing dark eyes, and complexion of "matté white," she was, according to Colonel T. Bentley Mott, "one of the most beautiful and intelligent women the United States has ever produced."[39] Huntington Wilson had met her in the lobby of the Grand Hotel in Yokohama. Watching her walk by in the company of her millionaire parents, he had turned to a companion from the American legation and remarked: "There goes the most beautiful girl I ever saw."[40] Plenty of people agreed. Lucy, after the wedding, charmed and dazzled one stolid politico after another in order to secure her husband's appointment as third assistant secretary in Washington. Even stonehearted Elihu Root, when he "watched her sweep across the room like a long-limbed Atalanta," seemed to Archie Butt a conquered man.[41]

J. Reuben Clark was one of the few who could maintain his composure in Lucy's presence, and this novelty seemed to commend him to her. Indeed, she found the unassuming assistant solicitor to be a nimble dancer and good conversationalist.[42] Gradually, Reuben's friendship with Huntington Wilson came to include Lucy as well. Although he was certainly no part of their world of luxurious clothes, high-powered cars, and social extravagance, his quiet stability offered the Huntington Wilsons a sort of safe anchorage—and occasionally they needed one.

Lucy did in particular. In addition to her keen mind and angelic face she was born with an arch and mercurial temperament, a streak of brittle arrogance, and an abiding contempt for all things ordinary. As the Huntington Wilsons' attorney, Reuben became familiar with Lucy's costly frivolities (like crystal whiskey decanters), her offbeat charitable causes (like the Seamen's Church Institute), and her strange enthusiasm for eugenics, or "race betterment" (she once funded lectures on this subject at three hundred universities).[43] Reuben

401

clearly recognized the instability in Lucy's makeup, and he was not surprised to learn of her eventual nervous collapse.

xiii

What *was* surprising was the pivotal role Reuben came to play in the events that followed. After Huntington Wilson recovered from the shock of his wife's breakdown, the first person he contacted was Reuben Clark. "Huntington ... made a sort of confidant of me," Reuben reported to Ransford Miller, "as the one close friend at hand whom he felt to call in."[44] Still, as well as Reuben had known the Huntington Wilsons he was unprepared for the details that his friend now proceeded to reveal in a long series of evening conversations. The most telling, perhaps, was that Lucy had survived the first year of their marriage only because she had kept a loaded revolver within reach and could end her life whenever she chose.[45]

It went without saying that most friends, however intimate, would have gracefully bowed out at that moment; and Reuben thought seriously of so doing. But there was the irrepressible fact that Francis Huntington Wilson had once put his neck on the block for him. Accordingly, long after Huntington Wilson had retired to the guest bedroom, Reuben paced the floor of his study and plumbed the depths of his conscience. This was a nasty business, he knew, and no one who grappled with it would be free from ultimate responsibility—yet the simple, primary, and obdurate fact still remained that Reuben Clark could not let his friend down.

This was not to say that Reuben could save the marriage; he knew that he couldn't. The barriers of personality and temperament were too great for rational people to overcome, and Lucy Wilson was no longer even that. What Reuben must do was help them to extricate themselves quickly and cleanly—and in such a way as to assure their individual survival. It was a very big order.

With Reuben gently shoring him up, Huntington Wilson set out for Reno and the divorce mill. At the same time, Lucy, who was in seclusion at her Newport cottage, also sought Reuben's advice. The "cottage" turned out to be a small mansion with seventeen rooms and eight baths, finished resplendently in woods and tiles. Outside, overlooking the foaming Atlantic surf, Lucy and Reuben sat at a glass-topped garden table and spoke of the days before her breakdown. Although dark whispers of melancholy still beset her, Lucy was more clearheaded now than she had been for some time. In a series of jolting non sequiturs, she described her own ambivalence of love and hatred for her husband, miserably confessing her powerlessness in the present situation.[46] Gradually Reuben came to realize that he and he alone must make the fateful decisions.

xiv

The hardest decision was that despite Lucy's ambivalence the divorce must go through. "A resumption without love," he explained to her,

> without respect, without anything that ethics, religion, sociology, or biology regards as essential to a marriage state, would be wrong to both of you and to society. From what you have said to me, it would on your part be soul suicide; it would be for him soul atrophy. You both owe it to yourselves, your friends, and your race, to get the best out of life that life has for you.[47]

Generally, Lucy agreed with this view—agreed with it nearly hysterically—but there were those moments when she discordantly changed her mind. On the day after her husband's departure for the West, she telephoned Reuben at one o'clock in the morning, frantically and tearfully imploring him to bring Huntington back, to stop him in Chicago, to track him down in Nevada, anything.[48] And for his part, Huntington Wilson wrote to Reuben with touching diligence, anxiously inquiring about his wife's health, hoping against hope that the situation would somehow reverse itself. Reuben alone could see that it would not reverse itself, and he firmly held the divorce proceeding on course.

Reuben also, perforce, became therapist. He corresponded daily with both parties, the numbered sheets of onionskin in his letterbook soon counting into the hundreds. Huntington Wilson, his ego demolished, needed constant transfusions of sympathy and encouragement. Lucy, on the other hand, was like dealing with high explosives. Reuben patiently humored her delusions and did his best to avert her impulsive tangents. When at one delirious moment she wanted to go to Europe and fight in the trenches, he soberly reminded her that "one Lucy living is worth, for the cause, many, many Lucys dead."[49] He also tried to focus her attention on the attainable, sending her off on eugenics, philanthropy, anything at all in which she could score some accomplishment. "I have a strong belief," he told her, "that you can get much good personally out of a vigorous wholesome amount of thought on that which is not personal."[50] And persistently, if carefully, he tried to orient her thoughts toward the spiritual. "I find age brings me a faith," he wrote, "that there ... is a great omnipotent force, power, being, whatever you will, who is the great reservoir of knowledge and wisdom from which humanity gets the little it has; and further, that its help may be had for the proper asking. But I had not thought of preaching."[51]

So it went. There were more letters, more tears, more trips to Newport, more appeals to extradite Huntington from Reno, more wild vacillations to and fro. But Reuben held firm. To Huntington Wilson he explained: "I think her conscience requires her to do everything possible to secure a resumption, which she admits would be all but a living horror to her."[52] Thus fortified, the couple went through with the divorce.

XV

Lucy Wortham—the name she now assumed—did not recover rapidly, and she continued to rely on Reuben. As counselor and therapist, he went on listening to her troubles and encouraging her to master them. As for her former husband, Huntington Wilson was very nearly washed up. He found a "comrade" in Reno and, against Reuben's almost frantic admonitions, married her—but only long enough to give her claim to his fortune.[53] With a second divorce on his hands he was politically dead. Friends turned their backs on him and one of them, Congressman Herbert Parsons, vowed to see that he never entered public life again.[54] He drifted aimlessly around the country—San Francisco, Palm Beach, New York, Savannah, Philadelphia—stopping occasionally in Washington to see Reuben. On these visits he drank nonstop, spoke wistfully of his vanished grandeur, and amused the Clark children by tying a black stocking around his eyes while taking his afternoon nap. He was an altogether pathetic figure.

404

Try as he might, Reuben could not arrest his friend's downhill slide. He lectured fervently about forgetting the past and starting anew. "She is as dead to you," he said grimly. "That part of your life must be sealed up, air tight."[55] He strove mightily to bring Huntington Wilson back to his career, too, interceding several times with the Democratic administration in an unsuccessful attempt to return the former assistant secretary to the State Department.[56] When Reuben did at length manage to land Huntington Wilson an executive position with Frank Vanderlip's National City Bank, things simply did not work out. "To me the bank was a gilded cage," Huntington Wilson recalled. After six months he resigned.[57]

xvi

The end of the story was as sad as its beginning. Huntington Wilson did eventually bestir himself, remarry, and resolve to make a comeback. The year was 1928, and the Kellogg State Department with its many offices and functions had come to fulfill Huntington Wilson's old dreams. "I thought I could expect at least a legation, on my record," he supposed; but more than any legation he wanted the job that he himself had invented: the undersecretaryship.[58] And it just so happened that in June of that year, with the resignation of Robert Olds, the undersecretaryship was vacant. Huntington Wilson decided to make a try for it.

There was only one ironic hitch: Secretary Kellogg did not want Francis Huntington Wilson for undersecretary; he wanted J. Reuben Clark. However, the desire was not reciprocal. Reuben, in fact, would have gladly given up the undersecretaryship if Huntington Wilson could be installed in his place, and he bent every political muscle to achieve that end. Huntington Wilson was thrilled. "It seems fairly obvious that if you were the Department's first choice I should be second," he wrote breathlessly. "I can hardly believe that my various definite achievements . . . have been forgotten."[59]

Yet forgotten they were. The only recollection at the Department of State was of the two divorces, and the puritan Coolidge would not even remotely consider appointing him. Reuben had the glum task of breaking the news, together with the announcement of his own appointment. It was a thoroughly unhappy scene.

xvii

In the diplomatic world of the twentieth century friendship was a tool, a device, a means to some kind of preferment. Once again Reuben was out of his time. Reading the files of his private correspondence, one does not encounter the stylish or smart words, the catch phrases, the recognition signs of the cognoscenti; rather one finds anachronistic words like "honor," "decency," "integrity," and "love." These were the currency of Reuben's personal relationships. An Alger figure with a difference, Reuben Clark never abandoned friends just as he never abandoned family. For him, friendship was neither rational nor self-interested. It was a thing apart, existing in the prelogical and ectoplasmic realm of the spirit. And it ran very deep.

Chapter 22

THE PERILS OF POLITICS

Men who scouted the forests for political timber early began to notice J. Reuben Clark. As early as August of 1906, in fact, when Reuben was commencing his first job, Luacine reported "wild rumors of your becoming Senator, and even the President."[1] Such rumors were wild indeed in 1906, but there was a certain basis for them. Reuben Clark had good political credentials, and in time they got better. He had deep and strongly held convictions and a close identification with the people of Utah. He was responsible and honest and of clearly evident integrity. His high-level experience and connections were abundant. He spoke well, wrote well, was handy with the appropriate quip or quote, and when necessary could wield his wit in a slashing repartee. With his silver-white hair and expressive features he looked like a man of account, and his fastidious dress bespoke confidence. In a word, Reuben Clark seemed to have the ideal political persona—and beneath the persona he was real.

Reuben himself seemed to believe that political destiny awaited him. After all, he had attended a prestigious law school and had sought to throw in with Reed Smoot. His close friends—Knox, Morrow, Huntington Wilson—all nursed political aspirations. And most importantly, he received a constant patter of encouragement from those who knew him. "In due time ... I shall expect to see you in the United States Senate, where men of your type are needed," wrote John Bassett Moore.[2] "I have long hoped that you would soon be in the Senate," said AIC executive William Franklin Sands. "You are needed there."[3] "When is the Senator coming home?" an acquaintance asked Luacine. "I often hear you called this," she added.[4]

In view of the promise that surrounded him, Reuben's actual political career was surprising. Twice he ran for the Republican Senate nomination in Utah and twice he was soundly defeated. Three times

407

he was promised that he would be made secretary of state, either by candidates for the presidency or by incumbents seeking reelection, and all three times the bids were lost. Every presidential election in which he personally invested himself was either a disappointment or disaster for him. Throughout the course of his entire political career, in fact, the wrong man always won.

ii

Actually there were solid reasons for Reuben's misfortune. The first of them was Reed Smoot. Political careers were made or broken by this man, and it was in mute testimony of this fact that Reuben had originally desired to serve as his secretary in Washington. The ensuing contretemps cast a long shadow over Reuben's public life. He seemed to become invisible to the ever more powerful senator. Although he could and did perform political favors for Smoot, the process never seemed to work the other way around; and after a while Reuben gave up entirely. Once, after venturing to see the Utah politician on his brother Frank's behalf, Reuben vented his frustration. "If we were dealing with an ordinary person," he said, "my request under the circumstances should get you the appointment; but we haven't an ordinary person to deal with, so I do not know what will happen."⁵ (Smoot declined.) Reuben kept on accommodating Senator Smoot and Smoot kept on refusing to reciprocate; it was the most lopsided relationship in Washington.

In consequence, Reuben Clark was never really able to get into the swing of politics. He could make end runs around Smoot to Philander Knox perhaps, or even to Democratic senator William King, but he could not connect himself to his party's logical source of patronage. Unable to dispense favors, Reuben had little chance to build up a constituency back home. Politically he remained a man of the East.

This, in turn, led to the second reason for Reuben's sterile luck. He became disillusioned about the very notion of politics. The idea of patronage—a legitimate and fundamental aspect of any political system—became increasingly distasteful to him. Of course, patronage in the area of foreign affairs always made for complications anyway. Judge Wilfley mixing into the Mexican Revolution, Madame de Prévost spoiling the Alsop settlement, William Jennings Bryan politicizing the American-British Claims Commission—these were all sources of discomfort and embarrassment to Reuben and he grew extremely wary of them. Once, when an unsuccessful lobbyist thundered at him, "Do you know who I am? I represent the Standard Oil!" Reuben, as solicitor, thundered back: "I don't give a damn who you are! So far as I am concerned you stand in the same situation as that peanut vendor outside the window there, and I would do no more for you than I would for him."[6]

In short, then, Reuben Clark simply never developed the practical side of a political personality. He never got the hang of making deals, of rolling logs, of switching positions, of striking poses, of slapping backs, of testing the winds, and, most importantly, of splitting the difference through compromise. Many people saw this as the man's great strength, and they had their point. "You know, Reuben," said millionaire Dwight Morrow, "you of all men are the least impressed by wealth that I've ever known."[7] He was equally unimpressed by power. When a certain spoilsman once visited his office in Mexico City and threatened to politically crush ambassador Dwight Morrow if that latter did not yield to certain interests, Reuben leaned back in his chair and fastened cold blue eyes on the visitor. "While I am not sure exactly how the Ambassador will express himself," Reuben enunciated slowly and deliberately, "if I were the Ambassador, I would tell you to go to hell."[8] Others, however, recognized that such high-mindedness did not make for success at winning elections. Susa Young Gates, the fiery suffragette daughter of Brigham Young, often lectured Reuben on the subject. "You get the idea ... that if you do great work the work itself is your best recommendation" she said. "That may be all right so far as lawyers are concerned, but it is a mighty poor way to play politics. Politics," she added, "is a game."[9]

iii

Reuben Clark never learned to play the game. And so, rather than becoming a practical politician he became a political idealist. Like his father before him, he came to view politics solely in terms of principles and to see in the principles a transcendent moral significance. By the time he graduated from college he possessed a fully developed political cosmology–or, more accurately, political faith–and he did not alter a great deal of it thereafter.

He believed first of all in the sanctity of the American experiment and in the inspired nature of the Constitution. Of the party system that grew out of the Constitution, Reuben adopted a compelling, if oversimplified, historical interpretation. He believed that the respective fathers of the two parties, Hamilton and Jefferson, were divided not by "mere arbitrary party affiliations" but by "deep fundamental differences of mind and political thought."

The Hamilton group wished a vigorous, virile people, and that people to be united under a great federal government that would bring the utmost possible development at home, by promoting and fostering agriculture, the arts, the sciences, and the industries, that would ensure peace among the people if necessary by force, and that should be able to protect itself from foreign aggression or dictation.

The Jeffersonians took quite the contrary view. They did not want a strong government; they believed we should encourage chiefly agriculture, and that we did not want the industries; that revolution was a virtue, not to be obstructed; and they seemed fatuous enough to think that no other power would be particularly interested in taking anything from us.[10]

So described, it was not difficult to distinguish the good guys from the bad. "The Hamilton thought," as Reuben put it, "has always been creative, constructive in its effect, the Jeffersonian thought has always been destructive."[11] It was the Jeffersonians, for example, whom Reuben saw as having dragged the United States into civil war in the 1860s, and it was a later generation of the same who had conceived the League of Nations. And there was worse. Reuben believed that it was the Jeffersonians who had given the country such doubtful innovations as labor unions, political machines, and spoilsmanship, or, simply put, the politics of interest. Williams Jennings Bryan was for Reuben the Jeffersonian par excellence.

Himself not a practical politician, Reuben might be pardoned for overlooking the interest politics of the Hamiltonians. For what he seemed to ignore was Hamilton's belief that the federal government should be the ally of the rich and the well-born, that it should openly favor the fortunes of the fortunate. Forgetting this fact, Reuben was free to romanticize the whole of American political history. He could point to the love of the Hamiltonians for the Constitution, to their solid, middle-class nature, to their heroism in saving the Union from secession, to their continuing public spiritedness. It was Abraham Lincoln who was the archetype of the Hamiltonian—and he happened to be Reuben Clark's political patron saint.

The martyred Lincoln, whom through the vista of retreating years we see clothed with so much of truth, honor, and wisdom, of love for right, of hatred for wrong and oppression, of charity for his fellow man and of deep unselfish, unpolluted, unalterable, affection and devotion for his country, that he stands before us the most solemn, glorious, Christ-like figure in all our history.[12]

Reuben thus came to see American politics in exceptionally elevated terms. He reduced most issues to questions of right and wrong. He spoke not of power but of principles. He vested an almost mystical faith in the wisdom of the people, believing that the people should seek out the candidate, rather than the other way around, and that their intuitive sense of choice was not to be constrained. He saw the "Hamiltonian Party"—the GOP—as the voice of the people and equated party loyalty to patriotism. Accordingly, he could neither understand nor sympathize with infighting. "Our bickerings," he implored fellow Republicans, "are our only weakness, they are our enemy's strength, his only strength."[13] For Reuben the ultimate dishonor was to forsake the party or, worse, to divide it as Theodore Roosevelt had done. Reuben had witnessed that unhappy event at close range, and he eventually came to blame five decades of misfortune on it.

iv

Such were the tenets of Reuben's political faith—a faith he brought with him to the State Department in 1906 and preserved as best he could through the years that followed. At the same time, however, Reuben embarked upon what can only be described as his political education. As he was to learn, faith and enlightenment did not necessarily agree.

The essential thing he learned was that the Hamiltonians of the Republican party had selfish interests of their own and rarely held back from acting on them. Like locusts, GOP spoilsmen descended on his office in the State Department, and they did not seem to know or care about the effects of their importunities on American diplomacy. The Harding scandals delivered another blow to Reuben. He wrote puzzled letters to Senator Smoot, asking why attorney general Harry M. Daugherty (who later turned out to be involved in the scandals himself) did not move faster with his investigations. "Corruption in public officials should be punished no matter where that corruption may lie," he said with dawning disillusionment, "and nobody should be exempt because he happens to be highly placed, either in the party counsels or in the public esteem."[14]

But it was the League of Nations fight more than anything else that undid him. Reuben could understand Democratic support for the League; Republican support, on the other hand, was absolutely incomprehensible to him, and in order to make sense of it he began looking for bogeymen. He first spoke of "the international law trust" as somehow controlling the party's foreign policy.[15] He then spoke of "the Republican Internationalists and International Bankers"[16] and, with increasing frequency, of "the interests."[17] By 1921, however, he had finally and permanently identified the malevolent influence in the party's counsels, and it was an influence that few Hamiltonians would have condemned. It was Wall Street.

> I have been convinced for a long time, as I think I have often told you, that what we know as Wall Street, is bending every effort, first to secure the ratification of the Versailles Treaty, or, that failing, to tie us up in some equivalent way with some new treaty. To me the purpose of this seems obvious, namely, to put us behind, as a guarantor, the German indemnity bonds, thus making them easily marketable. This would leave the tax revenues of France, Great Britain, and Italy more available for the service of their own bonds—some hundreds of millions of which Wall Street has.[18]

The notion of conspiratorial powers in American politics is of course an old one. Reuben, along with other Republican conservatives, had habitually groused about bolsheviks and their subtle doctrines, especially with respect to Democratic policies. To suddenly turn on Wall Street in this manner was more than a little surprising. After all, as an affiliate of the American International Corporation, J. Reuben Clark was a part of Wall Street himself.

At any rate, from the League fight onward Reuben's suspicions were directed not only to the Left but to the Right as well. For his friend Knox he summarized his new position.

The more experience I get and the more reflection I give, the more my conviction clarifies that there was something more behind the phrase than Rooseveltian exuberance in his characterization of "malefactors of great wealth." I am come to the point where I feel that those whom we usually designate as the "interests" are as inimicable to the safety of this country as the labor unions and that a sure way to wreck the country is to put it under the control of either of them.[19]

This insight amounted to the one departure from Hamiltonianism that Reuben allowed himself. Alexander Hamilton had wanted the federal government to represent the rich and the powerful; Reuben Clark wanted it to represent everyone. His hope was not unlike that of Herbert Croly, whose seismic *The Promise of American Life* he had read in the winter of 1916. Suddenly Reuben himself could share Croly's vision of an America devoted to a truly common commonweal. "I think the country can better stand," he said, "a radical for the people, than a radical for the interests."[20] This was what he meant in his repeated use of the term "Americanism."

So resplendent was the idea and so starkly did it contrast with the existing practices of both parties that it brought Reuben to the intellectual crisis of his life; by 1920 he was ready to duplicate the treason of Roosevelt and abandon the Republican party. "Sometimes I feel that the Party is so much and deeply under the control of capital," he lamented, "that it has lost the viewpoint of the Public (disregarding Labor) at large so that nothing but a new party can bring us salvation."[21] It was not so much that Reuben had changed his mind, he thought, as that the party had changed its principles. It was a matter of getting back to Lincoln.

v

This was where Reuben stood when he decided to take up politics seriously and run for office. He had preserved intact the idealism of his youth, but only by denying fundamental aspects of the American experience. He had come to the place where ideas no longer grew out of facts—where, indeed, facts grew out of ideas.

413

As a politician on the hustings Reuben could thank his political faith for both his strengths and his weaknesses. He charmed the voters by being precisely the kind of altruistic politician he believed in; but, because he was that kind of politician, he never came close to winning an election. To the man himself and to his followers, this circumstance made for bitter disappointment.

The charm beamed out in every direction when Reuben made his impromptu stump against the League in the summer of 1919. So simple, so wholesome, and so evident was the sincerity behind his message that listeners were swept along in spite of themselves. Reed Smoot perked up for the first time in their twenty-year acquaintance and realized that here before his eyes was a political property. Suddenly the senatorial talk of the Utah politicians lost its flippancy. Preston Richards promised that if Reuben would return to the state in 1920 and campaign for Smoot he was certain to be the Republican senatorial nominee in 1922.[22]

By the spring of 1921, the Clark-for-Senate movement was gaining momentum. Richards traveled to Washington and talked to several Republican heavyweights—including Knox, Smoot, and George Sutherland—finding the comment uniformly favorable.[23] The only conceivable difficulty was that Reuben had spent so much of his adult life in the East that he might be regarded as an outlander.[24] But this objection Richards deemed minor. "The way things are lining up," he reported, "it is absolutely inevitable that you will be the next Senator from Utah."[25]

The spirit of hopefulness carried through the year. James H. Anderson, a former editor of the *Deseret News,* began preparing articles and sending out favorable news releases about Reuben;[26] and "Aunt Susa" Gates brought her acute political mind into the advisory circle.[27] There were, she said, any number of little items that could be posted in the local papers relating to Reuben's business and social activities in the capital. At this juncture, however, Reuben's old political faith began to assert itself. "I feel that the office should seek the man and not the man the office," he submitted loftily. "This may be a trifle Quixotic, but nevertheless it is my feeling."[28]

The less quixotic were undeterred. Beginning in May of 1922, a group of Clark supporters began meeting weekly in the office of attorney John F. Bowman to lay out strategy.[29] Their main difficulty

414

was neither the disposition of the voters nor the threat of rival contenders, but the candidate himself, who was honestly and sincerely awaiting the call of the party. There was much that Reuben might have been doing to hasten the call along, yet he would stoop to none of it. He would not even stay in Utah but instead kept running back to the East on business. After repeated frustrations, the group had to settle for circulating two thousand copies of a personal letter from Bowman "To My Friends."[30] Even so, Utah Republicans seemed enthusiastic about Reuben's candidacy. The *Boston Transcript* predicted that he would unseat Senator King.[31]

vi

All of this, however, was reckoning without the opposition, which came to center in the person of Ernest Bamberger. Bamberger in 1922 was forty-five years old (several years Reuben's junior), but he had the smooth face and clean features of a man half that age. With steady hazel eyes, a long straight nose, and hair slicked to the side in the approved Rudy Vallee style, he looked as though he might have just stepped out of Eton. Bamberger was the scion of a wealthy Jewish family of mineowners and industrialists and was himself trained as a mining engineer. Educated at Williams College and Columbia, he had managed three mining companies and a coal operation, and he was only getting started. But his political experience was limited to a single term as Republican national committeeman.[32]

Bamberger and Clark represented portraits in contrast. Wealthy, powerful, and well connected locally, Bamberger belonged to all the right clubs and knew all the right people, while Reuben Clark was neither wealthy nor well known. In politics as well, Bamberger represented the obverse of Reuben's rational idealism. He simply believed that public office could be purchased, and in 1922 he decided to buy himself one.

This was to be accomplished by means of a political machine organized in Salt Lake City that year by Republican politico George Wilson and bankrolled by the Bamberger fortune. Taking a mystical number from the Old Testament, the founders of this organization called themselves "The Sevens" and made the most of it. An inner ring of seven principals each recruited seven satellites, who in turn

415

drafted seven of their own, and so on. The group held secret meetings and had a colorful ritual of recognition beginning with the question, "Which way are you going?" and ending the words "Jere" and "Miah" to form the name of the ancient prophet. Discipline and loyalty were mandatory, and punishment might consist of political blacklisting. A few of the Sevens, notably Wilson himself, were rumored to be involved in kick-back and protection rackets; but whether the charges were material or not, the Sevens unquestionably controlled the Republican politics of Salt Lake City, most of Salt Lake County, and a good deal of the state of Utah.[33]

Given Reuben Clark's approach to politics on the one hand and Ernest Bamberger's on the other, there was never much of a contest between them. Indeed, the Sevens had little difficulty dealing with the Clark campaign. They took note of the fact that Reuben had lived in the East for something like the last twenty years and promptly labeled him a carpetbagger. That stung. Reuben sat down to the typewriter and composed a reply that spared no use of the rapier. He called the charge "maliciously and wantonly false" and described it as a "blow from the back." Then, after setting out the facts of the case—his permanent residence in Salt Lake, his farm in Grantsville, the periodic summer visits of his family—he said,

> That in the face of all these facts and of the intent that lay always behind them to have and to hold Utah as my home, there should be those who have the hardihood to decry me as a "carpetbagger," to seek to expatriate me, and to attempt to outlaw me in my own land, in short, to deny to me my home and my birthright, is an affront, which, to face calmly, I find most difficult. It suggests the ends to which a needy aspirant for office will go to bolster a bad begging.[34]

Yet, after Reuben's anger cooled the political gentleman reemerged. As he read back over the typescript, it did not seem to reflect the right sense of himself. Ten days later, when the final draft of this announcement of candidacy appeared in the *Salt Lake Tribune,* there was not a word in it about the carpetbagger issue.[35]

Instead Reuben reaffirmed his belief that the office should seek the man. If the convention should conclude "that I may perhaps meet the necessary qualifications as well as any other," he said, he would carry the party's banner with pride. As for would-be opponents, the heaviest comment he could offer was an oblique observation. "The people of Utah learned long ago that political office is too vital a thing to be sought by or lightly bestowed upon the mediocre or the unworthy." When it came to issues and programs, Reuben, still in tune with Herbert Croly, offered something for everyone. He would cut taxes and build tariffs for the nation's industries; reduce freight rates and improve marketing facilities for the farmers; cut back "the improper dominating power of the great aggregations of wealth" for labor; and curtail government expenses for everybody.[36]

Reuben's announcement of candidacy set the tone for the rest of his campaign, which was short, simple, and utterly doomed. Unwilling to speak, write, or put in appearances in his own behalf, Reuben limited his activities to a single letter which he sent to each of the convention delegates in the belief that they would be free to choose whomever they wished. "I have no organization whatever and no workers except personal friends," it began.

Should yourself and your colleagues at the Convention conclude I should have the nomination, I should feel I was the choice of the whole Republican Party, and being elected, I would understand I represented the entire people of the State with a duty in the Senate to advance the interests of Utah and her people and to protect and foster the rights and interests of the United States among the nations.[37]

These were not the words of a man primed for victory, and Reuben Clark was not so primed. In fact, he knew he was going to lose. His one hope lay in a convention deadlock between Bamberger and the second leading contender, William Wattis, also well known and well financed. In such a case, Reuben might conceivably come forward as a dark horse. Otherwise, like the protagonist of a Greek tragedy who knows and accepts his fate, he steeled himself for the inevitable. "If . . . the convention shall decide, as I anticipate it will, that someone else shall carry the standard of the Grand Old Party in the approaching campaign, I shall be quite content," he promised himself. "I do not crave the glamor of Washington. I know its shallowness."[38]

vii

The delegates convened on Friday, July 14, at the old Salt Lake Theater. As soon as they were assembled it became painfully clear that the Sevens had done their work well. Using Bamberger's money they had hired precinct workers all over the state and employed them to rig the various county conventions. For the Salt Lake County convention, for example, the machine had held a trick primary and elected Bamberger men to a majority of the 206 state delegate slots; then they had passed a resolution instructing *all* the delegates, Bamberger men and others, to vote en bloc—which meant to vote for Bamberger.[39] The few remaining uncommitted delegates were wined and dined profusely as they stepped from the train in Salt Lake. One county chairman told Reuben that five members of his delegation had switched to Bamberger in the space of two days and that he himself had been assured that recent financial losses "need not be losses" if he voted for the right man.[40] Wired so well, the proceedings of the convention did not last long. Bamberger rolled up 357 votes on the first ballot, far more than enough for the nomination; William Wattis received 182½ votes; and Reuben Clark was left with 33, most of them cast by Salt Lake County renegades.[41] Had it not been for the bloc vote, which triggered an hour of bedlam in the hundred-degree heat, Bamberger and Wattis would have almost certainly deadlocked one another, leaving the convention wide open.

So much for the battle. As for the war, that did not go so well for Bamberger and the Sevens. Utah Republicans could be bought out or steamrolled under, but apparently they could not be made to like it. Delegates came away from the Salt Lake Theater fuming with indignity and threatening revenge. "A more disgraceful gathering I never attended in all my life," wrote one of them to Reuben.[42] Said another: "Six times I tried to get the floor, thinking that enough sanity might be in evidence to check the riot, but chaos ruled the day."[43] "The matter was decided before the convention assembled," observed a third correspondent, adding, "There was no reason to expect the humiliating spectacle that was presented."[44] Nor could Bamberger neutralize the effect of these schismatics with a forceful campaign style; as a public speaker he left much to be desired. Senator King, by contrast, was vibrancy itself, one of the great political orators of the Mountain West. Soon Reed Smoot had to step into the campaign in order to avert disaster. Smoot it was who fought the real battle, in fact, stumping the state for the candidate and trading blows with Senator King. Amid the fireworks Ernest Bamberger slipped quietly out of sight. One newspaper quoted him only twice.[45]

Reuben Clark also campaigned for Bamberger's election, although he told Fred Dearing that doing it was the hardest job of his life. "Were it not for the fact that my staying away would be charged to pique," he said, "I should never go near the place."[46] But there was more to the matter than that. Reuben's political faith, although severely tried, had not quite been shaken and it continued to govern his view of himself. He had not been chosen by the party, but he must pitch in with the same energy and dedication as if he had. Accordingly he traveled back to Utah from New York, whence the AIC had summoned him, and made more than a dozen speeches for Ernest Bamberger. Senator King, for one, was impressed by the speeches. "If you had run," he told Reuben, "I could not have defeated you."[47]

viii

This was a fate that could have befallen anyone. Bright and promising, Reuben Clark, like many another political aspirant, had been urged by his friends to run for Congress and had been trounced. That should have been that. Reuben should have returned to his law office, a chastened but wiser man, and left politics to the politicians. When never-say-die friends attempted to revive his candidacy at the next senatorial go-around, he should have met them with a sad, knowing shake of the head. Yet strangely enough, the scenario of 1922 was reenacted six years later in letter-perfect detail. Present in 1928 were the same parties and the same issues. Ernest Bamberger was back, not much the worse for wear; and so were the Sevens, more deeply entrenched and more powerful than ever. J. Reuben Clark again played the Galahad and William H. King the invincible foe. Where the practical politician would have learned from hard experience, Reuben Clark seemed determined to repeat it.

For what reason? Reuben's defeat, it seemed, had been interpreted by grass-roots Republicans as a defeat of the very politics for which he stood. "Personally," said one of them, "I was chagrined, saddened, humbled, [at] that which was designed to reflect and express liberty, becoming the instrument of a mob."[48] Wherever Luacine went people expressed their sorrow and dismay and their conviction that the nomination had been stolen. Reuben possibly came to believe that he could not be party to such a shameful transaction—even the wronged party. On his desk there reposed a bronze miniature of the martyred Abraham Lincoln, slumped moodily in the Lincoln Memorial pose and ever reminding the man before him of first principles. So great was Reuben's faith in the American political system that he may have imagined he had to run for the Senate a second time in order to vindicate it.

ix

The question was, what would be done differently the second time around? Clark supporters, at least, had learned some lessons. For example, in March 1927, a full year before the campaign was to begin, Preston Richards approached LDS church president Heber J. Grant with the possibility of Reuben's running again.[49] Grant was a nominal Democrat, but he had supported Wattis in 1922 on the theory that political office ought to be evenly divided between church people and nonchurch people.[50] And Albert Bowen, who was to become central to the Clark campaign, began thinking long and hard about financing. As a result of Bowen's concern, the Clark committee retained the services of a professional campaign manager by the name of Frank Kimball, who coolly estimated fifteen thousand dollars as the minimal cost of the nomination.[51] Furthermore, there was better coordination and timing in the matter of announcements, as well as a more effective use of the media. For example, less than a week after Reuben's official announcement of candidacy, Walter Lippmann, editor of the Democratic *New York World,* wrote a supporting editorial that fairly sparkled with superlatives—and a copy of it was telegraphed to Bowen the day before.[52]

But however they might refurbish the machinery, there was no refurbishing the candidate. Reuben still refused to join the clubs or show up at the affairs. And when he heard about Kimball's fifteen-thousand-dollar price tag, he almost went through the ceiling. "If you can get together fifty men who will invest $50 each in me," he wrote to Bowen, "you will have the strongest organization there is in the State."[53] Worst of all, Reuben would not come home to campaign. He was in Mexico with Ambassador Morrow throughout

420

most of 1927 and 1928, and he shrugged off the frantic appeals to return. "I am sure you will agree with me," he answered one, "that if my 'ambition' should get in the way of my duty, my duty must prevail."[54] This being the candidate's attitude, there could be little doubt of the final outcome. "Let's give up, Pa," wrote Luacine, "and save yourself needless worry—and a crushed feeling that is sure to come if defeated."[55] That he would not do, either. "I am not worrying about the situation," he wrote to John A. Widtsoe. "The whole thing is, as the ancients would say, 'in the laps of the Gods.' "[56]

Lacking Reuben's presence, the Clark committee did the best it could. Frank Kimball, disgruntled, resigned as chairman and his place was taken by Reuben's cousin Edwin D. Hatch.[57] A headquarters of sorts was opened in two rooms of the less-than-elegant Kenyon Hotel, and Hatch began sending out letters and pamphlets.[58] There were plenty of invitations for the candidate to speak before various civic groups, but with Reuben still in Mexico these had to go by the board. Poor Hatch spent more effort persuading his candidate than persuading the voters. "Supporters demanding your presence," he wired anxiously. "Believe imperative you be here immediately. Wire date of your return."[59] Thus demoralized, the efforts of the Clark people were neither well organized nor especially effective. Luacine put the matter insightfully when to Reuben she observed, "Your organization as they came out of the building [looked] too 'Mormonie' and not the hustler type enough for rotten old politics."[60]

In consequence, the real hustler types once again made short work of the Clark campaign. Rumor soon had it that Reuben was uninformed and uncaring about Utah's problems, that Dwight Morrow was paying a king's ransom to purchase the nomination for him, and that "all you came home for is to get a political job."[61] As the convention drew near, the Clark people once again intercepted the familiar signals of manipulation. "I find that the machine is doing what they can," said one correspondent, "and several of the boys that believe different are afraid to oppose them."[62] The machine was indeed doing what it could. The Sevens now had six years of experience behind them and some solid political successes. In 1924 they had succeeded in ousting Charles R. Mabey as governor, and by 1926 they had brought to terms every major Republican officeholder in the state.[63] Their bag of tricks had expanded too. In addition to the trick primary and the bloc vote, the Sevens had perfected such devices as ballot-box stuffing, voting repeaters, and voting aliens.[64] With mechanical certainty they began closing in on the senatorial nomination.

x

However, the Sevens had also made some enemies. Burton W. Musser, a prominent Democratic politician, had begun publicly attacking the Bamberger machine back in 1926, and by the summer of 1928 the attack had broadened. Spirited editorials began appearing in small tabloids like the *Sugar House Times* and even in the larger Salt Lake papers. Said one:

> There is a bigger and more important issue involved than the personal qualifications of J. Reuben Clark or Ernest Bamberger. The Republicans of Salt Lake City will decide next Monday as to whether or not a secret political machine, known as the "Sevens" is to dominate their state convention. They will decide as to whether or not the "Grand Kleagle" of this organization will name the next Republican candidate for the United States Senate or whether the rank and file of the party will retain that privilege. They will decide as to whether or not the Republican party is to be owned, controlled and voted by a small group of politicians, or whether it is to continue as a dominant factor in Utah politics. They will decide as to whether or not the voice of a clique and a well oiled and well nourished political machine is more potent than the voice of the people.[65]

Unlike the previous campaign, Reuben was now acknowledged as the leading challenger to the Sevens' monopoly and thus as the candidate of the rank and file. It was shaping up as a classic confrontation between the people and the interests.

xi

Reuben did not arrive in the state until July 12, only a month before the convention, but he came to campaign in earnest. He stoked up the Clark committee, gave radio addresses, placed a newspaper ad, and undertook a whistle-stop tour of the state.[66] Of even greater importance, Reuben ceased telling people that he was not seeking the Republican nomination. The time had come, he decided, to stop talking about the wisdom of the party and start doing something about it. By the eve of the convention he almost had a real campaign in progress.

The convention was held in Ogden's old Egyptian Theater. As the delegates settled in among the plaster pharaohs or slipped down to the speakeasy on west 24th Street for a free drink on the Sevens, they noted an atmosphere charged with expectancy.[67] One pundit had bet a new hat that there would be "at least one fist fight" on the convention floor and said that he had already bought the hat.[68] It was the culmination of what an observer called "one of the fiercest battles in the history of the Republican Party."[69]

When the delegates voted with their voices—shouting, cheering, applauding tumultuously—the tally appeared to be even: a "storm" for Ernest Bamberger versus a "tempest" for Reuben Clark.[70] Joshua, Sr., was listening to a broadcast of the convention in Preston Richards's parlor, and the sounds leaped out of the cathedral radio like bursts of static.[71] But when the voting proceeded to the ballots, the power of the Sevens became manifest. By a vote of 525¾ to 319, Bamberger was nominated once again on the first ballot.[72] Edwin Hatch, at a nod from Reuben, moved that the nomination be made unanimous and the motion carried. Then the defeated candidate took the floor himself. Looking out at the rows of faces and knowing that many of them had sold him out, Reuben was unexpectedly well composed. He wished to say, he began, that the party was bigger than any man in it and that the welfare of state and nation were more vital still. It was one of the "glories of our free institutions" that, though Americans engaged in spirited rivalries for political preferment, they happily abided the choice of the majority. "I then bespoke for Mr. Bamberger the support of all those who had honored me by working for my own nomination," Reuben recalled.[73] The delegates were deeply moved and some of them actually ashamed. "You stood head and shoulders above any one in the entire Convention Hall," one of them later wrote, "and by comparison made your successful rival look like a little dwarf."[74]

xii

And how did one campaign against the brilliant Bill King with a little dwarf? It was a serious problem. Smoot had stepped into the earlier campaign, but it seemed unlikely that he would do so again. Moreover, the bitterness of the disappointed Clark partisans was uncontainable: they would slash the party to ribbons, some of them, before they would countenance the election of Ernest Bamberger. But the Bamberger managers supposed that they had the answer to these difficulties: J. Reuben Clark himself. If it came down to the hard choice of seeing a Democrat reelected, thought they, the defeated aspirant could be counted upon to rally his shattered forces and even to make the same hard-hitting speeches as in 1922. However, the Bamberger managers were in for a surprise. The morning papers, instead of headlining Reuben's defeat at the Egyptian Theater, headlined his appointment as undersecretary of state—and announced that he would soon be leaving for Washington.[75]

This meant big trouble for the Bamberger campaign, and everyone knew it. In fact, no sooner had Reuben arrived at his State Department office in Washington than the first letter from the Bamberger people reached him. Campaign manager Carl Marcusen complimented Reuben for his sportsmanship at the convention and then got down to business. It was absolutely essential that the undersecretary return to Utah for the campaign, he said. Such was the state of the Republican party that Reuben Clark alone could pull it back together.[76] On September 22 Reuben responded politely to this entreaty and sent Marcusen some material that could be published over his name. He reiterated what he had said in Ogden about good losers and party unity. That would have to suffice.[77]

But it did not suffice. Indeed, the situation began to grow complex and volatile. In Utah a whispering campaign broke out to the effect that Reuben—sometime, somewhere—had told Senator Smoot that he would not support Bamberger and for that reason would not return to the state.[78] Reuben's credibility was now on the line. And, as if this were not enough, the Bamberger people steadily increased the pressure. They bombarded Reuben with supplications, wrote to the Republican National Committee, and then appealed directly to Secretary of State Kellogg.[79] The Utah senatorial campaign had literally followed Reuben to Washington.

Tighter and tighter the dilemma seemed to wind in upon itself. Reuben went to Secretary Kellogg and asked for permission to return to Utah. Kellogg replied that since he, the secretary, must leave

Washington on extended business the request would have to be denied.[80] Then Smoot got into it. He told Kellogg that if Clark were not allowed to return to Utah the loss of the senatorial campaign would be upon his, Kellogg's, head.[81] In long, agonized letters, Reuben attempted to spell out the intricacies of his problem to Harold P. Fabian, the national committeeman for Utah; but Fabian, like Marcusen, apparently did not believe him. They thought he was taking cheap vengeance on Bamberger.

Then came the counterpressure. Clark men all over the state began writing to Reuben and begging him to stay in Washington and keep quiet. Bamberger had made his bed, they argued; now let him sleep in it. Every time Reuben sent an endorsement of any kind to Marcusen, these diehards groaned in dismay. On October 10 Reuben wrote a second letter to Marcusen strongly endorsing Bamberger.[82] On the twenty-eighth he sent Fabian a wire urging Utah voters to elect "a full Republican ticket, National and State," adding that "Republican control of the Senate may depend upon whether or not Mr. Bamberger is sent from Utah."[83] Each syllable of these missives cut Reuben's own supporters like a knife. Could it be, they began asking one another, that Reuben Clark himself had sold out to the Sevens?[84]

By the end of October Reuben was disgusted and heartsick. "I have swallowed a great deal in this campaign in the form of misrepresentation, crooked political deals, corruption, et cetera, all aimed against me," he wrote to Harold Fabian, "but I have swallowed it all and smacked my lips as if I liked it."

I have tried to shape my course as if I had not been personally involved. You know what I did at the Convention; you also know what I did in my letter to Marcusen of September 22d, and what I again did in my letter to him of October 10th. These you have before you. I also made a contribution to the State Committee which, though small, was characterized by Marcusen as "extremely liberal." I have voted (absentee vote) a straight Republican ticket; I have urged others to vote a straight Republican ticket. These things are known in Utah; my telegram to Marcusen today is framed with the idea that he can make it public if he desires, thus restating my position.

Dr. Work and Senator Smoot this morning express themselves as if they thought that all I would have to do would be to go to Utah and wave my hand and the whole vote of Utah would change. Of course this is ridiculous as you know, as well as I. My going to Utah would scarcely change one vote. You know, and I know, that this movement is not founded upon my personal defeat at the Convention. I am only an incident in this situation, and so far as I can see, an incident in a way that may bring personal punishment. However, that is neither here nor there.[85]

Reuben did not know it but at the moment of this letter the future of Utah Republicanism hung in a critical balance. In Salt Lake the issue of machine politics had suddenly and dramatically come to the fore. There had been talk in the papers for some time about the Sevens and their doings, though most of it had been discounted as election-year froth. But on the eve of the election former governor Charles R. Mabey, himself a victim of the Sevens, had suddenly begun to arraign the Wilson-Bamberger machine in a cogent, specific, and unprecedentedly convincing way.[86] He had pointed up such damaging information as the fact that the Sevens' mailing address happened to be Ernest Bamberger's office on Main Street. On October 25 the attack was joined by *Deseret News* editor Joseph J. Cannon, and then by a series of anonymous chain letters.[87] Overnight, political secrecy had become not just *an* issue but *the* issue of the campaign—and all the while Reuben Clark was innocently casting forth his hearty endorsements of Ernest Bamberger.

"The publication and wide circulation of your letters and telegrams to State Committee causing furor in State politics," cabled Albert Bowen on the thirtieth; "Suggest you send nothing further until letter arrives which should by Friday."[88] This was Reuben's first clear hint that something was amiss. A second followed within the hour from Oscar W. Carlson. "The report is going around here that you favor and support the Sevens Organization stop Is this true? stop Reply immediately."[89] Reuben Clark did not pause to examine the implications of the Carlson telegram—or of his reply. He had had enough of politics. He had no more time and no further inclination to assess the subtle emanations of mood and feeling that might, through the course of a dozen tactical moves, redound to the benefit or detriment of this or that candidate. It was time to get back to first principles. Bless Bamberger Reuben might, if only for the sake of the party, but he would be damned if he would bless the Sevens.

So it was that Reuben Clark came to send the telegram that destroyed Ernest Bamberger, obliterated the Sevens, and dramatically altered the course of Utah politics. The telegram read:

Have always been and am now opposed to any and all secret political organizations whatever their name and however they are constituted, because in my view such organizations are contrary to the genius of our free institutions and dangerous to their perpetuity. I have never belonged and do not now belong to any such organization.[90]

The telegram appeared in Sunday's *Tribune* under the headline, "J. Reuben Clark Condemns Sevens."[91] It ripped the Utah Republican party cleanly in two and sealed the doom of the Bamberger campaign. Where Bamberger had lost by a mere six hundred votes in 1922, he now proceeded to lose by twenty thousand, almost all of them in Salt Lake County.[92]

xiii

There were, of course, any number of postmortems. Reuben's own retrospective, written to Fabian a week after the election, argued that what had destroyed the political machine was the righteous anger of the rank and file.[93] This judgment was hasty. Far more important than the rank and file had been J. Reuben Clark himself. He alone commanded a following wide enough and fervent enough to scotch the election, and he alone could have inspired them to do so. The outcome might better have been chalked up to idealism than to the sovereign will of the people, for in the last analysis Reuben's own ideals were the only real sticking point. He proved that he could "swallow," as he put it, almost anything in the way of personal gall and humiliation, that he could deliver stirring appeals to solidarity in the face of his own defeat, that he could repress and dissemble every natural human response to outrage save one: he could not deny his political faith. He could not bring himself to believe that the system brought forth by the Founding Fathers and saved from destruction by Abraham Lincoln could be, like the rest of political society, narrow, self-seeking, and corrupt. When it came down to choosing between his own world of responsible, disinterested politics and the real world of the practical politicians, Reuben steadfastly hewed to the one and rejected the other. This was no way to win elections, as Aunt Susa had suggested, but for J. Reuben Clark it was the way things had to be.

427

xiv

As the election of 1928 receded into history, Reuben turned away from politics and the notion of office, much as he had turned away from business and the notion of wealth. He would ever remain the avid spectator, but he would never again be the participant. Probably Reuben did not identify the flaw of his political career as a part of the East-West tension that had polarized his life, but in a sense it certainly was. Being a United States senator would have meant returning to the East permanently. In this connection, one of the condolences from disappointed friends took on special meaning. "I do hope that somehow affairs may permit you to do your work, your big work, here at home, among your own people, where strength will flow to you," wrote Elder John A. Widtsoe, after the earlier defeat. "You are needed here," he added, "—and there is a place for you."[94]

Chapter 23

STRANGER IN BABYLON

Going East was not the usual thing for Utah Mormons to do. To the eastern mind Mormonism at the turn of the century still defied everything decent and Christian in America. And the hostility was mutual. After all, Mormons told themselves, it was in the East that the Saints had been persecuted and the Prophet murdered,* that plural marriage had been outlawed, and, lately, that forces had been unleashed toward the very destruction of the church. Crossing the Mississippi, then, amounted to entering the camp of the enemy. It was like crossing over into Babylon.

Reuben accepted this state of affairs. He had grown up with it. The Merrill Anti-Bigamy Act had been passed shortly prior to his birth. He was eleven years old when the Edmonds Act was adopted, sixteen when the Edmunds-Tucker Act supplanted it, and nineteen when the Cullom-Strubble Act heaped final indignities on the church. He could remember when the First Presidency had gone underground, when federal marshals had ridden through the streets of Grantsville in pursuit of "cohabs," when numbers of the truly obstinate had packed up their goods and struck out for Mexico. Being nonpolygamous, the family of Joshua Clark, Sr., had not been one of the direct casualties of the "Mormon War"; but all church members were indirect casualties. All stood to lose the benefits of statehood and even American citizenship, and all became victims of the same siege mentality.

One aspect of that mentality was a deep-rooted identity crisis. In the beginning, Mormonism and Americanism had been synonymous.

---

*Joseph Smith, the founder of Mormonism, was murdered by a mob in Carthage, Illinois, in June of 1844. He is accepted by Mormons as a modern-day prophet similar to the prophets of the Old Testament.

Believers in the Book of Mormon had also believed in the divine nature of the United States and regarded its establishment as the fulfillment of ancient prophecy.* It was only when the persecutions began—when the Saints were driven out of Ohio, and then Missouri, and finally Illinois—that the sense of identity began to change. By the outbreak of the Civil War, no less a Mormon than Brigham Young could pronounce good riddance to the American republic; and in the postwar years there were such institutions as the "Political Kingdom," the "Gentile Boycott," and the "Mormon Party" to remind the faithful that they were different from other Americans.† But the old prophecies were still in existence and presumably still in force. Though America had spilled the blood of the prophets, who knew but what it was not still destined to be governed by them?

ii

Reuben Clark had grown up amid the Latter-day Saint orthodoxy of Grantsville. He had attended his church meetings and had received the necessary ordinances. As a holder of the priesthood, he had exercised sacerdotal authority in modest ways and had shown himself to be an animating preacher of the gospel.‡ So simple and well-rooted a faith was rarely ruffled by controversy, and life in small-town Utah generally remained placid. But the same was not true of Salt Lake City; in a confusion of Mormon versus Gentile, free market versus cooperative, and authority versus conscience, the metropolitan community seemed hopelessly torn and shivered. Here it was that the Latter-day Saints were beginning to come to terms with their uncertain identity, and the experience was an exceedingly painful one.

During his years in the city, Reuben evolved from the Grantsville boy of unalloyed faith into a far more complex, rational, and questioning individual. The change in him demanded a suitable

---

*See footnote on p. 4.

†These terms refer to the various political and economic organizations which attempted to institutionalize a sense of separate identity among Latter-day Saints.

‡In the Mormon church there is no paid or professional clergy. Male church members are endowed with priesthood authority at the age of twelve and are regularly upgraded in the possession of such authority until they reach the level of elder at about the age of nineteen. Elders are eligible to conduct most of the regular ordinances of the church.

explanation, and in time Reuben came up with one. Scientists and lawyers, he said, were not usually "blindly credulous or religious," because they of all people could accept nothing on faith. Scientists were always required to support their hypotheses through experimentation; lawyers were always responsible for facts. "[The lawyer] must consider motives, he must tear off the mask and lay bare the countenance, however hideous. The frightful skeleton of truth must always be exposed." This rule applied to religion, he continued. Here as elsewhere the scientist or the lawyer had to submit every conclusion to "the firey [*sic*] ordeal of pitiless reason," bringing to all doctrines, all preachments, and even the very scriptures themselves a final conclusive test. "What he can himself reason out according to his standards, he accepts unqualifiedly; whatever cannot stand his tests, he rejects as unfit."[1]

Later on, viewing Utah from a distance, Reuben applied his new-found skepticism broadly; and when he did so, the world of his Mormon childhood often came up short. In examining the career of Reed Smoot, for example, Reuben discovered much that displeased him. Smoot was at once a Mormon apostle and a United States senator—a rather visible linking of church and state. By 1914 Reuben regarded Smoot's dual affiliation as "unfortunate." Men who spoke with divine authority should be recognized ecclesiastically, he allowed; but in matters of civil government there could be no single holy mandate.

Religion having been established by a divine being, and civil government having been established by men for their own guidance and control, the two [are] entirely separate and distinct; and the qualifications essential to a great religious leader, [are] not necessarily those which must be possessed by a great civil leader.[2]

Polygamy was the next topic to come under scrutiny. Never quite happy with the practice in Utah and repeatedly embarrassed by it in Washington, Reuben was hard put for kind words. In his view, polygamists either violated the law as a matter of course or else they fled the country and forsook their American birthright; but worst of all they brought—and daily continued to bring—the entire church into discredit. When the Manifesto had come forth in 1890, there was a chance, as Reuben believed, for the church to rid itself of plural marriage once and for all. Yet there were those for whom opposition had become a way of life, and they would oppose the prophet himself in their willfulness. With such spirits Reuben Clark had little truck. "Why not rule," he scratched vehemently in a notebook, "cutting off all polygs. who have married since Manifesto."[3]*

In all sorts of smaller ways Reuben also made his independence known. Sacrament meetings, held biweekly at the Washington mansion of Senator Smoot, he found uninviting and increasingly easy to forego. The Smoots were gracious enough at these services, putting up rows of folding chairs and opening their doors to the entire Mormon community, but they still managed to remain austere and forbidding; and after the Clarks had taken a social chill once or twice Reuben began to find excuses for staying away. Once the umbilical of the sacrament meeting was severed, the concept of an inviolate Sabbath began to alter. Reuben continued to hold the family to a more or less rigorous observance of the day—no movies, bicycling, or skating, for example—but reserved for himself the old loophole of the ox in the mire. Indeed, J. Reuben Clark distinguished himself as the man on the job on Sunday.[4]

He also looked critically at the church's missionary program. Reuben himself had carried missionary credentials when first coming to the East, but the years blunted his evangelism.[5] By 1912, when brother Frank received his call to the Australian mission, Reuben was coldly objective. Frank was affiliated with the U.S. Geological Survey, Reuben pointed out in a letter to James Talmage, and in such a position he would be of far greater benefit to the church than proselyting in Australia. It was in the United States and to people of consequence that the church needed favorable representation. "By the way of giving point to this, I may say that I have had the opportunity for doing this kind of work with and from the Secretary of State down to elevator boys and messengers of the Department of State."[6] The intervention proved convincing and Frank was released from his missionary obligation. Not long afterward Frank drifted away from the church entirely.

---

*In 1890 church president Wilford Woodruff officially prohibited the further practice of polygamy. This manifesto, however, was not observed by all members, especially in the early years. Subsequent edicts and policies of the church gradually stiffened its opposition to plural marriage. By the 1920s only apostates persisted in the practice.

The exceptions to Reuben's orthodoxy continued to multiply. He objected to the wearing of temple garments, especially in Washington's insufferable heat, and frankly advised the First Presidency to modify or abolish them.[7] His tithing fell into arrears, especially under the burden of the Nelson debt, and he became ever less concerned about catching it up.[8] He adopted a liberal attitude on the church's Word of Wisdom observance, blasting William Jennings Bryan mercilessly for his crusading teetotalism.[9] He began sending his children to Protestant Sunday schools. In all these matters Reüben saw himself as reasonable and forthright. "Are we not only entitled, but expected to think for ourselves?" he asked himself approvingly. "Otherwise, where does our free agency come in? If we are to blindly follow someone else, we are not free agents."[10] This, in essence, was the voice of modernism in Mormon society, of the individual conscience, of self-conscious enlightenment, and of accommodation to the larger mores of American society. Yet it was on this selfsame issue of identity that Reuben Clark encountered the one difficulty that he could rationally surmount. For upon his arrival in the East, Reuben had to make a clear decision between Mormonism on the one hand and Americanism on the other.

iii

The source of the difficulty was again Reed Smoot. Duly elected to the United States Senate by the people of Utah, Smoot attempted to assume his seat at the same time that Reuben Clark was making his own Eastern debut. What followed upon the attempt was three years of acrimony as colleagues hurled objection after objection onto the Senate floor and investigated the church all over again. Smoot, although not himself a polygamist, became a convenient symbol of the Mormon satyr of popular imagination, about whom tabloid tales swirled in a fog. His trial before the Senate fed the public's appetite for sensuality and in turn fed upon it. Wherever the senator went he grew accustomed to the ladies lifting the hem of their garments in an unexampled gesture of contempt.

So there could be no shilly-shallying: Reuben had to make himself known as a Mormon and accept all of the consequences, or he had to deny his Mormonism completely. There was no middle ground. Here, as he discovered, the perceptivity of the scientist and the lawyer was not much help, for the problem was a moral one. It was one thing to question the church; it was quite another to betray it. Reuben found that, for all his questioning, the church was still very much a part of him and he a part of it. Like the biblical Joshua after whom he was named, he swallowed hard, stood up, and decided to be counted—as J. Reuben Clark, the Mormon.

This identity once established, Reuben immediately began to feel its effects. All of the rooms, it seemed, were filled with smoke. All of the teas involved tea. All of the cocktail parties presented guests with cocktails, and at any social gathering a glass of this or that was always being thrust into one's hand. Gracefully declining such amenities became a ritual that began with the words "No, thank you" and ended with the word "Mormon"—whereupon the conversation instantly turned to polygamy. Some people were accepting enough about Reuben's religion, while others had to drive every nail to the board. Assistant Secretary of State Alvey Adee was a nail driver. Every time he received a visit from Reuben Clark, Adee ceremoniously opened his drawer, took out a box of cigars, opened the box, and tendered it to Reuben, who, upon refusing as courteously as possible, was then faithfully regaled with the same one-liner: "Well, Clark, this is the cheapest treat I ever make."[11] In a myriad of such symbols, Reuben found himself not only owning up to his Mormonism but actually wearing it on his sleeve.

And how did one do that? The process of sorting things out—socially, philosophically, morally—seemed interminable. What, for example, did one offer to one's own guests? For a while Reuben tried grape juice. But when his nemesis William Jennings Bryan served his guests the same thing—and with excruciating ostentation—Reuben, as though seeing himself through the eyes of others, was horrified. He parodied his own predicament in a communication to Huntington Wilson.

It is reported that at a dinner which the Russian Ambassador gave in honor of the Secretary of State, Mr. Bryan upon their being seated at the table complimented the Ambassador very highly upon the beauty and brilliancy of the display of cut glass, etc. and calling attention particularly to the rather handsome, as Mr. Bryan thought, wine glasses upon the table, said "But Mr. Ambassador, in the return dinner which I shall hope to have the honor to give you, my table will be lacking the wine glasses, because you know I don't drink wine and don't serve it at my table." At this point, Mrs. Bryan broke in and said to the Ambassador, "Yes, you know Mr. Ambassador, we are teetotalers, Mr. Bryan does not drink, my father did not drink, and neither did my grandfather drink. We really come from a race of temperance people." Whereupon the Ambassador said "Is that so? Indeed! how very interesting. You know I don't care for wines myself and seldom drink them, but then, of course, I always serve them for my guests."

The thrust seems to have passed entirely over Mr. Bryan's head.[12]

Denouncing "Grape-Juice Willie," Reuben angrily switched to lemonade, but this beverage proved little more acceptable to most alcoholic tastes and it hardly removed the stigma of being "dry." Reuben was at a dead loss.

Inevitably the Clarks suffered their share of the general Mormonophobia too. No hems were lifted as Reuben passed by, but they scarcely needed to be. He was "different," and the fact was thrown back at him continually. Indeed, during his first year in the solicitor's office, Reuben lived in constant fear that his Mormonism would come to the attention of superiors and cost him his job.[13] Gradually the Clarks could count on their own safety but there were still any number of passes—as in the proposed hiring of Preston Richards—when the Mormon question sprang awkwardly to the fore. When being considered for admission to the Metropolitan Club in Washington, Reuben was quietly advised by Robert Lansing that it would be well not to mention his religion.[14] On another occasion, when he had introduced his father-in-law, C. R. Savage, to President Roosevelt, Reuben was dumbfounded when the president refused to accept a photographic print of Brigham Young made from an original Savage plate. To receive such a gift, stammered Roosevelt, would "not be wise."[15] The children were even less fortunate. They were regularly taunted on the playground and asked where their horns were.[16] To such treatment they gradually toughened in time, but there was no way to diminish the sense of isolation. Reuben confided to fellow assistant Cullen Dennis that he felt "separated by an intangible but real barrier" from those with whom he worked and that the loneliness had occasioned "many a moment of depression."[17] One reason that Reuben packed the family off to Utah every summer was to give them a respite from Babylon.

435

iv

Of necessity, it seemed, Reuben was compelled by the very anomaly of his situation to be a better, rather than worse, member of the church. Once having put himself on the line as a Mormon, he had to be the church's own representative. Though he privately scoffed at the punctilios of the Word of Wisdom, he publicly observed them to the letter. Though he objected to the temple garments, he dutifully wore them through the withering Potomac summers and shipped them back to Utah for laundering.[18] There were no easy answers, he found, to the riddle of life among the Gentiles, and occasionally he was forced into bizarre compromises. In the matter of diplomatic toasting, for example, Reuben settled on the practice of raising the wine to his lips and then setting it back untasted.[19] Friends shook their heads sadly.

v

His Mormonism now established, Reuben persisted in wondering about his status as an American. The sense of double identity was bothersome and ongoing. Much of the Utah-Mormon society was still turned inward upon itself, defying the eastern pressure for conformity. Its bunker mentality made Reuben's situation increasingly one of anomie. Friendly missives arrived from Pa Clark and others reminding him that he was residing among strangers.[20] His younger brother Sam admonished him in a citation from St. Matthew not to lay up for himself "treasures on earth, where moth and rust doth corrupt," adding, "I don't know why I should write this way to you. . . . But I know that you will take it in the spirit it is given."[21] Reuben answered them as best he could, composing his replies as carefully as state papers. He was dealing with the timeless dilemma of the city of God—how to maintain the integrity of sainthood in an alien society. Until he resolved it Reuben would feel comfortable neither as Mormon nor American. "We should not be like world:—" he penned at the head of a memorandum to himself, and followed with: "World wants us to be so."[22]

It took a good deal of thinking over a good many years before Reuben made sense of it all. Ultimately he did so by coming to grips with the two difficulties of Mormonism that had bothered him from the beginning—polygamy and theocracy. He took on polygamy first. "History of world shows," he outlined, "that whenever anybody [*sic*] of people have set themselves up in opposition to established habits—custom of thought or philosophy—they have suffered persecution."[23] The problem was not solely that such people dared to be different; it was that they dared to introduce new concepts of morality and then confused these with the immorality of the host culture. So it was that God's people always seemed to wind up being stiffnecked: they forgot about the moral rights of others. Reuben's solution for this malady was simple. "Does not mean that we shall have their immorality" he said, "but that we shall not do what they consider is immoral."[24] Polygamy, in other words, had to be abolished once and for all. Mormonism could not continue to exist in the United States with a radically different social and ethical order.

But stamping out polygamy would solve only half of the problem. The remaining half had to do with allegiance or, as Reuben put it, "obedience." Loyal Mormons were expected to be obedient in all things, and "all things" included the temporal as well as spiritual. The two kinds of obedience produced different results. Spiritual obedience was what had given Mormonism its verve and distinctiveness. But temporal obedience—the lockstep response of church members to economic and political directives—made for a very different situation. It set up a countervailing authority—a state within the state—and forced church members to choose between the two. Reuben's public experience had deepened his love for the United States and its constitution. He personally did not want to make such a choice. He believed that members of the church must therefore be citizens of the United States as well as subjects of God's kingdom—that they must render unto Caesar that which was rightfully his. "My position as to Church domination in politics," he concluded, was that

No Apostle—Presidency of Church, etc. including Presidents of Stakes—shall while holding such office be eligible for election to a political office.

Any person resigning a church office for political office shall be ineligible for re-election to a church office.

No person shall be eligible for election to a political office until five years after.

"Because," said J. Reuben Clark, "it is un-American."[25]

While Reuben was critically examining power relations in the church, his own rapport with church authorities was steadily on the rise. He had always been more or less well connected to the Latter-day Saint leadership. First through James Talmage, then through Joseph Nelson, and finally through Preston Richards, he had enjoyed essentially direct access to the Salt Lake headquarters. Possibly he was unaware that his career was being watched with interest by several of the church's general authorities and that among them he was regarded as a "comer." The signs, however, were unmistakable. On occasion he was an enthusiastically advertised speaker at the Tabernacle on Salt Lake City's Temple Square, and when the world war broke out he was asked to counsel the brethren about its implications.[26] His close friend Judge Ralston, visiting Salt Lake City in June of 1908, was surprised to find himself regally welcomed and personally received by the president of the church.[27] When Reuben was invited to go to Tokyo as legal counsel to the Japanese government, he happened to seek the advice of President Smith in the matter. The reply that there were "bigger and better things for [you] here at home" apparently did not strike him as prophetic[28] – nor did a remark, uttered to Luacine at a party in August of 1918, that Reuben Clark was believed to be "the greatest international lawyer in the United States."[29] He who made the comment was a comer in his own right – sixty-two-year-old Heber Jeddy Grant, one-time president of the Tooele Stake and now apostle of the church. Within three months he would be its president.

These encomiums were not unearned. Skeptical or not, Reuben had always regarded himself in a position to help the church and had never been slow to take advantage of it. When two Mormon missionaries were detained by authorities in Pennsylvania, he did not scruple to ask his friend Knox to intervene.[30] Reuben himself intervened when missionaries ran into trouble in Germany and served official notice that the persecution would not be tolerated.[31] And when the *Washington Post* came up for sale in 1915, Reuben hatched a fantastic scheme for bringing in the church as a silent purchaser.

In my view nothing would be more advantageous for our people than the control of the policy of the Post in a manner friendly to our people. The good that such a paper could do us is beyond measure, it being located as it is here in the Capital and being read by practically every member of Congress.[32]

Reuben Clark himself was good advertising for the LDS church. Wherever he went, whatever he did, whenever some new thrust of his career was made public, the press and wire services faithfully appended the codicil that he was a Utahn and a Mormon. As time went by Reuben became increasingly aware of his showcase value to the church. When one particularly tantalizing opportunity was offered him, the Washington lawyer made no decision until he had discussed the offer's public relations potential with President Smith.[33] And upon leaving the State Department in 1913, he wrote to Preston Richards,

I cannot tell you how really . . . grateful I am that opportunity has come to you and to me to show that some good can come from our people. I am inclined to believe that after all is said and done this constitutes my chiefest satisfaction for my government work, and for yours. I cannot help feeling that from this work of both of us will come benefit to our people—greater perhaps than either of us can now surmise. . . . I feel that we have been immeasurably honored in being allowed to do this work—that we have been abundantly blessed in its doing—that we have really been instruments in God's hands.[34]

As time passed Reuben's career took on ever more mythical qualities for fellow Utahns. He was not simply *a* Mormon who had made good in the East but, in many minds, he was *the* Mormon. "Few men," as a *Tribune* writer put it, "have ever been elected or appointed to a position of public trust with so exalted a reputation to live up to."[35] Although praise of this order might have been unfair to others, there was a certain rationale for it. The careers of a Reed Smoot or a James H. Moyle remained essentially western careers built upon local bases of support, while Reuben Clark had gone to Washington penniless and unknown and had carved out his own success. The difference was significant. Reuben had beaten the East on the East's own terms.

And once having beaten the East, Reuben found that he had also resolved his crisis of identity. Such was the symbolic significance of his breaking the barriers. In demonstrating that the obstacles to Mormon preferment could indeed be overcome, Reuben became the prototype of a new social phenomenon, the Mormon-who-makes-his-way-in-the-world; and in time the phenomenon would produce a brilliant constellation of success stories. But because Reuben Clark had no George Romney or Willard Marriott or Ezra Taft Benson to follow, he had to see his own feet across the barricade in order to know for a certainty that the barricade could be surmounted—that Mormonism and Americanism were compatible.

vii

The world war and the fight over the League of Nations marked a kind of middle passage in Reuben's religious development. He was still uncertain about many things, still cavalier about Mormon quaintness, still skeptical of the old verities. But his confidence in the rational world was now severely shaken. Nothing had worked out as enlightened men had expected, and all the fine theories about law and morality had not survived the German sweep through Belgium. Under these circumstances religion itself took on new meaning, and for Reuben Clark the apocalyptic battle over the League of Nations became a religious experience of first importance. No matter what his professed love for America had been hitherto, he had to see the United States under the perceived threat of actual peril in order to really understand the meaning of the ancient prophecies. When the Treaty of Versailles finally went to its doom in the Senate, Reuben knew how the Christians must have felt after winning the Battle of Tours.

Then, too, Reuben gradually acquired a different perspective on church policies and practices. It was one thing to discuss a Reed Smoot holding miter and scepter in the same hands; when it was Reuben Clark, however, who was pressing sacred causes before the public, as he regarded his own political campaigns, that somehow seemed different. And the polygamy issue took on a new aspect as well. True to their word, the church authorities began cracking down on the otherwise-minded—and one of the first to be cracked was saintly old Uncle John Woolley, who had been sealing plural marriages right along. "We all feel very sorry for him," reported Joshua.

A man that has been as solid and faithful in the church as he has been. . . . He expresses great faith in living to be restored to his former standing in the church. Few men in the church have done more for the cause than he.[36]

The issues had a way of losing their hard edges when seen close at hand.

So Reuben at midpassage was neither the faithful stalwart of his Grantsville youth nor the self-certain doubter of his State Department days. When his friend Milton Ross closed a letter with "trusting you are still in the Church and the Church is losing nothing on that account," Reuben replied in the words of John L. Sullivan, after ten rounds with Kilrain in New Orleans: "Slightly disfigured, but still in the ring."[37]

viii

In 1923, when the Clarks moved back to Utah, events conspired to resolve the situation for Reuben. For one thing, just being back in "God's country," as he described it, had an affirmative influence on him. His doubts about the church had had their not-too-distant relationship to a confused sense of belonging. Among friends once again, he could disentangle himself to some degree from aspirations born of Babylon. Eastern values, eastern perceptions, the whole eastern style had worked their enchantment on him. Crossing into the Salt Lake Valley and saying—as Brigham Young had said and for much the same reason—"This is the place" tended to break the spell. Reuben soon found his ambitions lapsing back into scale. Perhaps he was unaware that they had been distended.

But distended they had been. In his own way Reuben had been a prodigal seeking after the age-old seductions. To be sure, his had been a staid and crusty sort of prodigalism, but what it had lacked in wine and women it had pretty well made up for in lucre. Bewitched by his associations with the Knoxes, Morgans, and Vanderlips, he had very earnestly sought after riches. What he tacitly acknowledged by returning to Utah was that he would never succeed in that quest, that genteel poverty might well be his lot. At such a juncture he might have hearkened back to a letter from his father, sent in 1906 when the world was still young.

In looking back it doesn't seem very long since I was a young man, full of aspirations and hopes for the future and built air castles, which have proven to be only soap bubbles. And I realize that I have arrived at the station on life's journey when I can no longer hope to attain to anything more than what I am only I hope to become a better man. But I have one thing at least to be proud of and that is a good wife and a band of noble children. Many, many times do I thank the Lord for guiding my footsteps to the valley of the mountains, where I found a suitable companion, and had the courage and decision of character sufficient to embrace the great, grand and glorious gospel, and for the noble family that we have. The older I get the more I appreciate these great blessings.[38]

Joshua passed away in 1929. "This removes the last barrier between me and death," Reuben reflected.[39] And to his brother Frank he confessed that it was not pleasant to think of having lived out two-thirds of his useful life.[40]

Another person concerned for Reuben's soul was his wife, Luacine. Not content with her husband as a passive churchman, she had worked indefatigably to pull him off the fence. "I don't see why you can't do a little church work where you are," she chided, shortly before his return to the West.

Everyone loves to hear you talk, you would be such a big help if you would take hold. You have been nearly 20 years out of it. . . . However, we have thrashed this out before. I have hired you, I remember, more than once to go to church with me, but now you are of age. I will leave your religious training alone, and attend to my own.[41]

The strong words were not entirely justified. Reuben's church inactivity had been more a thing of the mind than the heart, and even before Luacine wrote her epistle his mind was beginning to change.

Finally, the Salt Lake City to which the Clarks returned in 1923 had significantly changed in their twenty-year absence. Things were more relaxed. Church leaders were more confident. Mormonism had navigated the rough water in its relations with the federal government, and the "us-them" dichotomy of the 1890s had passed into history. There was a much freer sense of identification with American cultural values too. Mormon children, dosed with the new mass media, were bobbing their hair and dancing the Charleston. At the Bijou on Saturday afternoon they were indistinguishable from youngsters anywhere. Moreover, without the constant baying of the

442

eastern critics, Mormons no longer felt that ranks had to be closed politically and economically. They now freely aligned themselves with Gentiles and found that the strain of internal factionalism eased up on its own. Senator Smoot hung on until 1933 as a reminder of the past, but he proved to be the last of the theocrats.

ix

These changes were not all brought about by Heber J. Grant, but he became the symbol of them. Tall and spare with a grandfatherly face and clipped white beard, he was at once heir to and a departure from the old patriarch-presidents. He had been a successful businessman and was well in step with the times. He had taken over a church economically devastated and socially outcast and had set about to repair both conditions. He resolved a number of doctrinal issues, streamlined church programs, expanded the administrative structure, and strengthened ties with the business community. Most importantly, Grant laid new stress on the church's missionary effort and told converts to remain at home rather than emigrate to Zion. Soon Latter-day Saints were talking spiritedly of a new era.

That J. Reuben Clark might usefully fit into such a risorgimento may or may not have been apparent. Quite beyond his experience and capabilities, however, Reuben happened to have "new era" stamped all over him. It was not so much that he had been an officer of the federal government, nor even that he had broken barriers; it was that he had convincingly demonstrated that devotion to God and devotion to country could once again complement one another. And that was to be the principal significance of the Grant presidency: to transform the Mormon church from a small sect cloistered away in the Rocky Mountains to a national, and eventually international, religious movement with a universal message. In order to accomplish such a transformation, the church first had to come to terms with the United States politically, socially, culturally (to some degree), and above all spiritually. It had to reconcile its own sense of mission with the existing sense of national purpose, to the end that it might become a working force in American life. Reuben Clark was one person who could bridge the worlds of church and nation and perhaps draw them back together. Indeed, in the new era of President Grant there was nothing more pressing than the need for an assertive Alma the Younger.*

x

By degrees Reuben found himself becoming involved in church affairs again. In June of 1925 he was appointed to the board of the Young Men's Mutual Improvement Association.[42] The following year he became a member of the advisory editorial committee of the *Improvement Era.*[43] He addressed the missionaries about emigration and foreign residency procedures and lectured tourists on basic Mormon beliefs.[44] In October of 1925 he delivered a talk from the fledgling KSL radio station in the basement of the Vermont Building.[45] The address was entitled "Divine Authority and Latter-day Saints," and President Grant later declared that it was one of the finest sermons he had ever heard on the subject of the priesthood.[46] But Reuben's abiding success in the church grew unpretentiously out of the Sunday school class he began teaching in the Twentieth Ward. The subject of the class was the life of the Savior; and Reuben, more or less pressed into service, commenced the series of lessons without visible enthusiasm. Soon, however, the subject took possession of him. He began putting in long hours of research and preparation for each lesson and drawing up lawyerlike briefs of the relevant facts. His adult pupils sensed his excitement. They began visiting from other classes, then from other wards, and soon they were trooping in from all over the county.[47]

Church activity was not compelling evidence of religious devotion, but the one did seem to grow out of the other. The Clark children began noticing shades of difference in Reuben's behavior. Where in the evenings one was accustomed to finding daddy in his study immersed in some technical problem, the trend gradually shifted toward theological matters, and in place of the legal reporters one increasingly saw the onionskin of the scriptures. From Mexico Reuben wrote to his son-in-law and requested the purchase of some

---

*Alma the Younger was among the most notable of Book of Mormon heroes. A Pauline figure, he was dramatically converted to the gospel, renouncing the waywardness of his youth, and became both high priest and judge of the Nephite civilization.

twenty religious volumes, including Bible dictionaries, scriptural commentaries, concordances, archeological and geographical works, and, most importantly, studies of the life of Christ.[48] Here began his work on *Our Lord of the Gospels,* to be published in 1947. In the book Reuben imposed upon the works of the four Evangelists precisely that passion for order which had distinguished his worldly career. There was something mechanical, perhaps, in the book's schematic layout of Jesus' life and ministry, but this was Reuben's way of discovering truth. The personal meaning of the experience ran far deeper than a reader might suppose. Indeed, in *Our Lord of the Gospels* Reuben Clark was grappling with the ultimate meaning of redemption. He was probing toward the very heart of the religious experience.

And here he found untold significance. His own life had been one of pursuit, of striving, of reaching beyond himself for attainments. He had been the trainbound wanderer, shuttling back and forth across the continent between conflicting poles of ambition and competing systems of value, never quite knowing the desires of his own heart. Now, with this new interest in matters spiritual, there came a mellowing, a deepening, an enrichment that seemed to impart new dimensions to the man. The Christian term for this transformation was humility. To his brother Frank, whose apostasy Reuben now regretted bitterly, he wrote, "My experience and observations tell me that as we grow older, we lose much, indeed most of our cocksureness, indeed a certainty about many matters, which in our youth seem beyond question."[49] To a college friend he explained that he had passed the time of his "higher criticism" and that, as he reflected back upon it, it reminded him of a story about Abraham Lincoln. While visiting with Grant before Appomattox, Lincoln was discovered by one of the general's staff sitting in the shade of his tent and reading the Bible. "What! Abe Lincoln reading the Bible?" exclaimed the officer. "Yes," the president replied, "I have learned to read the Bible. I believe all I can and take the rest on faith." Then Reuben wrote:

Substituting in substance the words "our Mormon Scriptures," you will have about my situation. I believe it all. I believe our whole scripture. Much of it I am not able to understand, but I take it on faith, because I am sure it is a living faith.[50]

The sojourner in Babylon had come home.

xi

In December of 1931 Charles Nibley, second counselor to President Grant, passed away. As Grant and his remaining counselor, Anthony W. Ivins, stood solemnly in the rain at the Salt Lake cemetery, the president suddenly whispered that he knew who could fill the vacancy. "This man Clark, the ambassador to Mexico," he said.

"You can't get him, Heber," Ivins replied, "because he is a $100,000-a-year man."

President Grant peered out from beneath his umbrella. "We can ask him," he said.[51]

PART V

GOOD NEIGHBOR

1926–33

THE LAWYER AS DIPLOMAT

J. Reuben Clark never meant to become a diplomat. Like others of his public service careers, the diplomatic one unfolded almost by accident, the final result of a chain of circumstance that began in 1903 with Columbia law school and continued its remarkable linkages. This being the case, Reuben did not possess two of the essential prerequisites of the diplomatic craft: a sense of vision and a store of experience. The want of vision, of an affirmative idea of what he might seek to accomplish, was the more disabling of the two. It left Reuben on the wrong side of history, confined by his conservative instincts, and committed to preservation above accomplishment. Even so, Reuben Clark's name somehow wound up on the side of progress—decisively so.

The want of experience was more visible. Discounting his inconsequential junket to Toronto with the American-British Claims Commission, Reuben had never been outside the United States. Nevertheless, he seemed to display an admirable self-possession. He was never spoken of as an upstart or outsider, and every new appointment brought forth a loud chorus of approval. It was as though the fates had decreed from the beginning that diplomacy, rather than law or politics, should become the capstone of Reuben's public career.

Chapter 24

IN THE WAKE OF THE
WHIRLWIND

"Is there any prospect of your being in Washington within the next two weeks?"[1]

Reuben Clark had received telegrams like this before, and when they came from high-ranking officials and made no mention of specific business, they usually spelled trouble. This wire, dated April 24, 1926, had been sent by Assistant Secretary of State Robert Olds, and its nonchalance seemed downright contrived. As matters turned out, it spelled something more than trouble.

ii

There was a certain poetic justice in the fact that Olds wanted Reuben to take charge of the American agency of the United States–Mexico Mixed Claims Commission. Throughout the dark years of the Mexican Revolution, when the Albert Falls and Henry Lane Wilsons had been ready to send the U.S. Army across the border, J. Reuben Clark had been the consistent voice of opposition. Time and again he had spoken of settling the differences with Mexico through "regular channels of diplomacy," of placing the responsibility for protecting American life and property on the shoulders of the Mexican government, of restoring order first and worrying about justice afterward. The mixed claims commission had been established for that exact purpose—to worry about justice afterward—and now, as Olds quietly explained to Reuben over a long afternoon's lunch, the commission was hanging by a thread. If Reuben wanted to rescue the cause of judicial settlement in the western hemisphere—not to mention the Mormon claims of Clark & Richards—he would have to step into the situation personally.

Of course, Reuben knew all about the Mexican claims commission. He knew that it had been established by treaty in 1924 as the

American price for recognizing the Mexican government then in power. He knew that the commission had recorded some 5,957 separate filings for an aggregate total of $934,994,399.58—or roughly half the total wealth of Mexico—and he knew that the commission had been plagued from its inception with volatile passions, undercurrents of intrigue, and a curious jinx of bad luck. He knew these things not because he was an international lawyer but because most Americans knew them. The Mexican claims commission was front-page news in the 1920s, and with good reason: it was judged to be the country's best hope for avoiding war with Mexico.[2]

The war that now threatened was not the military intervention debated by the Taft administration long ago, but it was similarly a by-product of the Mexican Revolution. The revolution had by now taken toll of much American life and property. But most injurious to the relations of the two countries was the fact that in its later phases the revolution had become increasingly radical and confiscatory. Beginning with the Querétaro constitution proclaimed by Carranza in 1917, revolutionary governments had progressively committed themselves to principles of nationalization and socialism. Oil, gas, and mineral rights, liberally granted by Díaz, were declared by this document to be essentially inalienable, belonging in perpetuity to the Mexican people; and laws had been passed to severely restrict the activities of American entrepreneurs. Lands, too, had been declared inalienable and, on paper at least, had been repossessed from American landlords for the benefit of the peasant *ejidos*. Moreover, the revolutionary regimes had all but broken with the Catholic church, which they viewed as a bastion of reactionism, and once again the church-state controversy threatened to explode at any moment into open violence. And beyond all this, American observers perceived a quiet but implacable determination on the part of this brave new Mexico to oust the *gringo* once and for all. Reported one diplomat: "There is one slogan at which all discordant elements rally; one banner under which the rich and poor, the politician and the peon, the Indian and the mixed breed gather at the call—that slogan is 'Mexico For Mexicans' and that banner is *Anti-Anglo-Saxon*."[3] The expulsion of the Americans was not being carried out by open warfare but by the unremitting pressure of laws that were never quite fair, by false arrests and detentions, by unequal taxation, and by a variety of other annoyances. There were tales of the American bank manager who kissed his wife as he climbed out of his limousine and was hauled into the *comiseria* for "public lewdness"; of the two American ladies who were bilked of their money and left stranded by a bus line; of the American owner of a hotel in Cuernavaca who was fined and persecuted until he resignedly handed over his keys and left the country.[4]

The mixed claims commission was charged with the task of straightening everything out. It was to punish the bandits and desperados (by punishing the authorities who tolerated them), to restore property seized, and to compensate for property lost. It was to adjudicate the grievances of the ranchers, mine-owners, and oilmen who believed that their rights under the new constitution were being grossly violated. And it was to serve notice upon the Mexican man-in-the-street that the revolution had not been fought for bolshevism. Responsibilities of such order called for unusual competence in handling the commission's work. For this reason J. Reuben Clark had originally been asked to take charge of the commission's American agency back in May of 1924, when it was first organized.[5] At that time Reuben had refused, explaining to Secretary of State Hughes that, as representative of the Mormon claimants, he lacked "that disinterested view necessary for directing the work."[6] Now, two years later, Robert Olds had him cornered; this time he accepted the job.*

Besides the sheer enormity of the task, there were personal reasons for Reuben's reluctance: he had committed himself to a law practice in Utah and his debts were still unpaid. He would take over the American agency, he told Olds, but only long enough to secure a competent replacement; thereafter he would switch over to general counsel, which would enable him to work out of his Utah office.[7] To this Olds agreed. Praising Reuben's patriotism and unselfishness, the ensuing State Department press release breathed an almost audible sigh of relief.[8] So did many of the letters of congratulation. "Somebody like you, who can combine quietness with forcefulness, is certainly needed there," wrote William Hard.[9] In broad terms he spoke for everyone.

---

*For a discussion of claims commission officers and functions, see note on p. 237.

On a bright June morning Reuben walked through the door of the American agency, with deepest misgivings. The offices were located in a large suite in the Investment Building on 15th and K streets. Busy at work were typists, clerks, stenographers, translators, and a sizable muster of lawyers. Case files and memoranda littered the desks, and research on the thousands of claims seemed to be proceeding apace. In contrast to the old American-British Claims Commission, where there were only a few lawyers and a more relaxed atmosphere, the size and bustle of this operation were impressive indeed. But Reuben knew that beneath the thrumming purposefulness there must lie some critical maladies.

As he thumbed through the manila file folders, Reuben glimpsed a veritable chamber of horrors. Cases in preparation included appalling breaches of contract (ninety-one locomotives delivered to the Mexican National Railway and never paid for) and numberless revocations of concessions (a five-hundred-thousand-dollar dredging operation at Port Frontera canceled and all its equipment taken over). There were millions of dollars' worth of defaulted bonds—federal, state, local, and private—all of them solemnly guaranteed in gold. Entire herds of cattle had been stolen, butchered, or just scattered loose to die. There were forced "loans" and "contributions," too; one American in Chihuahua City had had to put up eighteen thousand dollars' worth of them. Land patents had been revoked and title deeds nullified, the owners being forced to sell out at a few cents on the dollar and then accept worthless paper currency as payment. There were missing railway shipments, stolen bank deposits, stocks that were suddenly valueless. There was an American schooner that had been run down and sunk by a Mexican gunboat, and there was a cargo vessel that had put into a Mexican port in distress only to be confiscated for smuggling. Then there was the dreary procession of false arrests and imprisonments, of American citizens whisked off Mexican streets for this or that alleged crime and shut away without hearing. One had been kept in an outhouse and forced to pay for his own bread and water. Added to these were the personal injuries—people beaten, robbed, manhandled, kidnapped for ransom, some forcibly expelled from the country, and literally hundreds murdered. One particularly ingenious bandit had succeeded in snuffing out fifty-one lives at once, including those of fourteen Americans, by lodging a captured freight train in the Cumbre Tunnel, setting it on fire, and allowing a passenger train to plow headlong into the wreckage. But not all of the guilty parties were bandits. In one memorable case, three Americans surrounded in their house by a mob had appealed to Mexican civil authorities for help. When the soldiers arrived, it was they and not the mob who had fired into the house, killed the Americans, and then dragged their bodies through the streets.[10]

This reading made a stark contrast to the docket of the British claims commission, with its misshipped lumber and misplaced bridges. With the British claims, moreover, there had been much understanding among the judges, a shared heritage of the common law, and a long tradition of amicable settlement. Here, amid social upheaval, economic desolation, and hatred for all things Yankee, Mexico was supposed to settle claims in the amount of a billion dollars—claims that would bankrupt the country several times over—or face a crisis with the United States. And the mixed claims commission, whose clicking typewriters and office chatter could be heard through the open transom, happened to be the most demoralized and problem-ridden organization in Reuben's experience. But Reuben could only roll up his sleeves and plunge in.

iv

He learned that the first problem of the claims commission lay in the legal convention that brought it into being. In this document were some extraordinary weaknesses, most of them resulting from the strain of U.S.-Mexican relations. For one thing, the convention had set up two separate panels of commissioners to hear two different kinds of cases. The idea was that ordinary claims—those arising from the usual frictions between neighboring states—ought to be adjudicated by international law in the customary way, while the special claims—those arising specifically from the revolution—ought to be decided by different rules.[11] But as to what these different rules should be the parties could not agree. Just how such ambiguity might operate in an actual arbitration was soon illustrated in the notorious Santa Ysabel case, the first and last claim to be heard by the special commission. In 1916, a train carrying eighteen American mining engineers had been stopped by a contingent of Pancho Villa's ragged army at a forlorn cattle station in Chihuahua. The Americans had been marched outside and shot down like partridges as they tried to make a run for it.[12] When the case had come up for arbitration, Mexico claimed it was not liable because Villa had been a mere "bandit," and because the Mexican government had done all it could to bring him to justice. The Americans easily demonstrated that Villa was no mere bandit, but a powerful revolutionary, and that the Mexican government, in giving Villa political amnesty and a large *hacienda* some four years later, had done considerably less than "all it could" to bring him to justice. The case had been airtight from the standpoint of international law—but the special commission had still decided for Mexico.[13] Such a firestorm of outrage had arisen over the decision that the presiding commissioner, Rodrigo Octavio of Brazil, had resigned with the courtroom in bedlam.[14] Judge Perry, the American commissioner, had also resigned in the aftermath, and Henry Anderson had told Undersecretary Olds to find a new agent. The special claims commission was a total ruin.

v

So Reuben's first job was to see if any of the pieces of the special commission could be salvaged. He had to find a replacement for Commissioner Perry and a permanent replacement for Anderson. Most difficult of all, he had to find a new and acceptable presiding commissioner. In the meantime, he had to turn attention to the general claims commission, the one hearing the ordinary claims. Here the atmosphere was not much calmer. If the cases on the general commission docket lacked the emotional charge of Santa Ysabel, they included their fair share of violence; and, more ominously, they included the constituent difficulties of the great Mexican oil crisis. In the general commission also there had been discord and dissension; two weeks after Reuben took office, the American commissioner, Edwin B. Parker, added his resignation to the pile.[15] By the terms of the claims convention, all cases, general and special, were to be heard and decided within a period of three years. Almost two of the three years had now elapsed, and only seventeen cases had been settled. That left thirty-six hundred to go.[16]

Reuben's second task was to find out why the progress had been so slow. By the end of his first week he had the answer. It seemed that his predecessor, noting that the claims convention imposed a one-year deadline on filing, had despaired of evaluating the thousands of cases before him and simply filed them all. Then, in order to process so great a case load, Anderson had hired with abandon, choosing lawyers with little or no background in international law. He had correspondingly multiplied clerical and support functions, expanded the translation bureau, and doubled the number of secretaries. With so many claims and so many functionaries the work of the agency was being approached willy-nilly, counsel sequestering any available office help and tackling whatever cases came to hand. Lines of authority had become daily more confused, and through everything wound a skein of red tape. Worst of all, the agency's three-year operating budget was all but exhausted.[17]

It was almost as though process rather than product was the goal. For example, on his first day at the office Reuben received "feverish inquiries" from the Mexicans about his own credentials—a matter of mere protocol. What followed was all too typical.

I immediately telephoned Mr. Olds, who had the Commission prepared and sent to the White House for signature. Meanwhile, renewed inquiries came from the Secretariat. Then the Great Seal was not working for some reason, so we did not get the Commission on July 1st. On the following morning (Friday), they were at it again, but finally during the day we got it over here. I was not quite sure whether I ought to send it down by Butler or employ a brass band and have ceremony. I finally compromised on Dunn, who took the original and copies. They carefully compared original with copies, and everything seemed quiet on the Potomac. But the next morning (Saturday), they complained that I had not sent down a transmitting letter. So I sent a letter transmitting my own Commission. You will observe how decisive that procedure would be on whether I had forged the great document. What Tuesday has in store for us, I do not know.[18]

The tactics Reuben adopted to combat this inertia may have seemed extreme, but he judged them to be necessary. Beginning at the top of the agency and working downward, he interviewed every employee to determine whether training and skills matched job descriptions. By the end of the first month he had winnowed out twenty percent of the legal staff, and by the end of the second month he had cut it in half. There was another wave of resignations when Reuben dug into the budget and took to trimming salaries. With the office still in an uproar, the new agent next proceeded to reorganize everything, clarifying lines of responsibility and bringing all phases of activity under his own personal direction.[19]

Where necessary Reuben hired new personnel of whose competence and loyalty he could be certain. Old Mockahi brother Stanley Udy came aboard as counsel, and William Dennis, who was practicing law in the city, was retained as special counsel for the difficult cases.[20] From the judge advocate corps Reuben brought in General Walter A. Bethel, partially blind and officially disabled but a crack lawyer nonetheless.[21] Reuben also recruited Mexican expertise. Colonel Aristides A. Moreno, a Mexican-American whose English was as impeccable as his appearance, knew all about the atrocities of the revolution. Garbed in a serape and sombrero, he had led a somnolent donkey through northern Mexico as a spy for the United States Army. Among other accomplishments, it was said that he dissuaded Pancho Villa from a final murderous assault on the Mormons.[22] There were at least a half dozen others eventually lured into the agency, including some of the finest international lawyers in the country. Reuben assembled them together one day and delivered a short parable on how they were to conduct their work. The story was of Fred Dearing and himself stopping for a shoe shine in Detroit one day.

The man who was shining Dearing's shoes was one of these men who put a great many fancy touches to the job of shining shoes. He almost played a tune with the cloth. Dearing said to my man, who did none of this, "Why don't you give him a job like my man is giving me; why don't you play him a tune?" And the boy who was somewhat older and more experienced looked up and replied: "When he has been shining shoes as long as I have, he will know that nothing but the shine counts."[23]

Everyone seemed to get the point.

With a streamlined and revitalized organization, Reuben turned to the special claims, whose filing deadline was rapidly approaching. In the next two months his people reexamined forty-six hundred of these files and returned thirty-four hundred of them to the State Department as "closed." They then prepared and submitted memorials for the thousand or so cases remaining. Meanwhile, there were pleadings to mature, replies to formulate, and briefs to assemble. Some ninety of the cases already filed were found to be so shaky that extensive research was required before they could be placed on the calendar. And at odd moments Reuben attended to correspondence, some fifty items of it daily.[24] His days and nights were fully occupied, he wrote wearily to Vernon Romney: "It is a great job."[25]

Of crucial importance was the question of who would succeed Parker as American commissioner of the general commission. Even though the job was lucrative and prestigious, there were few available candidates. Those who possessed the necessary credentials, so it seemed, were understandably wary of the Mexican arbitration. After a good deal of soul-searching, Reuben finally decided upon Fred Kenelm Nielsen. Nielsen had been his own assistant solicitor back in the Knox State Department and had eventually succeeded Reuben as solicitor. Since then their paths had often crossed. Nielsen had been one of "Crowder's boys" in the judge advocate general's office and after the war had served with Reuben at the Washington arms conference.[26] Later he had become agent of the reactivated American-British Claims Commission and in that capacity had retained Reuben to write a series of memoranda for the landmark Cayuga Indian case.[27] Reuben knew Fred Nielsen as well as any lawyer in Washington—well enough to have grave doubts about him. Of the man's technical competence there was no question; but the fair Danish face with its square jaw and alert green eyes masked a dark and morose personality. Suspicious, fault-finding, and generally unhappy with the world, Nielsen was given to long bouts of sullenness, relentless personal vendettas, and lapses of out-and-out paranoia. He had succeeded in making enemies out of virtually every friend he had. Reuben Clark was one of the few upon whom the transformation had not yet been effected. With reluctance and foreboding, Reuben sent his name to the secretary of state.

A happier job was that of replacing himself. The man he selected as agent was Clement Lincoln Bouvé, a trusted friend of many years. Every inch the Massachusetts Brahmin, Bouvé was noted at the bar for his elegant tailoring, polished manners, and prolix style of expression. (He once invested 509 words in a single sentence.[28]) Outside the courtroom, however, there was something bluff and good-natured about him, a quality emphasized by his large frame, sweeping gestures, and free indulgence in billingsgate. He had been educated in Europe and had decided on a career in international law. He had served on claims commissions before and had recently been assistant agent under Henry Anderson. Having known one another as cub lawyers in the Cosmos Club, Bouvé and Clark got along famously.[29] Bouvé's one visible flaw, a certain want of tact in delicate situations, Reuben regarded as unimportant. He evidently did not think of Bouvé and Nielsen at the same time.

In a series of contracts worked out in late August, Bouvé agreed to become agent and take over the day-to-day operations of the American agency, while Reuben assumed the title of general counsel. Freed of the agent's administrative burden, Reuben could concentrate his efforts on legal problems, and he could do much of his work at home in Utah. Yet it was agreed that the two of them, Clark and Bouvé, would continue to run the agency as a team.[30]

When Reuben returned home in early September, he took with him the problem cases: the defaulted bond claims, the land expropriations, and, worst of all, the oil difficulties. Bouvé communicated with him weekly in long and detailed letters. Bouvé's first taste of the agent's job was apparently no more savory than it had been to Reuben. Before long, in fact, a plaintive note began creeping into his correspondence. "Ever since your departure," he said, "the Agency has lost its right hand, and most of its left."[31] Soon Bouvé was appealing for Reuben to return to the East—and there were increasingly cogent reasons for the appeal.

vi

Whatever the curse that had haunted the Mexican claims commission in times past, it returned now to hover over Clement Bouvé like an albatross. And Bouvé's problems, by joint custody, were Reuben Clark's as well. Their correspondence that autumn swelled drastically as the two of them tried to puzzle their way out of a bind that seemed to tighten by the week. In the end, Reuben indeed had to return to Washington and take charge. This proved to be the birth of his diplomatic career, and it could not have gestated under stranger circumstances.

First to be touched with the claims commission malady was the presiding commissioner, Cornelius Van Vollenhoven. As with Henri Fromageat on the old American-British Claims Commission, Van Vollenhoven was by definition the odd man out. When in the difficult cases each of the two national commissioners reverted from jurist to patriot, it was up to the presiding commissioner, as umpire, to decide the issue. For that reason his selection was a matter of the utmost importance. Cornelius Van Vollenhoven, a wizened little Dutchman with flawless English and a perpetually furrowed brow, was a distinguished professor, a practicing international lawyer, an associate justice of the Hague court, and a pioneer in the League of Nations movement.[32] But as presiding commissioner he was still a question mark.

Or he was until October 16. That afternoon Commissioner Van Vollenhoven handed each of his two colleagues a copy of some proposed new rules of procedure. Commissioner Nielsen began reading with interest—then alarm. He read the proposals over a second time. He read them a third. Van Vollenhoven, it seemed, had a plan to expedite the work of hearing and deciding cases, and the plan was simplicity itself. The commission would order up the filing of memorials in all cases to be heard. In those cases for which the memorials could not be immediately filed—which presently included perhaps ninety-nine percent of all the American claims—the case was automatically to be declared ready for hearing. Commissioner Nielsen, a little dazed, recited the proposed new rules back to Commissioner Van Vollenhoven and asked if he had understood them correctly. The reply was yes. Nielsen then took some hypothetical examples and worked them through to make doubly certain. Yes again. Nielsen then turned to the Mexican commissioner, Genaro Fernandez MacGregor, and asked if he concurred with the proposals. Yes, he did. Greatly perturbed, Nielsen returned to his office and began writing a long memorandum to Reuben Clark. If these rules were allowed, he pointed out, the result would be the immediate and permanent quashing of every American claim on the books.[33]

Reuben's receipt of the Nielsen memorandum was profoundly unsettling. He was still wondering what to do about it when more ill tidings arrived from Bouvé. The first of the big cases was presently being argued by Stanley Udy, and with no small apprehension

to the American agency.³⁴ The facts of the case were depressingly familiar. Janes, the American superintendent of a Chihuahua mining
company, had quarreled with Carbajal, a Mexican employee, who in
a fit of rage had emptied his revolver into the man. The murderer
had been taken into custody, treated with ostentatious leniency, and
then allowed to escape. A claim for damages was filed in behalf of
Janes's widow and four minor children, on the theory that he had
been the sole support of the family.³⁵

The facts of the case were uncontested, but to the Americans'
legal argument the Mexican agent entered a demurrer. The Mexican
government was not responsible for Janes's murder, he pointed out,
but only for the failure to bring the murderer to justice. But the
damages for which Mrs. Janes sought compensation were inflicted by
the murder itself, not by the failure to punish. Mexico therefore was
not liable.³⁶ The Mexican agent, Don Bartolemé Carbajal y Rosas,
was a small, square man with an enormous black mustache and an
expression of arch merriment. He was a good lawyer and an even
better legal obstructionist. When he flung down the demurrer at the
American lawyers, his eyes fairly sparkled with mischief.

Bouvé was on his feet immediately. According to certain well-
established principles of international law, he said with exasperation,
it was universally recognized that the state, by its failure to punish,
in effect condones and ratifies the wrongful act and therefore becomes responsible for it. For the next hour there ensued a battle of
authorities, with Bouvé hauling out Vattel, Pradier-Fodere, and Hall
while Carbajal, still smiling, referred to "certain eminent modern jurists" who considered the theory of condonation and ratification to
be passé.

I asked for the name of the eminent jurists in question and was given one name
which was obviously not a Spanish name and was very difficult for the young
gentleman making the argument to pronounce. Another young gentleman interrupted to ask me if I would like to see the quotation from the eminent jurist.
Upon my remarking that I should like to see it, he handed me a brochure on
international law written by no less eminent a commentator than C. Van
Vollenhoven.³⁷

Bouvé looked up in astonishment. There were Carbajal, MacGregor,
and the "eminent jurist" himself regarding him with expressions of
abashed mirth. The presiding commissioner, so it seemed, was about

462

to throw international law out the window and take the side of Mexico. Fortunately, however, Reuben Clark was expected to arrive from Salt Lake City within the week.

As Clark and Bouvé sat down to sort through the situation, there was not much comfort they could find. If Van Vollenhoven could turn his back on an established doctrine like condonation and ratification, what would he do with a controversial one? There was a temptation, then and there, to call the secretary of state and tell him that the Mexican claims commission was washed up. But Reuben counseled patience. After all, they still had Fred Nielsen, who, unstable though he might be, was a crack lawyer and a persuasive debater. If Nielsen were to put up a determined resistance, as he had against Van Vollenhoven's new rules, who knew but that the presiding commissioner might not come back to earth?

vii

But Nielsen himself was the next casualty. As had happened so often in the past, he abruptly changed into another person. Bouvé never knew how or why it happened, but Reuben Clark did. They were all in the courtroom one day and the Mexican agent, expounding on a fine point of the law, was rattling along in Spanish at breakneck speed. Suddenly Bouvé stopped him. He hoped, he said, that the American commissioner (the only member of the commission who did not speak Spanish) had been able to understand the point. Reuben winced. In all dealings with Fred K. Nielsen he had taken care to show forth an abundance of diplomacy, and he had avoided all reference to Nielsen's inability to speak Spanish. And now, as Carbajal resumed his discourse, Reuben saw a strange expression come over Nielsen's face.[38]

It was not for a couple of weeks that Bouvé learned that something was wrong. He breezed into Commissioner Nielsen's office one day in late December to ask the latter's opinion about trimming back the labor force in the translating bureau. The commissioner listened impassively and then slowly began shaking his head. "I won't abolish the translating bureau," he repeated over and over, and the strange expression was back. Bouvé tried to explain. He did not want to *abolish* the translating bureau, he said; he only wanted to cut excess spending. But Nielsen's responses grew increasingly cold and his eyes increasingly opaque. Finally, after two hours, he icily dismissed the American agent with the remark that he was sorry there had to be a translating bureau at all. He would be "very glad," he said, "to make way for a Commissioner who could speak the language."[39]

In the weeks following, the situation became ever more awkward. Despite Bouvé's almost frantic attempts at reconciliation, relations between himself and the American commissioner steadily deteriorated. Soon Nielsen began avoiding Bouvé, walking past him in the hallways, staring through him in the courtroom, snubbing him openly at social gatherings.[40] "I tell you frankly," Bouvé reported to Clark, "that I have never had to deal with what appears to me to be such a perfectly grotesque situation." He wondered aloud whether they should think of replacing "this strange creature of inexplicable moods."[41] But Reuben disagreed. To change commissioners now would be a disaster, he warned; and besides, who would they get? "We combed the field very thoroughly before." The better plan, said Reuben, was for Bouvé to keep his own counsel, give Nielsen a wide berth, and, above all, "lean over backward."[42]

viii

Fred Nielsen was not the only one to be jolted by the economies in translating: the head of the translating bureau suffered a nervous breakdown. Edith B. Newman was a good translator but a poor administrator; much of the extravagance of the bureau could be laid to her charge. Clark and Bouvé decided to advance Colonel Moreno to the bureau's directorship and return Mrs. Newman to her original job. When Bouvé broke the news to her there was a terrible scene. She "flew into a violent rage," he reported, "and was as impudent as any women could be. Had she been a man," Bouvé added, "I should have fired her out of the Agency at 12 o'clock on that day."[43]

As it turned out, the tantrum was only a start. Mrs. Newman began visiting everyone from Howard Locke, the commission's administrative officer, to Assistant Secretary of State Butler Wright. Then she went to pieces. Soon Bouvé's phone was ringing at all hours of the night, announcing the latest turn of Mrs. Newman's disintegration. Even in the Takoma Sanitarium, however, the disintegration was not so disabling as to prevent her from writing some effective letters to acquaintances in the Senate.[44] Before Reuben knew it, he was accounting to the Foreign Relations Committee for Edith Newman's demotion. Reuben wearily sent this correspondence back East to Bouvé. "Before you read it," he advised, "better put a cold pack on your head."[45]

ix

Bouvé needed more than a cold pack for the next installment of trouble, which came fluttering out of an envelope supposedly containing routine business matters. It was January 25, and the Newman affair of the nineteenth was still smoldering. Bouvé's secretary, Miss Jones, came to him in great embarrassment and explained that as she was opening the morning mail and removing an affidavit of citizenship from an envelope she found in it a carbon copy of three typewritten pages addressed:

To certain members of the House and Senate.
To certain newspapers.
To certain members of the New York and Washington bars.
To the Mexican Agencies and Commissioners.

In neat, professional typescript—marred only by the repeated misspelling of Bouvé as "Bouce"—the document began as follows:

When the affairs of Mexico are occupying so much of the public's attention it would be well to turn the search light on the American Agency of the United States-Mexican Claims Commission under the domination of one Clement L. Bouce, a neurotic self-confessed incompetent who however is past master in the art of feathering his own nest and raiding the Treasury in the name of those individual Americans who suffered heavy losses in Mexico, no one of whom is likely to benefit as long as Bouce is allowed to continue to do nothing but press the claims of corporations who add substantially to his princely salary—a salary equal to that of the Secretary of State.[46]

In keeping with this attention-winning overture, the memorandum poured out a cascade of invective that included: "long and frequent absences," "feigned illness," "attempts to demoralize the staff," "rape of the Treasury," "arbitrarily increased his [own] salary," "rewarded for his ability to cover up the tracks of," "engaged only in small time graft," "political appointee," "before the records are further doctored," and, finally, "there remain in the Agency two men who know details and who are not in the ring."[47]

More unnerving than the charges themselves was the eerie means of their delivery. Bouvé telephoned Chauncey Hackett, whose law firm had mailed the affidavit of citizenship, and innocently asked if he had also sent the mysterious document. Hackett arrived within minutes. Of course he had not sent such a document, he said; did they think he was out of his mind? Then, carefully inspecting the envelope, Hackett discovered evidence of its having been opened en route. But why commit a felony to deliver something that could just as well have been mailed separately? Obviously to draw attention away from someone in the agency proper. But who?[48]

Reuben Clark might have been as upset as Clement Bouvé. He was, as he put it, "given honorable mention" in two different places in the memorandum, once for collecting a government salary while serving his own clients' interests and once for running the agency puppeteerlike from behind Bouvé. Both allegations were technically true—if woefully misleading—but Reuben shrugged the whole thing off. "It reads more or less like the wanderings of a crazy man," he said, adding, "I do not know whether *our* crazy man has become that crazy or not."[49] Wanderings or not, within the week Bouvé was reporting "the sudden interest taken in Mexico by the Senate."[50] The interest may have been entirely coincidental, to be sure, but its existence was undeniable. On January 20 Bouvé learned that the Senate Foreign Relations Committee would soon commence hearings on the Mexican situation.[51]

x

It was the land and petroleum dispute that was leading the way in this interest. Since the beginning of the claims commission's work, the impasse over land ownership and oil rights in Mexico had deepened substantially. Suddenly, in the wake of the recent difficulties, ranking members of the Foreign Relations Committee wanted some hard answers. After all, literally hundreds of millions in oil and mining leases had been tied into knots by the Querétaro constitution, while the Mexican claims commission, which was supposed to untie them, apparently could not even deal with its own translators. Bouvé's people worked day and night through the weekend in order to have a comprehensive report on Senator Reed's desk by ten o'clock Sunday morning. Reed and several colleagues met with Assistant Secretary Olds for the remainder of the morning, and then only to request more information. Bouvé, in one of his encounters with the assistant secretary on Monday, noted how tired and strained he seemed to look and how different his own behavior had become. "I had noticed particularly," Bouvé reported, "that he had had very little to communicate to me with respect to what was going on."[52]

With this, Bouvé decided that it was time to pull the ripcord. On January 28 he asked for a meeting with Olds. He conceded that matters pertaining to the Mexican claims commission were indeed in a bad way. In a few months the convention was due to expire, and the sum tally of decided cases was still only sixty. The United States had managed to pull the Janes case out of the fire; but even granting this, the future looked grim. The commission could barely deal with simple matters, he pointed out; the difficult questions were quite beyond its reach. "I told him also that I thought it would be a pretty serious matter, and a pretty serious responsibility might arise there from, if claims involving the consideration of such cases and damages of millions of dollars were submitted to the [presiding commissioner]." In view of all this, the agent concluded, there was only one thing to do: bring back Reuben Clark.

> I told him that I felt that it was, of course, impossible to expect that you could drop your important personal matters and come to Washington for such purposes as I had roughly outlined for anything approximating a Governmental salary; that I did not know whether you would come or not, but that, feeling as I did and as I knew he did with respect to yourself, I thought it my duty to inform him that there were funds available in the Agency which justified making you a reasonable offer, in case the time had come.[53]

Olds hardly knew what to say. He had been entertaining the same fears as Bouvé, but he knew that Reuben Clark would return to Washington only at a high price, if he returned at all—and there would be the end of the commission's austerity program. The assistant secretary therefore decided to make do without Mr. Clark for the

467

time being—unless a crisis should arise. Bouvé left the interview un-mollified. "I am frank to state that I thought, and I think now," he confided to Reuben, "that a very distinct crisis has risen."

xi

In the meantime Reuben had been anything but idle in Utah. He had been burrowing steadily into the Mexican bond cases and wracking his brains over the oil and land conundrum. He was even having his own encounter with the strange malady that was haunting Bouvé in the East. While there were no mental collapses or ghost memoranda, the arrival of John W. DeKay in midwinter proved to be every bit as bizarre. Colorful, genial, and thoroughly eccentric, DeKay was a millionaire who wrote novels, published newspapers, spouted philosophy, tinkered with inventions, and, as it later turned out, cooked up frauds. Yet there was nothing fradulent in his claim against Mexico: he had lost a fortune in repudiated bonds and in the process had produced precisely the sort of test case that Reuben Clark thought he could win.[54] As DeKay met with him in Salt Lake City to go over the details it became apparent that the two of them got along exceptionally well. One day, in fact, John DeKay decided to share a little secret.

It seemed that he had taken an unusual interest in the late Otto-man Empire, and specifically in the empire's last ruler, Abdul Hamid Han II, the notorious "Bloody Sultan," whose personal fortune in real estate was said to have rivaled Genghis Khan's. John DeKay thought he had an inside track on that tidy bonanza. He hinted that Reuben Clark might share it with him.

All of this was the most vaporous sort of fantasy; but after the outlandish events of late, Reuben was almost a believer. Soon, in hushed tones, he and Bouvé were alluding to the "Turkish affair," and "that business," and "our friend." DeKay's plan was simple. He had rounded up Abdul Hamid's heirs—some nine widows and fifteen children—and formed them into a corporation for the purpose of se-curing their rightful inheritance. Since this inheritance was figured by DeKay at roughly half the wealth of the Middle East, the heirs' claim to it was not altogether uncontested—but DeKay had a secret weapon. He had arranged to split the Hamid superfortune with the

Banque de Turkie et d'Angora, or the Isch Bank, as it was commonly called, in exchange for using the bank's influence to speed his case through the Turkish courts. His only remaining problem was to travel to Constantinople and consummate his contract with the Isch Bank. DeKay himself was wanted in several countries in connection with financial arabesques of this same character, and it was inadvisable for him to travel abroad. That was where Reuben Clark would come in.[55]

Intrigue was piled on intrigue. One DeKay courier, a soldier of fortune named Huff, had returned from Constantinople empty-handed, the contract supposedly stolen from his trunk by agents of a rival syndicate. Others in the design included Samy Gunsberg, the sultan's former dentist, and an adventurer for hire named Schultz. None of them was trustworthy. Reuben, on the other hand, enjoyed DeKay's total confidence. He would be able to deal with the Isch Bank and the Turkish government and return triumphantly with the prize. And talk about money: there would be enough of it to expand Reuben's Grantsville estate to the Nevada border. DeKay's dark, beady eyes came alight when he spoke of the possibilities.[56]

Conceivably, had the jackpot been a bit less astronomical, Reuben might have been more tempted by it. As it was, he was fifty-six years old and had spent a good decade of that time on Wall Street; he had heard of pie in the sky before. Clement Bouvé, however, was totally and helplessly captivated by the whole incredible scheme.[57] Amid the strange misfortunes of the Mexican claims commission, he began packing for a trip to the mysterious Orient.

xii

Thus distracted, Bouvé increased the urgency of his appeals for help. By January 20 the agent was asking Reuben to name his price for devoting full time to the agency in Washington. Bouvé was certain, he said, that the claims commission would shortly inherit the full brunt of the oil and land imbroglio, and he was at a total loss for dealing with it. Reuben was less than electrified by the prospect of returning to Washington full-time and he still faced financial difficulties at home, so he set the price at a heady one hundred dollars a day for his services. He was certain that Olds was not yet desperate enough to pay that, he told Bouvé.[58]

But even as he discussed these possibilities, Reuben had begun to move beyond the idea of a claims commission as such for settling the big problems with Mexico. Had the commission functioned as intended, he might not have entertained these thoughts; but the nonstop upheaval had undermined his faith. The dereliction of Nielsen, the Newman affair, the Senate investigation, the mysterious memo, and, worst of all, the terrifying behavior of Van Vollenhoven had sent him in search of new alternatives. "A consideration of the Mexican situation," he wrote to Bouvé on January 25,

has raised a question in my mind as to whether or not the whole Mexican controversy is in such shape that all the companies can be said to have *claims* within the meaning of the General Claims Convention. If they have not, it would seem necessary to proceed to the arbitration of the petroleum controversy under a special agreement that would arbitrate the general questions and not particular claims. I therefore have a feeling that a special agreement should be made for the arbitration of the petroleum controversy, in order that all parties may be properly protected. This feeling becomes a conviction, when I think of the possibility that our estimable Presiding Commissioner might continue after August.[59]

The idea had immediate appeal. Instead of working through the petroleum and land problems one case at a time, the whole mess might be submitted to judicial settlement at the Hague. The petty politics of the commission would thus be circumvented by a single go-for-broke arbitration. There had been much talk in the newspapers of arbitrating the differences with Mexico, and even a recent Senate resolution had been made to that effect, but among international lawyers there was little hope that constitutional provisions (like the notorious Article 27) could ever be arbitrated. Reuben disagreed. He believed that if Mexico really wanted to avoid war some formula could be found for judicial settlement. Bouvé duly passed along Reuben's suggestion to the assistant secretary, reporting that "he was very glad to get it."[60]

xiii

The spring of 1927 found the Mexican claims commission verging upon collapse. Everything that had happened in the fall and winter had festered into a single canker of discontent, and progress on the claims had slowed to a near stall. By June, with summer coming

470

on and the treaty deadline only two months away, there was a pungent smell of disaster in the air. After all, the Mexicans were not obligated to extend or renew the claims convention, and they had very little reason to do so. Carbajal y Rosas, with thinly veiled satisfaction, was daily inventing new tactics of delay. He clearly believed that the treaty would not be extended and that the thousands of claims remaining would simply never be heard.[61]

Such a prospect was too awful to contemplate. Mexico *must* extend the treaty, the Americans kept saying. Nevertheless, nerves grew taut over the question, and various parties began looking for the escape hatches. Ordinarily the commission would have recessed for the summer months and everyone would have fled Washington's Bengal heat. But in the midst of preparations for the adjournment, Bouvé, on State Department instructions, suddenly declared that the recess would have to be foregone. If the treaty was not to be extended, the commission must push ahead and hear as many cases as possible.[62]

At this, everything fell apart. Commissioner MacGregor, who was especially sensitive to the heat, flew into a violent rage.[63] Commissioner Van Vollenhoven, in his own fit of pique, ordered that all written arguments be dispensed with and that each side limit its oral presentation to a single hour per case.[64] Commissioner Nielsen, after a terrible scene with Bouvé, seemed to wilt completely. "All his efforts were wasted—all is lost, he is tired out and in a state of despair,—he is going to resign, there is nothing worth living for—the Agency is an incompetent mess, and your return is looked forward to as the sole beacon in the sinister blackness," Bouvé reported to Reuben Clark on July 1.[65] In confirmation, Reuben received a telegram from Nielsen on the fifth stating that he was going to resign if Reuben did not return to Washington.[66] Nor was Nielsen the only one ready to depart. Bouvé himself was almost giddy with the prospect of embarking on his mission to Turkey and dropping the claims commission in Reuben's lap. "Your presence here," he wrote, "would more than make up for that of a dozen agents as far as the handling of the situation is concerned."[67] Even Robert Olds, who had now become undersecretary of state, was pondering how he too could escape from the Mexican claims mess and hand it over to the man from Utah. It was like a scene out of *Waiting for Godot*.

471

Even before he left for Washington on July 21, Reuben started trying to head off the commission's demise. He wrote to Olds and denounced the one-hour oral argument idea as judicial madness. He then telegraphed Nielsen and urged him not to resign under any circumstances. On the matter of Bouvé's projected errand to Constantinople, Reuben good-naturedly counseled business before pleasure.

I do not believe it would be wisdom for you to leave the Agency until the Commission has closed its sessions, and I say this in view of the fundamental fact which you delivered yourself of, namely, "that my presence there in this connection would more than make up for that of a dozen agents, so far as the handling of the situation is concerned." Of course you and I know this, freely admit it, one to the other; but the difficulty is that perhaps not everyone would be of our mind; some might be so misguided as to assume that you, the Agent, not only by right, but by fitness and ability, were the one to be on the job. People holding such a view of course would be sadly misled and undoubtedly would be inconsiderable in number, but still they might exist, and you should protect yourself against them.[68]

So it was that the fortune of Abdul Hamid Han II went glimmering. And just as well. The whole scheme fell through with a resounding crash, and John DeKay went on about his madcap career. Two years later they heard of him throwing money from the balcony of a Yugoslavian hotel—and then being jailed in a Munich bank swindle.[69]

Finally Reuben had commenced the process of pasting things back together. He consulted with the State Department on a possible treaty for extending the life of the claims commission for another two years. If the Mexican government accepted this proposal, well and good. If not, Reuben proposed to get tough. "I would withdraw our regular diplomatic representative on the ground that if it were impossible to conduct with Mexico so simple a piece of business as the extension of an ordinary Claims Convention, it was useless to maintain a diplomatic officer in that country."[70] And somehow, Reuben added, they had to get rid of Van Vollenhoven.

xv

By whatever fortune it is that links people with events, J. Reuben Clark seemed destined to take final charge of the Mexican problem. But he was not to do so by means of the claims commission. The first hint of this was received by Bouvé after a long afternoon's conversation with Undersecretary Olds on July 9. As Bouvé got up to leave the room, the undersecretary stopped him. Was it true, he asked, that Mr. Clark was soon planning to return? Bouvé replied that Mr. Clark would probably arrive in Washington around the middle of the month. That was fine, Olds answered; there were a great many matters he had to take up with him. Bouvé, mildly curious, threw out a small gambit. "If you want Clark to come here," he suggested, "why don't you telegraph him?"[71] Olds looked up from his papers and mumbled something perfunctory. Four days later he sent Reuben a telegram that read remarkably like the one of the previous year.[72]

xvi

Once again Reuben was altogether unprepared for what Olds had in mind, and it took a full hour for his mind to track it properly. The date was August 3, and the two men had returned to Olds's office after a leisurely lunch. Olds began by asking how long Reuben planned to remain in the capital. The latter replied that he must stay throughout the month, as all memorials had to be filed before the thirtieth. Olds then explained that he had to travel to Europe on official business and that while he was away there would be no one in the department specifically responsible for Mexico. Would he, Reuben Clark, consent to spend a part of each day sitting at his, Olds's, desk and taking charge of Mexican affairs?[73]

Reuben demurred with some vigor. Now, he objected, was no time to be leaving the post of undersecretary in the hands of an amateur. But Olds stood his ground. He had come to the State Department from a prosperous New York law firm in which he had accustomed himself to winning cases—and he was not about to lose this one. The Mexican problem had been dropped in his lap like an abandoned child and had made no more sense to him than a cuneiform

473

riddle. He was going to get rid of it. While Reuben was still lecturing expansively on the reasons why it would be impossible for him to stand in as undersecretary, Olds gently moved him through the door and into the office of the secretary of state. There the arrangement was concluded.[74]

It was a surreal enough ending to the Mexican claims affair, which had been touched with dreamlike qualities from the start. For two months Reuben dutifully sat at the desk of Undersecretary Olds, listening to complaints, giving advice, mediating with politicians, keeping the secretary informed, and toiling diligently on the difficulties of the Mexican claims commissions;[75] and in those two months a surge of progress was made. Mexico agreed to a two-year extension of the claims convention treaty, and the general commission finally adjourned.[76] Van Vollenhoven submitted his resignation and sailed back to the Netherlands.[77] Fred Nielsen snapped out of his melancholy. And Clement Bouvé joyously departed for a well-earned vacation.[78] By the end of September all that seemed to remain of the summer's difficulties was the oil crisis, and even here Reuben was determined to make some progress. He began combing through the files of complaints lodged by the oilmen in Mexico in a typically Clarkean effort to make sense of it all. By the time Olds returned from Europe, Reuben had readied a 145-page memorandum on the subject and was certain that he was beginning to see daylight down the tunnel.[79]

xvii

In the course of these events silent tumblers fell into place, locking Reuben into a new set of circumstances. By mid-October he would himself be in Mexico, on the firing line of the oil controversy, and by December he would be tendering his resignation to the mixed claims commission. So would end, at least for Reuben Clark, the attempt to settle the Mexican problem through arbitration, and so would begin the attempt to settle it through diplomacy.

Arbitration had unquestionably failed. Far from setting the Mexican turmoil in order, as the proponents of judicial settlement had promised, the United States–Mexico Mixed Claims Commission had turned out to be an unending tapestry of politics, petty squabbling, red tape, compromise, and betrayal. At the end of three years the score stood at 60 claims settled, 5,897 "continued."[80]

For Reuben personally the disappointment was acute. He had been a believer in arbitration. Time and again during the early years of the Mexican Revolution he had promised a day of judicial reckoning for Mexican wrongdoers, and he himself had labored assiduously to bring that day forth. But there was no time to pause over failure. As Reuben neared the end of his stay in the undersecretary's office, he unaccountably began reading up on what was for him a novel subject—the Mexican people.[81] He may or may not have guessed that he would soon be in their midst.

Chapter 25

WITH MORROW IN MEXICO

The difficulties that hamstrung the mixed claims commission grew as naturally out of the Mexican Revolution as did the Declaration of Independence out of the American. In fact, Article 27 of the revolutionary constitution was a sort of Mexican version of the Declaration of Independence—independence from her powerful northern neighbor. In this document the attempt was made to strike down the twin evils of the *hacienda* system and foreign domination of domestic resources. As to the *haciendas,* Article 27 empowered the state to expropriate land for the benefit of the peasants, compensating original owners in the process. As to the resources, the article put forward the doctrine that these were ultimately owned by the state itself and for that reason were legally inalienable. Article 27 thus threw down a direct challenge to the United States, for it was American ranchers who owned the finest *haciendas* and American mining and drilling companies who owned most of the subsoil mineral rights.[1]

For a time there was doubt that Mexican politicians were really serious about the new program. Both Venustiano Carranza (1916–20) and Alvaro Obregón (1920–24) seemed willing to mitigate the effects of Article 27 in return for diplomatic concessions. At the Bucareli conferences of 1923, Obregón promised that the new laws would not be applied retroactively and that those oil companies which had had good titles prior to 1917, when the constitution was approved, still possessed their drilling rights. For this concession, and for the agreement to set up the claims commission, Obregón's government had been accorded diplomatic recognition.[2]

But problems continued. Land was soon being expropriated faster than the Mexican government could pay for it, and bonds became the compensation instead of cash. There were nagging questions about mineral rights too, and the Bucareli agreements fell far short of outright ownership. Most unsettling of all was Plutarco Elias Calles, who ascended to the presidency in 1924. Initially Calles seemed as flexible as his predecessors, but with time he grew increasingly assertive. Relations between the United States and Mexico steadily deteriorated throughout 1925, even without official changes in policy; and then in December the official changes came like a pair of pistol shots. The first was a new petroleum law, passed on December 18, requiring that all companies working Mexican oil lands apply for new fifty-year concessions before January 1. The second was an alien land law, passed on December 23, with across-the-board restrictions on all foreign property holding. The petroleum law seemed to negate the Bucareli agreements, apply Article 27 retroactively, and force the exchange of outright ownership for mere "concessions." The alien land law discriminated against Americans while ignoring the problem of paying for expropriated properties. Secretary of State Kellogg forthwith branded the new legislation "confiscatory."[3]

President Calles, however, saw these laws through entirely different eyes. He was often more concerned with symbols than substance. He wanted to demonstrate that Mexican law and the Mexican government were sovereign in their own land and that Porfirian economic vassalage had come to an end. Thus, for him the dispute was not so much diplomatic as legal—even constitutional. It reached toward the very meaning of the Mexican Revolution.

Throughout the summer of 1926, while Reuben Clark and Clement Bouvé were clinging to the tatters of the claims commission, "the great oil controversy," as it was coming to be known, gradually deepened. Phrases like "Mexican bolshevism" rang through the American press with ever greater frequency while dark rumors circulated that Mexico was exporting revolution and subversion all over the hemisphere.[4] Familiar names like Albert Fall of the Senate Foreign Relations Committee and Edward L. Doheny of Pan-American Petroleum again began appearing in support of military intervention. While few diplomatic officials advocated such extreme measures, it was clear that the spirit of Henry Lane Wilson survived among certain of them. James R. Sheffield, who had become ambassador to Mexico in 1924, was a leading proponent of firmness toward the Mexicans. His strident diplomacy alienated Mexican leaders to a degree unusual even for the time. Setting his face against the Calles government, Sheffield aligned himself with old Henry Lane Wilson affiliates in Mexico City, with out-of-favor Mexican conservatives, and, of course, with the oil companies. While Sheffield occupied the American embassy, Doheny's National Association for the Protection of American Rights in Mexico exercised great influence on the course of American diplomacy.[5]

But not enough influence for the oil men. They wanted a clear-cut victory over Calles and the Mexican nationalists, and they wanted it immediately. Some of them, in fact, decided to take on their adversary directly. By December of 1926 several companies were involved in legal challenges to the hated petroleum law, while others simply ignored it entirely and refused to apply for concessions. When President Calles declined to extend the January 1 deadline, a few companies moved their equipment into the fields and began drilling without permits. Calles threatened to call out the army, and he meant it.[6]

Then some fortunate developments intervened. On the Mexican side, Calles suddenly faced the reality of declining oil revenues and the prospect of severe economic dislocation.[7] He was prepared to go to the wall, if need be, to win the battle for Mexico's national pride; but if a way could be found to sheathe his sword gracefully, he had every disposition to do so. On the American side, the notorious Teapot Dome scandal implicated both Doheny and Fall and made several of the major oil companies appear to be selfish and conniving. Senator Borah's resolution to arbitrate with Mexico, the appointment of the peaceable Robert Olds as undersecretary of state, and the ill-starred landing of the marines in Nicaragua all contributed to an American mood of conciliation.[8] Presient Coolidge spoke for the new temper when on April 25 he said, "[We] do not want any controversy with Mexico. We feel every sympathy with her people in their distress and have every desire to assist them."[9] Such sentiments offered Calles an important opening, and within two months he was able to effect the resignation of Ambassador Sheffield.

ii

This was where the situation stood when Reuben Clark assumed what he termed the "unconventional, irregular, and possibly illegal" role of undersecretary substitute.[10] Mexican-American relations had thawed somewhat, but the ice had not yet broken. There was a fresh sense of urgency in the air and an unvoiced assumption that the new face behind the undersecretary's desk presented an opportunity to break everything loose. Such, at least, was the spirit of Reuben's first encounter with the oil men on August 9. The position of the companies was quite simple. There was an airtight legal and moral case against the Calles government, they said; this case had been accepted by the U.S. State Department, and all that remained was the application of enough diplomatic pressure to bring about its acceptance in Mexico City. J. Reuben Clark merely had to do his job, in other words, and the oil crisis would be resolved.[11]

Reuben was a little shaken. In this and subsequent meetings with the oil attorneys he was repeatedly struck by their smug self-assurance and contempt for things Mexican. But he believed their case to be fundamentally sound, and he immediately set to work on it. The first item of business was the usual Clarkean investigation of precedent. Reuben ransacked the files of the department and culled out every document bearing on the oil situation. He then arranged the various dispatches, communications, transcripts of Mexican oil laws, and summaries of oil company complaints in narrative sequence, to give a "complete and chronological story" of the controversy.[12] This, of course, had never been done before and it yielded some surprising results. In the first place, Reuben discovered that legal officers of the State Department had never stopped to assess their own responsibility in the oil difficulty, nor had they investigated the Mexican laws that supposedly governed the situation. The department, in other words, had simply adopted the brief of the oil men. "We had come to the point," Reuben recalled,

where in effect we were saying that the Executive of Mexico did not know the law of Mexico, neither did the Legislature of Mexico, neither did the Courts, and that the only people who knew what the law of Mexico was, were the oil attorneys.[13]

In the second place, Reuben learned that, despite the general hue and cry of the companies, no actual confiscation of oil lands had yet taken place. He happened to believe that state departments should not intervene to prevent *threatened* injury, but only to redress *actual* injury. So both discoveries changed the situation. If the oil men, as

Reuben suspected, "[thought] that they could rush things through" with this new man in Washington, they were to be disappointed. By the time the undersecretary had returned, Reuben Clark had aligned the State Department with the forces of conciliation.[14]

iii

While Reuben was winding up this work in late September and preparing to return to Utah, news broke that Dwight W. Morrow

Dwight W. Morrow: A tough sense of the practical.

Courtesy of the *New York Times.*

480

had been appointed to succeed Sheffield as ambassador to Mexico.[15] Reuben was delighted. He had known Morrow since the fall of 1915 when they had met in New York.[16] Morrow had joined J. P. Morgan & Company the previous year and, both as corporation lawyer and international financier, had already acquired legendary status. Short of stature, with gray disheveled hair and a myopic squint, he was altogether unimposing. He had about him the well-worn and perpetually rumpled look of an Ivy-League professor (he was offered the presidency of Yale in 1921) and a detached air that many took to be absentmindedness. He could sit at a dinner table wrapped in thought and scarcely know he was eating; in fact, he could pause in the middle of taking a bite, his fork poised in the air, his mind transfixed by some idea, until a sharp "Dwight!" from Mrs. Morrow brought him to his senses.[17] Yet Morrow's mind was of an extraordinary caliber, and coupled with it was a tough and agile sense of the practical. But Morrow's most striking characteristic was the personal charm that radiated from him like a nimbus. Neither friend nor foe, it seemed, could hold out against it. Needless to say, this unique combination of qualities made for an ideal negotiator and problem solver.[18] From the very first, Reuben felt the Morrow magnetism at full strength.

In many ways the two were kindred spirits. They had learned similar lessons from the world war and had come to share the same vision of a moral diplomacy. Morrow's postwar efforts to revitalize the sagging economy of Cuba had run counter to the established practice of landing troops in bankrupt American republics, scoring a victory for negotiation over intervention.[19] Then in 1924, still wrestling with the gunboat ethic, Morrow had retained Reuben Clark to prepare a memorandum on the forceful collection of foreign debts. From this document the convergence of their ideas was readily apparent; and when Reuben, in thumping campaign-style rhetoric, proclaimed that the American people "could not willingly offer the life of one American boy for all the gold we have lent to all the powers," it was Morrow's turn to be captivated.[20] He distilled blocks of the 281-page memorandum into a speech he delivered in Chicago in 1926.[21]

When Morrow was first approached about the ambassadorship, he wrote to Reuben and asked about the claims commission as an instrument for settling the oil and agrarian disputes. Reuben replied, as he had to Olds, that a special agreement to arbitrate offered better chances than the existing commission. Morrow was impressed enough to forward Reuben's letter to the president.[22]

On July 19, Morrow received a letter from his old Amherst classmate officially offering him the appointment. "I would prefer to trust you with this place above anyone else," said Calvin Coolidge.[23] But others were less sanguine. In addition to its immense financial sacrifice, the ambassador's job might well lead to the political boneyard; for if Mexico City was the most prestigious diplomatic post of the United States, it was also the most difficult and dangerous. Sighed one friend: "[Dwight] can't accomplish anything and it will break his heart."[24] Despite such fears, Morrow was intrigued by the Mexican challenge, and on August 19 he notified the president of his acceptance. "My only instructions," Coolidge is reported to have said, "are to keep us out of war with Mexico."[25]

Meanwhile Reuben was finishing up his work in Washington, including a summary of the agrarian dispute similar to his summary of the petroleum issue.[26] His letter of congratulation to the new ambassador neatly capsulized his thinking on the Mexican situation.

My dear Mr. Morrow:

Allow me to congratulate you on a great opportunity for a great service. I think that is about the only thing you get out of it. The honor and prestige adds nothing to what you already have; the pleasure is likely to be nil; and, financially, it must mean a tremendous sacrifice. But the country is to be congratulated that such marked wisdom and ability, accompanied by the full Presidential confidence, has been brought into this difficult situation.

No one needs to tell you that you will be the victim of every wile and artifice which an astute and practiced group of Bolshevist politicians can bring to bear upon you, for it is vital to that group that Mexico be saved to that cause on this hemisphere, for that cause finally succeeding there, strong reason appears for believing other of the Latin Americas will follow.

Personally, I feel there is no safety for Americans or their capital in Mexico while the present regime or its allies rule there. Of course, if revolution shall threaten them (as seems now probable), they will promise anything for our assistance,—promises they will break as they have broken all others.

Mexico is a country of great undeveloped resources; she cannot develop them herself because of lack of capacity, economic and intellectual; she has put perhaps not more than one to five per cent of the actual money that has gone into oil development in that country; she has taken lands for ejidos from Americans for the poor Mexicans, but reports indicate that such lands have in good part either fallen into the hands of a new group of large Mexican landholders—of the Obregon type—or after a year or two or three, have lapsed back to the wild state. The World will soon need Mexico's resources. History shows that what the World needs, it takes. Mexico's farming and grazing and timber lands, its minerals, lying alongside of us, will be indispensable within the next few decades at most. It seems to me that a far-sighted policy for us will preserve these great resources for development by ourselves rather than for development by some other power which, under such circumstances, must be hostile to us. It seems quixotic to believe that the World can wait for Mexico's riches until the Mexican people have developed to the point where they can bring them to the service of the World's wants.

However, I did not intend to write a dissertation, but only a congratulatory note.

I wish you the fullest measure of success.[27]

This, very clearly, was the old dollar diplomat speaking—and speaking from the perspective of the dispossessed Americans. Reuben had been in contact with Noble Warrum, a diplomat in Mexico City and a blatant national chauvinist. Warrum's reports of the evil and sinister in Mexican politics—which pretty well encompassed the whole of it—confirmed Reuben's earlier idea of the revolution as part comic opera and part spreading cancer. Reuben's own preliminary study of the Mexican people had zeroed in on their poverty, their illiteracy, their racial promiscuity—in a word, their candidacy for despotism. Though he may have had his suspicions of the oil magnates and *their* motives in Mexico, even greater was Reuben's mistrust of the Mexicans themselves. He wished well to Morrow in the spirit that Abraham had wished well to Lot.[28]

iv

Cryptic telegrams from Robert Olds were becoming commonplace. This one arrived in the Salt Lake City station a bare three days after Reuben's own return.

Have just returned and found your extremely valuable memoranda. Have conferred with Morrow and we both consider of the utmost importance to have a conference with you here before Morrow leaves for Mexico on the fifteenth of this month. Can you not arrange to be in Washington for a day or two early next week beginning October tenth?[29]

483

Wearily Reuben retraced his route across the American continent and arrived in the capital on October 1, where he conferred immediately with Olds and Morrow. The conferences stretched into the next several days and gave Reuben a chance to share his views on Mexican problems.[30] At some point in these conversations the suggestion was put forward that Reuben Clark accompany Dwight Morrow to Mexico as legal advisor, at least for the first critical weeks. Considering the state of Morrow's thinking on the oil and agrarian controversies, such a move seemed only natural. But Reuben's own thinking, as he recalled, was not much more advanced. "I had almost a virgin mind on the subject."[31]

There was little haggling over money. Reuben had recently demanded one hundred dollars a day from the claims commission, and that sum had seemed immoderate to everyone. (Only in the heyday of the American International Corporation had he been paid so much.) Dwight Morrow now cheerfully offered him double that amount—to be paid out of his pocket. Morrow's friend Will Rogers recalled the logic of the situation.

Morrow was the best Ambassador that ever lived for he admitted that he wasn't one, and knew nothing about it. But if you send me out on a job where I have to play a mouth organ (and I know I can't play it) I will go hire me the best player in the country that can play it.[32]

That the best player in the country might come at the staggering fee of twelve hundred dollars a week seemed unimportant to the new ambassador. He had a job to do.

And so Reuben returned to Utah only long enough to pack his bags and say goodbye once again. As he planned on only a brief absence, the parting was not difficult. After granting a hurried interview to the press, he boarded the *Continental Limited* on October 17 and set out for St. Louis.[33] The Morrow party, consisting of the ambassador, Mrs. Morrow, fourteen-year-old Constance, and several others, pulled into St. Louis on October 20 aboard the Missouri Pacific *Sunshine Special.* Reuben joined them in their private car and the train headed for Laredo.[34]

Aboard the *Sunshine Special* there quickly developed a strong rapport between Clark and Morrow. The ambassador was interested in general problems rather than specific details; he wanted to reconstruct friendly relations between the United States and Mexico. Reuben Clark, on the other hand, was the technician who could puzzle for hours over the tiniest of intricacies. The complement was perfect: Morrow could wave his hand over spacious contours of policy and his legal aide could translate them into tangible increments of activity. Reuben soon came to appreciate in his boss an acumen and sagacity rivaling Philander Knox's; and for his part, Morrow took up the old Knoxean practice of bouncing ideas off Reuben in order to test their qualities. There were shades here of the old days at Valley Forge. Young Constance remembered the atmosphere as exceptionally "cheerful and friendly."[35]

"Such a contrast!" wrote the ambassador's wife of their drive across the international bridge. "Bad streets, poor houses, rubbish, dirt, many Indians, but much picturesqueness in the faded green doorways and windows."[36] It was Reuben's first look as well at the land of revolution and turmoil he had imagined so often from afar. At least one member of the group thought better of venturing into it. Daffin, Constance Morrow's white highland terrier, took one look at Mexico, leaped from the car, and made a beeline back for the United States, with Constance, assorted American dignitaries, and a crowd of Mexican bystanders in full pursuit. He was corraled halfway across the bridge by a small Mexican boy. "That dog," remarked Reuben dryly, "has more sense than any of us."[37]

There was little in the ensuing leg of the journey to brighten the initial impression: wide and barren desert, dreary villages, now and then some large *hacienda* off in the distance. Anne Morrow would make the same journey two months later and would render it in the imagery of gloom.

We stop at little stations; mud-built houses, sticks and stones; standing outside, a man, dark, savage-looking, a blanket around him, covering his nose and mouth, showing just those sullen dark eyes. Pigs and thin, tail-lowered dogs run in and out of his house. A woman in the door—a great blanket around her, too—her eyes only showing above the rim. It is so cold.

There is nowhere any color. It is all just the same, this dull gray green: the sand, the bushes, the sky even—cold and cloudy—seemed washed with the same color; no reds, no yellows or tans, just this cold enveloping dry gray. It is terribly depressing. We have traveled three days seeing nothing lovely: flat fields first, of cornstalks, then of cotton, now today *nothing* but this gray cactus. It looks like one vast mildew![38]

The trip was not without its drama, though. Mexico was in the midst of one of its periodic upheavals, and the country wore the aspect of an armed camp. Two carloads of federal soldiers were coupled to the ambassador's train at Laredo and more troops lined the route to Mexico City. Nevertheless, at each whistle stop government and military officials solemnly greeted the train, bands played, and reporters crowded around the new ambassador with anxious queries. Throngs of Mexican people cheered the train's progress toward the capital. There was an air of triumphal procession to it all.[39]

The red carpet, though perhaps trite, was no joke. As the embassy limousines pulled through the eagle-crested gate and drew up to the magnificent granite building, there it was—a swath of brilliant scarlet flowing regally down the steps to greet the new ambassador.[40] It seemed a fitting enough climax to the pageantry of the preceding week (which had begun with a nineteen-gun salute in Laredo) but a reminder as well of the awesome responsibilities awaiting them. Reuben stepped from the car and took his first unhurried look at Mexico. The embassy was situated in the heart of the city, some three miles from the National Palace. It was an imposing Palladian structure with colonnaded portico and balustrade running the entire length. It looked out over a walled garden and manicured grounds which gave a feeling of peace and seclusion. Strange tropical flora stood everywhere, reaching exotic limbs around corners and spilling bright foliage out of unexpected places. Colored birds called mockingly from the trees high above. Across the garden was located the chancery, also Palladian but a little more businesslike; it was here that the real work of the embassy was carried on. The street side of the chancery faced the Paseo de la Reforma, the boulevard down which Maximilian and Carlota had been driven to be crowned emperor and empress of Mexico. It was sobering to gaze out at the Paseo at twilight and recall their tragic fate.[41]

v

Tasks of organizing and settling in were substantial. There were staff members to hire, assignments to alter, and routines to establish. The new ambassador had to pick up the reins of his power one at a time and see what happened when he pulled them, while his wife had to launch into wearisome preparations for entertaining. Morrow had been warned that two obstacles would stand in the way of improved relations with Mexico: the city's American community and the embassy's own staff.[42] In particular, the counselor of embassy, H. F. Arthur Shoenfeld, was an advocate of firmness out of the old Sheffield mold. Morrow's solution was to let Shoenfeld supervise the daily routine of the embassy while the ambassador himself and a few trusted advisors attended to the oil controversy and the agrarian problem.[43] George Rublee, Washington lawyer and longtime personal friend of the Morrows, was one such close advisor. Captain Lewis B. McBride, thinly disguised as naval attaché, was another. But it was J. Reuben Clark who would sit on the ambassador's right hand in the days that followed. While the offices of Shoenfeld and the titled secretaries hummed with activity on the chancery's ground floor, it was upstairs that the real work was carried on. Reuben's office was in a secluded corner on the second floor.[44]

Morrow had to labor against a vast accumulation of mistrust created by his predecessor. "After Morrow," as one Mexican newspaper put it, "come the marines."[45] But he assailed the task cheerfully. He changed the sign over the gate from "American Embassy" to "United States Embassy," a small but significant token. He attempted assiduously to learn Spanish, never quite mastering the distinction between *Señora* and *Sonora* but charming the Latins nonetheless. Above all, he showed a warmth for the common people and a respect for things Mexican. He was a master of symbolic communication.[46]

And it was through symbols, largely, that Morrow proceeded to deal with the Mexican government. Violating one Sheffield tradition after another, he conducted negotiations orally instead of in writing, approached high officials directly instead of through channels, and wore morning clothes instead of diplomatic regalia to his presentation of credentials.[47] Within the first week, in fact, Dwight Morrow had established himself as a very different sort of ambassador. And fortunately enough, Morrow's bluffness and candor sat well with Plutarco Calles. Calles was a stone-faced, hard-bitten veteran of the revolution who had risen through the ranks under Carranza and Obregón. An ex-bartender, he could have still passed for a saloon bouncer, and in politics he had the pugnacity that accompanied his looks. In some ways he was the typical iron dictator. But Calles had learned the great lesson of the revolution—that no Mexican leader could long remain in power while ignoring the will of the people—and he pursued vigorously the ideals of nationalism and social justice for which they had fought. What he wanted now was a means of preserving and strengthening those ideals while avoiding a rupture with the United States. Between such alternatives the balance was often precarious. Calles looked to Morrow with hope.[48]

The new ambassador had no predetermined policy. He wanted Calles to make the first move. And on October 31 the Mexican president, having already dropped several diplomatic handkerchiefs, invited Morrow to breakfast at his ranch on the outskirts of Mexico City. Morrow quickly accepted. An informal breakfast in a relaxed setting was exactly his kind of encounter. The ambassador also decided not to take along Arthur Shoenfeld as interpreter in the usual way, but to rely on Calles's interpreter instead. (This was James Smithers, an American and a lifelong friend of the Mexican president, who was so facile with the Spanish tongue that he could translate Will Rogers's jokes with their hilarity intact.) It was another of those extremely important symbolic gestures.[49]

The breakfast went well. President Calles proudly guided his guest on a tour of the four-hundred-acre ranch, and Morrow displayed appropriate fascination with the blooded cattle, the extensive irrigation system, and virtually everything else he saw. During the meal itself Calles talked freely about his programs for improving Mexico, and Morrow, through some shrewdness of his own, purposely avoided any mention of oil or land. After two hours of cordial conversation, the ambassador thanked his host warmly and returned to Mexico City. Accustomed to Sheffield's blunt demands, Señor Calles did not know what to make of the visit. "Ham and eggs diplomacy," like Morrow the diplomat, was something new.[50]

vi

While Morrow was chipping away at the diplomatic ice, Reuben Clark was at work on the problems frozen beneath it. So busy was he so soon after his arrival that his experience with the City of the Aztecs was confined to the view from his chancery window. "The atmosphere of the place is unlike anything I have ever experienced be-

Clark and Dwight Morrow greeting President Ortiz Rubio: Ham and eggs and homework.

fore," he reported to Clement Bouvé. "Everything seems mysterious and, to me, unfathomable." But the sky was clear, the air sparkled, and the mountains reminded Reuben of home. As for the Mexican people, whose "indifference ... amounts practically to fatalism," Reuben said that he would reserve judgment for the present.[51] It was clear that he did not, as he had once supposed, have Mexico all figured out.

First on the agenda was the oil problem. "Before we can settle the oil question," Morrow said, "we must know as much about the oil question as anybody on earth."[52] This was a uniquely Clarkean challenge and Reuben accepted it literally. He began collecting everything ever written about Mexican oil and land laws. He deputized the embassy staff to forage through the secondhand bookstores of the city for whatever might further the research. Government publications, legal commentaries, rare old volumes, obscure works by long-forgotten authors—anything and everything of pertinence was dutifully hauled in.[53]

Then came the tasks of reading, translating, assembling, organizing, and distilling the material into precise and coherent memoranda.

489

It was fortunate that Mr. Clark was no society man, remarked staff members on their way to the country club, for he always seemed to have a mountain of work before him. But he hacked into it with gusto. While George Rublee squired Mrs. Morrow about the golf links on lazy afternoons, Reuben pored over dusty tomes of Mexican mining laws, and the light in his chancery office burned late into the night. He eschewed sightseeing, avoided the cocktail parties, took many a meal with young Constance in the embassy kitchen, and became famous for devotion to his labors.[54] But by the first week of November he was beginning to make sense of the oil controversy.

The chief difficulties stemmed from differences in legal culture between the United States and Mexico. For example, in Mexican law, which derived from the old Spanish colonial law, there was a distinction clearly drawn between ownership of the surface of the land and ownership of the minerals below. Possession of the one did not necessarily confer possession of the other. Thus, the king might grant the surface to one individual and the subsurface to another, with entirely different rules governing each. In particular, the grantee of subsurface rights was obligated to perform a certain amount of work, a "positive act" (roughly the equivalent of assessment work in American mining law) before the mineral rights actually belonged to him; otherwise the grant would revert back to the king. By contrast, the American oil companies, accustomed to principles of Anglo-American law, thought of ownership in terms of fee simple, where the owner of the land owned everything from the surface to the center of the earth. They had not often troubled themselves with the required positive acts, for in their view they owned the lands outright. They had also undertaken to have the troublesome laws changed. Back in the days of Díaz they had succeeded in Americanizing the ancient law of Mexico to their own private advantage. With the revolution and the new constitution, the Mexicans had changed the laws back and with a vengeance. If they now chose to apply the changes retroactively, many oil and mining properties would simply revert back to the government. For Mexican radicals, of course, this was eminently desirable, and they would construe the definition of positive acts so narrowly as to dispossess *all* the Yankees. But for the more thoughtful Mexicans—like Calles—it was more important to retain the American developers and their know-how, but subject to Mexican control. Unfortunately, the oil men wanted no changes at all. They wanted the laws which, under Díaz, they themselves had written. The real point of the controversy, then, was whether Mexican law or American muscle was to be supreme in Mexico.[55]

These discoveries had a pronounced effect on Reuben. He had arrived in Mexico expecting to find bolshevism run amuck. What he had actually found was misrepresentation by American lawyers. From the days of the League of Nations fight, Reuben had suspected the interests and their motives. Suddenly he began to wonder about the dealings of the oil interests in Mexico.

vii

Reuben's changing viewpoint dovetailed with that of Dwight Morrow. When the two of them sat down after the breakfast visit and compared notes, it was clear that Morrow had been greatly impressed by Calles. He described the Mexican president as dignified and forceful in his personal relations, able and honest as an administrator.[56] It was time, said the ambassador, to discard the legalism of the Sheffield era and meet the president's sincerity in kind. The oil controversy need not be a confrontation of ideologies, he believed; it might just as well be a practical problem that reasonable men could solve.

The approach they worked out was simple and direct. Since neither diplomacy nor power politics had been effective, why not commit the problem of the oil lands to adjudication by the Mexican courts? (As solicitor, Reuben had given claimholders that same advice a thousand times.) If President Calles really desired an equitable solution, there was every reason to expect a fair decision. And the settlement would be wholly local, wholly legal, and wholly mindful of Mexican sovereignty. Moreover, Reuben's research had uncovered a persuasive precedent. In the Texas Oil Company cases of 1921, the Mexican supreme court had ruled that Article 27 of the constitution was not retroactive and could not abrogate property rights already vested. If this decision could now be affirmed by the court and applied to the new petroleum law, it would effectively confirm the oil rights purchased before 1917 and thus remove the chief obstacle to a settlement.[57]

A chance to play the Texas Oil card presented itself on November 8, when Calles once again invited the ambassador to breakfast. This time they discussed business. President Calles asked Morrow what solution he might suggest to the oil controversy, and Morrow, without so much as a pause, replied that a "clear decision" following the Texas Oil cases was the place to begin. Calles sat up in his chair. "You mean to tell me," he said, "that if the Supreme Court should hand down a decision reaffirming the Texas decision that the oil question would be settled?"

"Well," Morrow replied, "it would be a long way toward it."

"The oil question is settled," said Calles. "Within two weeks the Supreme Court will hand down its decision reaffirming the Texas decision."[58]

The Mexican supreme court was as good as the president's word. On November 17 it ruled that the petroleum law could not impair oil rights held before 1917. Those who had secured title prior to that time in conformity with existing Mexican law were entitled to ownership in perpetuity. Two days later Señor Calles summoned Morrow to the National Palace, this time to express his pleasure with the decision. He was certain, he added, that the legislative and executive branches of government would comply with the ruling; and within the next few weeks the congress, at Calles's request, began amending the objectionable portions of the petroleum law.[59] Several aspects of the problem remained unsettled—among them the working definition of positive acts—and Reuben Clark was still cautious about the results. Still, no one could deny that Morrow and Clark had broken the great oil controversy wide open.

viii

For the time being, they were free to turn attention to the second great difficulty before them: the agrarian dispute. When Morrow arrived in Mexico, there were some two hundred fifty cases of land seizure awaiting his attention.[60] He initially attempted to deal with them on an individual basis, detailing embassy staff to investigate the facts of each case and then making representations to the appropriate government officials. Soon, however, it became apparent that the problem was far too large for ad hoc solutions, and

Morrow began to think of the difficulties in general terms. No socialist and certainly no bolshevist, Morrow approached the land problem with the same sympathy and understanding that characterized his attitude on oil. He tried to see the nationalization of land through Mexican eyes. After all, as Morrow well knew, the land now being expropriated for the peasant *ejidos* was land fairly stolen from them back in the time of Díaz. So the ambassador's position was that the Mexican government possessed the right to seize lands in the interest of reform, so long as the action was not confiscatory or discriminatory.[61]

His aide Reuben Clark was appreciably less sympathetic. As in the oil controversy, Reuben's initial attitude was close to that of the imperiled American interests. Before leaving for Mexico he had publicly alluded to the mismanagement of the agrarian bureaucrats and the negligence of the peons. Land titles and procedures of taxation were in a woeful mess, he had pointed out, and the practice of paying for expropriated lands with bonds instead of cash was little short of economic mayhem.[62] Nor were these sentiments much altered during Reuben's early weeks in Mexico, for in his first memorandum on the subject Reuben still spoke of waste and inefficiency in the land program. The way to insure good management of land, he said, was to make people pay for it.[63]

But Morrow remained moderate. His suggested remedy for the agrarian controversy was to slow down the rate of expropriation and concentrate on improving the lands already taken over. He agreed with Reuben Clark that rapid nationalization of lands, coupled with payment in bonds, was undermining the already tottering financial structure of Mexico. If the Mexicans tried paying as they went, Morrow suggested, they might begin working toward a balanced budget.[64]

Such observations were not unwelcome. After all, Morrow represented the genius of the house of Morgan and he had had wide experience in Latin American finance. Finance minister Luis Montes de Oca, for one, accepted whatever advice Morrow had to offer, and President Calles suggested that the ambassador look into other departments of the government as well.[65] As for Morrow's particular ideas on the agrarian problem, here Calles and the Mexicans wanted to go slowly. The cry for land had been one of the animating forces of the revolution, and few Mexican politicians were likely to back away from their commitment to reform.

ix

As Thanksgiving drew near, Reuben was preparing to journey to Washington and report to the administration. For the embassy Thanksgiving celebration Mrs. Morrow composed short poems in honor of the principal guests.

> Our Reuben Clark has learned to make
> One good meal do for three,
> But when it comes to stuffing work,
> A glutton sure is he!
>
> Now if he ate *three* meals a day,
> Or even swallowed *two,*
> There isn't anything I'm sure,
> Our Reuben couldn't do![66]

The allusion was to a massive memorandum summarizing the work of the Morrow mission to date.[67] In Washington, Reuben presented this information to Undersecretary Olds on December 6 and to Secretary Kellogg the following day. On December 8, Reuben accompanied Olds to the White House for a firsthand report to the president.[68] As the two of them entered the Oval Office, Reuben was struck by the tidiness of the room, the absence of work on the great oak desk, and the evident repose in the president's demeanor. "Mr. Coolidge," he recalled,

sort of straightened himself up in his chair, wheeled half way around, and leaned back in his chair, put his hand in his pocket, pulled out a set of keys, picked out a key, opened the upper right hand drawer of his desk, took out a box of first class Havanna cigars. They smelled good. He took out one, put it in his mouth, carefully closed the box, put it back in the drawer, locked it and put the keys in his pocket, lighted the cigar, and then we were ready to proceed. He did not know that I did not smoke, and he did know that the Under Secretary did![69]

After this unpromising start, however, the audience with Calvin Coolidge stretched into a pleasant two hours and proved to be invaluable. The president agreed that amazing progress had been made in a very short time.[70]

Reuben Clark had gone to Mexico with the expectation of a brief stay, and when he now rejoined his family in Salt Lake City it was with the understanding that his mission was accomplished. Indeed, as the Clarks journeyed to Los Angeles to spend the holidays with Louise and Mervyn, they spoke of the Mexican sojourn as past history. Still, it was interesting to follow Morrow's continuing exploits in the California newspapers. When Will Rogers made a visit to the embassy and toured the Mexican countryside with the ambassador and President Calles, the event created a gust of favorable commentary. Even more newsworthy was the visit of Charles A. Lindbergh on December 14. Morrow had arranged for the Lone Eagle to fly nonstop from Washington to Mexico City as a gesture of goodwill; and wherever the two of them went in the days following, goodwill abounded in the cheering throngs. (Goodwill of a different sort began to develop between Colonel Lindbergh and the ambassador's brilliant daughter Anne. It was to be the match of the decade.) But the enduring symbol of Mexican-American friendship remained the ambassador himself. Whether in the company of celebrities or shaking hands with ordinary Mexican citizens, Dwight Morrow continued to pour forth his special charm.[71]

Just before the New Year, Morrow requested Reuben Clark's return. Both men knew that the oil controversy had not been laid to its final rest, and Morrow had remained in touch with Reuben over technical details of the settlement. It was only half in jest that Reuben ended one communication with the words, "My respect for the intuitive wisdom of Daffin [Constance Morrow's patriotic terrier] has not lessened."[72] Now a new crisis seemed to be approaching, and Morrow was eager to have Reuben on the firing line before he himself had to depart for Havana and the Pan-American conference on January 10. Reuben readily answered the request. "I do not know how long I shall be in Mexico City," he wrote to Clement Bouvé. "Conceivably it will be several weeks, stretching into a month or two, perhaps."[73] His estimates were steadily growing longer.

This time Reuben took Luacine along. It was the nearest thing to a real vacation that the two of them had ever known, complete with sightseeing, shopping, and spending an occasional evening

Relaxing at the Morrow retreat in Cuernavaca: Almost a real vacation.
Seated at the far right are Reuben and Luacine Clark; Morrow is seated fifth from the right; second from the left is Rudolf Hess, soon to become Hitler's henchman in the Third Reich.

together at the Mexico City Country Club.[74] Still, these moments were but punctuation in Reuben's tedious labors, and Luacine regarded herself as an uninvited guest. "I am very anxious to see all the sights," she wrote to her son, "so I can get back home." Withal, the Morrows were gracious, the days languidly pleasant, and the new sights and sounds exciting. "We eat something each day that we have never seen before," she remarked.[75]

x

The oil controversy plodded on. As Reuben had predicted, the supreme court's affirmation of the Texas Oil cases resolved some problems and created others. The favorable ruling and the amended petroleum legislation removed the substance of the oil men's complaint; what remained was mostly shadow. For example, the new law (passed in December) still required oil companies to take out concessions, but these were now described as confirmatory concessions of unlimited duration, and they would issue from existing rights of the petroleum producers rather than being granted by the government. For Calles the rather meaningless distinction between these concessions and outright ownership was important symbolically, for it once again reaffirmed the supremacy of Mexican law. For the oil men the distinction also meant something: that their ownership was still less than outright. A concession was a concession, they said. Both sides were trading in symbols.[76]

And with Morrow in Havana, it was Reuben Clark who had to bear the brunt of the oil companies' complaints. He agreed with Morrow's often-stated rule that the government must confine itself to defending property rights in the broad sense, not serving as counsel for particular interests. The more Reuben dealt with the oil companies, in fact, the less he seemed to admire them. He grew wary of their demands for Mexican blood. He grew even more wary of the motives of their attorneys, who stood only to lose if the difficulties with Mexico were ironed out and only to gain if the whole thing fell apart. "The oil business," Reuben confided to one Mexican official, "seems to attract more than its share of lawless men."[77]

As a result of his disaffection, Reuben turned upon the oil representatives the very weapons he had been honing for their defense.

Soon it was they, and not the Mexicans, who became the subject of a Clark memorandum. Reuben assessed their arguments in exhaustive detail and concluded that these boiled down to a "legal and logical dilemma." "The companies appear to contend that they wish the Government to *confirm* their titles," he wrote, "although they insist the Government has nothing to give and they want nothing from it." Furthermore, the memo spoke out against the oil men's general presumptuousness. "The Standard Oil Company," Reuben charged, "leaves the matters which are before the Ambassador and State Department with reference to Mexico, and enters the domain of statesmanship." Reuben termed this "the spirit of oil super-sovereignty."[78]

With this most recent memorandum in hand, Morrow was unlikely to bend much in the direction of oil company demands, and bend he did not. He continued to work for a settlement fair to both sides, and he steadfastly refused to plead individual cases. Many oil representatives were displeased with such neutrality, and a few of them determined to push ahead with or without Morrow's assistance by approaching commerce minister Luis Morones directly and attempting to negotiate on their own account. Morones's department was charged with putting the new petroleum law into effect, and the oil men hoped to press upon him their own draft of amended regulations. But Morones would not play ball.[79]

And so, in effect, the Mexican government and the American oil companies were deadlocked once again. Yet Morrow and Clark were able to go back to the drawing board with renewed confidence. Their experience together in Mexico was now stretching toward the six-month mark, and the ease with which they had initially approached each other had ripened into a deep friendship. Beginning with Morrow's trip to Havana, Reuben had assumed greater and greater responsibility in the oil controversy. By February, in fact, he had practical charge of all negotiations, holding daily meetings with petroleum department *jefe* Ingeniero Paredes while Morrow confined his own involvement to questions of policy.[80] They made a good team. For Dwight Morrow, jaded in the confines of the Morgan empire, Mexico and its challenges offered new worlds to conquer—and this portly Mormon lawyer was his faithful Sancho Panza. For Reuben Clark, having supposedly exhausted his international career, this experience had the romance and excitement of the old fight against the League—and this rumpled and dowdy little millionaire was the new knight in shining armor.

xi

It was Reuben who finally broke the stalemate. His method was uniquely Clarkean. He pulled together drafts of all prior oil regulations in order to get the feel of the Mexican commerce department's approach to petroleum management. Then, with this material in view, Reuben set about to determine the minimum number of regulatory amendments necessary to give the oil men what they wanted. Carefully comparing the new statutes, the record of the Bucareli negotiations, the Mexican-American oil correspondence, and the drafts of new regulations proposed by both sides, Reuben then worked out his own set of regulations. In every instance where change was called for, Reuben employed language as close as possible to the actual pronouncement of some official Mexican source and duly noted the source in the margin.[81] These proposed compromise regulations thus exhibited both respect for Mexican law and regard for Mexican sensibilities. Reuben Clark was learning from his boss.

By March 1 the new proposals were ready. Response from the Mexicans was surprisingly favorable and, after some jockeying over details, virtual agreement was reached. Reuben's compromise formula embodied the idea of confirmatory concessions as described in the new petroleum law, but these concessions were defined in such a way as to guarantee the vested property rights of the oil men. There were still a few loose ends sticking out, but in the atmosphere of mutual accord these were handily tucked into place. Positive acts were liberally defined so as to assure title to most of the pre-1917 oil lands. The "untagged lands" (upon which no positive act had been performed prior to 1917) remained a possible sticking point, but Reuben set himself to work on the problem and there was every hope for ultimate success.[82] On March 27, 1928, after ten years of active and heated debate over petroleum, the amended regulations were signed by representatives of both governments. The great oil controversy was at an end.[83]

Press reaction was immediate and enthusiastic. Of all of Dwight Morrow's achievements, this would be best and longest remembered.

What he had accomplished, almost incredibly, was the resolution of concrete issues while allowing both sides to maintain their principles. If the petroleum companies gained less than they had hoped for, they had clearly won on the essential point of vested property rights; and if the Mexicans had surrendered on that point, they had preserved the symbols of their national sovereignty. There remained, of course, the manifold difficulties of implementation, and no one expected these to be small; but the really rough water lay behind. On March 29 the embassy held a little celebration of its own.[84]

xii

Reuben was digging into new aspects of the Mexican imbroglio when a letter arrived from Secretary Kellogg at the end of March. In preparation was the last and largest of the oil memoranda, a massive summary of all work on the subject to date. (One appendix alone ran to 543 pages.[85]) In the light of Reuben's obvious enjoyment of himself, Kellogg's request was not without its irony. He wanted Reuben to succeed Robert Olds as undersecretary of state. The letter was followed by a phone call from Olds, and there was a certain amount of haggling back and forth.[86] There appeared to be little doubt, however, that Reuben would accept the position, and on April 2 newspapers across the country reported the appointment as all but certain.[87] The reports were premature.

Reasons ran for and against the proposed new assignment. It was a logical extension of Reuben's Mexican work, and it would enable him to better coordinate Morrow's activities with the department and administration. It had its obvious social and pecuniary benefits. On the other hand, it was an executive post—one for which Reuben had no particular enthusiasm and one apt to be long on headaches and short on creativity. Besides, it was essentially a lame duck's nest, for Coolidge was not running for reelection. But the most important consideration was Reuben's own itch for politics and the knowledge that 1928 offered him one last try for the Senate. So for the present all parties decided on a holding pattern. Reuben would make his bid for the Senate nomination first.[88]

xiii

Meanwhile, the pace of the Mexican work never slackened. On April 20 Reuben traveled to Washington for another round of reports to the department. After a brief visit home he returned to the capital for meetings with several of the oil companies.[89] Recalling the happy days of Sheffield, these oil men were still unwilling to make their peace with Mexico and seemed to regard compromise as unbusinesslike. Reuben's patience with them was by now wearing thin. They could not expect the State Department to take action, he said, unless advised of an actual injury. No such injury had occurred so far, and if the oil people applied for their concessions and got back to the business of producing oil it would not occur in the future. When the meeting broke up, tempers were steaming on both sides, and some of the oil attorneys complained bitterly to the department.[90]

By June Reuben was back in Mexico City and hard at work on the agrarian controversy. He was also able to address the work of the claims commission.[91] The slow pace of settling the claims was of concern to the Mexicans as well as Americans, and at one point an en bloc settlement was proposed by the Mexican government. Reuben participated in these as well as the agrarian negotiations (the two were closely related), but progress on both of them went very slowly.[92] In the meantime he prepared a journal article on the oil settlement. Reuben's library in the embassy now occupied two large rooms in the chancery and threatened a third; young secretaries joked about returning from lunch to find their desks replaced by bookshelves.[93] It was from these archives that Reuben proceeded to draw the material for his essay, which was published in *Foreign Affairs* as "The Oil Settlement with Mexico."[94] If doubts existed as to the technical genius behind Morrow's accomplishment, they were cleared away now.

Reuben ended this third, and presumably final, trip to Mexico with mixed emotions. Behind him he was leaving work as satisfying as the League fight and a friendship as vital as Philander Knox's. And Mexico itself had worked a subtle charm upon him. It no longer seemed a land of comic-opera politics and certainly not a land of rapacious communism. The change of mind was evident in Reuben's new regard for Plutarco Elias Calles, whom he saw as strong, soft-spoken, arbitrary at times, but utterly devoted to his fearsome responsibilities and profoundly wise about human affairs. "General Calles was one of the great men, the very, very great men that I have

501

ever met," Reuben would someday recall. "He was a real statesman."[95] Similarly, Reuben had had an inside view of Mexican problems, and from that perspective they did not look as easy as they had
from Washington. "When I went to Mexico with Mr. Morrow,"
Reuben later confided to Frank Kellogg's biographer,

I had a definite, strong prejudice against Mexico and the revolutionary regime in
control. I thought they were a group of adventurers, dictators, thoroughly lawless,
really despots. I am afraid this was a reflex of the Department's attitude. When I
got to Mexico, I began my first independent study of the situation. . . . As I went
forward in my work and learned more about the facts involved, the law of Mexico,
the centuries of inflictions made by Church and State upon the great Indian
(Mexican) population, and got a better understanding of the purposes and activities of the revolutionists (guilty of many excesses, some of them tragically cruel), I
found it necessary to reappraise my views and modify my prejudices.

I recall that one day as I reflected, I said to myself, almost orally, "Well, you
have thought you were pretty smart in your appraisals of the Mexican Government and its activities in this revolution, which, after all, did away with the curse
of peonage, practical slavery, and what would you have done to work out the
Mexican problem without the bad elements that occurred?" After a good deal of
thought I concluded that I could not have worked out the revolutionary purpose
with less bloodshed, less hardship to the people, less injury to the great landed
class, than had the revolutionary leaders.[96]

The lesson marked another kind of turning point in Reuben Clark's
career. It gave him a new access of humility. Like Dwight Morrow
himself, Reuben was becoming *simpático.*

Ahead of him lay the agonizing campaign against Bamberger
and the understanding that, if defeated, he would accept Olds's job
as undersecretary. The uncertainty of it all made a fitting backdrop
for the long ride across the gray desert. There was uncertainty behind
him, too. When reporters in San Antonio asked him about the situation in Mexico, he replied, "I do not know. I left there last night."[97]
Beneath the flippancy lay an awareness that the struggles over oil,
land, claims, finances, and the Catholic church were far from over.
And it happened that J. Reuben Clark was far from finished with
them.

Chapter 26

UNDERSECRETARY

Ever afterward, J. Reuben Clark referred his ten months as undersecretary of state as an "interregnum." The choice of terms was revealing. At the outset Reuben had predicted that the job would be one of "many irritating experiences" and "many unhappy hours" and it would be a distraction from his real work in Mexico.[1] The thought of his snug corner office in the Mexico City embassy, his amiable boss, and the "high thinking" that had been interrupted occasionally plunged Reuben into gloom.[2] Undersecretaries, by contrast, did little that was exciting or creative, as attested by the quiet desperation of Robert Olds. Interregnum was not a felicitous word.

The congratulatories were brighter. John Bassett Moore, a little mischievously, termed the undersecretaryship a "happy rest."[3] Chandler Anderson, another one-time counselor of state, enthusiastically pointed out that Reuben would constructively be secretary of state.[4] Enoch Crowder was positively excited about the appointment,[5] while Ingeniero Paredes, head of the Mexican petroleum department, noted approvingly that it was about time for an undersecretary "[whose] course of conduct is straight."[6] On one point, at least, all of the congratulatories agreed. President Coolidge had found, "bar none, the best man in this country" for the post.[7]

ii

Still, Reuben's dour assessment was in some ways the more accurate one. Frank Kellogg's State Department was not a particularly agreeable place to work. As in the days of Root and Knox, it was shot through with squabbles and jealousies; and the secretary, rather than moderating them, often seemed to be their cause. This was not entirely his fault. Kellogg had little experience or expertise in foreign affairs. After a somewhat scanty education he had studied law, built a successful corporate practice in Minnesota, served as president of the American Bar Association, and then been elected to the Senate. President Coolidge had sent him off to London as U.S. ambassador in 1924 and recalled him to be secretary of state the following year. Rumor had it that this was in payment of a political debt. Whatever the case, the president seemed to enjoy putting Kellogg down, dwelling on his shortcomings, and going so far as to declare at one point that he would have much preferred Reuben Clark for secretary. H. L. Mencken dismissed Kellogg as a "doddering political hack from the cow country."[8]

The problem was not the secretary's intelligence—which was high—nor his devotion to duty—which was martyrlike—but rather his temperament, which was strung almost to the snapping point. Gaining the sobriquet "Nervous Nellie," Kellogg was afflicted with a tremor of the hands and head and with a temper that flared violently without warning. In making decisions he vacillated erratically, and when under strain he was nearly impossible to deal with. A typical Kellogg response to some bit of ill tidings was to summon all aides to his office at once and subject them to blistering fulminations of wrath. The ordinary course of diplomacy wore hard enough on him; the intervention in Nicaragua and the threat of war in Mexico drove him to the brink of nervous exhaustion. Finally, in February of 1928, President Coolidge had to step in and order the secretary to take a rest. As Kellogg obediently prepared to board the train for Virginia's Warm Springs, he presented to his assistant the specter of a "sick and broken man."[9] When he returned, he asked for Reuben to come to Washington and help him. "If I can not get Mr. Clark," he wrote to Morrow, "I have not much idea what I shall do."[10]

There was a reason for specifically requesting Reuben. When Frank Kellogg had originally come to the State Department, the Rogers Act had just signaled the final victory of the career diplomats over the political spoilsmen. Thereafter the career men, many of them bluestocking aristocrats from Beacon Hill and the North Shore, effectively seized control of the State Department and created an engine of favoritism for their own kind. At the throttle was Joseph Clark Grew, scion of the Boston Cabot family and undersecretary of state. Kellogg, unsure of himself, had relied on Grew, with the result that State Department affairs continued to be monopolized by the career clique. Eventually there was an explosive political reckoning, and the clique had to be scattered abroad.[11] Secretary Kellogg, badly singed, had at that time requested Reuben Clark to take Grew's place.[12] He wanted an experienced and knowledgeable diplomatist, he said, but definitely not of the "career" variety. Now, a year later, he finally had his man.

And just in the nick of time. On August 17 Kellogg had to leave for Paris and the signing of the Kellogg-Briand peace pact, immediately placing the new undersecretary in charge. The tensions and frictions of the early Kellogg years were still much in evidence. In fact, Reuben sensed that what the department needed most was a calm and steady hand, someone to moderate the excitable secretary of state, to mediate between the various uneasy factions, and to provide cohesion to the entire organization. "If I had my own personal preference," he wrote plaintively to Morrow, "I would now be in Mexico rather than here."[13]

Outwardly, the State Department had changed little since the days of Philander Knox. Its headquarters were still in the old State, Navy, and War Building. The same sense of timelessness hovered in the marble halls and the same black messengers dozed or worked crossword puzzles at their stations (one of them could trace his service back to the administration of Ulysses Grant). But in truth, a great deal had been altered. There were now some six hundred officers and clerks in the Pennsylvania Avenue operation. They were divided into six major geographical divisions, plus divisions for passports, visas, protocol, historical data, law, foreign buildings, personnel, treaties, economics, accounts, publicity, and archives. Each day they mailed out 3,400 letters to all parts of the world, and each day they received 50 pouches of reports from 4,000 representatives in 425 posts. Despite a lingering aura of tradition-bound inefficiency, the State Department was now doing its job as well as any other. Reuben had to toil mightily to keep up with it.[14]

Below the undersecretary were four assistant secretaries, and they did much to make the job tolerable. Owing to the exodus of Butler Wright and Leland Harrison (both members of the discredited career clique), three of the four assistants were comparatively new on the job. Two of them, Francis White and Nelson T. Johnson, were quiet, unassuming, and ultracompetent, despite their "career" status. The third was Wilbur Carr, looking older, grayer, more tired, but still rather like a Keystone Cop. The invalid wife he had supported for years on his meager salary had gone to her final rest, and Carr had remarried into wealth. Now he directed most of the department's support functions and had become indispensable.[15]

It was the remaining assistant of whom Reuben had to be wary. William R. Castle possessed credentials for the undersecretaryship himself—including charm, good looks, and a high order of intelligence—and he believed that the job might better have gone to him. Not specifically one of the errant career men, Castle shared their wealth and high-level connections. The Castle family had been missionaries-turned-capitalists in the Hawaiian Islands, and their fortune had come to rest on an impressive segment of the Hawaiian economy. William's father was among those who had overthrown Queen Liliuokalani and then ventured to Washington in search of American annexation. Owing to his distinguished career at the State Department, Castle had acquired an unofficial mantle of leadership that Kellogg sometimes acknowledged and sometimes ignored. Castle's office, rather than Reuben Clark's, was the one adjacent to the secretary's, and the two of them took long morning jaunts together. On the other hand, Kellogg had passed over Castle twice for promotion to undersecretary, and his first choice on both occasions had been Reuben Clark. This fact alone put a strain on Clark-Castle relations.[16] When Reuben learned of the situation, as eventually he did, he sharpened his vigilance a little; but it was his own lack of enthusiasm for the undersecretaryship that most likely saved him from a head-on collision.[17]

iii

Assuming the role of acting secretary was like stepping onto a moving train: it resembled anything but Reuben's cloistered life in Mexico City. Research, contemplation, systematic thought of any kind were suddenly thrown to the wind, and Reuben sat behind his desk while visitor after visitor passed before him in kaleidoscopic succession. Within the first weeks alone, he dealt with the kidnapping of an American executive in Mexico; a case of noxious fumes crossing the border from a Canadian chemical plant; a spectacular extradition proceeding in France; a falling out with Colombia that had all the earmarks of another oil controversy; dealings with pirates on the Yangtze River; the Geneva Conference on Opium; a new installment of the endless Tacna-Arica dispute; the notorious "Black Tom" case in which the German claims commission was attempting to buy evidence from a former spy—and the parade went on. Weaving in and around these difficulties were examples of what Reuben would soon recognize as the standard fare of his job: claimants seeking to short-circuit the judicial process, party hacks looking for patronage, and bureaucratic climbers hitchhiking a ride up. It was an altogether dizzying experience.[18]

And Washington was becoming increasingly hospitable to dizziness. This was the high jazz age, and there was madness in the air. For the diplomatic "smart set" Great Britain's Sir Ronald Lindsay, Germany's Friedrich von Prittwitz und Gaffron, France's Paul Claudel, Italy's Nobile Giacomo de Martino—life was a succession of high-voltage social affairs. And even around the lesser dignitaries there coursed a nightlife to rival Hollywood's: Count Szechenyi, the Hungarian minister, regaling guests with a Slavic rendition of the highland fling; Charles Davila, the Rumanian minister, courting the daughter of Bernard Baruch while landing in the gossip columns with a certain chorus girl; Major General Prince Kridadara, minister of Siam, being caught with a truckload of bootleg bound for his legation. Although Reuben had daily contact with these people, he assiduously avoided their world. As opposed to what Drew Pearson called the "diplomats who dine out," Reuben remained a diplomat who dined at home and gave all attention to his work.[19]

With competent men like Castle and Johnson to oversee Europe and the Far East respectively, with Francis White to superintend the "Nicaraguan affair," and with the faithful Wilbur Carr to work through the administrative red tape, Reuben was gradually able to shift the focus of his work back toward Mexico. Here he was assisted by Arthur Bliss Lane, chief of the Mexican division and a competent man in his own right. Most of the Mexican troubles were familiar enough, and Reuben had no difficulty in picking up on them. The first one was especially familiar. Indeed, Reuben had been in office barely a few hours when Clement Bouvé called him on the phone to discuss Fred Kenelm Nielsen. Since the termination of Reuben's own affiliation with the Mexican claims commission almost a year before, much had transpired. After an agony of seesawing, a new presiding commissioner had been chosen by the Hague court: Kristian Sindballe of Denmark. Preparations were now underway for a resumption of the commission's work in Mexico City. But in the midst of this progress, Commissioner Nielsen had once again slipped off the rails. His relations with Bouvé were now totally beyond reclamation. Though Bouvé had tried again and again to repair the damage, each attempt had only worsened it, with the result that Nielsen had denounced the American agent to his Mexican colleagues and had openly snubbed him in Sindballe's presence. The matter was rapidly approaching impasse.[20]

Like Bouvé, Nielsen had remained in touch with Reuben Clark and at one point had again threatened to resign. Reuben had tried to keep the lid on the pot, but circumstances were obviously running against him. Finally, in early August, he had sent a wire from Salt Lake City to the secretary of state and explained what was going on. Kellogg, taken aback, promised to speak to each of the principals personally and did so. But he too could see how hopeless the situation was and, anyhow, he was preparing to leave for Paris within the week. The problem was left for the undersecretary to solve.[21]

And in a long letter to Reuben the day after the phone call, Bouvé pressed hard for a solution. It was intolerable, he said, that things should continue thus, that Nielsen should be allowed to snub and belittle him in public. In eight pages of single-spaced type, Bouvé proceeded to set down indignity after indignity, ending with the transcript of a dreadful tongue-lashing from Nielsen. He closed by asking Reuben to cut the knot once and for all.[22]

While taking this request under advisement, the acting secretary picked up on other strands of the Mexican situation. The special claims commission was still defunct, but Reuben compulsively tinkered with it as with a broken watch. He also held some long-distance telephone conversations with Morrow on the idea of a lump-sum settlement for the claims. When he could, Reuben stole a few hours from his office—as one might do for a round of golf—and delved into the Mexican oil and agrarian archives. He continued to discuss the oil settlement with company representatives as well, and his relations with them were no better than before. (He came upon one memorandum that spoke of the "ill feeling" of the oil men "towards Mr. Clark," and decided that the sentiment was fully mutual.[23]) But in this matter, like the one between Nielsen and Bouvé, he was obliged to continue the holding action as best he could.

iv

In the Mexican "church-state controversy," however, Reuben came to the fore and remained there throughout his tenure. In Mexico Reuben had had little to do with the religious problem, which had been the responsibility of another Morrow aide, George Rublee. Yet Reuben had maintained a lively spectator interest. Morrow had been every bit as interested in this difficulty as in the oil and agrarian disputes, and the difficulty itself had been no more readily resolvable.

The church-state controversy was as old as Mexico itself. From colonial times the church had owned vast properties in Mexico and had never quite acknowledged the sovereignty of the temporal government. Moreover, many Catholic priests—often either European-born or European-educated—were not such as to remain quietly within their churches while political questions were abroil; they were active interventionists in the spirit of Ignatius Loyola himself. Accordingly, in a land struggling for self-government, self-respect, and self-renewal, the Catholic church seemed to symbolize all the wrong things.[24]

Nor was the problem merely one of symbols. The churchmen had fought the revolution tooth and claw, dug in their heels against every proposed reform, teamed up with whatever party represented reaction, and generally provided as much obstruction as possible. Then, as a final indignity, a Catholic fanatic had assassinated President-elect Alvaro Obregón, the great hero of the revolution, only weeks before Reuben became undersecretary. The revolutionary regimes had hit back, of course, and hit back hard. Various generals had closed churches, jailed priests, and dealt violence to the entire Catholic establishment. They had melted down the church's gold icons for army payrolls and used its magnificent cathedrals for horse stables. It was not, however, until the Querétaro constitution was adopted in 1917 that the full extent of the church-state rift became apparent. The constitution dealt as harshly with the church as it did with the American development companies, and Plutarco Calles implemented it with the same heavy-handedness. "Calles Law," as the enabling legislation became known, nationalized church property, closed parochial schools, disbanded the monastic orders, and sweepingly subjected the church to civil authority.[25]

To the clergy this seemed like nothing less than doom. They proclaimed a clerical strike that effectively closed the Mexican churches. This action triggered violence almost immediately, and by 1927 rebellion was flaring sporadically in more than a dozen states. Then Catholic guerrillas, sounding the cry, *"¡Viva Cristo Rey!"* began mustering in the Mexican hinterlands, often under the generalship of a priest. These *"Cristeros"* soon welded themselves into an effective fighting force and set about to challenge the government. For its part, the government rounded up most of the twenty-nine Mexican bishops, charged them with incitement to rebellion, and dumped them unceremoniously across the Texas border. As the *Cristeros* intensified their military campaign, the casualty figures began to recall the days of Pancho Villa. Mexico was embroiled in civil war once again.[26]

All of this was bad enough for U.S.-Mexican relations, but American Catholics made it even worse. They believed that the State Department could and should do something. It was in response to pressure from the National Catholic Welfare Conference, in fact, that Secretary Kellogg had begun to consider some form of diplomatic intervention and that Dwight Morrow had originally been instructed to approach Calles.[27] Now, on the eighth of September, Reuben looked across his desk at the man who had effected this activity, Father John J. Burke.[28] He was a mild-looking man, with a smooth, saintly face and an aura of Christian peace about him. But beneath the Benedictine countenance (he was actually a Paulist), Burke was a man who got things done. He had edited *Catholic World* before the war and had organized the Chaplain's Aid Association when the army went to France. Under his leadership the National Catholic Welfare Conference had come into being after the war, and in a few short years it had become a remarkably influential organization. One of the embattled Mexican bishops, Mora y del Rio, had appealed to the NCWC and Father Burke for assistance against "the Turk" who ruled Mexico.[29]

Reuben needed little catching up. He knew that the essence of Morrow's church-state diplomacy had been to arrange a meeting between Calles and Burke in Veracruz in April. Things had gone off well. The Mexican president had not promised to abolish Calles Law but he had promised to apply the law in a spirit of reasonableness.[30] After the Veracruz meeting, however, matters had deteriorated on both sides. Father Burke, although acting on papal authority, could not speak for the Vatican itself, nor could he prompt the Holy See to support his informal bargain with Calles. Still less could the Paulist father control the exiled Mexican bishops, some of whom actively supported the gun-wielding *Cristeros*. And Calles could not control events in Mexico. The assassination of Obregón finished off anything that remained of the Calles-Burke agreement.[31]

In the weeks following Burke's first visit, he and Reuben Clark tried to put the agreement back together again. Their first meeting was a bit rocky. Reuben no longer spoke instinctively against the fathers of the Mexican Revolution; he spoke instinctively *for* them. When Burke portrayed the humiliation of Archbishop Ruíz y Flores, whose palatial house had been taken over by the Mexican government, Reuben was something less than moved. "I told Father Burke that I appreciated that," he reported, "and yet, if I might be permitted to say so, speaking in a religious way, the humility which the Master had taught would perhaps not forbid the Bishop to make such a sacrifice."[32]

What Reuben was actually trying to do was alter the terms of the controversy. He agreed with Dwight Morrow that the church-state conflict, if presented as a clash of ideologies, could never be resolved. What was needed, as in the oil dispute, was a reduction of ideology to practical problems which could be adjusted politically. When Burke, for example, spoke hopefully of inducing the Mexican government to recognize an apostolic delegate, Reuben stopped him again.

I intimated to Father Burke that perhaps too much emphasis was being laid on designations. I told him that in my own church we had what we called the Mexican Mission and we had a man in charge of it, but that he had nothing to do with politics, his sole business having to do with the Mormon native colonies that were in Mexico. I told him that it seemed to me that the way to look at this thing was that the Catholic church wanted to appoint a man who would have charge of the 29 bishops in Mexico with reference to their church work, a man to whom the bishops would look for instructions; that it was not the State's affair at all who it was or that he was there; he had no connection with the State; that as a matter of convenience the President of Mexico would naturally prefer to deal with one man than with 29 men, and that too much importance should not be placed in a mere name.[33]

In time this approach began to have its effect. Father Burke gradually viewed the religious controversy in less exalted terms. He came to agree that hard, practical, limited steps were necessary if peace was to be achieved.

But Father Burke could not see that a good half of the problem was in Rome. He supposed that Calles, through a simple act of will, could put an end to the religious controversy, and he constantly sought ways to make the Mexican president move. Reuben, on the other hand, could see rather clearly that this was not the case, that Calles could not simply offer peace to those who were waging war against him, and that the Holy See was making matters worse by not taking a position of its own. It was the Vatican, not Mexico City, that had to move, and Undersecretary Clark had to find some way of moving it.

In the meetings throughout October the impasse continued. As delicately as he could, Reuben explained over and over again that Calles would not budge. Yet Burke, the faithful priest, was loath to appeal back to the Holy See. Then on November 11, Reuben Clark and Arthur Bliss Lane put their heads together. They agreed that nothing was likely to happen so long as the State Department sat back passively. There was a meeting with Burke scheduled for that afternoon, and Reuben promised that he would make the necessary point convincingly.

At the crucial pass, however, the undersecretary was unexpectedly called out of the meeting. Arthur Bliss Lane stepped adroitly into the breach. To each suggestion of Burke's for the possible action of the Mexican government, Lane quietly explained why it would not work. Eventually Burke ran out of suggestions. He then seemed to grasp the point. Perhaps, he said haltingly, he himself should make the next move, requesting papal permission to try another overture to President Calles. Reuben reappeared in time to receive the good news. Mr. Morrow, he said, would be informed immediately.[34] Meanwhile, the state of Jalisco was aflame, and in Colima the *Cristeros* had demolished a large government force.

v

The undersecretary and the four assistants were standing on the platform at Gate 18 when the train pulled in. The man who stepped from the coach to reassume direction of the State Department was small and stoutly built, with snow-white hair and an artificial eye. And for once in his life Frank Kellogg was jubilant. The peace pact, his great dream of two years and more, had been signed by representatives of the world's great nations: aggressive war was henceforth and forevermore declared unlawful. Kellogg showed them the gold pen with which he had signed the treaty.[35]

J. Reuben Clark congratulated the secretary warmly, but he was not unaware of the occasion's ironies. Cynically, perhaps, Reuben himself had done much to keep the outlawry movement afloat during its less fashionable days—and now here before him was the product of that labor. (Few of Reuben's *real* projects ever turned out so well.) Moreover, as the secretary made clear, it was to be Reuben Clark's job to see that the great treaty was ratified and that the Senate did not attach reservations as it had to the Treaty of Versailles. One ally on Capitol Hill promised to be indispensable to this effort— William Borah.[36]

Two weeks later Secretary Kellogg spelled out Reuben's mandate in greater detail. The chief problem, he explained, was the Monroe Doctrine. Over the years that historic proclamation had acquired a mystique almost religious in nature, and whenever some new direction in foreign policy was contemplated, Monroe cultists could be counted upon to raise objections. Accordingly, Kellogg thought it would be well to make a speech in which the Monroe Doctrine might be shown to be wholly consistent with the Kellogg-Briand Pact. In order to do this, it would be necessary to shear off the notorious Roosevelt Corollary of 1905 and deny any connection between the Monroe Doctrine and foreign intervention.[37]*

This was a journeyman's assignment. It contemplated no great shift in American foreign policy, no epoch-making diplomatic pirouette, no renunciation of the past. Kellogg had no thought whatever of condemning the *practice* of intervention. (After all, he himself had launched the recent four-alarm intervention in Nicaragua.) He merely believed that the practice could be justified in other ways. Indeed, so prosaic was the job Kellogg had in mind that Reuben need not even attend to it personally. A researcher under his guidance had only to sift through the accumulated restatements, analyses, and explanations of the Monroe Doctrine and conclude that certain of them, right around 1905, had gone a little off the track.[38]

It was entirely fitting that the *Memorandum on the Monroe Doctrine,* which had these humble beginnings and which would place Reuben Clark's name decisively in the textbooks, should have been a compilation of historical precedent. But it was strange that this of all such undertakings should have resulted in public recognition. For no more than his boss did Reuben contemplate writing a historical document or putting an end to an established practice. For one thing, he would not have dreamed of condemning intervention while serving under Frank Kellogg. (At the Havana conference in February, Kellogg had forbidden delegates even to discuss the subject.[39]) For another thing, neither Reuben Clark nor Frank Kellogg, both staunch conservatives, believed in the efficacy of altering foreign policy by executive fiat. Foreign policy, like the law, had a life of its own, a life that depended on broad consensus and many variables; it waxed or waned by processes of gradual evolution, not by the whims of individuals.

---

*The Monroe Doctrine, as originally enunciated in 1823, had addressed itself primarily to the fear that Spain would attempt to reassert its authority over recently liberated colonies in Latin America. The heart of the doctrine, therefore, was Monroe's statement "that the American Continents, by the free and independent condition which they have assumed and maintain, are henceforth not to be considered as subjects for future colonization by a European power." By the end of the century, of course, recolonization was no longer the problem. The main danger now was that chronic Latin American instability invited, and sometimes nearly required, European intervention, especially with regard to financial obligations. In the so-called Roosevelt Corollary to the Monroe Doctrine, President Roosevelt pledged that the United States would itself intervene in Latin America whenever a situation threatened to become so disorderly as to provoke European action. The way to maintain the Monroe Doctrine, so it seemed, was to become policeman of the hemisphere.

And yet, all of this granted, the Clark Memorandum project tended from the outset to take unexpected turns. After the secretary and undersecretary had discussed the proposed assignment on September 25, they somehow got off onto the corollary subject of interference in Latin American affairs. "I told him," Reuben reported, "that I felt we were becoming altogether too meddlesome." This gambit, far from provoking one of Kellogg's famous explosions, triggered instead a kind of cathartic release. "He instantly agreed with me and said that he tried all he could to keep the matter down but was unable to control it." Once broached, the untouchable subject led to quite a discussion all around, with both Clark and Kellogg unburdening themselves.

I told him that although I had said nothing about it, I thought we had made a mistake in the Barco matter with Colombia. He said he wished I had "butted in." I told him that I did not feel I could do that under the circumstances. He said that he had been assured that the legal situation with reference to the Barco case was all that could be desired. I told him I seriously questioned that fact. I had not gone into the matter with great care but I had talked about it somewhat with representatives of the company and also with men in the Department who had been handling it and I thought there might be a serious question as to whether the Colombian Government wasn't right in its assertion that it could cancel the contract.[40]

Reuben was in the same mood of unburdening a few minutes later when he met Francis White. The two of them went over the Barco case again, this time from the viewpoint of the Colombians. (An oil concession had been granted to an American firm, and the grant had been subsequently rescinded. Colombia claimed that Barco had not kept its side of the bargain.) Suddenly, Reuben Clark, the State Department lawyer, was no longer defending his client; in fact, he was beginning to question the whole adversary approach to diplomacy. "I told [White]," he said, "that sometimes mistakes were made in looking merely for the strong points of our side instead of for the weak points; that I felt when we dealt between nations we must always look for the weak points in order to be sure we made no mistakes."[41] This conversation, with its overtones of introspection and self-doubt, could not have occurred at a more significant moment than on the eve of the Clark Memorandum.

vi

The ensuing weeks were hectic. Kellogg was away again for much of the time, and Reuben found himself saddled with ceremonial as well as administrative responsibilities. On October 19 he had breakfast with the president in honor of Dr. Eckener, commanding officer of the *Graf Zeppelin,* which had just crossed the Atlantic.[42] He and the president also conducted ceremonies opening telephone service between the United States and Spain and the United States and Austria.[43] Mostly, however, the work was of the sleeves-rolled-up variety. In both Haiti and Cuba there were "situations" simmering along that threatened to boil up into "incidents." The oil companies were still hounding the department about their rights in Mexico, and Bouvé wrote from Mexico City to say that the new presiding commissioner was every bit as bad as Van Vollenhoven.[44] A complicated imbroglio arose from President-elect Hoover's proposed tour of Latin America, for no one could decide whether he should travel as a president or private citizen. The Soviet Union, a perennial gadfly at the State Department, sent its representatives sniffing around about possible diplomatic recognition, now that a new and presumably more civilized revolutionary by the name of Stalin had come to power. Various countries were ratifying the Kellogg-Briand Pact, and someone had to evaluate the legal status of each. There was another Geneva conference to be readied for 1929, and another round of talks in the European debt triangle. John DeKay was in trouble again, this time in Switzerland, and his brother Henry came to ask if

Acting secretary of state, in the company of President Coolidge and Walter S. Gifford of American Telephone and Telegraph, opening telephone service to Spain: "Interregnum" was not a happy word.

Reuben could bail him out. All the while conversations with Father Burke continued.[45]

In the midst of these distractions research was begun on the Monroe Doctrine memorandum. It was undertaken by Anna O'Neil, a capable lawyer in her own right and former assistant solicitor. Her task was to dig up everything that had been said about the Monroe Doctrine by presidents, secretaries of state, and other high officials. In the search she relied on Moore's *Digest* and on Reuben's own occasional suggestions.[46] The undersecretary felt uneasy about this particular delegation of authority, and he constantly tried to get his own hand into the operation; but the pace of other business would not allow it. By November 24 some forty-five pages were completed, and Reuben showed them to Kellogg. The secretary was "entirely satisfied."[47]

Events were moving more swiftly than the research, however. By December 4 the Kellogg-Briand Pact was referred to the Foreign Relations Committee, and three days later the secretary of state was scheduled to testify.[48] On Wednesday the fifth he pressed Reuben for the finished memorandum, and Reuben had to explain the delays. There was no time left for a polished speech to be drafted, yet something concise and to the point had to be placed in Senator Borah's hands immediately. So it was decided that Reuben should quickly throw together a short summary of the work—now well over two hundred pages in length—which Kellogg could use as the basis of his statement and which Borah could circulate among fellow senators. It was this seventeen-page summary, dashed off by Reuben Clark that same afternoon, which came to be known as the Clark Memorandum.[49]

With time for reflection, Reuben might not have written precisely as he did. This was a quick draft and it put matters a little too baldly perhaps. Inspecting Miss O'Neil's work, Reuben discovered that while the compilation itself was comprehensive it contained no explicit disavowal of the Roosevelt Corollary, as Kellogg had wished. This Reuben inserted into his summary. On a hurried rereading, he was satisfied.

And indeed, on a hurried reading, the memorandum apparently *had* fulfilled its purpose. By examining the accretion of interpretive statements about the Monroe Doctrine, Reuben could demonstrate convincingly that certain of them had strayed from the doctrine's original meaning. That meaning had had no reference whatever to intrahemispheric relations but had been intended to ensure the continued separation of Europe and the Americas. "The Doctrine," as Reuben put it, "states a case of United States *vs.* Europe, not of United States *vs.* Latin America."[50]

This, of course, was exactly the point Secretary Kellogg wanted to make. If sanctions needed to be applied, they lay against the *European* power offending the Doctrine, not against the *Latin American* power; and thus there was no excuse whatever for paternalistic intermeddling. "The so-called 'Roosevelt Corollary,'" said Undersecretary Clark, "is not ... justified by the terms of the Monroe Doctrine, however much it may be justified by the application of the doctrine of self-preservation."[51]

The last clause was meant to ensure the conservative nature of the memorandum. It was all right to intervene in Latin America, Reuben was saying, as long as the intervention was a matter of self-defense rather than paternalism. In order to establish that point, the undersecretary quoted extensively from his own *Right to Protect Citizens* memorandum of 1912. But such things hardly needed spelling out. That the United States could intervene militarily in Latin America, and especially in the vicinity of the Panama Canal, as a matter of self-preservation was a central assumption of American diplomacy. Reuben merely restated it to ensure that there was no misunderstanding about the purposes of the present document. It was no manifesto.

But then came the conclusion, and that somehow did sound like a manifesto. Its whole spirit seemed strangely out of keeping with the rest of the memorandum. One historian observed that it read "like a criminal lawyer's closing statement."[52]

The fact should never be lost to view that in applying this Doctrine during the period of one hundred years since it was announced, our Government has over and over again driven as a shield between Europe and the Americas to protect Latin America from the political and territorial thrusts of Europe; and this was done at times when the American nations were weak and struggling for the establishment of stable, permanent governments; when the political morality of Europe sanctioned, indeed encouraged, the acquisition of territory by force; and when many of the great powers of Europe looked with eager, covetous eyes to the rich, undeveloped areas of the American hemisphere. Nor should another equally vital fact be lost sight of, that the United States has only been able to give this protection against designing European powers because of its known willingness and determination, if and whenever necessary, to expend its treasure and to sacrifice American life to maintain the principles of the Doctrine.[53]

Talk of shields of protection, territorial thrusts, weak and struggling nations, covetous eyes, designing powers, and the sacrifice of American life was far more affective than the rest of the document. Yet these were the phrases that led to the concluding statement and suffused it with tone and meaning.

So far as Latin America is concerned, the Doctrine is now, and always has been, not an instrument of violence and oppression, but an unbought, freely bestowed, and wholly effective guarantee of their freedom, independence, and territorial integrity against the imperialistic designs of Europe.[54]

One has trouble reading this paragraph to mean anything except a condemnation of intervention. The Monroe Doctrine, stripped of its accretions and encumbrances, was not, said Reuben Clark, "an instrument of violence and oppression."

In the haste of the moment, Reuben was condemning intervention in spite of himself—just as he had to the secretary on September 25—and allowing carefully controlled feelings to slip out. The ancestry of those feelings went back a long way. By 1928, in fact, J. Reuben Clark had become one of the most experienced officials in Washington in the business of intervention. His early career in the State Department had touched upon virtually every American intervention in the twentieth century. He had had dealings with the Honduran intervention, the Colombia-Panama intervention, the Cuban intervention, the Haitian intervention, and, for good measure, an intervention in China.[55] He and Huntington Wilson had masterminded the Nicaraguan interventions of 1910 and 1912 largely by themselves.[56] Having been party to the behind-the-scenes deliberations, Reuben well knew what each of these undertakings was supposed to have achieved—and how hopelessly each had failed. At the time of the Clark Memorandum evidence of the failures lay all around. Honduras was still wretched and unstable. Bitterness still rankled in Colombia. Haiti was in a shambles and wracked by civil strife. Cuba was in a permanent slump and would someday be ripe for communism. And in Nicaragua, the *pièce de résistance* of U.S. interventionism, action and reaction had impinged upon one another with mounting strain until the thing had sprung closed like a giant steel trap. President Coolidge had finally been obliged to send in the marines, and now the marines were obliged to deal with Sandino.[57] Yet an even more explicit lesson had been taught by Mexico. It was here that Reuben, largely for practical reasons, had first taken a stand against intervention, had seen that stand undermined and overthrown, and then, in helpless expostulation, had watched the results unfold. Reuben Clark knew all about intervention.

And what he knew had changed him. By the time he wrote his memorandum for Morrow on the forcible collection of debts, Reuben was no longer detached and unflappable about diplomacy by the sword. "If I read aright the temper of the American people it is this," he said," – they are willing to make every sacrifice for the sake of international justice and right as it affects the safety and progress of the world and its peoples, but they could not willingly offer the life of one American boy for all the gold we have lent to all the powers."[58] This was a far cry from the dollar diplomacy of his earlier days. Indeed, it was an explicit renunciation of it.

Taking charge at the Department of State seemed to have brought these feelings to the dew point. When the Barco affair in Colombia threatened to flare into real trouble, Reuben suddenly became uncompromising in his attitude. He instructed the new minister "that we were not going to land troops in Bogotá on account of any oil concession ... and that therefore whatever we did down there with reference to the oil concessions must be with that fact in view."[59]

If Reuben could not see his own indignation in the Clark Memorandum, there were others who could. In some quarters the document seemed to engender acute unease. Herbert Hoover, for example, although himself formally committed to principles of nonintervention, looked askance at the Clark Memorandum for the first half of his administration.[60] Only belatedly and with some foot shuffling did he co-opt the document as his own.[61] Similarly, Franklin Roosevelt, who took credit for the Good Neighbor policy with Latin America, was not prepared to regard the Clark Memorandum as official.[62] Every so often, it seemed, one had to resort to at least a hint of intervention in order to preserve Latin American respect.

Such being the official attitudes, the Clark Memorandum had a rugged and ultimately futile career as public policy. The career began in February of 1929, when Secretary Kellogg asked Reuben to redraft the document and transmit its essentials to all Latin American missions for eventual delivery. This letter wielded the same indignity as the original memorandum. "The [Monroe] Doctrine is not a lance; it is a shield," it proclaimed. But Hoover never gave the signal and the note was never delivered.[63] The original Memorandum was published in March of 1930, but not as official policy. Attempts by Kellogg's successor, Henry Stimson, to make it official, or even official-sounding, were squelched by the president. The Clark Memorandum, said the government, was merely the private opinion of a former undersecretary.[64]

Journalists and other commentators, however, were not nearly so sheepish. For some time they had been awaiting an official redefinition of the Monroe Doctrine, long rumored to be in the works. What appeared in print as J. Reuben Clark's *Memorandum on the Monroe Doctrine* was quite obviously the document in question and most analysts treated it as such. Their comments picked up on the memorandum's enthusiasm and made it appear to be a reflection of official enthusiasm.[65] So even though the Clark Memorandum never became official, it did assume a kind of power of its own and helped catalyze a new ethic in inter-American affairs. Reuben himself, who had not intended to alter foreign policy, looked back on the memorandum with new perception. "It will probably all be soon forgotten," he commented wistfully to Tyler Dennett, "and the press generally will recur to the Imperialistic conception and misinterpretation of the Doctrine."[66]

vii

Meanwhile, the undersecretary's work seemed to escalate. There was a barley tariff in Germany and a lard tariff in Poland, and representatives of both interests visited Washington regularly. There were also regular visits from Italy's ambassador, Nobile Giacomo de Martino, complaining of unkind references to Mussolini in the American press, and from Portugal's Viscount d'Alte, simply complaining. Things were still not going well in Cuba, nor in Haiti for that matter, and the Barco business in Colombia needed constant attention. Affairs of the German claims commission seemed to be spinning toward the same fate as the Mexican claims commission, and the French war debt problem posed an unremitting worry. In the midst of these concerns Reuben became involved in the question of who would succeed Kellogg as secretary of state. Justice Stone was trying to secure the bid for Dwight Morrow and doing a rather poor job of it.[67]

Reuben was also becoming concerned about the department itself and about the curious uncertainty of its loyalties. Fully aware now of the various power struggles and their implications, Reuben decided to take a hand. On November 15 he delivered an address at the monthly Foreign Service Association luncheon, and in it he advised the diplomats that problems of preferment were not best handled by the methods they were using.[68] The next day Arthur Bliss Lane stopped by Reuben's office to report that the association had decided not to publish the address. Clark and Lane discussed the "inner group" mentality of the diplomats, and the undersecretary voiced his concern. "As [Lane] left the room," Reuben recorded, "I suggested to him that the Foreign Service group had better watch its step."[69]

A week later Reuben was after the diplomats again, this time in the company of Gardiner Shaw of the Foreign Service personnel board.

I told him that if I were King I would require every Secretary stationed at a foreign post to write in to the Department a dissertation on some point of history or otherwise connected with the country in which he was stationed, and that the results of that requirement would figure largely in the promotions which he obtained. He stated that they would regard it as a great imposition because they were already fully employed during the day. I stated that much that they were doing was unnecessary, and that furthermore they had their nights, and that any man who is not prepared to spend his nights at his work was not going to make any particular advancement in this world.

"The conversation," said Reuben, "was perfectly pleasant and good natured, but I was clear in my observations."[70]

viii

Reuben also moved to resolve the Mexican claims muddle. Fred Nielsen paid him a visit on January 25, and it was immediately evident that a new chapter in the commission's troubled history was about to be written. It seemed there was another delicate case in hearing, and Clement Bouvé, according to Nielsen, had written a pointless, offensive, and totally wrongheaded brief in support of the American position. Reuben discussed the law in question with the commissioner, noting with uneasiness how difficult the conversation seemed. But he promised to take the matter up with Bouvé, and later in the afternoon he did. The troublesome brief was withdrawn.[71]

But a month later there was another visit and another complaint. This time Reuben decided to deal with the Nielsen problem frontally. Their conversation was long and disjointed, veering erratically back through the translation bureau incident, the adjournment incident, the blasts and counterblasts that echoed down through the years. Over and over, Reuben tried to make the commissioner see reason.

I told him that Bouvé had assured me time and again that he had not applied to him (Nielsen) the epithets which he (Nielsen) understood had been applied; that Bouvé was anxious to get along; that as the friend of each of them I sincerely regretted this situation in which they had worked themselves because I thought that it was the worst thing that could happen for both of them.[72]

Reuben also pointed out that Nielsen had not felt kindly toward others in his day, and that there was perhaps a sort of pattern to it all. Here he was walking on dangerous ground. Nielsen soon lapsed into the familiar litany of resignation, with the same flatness of the voice and opacity of the eyes that Bouvé had seen two years earlier. The undersecretary hoped, a little apprehensively, that the interview had accomplished its purpose. What he did not know was that, in Fred Nielsen's troubled eyes, he himself had now gone over to the enemy.

ix

As the clammy Washington winter yielded to spring, Reuben found himself looking forward to March 4. He talked with Morrow in February, and it was immediately agreed that Reuben should return to Mexico City as soon as the department changed hands. Morrow warned, however, that "a great deal of pressure" would be applied to keep the undersecretary at his post in the new administration.[73] The presssure was not long in materializing. It soon developed that the new secretary of state designate, Henry L. Stimson, who had been serving as governor-general of the Philippines, was not expected to arrive in Washington by inauguration day. So, of all the State Department resignations neatly arrayed on President Hoover's desk, Reuben Clark's alone was not accepted. Eager to rejoin Morrow, he felt like the last rose of summer as all around him desks were being emptied and papers crated up. He was to be acting secretary once again.[74]

x

And just when this responsibility became final, all hell broke loose. First of all, another revolution erupted in Mexico, on Sunday, March 3. A number of old *Obregónista* generals were not persuaded that Plutarco Calles really meant to retire from politics; they imagined rather—and quite rightly—that he meant to continue his rule behind such stagemen as the recently elected Emilio Portes Gil. Under the leadership of José Gonzalo Escobar, these "Renovators," as they called themselves, struck ferociously in northern Mexico and soon controlled the crucial border states.[75]

Michael McDermott, the public information chief, was the only State Department officer on duty when the telegrams began arriving. He was about to panic when he looked up to see the acting secretary coming through the door. Reuben read over the first dispatch, pondered for a moment, and sat down to the nearest typewriter. Soon he was banging out instructions left and right, this one to the officials at Ciudad Juárez, that one to Morrow in Mexico City. He warned the border consuls of an impending occupation of the customhouses and instructed that they inform the interior, where the Mexican government would set up new customhouses, that duties would not be paid twice. He then notified the American embassy of this action and explained what to expect by way of Mexican reaction. He was moving on to a third set of dispatches when he looked up to see

McDermott staring in blank amazement. Mr. Clark was reacting to events which had not even transpired yet![76]

The steady hand on the helm reassured more than McDermott. Herbert Hoover, who was not yet legally president, approved all State Department actions as a matter of course and continued to do so.[77] With little to fear by way of oversight, Reuben was thus, for better or worse, on his own. In his hands lay the fate of the Mexican government.

Had the Renovator revolt occurred before, rather than after, Reuben's own Mexican sojourn, there might have been a temptation to give the rebels full rein. Indeed, had Reuben followed his own policies of 1910–12 and allowed the rebels to purchase American arms, it might have been all over for Portes Gil. (As it was, there was a frantic scramble in Mexico to hold things together, with Calles taking personal command of the federal army.) But much had transpired in twenty years, and the man who was now acting secretary had changed fundamentally from the one who had been solicitor. Reuben's laissez-faire ideas had been supplanted by a broader if less clear-cut feeling of the wisdom of supporting Calles and the Mexican Revolution. In the name of this support Reuben pulled out all the stops.

During the first week of the revolt, Reuben announced through the president that the United States would continue arms shipments to the Mexican government and would even allow Mexico to purchase arms directly from U.S. arsenals. The next day the United States arranged to deliver ten thousand Enfield rifles and ten million rounds of ammunition to the Mexican army. If this assistance failed to do the job, the American government stood ready to supply machine guns, bombs, and aircraft ammunition too, and a sale of war planes was announced on March 30. As for the insurgents, the acting secretary dismissed them with a wave. They had no status in international law, he said, and must be classified as common bandits.[78]

Such ex parte diplomacy might well have angered Señor Escobar, and the anger might have translated into American casualties. Here again, however, Reuben had learned from the past. Knowing that the *insurrectos* would always fight with one eye on their escape routes, the undersecretary made one simple diplomatic point: that there would be no asylum for them in the United States if Americans in Mexico came to harm. Then, in order to eliminate that other complication, Reuben had the State Department announce that Americans who fought with the rebellion would be wholly subject to Mexican law. "Mexican law" meant "firing squad."[79]

The combination worked like magic. In contrast to the old days, the rebels gave resident Yankees extremely wide berth. "No previous major Mexican revolution has caused so little loss to Americans," reported the United Press. "It probably will not even be necessary to convene a mixed claim commission to settle such affairs."[80] For that Reuben was especially thankful.

xi

When the Renovator revolt was just hitting its stride, more trouble broke out in the Gulf of Mexico. A British rum-runner, the *I'm Alone,* was about to close on the swampy coast of Louisiana with a cargo of bootleg when the Coast Guard cutter *Wolcott* suddenly hauled into view and ordered her to heave to. Instead of obeying, the *I'm Alone* made a run for it. What followed was a two-day sea chase, each knot of which took the vessels farther and farther from American territorial waters, before the smuggler was sent to the bottom in a blaze of gunfire. One crewman drowned.[81]

All sorts of questions were raised. Where had the ship actually been hailed? Had it been within American jurisdiction? Had the chase been legal under the doctrine of hot pursuit? Had excessive force been used? No one—and least of all Reuben Clark—wanted to contend with another *Trent* affair;* but the master of the *I'm Alone,* his ship sunk and his pride hurt, delivered himself of a series of newspaper interviews that were not calculated to lay the matter to rest.[82]

In the midst of the controversy Henry Stimson finally arrived at his post. But the new secretary, far from taking command, behaved rather dreamily, as though still in the tropics. At sixty-two, Stimson was a cool and sometimes brusque individual with an aristocratic bearing, military ideas, and a disposition to give orders. In the days of the Knox State Department Stimson had been secretary of war.

*See note on p. 236.

His diplomatic experience was limited to Nicaragua, where he had played a decisive role as special envoy, and the Philippines, where he had played *pukka sahib*.[83]

Shaken from his somnolence, the new secretary seemed bewildered by the pace of State Department activities. It might take weeks, even months, for him to take hold of the manifold events and shape them purposefully. Like the president, Stimson was impressed by Reuben's adroit crisis management. He joined with Hoover and Senator Smoot in strongly urging that Reuben stay on as undersecretary. And when Reuben made it clear that he must return to Mexico, Stimson had a fallback proposition. Would Mr. Clark stay on, he asked, until he himself could get the hang of things?[84]

xii

It was fortunate that Reuben stayed. There were indeed many things for the new secretary to get the hang of, and in the ensuing weeks Reuben was as much the acting secretary as ever. Stimson, in fact, institutionalized that arrangement by making all bureau chiefs and department assistants report directly to the undersecretary rather than himself.[85] And there was a great deal to report. In Europe the Young Plan had been slowly taking shape and now was about to come forth. In the Far East, China, ever on the brink of dissolution, was under constant diplomatic watch, while Japan looked on covetously. Yet it was in Mexico, once more, that the real movement occurred. On May Day the church-state controversy suddenly broke wide open.[86]

Few people expected any progress. The initiative ignited in November by Father Burke had fizzled out. Calles's term as president had then expired, and the old general had not thought it wise to immediately press his successor, Emilio Portes Gil, for action. Early in January, Clark, Burke, and Morrow—who was home for a visit—had put their heads together and discussed another possible overture, but the problem once again was the Holy See. What use was it, asked Morrow, to approach the Mexican president with a new proposal if the Vatican would not stand behind it? They had adjourned in low spirits.[87]

Then, on May first, Portes Gil was holding a press conference when a foreign correspondent asked him whether Catholics as such had been involved in the Renovator rebellion. Phrasing his response carefully, the Mexican president exempted Catholics as such from blame, and then went on to make some conciliatory remarks. "No religion will be persecuted," he said, "nor is the government guilty of persecuting any sect. Liberty of conscience will be respected, as heretofore. The Catholic Clergy, when they wish, may renew the exercise of their rites with only one obligation, that they respect the laws of the land."[88] In Washington the next day Archbishop Ruiz y Flores, president of the exiled episcopal committee, answered Portes Gil with a conciliatory statement of his own. After years of acrimony, the two sides were suddenly talking to one another. The only question remaining was Rome.[89]

Reuben had not seen Father Burke for several months, for the priest had traveled to the Vatican for further talks. However, William Montavon, legal counsel for the National Catholic Welfare Conference, had continued the weekly visits, and on May 9 he brought Reuben another bolt of lightning. Bishop Ruiz's reply to the Mexican president had been authorized by the apostolic delegation to the United States and hence could be regarded as official.[90]

The task now was to get the right people in the right places to agree. This was not easy. The parties to the dispute had been frozen in their respective positions for so long that they seemed unable to navigate beyond them. But both Morrow and Clark recognized that the moment of truth had arrived, and they each began to urge fast action.

Morrow worked with President Portes Gil, arranging for Archbishop Ruiz to come to Mexico and talk matters over. Reuben Clark worked with William Montavon and through him with the Holy See, expediting communications wherever possible. When, at one point, Montavon lacked the funds to transmit the text of a long dispatch to the Vatican, the American undersecretary put the message out over the State Department cable, together with his own plea for urgency.[91]

All the while the war ground on. *Cristero* forces, resenting what they saw as the intermeddling of the bishops, were the more anxious to settle their question on the battlefield and stepped up their attacks accordingly. For its part, the government launched a major counteroffensive. By the middle of May some five thousand troops had been thrown into Colima and were dealing with the guerrillas systematically. On the twenty-eighth they captured Cerro Grande. The following week they battled the hymn-singing *Cristeros* on the slopes of the Colima volcano. The week after that they were at it again, at San José del Carmen. Combat deaths for the month of May totaled 1,250.[92]

On May 22, Father Burke, back from Rome, called Reuben with tidings of another breakthrough. Bishop Ruiz had been named apostolic delegate to Mexico, with powers to settle the church-state controversy. Reuben flashed out the word to Morrow, and the ambassador conveyed it to the Mexican authorities. In the company of another Mexican prelate, Pascual Díaz, Ruiz y Flores left Washington by train on the evening of June 4. Montavon had telephoned Reuben that morning to assure him that the bishops would not demand a change in the laws, but only moderation in their enforcement. Everyone held his breath.[93]

Three months had now passed since Reuben was to have resigned from the State Department. Even amid the excitement of the church-state denouement, the undersecretary was growing impatient with his boss's procrastination in replacing him. Reuben dropped hints, then made inquiries. Finally the two of them had a scene.[94] Stimson recognized that the game was up and submitted the name of New York attorney Joseph P. Cotton for Senate approval.[95] Reuben was pleased, of course, for his job was now finite at last. Appreciably less pleased was assistant secretary William R. Castle.

The final fortnight in Mexico was excitement itself. By June 9 Ruiz and Díaz, the two exiled prelates, were in Mexico City, and Morrow was preparing for their meeting with Portes Gil. This took place at noon on the twelfth, in Chapultepec Castle.[96] Things seemed to go well; but a subsequent exchange was less satisfactory, and Morrow had to move fast in order to prevent a backslide. The ambassador took to preparing written statements for each of the parties and submitting them to the other for approval. By June 18 the agreement was essentially complete. Now it was only a matter of securing the Vatican's ratification.[97]

It was Reuben's turn to prod. Back and forth between himself and Morrow flew the anxious inquiries about papal action—or inaction, as it turned out. Reuben cornered William Montavon and turned on the pressure as never before in his career. By June 19 Morrow, almost desperate, wired Reuben the final texts of the agreements and implored that something be done to make the papacy move. There was yet another session with Montavon and yet more stony silence from Rome.[98]

Then finally, on the twentieth, like a sunburst breaking through the storm, the long-awaited telegram from the Vatican arrived and the negotiation was complete. The Catholic clergy agreed to return to Mexico, reopen the churches, and abide by the laws of the land. The government promised to interpret those laws fairly, to respect the identity of the church, and to remain in contact with the clergy regarding problems that might arise.[99] It was the first day of summer,* and the church-state controversy was at an end.

xiii

On June 28, a week later, Undersecretary Clark paid a final visit to the State Department to bid friends and colleagues farewell. From the press room where he shook hands all around, three cheers were shouted into the decorous marble corridors. And if there was corresponding sentimentality for the occasion, none of it showed. Reuben Clark, for one, was beaming.[100]

Somewhat less ebullient were the correspondents themselves. "Mr. Clark's resignation," wrote one of them, "is a distinct loss."

Though he has abundantly earned the right to retirement, it is to be hoped that he will be returned to office again either by presidential appointment or by election from Utah, his native state. His learning in the law, his common sense, his gift of counsel, his profound knowledge of the principles on which our government was founded and his talent for applying them to problems at home and abroad make this truly unconditional American too valuable to be long spared the services of the nation.[101]

Of course, Mr. Clark was not sparing his service to the nation at all. He was heading back to Mexico.

---

*Last-minute details delayed the final consummation of the agreement until the following day, June 21.

Chapter 27

KING FOR A DAY

As J. Reuben Clark, in the company of his wife and daughter, returned to Mexico City in mid-July of 1929, it was with an air of triumph. After all, when the Morrow-Clark mission had begun some two years earlier, it had faced three extraordinarily difficult problems; and now two of the three were resolved and substantial progress had been made on the third. Reuben was returning to help polish off that third problem and his mood was one of buoyancy. For the pleasure of this experience he had turned down a partnership in one of the largest law firms in New York.[1]

Yet the Mexican idyll of Reuben's memories had unquestionably changed in his absence. Even though things were much as he had left them, they reflected small differences. Pests had ravaged the silken lawn of the embassy compound, and the whole thing had had to be rooted up. The edifice itself had been damaged in one of Mexico City's periodic earthquakes, and some structural reinforcement had been necessary.[2] Most changed of all was the ambassador himself. He appeared smaller and more shrunken than ever, and the circles under his eyes had thickened into pouches. These developments had taken place slowly, incrementally, largely escaping daily notice; but they were nonetheless real. Dwight Morrow was no longer well.[3]

Reuben's old office was still on the second floor and his bookshelves still folded around it protectively. Most of the embassy staff presented familiar faces, and outwardly they still seemed confident of their mission. At one gathering Reuben Clark, Joseph Satterthwaite, and Arthur Bliss Lane, who had accompanied Reuben as the new counselor of embassy, donned charro costumes and regaled guests with flute and harmonicas.[4] Luacine remembered it as "a very carefree winter, nothing to worry about and Reuben drawing a large salary. Everyone was very kind to us, entertained us constantly."[5]

The Morrow achievements were still in place and still the subjects of exuberant press commentary, but even here things had subtly altered. The assassination of Obregón had thrown Mexican politics into spasms of recoil, and no one knew exactly what the end result might be. Morrow, for one, was concerned. He seemed to sense that somehow, below the surface, the structure of U.S.-Mexican accord was slipping ever so slightly.

ii

Most noticeable, perhaps, was the slipping of the petroleum agreement. The American oil companies had finally resolved to buck up and apply for their confirmatory concessions. The result was not the happy ending envisioned by Morrow and Clark, but a new set of difficulties as the overwhelming majority of the applications now became stalled in the Mexican courts.[6] Beyond the usual bureaucratic snarls there were some ungauged problems. The Mexican commitment to resolve the oil controversy had not always run beyond Plutarco Calles, and even though he was still indisputably *jefe máximo,* his Revolutionary party was of two minds on the subject of accommodating American oil interests. The other mind was steadily gaining ascendency.

Morrow had put off facing the problem until Reuben Clark returned.[7] These were not the happiest of homecoming tidings, but Reuben rolled up his sleeves. On July 26 he paid a courtesy call on Ingeniero Paredes of the petroleum department, the man with whom he had hammered out the original agreement. None of their old rapport had slackened. When Reuben suggested that confirmatory concessions be issued at once on all uncontested applications and that one of the major contested cases be settled as a token of good faith, Paredes seemed entirely agreeable. However, bottlenecks, inefficiency, and governmental corruptions conspired to frustrate the best of efforts. All through the summer and into the fall Reuben continued to meet with Paredes, with Enrique Estrada, the foreign minister, and with provisional president Portes Gil* himself, but no amount

---

*At the assassination of President-elect Obregón, Portes Gil was chosen by congress to succeed Calles on December 1, 1928, as Obregón would have done, but with the designation of "provisional president" and the promise that a new election would soon be held. It was in the subsequent election that Pascual Ortiz Rubio was chosen to become Calles's legitimate successor. He was inaugurated in February of 1930.

of energy seemed capable of overcoming Mexican inertia. This was clearly not the "high thinking" he had dreamed about while back in Washington.[8]

iii

There had never been a hard and fast agrarian agreement, but such an agreement as there was also began to slip. To the extent that Portes Gil possessed a mind of his own, it happened to be on this subject. He accelerated the rate of land expropriation and opposed Morrow's idea of paying cash for the lands taken over.[9] Pascual Ortiz Rubio, who succeeded Portes Gil in February of 1930, was more amenable to American persuasion and trimmed land reform back considerably, but then another difficulty reared up. Mexico's foreign indebtedness, which was closely connected to the agrarian problem, became the subject of a bitter new controversy. Morrow had sought to overhaul the entire financial structure of Mexico in order to assure responsibility for foreign bonds, fair payment for expropriated lands, and long-term fiscal stability. However, his efforts were undermined by a close personal friend and Morgan associate, Thomas W. Lamont, who, representing an association of American bondholders, pressed for immediate service on Mexico's bonded indebtedness regardless of the ultimate consequences.[10] Once again, Mexican finances threatened to run out of control. Although this situation was mainly the worry of Lewis McBride, the ambassador's financial advisor, Reuben Clark was thrown into the breach as well. As of December, 1929, his work was " 'nothing else but' bonds."[11]

iv

Against these tribulations the Morrow mission was more or less holding its own and might have continued to do so but for one final difficulty. At the end of November word arrived that Governor Larson of New Jersey wished to appoint Dwight Morrow to fill the unexpired Senate term of Walter E. Edge, recently named ambassador to France. There were a number of complications, and the decision was difficult for Morrow to make. Finally, on the advice of Clark and Rublee, the ambassador decided to go instead to the London naval conference, where he was to be a principal U.S. delegate, and then make a try for the vacant Senate seat in the regular election.[12] Both activities, of course, would take him away from Mexico.

So it was that J. Reuben Clark found himself, for all intents and purposes, U.S. ambassador to Mexico—and at a time when things were coming apart. It was a frightening experience. "There will be some extremely hard sledding for the man who follows the present Ambassador," Reuben wrote to Walter Lippmann in January. "So hard, indeed, that no one who understands it would be likely to take it on with anything else than keen misgiving."[13] Under Morrow's aegis Reuben had undertaken some tough bargaining in his day. He had assumed virtually full responsibility for the oil negotiations. But acting under the guidance of a strong, charismatic leader was not at all the same as acting on one's own. The prospect filled Reuben with foreboding.

v

The first order of business was to pry loose some oil concessions, if only to demonstrate that it could be done. Reuben approached Paredes with new earnestness on February 7 and told him that here was a chance to make certain that Dwight Morrow gained full credit for the oil settlement before he left Mexico for good.[14] Nothing happened. Reuben decided to raise the ante. In April he called on Calles at his Santa Barbara ranch. There was no telling, he intimated to the gnarled old *jefe,* what might happen to the concession situation under a less sympathetic ambassador; the Mexicans had best act while there was still time for a favorable solution.[15] Nothing happened. Finally, in desperation, Reuben went to President Ortiz Rubio and applied strong-arm tactics. The senatorial campaign was bowling along in New Jersey at this time, and Senator Frelinghuysen was threatening to investigate Morrow's record as ambassador. "I pointed out," reported Reuben,

that any discussion of Mr. Morrow's work in Mexico would undoubtedly include oil matters; that there were some men in the States who were anxious to prove that Mr. Morrow had been wrong in all he had done in that matter and to cast reflections upon the Mexican government, and that it seemed the best answer to any criticism that might be made would be the issuance of the concessions.[16]

But even this ploy failed. On July 30 Reuben's box score stood at seventy-three concessions still pending, and only ten of them were granted during the next two months.

In this flurry of activity there was little concern for the oil companies themselves. As Reuben had explained to Calles in April, he "held no brief" for the oil producers. "But . . . I thought they had a certain trouble-making power which it would be well to eliminate."[17] Soon that power became all too evident. In September Reuben was visited at the embassy by a certain E. H. Bell of Boston who carried a letter of introduction from New Jersey congressman Randolph Perkins.

Mr. Bell then said, "You know Mr. Morrow got a very large vote in the primaries." I said I knew that. He said that was a forced vote and intimated that Mr. Perkins and the "interests" behind him were responsible for it; he stated that Mr. Perkins, before Mr. Bell came down here, had told him (Bell) that he (Bell) was to go to Mexico and get these confirmatory concessions. It was immaterial how he got them, but he must get them. Mr. Bell then continued (intimating that this was Perkins' attitude), that if these concessions were not obtained, the interests behind them were not sure that they could deliver this forced primary vote in the election.[18]

Meanwhile, three separate committees were studying the oil problem for the Mexican government, none of them completely sure of what it was supposed to be doing or how it related to the others, and the bureaucratic brambles were growing more prickly by the week. The job was "hard sledding" indeed.

vi

Shocks from the New Jersey senatorial campaign also toppled Morrow's financial agreement. During a speech for Morrow in April, Colonel Alexander McNab, a former military attaché at the embassy, told a Newark audience that the American ambassador "put Mexico on her feet and [gave] her a strong Government." McNab went on to assert that there was "no department of government in Mexico which [Morrow] has not advised and directed. He took the Secretary of Finance under his wing and taught him finance."[19] However true and well meant, McNab's words created a terrible debacle for Morrow's diplomacy. Mexicans were sensitive to just such paternalism as this, and the birdlike Montes de Oca, who was specifically mentioned in McNab's boast, was more sensitive than most. The embassy tried to avert disaster. Reuben made a trip to see Calles and beseeched him to intervene, but the old general was warily non-committal. "Mr. Morrow is a smart man," he said. "He will know what to do."[20] The result was predictable. Montes de Oca veered sharply toward the Lamont plan of financial readjustment and sharply away from the Morrow. On July 25 an agreement was signed that dealt the ambassador his first capital defeat.[21] The Morrow people kept a stiff upper lip, but there was no denying the effect of McNab's gaffe. Reuben confided to Mrs. Morrow that the speech had been devastating.[22]

vii

Curiously though, as Dwight Morrow's stock began to fall in Mexico, Reuben Clark's began to rise. He had learned a great deal from the ambassador, and the recent experience of walking in Morrow's shoes had enabled him to put the learning into practice. For example, if the Mexicans challenged certain American statistics, Reuben would quietly go back and research the statistics over again, often discovering that the Mexicans were right and occasionally discovering that their case was even stronger than they thought. Then, ingenuously enough, he would tell them so, enormously adding to their confidence in him. From that practice, Reuben took to advising the Mexicans of their own legal rights and pointing out technicalities of the law that worked to their advantage. "They know him to be honest and implicitly trust him," was the judgment of one American observer.[23] True, he could not move mountains nor sometimes even diplomatic molehills, but he could unerringly win Mexican respect.

Unsurprisingly then, Reuben Clark, along with George Rublee and Senator George E. Moses (the old bitter-ender), was mentioned with increasing frequency as Morrow's possible successor. Owing to the duration of Morrow's political absence, speculation about the successor was both wide and intense. And for once Reuben himself was interested. "It would not fall far short of a calamity," he wrote to Susa Young Gates, "for one of us [Mormons] to decline such a position if it were offered."

Not one of our people has yet held a position in any branch or division of our government of the rank, dignity, and estimation in the eyes of the world of an Ambassador, particularly of Ambassador to a country of the importance of Mexico to the United States, for the Ambassadorship to Mexico is the most difficult and probably the most important of any Ambassadorship of the United States.[24]

Still, Reuben held off on the purchase of any swallowtail coat. There were, as he explained to Walter Lippmann, "at least a score of vociferous, wire-pulling, political sand-bagging, two-legged reasons" why the post would not be offered to him.[25] There were some less anthropomorphic reasons too, chief among which were his Mormonism and his uncertain finances. The latter was especially crippling and the newspapers stewed about it fretfully. "I seem to have the best advertised poverty in the United States," Reuben quipped.[26]

There was at least one other reason, less well advertised. In the middle of February, Fred Nielsen finally coiled himself and struck. The blow had been some time in the offing. Relations between Clark and Nielsen had deteriorated steadily throughout 1929, dating from their conversation about Bouvé. As with others on his hate list, Nielsen had stopped speaking to Reuben; then he had openly snubbed him.[27] This course of action had apparently seemed appropriate to the commissioner—until all the talk of Reuben Clark replacing Dwight Morrow. Then, suddenly, it seemed rash. With the claims commission now meeting in Mexico City, Nielsen would have to report directly to the ambassador. To avert such poetic justice, he reacted in the only way he could—with a cold-blooded attempt at character assassination.

His charge was that Reuben Clark had disqualified himself for the ambassadorship back in 1927 by writing a scathing editorial about Mexico in the *Washington Post*. The charge was made to Arthur Bliss Lane for transmission to the "right people." Lane transmitted it to the wrong people. He took it first to Clement Bouvé, who fairly exploded with anger, and then he took it to Reuben personally, whom he met in Laredo. Lane then did a little checking on his own and discovered that the editorial writer, whose identity Nielsen claimed to have known for certain, was definitely not Reuben

Clark and that Nielsen definitely *knew* it was not. That ended the matter insofar as the State Department was concerned.[28] But with Nielsen heading for Mexico City at the same time as Clark, disaster loomed again for the luckless claims commission.

viii

Against these liabilities, Reuben possessed a single powerful asset: Dwight Morrow. And Morrow had already made up his mind. He had resolved that the Utah Mormon was the one who must succeed him and that neither his Mormonism nor his isolationism nor his personal finances must be allowed to stand in the way. "Morrow left Mexico because he trusted Reuben Clark to carry on," was the way Will Rogers put it. "Had there been no Clark to take up that work, Morrow would have stayed there and not gone to the Senate."[29] Mexico watchers discerned the portents of this mandate in the fact that it was Reuben, rather than Rublee or some other, who was appointed ambassador extraordinary and plenipotentiary to attend the February 5 inauguration of President Ortiz Rubio. Reuben joked about being "king for a day" and "[getting] front seats at the ceremonies," but he too could now see the appointment coming and he began bracing himself for it.[30]

ix

For the family, however, the ambassadorship was still an impossible dream. They had not moved into the embassy, as on Luacine's earlier visit to Mexico, but instead rented a comfortable suite at the Genève, a block or so away. The hotel was owned by an Englishman, Thomas Gore, and his wife, Pauline, both of them former opera singers. Friendship with the Gores was a natural. Young Luacine even found a companion in Marie Gore who, like Luacine, loved music and was studying to be a concert pianist. The girls enrolled together at the American school where Luacine came to realize that, because her father was known as Morrow's right-hand man, *she* was somebody too.[31]

Otherwise, though, the Clarks witnessed embassy life at a distance. Reuben bought a new car and hired a chauffeur—he himself

538

was a danger behind the wheel—to deliver them to the diplomatic functions. But mostly they just picnicked. At Christmas time Reuben brought the entire family together for an unforgettable Mexican holiday. Now the picnicking went on continually, with and without Reuben, and Marianne and Louise became so enchanted with Mexico that they stayed on until March. It was the nearest thing they had known to affluence since the world war, and they made the most of it. Even so, the embassy, with its classical elegance and throbbing social life, seemed a very long way off.[32]

x

Morrow's political fortunes piled success upon success. In June he won the Republican nomination by a plurality of three hundred thousand votes, defeating incumbent Senator Frelinghuysen in the process.[33] Thereafter the election was little in doubt. Nevertheless, it was a tired and lonely man who returned to Mexico City in July for his last brief season as ambassador. The long naval conference and the free-swinging campaign had left Morrow exhausted, and the compromises forced upon him by New Jersey politicians had been morally enervating. The Mexicans, moreover, appeared to have lost their old enthusiasm for the ambassador and seemed immunized at last against the Morrow charm. The oil agreements were as tangled as ever, and the bond agreements were a bitter disappointment. The Catholic church was back in operation and the *Cristero* revolt had come to an end, but even here the two sides were eyeing one another warily and small matters made them bristle. Reuben Clark at this point had been unofficially superintending U.S.-Mexican relations for almost a year, and he knew how fragile they were. As he looked to the future, he saw little reason for hopefulness. His mood matched that of Morrow.

In May, with the end of school, Luacine and her daughter returned to Utah, and in the dog days of August Reuben prepared to follow them. There were last-minute details to attend to, papers to file, books to box up—"a strenuous and generally upsetting performance."[34] He left Mexico on the seventeenth of September with much of the uncertainty that had attended his first coming. Doubtless he agreed with Morrow's final assessment of their mission, that "while we did not accomplish all that we had hoped for, we probably got more done than we had the right to expect."[35] Warm letters of appreciation were exchanged between himself and his recent boss, but the most significant words were scrawled by the latter in a postscript.

Since dictating the above I have talked to the President. I told him what I thought of you. I cannot quote him; but I think the appointment will be made, and quickly![36]

It was. Barely had the letter arrived, in fact, before the Clarks' telephone began ringing with long-distance calls. Two days later, October 3, Reuben stopped at a newsstand and saw his name spread across the headlines in bold, black capitals. He was United States ambassador to Mexico.

xi

After that day, the world was never the same for the Clark family. Reuben had received congratulations before, but now he received a deluge of them—sheaves of letters and telegrams. The Clarks had talked to reporters before, but now the reporters trooped into the D Street parlor and began raising all sorts of impertinent questions. (Luacine could be equally testy. When asked if Reuben had money enough for the ambassadorship, she snapped back: "Of course he has. You can say that he will take it.")[37] Young Luacine had been a person of account before, but now she found herself a celebrity. Heady as all this was, it was also frightening. Luacine approached her husband nearly in tears one night. How could she possibly be an ambassador's wife? she asked. How could she entertain presidents and potentates? How could she acquire the grace of an Astor or a Vanderbilt? Reuben smiled at her tenderly. She would do fine, he assured her; and then, remembering their betrothal long ago and his mild sense of pique, he added: "Why, you've been to California!"[38]

And, frightened or not, Luacine was going to Mexico too. A week later she and her daughter were wandering dazedly through ZCMI in Salt Lake City and buying silverware, linen, and evening clothes as casually as the Morrows. Purchases included tea service, candelabras, and a twenty-four-place setting of the finest sterling available, complete with fish knives, cream spoons, and grape scissors. By day's end the bill tallied a thousand dollars.[39]

Reuben, however, was a bit more down to earth. How indeed was he to maintain himself as ambassador? The newspapers were still fretting over this point and so, in secret, was he. There was even a scandal of sorts when word got around that Morrow had offered to foot the bill.[40] After all, it was publicly known that the ambassador's job paid but $17,500 a year, that the expense budget amounted to a meager $2,500, and that Dwight Morrow had laid out as much as $75,000 a year for entertainment alone.[41] These figures, observed Marshall Morgan from the Mexican claims commission, "[place] you substantially in the position of the Comanche Indian who lassoed a locomotive."[42]

Nevertheless, Reuben was determined to be his own man in Mexico City. He wrote to counselor Arthur Bliss Lane at the embassy and asked for a peso-by-peso estimate of the monthly expenses he was likely to incur.[43] When it came back, itemized right down to wax and brooms, Reuben shuddered at the totals but presented a face of defiance. "I'm paying my own way," he declared. "When I can no longer finance myself I'll come home."[44] He had hoarded the small fortune that Morrow had paid him for legal services, and he stood ready to draw upon it. At need, Reuben could be tightfisted as well, slashing and trimming viscerally if he had to. Finally, he was prepared, if necessary, to mortgage the Grantsville farm. He was determined to succeed as an honest poor ambassador, one of the first in American history; but it would be touch and go.[45]

Meanwhile, Reuben traveled to Washington to confer with the president and secretary of state. Public response to his appointment had been favorable—possibly a little too favorable. The editorials had fairly gushed about Mr. Clark and his qualifications, styling him "a most obvious power behind the [Morrow] throne" and predicting him "an abler diplomat than Morrow."[46] "Few men have been so warmly liked in the State Department by all comers, ambassadors, career men, legislators and journalists alike," said one editor.[47] "Mr. Clark is well liked by all factions in Mexico and is noted for the charm of his personality," said another.[48] Such blanket approval ran the gamut from radical to ultraconservative newspapers. "The ideal ambassador may not exist," spoke the *Boston Transcript* for everyone, "but Mr. Clark will measure up very close to him."[49] This was all very gratifying, of course, and Reuben himself would like to have been carried along by it, but cool intellect prevailed. "As we get nearer the job," he said, "the difficulties of it loom so large that I think neither Lute nor myself will have any trouble in wearing our ordinary-sized hats."[50]

Secretary Stimson, however, seemed to accept the newspapers' view of the matter and blandly assumed that Reuben, like his predecessor, would be in charge of making, as well as executing, Mexican policy. When the new ambassador asked for instructions, the secretary absently replied that if Reuben wanted any he should go and write them out himself. "I told him," Reuben recorded crisply, "if he did not want to give me any instructions I did not wish to give any to myself."[51] Yet the new ambassador was far from on his own. He was a prisoner of the Morrow legacy as surely as John Adams had been a prisoner of the Washington legacy or Andrew Johnson a prisoner of the Lincoln.

I had been more or less a party to, and more or less responsible for . . . the work of Mr. Morrow in Mexico; I felt that the work was moving along the right lines; I was willing to continue along those lines, thoroughly appreciating that if I succeeded in getting through without trouble it would be credited to Mr. Morrow's work, and that if I failed to get through without trouble it would be charged to inept dumbness on my part.[52]

In this statement was to be found a massive paradox. Reuben Clark, in publicly vowing to carry on the work of Dwight Morrow, was already making such a task impossible. Morrow's diplomacy had been creative, assertive, and unpredictable, never a mere formula that successors could imitate. What Reuben was really saying, then, was that he would never and could never be the kind of diplomat that he was succeeding. "I am not Morrow," he confided solemnly to Lennie Riter, "and therefore it must not be expected that I shall do so well."[53] So the dilemma was complete. Reuben could not break new ground as Morrow had done, for that violated his conservative nature; yet if he remained content only to preserve the Morrow accomplishments, he would defeat everyone's—including Morrow's—hopes for his success. "Few men," observed O. N. Malmquist in the *Salt Lake Tribune,* "have ever been elected or appointed to a position of public trust with so exalted a reputation to live up to as J. Reuben Clark."[54] The question was whether he would live up to it.

542

xii

The dreamlike aura carried the Clark family through the next weeks. There was shopping and packing, farewells of assorted descriptions, a public reception at the Salt Lake Twentieth Ward (which was held, unfortunately, three days after their departure), a train ride across the continent, a formal dinner at the White House, and the same sort of procession into Mexico that had attended the Morrows three years earlier. Reuben was not yet quite comfortable with the pomp and circumstance. When President Ortiz Rubio sent a private coach to the border to be spliced into the ambassador's train, Reuben gracefully declined the favor. He knew Ortiz Rubio as an old friend—what was this? By degrees, however, the logic of diplomatic pageantry settled upon him, and by the time they were clattering down the Paseo de la Reforma under military escort he was evidently enjoying himself. When their blue limousine pulled through the eagle-crested iron gates and young Luacine saw the red carpet flowing down the steps in greeting, the poignancy of the occasion was complete.[55]

Indeed, as the Clarks approached the grey stone palace that was to be home, the magical, improbable, Cinderella quality transcended all else. The poor man had become ambassador. The hireling had taken charge. The Mormon had broken the topmost barrier. And the world, so it seemed, was applauding in unison. With such a remarkable turn of fortune, J. Reuben Clark was more than a little uneasy. Like winning the Irish Sweepstakes, like finding pirates' gold, like being king for a day, it all seemed too good to be true.

Chapter 28

AMBASSADOR

The American embassy was never more beautiful than on that November morning, and the Clarks beheld it as if for the first time. A fire burned brightly in the carved stone fireplace, and great calla lilies stood on the mantle above. The room opening before them was of baronial splendor, with gleaming checkered tiles, rose marble columns, tapestries gracing the walls, oriental carpets, richly polished mahogany, here and there the glint of Mexican silver, and the air pungent with the scent of tuberoses. To Anne Morrow, when she had first seen it, it had seemed like a stage setting straight out of Hollywood.[1]

As with the Morrows before, there came the period of settling in. Reuben had an easier time of this than Luacine, for he knew the staff members personally. They varied widely, as he also knew, in their interests and capabilities. On the one hand, there were men of the caliber of Arthur Bliss Lane, counselor of embassy, whose diplomatic career had stretched back to the Treaty of Versailles and who was in fact as well as in name the mainstay of the embassy staff.[2] On the other hand, there were several staffers who struck Reuben as having been in the Foreign Service too long. To a man, it seemed, this latter group hailed from the distinguished diplomatic families and listed Harvard, Yale, and Princeton on their vitas with deadly uniformity. Diplomacy for them seemed to consist of tea-drinking and party-throwing, and they executed it with gusto. Reuben much preferred the likes of amiable Joe Satterthwaite, who hailed from Tecumseh and had attended the University of Michigan. In group pictures, this third secretary, with his owlish spectacles and hair parted down the middle, looked altogether outclassed by First Secretary John Farr Simmons and Second Secretary Stanley Hawks, but in actual influence he outranked them.[3] Like Satterthwaite, Reuben

Clark's people were the ones who got things done. One of them was a two-fisted lawyer named Steven Aguirre, who in the rough-and-tumble of protection work—springing Americans out of Mexican jails, mostly—outperformed the embassy and consular staffs combined but who, because he happened to have a Mexican wife, could never quite seem to merit a promotion. (The aristocrats of the State Department frowned upon mixed marriages.) Reuben had first encountered him in Nuevo Laredo, where on an early morning in 1928 Aguirre had met the undersecretary's train and taken him to Mrs. Riser's Waffle House for pecan waffles. Unable to forget either the waffles or the young vice-consul, Reuben now went to bat for him. "I hope," he wrote to Wilbur Carr, "that the spats, the accent, the tailoring, etc., etc., can be forgotten in this instance, and real worth ... be given decisive consideration."[4] This was Reuben's administrative philosophy in a nutshell.

His administrative practice was less direct. There was no wholesale house-cleaning of the embassy. Reuben simply allowed the socialites to attend to social functions and the workers to attend to diplomacy. When he could, he augmented the working staff with especially competent recruits, like Colonel Moreno from the claims commission. In time he was said to have the finest staff in the United States Foreign Service.[5]

Luacine's orientation took more time, but she had the assistance of her social secretary, Elizabeth Lewis. Miss Lewis was genteel in the way that only Smith graduates could be and was endowed with common sense besides. She it was who decided whom to invite and to which functions, who made elaborate seating charts to ensure that rank and protocol were strictly observed, who wrote out the invitations and menus and delivered them to the printer for engraving, and who, in consultation with Luacine, decided what to serve and what the entertainment should be. Luacine also had to keep track of a platoon of servants, sixteen in all. There was Fernando, the chauffeur, who lived just off the garage and spent his days endlessly polishing the navy-blue Lincoln. There were the two butlers, Sabino and Miguel, who bustled around officiously in their daytime starched whites and resplendently in their evening tuxedos. There was the chef and his staff, a corps of gardeners, a laundress or two, a private maid for Luacine and her daughter, and below the eagle-crested iron

Interior views of the embassy: Calla lilies and the glint of Mexican silver.

gate a gateman in full livery. It all took a little getting used to. When Luacine's napkin chanced to slip from her lap, she had to learn never to reach down for it lest Sabino, who would materialize instantly with a new napkin on a silver tray, be utterly devastated.[6]

But the mansion itself required no acclimatizing. With all its wonder, it was home from the start. One entered it from the colonnaded veranda through massive oak doors. The living room was spacious and airy, mounted by twenty-foot ceilings and ringed by alcoves for quiet conversation. Tall French doors led to more rooms: a *sala,* much like the living room with conversational groupings; a dining hall, long and elegant, its palladian windows looking out over the garden; a kitchen that would have done a hotel proud where Juan and his assistants prepared continental cuisine. The private wing of the embassy was much more homelike. Here too was a living room—smaller in scale—along with separate master bedrooms for the ambassador and ambassadress, and three guest bedrooms. The family bedrooms were each equipped with a marble bath, a vast walk-in closet, and private fireplace, and each opened onto the veranda. It was in this wing of the house that Miss Lewis had her office as well, outside of which were located two telephones. Mexico City happened to have two competing phone companies, and it was necessary to subscribe to both of them.[7]

As she surveyed all of this, Luacine had mixed emotions. She, too, possibly felt that she had lassoed a locomotive. Yet, as she said, it was "the most thrilling adventure in our checkered married life."[8] Like the ambassador, she plunged in.

ii

The official commencement of the adventure was something like a page out of Walter Scott. On November 28, three days after their arrival, there was a clatter of hooves in the street outside. A troop of the presidential cavalry had arrived to escort the ambassador to the National Palace for the presentation of credentials. Down the Avenida de los Insurgentes rolled the caravan of limousines, flanked by motorcycles and headed by the cavalrymen, their silver and brass glittering in the sun. They turned onto the Paseo de la Reforma and trotted sedately through the midday traffic toward the Zócalo.

Ambassador Clark leaving the embassy to present his credentials: Ruffles and flourishes were still rather new.

Through the high vaulted gate of the palace they went, the horses stepping as if synchronized, and into the colonnaded inner court; then down a file of soldiers stiffly at attention as trumpets blasted out an earsplitting fanfare and to a stop before the lavish baroque entranceway.[9] This was the twilight of the old diplomacy of ruffles and flourishes, and J. Reuben Clark would be one of the last ambassadors to know its pageantry.

Reuben's address to President Ortiz Rubio was short and perfunctory, but it set the tone for his ambassadorship perfectly.

I come with a message of friendship and goodwill from the people of the United States to the people of Mexico. The President of the United States has

The ambassadorial procession clatters into the National Palace: Twilight of the old diplomacy.

particularly charged me to convey to Your Excellency the best wishes of the Government of the United States for the continued welfare and prosperity of the Mexican people and for the personal happiness and well being of Your Excellency.

To these messages I hope I may be permitted to add a personal word of true friendship for the Mexican people, a friendship I have gained fom a considerable residence among them. I have a real sympathy for their struggles and their aspirations, and a deep respect for their lofty ideals and their sterling virtues.

History records and experience demonstrates that there are no questions arising between nations which may not be adjusted peaceably and in good feeling, as well as with reciprocal advantage, if those questions are discussed with kindly candor, with a mutual appreciation of and accommodation to the point of view of each by the other, and with patience and a desire to work out fair and equitable justice.

It is in this spirit that I take up the performance of my official duties.[10]

These words encapsulated Reuben's attitude toward Mexico. "Mexico is our neighbor," he had told a Mormon general conference on the eve of his departure. "We should treat Mexico as a neighbor."[11] In two sentences he had enunciated a new Latin-American policy for the United States, and he meant to put it into practice.

549

Later that afternoon, to a throng of well-wishers at the embassy the new ambassador served punch and cookies, which neither the seasoned diplomats under his charge nor the American community of Mexico City found particularly to their taste.[12] There was a worse disappointment in store for them. Reuben smilingly announced that punch and cookies would be the fare from then on. "Whether alcoholic beverages shall be served in American Embassies and Legations is a question regularly determined by the various chiefs of missions concerned," he said. "I have decided not to serve alcoholic beverages in the Embassy in Mexico City during my term at this post."[13] There was, of course, a certain reaction to this, and it flashed out immediately in the papers back home. Intoned the Baltimore *Sun*:

> The perfect diplomat, one would think, is one who is careful to observe every delicate aspect of the traditional relation between guest and host. Certainly, in a Latin country, to start by ignoring one of the chief of those aspects is a very poor start indeed.[14]

And just as predictably the voices of temperance came back with a loud defense. In the editorial tug-of-war that ensued, Reuben's motives were assessed from both economic and religious perspectives, but neither economics nor religion explained his decree. (Morrow had bequeathed him an eight-hundred-thousand-dollar-cache of liquor in the embassy basement, and before the days of Prohibition Reuben himself had poked fun at Bryan's missionary teetotalism.)[15] For Reuben the question was simply one of representation. Did one adequately represent his country, he asked, by flouting its laws abroad? As an El Paso editor who took Reuben's part reasoned: "To see the constitution ignored within the embassy walls is scarcely an effective way to obtain its respect from the nation to whom the ambassador is accredited."[16]

Most disconcerting about the new edict was the implication that Reuben Clark was going to abandon the Morrow tradition and be his own man in Mexico. (After all, had not Morrow campaigned for the Senate on a platform of militant wetness?) This was a difficult question. Reuben, surely, had been Morrow's man. He had done Morrow's bidding, had helped engineer his successes, and had approved of his accomplishments. At the same time, though, Reuben understood the altered nature of his own task. Morrow's diplomacy had resolved the major problems with Mexico. What was called for now, Reuben believed, was not more Morrow, not more dynamic reshaping of an unfavorable state of affairs, but a wholly new and essentially conservative task—to preserve the gains that Morrow had made. Reuben Clark did not intend to roll up his sleeves and begin buttonholing the Mexican politicos as his predecessor had done. He intended, as he had said, to treat them with new respect and dignity. This was what he had meant when he said, "I am not Morrow."

Yet Reuben did not want to stand pat either. He had recently made some discoveries about diplomacy—and about himself—and these had profoundly reshaped his thinking. From the Morrow mission he had discovered the truly progressive character of the Mexican Revolution—and how that character had escaped the notice of the State Department. From the Clark Memorandum experience he had discovered that hemispheric relations were generally unhappy, unjust, and unwholesomely dominated by the United States. There was a logical coherence to these revelations, one that seemed to impose a new kind of obligation on Morrow's successor. Ambassador Clark decided that he wanted to move United States-Mexican relations not only beyond specific confrontations but beyond confrontation itself.

The new ambassador at his desk: The shadow of his predecessor lay everywhere.

He resolved to do away with the old diplomacy once and for all: to generate an aura of North American goodwill so tangible that a recurrence of the days of Henry Lane Wilson—or even James R. Sheffield—would become unthinkable.

In some ways the new plan unfolded evenly enough. The slipping of U.S.-Mexican understanding that had occurred over the spring and summer mercifully relented in the fall. The oil and bond agreements, at least, seemed stable for the time being. The church-state armistice, it was true, did not seem quite as stable. Miscommunication had once again begun to flicker in the press, and evidence lay all around of continuing hostility. Reuben could not drive through the old city west of the Zócalo without noticing scars. The Cine Mundial, for example, had once been the Convent of Jésus María. The government library had once been the Bethlehemite's Church. There was a warehouse that used to be a Catholic college; a shop, a garage, and a newspaper office still presented forlorn baroque facades. It was an eerie sight.[17]

iii

For the present, though, the new ambassador clenched his teeth and determined to hold a steady course. To the extent that he would seek objectives, they must be hard, specific, and limited. One of them, of course, was the settlement of the claims. The claims commission had fortunately adjourned its Mexican session barely in time to miss Reuben's arrival. Fred Nielsen was still in the American commissioner's chair and more restive than ever. As long as he remained with the commission, the going would be ever more rocky and the prospects ever more slim. Reuben set about with renewed determination to stump for an en bloc settlement of the claims.[18]

Reuben's second task concerned the U.S.-Mexico boundary. Unhappily for the two countries, their common border posed endless problems. In the west it knifed across Baja California precisely at the point where Arizona would be denied access to the sea and Sonora access to the Colorado River. Even worse difficulties lay further south on the Rio Grande. No river in the world could have provided a less desirable boundary. Wide, shallow, and sometimes almost dry, the river at flood time could alter its course dramatically, now coil-

Ambassador Clark with President Ortiz Rubio and Foreign Minister Estrada: Beneath the pomp lay the problems.

ing like a python over Texas range land, now plunging southward into Chihuahua. Any two countries but the United States and Mexico might have overlooked this perfidity and hoped that the transfers of real estate would average out. It happened, however, that these particular neighbors had once fought a war over real estate, that memories of the war still lingered, and that politicians in Mexico had found that they could win enormous favor by crying, "Not another inch!" Accordingly, out in the dry chaparral where land would scarcely bring a dollar an acre, Mexicans and Americans argued over it as over Montezuma's gold; and where the river cut through downtown El Paso–Juárez they had something to argue about, for here the land was really worth Montezuma's gold. This was the so-called Chamizal district, and its name had rung through U.S.-Mexican relations like the Alamo. An aerial map of the Rio Grande's various courses through the Chamizal resembled a box full of snakes, and every few years a new snake had to be added. An international boundary commission had taken this map and carefully pieced out the six hundred acres of disputed territory, deciding which of them ought to be Mexican and which American. Then, in the interests of controlling the floods and stabilizing the boundary, the commission had proposed that the river be straightened artificially, that its course be shortened by some seventy miles, and that a dam be constructed below the two cities.[19] All of this had come about before Reuben's ambassadorship, yet he had been well aware of it. Under Morrow he had traveled to El Paso with the boundary commissioners to look over the disputed properties.[20] Now only the details remained to be worked out. But Reuben knew that the working would be difficult.

Reuben's third objective was the most important of all: doing away with the historic American posture of "Colossus of the North." There were two ways to accomplish the task. The first was by applying the principles of the Clark Memorandum and adhering to a rigid policy of noninterference in Mexican affairs. The second was by carrying forward Morrow's campaign of public relations: meeting the Mexicans, entertaining them, showing enthusiasm for their way of life.

Both techniques had their obstacles. There were endless temptations to intrude oneself into Mexican domestic affairs. For example, when Ortiz Rubio, who had taken special pains to befriend Reuben, was threatened with a political crisis, the Cuban ambassador, Márquez Sterling, called upon Reuben to step into the situation. Márquez Sterling was a suave little man with unctuous manners and an itch for playing the busybody. In his day he happened to have written a book excoriating Ambassador Henry Lane Wilson for the very sort of interventionism he was now urging upon Reuben Clark. Reuben could not help savoring the squelch. "Mr. Ambassador," he said with a sad, slow shake of the head, "you know the amenities of this situation. You are the last man in the world who should come to the American Ambassador and ask him to intervene in Mexican politics."[21]

Showing forth love had its moments of difficulty too. President Ortiz Rubio was quite visibly a Calles puppet without real power of his own, and he had ways about him that were odd, to say the least. Calles himself was distant and often inaccessible. And Enrique Estrada, the foreign minister, had apparently been sent by Providence to teach diplomats in Mexico humility. He had a habit of arriving hours early or hours late to formal soirées in order to see what damage he might inflict upon diplomatic etiquette. Smiles grew forced over the punch and cookies, and gourmet delights grew cold in the kitchen while awaiting the foreign minister's arrival. As an encore, he would then stay late—or leave early—to see what effect *that* might have. Since no one could leave before he did and no one could stay afterward, the effect was routinely devastating. Even the charitable Morrow referred to Estrada as "a three-ply s.o.b.—once on his mother's side, once on his father's, and self-made."[22]

Nevertheless Reuben Clark persevered. He knew he had much to learn about black-tie diplomacy. A man who could ride in from a hard day in the saddle and devour congealed gravy, as Reuben had often done in his Grantsville youth, obviously worked under a certain handicap; but he was an apt pupil. He secured a first-class protocol officer in the person of John M. Cabot, who became third secretary in December of 1930. Cabot's was a family acknowledged in a rhyme of the day:

> Here's to good old Boston,
> The home of the bean and the cod,
> Where the Astors speak only to the Cabots,
> And the Cabots speak only to God.[23]

As a Boston Cabot, John knew his protocol. He was the perfect counterpart to Elizabeth Lewis, and the two of them struck it off so well that a romance was soon in flower. But their marriage—which, to say the least, was performed in style—did not disable the ambassador. By that time he had mastered the diplomatic arts as well as sciences and could make protocol decisions on his own.[24]

Regarding his intuitive response to things Mexican, the ambassador needed no tutelage. "I have come to have for [the Mexicans]," he told a Salt Lake audience, "a sympathy and love I have not felt for any other people."[25] And he constantly worked to improve it. In an evening's spare moment, for example, he penned these lines.

Mexico—where the shadows of giant monuments of the greatest antiquity fall upon the culminating achievements of our most modern science.

Where art, so old there is no record of its creations, makes its impress upon the most modernistic of artistic conceptions.

Where an astronomy of unknown antiquity has left instruments of observation of an accuracy that rivals modern equipment.

Where an architecture as beautiful and characteristic as Greek at its best lies hidden and buried in primeval forests, while a new architecture itself centuries old, adorns the landscape.

Where the memories of a century old literature of great beauty and of a philosophy with profound truths still are the pride of a race which cherishes the traditions of a former culture while now developing a new literature and fostering a new philosophy.

Where deep-seated concepts of law and jurisprudence and government, the heritage of centuries gone, still influence and at times direct the course of legislation and governmental administration in what is characterized as the most progressive of modern thought.[26]

No envoy with pastimes such as this could fail to reach across the chasm of nationhood.

iv

Few people who saw Reuben Clark in action doubted his effectiveness. It hit the visitor full force, observed Howland Cox of the *Christian Science Monitor,* when he walked into the chancery and noted the striking resemblance between the man at the desk who was the American ambassador and the man in the picture on the wall who was the American president. Indeed, with his silver-white hair, finely tailored coat, and obligatory striped trousers, J. Reuben Clark cut a memorable diplomatic figure. Behind the broad mahogany desk in an office furnished like a fine old mansion, he might well have been the president.[27]

Reserved and yet accessible, the ambassador was ready to talk to anyone. When groups of Americans pressed him with difficult questions, he gave them their money's worth in answers. One group, meeting in the lecture hall of the Banco de México, was described by a reporter as being in a particularly skeptical frame of mind.

> Perhaps the ambassador sensed the questioning attitude of his fellow Americans. As he sat there listening to the introductory words of the presiding officer his rather quizzical gaze studied those whom he was to address, and when he arose to speak there flashed across his lips a smile that seemed to ask, "Well, what do you want me to say?"
>
> It was a friendly smile, a smile so genuine that before it faded his audience smiled back at him. Then he spoke of the country and its problems in such fashion that, for the first time, perhaps, his audience got the other fellow's side of the picture, and when he had concluded they applauded for two minutes, the man they had come to criticize. Minutes later, after he had gone, a tall serious American announced loudly: "If that man ever runs for President he will get my vote."[28]

This kind of performance was repeated over and over again, to clubs, to civic groups, to churches, to business associations, to politicians, to the diplomatic community. Indeed, the ambasssador seemed ubiquitous. He spoke to the Press Congress of the World; he delivered the commencement address at the American School in Pachuca; he officially opened the baseball season in Mexico City; he hosted the Boy Scouts of North America; he presented prizes at the country club golf tournament; he guided VIPs about the capital; he attended to political mail from Washington–and always with a message of peace and understanding between the two neighbors. "Our country, right or wrong," was a fine maxim for military men, he said to one distinguished gathering–but it had no place among diplomats.[29]

Reuben was equally impressive on the social front. There were luncheons at noon, teas at four, and dinners at eight–an endless whirl of them. Whether guests or hosts, the Clarks were not infrequently the couple of the hour, ranking alongside the president and first lady of Mexico. At the Opera Mexicana, for example, they were received with great enthusiasm, the opera glasses converging on the ambassadorial box when Reuben and Luacine took their places. Once a month there was a large reception at the embassy for the American community or the diplomatic corps, the guests numbering up to a thousand. Interspersed were smaller gatherings in honor of another diplomat, a Mexican official, a visiting dignitary, or a personal friend. Finally, there was the club life: the country club, the

Officially opening the baseball season in Mexico City: Military maxims had no place among the diplomats.

American Club, the Pan American Club. If between entertainment and speech-making a night somehow remained open, Reuben would fill it by bringing the embassy staff together, forcing the usual punch on them, and subjecting them to an opera on the Graybar phonograph. Only on the rarest occasions would the Clarks sit home by the fireplace and relax.[30]

Embassy affairs were noted for their brilliance. They usually began with a reception. Guests would move in file past the ambassador and ambassadress, their names and titles spoken softly by Counselor Lane. Reuben would greet them with great animation, his face

Diplomatic reception at the embassy, July 4, 1931: Showing forth an abundance of goodwill.

breaking into wreaths of smiles. Later on he would move among the guests like a down-home politician, greeting them informally, passing on a good story, revealing a diplomatic tidbit. From off in a corner an orchestra would play, lilting demurely over the sea of chatter. Or if it were a garden affair there might be a charro or marimba band thumping away amid the palm trees while the guests danced on the broad terrace. Through a doorway the table would be visible, loaded to creaking with rich buffet offerings. The poor of Mexico City might occasionally be found among the throng, quietly filling their pockets with food. Reuben Clark would manage to look the other way.[31]

If the entertainment in question was a formal dinner, its tone was appreciably more austere. The long table was spread with fine crystal and china. Baskets of flowers reflected brightly in the polished surfaces of the silver. Printed menus, rolled and tied, rested on each plate, and beside each lady's place was a wrapped favor. The seating of the guests was according to painstaking diplomatic architecture, one of whose axioms was that men and women were seated alternately but husbands never next to their own wives. The cocktail

Luncheon at the San Angel Inn: Dindonneau rôti *and* pommes dauphine *on a poor man's retirement.*

hour in the *sala,* what with the punch and all, was never the liveliest part of the evening, but when the guests assembled at the table the Clarks came into their own. First to be served was a thin soup. Then came the fish course. Then in succession followed the entree, the main course, the salad course, the dessert course, fresh fruit, cheese and crackers, and at the end coffee. All but the hardiest of appetites tended to falter somewhere into the salad course, with the result that Juan's elaborate sculptures of French ice cream often melted peacefully at the end. For the coffee there was a rigidly prescribed ritual. Luacine would rise and lead the ladies from the room to take their coffee elsewhere, leaving their consorts in command of the table. After a good cigar's length of informal discourse, the sexes were reunited for more decorous conversation. Reuben Clark, the Grantsville boy, did not exactly revel in the dancelike solemnity of it all, but he directed it with increasing sure-handedness and savoir faire. And he eventually preferred caviar to cold gravy.[32]

Diplomatic business was discussed at these gatherings, but never formally. There was an unwritten rule aginst such gaucherie and everyone would strain mightily not to break it. One day, for example, Reuben was informed that President Ortiz Rubio had weathered one crisis too many and was about to be forced out of office. As it happened, the fateful cabinet meeting was scheduled for the same afternoon on which Ambassador Clark was supposed to host the president and Mrs. Rubio at an embassy luncheon. Yet no one faltered. Promptly at one o'clock the limousines drew up to the embassy and the presidential party strolled in. Aside from the "healthy bulge" on the president's hip where he was obviously carrying a gun, nothing seemed amiss and everyone affected perfect nonchalance. "I was careful to see that I was never alone with the President," Reuben recalled. "I always had either the Ambassador with me, or Duplan, the undersecretary." After two hours of light pleasantries—and exquisite tension—President Ortiz Rubio amiably took his leave and was driven to the rendezvous that snuffed out his political life. This was old-time diplomacy at its best.[33]

v

Beneath the smiles the new ambassador was all business when it came to his diplomatic work. An old Mexican hand, he had come to

A visit to the jefe máximo: *A simple matter of knowing where the power lay.*

know a great deal about the inner workings of Mexican politics; and he implemented the knowledge skillfully. He knew, for example, when to go to the foreign minister, when to go to the president, and when to go to the *jefe máximo* himself. In the latter circumstance he would have to take the winding road to Cuernavaca where Calles ranched in ostensible isolation. The two of them got along well enough, and with every new encounter Reuben's admiration for the onetime president increased.

> On one occasion I was talking with him through an intepreter there, and I was expressing some apprehension ... about what might happen in Mexico. He said, "I am not worried about Mexico; I am worried about the United States." There was not a cloud on the horizon at that time, but he had fear that we were going to wander a bit. I repeat, he was a great man.[34]

Reuben was also sophisticated about political information and its uses. Most intelligence gathering of diplomats was, as he knew, relatively worthless, and he complained to the State Department about its quality. As a result of this wariness, Reuben was rarely taken in by the stories and rumors that colleagues swallowed whole. And Reuben had his own sources of information, some of them rather subtle. When his son returned from his church mission to France and chanced to be visiting the embassy, the ambassador posted him routinely in the room where high-level discussions were taking place. Reuben himself spoke no Spanish and he often relied on the Mexican translators, as Morrow had done. Reuben III, for all appearances, also spoke no Spanish, and he could affect an expression of bored abstraction that was entirely convincing. Actually the boy was fluent in Spanish and was monitoring every word of the Mexican officials—translated and otherwise—and after the meeting he would carefully write down everything he could remember. In time, his father acquired a reputation for clairvoyance.[35]

One needed such gifts and others too in dealing with Mexican politics on the one hand and American politics on the other. Often Reuben was simply caught in the crossfire. No American in Mexico, it seemed, could understand that the domestic laws of the United States did not fully protect him, and whenever there was trouble he would appeal to the politicians back home rather than to the American ambassador. As a result Reuben found himself defending, ad nauseam, the sovereignty of Mexican law in Mexico. But this was only the beginning of his troubles. Every point on Reuben's diplomatic agenda sooner or later ran afoul of American domestic politics. On the claims issues, for example, the ambassador was making hopeful progress on his lump-sum program when, in February of 1931, a resolution was introduced by Senator Borah and passed by both houses requiring Reuben to negotiate yet another extension of the claims commission. In point of fact, the claims commission had clearly failed in its mission. Fred Nielsen was behaving ever more erratically and the machinery grinding ever more creakily. Bouvé was laying plans for his own escape and defeat hung over the commission's proceedings like a pall. Nevertheless, Reuben Clark and the Mexican leadership wearily embarked on a new round of negotiations to renew the claims convention.[36]

With the Chamizal discussion too, American politics got in the way. Early in 1931, just at a point where the negotiations seemed to be moving, Senator Henry F. Ashurst of Arizona introduced a resolution in Congress proposing the purchase of nothing less than the whole of northern Mexico.[37] A hand grenade lobbed into the conference room would have done less damage. No sooner had the furor died down than the Arizonans were at it again, this time debating a petition for tidewater port privileges on the Gulf of California and overland rights-of-way across the Sonoran desert. Reuben reacted with quiet vehemence. "That such irresponsibility may sometimes actually shape the relationship of two nations," he wrote in cold anger, "seems not to be appreciated always by the *irresponsibles.*"[38]

But the ambassador was only beginning to hear from people back home. On February 3, 1931, he received a letter from Father John Burke. The religious settlement, said Burke, was not going at all well. Mexico had neither repealed the anticlerical laws nor amended the constitution. "The very fact that they stand unaltered," he wrote, "is evidence that the Government has by no outward sign at least receded from its old position." The Paulist father closed with an appeal for Reuben to step in and settle the matter once and for all.[39]

This was the moment of truth for Reuben's Mexican diplomacy. Dwight Morrow, as the ambassador well knew, would have readied his guns at this moment and sailed into the controversy once again; and Reuben Clark was obviously expected to do the same. Yet it was precisely at this point and over this question that the objectives of Morrow and Clark diverged. Morrow would settle the religious issue first and talk about diplomatic propriety later; Clark would behave properly first and talk about the church and state later. The success or failure of his own diplomacy absolutely depended on this point. "I am inclined to believe," Reuben replied to Father Burke,

that we must all have the proverbial patience of Job to work the situation out satisfactorily.... I am convinced that what the situation here now requires more than anything else is mutual patience, mutual forbearance, mutual charity, and a mutual disposition peacefully to get along.[40]

At least one Mexican agreed with this analysis. The hope that the ambassador "would not interfere as Mr. Morrow had done" was fervently expressed by Plutarco Elias Calles.[41]

For young Luacine Clark—or "La Señorita" as she now came to be known—embassy life was a fairy tale come true.[42] She was a sensitive, sloe-eyed child with winsome manners, a shy smile, and versatile giftedness; and at sixteen she was in love with love. If the vast granite mansion dazzled her mother, it fairly overwhelmed Luacine's scale of things. She had formed her ideas of the universe from 80 D Street, and that universe had not included San Simeon or The Breakers. Suddenly here were servants to dote on her and chauffeurs to drop her off at the American school where she found herself ex officio Queen of the May. It was true that her parents moved in a higher realm still and that their responsibilities tied them up much of the time. Still, if she had to sit alone several nights a week it was nice to have a palace to sit in, and her solitary meal was less forlorn at the end of a very long table. Occasionally La Señorita herself was the one to go out, and it was she, rather than her mother, who walked resplendently down the granite steps with her escort. The triumph of such evenings was denatured a little by the litany required before her departure.

> I am a Latter-day Saint.
> I am the ambassador's daughter.
> I will be home by midnight.

"Don't you trust me?" she once cried out in exasperation. "My dear," replied her father, "I don't even trust myself." Surprisingly often, Luacine was not excluded from official nightlife. Her father even allowed her to bring friends to embassy functions on the promise that they behave themselves. Seated discreetly behind the potted palms, these youngsters kept time to the orchestra and watched the fashionable ladies in their billowy dresses and cloche hats. Luacine went on most of the family excursions besides, and she came to know the magical city of Mexico as a resident, not just as a tourist. At school she fell in love—or thought she did—and that circumstance put a glow on her Mexican years that decades would never efface. But the heart of the experience was still the embassy. Her private bedroom and bath was a world of its own, complete with a wall safe onto the sweeping veranda, with a view of her own tropical garden beyond; and on moonlit nights she could sit out amid the dark shadows and see the lights burning in her father's chancery window. Or if her mood was really romantic, she could sit down to the Steinway piano Reuben had bought for her and play some Debussy. The sensuous melodies went perfectly with the muted pastels of the *sala,* with the marble columns and towering archways. The dullest servant on his nightly rounds would have been struck by the sight of La Señorita there at the keyboard. For who could fail to notice that she was Miranda?

Luacine Savage Clark also came into her own. As the days of the Mexican adventure steadily lengthened, she grew more and more confident in the exercise of her responsibilities. She planned menus, pored over guest lists, marshaled the servants, and stepped forward brightly to perk up a lagging conversation. And often she had high-velocity house guests to look after. Will Rogers could not resist another fling in Mexico, and Leopold Stokowski traveled down to conduct the Mexican National Orchestra. Bud Abbott of Abbott and Costello; Admiral Richard Byrd, the arctic explorer; and Cyrus McCormick of International Harvester all visited the Clarks—and there were many more. Even with her long apprenticeship in Washington, Luacine found that it took dogged effort to become first lady of an embassy. But she kept at it. By the time Elizabeth Lewis resigned to join the Boston Cabot family, the embassy no longer needed a professional social secretary; Luacine Clark could handle the job herself.

And not all of the job was confined to the embassy. Luacine found herself making speeches, visiting hospitals, touring orphanages, and directing welfare projects. Periodically she called upon Señora Ortiz Rubio, and the two of them went out together. As the ambassador's wife stepped from her limousine into the canopied entrance of the country club or the midday throng of the marketplace, all eyes turned respectfully toward her. She was the recluse of D Street no longer.

On Luacine's first trip to Mexico City she had been the humble tourist. Now, with that curious panache that only rank can bestow, she came to feel that the capital belonged to her—and she regarded the property lovingly. In time, through excursions with Reuben and on her own, she got to know the city well. To the east of the embassy lay the Zócalo, the National Palace, and the Cathedral Metropolitana. To the west lay Chapultepec Park and the fortresslike castle in which Maximilian had brooded over his Mexican empire. Less conspicuously than the landmarks, the individual sectors of the city also began to reveal their distinctiveness. Chapultepec Heights was where the mansions stood shoulder to shoulder, where pure-blooded Spanish *criollos* roared through the streets in high-powered American automobiles, where the flood tide of the revolution seemed not to have reached. The university quarter, by contrast, was where the streets were steep, dark, and stony, where tramways and dingy shops masked sleazy brothels, where Indians drove dogcarts through the narrow byways and herded turkeys to market. Then there was the shopping district, where Cinco de Mayo and Francisco Madero ran parallel like Broadway and Fifth Avenue through fashionable Mayfair stations, exclusive antique shops, and bastions of Americana such as Sanborns. There was the tourist district, featuring the Palace of Arts and the Alameda, where curio shops and confectionary stalls jammed the Avenidas Juárez and Hidalgo. Finally, there was the diplomatic district along the Paseo de la Reforma, where great monuments towered above tree-shaded boulevards, where smart pastel houses lined the manicured streets, and where President Huerta had drunk himself into a nightly stupor at the Colón Cafe.[43]

Luacine loved all of it. She traipsed through it like a schoolgirl on summer vacation, often with a reluctant ambassador in tow. They went to the clubs. They went to the American tea shops. They went to the open-air markets. They went to Sanborns. One weekend they went to Chapultepec Park, where authentic charros still clattered along the bridle paths in their knight-errant habiliments, and at the behest of the Mexican president they toured Chapultepec Castle. Unbeknown to them, their host had sent instructions that the ambassador should be given anything that particularly caught his eye. Sure enough, he took a fancy to an elegant silver bowl and picked it up admiringly. The following day it was delivered to the embassy.

They went to the national pawn shop and saw the warehouse full of jewelry pawned by the wealthy during the revolution. They went to the national museum and gazed at the underground ruins of Tenochtitlán, where the Aztecs had butchered their sacrificial victims and where troughs cut in the stone altars had carried away the blood. They visited the thieves' markets and the flower markets, and Reuben bought La Señorita a *china poblana* costume with embroidered blouse and sequined skirt.

Excursions out of town were doubly exciting. Of course, one ventured into the Mexican countryside only at some risk. Once the Clarks came upon three Americans who had been robbed of everything, including their clothes, by a wayward platoon of federal soldiers. But ambassadors were comparatively safe, and with Fernando resolutely at the wheel they went to Teotihuacán. Here it was that the Aztecs, upon settling the Valley of Mexico, had found the majestic ruins of two ancient pyramids, one of the sun and one of the moon. Traveling along the broad Highway of the Dead, the Clarks inspected these ruins with the awe of the first discoverers. The ambassador hazarded a theologically inspired guess that the arrangement of pyramids and altars might have corresponded to the buildings in Solomon's temple.* "If you have imagination you could really build something from this," he offered.

Their favorite picnic spot was Xochimilco, the floating gardens. Here they would hire a gondola and ply the labyrinth of canals separated by flower-banked islands. While punting placidly among the lily pads, they would open their picnic basket to discover what delicacies Juan had put up for them. Centuries ago the Aztec nobility had come to Xochimilco for just such relaxation as this. And Reuben Clark reflected upon such things. Indeed, the subject of the Aztecs and their civilization grew steadily in his awareness as in odd moments he still grappled with the riddle that was Mexico.

One sort of excursion made no sense at all to Fernando. On an occasional Sunday, the family rode out to San Pedro to attend services in the desolate little Mormon church there. The chapel was a whitewashed adobe room twenty by thirty feet. Worshipers sat on backless benches. Some came barefoot; others wore sandals. The men were dressed in their white cotton *pantalones* and coats, their dog-eared scriptures resting on their laps, while the women came draped in colorful serapes. Only the hymns were familiar.

---

*Mormons widely assumed that these ruins were those of the ancient civilizations chronicled in the Book of Mormon.

Nevertheless the service was unquestionably Mormon. There was a rickety wooden sacrament table and three folding chairs for the branch presidency. To the side stood an old pump organ on which a *mestiza* sister earnestly squeaked out "Come, Come, Ye Saints." Sometimes Reuben addressed the congregation after regular services were ended, for the law strictly forbade "foreign preachers." After that there were *abrazos* and kisses and adjournment to the shade outside for a feast of turkey and *mole*. As the ambassador, sitting crosslegged on the ground, deftly folded his tortilla and scooped up the spicy *mole* peon-style, Fernando rolled his eyes heavenward.

But the best excursion of them all was to Cuernavaca. Dwight Morrow, so it seemed, had left a few things behind. One of them was a villa named Casa Mañana in this, the favorite resort town of the Mexican men of state. Democratically, Ambassador Clark rotated the use of the dwelling among embassy personnel, taking his own turn along with the others. When a Cuernavaca weekend happened along, the diplomats, including Reuben, would move heaven and earth to break free for it. For, as the name Casa Mañana implied, it was a little world unto itself—and a distinctly agreeable one.

The ride to Cuernavaca was fifty miles of bad road—some of it still consisting of the volcanic blocks laid down in patterns by the Aztecs—winding, twisting, veering, descending from the heady altitude of the capital down to the langorous air of the tropics. The highway snaked its way through a dozen dusty towns, each with its

Ambassador Clark with the Mormon congregation of San Pedro: Turkey and mole, *peon style.*

569

Two vistas of Casa Mañana: Church bells on the blossom-scented air.

plaza, its marketplace, and its gingerbread cathedral. Beggar children ran to the roadside and cried for pesos. Dogs yapped fearfully from the safety of the banana trees. The sickly sweet smell of *pulque* filled the air with intoxication.

And then there it was—Cuernavaca—with the turrets of its rose pink cathedral rising into the Friday evening sunset; and down a narrow, winding lane was Casa Mañana. It was the kind of place that one imagines when dreaming of the Latin tropics: all white stucco, bright tiles, and gleaming parquet inside; and terraces, fountains, and foaming bougainvillea outside. In the coolness of its rooms one could sleep in carelessly on a Sunday morning and listen to the soft peal of church bells in the blossom-scented air.

Not to say that the ambassador was disposed to sleep in. He was up at dawn, Grantsville-style, with his briefcase open and his papers spread before him. But others were more mellow. They would stroll about the lawns and gardens or go for a dip in the pool. Beside the pool was a warm brick patio filled with lounging furniture and large jar planters of petunias—perfect for a lazy afternoon. On a terrace below there stretched a long narrow lawn bordered by flowers and shrubs. At one end was a blue-tiled fountain, its water trickling perpetually from a mossy wall above, and through a gate by the fountain opened a secret garden of tropical delights. One visit to Casa Mañana was enough to show why Charles Lindbergh fell in love there.

At the end of a day of lolling about this sleepy paradise, dinner was served in a vine-covered bower. Then, after La Señorita and her guests had retired to their bedrooms, Reuben and Luacine would sit out under the stars with their own guests and talk of things that made life worthwhile. It was a nice respite from the world of ambassadorial responsibility.

vii

The full measure of that responsibility could only be assessed in due time and from some distance. Reuben worked indefatigably throughout the twenty-eight months of his ambassadorship, but in the end he had no single stunning achievement to place beside those of his predecessor. Indeed, his life in Mexico was marked by a striking calm in the diplomatic weather. Dwight Morrow had braved one crisis after another. Josephus Daniels, Reuben's successor, would have an even worse time of it. But Reuben Clark saw only peace and goodwill. Perhaps that was an assessment in itself.

With the claims imbroglio there was no final victory. Reuben ultimately succeeded in extending the claims convention for another two years, but the victory was a hollow one. Congress failed to ratify the extension of the special commission, possibly on account of an exceedingly unfortunate exchange between Commissioner Nielsen and his two colleagues in June of 1931. The general commission fared little better; it met in Washington between May 5 and July 15 of 1931, until something else happened. "As a consequence of an incident provoked by the American Commissioner," reported the *Memoria* of the Mexican secretariat of foreign relations, "the ninth session of the Commission was, at first, suspended, and then declared terminated in August 1931." The Mexican claims commission never convened again. Eventually, there was a settlement—or, more accurately, half a settlement—based on the lump-sum principle.[44]

On petroleum and agrarian matters Reuben held the line, which was the best he had hoped to do. Yankee exploitation continued to be a matter of controversy among the Mexicans; and, while that was the case, oil licenses and drilling permits had a way of sinking into the bureaucratic quagmire. Reuben Clark could not rescue all of

The National Agrarian Commission on the steps of the embassy: A far cry from Tlahualilo.
Principal officers of the embassy shown: Arthur Bliss Lane, far left in front row; Stanley Hawks, far left in back row; John Farr Simmons, third from left in back row; and Joseph Satterthwaite, far right in back row.

them, but he rescued enough to keep oil out of the headlines. The business of land expropriation was handled systematically by the National Agrarian Commission, consisting of agriculture minister Manuel Pérez Treviño and ten principal Mexican *potentes.* The commission met regularly with the American embassy staff and threshed out troublesome cases. The group once posed for a photograph on the front steps of the embassy, and Ambassador Clark, in his dark coat with satin piping and his natty striped trousers, looked every inch the diplomat. Yet he was never quite able to convince the folks back home that Mexican agrarian reform was legal, moral, or constitutional. Mexican ways were different, he said over and over again, but they were not necessarily inferior.[45] He had come a long way from his role as counsel for Tlahualilo.

A decidedly unhappy ending came for Reuben's church-state diplomacy. During his ambassadorship, relations between Catholics and the Mexican government slid steadily from bad to worse. If there was no open warfare, as in the days of the *Cristeros,* there was a good deal of abject surrender. Churches, rectories, and seminaries that had been confiscated during the controversy were restored tardily or not at all. *Cristero* leaders were systematically hunted down and killed by vigilantes, some forty-one of them in a single Jalisco execution. When the apostolic delegate, Ruiz y Flores, urged the president to honor the promises made by his predecessor, Ortiz Rubio replied that Portes Gil had made no promises.[46]

The dilemma posed by this situation for Reuben Clark was acute, and his old friend Father Burke made it even more so. But Reuben had set his course. He replied to Burke, as he had to Calles earlier, that the problem was entirely domestic and, this being the case, that he as ambassador could make no representations concerning it. Reuben Clark the lawyer had another reason for keeping hands off. The statements which had been issued by Portes Gil and Archbishop Ruiz on the afternoon of June 21, 1929, were nothing more than that: statements. They could hardly be regarded as contracts in law.[47]

Even so, the ambassador worried considerably about the downhill plummet of church-state relations. As an architect of the original settlement he was concerned about Mexico gaining a bad press in the United States, and as a human being he was concerned about the peace of the land. Both concerns took a quantum leap in June of 1931 when Catholics prepared to celebrate the four hundredth anniversary of the appearance of the Virgin of Guadalupe.[48] Devotees of the Virgin worked themselves to the brink of religious frenzy. The atmosphere grew tense. Then somehow a rumor caught fire that the government was planning to remove the Virgin's sacred shawl from the Cathedral of Guadalupe and transfer it to the old palace on the Zócalo. Mexico City trembled as if anticipating one of its famous earthquakes.[49]

Unfortunately, the man who held the title of president, Ortiz Rubio, and the man who held the powers of state, Plutarco Calles, were not on speaking terms at the moment. And Ortiz Rubio was worried. He sent his majordomo to the American embassy to ask Ambassador Clark to intervene. Reuben was worried too. He wondered if the time had not come to temper diplomatic purism with some Yankee common sense. To avert the riot and massacre feared by the president, he set out at once for Cuernavaca to see General Calles.

I stated that whether or not this mantle was removed from the Cathedral to the Museum was none of my business and none of my Government's business—I appreciated that; nevertheless, I wished to point out to him that if this were moved and there was a riot and a great many people killed, that it would present a problem because of the trouble which the Catholics in the United States would make, declaring that the situation was out of hand and of course asking for intervention. I said that was my sole interest in the matter and I presented that merely for his consideration.[50]

The old *caudillo* smiled indulgently, possibly at the ambassador's string of disclaimers. There was no intention of removing the sacred shawl from Guadalupe cathedral, he said. But as Reuben arose to take his leave, there was a follow-up remark that could only be called chilling. "I am told," said the man who ruled Mexico, "that there are some Americans who would pay a large price for it."[51]

From that point onward, church-state relations unraveled ever more rapidly. In June, Adalberto Tejeda, *potente* of Veracruz, signed a law limiting the number of priests to one per hundred thousand inhabitants, whereupon the churches of the state again closed their doors. Congress then passed a similar law restricting to twenty-five the number of priests in the Federal District. By September things were in a desperate state once again, and Pope Pius XI broke all precedent to speak out publicly. President Rodriguez, who was now in office, accused the Pope of trying to foment rebellion. An even more forceful reply was entered by the Chamber of Deputies, which ordered the arrest of apostolic delegate Ruiz y Flores and summarily expelled him from Mexico.[52]

Over all of these proceedings the spirit of Dwight Morrow brooded accusingly. No one publicly charged Reuben Clark with a failure to measure up to expectations, but no one had to. Morrow himself passed away quietly in October, just as Archbishop Ruiz was stepping from the train in El Paso. His career in politics had been a disappointment. "I find the work in the Senate somewhat puzzling for me," he had written to Reuben in a last gloomy letter. "I am not enjoying it very much."[53] Neither was Reuben. He may or may not have heard about the remark made by Father Walsh to Archbishop Orozco y Jimenez, who, exiled in Rome, chanced to ask one day what had been the guarantee that the 1929 agreement would be honored. "Morrow," the Jesuit replied, "but Morrow died on us!"[54]

Nevertheless Reuben held to his course. There was more at stake here than the well-being of the Catholic church. It was imperative, as he believed, to destroy the mentality of knee-jerk interventionism, and his restraint in this matter went far toward doing just that. Never again would a U.S. ambassador deal with the Mexican government in terms implying the threat of war. In fact, later on, when teachers in Yucatán were required to profess atheism and when Archbishop Díaz was thrown into jail like a common criminal, Reuben's successor, following his lead, remained pointedly silent and aloof.[55] This, in truth, was Reuben's major diplomatic achievement—the fulfillment of his wish to abolish intermeddling—but it came at the price of turning his back on Mexican Catholicism. With unconscious symbolism the ambassador purchased a vestment cloth on the street corner one day and hung it on his wall—where its crimson brilliance gradually faded to a dusty pink.[56]

In the river rectification negotiations, Reuben had cause for pride. After the two disastrous proposals from Arizona, the Rio

Grande talks very nearly broke down. Only by the most determined of efforts did the ambassador manage to salvage them. Throughout 1931 and most of 1932 he continued the discussions in that same spirit, quietly pledging not to take no for an answer. He received one boost when the abrasive Estrada resigned as foreign minister and was replaced by cool and sophisticated Manuel Tellez, whom Reuben had known well as Mexican ambassador to the United States. Finally, on August 25, 1932, Ambassador Clark was able to telephone Washington with the happy news that he and Tellez had reached an agreement on the Chamizal question. All that remained was the approval of the two governments.[57]

It was just at that point, however, that Ortiz Rubio was forced from the presidency; during the ensuing confusion the boundary negotiations were temporarily set aside. "Reuben was disappointed over his case," Luacine reported. "Another delay—Plenty of mañana about his work."[58] Plenty indeed—just as executive administration began to rally under the leadership of Abelardo Rodriguez, the presidential cabinet decided to assert itself. On October 11, Tellez reported that some cabinet members "indicated a disposition to be inquisitive" about the Chamizal and wanted to know exactly how much land would be transferred in the proposed settlement. When Reuben replied that the amount was impossible to determine exactly, the Mexicans broke off negotiations.[59]

Here was where the American ambassador's intelligence network came into play. He learned through his sources that the motives of the cabinet were not entirely unmixed. One member, it seemed, stood "to shine as an international lawyer" by the interruption of the talks. Another member had his own personal political reasons, and a third had acted out of spite for Tellez. As if to confirm this last report, Tellez, who almost alone had promoted the Chamizal settlement, notifed Reuben on December 20 that he was being forced to submit his resignation. Most of the cabinet members, however, were simply stalling in hopes of winning a better bargain from the soon-to-be-inaugurated Roosevelt administration in Washington. Reuben saw his time running out.[60]

He resorted to his secret weapon—Calles. After touching the proper bases, Reuben, at the end of December, made the tortuous drive over Ajusco Pass to Cuernavaca. There, in the company of the president and the new foreign minister, J. M. Puig Casauranc, he confronted the grizzled old *jefe máximo* with the extremity of the case. They were seated comfortably in Calles's living room, and the night air was heavy with Mexican fragrance. Reuben, counting the final days of his ambassadorship, was not unmindful of a parallel circumstance four years earlier when, in the anguish of the oil controversy, he had come to Calles with the same gentle threat that he was about to redeploy. At that time it had backfired.

The Democrats were coming into office, Reuben began. It was true that they might do better for Mexico in settling the Chamizal, but they might also do worse. "I said," the ambassador later recorded, "that inevitably the new Administration . . . would reexamine the entire foreign policy of the United States, including the policy with Mexico." Who knew, he hinted, but what the golden age of Morrow might not just fade away? General Calles thought for a long moment; then he bestirred himself. Perhaps it would be possible, he said, to base a settlement on the river rectification alone, without opening the Pandora's box of Chamizal. It was the territorial transfers that rankled with his countrymen, but if the river could be straightened without ceding land "the adjustment could be concluded at once."[61]

Now Reuben had to decide whether to settle for half a loaf. He was aided by the American boundary commissioner, who wrote him in January of "the great anxiety of the people of El Paso to have the river rectification and flood control provided for, either with or without the adjustment of the Chamizal controversy."[62] On January 14 Reuben decided to go for the settlement. Lives and property in the El Paso–Juárez Valley had to be the first consideration.

From this point the negotiations proceeded apace. Drafts of a settlement were drawn up, exchanged, revised, and agreed upon, all within the next two weeks. By February 1, 1933, Ambassador Clark and Foreign Minister Puig Casauranc were able to sign a convention providing for the rectification of the river and the stabilization of the international boundary.[63] In April the treaty sailed through the Senate and soon afterward the bulldozers began their work. The troublesome issue of the Chamizal would remain unresolved for the next thirty years, but the Rio Grande itself was subdued. Two years after he left Mexico, Reuben received a letter from the El Paso boundary commissioner and a photograph of the completed construction. "At least," quoted the letter, "we have the river fixed thanks to you."[64]

Ambassador Clark had fixed more than the river. In broad and amorphous terms that do not lend themselves to newspaper head-lines, he had fixed U.S.-Mexican relations as well. Texas oil man Mi-chael Hogg put the case succinctly to his friend Colonel House, while the two of them were conspiring to keep Reuben in Mexico for another four years.

In the old days, before the coming of Morrow and Clark, our Government and our citizens in Mexico moved under a constant cloud of fear, suspicion and resentment, both in official and business circles. In recent years there has been a pronounced change. The old haunting fears of the "Colossus of the North" have given way to a feeling of mutual confidence and respect. As we all know, there has been harmony, understanding and cooperation between the two Governments as never existed before.... All of this is the result of slowly built up confidence, based upon an American policy of frank, fair and courteous dealing.[65]

If this was an odd sort of blessing for a conservative Republican to be receiving from a liberal Democrat, it was surely not undeserved. A policy of "frank, fair and courteous dealing" had been Reuben's main objective from the beginning.

viii

Christmas of 1932 was the most poignant of the four the Clarks spent in Mexico. The Republicans had lost the election. The depres-sion had taken on nightmare proportions. Reuben, perforce, would soon be leaving Mexico as U.S. ambassador; his resignation was timed to coincide with the changing of the guard in Washington. There was a sense of finality in the air, a suggestion of things com-ing to an end, a locking away of history. As Luacine Clark surveyed her palace by the light of a winter's day, it still seemed to her the most beautiful place on earth. She began packing up her fine silver.

The ambassador himself was strangely quiet. He was, after all, sixty-two years of age and, as he had been saying for some time, ready to step down.[66] But down to what? As Morrow's legal aide he had amassed substantially the retirement of his dreams—several hun-

Farewell banquet for the ambassador: A violation of fundamental precepts.

dred thousand dollars' worth of it. And now it was gone for parties and dinners and luncheons and teas–scores of them–and for the cigarettes he had furnished to the embassy by the thousands, only to watch the Mexicans pocket them in handfuls because they were American. Any guess of his net worth at that moment might well have occasioned Reuben's peculiar moodiness–he was flat broke. But he was not worrying about personal finances. He was inwardly marking the anniversary of an event that had changed his life dramatically and would soon change it even more. A few days before Christmas of 1931 a large manila envelope had arrived special delivery for him from LDS church headquarters in Salt Lake City. Reuben had retired to his study with the envelope and had made no mention of it afterward. For precisely a year now he had been guarding its secret, but the time was approaching when the secret would have to be divulged. His son had an inkling of what was coming; he had chanced to stop by church headquarters one day and had suddenly found himself privy to a remarkable confidence. Like his father, young Reuben knew how frightening the secret was.

It was not long, though, before the send-off syndrome seized hold of them all. If life in the embassy had been gay heretofore, now it was downright frenetic. Farewell luncheons were given by the country club, the American Club, the University Club, the Foreign Correspondents Club, the Chamber of Commerce, and President and Señora Rodriguez. Banquets were lavished upon them by the ministers of China, Spain, and Great Britain, and the ambassador of Japan. The Pan American Round Table could fit neither luncheon nor banquet into the ambassador's hectic schedule, so it gave him a reception instead.[67]

Not to be outdone by foreigners, Puig Casauranc put on an evening's entertainment that surpassed them all. It began with a dinner for the diplomatic corps and ended with a reception for the elite of Mexico City.[68] Arthur Bliss Lane, who had seen a number of soirées in his day, reported this one as the most brilliant in memory. Both Calles and the president, it seemed, wanted nothing spared for the retiring ambassador, for they too were privately attempting to retain him at his post.[69] In its own romantic way, official Mexico was clearly trying to say something.

To Puig Casauranc's flowing toasts and tributes, Reuben responded with one of his own. It was an apt farewell. It began in the ordinary way with manifestations of love and respect. The old diplomacy, said the ambassador, was supposed to have two fundamental precepts: that the ambassador should despise the minister of foreign affairs and that he should hate the people to whom he was sent. "Both of these precepts," said Reuben, "I have grossly violated."

But the speech at that point swerved away from cocktail grandiloquence and turned to a subject that had occupied Reuben Clark's thoughts for a great while. "Mr. Minister," he said,

the mists that obscure the history of the past of your people hang very near and very heavy, but through them we dimly perceive civilization after civilization rise, flourish, and decay. We glimpse monuments of civilizations greater than any heretofore known; we hear echoes of desperate conflicts in which were forged the iron qualities that characterize the people.

History records a patient, indomitable racial will to hold the heritage of this past, a heritage of culture, of character, of experience, and of wisdom, which is a graven record upon the mind and heart of those remnants of former peoples that make the present race.

It has seemed to me, Mr. Minister, that all this past is an integral and vital part of the present, and that, therefore, to understand the present we must comprehend something at least of the past.

It is in this view and in this spirit that I have approached my work in Mexico; and this view and this spirit have given me a tolerance for the ardent zeal with which at times the race has surged to and fro; they have given me a sympathy with the aspirations and ideals proclaimed in your revolution; they have accounted, and have given excuse, if not reason, for the measures which always mark a rebellion, when a people, downtrodden for generations, grope upwards for the light of the sun. This view and this spirit have given me the faith that, coming down through the generations, there lies somewhere in the deep recesses of the racial mind of Mexico, a spark of that cumulated wisdom and experience, descended from former ages and greatness, that shall in due time blaze forth and light the race along a new path, leading to greater glories.[70]

This was Reuben Clark's public benediction upon the revolution he had once damned—and it was his final assault on the mystery that was Mexico.

x

After that evening, February 10, everything was a blur. There were goodbyes and tearful embraces exchanged with the embassy staff. There was the last drive down the Paseo de la Reforma. There were friends at the railroad station—some three hundred strong—and the platform piled high with flowers. There was a private car named *Hidalgo*—and this time the ambassador did not decline the use of it. There was a Mexican orchestra playing above the hubbub, and as the train pulled away it swung moodily into "La Golondrina" ("When the Swallows Return").[71] There was the ride across the desert, the report to the president, and the official submission of the resignation. There was a briefing with the president-elect, too. He had been reading the reports from Mexico, and when he said he regretted Mr. Clark's resignation there was genuine sincerity in his voice.[72] There were homecoming parties—an endless cycle of them—rounded off by a grand reception in the Salt Lake Twentieth Ward at which general authorities of the church were strangely prominent.[73] And finally there were the newspaper tributes, most of them a little grandiose

but every once in a while one that displayed real insight. "Mr. Clark
... has distinguished himself," editorialized the *Mexico City Excelsior,*
"by a virtue which is not common among diplomats: that of not
putting himself forward, of not calling attention to himself, of observing a prudent reserve that has won for him the esteem of all social classes in Mexico."[74] That was the quietest one. Reuben liked it
the best.

xi

But none of these events really marked the end of the Mexican
adventure for J. Reuben Clark. Rather, the memory that lived on,
the moment of supreme triumph, turned out to be a private one. It
was of an early evening at the embassy in the twilight of autumn.
The Clarks were preparing to entertain. Servants were still bustling
around starchily, and Sabino was waiting mannequinlike for the arrival of the first guests. Reuben, resplendent in his Prince Albert,
had paused in the *sala* to fumble with an errant cufflink when he
looked through the vaulted archway to see what he described as an
apparition. It was Luacine Savage Clark, standing in a floor-length
blue gown, arranging some calla lilies on the piano—easily at that
moment the most beautiful woman on earth.

This, Reuben told himself, was it. For this he had slaved and
sacrificed his entire life. For this he had gone to the Grantsville
eighth grade over and over again, and then to the university, and
then to Columbia law school, and then to the State Department.
This was the dream that lay behind those endless pilgrimages back
and forth across the continent, that had taken him in and out of
public service, in and out of private practice, up and down through
boom and bust looking for El Dorado. Here was the imposing mansion. Here was the well-stocked library with its crackling hearth.
Here was the man of account and here were the people coming to
honor him. And here, vastly more important than all else, was the
woman whose sacrifice, whose gallantry, whose quiet self-abnegation
had made it all possible. Was it a dream still, or was it reality? A case
could be made either way.

Reuben thought of a song, one of his favorites, by Jessie Evans
Smith. He listened to Verdi and Wagner any night of the year, but

in the few sentimental moments of his life he liked Jessie Evans Smith.

> Four ducks on a pond,
> The grass bank beyond,
> The blue sky of spring,
> White clouds on the wing.
>
> What a little wee thing
> To remember with tears;
> To remember for years,
> With tears, with tears. . . .

Tears filled the ambassador's eyes. But this was no way to behave! Tough and cynical Puig Casauranc would be walking through that door any moment, a cigar clamped in his teeth, and it would not do for him to see the U.S. ambassador wiping tears.

The moment passed quickly and Reuben hurried to receive his guests. But he never forgot it. And Jessie Evans Smith could always bring it flooding back upon him with her Victorian sentimentality. It was the point in life when J. Reuben Clark knew that he had found success.

EPILOGUE:

BETWEEN EAST AND WEST

On a summer day in the late 1950s, Rowena Miller, clearing up some odds and ends in the office where she worked, decided to clean out the old closet. As she pulled the dusty items from the shelf, she could see through the open doorway her employer, J. Reuben Clark, writing busily at his desk. He was second counselor to the president of The Church of Jesus Christ of Latter-day Saints, and his office looked out across a placid setting of trees and flowers, with the spires of the temple in view. He was an important man in this billion-dollar organization; his was the genius behind its daily operations. He had held this position and similar ones ever since the spring general conference of 1933, when President Heber J. Grant had stunned the faithful by naming Brother Clark—who had never even been a bishop, much less a general authority—to the First Presidency of the church. But all that had happened a quarter of a century ago.

Amid the rubble and refuse of the closet, Rowena found some unmarked cans of movie film. Should she keep them or throw them away? She decided to find out for herself. A short while later she was back with a sixteen-millimeter projector, adroitly threading the film through a maze of wheels and sprockets. She switched off the room lights and turned on the machine. There were flashes of one scene and then another, both of them unfamiliar, and then the camera settled on a sweeping stone edifice, colonnaded like a Roman temple and surrounded by tropical vegetation. Two people walked through massive French doors and down the granite steps. One of them was President Clark himself, looking a good deal younger and distinctly ambassadorial; the other was Sister Clark, dressed in the dimly recollected style of the depression, smiling shyly at the camera and shielding her eyes from the sun. Sister Clark had been gone now for more than a decade.

585

Rowena looked up to see President Clark standing in the doorway behind her, his arms folded and a strangely distant expression on his face. He closed the door to the hall and pushed up a leather chair. "Rowena," he said in a voice audibly shaken, "let's see that one again."[1]

ii

J. Reuben Clark was a general authority with a difference, and in some obscure way it was understood that the difference related to the images that now flickered before them on the screen. This was true. The legacy of Reuben's worldly career had profoundly affected the development of his religious career afterward. It had made him a church leader quite like no other.

In the first place, he had continued in some fashion his tradition of public service. Franklin Roosevelt had meant what he said about not wanting Reuben Clark to retire. In the fall of 1933, some months after Reuben had joined the First Presidency, Roosevelt inquired whether he might be available for an assignment of considerable importance.[2] What the president had in mind was the Seventh International Conference of American States to be held at Montevideo in December. Some rather weighty issues would be up for discussion. Would Reuben be free to attend as a delegate? The offhand reply had to be negative, of course, and in conversing with President Grant Reuben made fully clear his devotion to church responsibilities. Unexpectedly, however, President Grant took a different view. "Go, by all means," he said. "We need every good connection we can get to the Federal Government."[3]

Montevideo was only the first of several assignments. The following year Reuben was asked to serve on the quasi-official Foreign Bondholders Protective Council, charged with the task of salvaging several billion dollars' worth of defunct bonds. Once again, Reuben saw the matter in terms of patriotism and President Grant saw it in terms of public relations. Work on the foreign bondholders council occupied Reuben's time intermittently for half a decade.[4]

Other tasks included service on the Committee of Experts on the Codification of International Law, 1936, and the Commission of Experts on Codification of International Law of Phi Delta Phi, 1945 to

President J. Reuben Clark and Rowena Miller in the Clark library at 80 D Street: A general authority with a difference.

1950.⁵ And there were public addresses of one kind and another and a good many opportunities for consultation. Reuben Clark had remained very much a public figure.

iii

In the second place, the events of Reuben's public career had had a way of reasserting their relevance from time to time, and President Clark was not slow to apply the necessary lessons. He cut a princely figure as he stood before the semiannual general conferences of the church, and he knew how to lay down the law. That the law was often mirthless was reflected in the titles of his addresses: "Slipping from Our Old Moorings," "Our Dwindling Sovereignty," "The Awesome Task of Peace."⁶ There was little here of cheery optimism.

These addresses recapitulated the great battles Reuben had fought. One of them was isolationism, which Reuben defined not as a withdrawal from the world but as the reassertion of America's moral leadership. "I believe that President Wilson had the true principle when he spoke of the strength and power of the moral force of the world," he said. "I believe that moral force is far more potent than physical force."⁷ A second theme was interventionism, which Reuben saw as having been blown by the Second World War into a monstrous national conceit. Not only was the United States now aiming to run the world, he asserted, but it was aiming to reshape the world in its own image.

We must give up this idea too many of us have, that our way of life and living is not only the best, but often the only true way of life and living in the world, that we know what everybody else in the world should do and how they should do it. We must come to realize that every race and every people have their own way of doing things, their own standards of life, their own ideals, their own kinds of food and clothing and drink, their own concepts of civil obligation and honor, and their own views as to the kind of government they should have.⁸

Understandably, Reuben fought the United Nations as he had fought the League of Nations two decades before. "We are entering this [organization]," he said, "with the blind infatuation of a nation of Darius Greens, ignoring all laws, disregarding all experiences, and blindly and blithely moving out with the confidence of a set of ignoramuses."⁹

The atomic bomb shocked him terribly. In view of feelings that recoiled from the use of poison gas or submarines, he could barely find words for Hiroshima. It was the "crowning savagery of the war," he said; it was "world tragedy."¹⁰ And he viewed the bomb as but a prelude to the holocaust to come—a holocaust he perceived as being carefully planned by the American military establishment. "If the plans of the militaries carry," he predicted in 1945, "we shall become as thoroughly militarized as was Germany at her best, or worst."¹¹ Reuben Clark interpreted the whole of the cold war in that light. "We are becoming a blaspheming, unchaste, non-Christian, Godless race," he would declare in a final message to the Church. "Spiritually we seem ripe for another war."¹²

There were other themes in his public discourse. He lashed out at the New Deal and defended the individual from what he saw as omnivorous government encroachment. He continued to speak for the power of law—international law specifically—and labored indefatigably to bring about the old dream of codification. He saw American constitutionalism as being imperiled by such abuses as the "war powers doctrine"—this, significantly, on the eve of Vietnam—and he wrote a book, *Stand Fast by Our Constitution,* in an energetic effort to defend it.¹³ His constitutionalism, like that of the Founding Fathers, was of a dark and defensive nature, and it placed all hope on the continued balancing of one human weakness against another. Thus, for him, the "great fundamental" of the Constitution, the separation of powers, was directly inspired by God. The overturning of this principle, he said in a voice of warning, "would ... do violence to my religion."¹⁴

Yet for all his pessimism, Reuben never came close to writing off the United States. When he donated some book royalties to the church's Relief Society and the money was used to erect a magnificent flagpole outside Relief Society headquarters, President Clark happened by at the dedication. As he looked up at Old Glory snapping in the breeze, he was all but speechless. "You couldn't have pleased me more," he said quietly to President Belle Spafford. "I love my country."¹⁵

589

United States delegates to the Montevideo conference: Tough questions and diplomatic swordplay.
From left to right: Spruille Braden, Alexander W. Weddell, J. Butler Wright, Sophonisba Breckinridge, Ernest Gruening, Cordell Hull, and J. Reuben Clark, Jr.

iv

This was the J. Reuben Clark that the Mormons knew, the one they saw standing behind the pulpit at general conference. The extent to which his words of warning had grown out of his eastern experience they never fully appreciated, but the messages themselves were plain enough. Yet there was another J. Reuben Clark, one that was not so much in public view, and he too remained tied to his eastern past. In the world of experience quite as much as the world of exhortation, Reuben's life continued to unfold from his bygone public career.

His work at the Seventh Pan-American Conference in Montevideo represented such an unfolding. Reuben was invited to attend the conference as one of the five American delegates. Important work was on the agenda—including a discussion of the right of intervention. Reuben was not certain that he wanted to take up such an issue with Latin Americans on one side of the table and New

Dealers on the other; but when he learned that staid and conservative Cordell Hull of Tennessee (Roosevelt's secretary of state) would head up the delegation, he decided to come aboard.[16]

With most of his colleagues in the American delegation Reuben was well pleased. Alexander W. Weddell, U.S. ambassador to Argentina, and J. Butler Wright, now minister to Uruguay, were the principals, joined by New York attorney Spruille Braden and a delightful spinster with the improbable name of Sophonisba P. Breckenridge, whose concern with the conference was strictly humanitarian and whose horrified fascination with diplomatic swordplay provided comic relief.[17] With all of them on board the *American Legion,* chatting amiably in the lounge or on deck chairs, the New Deal seemed far away—except, that is, for Ernest Gruening. Gruening was not an official member of the U.S. delegation, but as a self-styled expert on Latin America he had attached himself to the group as an advisor and was making the most of it. There were shades of James Brown Scott about Gruening, too. He was a firm adherent of the principle, announced by Scott's International Commission of American Jurisconsults in Rio de Janeiro in 1927, that "no state has the right to intervene in the internal or external affairs of another."[18] Gruening, in fact, was traveling to Montevideo to translate that principle into action.[19]

Reuben himself was an opponent of intervention, but he vehemently disagreed with Gruening on one crucial point. Reuben believed that if a strong nation like the United States pledged itself in law not to intervene, it then became a target for every kind of insolence and spite—and invited retaliation for the wrongs of the past. "We know we're not going to intervene," he once explained to his son, "and they know we're not going to intervene, and we know they know—but you just can't bind yourself legally."[20] This was Reuben's typically cautious way of backing forward. He had counted too many American dead in his day to reason otherwise.

So Clark and Gruening established themselves as adversaries from the outset. It was a fascinating duel. On his side Gruening had the advantage of temerity. "Mr. Secretary," he said to Hull on the first day at sea, "the one issue that concerns every Latin-American country is intervention. We should come out strongly for a resolution abjuring it." When Hull objected that such a resolution would get him pilloried in the Hearst newspapers, Gruening replied: "Mr. Secretary, if I could achieve that for you, I would feel that I had not come in vain."²¹ And this was only the warm-up. By the time the *American Legion* pulled into Montevideo harbor, Ernest Gruening had gone on record for scrapping the Platt Amendment, continentalizing the Monroe Doctrine, renouncing the theory of interposition,* and, for good measure, forcibly ending the Chaco War between Bolivia and Paraguay.²² This last item did not strike him as inconsistent with nonintervention.

On his side Reuben had the advantage of experience. He was the elder statesman of the delegation, and Hull seemed to lean on him instinctively. After many a lively discussion in which Gruening would hold forth grandiloquently—and Sophonisba Breckenridge would marvel—Secretary Hull would quietly ask Reuben Clark to remain behind and the two of them would make policy decisions. "I asked him," Reuben recorded, "if he objected when I butted into his conversations, such as the one he had with Gruening this morning. He said he would like to have me come in whenever I wanted to. He said Gruening was a wild man."²³

The tug-of-war continued at the conference proper. From the pageantlike inaugural session in the Legislative Palace on December 3 to the division of work among the conference's ten commissions and twenty-four subcommissions to the behind-the-scenes diplomacy of all parties concerned, the intervention issue hung in the air like an electrical charge. No question was seemingly detached from it. Much as he would like to sign Mr. Hull's declaration on tariffs, boomed out Haiti's Antoine Pierre-Paul in thick Gullah French, he could not do so without permission from the American fiscal comptroller who ruled his island.²⁴ There was clearly a showdown in the works.

Reuben Clark had never scrambled so hard or so fast since the days of the League fight. After a week of heavy politicking, he succeeded in assembling a cabal of delegates pledged to defeat the issue. Everything was mapped out meticulously and perfectly timed, the plan to be activated by Argentina's Saavedra Lamas moving to refer

---

*This was the doctrine of Reuben Clark's 1912 memorandum on *Right to Land Forces,* by which the practice of protecting the lives and property of nationals in a foreign country was declared to be lawful and proper.

the question of intervention to the Subcommission for Codification of International Law, where J. Reuben Clark would quietly destroy it.[25]

But at the critical moment everything went wrong. The delegates were assembled in plenary session and the hour was marked for the fateful decision, but just when the Americans and their allies were ready to execute their plan the cogs began to slip. Reuben's old friend from Mexico, Puig Casauranc, in the midst of what was supposed to be only a pro forma denunciation of interventionism, quite lost control of himself and launched out into impassioned oratory. Striding over to where the American delegation was seated, the Mexican foreign minister, who disconcertingly resembled Mussolini, pointed a chubby finger at the secretary of state and cried, "Señor Hull, what would the Roosevelt administration lose by a great new policy?"[26] Other defections followed. When the moment arrived for Saavedra Lamas to move for referral of the question to the subcommission for codification, he moved instead for its adoption![27]

The moment of truth had arrived for Cordell Hull. He was pinioned between Clark on the one side and Gruening on the other,

Entering the Legislative Palace in Montevideo: At the critical moment everything went wrong.

593

and both of them were passing him notes and whispering vehemently in his ear.[28] Reuben, of course, was urging him to stand up and denounce the resolution, while Gruening was urging him to embrace it. Hull rose to his feet, looked around at the assembled representatives of the western world, swallowed hard, and then, in his somnolent bluegrass drawl, threw in with Ernest Gruening and the noninterventionists.

The United States is determined that its new policy of the New Deal—of enlightened liberalism—shall have full effect and shall be recognized in its fullest import by its neighbors. The people of my country strongly feel that the so-called right-of-conquest must forever be banished from this hemisphere and, most of all, they shun and reject that so-called right for themselves. The New Deal indeed would be an empty boast if it did not mean that.[29]

The assembly broke into thunderous cheering.

Cordell Hull, however, had not been entirely deaf in the other ear. While making the momentary decision to vote for the proposed new treaty, he had received from Reuben Clark the tiny legalistic implement enabling him to do so. In the final report of the conference, the United States attached a mild and seemingly innocuous reservation to its vote. America would continue to be bound, said Hull, by "the law of nations as generally recognized and accepted."[30] The victorious Latin delegates did not much concern themselves with those words, and the toasting and congratulating went on and on. It was only J. Reuben Clark who, on the way home aboard the *American Legion,* could look out to sea and smile with satisfaction. For "the law of nations," as he had whispered to Secretary of State Hull at that crucial moment, fully recognized the right of interposition.[31]

v

Reuben retained his predilection for lost causes. His prodigious labors for the Foreign Bondholders Protective Council clearly answered this description. Officially, the bondholders council was charged with curing one of the salient maladies of the Great Depression: the two billion dollars' worth of bonds which had been issued or backed by various foreign governments and purchased by American citizens—all in default. Unofficially, as Reuben seemed to believe, the council was charged with preserving the canons of responsibility which underlay modern society. This was a big task. And like so many that Reuben took on, it was on the wrong side of history.[32]

On the council sat eighteen of the most influential men in America. Their blue-ribbon qualities stood in lieu of formal diplomatic powers, for the FBPC possessed only quasi-official status. There was, as its members well knew, no legal remedy for defaulted international bonds; the creditor left in the lurch could appeal only to the debtor nation's reputation, credit rating, or national honor. Reuben himself was no Wall Streeter. He had never so much as owned a foreign bond. But he knew international law, had had experience with financial tangles, and enjoyed a distinguished reputation. Besides, as Herbert Feis remarked, he was "a really hard-fisted Mormon."[33] He was made general counsel of the bondholders in October of 1933.

Reuben took the assignment seriously. On his way to the Pan-American conference in Montevideo he stopped off in Rio de Janeiro and held talks with Brazil's finance minister, Dr. Oswaldo Aranha. These talks were extremely productive. Aranha virtually committed his government to the entire agenda of council proposals and pointed the way for other Latin American states to follow. That they would follow indeed was indicated when Reuben stopped at the Dominican Republic on his return voyage and scored an equally impressive triumph with President Trujillo. At the end of February, 1934, council president Raymond Stevens, who had never been in the best of health, effectively resigned, and J. Reuben Clark took charge.[34]

For the next five years Reuben *was* the foreign bondholders council, dividing his time between its New York offices and church headquarters in Salt Lake City. The East-West shuttle, of course, was thoroughly familiar to him—every mile of it—and so was the confusion of loyalties it produced. But the attractions of the bondholders council were few. Reuben's salary of fifteen thousand dollars was flush enough by depression standards, but it was nothing like the halcyon days of international law. This was public service at its purest, the kind of thing into which Reuben Clark seemed to fall most readily.

Only a veteran of the Mexican claims commission could have borne the reversals of the bondholders council with Reuben's equanimity. First of all, there was bickering between the FBPC and the

595

forty-odd independent agencies which were also attempting to collect the bonds. Then there was internecine warfare over council authority, with the complaint that Clark and the executive committee had usurped the powers of the directors. Next there ensued a crisis over finances. The big eastern houses of issue were entirely willing to underwrite the costs of council operations, but others objected to Wall Street domination. To further complicate matters, the State Department was never certain just how closely it wanted to stand behind the activities of an essentially private organization, especially such a controversial one, and it fretted constantly over the alternative of converting the bondholders council into a federal agency. Even the Securities and Exchange Commission got into the act, worrying that the council was becoming elitist and plutocratic and forgetting the small investor. SEC hearings were held throughout October and November of 1935 in which Reuben Clark and William O. Douglas squared off against one another with wearisome regularity. Reuben ultimately won this bout with the New Deal. In fact, one at a time, he triumphed over every obstacle met by the Foreign Bondholders Protective Council—save one. He never found the way to make defaulters pay their debts.[35]

He pled with the defaulting governments. He argued with them. He pointed out that the issue before them was one of will, not capacity, and that the will to repay was what counted. He scored them mercilessly for diverting revenue into such frivolities as public works while allowing honest debts to go unpaid. Finally, he condemned them—all eighteen of them—as one would a common deadbeat. Back and forth across the United States he journeyed, tirelessly pursuing his quest. He even traveled to Europe and confronted the rulers of the Third Reich eyeball to eyeball.[36] But all to no avail. New defaults appeared faster than Reuben and the FBPC could address themselves to the old ones.

J. Reuben Clark himself knew about hard times. He had overextended himself in the panic of 1920 and had fought for a decade to make good on his losses. Thus tempered in the crucible of experience, he could hardly conceive of national statesmen who would—or could—do less. In his world it took hard work and guts to survive, and now it seemed that both commodities were in short supply. So, despite herculean efforts, the bonds remained in default and the world drifted aimlessly toward another global war. The old order was beyond recovery.[37]

vi

Montevideo and the Foreign Bondholders Protective Council were not the only bridges to the past. Reuben had thought seriously about running for the Senate again in 1934, and with even greater enthusiasm friends had thought about it for him. This time, with the Sevens demobilized and President Grant in his corner, Reuben believed he could win. The matter reached the point where the new counselor, his scorn for theocracy still incandescent, was typing up letters of resignation from the First Presidency.[38] But his heart was not really in it. His work in the church had resolved the main conflicts in his life and brought him to a new steadiness. He no longer needed the Senate.

Reuben had returned to Mexico too, but the trip was a sad postscript to his ambassadorship there. By 1934 the fire-breathing Lázaro Cárdenas was consolidating his hold on the Mexican presidency. Friction between himself and the American oil magnates was immediate and relentless, and no more than a few months of it elapsed before someone got the idea of bringing back J. Reuben Clark and the good old days. The oil men approached Ambassador Daniels, who was rightfully miffed by the whole idea, and then they went to the Department of State. Even Reuben thought the plan unwise. Eventually he agreed to come in a totally private capacity, his expenses to be paid by the petroleum industry. For the most part the trip was futile. Reuben pulled every wire in his recollection, including the one that ran to Calles's door in Cuernavaca, but to little avail. Lázaro Cárdenas was a Mexican politico of a different sort. He would soon nationalize the entire Mexican oil industry.[39]

One of these oil clients, however, came out well in the Clark mission. Royal Dutch Shell was so benefited by Reuben's diplomacy, in fact, that it paid over to him the princely sum of $108,000. That sort of fee must have put him in mind of the Alsop days and of his dream of cashing in on a tidy fortune. Yet, like the Senate campaign, the old fires of ambition were decidedly banked down. Instead of building a country estate or buying blooded horses, Reuben neatly divided the Shell money among his four children, buying the three girls houses on D Street and putting his son through Columbia.[40] Here was more evidence of the change brought over him by the church.

Reuben eventually had cause to regret his Far Eastern diplomacy. The agreements signed in Washington in 1921 did nothing to stem the tide of Japanese expansionism, and they did a great deal to curb American naval power. Japan attacked Manchuria in 1931 and set a course that proved to be tragic. On December 7, 1941, when the Japanese bombed Pearl Harbor, Reuben's son-in-law, Commander Mervyn Bennion, who had repeatedly warned of a surprise attack in the Pacific, was on the bridge of his ship, the *West Virginia*.[41] His death marked the beginning of World War II for the United States—and helped justify the use of the atomic bomb later on.

Reuben never abandoned his fight against the World Court, which he persisted in identifying with the League of Nations. There was another big push for the court in 1935 and another decisive vote against it. Reuben Clark testified before the Senate Foreign Relations Committee and supplied a ponderous brief that Senator Johnson described as the backbone of the opposition.[42] Sighed Reuben during the battle: "The World Court, and the League will go down to posterity as the 'maniest [many-est] lifed' international cat that the history of the world has ever known."[43]

vii

All of these activities tied Reuben to the past. So too did his lifelong friendships.[44] William Dennis, his old fellow sufferer under Scott, remained a friend to the last. Dennis became president of his alma mater, Earlham, in 1929 and prevailed upon Reuben to deliver a commencement address or two. Others of the old Mockahis made good as well. Harry Armes, "The Shadow," was made attorney-examiner for the Interstate Commerce Commission, where he had a distinguished career. Hugh Gibson, the "Wild Indian," represented the United States in something like a quarter of the nations of Europe. He was ambassador to Brazil when Reuben stopped off in Rio on his way to Montevideo. Gibson's hair had turned to silver-grey and he had grown decidedly stout, but something of the old Mockahi mischief still gleamed in his eye. The two of them enjoyed an old-style talkfest.[45]

Scott himself, the Mockahi nemesis, never came back down to earth. The longer he lived, it seemed, the busier he became with what Reuben called his wild projects.[46] When at Montevideo a delegate alluded to Scott's American Institute of International Law, Reuben, in his own words, "launched out into a perfect tirade."[47] But James Brown Scott was never deterred. He moved ever onward and upward, with new and better ways of establishing world peace. He died in 1943, in the midst of a world war.

Fred Morris Dearing's public career was also a success. He became minister to Portugal in 1922 (after his tour as assistant secretary), and ambassador to Peru in 1930. Henry Lane Wilson, on the other hand, lapsed into oblivion, his once-promising diplomatic career in ruins. Wilbur Carr stuck doggedly to his administrative post in the State Department and finally obtained a diplomatic appointment of his own. In 1937 he became minister to Czechoslovakia—just in time to see Czechoslovakia carved up at Munich. Enoch Crowder retired from the army to become a diplomat himself. After rescuing Cuba from a spate of fiscal catastrophes, he became the first U.S. ambassador to that country in 1923.

Charles Evans Hughes returned to the Supreme Court, this time as chief justice, where he served with great distinction—and occasional obstruction—until the outbreak of the Second World War. He was the third of Reuben's acquaintances to serve on the high court, the others being Harlan Fiske Stone and William Howard Taft. All three served as chief justice.

Francis M. Huntington Wilson never found the combination to public life again. After making his futile bid for the undersecretaryship in 1928, he satisfied himself with such tasks as manufacturing automobile horns—"signally devices," as he called them—and directing the moribund Philadelphia Commercial Museum. "There is something pathetic about our old friend and his clinging to his vanished importance," Dearing wrote to Reuben in 1943, "but for all his willingfulness [*sic*], he is the most loyal friend in the world and [my wife] and I are glad we can remind him of the days of his prime."[48] On New Year's Eve of 1946, at the age of seventy-one, Huntington Wilson died of cancer in a New Haven hospital.

599

Reuben remained on good terms with all of the surviving bitter-enders—Johnson and Borah especially—but he fell to quarreling, good-naturedly, with Salmon O. Levinson over the World Court. In arguing with Clark, the father of outlawry was beyond his depth. When he thought to be ironic one day by referring to Reuben's position as an "oasis in the desert," this was the reply.

I know of nobody who needs such an oasis worse than yourself. I feel this is particularly true in view of the fact that at one time I thought you were on the oasis with me, and I was really surprised and grieved to find you had wandered off into the desert—the victim of hallucinations and mirages.[49]

The people associated with Reuben's Mexican adventure also fared pretty well. Clement Bouvé resigned from the Mexican claims commission in 1931 to become register of copyrights in the U.S. Patent Office. Fred K. Nielsen went on to serve as legal advisor at the London Economic and Financial Conference in 1933, after which he lapsed into obscurity.

Frank Kellogg was awarded the Nobel Peace Prize in 1929 for his work on the Kellogg-Briand Pact. Thereafter, until his death in 1937, he served as a justice on the World Court. William Castle finally achieved his dream of becoming undersecretary, replacing Joseph Cotton in March of 1931, only to go down with the Hoover administration two years later. Another assistant secretary, Francis White, joined Reuben on the Foreign Bondholders Protective Council as executive vice-president and secretary. He and Reuben labored in tandem throughout the remainder of the decade. Henry Stimson finally got the secretaryship figured out and ran the Department of State moderately well. He became Franklin Roosevelt's secretary of war in 1940, soon after which he found himself with a world war on his hands. That made his old days at the State Department seem easy.

Oddly enough, Herbert Hoover and J. Reuben Clark, who had barely been on speaking terms throughout the 1920s, became fast friends upon the termination of their public careers. Of course, in the New Deal they had a common enemy. Judging by their correspondence, each seemed to regard the other as a symbol of lost individualism and self-reliance.[50]

Several of Reuben's embassy staff members went on to distinguished careers. Joseph Satterthwaite represented the United States

600

on five continents, retiring as ambassador to South Africa. Steven Aguirre, with Reuben's backing and blocking, finally advanced in the consular ranks and went on to become a consul general. Arthur Bliss Lane achieved ambassadorial rank in Europe, where in the aftermath of Yalta he was made U.S. ambassador to Poland. Three years later he scored a bull's-eye in the cold war with his electrifying memoir, *I Saw Poland Betrayed.*

Plutarco Elias Calles was in bed one night in 1936 reading the best-seller of the day, *Mein Kampf,* when something rather like storm troopers burst in upon him. The next thing the old *jefe* knew, he himself was being dumped across the border in El Paso. He thus learned the lesson that Reuben Clark had learned a few years earlier: that Lázaro Cárdenas, supposedly one of his own hand-picked puppets, had a mind of his own.[51]

Of all the friendships that linked Reuben to the past, easily the most remarkable was with John W. DeKay. After 1927, when Reuben had bowed out of the "Bloody Sultan" scheme, DeKay's behavior became increasingly erratic. In Yugoslavia, for example, he reportedly bought the Raguza Hotel in order to fire an obnoxious waiter.[52] His checks, moreover, had a curious way of bouncing, and DeKay's life became one of ever greater harassment. Periodically he made whirlwind visits to Salt Lake City where, in hotel rooms with drawn shades, he breathlessly spelled out to Reuben the latest million-dollar proposition. Once or twice the propositions concerned Utah. DeKay liked the Mormons. He felt a peace in the Tabernacle, he said, like unto that of the Sistine Chapel in Rome. Somehow he hatched the idea of boring an aquatic tunnel through the Oquirrh Mountains and into Tooele Valley and then using the water to establish a utopian community in the desert.[53] That plan never quite took off, but DeKay had another one. He named J. Reuben Clark executor of his estate and left a sizeable chunk of it (16½ percent) for the establishment of a foundation at Brigham Young University. "Intellectus et Labor," as the foundation would be called, was a hodgepodge of religion, education, and democracy. It too never quite got off the ground, mostly because 16½ percent of nothing was also nothing.[54] In fact, after John DeKay would issue forth one of these earth-rocking prospectuses, Reuben would usually have to stroll down from church headquarters and foot the bill for his hotel room.

"I do not need to tell you that he was brilliant to the point of genius," wrote Reuben to John's brother Henry when John passed away in 1938. "I shall never forget him, I am sure, while I live."[55]

viii

When it came to explaining J. Reuben Clark himself, no one ever really tried, then or since. One could make observations about him—and many people did—but the observations had a way of raising questions, and the questions raised further questions. Ultimately, the conclusion asserted itself that the man was a complete and unfathomable paradox. Counting only a few of the particulars, there were these:

1. He was a thoroughgoing conservative, an avowed Hamiltonian, a servant of Wall Street, at times even a reactionary—yet he entertained some startlingly progressive ideas. Antimilitarism, antiimperialism, support for popular government, espousal of human rights, hostility toward big business, fear of corruption, respect for foreign values, defense of violent revolution, sympathy for the underdog—these and other ideas often put him out of step with fellow conservatives.[56]

2. He was consistent, sometimes even inflexible; yet on pivotal issues he changed his mind. He unashamedly reversed himself on the rule of international law, on support for world organization, on pacifism, on the value of an international judiciary, on the codification question, on internationalism, on interventionism, even on such fundamentals as religion. At one point he considered abandoning his Republican moorings, which for him was tantamount to intellectual suicide.

3. He was an intensely political man, one who cherished his party; but he was constantly out of sorts with its leading men and ascendant ideas. He opposed at one time or another—usually most inopportunely—virtually every figure of power with whom he had political relations: Roosevelt, Root, Taft, Lodge, Wilson, Bryan, Lansing, Harding, Hughes, Hoover, Stimson, Lowden, Wood, Roosevelt, and, continuously, Reed Smoot. Still, incredibly, all of these men seemed to like and respect him, and one searches in vain for evidence that they ever returned his brickbats. Reuben was not with-

out his own officeholding aspirations, yet so set was he against playing the political game that the aspirations were utterly foredoomed.

4. He was a self-effacing man. He worked most happily behind the stage. On any number of occasions he turned his back contemptuously on administrative opportunities. He had no taste whatever for power and prestige. Yet powerful and prestigious responsibilities were constantly being thrust upon him, and he found himself grudgingly obliged to accept them. Wealth, on the other hand, was something he unabashedly pursued throughout his life, endlessly watching for the main chance. But for gaining and holding onto wealth he seemed to have no talent whatever.

5. He found joy and meaning in work. Of interests, pastimes, and hobbies he had virtually none. And yet, far more than any of his accomplishments he prized the noneconomic, nonprofessional things of life: his friendships, his children, his marriage, his Mormonism. Indeed, since he hungered neither for power nor material possessions, the work itself often seemed pointless.

6. His life was literally strung out between two poles of identity, one of them in the West, where he was born and raised, and one of them in the East, where his dreams of fulfillment lay. In neither place, it seemed, could he find final peace, nor could he long establish himself at either before experiencing the lure of the other. His real life, perhaps, was spent in shuttling to and fro.

7. He was an affirmative man, bright and witty, known for the one-line quip which he tossed off almost thoughtlessly and for the merry twinkle in his eye. No one who knew him doubted that he had found happiness. Yet virtually every one of the crusades that formed the substance of his life ended in defeat and sorrow. He fought against international organization. He fought for fiscal responsibility. He fought against militarism. He fought for international law. He fought against the nightmare weapons. He fought for public morality. He fought against the welfare state. He fought for individualism. He believed in an America of innocence and righteousness; an America whose diplomacy would be fair, open, and disinterested; an America that would exert moral leadership in the world and that alone. He would die during the Bay of Pigs fiasco, and he would see little prospect for America but slow ruin or atomic doom. For a man of hope, there was something undeniably tragic about his life.

603

Some of these contradictions were not personal—they were aspects of the clash between the nineteenth and twentieth centuries. But a great many of them *were* personal and they invite explanation. J. Reuben Clark seemed to have two distinct sides to his personality, and they sometimes got in one another's way. One side of him was the Grantsville farmer, the boy who had milked cows and pitched hay, the man who had bought land and prize Herefords. Like many a farmer, he had an essentially hardheaded view of the world. The ultimate realities for him were the day-to-day realities: storms, frosts, droughts, pestilence, things that needed to be attended to—and could be. Thus he was tough, practical, and down-to-earth, or, as Herbert Feis described him, "stubborn and acquisitive."[57] He was appreciative of the practical limits of the possible and ever mindful of the value of experience.

At the same time, Reuben was born and raised a Mormon and, whether close to or away from the church, he lived in the Mormon universe. In this universe God was not an aloof abstraction but an actual living being concerned over man's fate, interventionist in history, and Old Testament—like in solicitude for His people. In such a universe angels ministered to men, prophets received daily guidance, and divine miracles were commonplace. The potential for human society was correspondingly unmeasured.

These, then, were the two substantively dissimilar sides of Reuben Clark: realism and idealism. One pointed toward hardheadedness, practical-mindedness, and ultimately a doctrinaire conservatism, while the other pointed toward open-endedness and possibility. The two interfaced in complex ways and addressed themselves differently to different issues. But one of them responded to the power politics of a John Bassett Moore or a Philander Knox and the other to the visions of a James Brown Scott or an Elihu Root—occasionally at the same time. In an early speech to be delivered at Lake Mohonk, Reuben, discussing unlimited compulsory arbitration, dissected the subject with vehemence, showing its practical limitations, its logical absurdities, its hopeless impossibility. Then he said,

Nothing that has been said means or is intended to mean that merely because the ideal may now be unapproachable we should cease to reach after it; on the contrary, we should still hitch our wagon to the star.[58]

Like this kind of paradox, Reuben Clark himself could be interpreted in either of two ways. To the tough-minded and practical he often seemed abstracted, quixotic, a man out of his time. To the high-minded and intellectual, he seemed unimaginative and hidebound. On one point, however, both sides agreed: that J. Reuben Clark had a mind of his own.

Indeed he did. He was ever out of step with his time and ever disappointed with immediate outcomes—yet he seemed strangely capable of apprehending larger or more distant truths. Quite apart from his formal religious calling as a prophet,* there was something eerily prophetic about the things he said. In 1919 he predicted another war growing out of the peace of Versailles, a war in which resurgent Germany would join hands with Japan and a third power in an irredentist apocalypse. In the early 1930s he added that the United States would become involved in such a war. He foretold the cold war as well, and the binge of American do-goodism that exacerbated it. He prophesied the rise of a military-industrial complex and the corollary rise of McCarthyism; and while he did not use the term "imperial presidency," he incessantly warned of its dangers. He said that human nature would never change and that human problems would not be solved by bigger armaments, better parliaments, or improved collective security. He predicted that physical force would be no more and probably a good deal less effective than moral force in resolving the world's difficulties. He foretold the moral relativism in postwar American diplomacy by which the United States would agree to support its "friends" no matter what their vices and to oppose its "enemies" no matter what their virtues. Without delving into the specifics of a Mai Lai or a Watergate, he predicted, over and over again, that the United States, with its busybody internationalism, stood in danger of losing its own soul. And lastly, he forecast that final day of reckoning when America must frankly acknowledge that it could play the good uncle no longer. This all sounded strange in the thirties and forties, like a lone voice crying in the wilderness. Forty years later it would read like history.

---

*General authorities of the LDS church are called and sustained by the church membership as "prophets, seers, and revelators."

ix

The final reel of film wound through the movie projector. Before the concluding blaze of white light, the machine had cast out images of Mexican horse soldiers escorting a file of black limousines down a wide boulevard; of a charro band; of fashionable men and women at a lavish garden affair; of a labyrinth of idyllic canals banked by walls of brilliant flowers; of Ambassador Clark clowning before the camera; and finally, of Luacine Clark smiling at her husband in shy adoration. In one final scene she was wearing a well-remembered blue gown, and she looked not only beautiful but regal.

Rowena walked over and switched on the lights. She started back toward the movie projector but then stopped short. She had known President Clark for a quarter of a century. She had seen him in triumph and she had seen him in defeat—yet never, until this moment, had she seen him in tears. But then, President Clark was not a weeping man. He was the anchor of the church, the genius behind its temporal affairs, the symbol of strength to which Mormons the world over could look and hold, the man who stood ever staunch, ever faithful, ever true. Rowena Miller understood this well. Sensitive woman that she was, she stepped through the door and discreetly closed it behind her.[59]

NOTES

The J. Reuben Clark, Jr., Collection, which is housed in the archives of the Harold B. Lee Library at Brigham Young University, is numbered MS 303. Box numbers are provided in the individual footnotes.

Rowena Miller, Reuben Clark's private secretary, combed through his papers and selected many of the most important for biographical purposes. Items in this collection, listed in the notes as RM, as well as many of the newspaper clippings found in the Clark scrapbooks, are often devoid of page numbers. Thus, where page numbers are missing in a notation it may be assumed that they are not available.

"JRC" as it appears in the notes refers only to J. Reuben Clark, Jr. The names of his father, Joshua Reuben Clark, Sr., and his son, J. Reuben Clark III, are spelled out in full.

Prologue BETWEEN WEST AND EAST

1. Diary of J. Reuben Clark, Sr., 19 September 1903, Harold B. Lee Library, Brigham Young University, Provo, Utah.

2. Luacine Savage Clark, Handwritten autobiographical account (hereafter cited as Luacine's Autobiography), Box 474, p. 10.

3. This account of the trip westward was supplied by J. Reuben Clark III, who often traveled this route with his father.

4. "Modern Representatives of Ancient Families," *Utah Genealogical and Historical Magazine* 24 (October 1933): 151.

5. Diary of J. Reuben Clark, Sr., 14 June 1864 to 5 September 1864.

6. Ibid., 10 March 1867, 14 April 1867, 15 April 1867.

7. Ibid., 3 November 1868.

8. Visitors to Grantsville today find it little changed from the time of Joshua's first visit.

9. Autobiography of John Clark, typed manuscript supplied to the author by Clark family, pp. 5-6.

10. Ibid., p. 23.

11. JRC to Roscoe A. Grover, 18 April 1934, RM.

12. Interview with J. Reuben Clark III, 20 July 1977.

13. Marianne Clark Sharp, "Born to Greatness: The Story of President J. Reuben Clark, Jr.," *Children's Friend* 53 (September 1954): 360.

14. Bryant S. Hinckley, "President J. Reuben Clark, Jr.," *Improvement Era* 36 (September 1933): 643.

15. JRC, Memoir of 31 January 1959, RM.

16. Autobiography of John Clark, pp. 6–8.

17. Diary of J. Reuben Clark, Sr., 29 September 1887 to 27 October 1887.

18. Ibid., 15 October 1883 to 15 December 1883.

19. Ibid., 25 March 1886.

20. Ibid., 7 January 1890.

21. Autobiography of John Clark, p. 17.

22. Diary of J. Reuben Clark, Sr., 2 September 1879, 7 September 1879.

23. Ibid., 1 May 1881.

24. Ibid., 7 May 1889, 24 November 1889, 13 April 1890.

25. J. Reuben Clark, Jr., "What I Read as a Boy," *Children's Friend* 42 (March 1943): 99.

26. Diary of J. Reuben Clark, Sr., 2 January 1882.

27. Ibid., 29 November 1882.

28. Ibid., 13 February 1884.

29. JRC, Speech to Emigration Stake High Priests, 14 January 1952, RM.

30. Diary of J. Reuben Clark, Sr., 4 December 1881, 27 December 1881, 19 October 1882, 17 October 1885.

31. Ibid., 9 December 1880, 24 December 1882, 22 December 1886.

32. Ibid., 25 July 1887, 24 July 1889.

33. Ibid., 26 July 1883, 18 August 1883, 12 September 1883, 17 March 1884, 21 June 1884, 5 June 1886, 14 August 1886.

34. Ibid., 13 April 1881.

35. Ibid., 21 March 1884, 1 December 1884, 24 December 1884, 17 February 1885, 23 June 1885, 23 August 1885.

36. Ibid., 1 January 1889, 30 November 1889, 24 December 1889, 10 January 1890, 22 March 1890.

37. Speech to Emigration Stake High Priests.

38. Diary of J. Reuben Clark, Sr., 1 November 1890.

39. Speech to Emigration Stake High Priests.

40. JRC, Memoir of 26 January 1949, RM.

41. Diary of J. Reuben Clark, Sr., 17 January 1891.

42. JRC, Memoir of 26 January 1949.

43. Ibid.

44. Ibid.

45. Anecdote related by JRC to Rowena Miller, 10 September 1945, RM.

46. JRC, Memoir of 26 January 1949.

47. Diary of J. Reuben Clark, Sr., 14 June 1894, 19 June 1894.

48. JRC, Memoir of 26 January 1949.

49. Diary of J. Reuben Clark, Sr., 15 June 1898.

50. Interview with Louise Clark Bennion, Marianne Clark Sharp, and J. Reuben Clark III, 8 and 15 June 1977.

51. Ibid.

52. Luacine's Autobiography, p. 6.

53. Sharp, "Born to Greatness," p. 361.

54. Interview with Louise Clark Bennion, Marianne Clark Sharp, and J. Reuben Clark III.

55. Luacine's Autobiography, p. 6.

56. Ibid., pp. 7–8.

57. Interview with Louise Clark Bennion, Marianne Clark Sharp, and J. Reuben Clark III.

58. Diary of J. Reuben Clark, Sr., 14 September 1898, 15 September 1898.

59. Luacine Savage Clark, "Notes on My Life," Box 474, p. 7. This painful initial separation was only the first hint of what would soon emerge as an abiding theme of the Clark marriage. "I did not know it at the time," Luacine would later write, "but this was the beginning of his leaving me, which he has continued ever since" (Ibid.).

60. Ibid.

61. JRC to Frank Conrad, James R. Smith, John W. McDonald, Henry Moulton, Elizabeth F. Lindsay, and Lottie Moulton Giles, 22 September 1955, Box 392.

62. Luacine S. Clark, "Notes," p. 7.

63. Ibid.

64. JRC to Reed Smoot, 22 November 1902, Box 1.

65. John Henry Evans, "An Historical Sketch of the Latter-day Saints University," 1913, excerpt in RM.

66. Speech to Emigration Stake High Priests.

67. Luacine's Autobiography, p. 9.

68. Speech to Emigration Stake High Priests.

69. JRC to Milton Bennion, 3 May 1901, Box 1.

70. *Deseret Evening News,* 15 December 1900.

71. JRC to William M. Stewart, 13 November 1900, Box 1.

72. JRC to J. T. Kingsbury, 5 April 1901, Box 1.

73. A copy of this petition can be found in RM.

74. Sharp, "Born to Greatness," p. 361.

75. See, for example, JRC to Dean, Harvard Law School, 26 September 1901, Box 1.

76. Luacine's Autobiography, pp. 9–10; Luacine S. Clark, "Notes," p. 7.

77. JRC to Reed Smoot, 22 November 1902, Box 1.

78. Ibid.

79. Speech to Emigration Stake High Priests.

80. Recollection of JRC, related to Rowena Miller, RM.

Chapter One   MORNINGSIDE

1. *New York Times,* 14 June 1906.

2. H. R. Steeves, "Memories of Goatville Days," in *University on the Heights,* ed. Wesley First (New York: Doubleday, 1969), pp. 137–38.

3. John William Robson, ed., *A Guide to Columbia University* (New York: Columbia University Press, 1937), p. 36; Edwin E. Slosson, *Great American Universities* (New York: Macmillan, 1910), p. 449.

4. Francis Marion Burdick, "The School of Law," in *A History of Columbia University, 1754–1904* (New York: Columbia University Press, 1904), pp. 335–47.

5. R. Gordon Hoxie et al., *A History of the Faculty of Political Science, Columbia University* (New York: Columbia University Press, 1955), pp. 256–67.

6. Barbara W. Tuchman, *The Proud Tower: A Portrait of the World before the War, 1890–1914* (New York: Macmillan, 1966), pp. 229–67.

7. C. Roland Marchand, *The American Peace Movement and Social Reform, 1898–1918* (Princeton, N.J.: Princeton University Press, 1972), pp. 39–70.

8. Hoxie, *History of the Faculty,* pp. 5–6, 42, 257–60.

9. Ibid., p. 8.

10. Horace Coon, *Columbia, Colossus on the Hudson* (New York: E. P. Dutton, 1947), p. 230.

11. Alpheus Thomas Mason, *Harlan Fiske Stone: Pillar of the Law* (New York: Viking Press, 1956), pp. 71–72.

12. Marchand, *American Peace Movement,* pp. 39–40.

13. *National Cyclopaedia of American Biography,* Current Series (Clifton, N.J.: James T. White & Co., 1898–   ), C:69–70.

14. Richard Megargee, "The Diplomacy of John Bassett Moore: Realism in American Foreign Policy" (Ph.D. diss., Northwestern University, 1963), pp. 3–6, 20–69.

15. J. Reuben Clark, Jr., *Stand Fast by Our Constitution* (Salt Lake City: Deseret Book, 1962), pp. 138–45.

16. Slosson, *Great American Universities,* p. 450.

17. Memoir of 14 January 1949, Box 2.

18. JRC to John J. Massey, 10 January 1959, RM.

19. This exchange is familiar to most law students. The case, an ancient and famous one, is still taught in first-year torts classes.

20. Coon, *Colossus on the Hudson,* pp. 228–29.

21. Kenneth S. Davis, *FDR: The Beckoning of Destiny, 1882–1928* (New York: G. P. Putnam's Sons, 1971), p. 191.

22. Fon W. Boardman, "After Class," in *A History of Columbia College on Morningside* (New York: Columbia University Press, 1954), pp. 169, 181–82.

23. Luacine's Autobiography, p. 10.

24. Luacine S. Clark, "Notes," p. 8.

25. Memoir of 14 January 1949, Box 2.

26. Ibid.

27. Ibid.

28. Ibid.

29. Report of Carr Morrow, 1905, Box 2.

30. Diary of J. Reuben Clark, Sr., 30 July 1905.

31. Reuben never forgot this injustice at the hands of Scott. He was still brooding over it when he went to South America in 1933. See Montevideo Conference Diary, 7 December 1933, Box 144.

32. Thomas A. Bailey, *A Diplomatic History of the American People* (Englewood Cliffs, N.J.: Prentice-Hall, 1970), pp. 433–35, 438–47, 462–64, 468–70, 480–84, 488–98, 504–6, 511–12, 516–19.

33. Marchand, *American Peace Movement,* p. 69.

34. JRC to James Brown Scott, 4 March 1906, Box 346.

35. *New York Times,* 14 June 1906.

36. Luacine's Autobiography, p. 10.

37. Diary of J. Reuben Clark, Sr., 6 November 1905, 2 May 1906.

38. Ibid., 29 April 1906.

39. Luacine S. Clark, "Notes," p. 8.

Notes

Chapter Two ASSISTANT SOLICITOR

1. George F. Kennan, *American Diplomacy, 1900–1950* (Chicago: University of Chicago Press, 1951), pp. 91–92.

2. Luacine's Autobiography, p. 10; Luacine S. Clark, "Notes," p. 10; George D. Parkinson, "How a Utah Boy Won His Way," *Improvement Era* 17 (March 1914): 559.

3. Francis M. Huntington-Wilson, *Memoirs of an Ex-Diplomat* (Boston: B. Humphries, 1945), pp. 151–52.

4. Kennan, *American Diplomacy*, p. 92; Katherine Crane, *Mr. Carr of State: Forty-seven Years in the Department of State* (New York: St. Martin's Press, 1960), pp. 21–22, 25; James Brown Scott, "Elihu Root," in *The American Secretaries of State and Their Diplomacy,* ed. Samuel Flagg Bemis, 10 vols. (New York: Pageant Book, 1958), 9:243–44.

5. Crane, *Mr. Carr of State,* pp. 18–21, 25; William Phillips, *Ventures in Diplomacy* (Boston: Beacon Press, 1952), p. 35.

6. Graham Stuart, *American Consular and Diplomatic Practice* (New York: D. Appleton-Century, 1936), p. 105.

7. Frederick Van Dyne, *Our Foreign Service: The "ABC" of American Diplomacy* (Rochester, N.Y.: The Lawyers Cooperative Publishing Co., 1909), p. 30.

8. Stuart, *Consular and Diplomatic Practice,* p. 104.

9. Ibid., p. 105; Van Dyne, *Our Foreign Service,* p. 31.

10. Stuart, *Consular and Diplomatic Practice,* p. 106; Van Dyne, *Our Foreign Service,* p. 30.

11. William C. Dennis to JRC, 16 August 1910, Box 343.

12. Philip C. Jessup, *Elihu Root,* 2 vols. (New York: Dodd, Mead & Co., 1938), 2:59.

13. Gaillard Hunt to James Brown Scott, 7 December 1907, Box 59.

14. The final report was entitled *Citizenship of the United States, Expatriation, and Protection Abroad,* House of Representatives, Document No. 326, 59th Congress, 2d Session. The bill was designated H.R. 24122.

15. Scott contributed nothing of his own to the study. JRC, Memorandum of June, 1951, RM.

16. *Who's Who in America, 1906–7* (Chicago: A. N. Marquis & Co.), p. 465. (Hereafter, only the title, date, and page numbers for references to this series will be cited.)

17. Marchand, *American Peace Movement,* p. 69.

18. Interview with Louise Clark Bennion, Marianne Clark Sharp, and J. Reuben Clark III.

19. "The Daily Grind, or, The Missing Papers. A Farce," Box 2. This undated and unsigned memorandum, probably composed by W. Clayton Carpenter, contains a tongue-in-cheek look at life in the solicitor's office under Scott.

20. Ibid.

21. Crane, *Mr. Carr of State,* pp. 78–79.

22. Ibid., p. 99.

23. Jessup, *Elihu Root,* 1:456.

24. "Departmental Trickery," Box 36. For more on this intriguing memorandum, see chapter four.

25. Ibid.

26. Crane, *Mr. Carr of State,* p. 99.

27. "Departmental Trickery."

28. Ibid.; Huntington-Wilson, *Memoirs,* p. 165.

29. "Outline of the Organization and Work of the State Department," Box 63.

30. "The Daily Grind."

31. O. T. Carpenter to JRC, 15 July 1910, Box 2.

32. "The Daily Grind."

33. William C. Dennis to JRC, 27 December 1916, Box 343.

34. "The Daily Grind."

35. Parkinson, "How a Utah Boy Won His Way," p. 560.

36. *Papers Relating to the Foreign Relations of the United States* (hereafter cited as *FRUS*) (Washington, D.C.: Government Printing Office, 1909), pp. 512–13. (Only the abbreviated title, date, and page numbers for further references to this series will be cited.)

37. *New York Times,* 23 October 1908.

38. Maruta Karklis et al., *The Latvians in America, 1640–1973* (Dobbs Ferry, N.Y.: Oceana Publications, 1974), p. 3.

39. Alfreds Bilmanis, *A History of Latvia* (Westport, Conn.: Greenwood Press, 1970), pp. 215–20, 258–82; Sidney S. Harcave, *First Blood: The Russian Revolution of 1905* (New York: Macmillan, 1964), p. 107.

40. *The Outlook* 90 (5 September 1905):2; *New York Times,* 7 November 1908, 10 November 1908, 13 November 1908.

41. *New York Times,* 13 September 1908, 21 September 1908, 18 October 1908, 22 October 1908, 18 April 1909.

42. Jessup, *Elihu Root,* 2:66–67.

43. Reuben's most important conclusions on these procedural matters are contained in two memoranda: "Questions of Furnishing Copies of Department's Archives," 11 September 1908, and "Reply to Attorneys," 18 February 1909, both in Box 61.

44. "Departmental Trickery."

45. "Reply to Attorneys."

46. "The Nature and Definition of Political Offenses in International Extradition," Box 61.

47. Ibid. For a fuller discussion of Reuben Clark's views concerning the right of revolution, see Epilogue, note 56.

48. *New York Times,* 31 March 1909.

49. *Proceedings of the American Society of International Law* (New York: Baker, Voorhies & Co., 1909), p. 13.

50. "The Nature and Definition of Political Offenses in International Extradition."

Chapter Three FRIENDSHIP AND ALLIANCE

1. Crane, *Mr. Carr of State,* p. 16.

2. Jessup, *Elihu Root,* 1:456–57.

3. Marchand, *American Peace Movement,* pp. 45–46.

4. James Brown Scott, "Robert Bacon" in *The American Secretaries of State and Their Diplomacy,* ed. Samuel Flagg Bemis, 10 vols. (New York: Pageant Book, 1958), 9:284–88; Graham Stuart, *The Department of State: A History of Its Organization, Procedure, and Personnel* (New York: Macmillan, 1949), pp. 203–5; Huntington-Wilson, *Memoirs,* pp. 153–54; Jessup, *Elihu Root,* 1:455.

5. Walter V. Scholes and Marie V. Scholes, *The Foreign Policies of the Taft Administration* (Columbia: University of Missouri Press, 1970), p. 17; Crane, *Mr. Carr of State,* pp. 38–43; Huntington-Wilson, *Memoirs,* p. 154; Jessup, *Elihu Root,* 1:454–55.

6. Jessup, *Elihu Root,* 2:13.

7. Richard W. Leopold, *Elihu Root and the Conservative Tradition* (Boston: Little, Brown & Co., 1954), p. 50.

8. Julius W. Pratt, *Challenge and Rejection: The United States and World Leadership, 1900–1921* (New York: Macmillan, 1967), p. 5.

9. Jessup, *Elihu Root,* 2:111.

10. Ibid., 1:460.

11. Ibid., 1:505–7, 523, 526.

12. Huntington-Wilson, *Memoirs,* pp. 150–52.

13. Jessup, *Elihu Root,* 1:459.

14. Huntington-Wilson, *Memoirs,* pp. 47–48, 165.

15. Ibid., p. 62.

16. Crane, *Mr. Carr of State,* pp. 100–101; Huntington-Wilson, *Memoirs,* pp. 62, 195, 229, 241; Jessup, *Elihu Root,* 1:457; Scholes and Scholes, *Foreign Policies,* pp. 16–17; Stuart, *Department of State,* p. 204.

17. Richard Jay Eppinga, "Aristocrat, Nationalist, Diplomat: The Life and Career of Huntington Wilson" (Ph.D. diss., Michigan State University, 1972), p. 328; Huntington-Wilson, *Memoirs,* pp. 47–48.

18. Huntington-Wilson, *Memoirs,* pp. 156, 159, 170.

19. Ibid., pp. 135–45.

20. Jessup, *Elihu Root,* 2:103–4.

21. Crane, *Mr. Carr of State,* p. 51.

22. Huntington-Wilson, *Memoirs,* pp. 62, 156, 166, 204.

23. Ibid., p. 165.

24. Ibid., p. 235.

25. Joseph Grew, *Turbulent Era: A Diplomatic Record of Forty Years, 1904–45,* 2 vols. (Boston: Houghton Mifflin, 1952), 1:77.

26. Huntington-Wilson, *Memoirs,* p. 165.

27. Charles Toth, "Elihu Root," in *An Uncertain Tradition: American Secretaries of State in the Twentieth Century,* ed. Norman A. Graebner (New York: McGraw-Hill, 1961), p. 56; Crane, *Mr. Carr of State,* p. 98; Huntington-Wilson, *Memoirs,* pp. 155–56; Jessup, *Elihu Root,* 1:563, 2:250.

28. Paige Elliott Mulhollan, "Philander Knox and Dollar Diplomacy, 1900–1913" (Ph.D. diss., University of Texas, 1966), pp. 78–79; Jessup, *Elihu Root,* 1:559–60.

29. Jessup, *Elihu Root,* 1:468, 491.

30. Ibid., 1:471–74, 490–91, 530; Stuart, *Department of State,* p. 208.

31. Salvatore Bizarro, *Historical Dictionary of Chile* (Metuchen, N.J.: Scarecrow Press, 1972), pp. 155–56; Dana Gardner Munro, *The Latin American Republics: A History* (New York: D. Appleton-Century, 1942), pp. 3–7; Alfred Barnaby Thomas, *Latin America: A History* (New York: Macmillan, 1956), pp. 396–98.

32. J. Reuben Clark, Jr., *The Alsop Claim. The Case of the United States of America* (Washington, D.C.: Government Printing Office, 1910), pp. 3–11.

33. Ibid., pp. 12–14, 18–38, 209; J. Reuben Clark, Jr., *The Alsop Claim. The Counter-case of the United States of America* (Washington, D.C.: Government Printing Office, 1910), pp. 16–17.

34. Clark, *Alsop Claim Case,* pp. 26–33, 38–39.

35. Testimony of J. Reuben Clark, Jr., in the Case of the Estates of Prentiss and Boutwell v. Estate of Edward McCall, Box 6.

36. This report has apparently been lost. The correspondence with Nathaniel Prentiss is preserved in Box 6.

37. J. Reuben Clark, Jr., "Legal Aspects Regarding the Ownership and Distribution of Awards," *American Journal of International Law* 7 (1913):383–86.

38. Clark, *Alsop Claim Case,* pp. 40–41.

39. "I drew [up] all the correspondence between the United States and Chile on the Alsop Case," Reuben would later recall. Undated memorandum, RM.

40. Memorandum on the Alsop Case, 15 May 1947, Box 6.

41. Harry B. Armes to JRC, 15 April 1913, Box 6.

42. Memorandum on the Alsop Case.

43. Ibid.

44. Clark, *Alsop Claim Case,* p. 41.

45. Ibid., p. 42; JRC to John Bassett Moore, 23 August 1911, Box 345.

46. Memorandum on the Alsop Case.

47. Huntington-Wilson, *Memoirs,* pp. 160–61.

48. Ibid., pp. 173–74.

49. Ibid., pp. 176–77.

Chapter Four DARK HORSE KICKING

1. Scholes and Scholes, *Foreign Policies,* pp. 4–5.

2. Ibid., pp. 27–31.

3. Walter V. Scholes, "Philander Knox," in *An Uncertain Tradition: American Secretaries of State in the Twentieth Century,* ed. Norman A. Graebner (New York: McGraw-Hill, 1961), pp. 73, 75–77.

4. Herbert F. Wright, "Philander Knox," in *The American Secretaries of State and Their Diplomacy,* ed. Samuel Flagg Bemis, 10 vols. (New York: Pageant Book, 1958), 9:309–10; Huntington-Wilson, *Memoirs,* pp. 175, 236; Mulhollan, "Philander Knox," pp. 8–19; Scholes and Scholes, *Foreign Policies,* pp. 8–10, 22; Scholes, "Philander Knox," p. 60.

5. Mulhollan, "Philander Knox," p. 34.

6. Huntington-Wilson, *Memoirs,* pp. 178, 180.

7. The main feature of Huntington Wilson's reorganization plan was the creation of an "under secretary" to play a role analogous to the chief of staff in a military organization. All assistant secretaries and bureau chiefs would report directly to the undersecretary, freeing the secretary himself for broad considerations of policy. The title "under secretary" (or "undersecretary," as later usage preferred) proved rather awkward on account of its prior use by the British. Nevertheless, Huntington Wilson, as first assistant, was in fact if not in name the undersecretary of state.

8. Huntington-Wilson, *Memoirs,* pp. 179–80; Scholes, "Philander Knox," p. 66.

9. Huntington-Wilson, *Memoirs,* pp. 183–85.

10. Scholes and Scholes, *Foreign Policies,* p. 27.

11. Huntington-Wilson, *Memoirs,* p. 187.

12. Ibid., pp. 185–86.

13. Wilbur J. Carr Diary, 20 April 1907, Carr Papers, Library of Congress, Washington, D.C.

14. Huntington-Wilson, *Memoirs,* pp. 190–91; Otis T. Cartwright to JRC, 15 July 1910, Box 2. The counselor was not a competing solicitor, but he did wield considerable informal authority and his salary was significantly higher than that of the solicitor or the assistant secretaries. In Woodrow Wilson's time the counselorship would become a position much

like the undersecretaryship which Huntington Wilson had envisioned and would be filled by no less a luminary than John Bassett Moore. Under William Jennings Bryan, Moore effectively ran the State Department. It was this position which in the 1920s evolved into the undersecretary of state.

15. "Departmental Trickery," Box 36.

16. Huntington Wilson, Memorandum of 7 December 1909, Box 2.

17. JRC to Luacine, August 1909, Box 329.

18. Wright, "Philander Knox," p. 325.

19. Knox was often criticized for being blunt, impatient, and preemptory. See Jessup, *Elihu Root,* 2:251; Scholes and Scholes, *Foreign Policies,* p. 24; Wright, "Philander Knox," p. 304.

20. Huntington-Wilson, *Memoirs,* pp. 178–79; Mulhollan, "Philander Knox," pp. 20, 23, 34, 752.

21. Jessup, *Elihu Root,* 2:250–51.

22. Arthur Deerin Call, "The Friendly Composition of International Disputes: Can the Opposition to Arbitration Be Lessened?," in *Proceedings of the Fourth National Conference of the American Society for Judicial Settlement of International Disputes,* ed. James Brown Scott (Baltimore: William & Wilkins Co., 1914), pp. 222–26.

23. Parkinson, "How a Utah Boy Won His Way," p. 560.

24. JRC, Memorandum of Personal and Informal Conversation, 5 May 1910, Box 71.

25. Clark, *Alsop Claims Case,* pp. 315–52.

26. Untitled memorandum, Box 71.

27. Award Pronounced by His Majesty King George V, Box 71.

28. Distributing the Alsop award among the heirs and creditors of nine estates proved to be almost as big a job as winning it. It was impossible, of course, to cut the pie in such a way as to please everyone, and when Reuben was handed the knife he knew he was in for another thankless task. His eighty-seven-page opinion, published in August of 1912, provided for awards ranging from $500 to $167,628 to fifteen different parties, while referring fourteen disputed or contested claims to the courts. This work was widely applauded. It did not, however, avert the clash of interests which had been building so long. Litigation over the Alsop award stretched on for years.

29. Memoir of 19 August 1960, RM.

30. JRC to John Bassett Moore, 23 August 1911, Box 345.

31. Huntington-Wilson, *Memoirs,* pp. 212–13.

32. Crane, *Mr. Carr of State,* pp. 95–96.

33. Ibid., p. 124.

34. JRC, Lecture Notes, 19 June 1909, Box 61. Besides the "consular school," Huntington Wilson set up a "diplomatic school" to furnish the same kind of training for new diplomats. Reuben lectured here as well.

35. Huntington-Wilson, *Memoirs,* pp. 187–88.

36. Reuben Clark was well suited for this work. He represented an almost perfect hybrid of the political appointee—who happened to be "connected" to the right people—and the qualified professional. At one time or another, the newspapers referred to him as both.

37. Huntington-Wilson, *Memoirs,* p. 185.

38. Jessup, *Elihu Root,* 2:74–75.

39. Memorandum of Matters Handled while Solicitor, RM.

40. Ibid.; Huntington-Wilson, *Memoirs,* p. 233. John Bassett Moore, who became counselor under Secretary of State William Jennings Bryan, reported to Green Hackworth that

he was "amazed" at the sheer amount of creative work that Reuben Clark had done in the department (JRC, Memorandum of 29 September 1955, RM).

41. Alvin C. Gluek, Jr., "The Passamaquoddy Bay Treaty, 1910: A Diplomatic Sideshow in Canadian-American Relations," *Canadian Historical Review* 47 (1966):1-3, 18, 20.

42. Huntington-Wilson, *Memoirs,* p. 237.

43. Gluek, "Passamaquoddy Bay Treaty," pp. 7-20.

44. "The International Prize Court and the Proposed Court of Arbitral Justice," 14 April 1911, Box 69.

45. JRC to James Brown Scott, 14 August 1909, Box 346.

46. Diary of J. Reuben Clark, Sr., 29 April 1910.

47. Ibid., 19 March 1909.

48. William C. Dennis, "The Orinoco Steamship Company Case before the Hague Tribunal," *American Journal of International Law* 5 (January 1911):35-40; Jessup, *Elihu Root,* 2:83-92.

49. "Departmental Trickery."

50. Grew, *Turbulent Era,* 1:76-77.

51. Otis T. Cartwright to JRC, 16 June 1910, Box 343.

52. "Departmental Trickery."

53. Clark Papers, Box 343.

54. William C. Dennis to JRC, 16 August 1910, Box 343.

55. *New York Times,* 2 April 1911.

56. William C. Dennis to JRC, 16 August 1910.

57. Otis T. Cartwright to JRC, 16 June 1910, Box 329.

58. Otis T. Cartwright to JRC, 15 July 1910, Box 2.

59. William C. Dennis to JRC, 16 August 1910.

60. Otis T. Cartwright to JRC, 15 July 1910.

61. William C. Dennis to JRC, 16 August 1910.

62. James Brown Scott to JRC, 13 July 1910, Box 2.

63. There is some uncertainty as to Dennis's actions at this time. The best guess seems to be that the first assistant solicitor, being fed up with Scott and finding an opportunity to take the Venezuelan arbitration to the Hague, resolved to resign from the State Department at that time and made his intentions known *before* sailing for Europe. This may account for his gracious acceptance of Reuben's promotion.

64. JRC to William C. Dennis, 30 June 1910, Box 343.

65. Otis T. Cartwright to JRC, 15 July 1910.

66. Ellery C. Stowell to JRC, 8 August 1910, Box 2.

67. Mary Gibson to JRC, 6 July 1910, Box 2.

68. William C. Dennis to JRC, 27 December 1916, Box 343.

Chapter Five   DOLLAR DIPLOMAT

1. "Outline of the Organization and Work of the Department of State"; JRC to Dallas Townsend, 4 January 1916, Box 8; interview with Louise Clark Bennion, Marianne Clark Sharp, and J. Reuben Clark III.

2. See, for example, JRC to Harlan Fiske Stone, 1 August 1910, Box 2.

3. "Outline of the Organization and Work of the Department of State."

4. JRC, Remarks at Funeral Services for Preston D. Richards, 4 February 1952, Box 245.

Notes

5. Ibid.

6. "Outline of the Organization and Work of the Department of State"; *Register of the Department of State* [periodical], 15 October 1912, p. 21.

7. Memorandum of Matters Handled while Solicitor, RM.

8. Two factors seem to have contributed to Reuben's enhanced stature. First, due to the effective absence of the secretary from the Department of State, every subordinate officer received a constructive appointment. Huntington Wilson became, for all practical purposes, secretary of state, and Reuben Clark was called on to function as assistant secretary. Second, there was something of a power struggle during the second half of Knox's administration. Chandler Anderson, who became counselor upon the death of Henry Hoyt in 1910, did not get along with Huntington Wilson; each jealously guarded his own prerogative and warily eyed the other. Meanwhile, Knox, persuaded at last that he had been hasty to give Huntington Wilson such sweeping authority, began conspiring with Anderson to send the assistant secretary abroad so that he could give his duties to the counselor. Solicitor Clark was virtually the only ranking officer in the department who was on good terms simultaneously with the secretary, the assistant secretary, and the counselor; they were not on good terms with one another.

9. Dana Gardner Munro, *Intervention and Dollar Diplomacy in the Caribbean, 1900–1921* (Princeton, N.J.: Princeton University Press, 1964), pp. 65–66, 161–62; Mulhollan, "Philander Knox," pp. 166–69.

10. Mulhollan, "Philander Knox," pp. 50–55, 77, 82.

11. In securing these funds, Knox also had to be certain that interest rates were not exploitive, which, in view of the risk involved, was often simply impossible. For this reason alone, dollar diplomacy was foredoomed.

12. Article on U.S. Foreign Policy under Knox, Box 90. This document was originally intended for publication in the *Saturday Evening Post* (Diary of Wilbur J. Carr, 8 February 1912).

13. Article on U.S. Foreign Policy under Knox.

14. Thomas A. Bailey, *Theodore Roosevelt and the Japanese-American Conflict* (Gloucester, Mass.: Peter Smith, 1964), pp. 28–84.

15. Payson Treat, *Japan and the United States, 1853–1921* (Stanford, Calif.: Stanford University Press, 1928), pp. 206–7.

16. Memorandum on Termination of Treaties, June 1909, Box 59.

17. Memorandum on Treaty of Commerce and Navigation with Japan, 24 January 1911, Box 62.

18. Ibid. For example, Reuben argued that the right to restrict immigration was so intimately connected to sovereignty that nothing short of an explicit waiver of the right in the treaty could prevent congressional power from being exercised. In other words, although the treaty itself might say nothing at all about restricting immigration, the authority to do so would still exist. Clearly, Knox and Clark were thinking along the same lines.

19. Huntington-Wilson, *Memoirs*, p. 179.

20. Mulhollan, "Philander Knox," pp. 191–216.

21. Memorandum on Chinese Hukuang Railway Bonds, 24 January 1913, Box 62.

22. John Gilbert Reid, *The Manchu Abdication and the Powers, 1908–12: An Episode in Prewar Diplomacy* (Westport, Conn.: Greenwood Press, 1973), pp. 203–41.

23. *FRUS*, 1912, pp. 169–71.

24. Memorandum on Political Disturbances in North China, 30 January 1912, Box 62.

25. Jessup, *Elihu Root*, 1:493–99.

26. Memorandum on Kunhardt Claim, 19 October 1906, Box 59.

27. Munro, *Intervention,* pp. 24–33.

28. Jessup, *Elihu Root,* 1:317.

29. JRC to W. T. S. Doyle, 17 March 1911, Department of State Files 837.156/29, National Archives, Washington, D.C. (hereafter cited as DS).

30. Ibid.

31. J. B. Jackson to Secretary of State, 22 April 1911, DS 837.00/473. Jackson was the United States minister to Cuba.

32. JRC to W. T. S. Doyle, 17 March 1911.

33. Knox to Jackson, 6 May 1911, DS 837.00/473. Circumstances and style indicate that Reuben Clark probably authored this dispatch.

34. The most notorious of these was the Zapata Swamp concession, which, as U.S. minister Arthur M. Beaupré complained, would give away "incalculable millions" in timber and charcoal wood in "a gigantic and barefaced steal." The reaction of the State Department was nearly identical to its reaction in the Ports Company affair (Munro, *Intervention,* pp. 480–83).

35. *FRUS,* 1912, pp. 242–68.

36. JRC, Memoir of 19 September 1960, RM.

37. Ibid.

38. Memorandum on Intervention in Cuba under the Platt Amendment, 12 July 1912, Box 62.

39. Munro, *Intervention,* p. 481. The nexus between this note and Reuben's memorandum of 12 July is clear from the Clark Papers.

40. Munro, *Intervention,* pp. 245–55.

41. Memoranda of 4 January 1911, 9 January 1911, and 13 May 1911, DS 835.51/229 and 828.51/243.

42. E. Taylor Parks, *Columbia and the United States, 1765–1934* (Durham, N.C.: Duke University Press, 1935), pp. 395–403.

43. Jessup, *Elihu Root,* 1:521–27.

44. Huntington-Wilson, *Memoirs,* pp. 185–86.

45. Memorandum on Efforts to Settle Difficulties between Columbia and Panama, 1912, Box 62.

46. Memorandum of Matters Handled while Solicitor, RM.

47. John Richard McDevitt, "American-Nicaraguan Relations from 1909 to 1916" (Ph.D. diss., Georgetown University, 1954), p. 45; Munro, *Intervention,* pp. 167–69; Scholes and Scholes, *Foreign Policies,* pp. 45, 50.

48. Jessup, *Elihu Root,* 1:500–504.

49. Anna I. Powell, "Relations between the United States and Nicaragua, 1898–1916," *Hispanic American Historical Review* 8 (1928):44–45.

50. Charles A. Beard, in collaboration with G. H. E. Smith, *The Idea of National Interest: An Analytical Study in American Foreign Policy* (New York: Macmillan, 1934), pp. 171–72.

51. This notebook is preserved in the Clark Papers, Box 61.

52. *FRUS,* 1909, pp. 460–67.

53. Munro, *Intervention,* pp. 161–62; Parkinson, "How a Utah Boy Won His Way," p. 561.

54. Munro, *Intervention,* pp. 171–73.

55. Ibid., p. 174; Mulhollan, "Philander Knox," p. 126.

56. Munro, *Intervention,* p. 175; Scholes and Scholes, *Foreign Policies,* pp. 52–54.

Notes

57. Lowell J. Thomas, *Old Gimlet Eye: The Adventures of Smedley D. Butler as Told to Lowell Thomas* (New York: Farr & Rinehart, 1933), pp. 130–31.

58. Munro, *Intervention,* p. 175.

59. Memorandum to Thomas Dawson, 4 March 1910, DS 817.00/793½.

60. *New York Tribune,* 21 November 1910.

61. Munro, *Intervention,* p. 176.

62. Ibid.; Scholes and Scholes, *Foreign Policies,* p. 53.

63. *FRUS,* 1909, pp. 455–57.

64. In view of what happened later on, it is worthwhile to consider whether Madriz was indeed only a Zelayist puppet. He came from Zelaya's Liberal Party and from Zelaya's home town of Granada. He had held office in Zelaya's government, and he was appointed by Zelaya's congress. Yet Madriz stoutly claimed—with some evidence—that he had quarreled with Zelaya and that relations between them were ruptured beyond repair. Several European governments accepted this view and recognized the new regime. So many of Madriz's subsequent appointments, however, went to prominent Zelayist politicians (like Julián Irías) that the doubts of Knox and Huntington Wilson seem well justified.

65. Munro, *Intervention,* p. 179; Mulhollan, "Philander Knox," pp. 132–33.

66. Munro, *Intervention,* pp. 180–81; Thomas, *Old Gimlet Eye,* p. 127.

67. Harvey K. Meyer, *Historical Dictionary of Nicaragua* (Metuchen, N.J.: Scarecrow Press, 1972), p. 38; Thomas, *Old Gimlet Eye,* p. 127.

68. Moffat to State Department, 12 April 1910, DS 817.00/902.

69. *FRUS,* 1910, p. 745; Munro, *Intervention,* p. 183.

70. Thomas, *Old Gimlet Eye,* pp. 127–28.

71. JRC to Thomas Dawson, 18 May 1910, DS 817.00/943.

72. *FRUS,* 1910, pp. 747–48.

73. Charles G. Fenwick, *The Neutrality Laws of the United States* (Washington, D.C.: Carnegie Endowment for International Peace, 1954), pp. 81–87.

74. Dawson and Doyle to Huntington Wilson, 26 April 1910, DS 817.00/910.

75. *FRUS,* 1909, p. 455; 1910, p. 746.

76. Questions of neutrality, such as the *Venus* decision, posed an especially difficult problem in international law. The general rule was stated in terms so broad and vague that it was subject to absurd interpretations. One judge allowed an obvious filibustering expedition on the grounds that "it [is] possible that the men might intend to act merely as individuals and simply as porters of the arms" (*United States* v. *O'Brien, Federal Reporter,* National Reporter System—United States Series [1st Series], permanent ed. [St. Paul, Minn.: West Publishing Co., 1880–1925], 75:901). Such being the state of the law, Reuben's decision in the *Venus* case does not look quite so bad.

Still, it was wrong. The ship had been neither built nor armed in the United States. It was carrying guns and ammunition when it cleared New Orleans; but, as Reuben himself had repeatedly emphasized, "international law favors the continuance of commercial transactions and holds them innocent until those transactions become really a part of the military operation against a friendly government" (William Howard Taft to Secretary of Treasury, 12 May 1911, paraphrasing "List of Prospective Questions," cited below). When it sailed, the *Venus* was still under British flag and registry, and its guns were stowed safely below. It was not until the ship had *completed* its voyage from New Orleans to Greytown that the crew was changed, the guns mounted, and the identity as the *Máximo Jérez* begun. The integrity of the completed voyage was crucial in determining the ship's legitimacy as a blockader.

Before the *Venus* left the United States, its British captain had been required to promise that he would not undertake belligerent operations. Later, much was made of the fact that this promise was "broken." This seems particularly strange. Either the ship could lawfully clear port or it could not. If it could not, it should have been detained; if it could, no condition on its exit made any sense at all.

Perhaps the most trenchant commentary on the case is to be found in a legal postscript. On May 11, 1910, one Albert J. Oliver brought suit in federal court for forfeiture of the *Venus* by reason of its alleged violations of U.S. neutrality laws. (Half of the proceeds would go to him as "informer" if he won.) Without explanation, the United States attorney appeared in court, intervened in the suit, and moved to dismiss. Over Oliver's loud objections the case was dropped. (The account of this case, brought in federal court for the eastern district of Louisiana, was published in the *Federal Reporter*, 180:635.)

77. *FRUS*, 1910, pp. 748–50.

78. Scholes and Scholes, *Foreign Policies*, p. 58. The customhouse game, as it might be called, was a familiar feature of Latin American revolutions. One side was always trying to capture the other side's customhouse, and the natural response upon being so deprived was to set up a rival customhouse and continue doing business. Reuben always decided such cases in favor of the group holding the bona fide government customhouse, whether it was composed of rebels or government forces. Customs would continue to be paid at the regular location, he said, and not at some other hastily contrived port in the interior; and customs would only be paid once. Such decisions, which incidentally ran counter to the Latin legal tradition, tended to make the customhouse game more rather than less dangerous, as Reuben would soon discover. In the case of Bluefields, Reuben reversed his customary decision and held that the rival customhouse was equally legitimate. Here, however, the geography was a little different from the usual. The customhouse set up by the Estrada rebels on Schooner Key was actually closer to Bluefields proper than the regular customhouse out on The Bluff. Ships were thus able to choose freely between the two. Since Reuben always held that a warring faction had the right to collect customs for the area which it controlled, his decision here might not have been as biased as it appears.

79. See, for example, *New York Times,* 1 June 1910, 2 June 1910, 6 June 1910.

80. "Outline Nicaragua," 8 June 1910, and "Specific Congressional Authorization for the President to Use Military Force," 20 June 1910, both in Box 59. The "Outline Nicaragua" memorandum demonstrates the extent to which Reuben had departed from purely legal concerns and entered the realm of policy-making. After analyzing the background, causes, and probable outcome of the Nicaraguan muddle, Reuben recommended a joint intervention by the United States and one other government. He then carefully sifted through the possibilities in search of a partner, deciding in the end on Chile. His reasons for doing so are illuminating. The Tacna-Arica dispute was still simmering, and Chile was in a position to do great damage if things heated up again. Then too, Santiago was presently embroiled with Washington over the Alsop claim and perhaps needed to be shown "that the United States does not desire to isolate that Government." Finally,

> having little or no direct interest in Central America (as it is understood she has not) Nicaragua being so far away from Chile, and Chile not having money to expend in [peacemaking] operations of this sort, it would doubtless result that this Government would be given practically free hand in the matter subsequent to the first intervention, that is, in matters relating to the establishment of a proper government. If this were true, this Government might gain all that it desired to gain (or practically all) by sole intervention and at the same time increase its good relations with Chile.

One further point in the memorandum is significant: once again, the dollar diplomat seemed to be having his doubts. If Nicaragua were really to be set aright, said Reuben, the "troublesome monopolies" held by Americans would have to be eliminated. This was as close as anyone in the Knox State Department ever came to a confession of error.

81. Thomas, *Old Gimlet Eye,* pp. 128–29.

Notes

82. Mulhollan, "Philander Knox," pp. 139–40; Parkinson, "How a Utah Boy Won His Way," p. 561.

83. Thomas, *Old Gimlet Eye,* pp. 130–31.

84. Mulhollan, "Philander Knox," pp. 140–41.

85. Ibid., pp. 153–54.

Chapter Six   DARKENING SKIES

1. William Weber Johnson, *Heroic Mexico: The Violent Emergence of a Modern Nation* (Garden City, N.J.: Doubleday, 1968), pp. 3–5.

2. Ronald Atkin, *Revolution!: Mexico, 1910–20* (New York: John Day Co., 1970), pp. 5–6, 7–9.

3. Ibid., pp. 12, 24–31; P. Edward Haley, *Revolution and Intervention: The Diplomacy of Taft and Wilson with Mexico, 1910–17* (Cambridge: Massachusetts Institute of Technology Press, 1970), p. 11.

4. Atkin, *Revolution!,* pp. 12–16.

5. Ibid., pp. 10, 18–23; Haley, *Revolution and Intervention,* pp. 11–12; Peter Calvert, *The Mexican Revolution, 1910–14: The Diplomacy of Anglo-American Conflict* (Cambridge, Eng.: Cambridge University Press, 1968), p. 19; Henry Bamford Parkes, *A History of Mexico* (Boston: Houghton Mifflin, 1960), p. 309.

6. Atkin, *Revolution!,* pp. 20–21.

7. James Morton Callahan, *American Foreign Policy in Mexican Relations* (New York: Cooper Square Publishers, 1967), p. 452.

8. Frederick C. Turner, "Anti-Americanism in Mexico, 1910–13," *Hispanic American Historical Review* 47 (November 1967):502–3.

9. Johnson, *Heroic Mexico,* pp. 19–30, 32–35.

10. Atkin, *Revolution!,* pp. 54–55, 303.

11. Calvert, *The Mexican Revolution,* pp. 29–32; Johnson, *Heroic Mexico,* pp. 36–46.

12. Atkin, *Revolution!,* pp. 3–5.

13. Ibid., p. 5.

14. See chapters four and five for details of these various crises.

15. "Work of the Solicitor's Office," 28 January 1911, Box 63. The Justice Department shared responsibility for political exiles in the United States. The solicitor concerned himself primarily with questions of extradition.

16. *FRUS,* 1911, pp. 354–58; Turner, "Anti-Americanism," pp. 504–5.

17. *FRUS,* 1911, p. 356.

18. *New York Times,* 22 May 1910.

19. Knox to De la Barra, 28 November 1910, DS 812.00/499.

20. Knox to De la Barra, 24 January 1911, DS 812.00/654.

21. Atkin, *Revolution!,* p. 50.

22. *New York Times,* 22 November 1910.

23. Atkin, *Revolution!,* pp. 50–51.

24. *FRUS,* 1911, p. 367.

25. Henry Lane Wilson to Secretary of State, 12 December 1910, DS 812.00/563.

26. *New York Times,* 23 November 1910.

27. Henry Lane Wilson to Secretary of State, 16 November 1910, DS 812.00/447.

28. Henry Lane Wilson to Secretary of State, 18 November 1910, DS 812.00/388.

29. De la Barra to Secretary of State, 19 November 1910, DS 812.00/476.

30. *Congressional Record,* 62d Congress, 1st Session, p. 118 (10 April 1911).

31. The assumption here is that the basic policy decision was made by Knox or Taft and that Reuben Clark was merely asked to carry it out. There is some evidence pointing to an alternative explanation: it may be that Reuben himself essentially determined the policy and that Knox and Taft simply acquiesced in it.

32. JRC, Draft of Message to Mexican Ambassador, 7 March 1912, Box 63.

33. Ibid.

34. Knox to Henry Lane Wilson, 14 December 1910, DS 812.00/447.

35. "List of Prospective Questions Likely to Arise under Present Conditions in Mexico," 11 May 1911, Box 63.

36. There must be a reasonable suspicion here that Reuben Clark and the others were using the law rather than simply observing it. Reuben repeatedly told the Mexican ambassador that the American neutrality statutes imposed no international rights or obligations. Later on, however, when the Mexican ambassador, a distinguished international lawyer in his own right, brought up the case of the *Alabama* in condemnation of American policy, Reuben replied that the United States had won the *Alabama* claims not because the ship had violated international law but because it had violated the domestic neutrality statutes of England. It is hard to see this as anything but double-talk.

37. Knox to Henry Lane Wilson, 14 December 1910, DS 812.00/447.

38. Carr to Consul Ellsworth, 25 January 1911, DS 812.00/672a.

39. Knox to De la Barra, 24 January 1911, DS 812.00/655.

40. Carr to Consul Ellsworth, 25 January 1911.

41. *National Cyclopaedia of Biography,* Permanent Series (Clifton, N.J.: James T. White & Co., 1898–   ), 4:441.

42. Anecdote related by JRC to Rowena Miller, RM.

43. Edward J. Berbusse, "Neutrality-Diplomacy of the United States and Mexico, 1910–11," *The Americas* 12 (January 1956):274–76; Calvert, *The Mexican Revolution,* pp. 47–48; Haley, *Revolution and Intervention,* pp. 24–25.

44. "List of Prospective Questions."

45. Taft to Secretary of Treasury, 12 May 1911, DS 812.00/1808.

46. Official or de jure neutrality would have been a mortal blow to the Díaz government and may well have sufficed to topple it. Moreover, it would have removed all grounds for holding the Mexican government liable for damage done by the *insurrectos.* Reuben's approach had most of the assets of actual neutrality and few of the liabilities.

Chapter Seven   HAWKS AND DOVES

1. Huntington Wilson found room in his autobiography for only one paragraph on the Mexican Revolution (Huntington-Wilson, *Memoirs,* p. 242).

2. *Register of the Department of State,* 15 December 1916, p. 86.

3. Huntington-Wilson, *Memoirs,* p. 210.

4. This compilation is preserved in the Clark Papers, Box 4.

5. "Resume of the Revolutionary Disturbances in Mexico since September, 1910," 29 July 1912, Box 4.

6. Diary of J. Reuben Clark, Sr., 29 March 1911.

7. Reuben's copy of Moore's *Digest* is preserved in the Special Collections Department, Harold B. Lee Library, Brigham Young University. His handwritten notes on neutrality,

found in Box 63 of the Clark Papers, were made in the same distinctive red ink he used to annotate his *Digest.*

8. JRC, Memorandum, 31 March 1911, Box 63.

9. Henry Lane Wilson to Secretary of State, 29 December 1910, DS 812.00/622.

10. Atkin, *Revolution!,* pp. 6, 55, 60.

11. Ibid., pp. 51–52, 53, 56.

12. Consul Edwards to Secretary of State, 23 January 1911, DS 812.00/661.

13. Atkin, *Revolution!,* p. 63.

14. Ibid., pp. 65, 66; Turner, "Anti-Americanism," pp. 507–8.

15. Turner, "Anti-Americanism," pp. 507–8.

16. "American Citizens Killed in Mexico," 26 July 1912, Box 4.

17. *FRUS,* 1911, pp. 605–14.

18. "List of Prospective Questions."

19. *New York Times,* 17 February 1913.

20. Ibid., 2 March 1911.

21. Ibid., 30 May 1911.

22. Lowell L. Blaisdell, *The Desert Revolution: Baja California, 1911* (Madison: University of Wisconsin Press, 1962), pp. 165–67.

23. *Congressional Record,* 62d Congress, 1st Session, p. 451 (20 April 1911).

24. Whenever congressional critics like Stone spoke out, Reuben Clark seemed to draw the assignment of answering them. These replies usually took the form of notes and factual data from which a pro-administration speech might be written by a friendly congressman. Occasionally Reuben himself was called upon to write the speech.

25. Atkin, *Revolution!,* p. 104.

26. Haley, *Revolution and Intervention,* p. 28.

27. *New York Times,* 7 February 1911.

28. John Reed, *Insurgent Mexico* (New York: D. Appleton & Co., 1914), p. 170.

29. Milton B. Kirk to Henry Lane Wilson, 1 May 1912, DS 812.00/3823.

30. Turner, "Anti-Americanism," p. 515.

31. Haley, *Revolution and Intervention,* pp. 15–20.

32. *New York Times,* 4 February 1911, 6 February 1911.

33. Blaisdell, *Desert Revolution,* pp. 53–55; Callahan, *American Foreign Policy,* pp. 461–67.

34. JRC, "Right of this Government to protect . . . the Colorado River levee . . . ," 14 February 1911, Box 63.

35. *Congressional Record,* 62d Congress, 1st Session, pp. 306–7 (17 April 1911), 448–52 (20 April 1911).

36. Atkin, *Revolution!,* p. 104.

37. Blaisdell, *Desert Revolution,* p. 55.

38. "The Right of this Government to protect . . . the Colorado River levee. . . ."

39. Blaisdell, *Desert Revolution,* pp. 163–87.

40. Scholes and Scholes, *Foreign Policies,* p. 84.

41. Haley, *Revolution and Intervention,* p. 25.

42. Ibid., pp. 25–28.

43. Scholes and Scholes, *Foreign Policies,* p. 85.

44. Atkin, *Revolution!,* pp. 56–57.

45. Archie Butt, *Taft and Roosevelt: The Intimate Letters of Archie Butt, Military Aide,* 2 vols. (Garden City, N.J.: Doubleday, 1930), 2:602–3.

46. Haley, *Revolution and Intervention,* p. 30.

47. Diary of J. Reuben Clark, Sr., 16 March 1911.

48. A beautifully printed copy of this stillborn 1911 proclamation can be found in the Clark Papers, Box 4.

Chapter Eight   BLOOD ON THE BORDER

1. Photo File, Clark Papers.

2. *New York Times,* 15 April 1911.

3. Ibid., 14 April 1911.

4. Howard F. Cline, *The United States and Mexico* (Cambridge, Mass.: Harvard University Press, 1963), p. 122.

5. [Walter Blaine Kelley, comp.], *Arizona* ([Los Angeles: W. B. Kelley and R. A. Kirk], n.d.).

6. *New York Times,* 15 April 1911.

7. Ibid., 14 April 1911.

8. Ibid., 15 April 1911.

9. Scholes and Scholes, *Foreign Policies,* p. 85.

10. Henry Lane Wilson to Secretary of State, 19 April 1911, DS 812.00/1458.

11. Calvert, *The Mexican Revolution,* pp. 64–65.

12. Ibid., p. 64.

13. *New York Times,* 15 April 1911.

14. Scholes and Scholes, *Foreign Policies,* p. 88.

15. S. Res. 19, *Congressional Record,* 62d Congress, 1st Session, pp. 306–7 (17 April 1911).

16. Calvert, *The Mexican Revolution,* p. 64.

17. Memorandum on Customs Duties, 16 April 1911, Box 63.

18. "Closure of Ports," 12 May 1911, Box 63.

19. *New York Times,* 18 April 1911.

20. Atkin, *Revolution!,* pp. 63–64.

21. *New York Times,* 18 April 1911.

22. Ibid.

23. Diary of Wilbur J. Carr, 17 April 1911. In possession of Mrs. Wilbur J. (Edith) Carr.

24. Atkin, *Revolution!,* p. 64.

25. *New York Times,* 6 February 1911.

26. Ibid., 9 May 1911.

27. Atkin, *Revolution!,* pp. 64–65.

28. Ibid., pp. 68–71; *New York Times,* 10 May 1911, 11 May 1911.

29. Butt, *Taft and Roosevelt,* 2:664–65.

30. *Dictionary of American Biography,* s.v. "Stone, William J."

31. *Congressional Record,* 62d Congress, 1st Session, pp. 1131–34 (9 May 1911).

32. Ibid., p. 452 (20 April 1911).

33. Atkin, *Revolution!,* pp. 74–78.

Notes

Chapter Nine   JUÁREZ

1. Henry Lane Wilson to Secretary of State, 22 September 1911, DS 812.00/2384.
2. JRC to Judge L. R. Wilfley, 22 August 1912, Box 4.
3. This claims commission is mentioned in an untitled memorandum, Box 63.
4. JRC to Delbert J. Taft, 12 December 1912, Box 4.
5. Reuben met with Garner and Sharp on March 8, 1912 (Memorandum, Box 4).
6. Confidential memorandum for Secretary of State, 22 January 1912, Box 4.
7. Huntington-Wilson, *Memoirs,* p. 242.
8. Atkin, *Revolution!,* p. 48; Johnson, *Heroic Mexico,* pp. 73–77.
9. Atkin, *Revolution!,* pp. 84–87.
10. Ibid., pp. 87–88.
11. Ibid., pp. 93–94.
12. Ibid., pp. 95–96.
13. Henry Lane Wilson to Secretary of State, 24 February 1912, DS 812.00/2884.
14. Haley, *Revolution and Intervention,* p. 42.
15. Huntington Wilson to William Howard Taft, 24 February 1912, DS 812.00/2884A.
16. Memorandum, 26 February 1912, Box 63 (DS 812.00/3292).
17. The copy of this memorandum in the State Department files bears a notation indicating that it was read (and presumably approved) by Huntington Wilson.
18. Henry L. Stimson to State Department, February 1912, DS 812.00/2733.
19. Huntington Wilson to De la Barra, 26 February 1912, DS 812.00/2825.
20. Ellsworth to State Department, 14 February 1912, DS 812.00/2834.
21. Henry L. Stimson to State Department, 24 February 1912, DS 812.00/2859.
22. Garrett to State Department, 24 February 1912, DS 812.00/2882.
23. *New York Times,* 25 February 1912.
24. *Register of the Department of State,* 15 October 1912, p. 70.
25. This construction of the facts is based on admittedly circumstantial evidence, but it seems far and away the most plausible one. Huntington Wilson was in Washington on February 24, when he authored a major policy letter to the president and a dispatch to Ambassador Henry Lane Wilson (DS 812.00/2884A). On February 26, however, when the crisis broke, Clark and Dearing represented the State Department at the White House. Huntington Wilson would never have allowed such a breach of protocol had he still been in Washington.
26. Ellsworth to State Department, 25 February 1912, DS 812.00/2883.
27. Huntington Wilson to William Howard Taft, 24 February 1912, DS 812.00/2884A.
28. We will never know for sure, of course, just why Clark and Dearing did what they did. But somewhere in the background they very likely heard the voice of Senator Stone charging them with treasonable faintheartedness.
29. JRC, Speech at Grantsville, Utah, 5 May 1950, RM.
30. Fred M. Dearing, Memorandum of 26 February 1912, DS 812.00/2912.
31. Ibid.
32. Huntington Wilson [per JRC] to American Consul at Juárez, 26 February 1912, DS 812.00/2912.
33. Huntington Wilson [per JRC] to Henry Lane Wilson, 26 February 1912, DS 812.00/2912.
34. Dearing, Memorandum of 26 February 1912.

35. Atkin, *Revolution!*, p. 93; Calvert, *The Mexican Revolution,* p. 113.

36. Mexican Ambassador to Acting Secretary of State, 11 March 1912, DS 812.00/3194.

37. JRC, Memorandum of 1 April 1912, Box 4.

38. Mexican Ambassador to Acting Secretary of State, 11 March 1912, DS 812.00/3194.

39. JRC to Fred M. Dearing, 7 March 1912, Box 63.

40. JRC, Memorandum of 7 March 1912, Box 63.

41. *FRUS,* 1912, pp. 745–46.

42. Huntington Wilson to Henry Lane Wilson, 2 March 1912, DS 812.00/3005C.

43. See Reuben's handwritten notes in support of the proclamation, Box 4. These afford a glimpse into the workings of Taft's diplomacy. The solicitor carefully laid out the advantages of the proclamation to both sides in the revolution, but his first comments were addressed to American domestic politics and how the proclamation would impinge upon them.

44. JRC to Fred M. Dearing, 7 March 1912, DS 812.113/221.

45. *FRUS,* 1912, pp. 745–46.

Chapter Ten THE MORMON TRAVAIL

1. Atkin, *Revolution!*, p. 95.

2. Thomas Cottam Romney, *The Mormon Colonies in Mexico* (Salt Lake City: Deseret Book, 1938), pp. 51–148, 180–83, 195.

3. Ibid., p. 217.

4. Ibid., p. 157.

5. Ibid., pp. 157–60.

6. Ibid., pp. 161–68.

7. Atkins, *Revolution!,* p. 93.

8. Ibid., pp. 96–97.

9. Ibid., pp. 86–87, 97.

10. Michael C. Meyer, *Mexican Rebel: Pascual Orozco and the Mexican Revolution, 1910–15* (Lincoln: University of Nebraska Press, 1967), pp. 81–83.

11. This curious pattern of logic obtained in virtually every insurrectionary situation faced by the State Department. As long as rebel forces stood a good chance of success, they tended to behave themselves; but when they were beaten and retreating, they had nothing to lose and everything to gain by venting their wrath on foreigners. It took Reuben nearly twenty years to devise an effective response to the problem, but eventually he did. See p. 524.

12. A. W. Ivins to Reed Smoot, 28 July 1912, Box 4.

13. Diary of Reed Smoot, 20 April to 29 July 1912, Smoot Papers, Harold B. Lee Library, Brigham Young University, Provo, Utah.

14. Ibid., 12 April 1912, 14 April 1912.

15. DS 312.11/237.

16. See, e.g., *Congressional Record,* 62d Congress, 2d Session, pp. 11512–18 (22 August 1912).

17. Diary of Reed Smoot, 20 April 1912.

18. Ibid., 14 April 1912.

19. DS 812.113/311, 352.

20. Diary of Reed Smoot, 15 April 1912 to 24 April 1912. The supplies were shipped to Casas Grandes on April 15 (DS 812.113/426).

Notes

21. Romney, *Mormon Colonies,* p. 172.

22. Ibid., p. 176.

23. Ibid., p. 177.

24. Ibid., pp. 179–84.

25. Ibid., pp. 186–91.

26. JRC, Untitled memorandum on claims, Box 4.

27. Romney, *Mormon Colonies,* p. 219.

28. David Stratton, "The Memoirs of Albert B. Fall," *Southwestern Studies* 4 (1966):5–6.

29. *Congressional Record,* 62d Congress, 2d Session, p. 9411 (22 July 1912).

30. Fall himself happened to be one of those difficult and powerful claimholders against Mexico with whom Judge Wilfley was connected. He was also, oddly enough, a personal friend of Pascual Orozco.

31. *Congressional Record,* 62d Congress, 2d Session, p. 9414 (22 July 1912).

32. Reuben was particularly stung by the tone of Fall's rhetoric: "We could take up claims for injuries by jack rabbits and coyotes to fruit trees and sheep, but an American citizen was not worthy of diplomatic considerations" (Ibid., p. 9421).

33. There is no direct evidence on this point, but there are some enticing possibilities. Reuben was in the colossally ironic position of opposing those very measures which were ostensibly designed to protect the Mormons. It is possible that he found himself working under still another handicap: the suspicion on the part of his fellow Saints that he had deserted them.

34. Diary of Reed Smoot, 2 August 1912, 6 August 1912.

35. A. W. Ivins to Reed Smoot, 28 July 1912, Box 4.

36. Romney, *Mormon Colonies,* pp. 195–96.

37. Ibid, p. 197; JRC, "The Mexican Situation," 1 October 1912, Box 63. (More on this critical memorandum below.)

38. DS 312.11/760, 770, 780.

39. Romney, *Mormon Colonies,* p. 121; see Karl E. Young, *Ordeal in Mexico: Tales of Danger and Hardship Collected from Mormon Colonists* (Salt Lake City: Deseret Book, 1968), for a map clearly depicting the geographical relationship of the colonies to the railroad lines.

40. Huntington Wilson to Henry Lane Wilson, 10 September 1912, DS 812.2311/53.

41. Romney, *Mormon Colonies,* p. 198.

42. Ibid., pp. 197–98.

43. David D. Joyce, "Senator Albert B. Fall and United States Relations with Mexico, 1912–21," *International Review of History and Political Science* 6 (August 1969):75.

44. "The Mexican Situation," 1 October 1912, Box 63.

45. Ibid.

46. Ibid.

47. See chapter six for details.

48. Mulhollan, "Philander Knox," pp. 154–55.

49. Ibid., p. 158.

50. The Acting Secretary of State to the American Minister, 4 September 1912, DS 817.00/1940b.

51. *FRUS,* 1912, pp. 1032, 1039, 1046.

52. These handwritten notes which became the instructions to Sutherland are contained in Box 4.

53. *FRUS,* 1912, p. 1049.

54. Acting Secretary to the American Minister, 26 September 1912, DS 817.00/2033; see also Huntington Wilson's policy statement of 4 September 1912, DS 817.00/1940b.

55. Mulhollan, "Philander Knox," pp. 157–58.

56. *FRUS,* 1912, p. 1055.

57. B. H. Roberts, *A Comprehensive History of the Church of Jesus Christ of Latter-day Saints,* 6 vols. (Provo, Utah: Brigham Young University Press, 1965), 6:270.

58. "The Mexican Situation."

59. Romney, *Mormon Colonies,* pp. 188, 200.

60. Ibid., pp. 202–5, 211.

61. Roberts, *Comprehensive History,* 6:268.

Chapter Eleven AN END AND A BEGINNING

1. Elting E. Morison, ed., *The Letters of Theodore Roosevelt,* 8 vols. (Cambridge, Mass.: Harvard University Press, 1954), 7:266–67.

2. *New York Times,* 23 February 1912.

3. Ibid., 23 June 1912; William H. Harbaugh, *The Life and Times of Theodore Roosevelt* (New York: Oxford University Press, 1975), pp. 402–9.

4. *New York Times,* 14 April 1912.

5. The first salvo of this new offensive had been fired by Reuben on April 15, after the arms embargo. He dictated identical notes to be sent to Orozco and the Mexican government, warning both in minatory terms to protect American life and property. The Mexican foreign office bridled at the unwonted harshness of the note. Orozco ignored it. Virtually all of the official correspondence that followed was the work of Solicitor Clark.

6. "The Mexican Situation."

7. Haley, *Revolution and Intervention,* p. 47; Scholes and Scholes, *Foreign Policies,* p. 95.

8. Scholes and Scholes, *Foreign Policies,* pp. 92–93.

9. Ibid., p. 95.

10. Reuben issued opinions on various technical aspects of the proposed invasion. See Box 4.

11. So popular did this work become that it was published as a hardbound volume by the Government Printing Office in 1910.

12. Daniel James, *Mexico and the Americans* (New York: Praeger, 1963), p. 150.

13. JRC to Mrs. Dwight Morrow, 28 May 1933, RM.

14. Calvert, *The Mexican Revolution,* p. 39; Johnson, *Heroic Mexico,* pp. 108–9, 111.

15. Henry Lane Wilson, *Diplomatic Episodes in Mexico, Belgium, and Chile* (Garden City, N.Y.: Doubleday, 1927), p. 248.

16. Henry Lane Wilson to Secretary of State, 23 June 1911, DS 812.00/2181.

17. Henry Lane Wilson to Secretary of State, 17 April 1912, DS 812.00/1364.

18. Henry Lane Wilson to JRC, 2 October 1912, Box 4.

19. Calvert, *The Mexican Revolution,* p. 38.

20. Henry Lane Wilson to Secretary of State, 28 August 1912, DS 812.00/4899.

21. Haley, *Revolution and Intervention,* p. 56.

22. Calvert, *The Mexican Revolution,* p. 115.

23. Wilson, *Diplomatic Episodes,* p. 250.

24. Haley, *Revolution and Intervention,* p. 53.

25. Henry Lane Wilson to Secretary of State, 18 January 1913, DS 312.11/1048.

26. Knox to Taft, 27 January 1913, DS 812.00/7229A.

Notes

27. JRC, Undated memorandum, Box 63.

28. *New York Times,* 20 December 1912.

29. JRC, Undated memorandum, Box 63. See also Memorandum by Huntington Wilson, 7 January 1913, DS 312.11/1240.

30. Atkin, *Revolution!,* p. 105.

31. Ibid., p. 106.

32. Ibid., pp. 100–101, 106.

33. Ibid., pp. 107–12.

34. Ibid., pp. 112–13.

35. Ibid., pp. 113–14.

36. Henry Lane Wilson to Secretary of State, 9 February 1913, DS 812.00/6058.

37. Henry Lane Wilson to Secretary of State, 11 February 1913 and 12 February 1913, DS 812.00/6092.

38. Haley, *Revolution and Intervention,* pp. 64–66.

39. Atkin, *Revolution!,* p. 114.

40. Knox to Henry Lane Wilson, 14 February 1913, DS 812.00/6170A.

41. Henry Lane Wilson to Secretary of State, 17 February 1913, DS 812.00/6225.

42. Atkin, *Revolution!,* pp. 115–16.

43. Ibid., p. 117; Calvert, *The Mexican Revolution,* pp. 147–48.

44. Calvert, *The Mexican Revolution,* p. 153.

45. Henry Lane Wilson to Secretary of State, 19 February 1913, DS 812.00/6271.

46. Knox to Henry Lane Wilson, 20 February 1913, DS 812.00/6271.

47. Atkin, *Revolution!,* p. 121.

48. Ibid., pp. 122–24.

49. Ibid., 140–42; Johnson, *Heroic Mexico,* pp. 129–36.

50. "Suggestive Points on the Mexican Revolution," no date, Box 90.

51. For a discussion on Reuben's views concerning the right of revolution, see Epilogue, note 56.

52. "Suggestive Points."

53. Ibid.

54. Ibid.

55. Ibid.

56. Huntington-Wilson, *Memoirs,* p. 249.

57. Ibid., p. 246.

Chapter Twelve   TO REAP THE WHIRLWIND

1. Fred M. Dearing to JRC, 10 January 1914, Box 90.

2. Fred M. Dearing to JRC, 10 March 1929, Box 343.

3. Fred M. Dearing to JRC, 7 July 1944, Box 371.

4. Atkin, *Revolution!,* pp. 129–86, 203–73.

5. Ibid., pp. 187–202.

6. Ibid., pp. 274–92.

7. JRC to Mrs. Dwight Morrow, 28 May 1933, RM.

8. Atkin, *Revolution!,* pp. 268–69.

9. Ibid., p. 169; Thomas Edward Gibbon, *Mexico under Carranza* (Garden City, N.Y.: Doubleday, 1919), p. 261.

10. Romney, *Mormon Colonies,* pp. 238–40.

11. JRC to Philander C. Knox, 5 January 1916, Box 22.

12. "Suggestive Points."

Chapter Thirteen THE NEW LAWYERS

1. *Proceedings of the American Society of International Law,* 1907, p. 28.

2. Marchand, *American Peace Movement,* pp. 41–43.

3. John Bassett Moore, *History and Digest of International Arbitrations to Which the United States Has Been a Party,* 6 vols. (Washington, D.C.: Government Printing Office, 1898), 1:liv-lv.

4. Tuchman, *Proud Tower,* pp. 264–67.

5. Marchand, *American Peace Movement,* pp. 18–38.

6. Philander C. Knox, "The Spirit and Purpose of American Diplomacy," Box 88.

7. Marchand, *American Peace Movement,* pp. 39–41, 45–51.

8. Ibid., pp. 68–70.

9. James Brown Scott, *The Status of the International Court of Justice* (New York: Oxford University Press, 1916), pp. 3–4.

10. Leopold, *Elihu Root and the Conservative Tradition,* pp. 54–59.

11. Marchand, *American Peace Movement,* p. 66; Wright, "Philander Knox," pp. 346–48.

12. George A. Finch, "James Brown Scott, 1866–1943," *American Journal of International Law* 38 (January 1914):184–85.

13. Ibid., p. 22.

14. James Brown Scott, *The American Society for Judicial Settlement of International Disputes—Its Scope and Work* (Baltimore: Williams, 1910), p. 1.

15. Finch, "James Brown Scott," pp. 201–9, 215–17; Marchand, *American Peace Movement,* pp. 66–69.

16. Scott, *American Society for Judicial Settlement,* pp. 8–9.

17. Ibid., pp. 7–8. One of Scott's books was significantly entitled *James Madison's Notes on Debates in the Convention of 1787 and Their Relation to a More Perfect Society of Nations* (n.p., 1918).

18. Reuben joined the American Society of International Law in April of 1907 (Diary of J. Reuben Clark, Sr., 28 April 1907). He joined the Judicial Settlement Society in October of 1912 and was immediately appointed its representative on the board of directors of the American Peace Society (Theodore Marburg to JRC, 23 October 1912, Box 343).

19. JRC, "Difficulties in Unlimited Compulsory Arbitration," Box 62. This speech was never delivered in public.

20. JRC, "Rough Draft of International Court System," 30 September 1910, Box 61.

21. JRC, "The International Prize Court and the Proposed Court of Arbitral Justice," 14 April 1911, Box 69.

22. William Howard Taft to JRC, 10 June 1912, Box 7.

23. Memorandum for American Preparatory Committee for Third Hague Conference, September 1913, Box 76; "The Next Advance in the Judicial Settlement of International Disputes," 3 May 1915, Box 343.

24. Montevideo Conference Diary, 21 November 1933, Box 144.

25. Memorandum to Huntington Wilson, 8 September 1910, Box 62.

26. "Difficulties in Unlimited Compulsory Arbitration." See also Memorandum for American Preparatory Committee.

Notes

27. Jessup, *Elihu Root,* 2:83.

28. Ibid., 2:83–96, 160.

29. Montevideo Conference Diary, 21 November 1933, Box 144.

30. Article on U.S. Foreign Policy under Knox, Box 90.

31. Diary of J. Reuben Clark, Sr., 27 November 1911.

32. Memorandum to Huntington Wilson, 8 September 1910.

33. Memorandum for American Preparatory Committee.

34. JRC to John Bassett Moore, March 1913, Box 345.

35. JRC to Theodore Marburg, 3 May 1915, Box 24.

36. "The Next Advance in Judicial Settlement." Like the Lake Mohonk speech, this article was never published.

37. "International Cooperation to Prevent War," speech delivered to League of Women Voters, August 1916, Box 90.

38. JRC to Philander C. Knox, 7 May 1920, Box 91.

39. Marchand, *American Peace Movement,* pp. 144–81.

Chapter Fourteen   CLAIMS AND CONTROVERSIES

1. *New York Times,* 5 March 1913.

2. Marchand, *American Peace Movement,* pp. 42–44.

This sense of Anglo-American partnership was fraught with racial overtones. The confident world of the Victorians was, after all, the world of Rudyard Kipling and Josiah Strong—the world of the "white man's burden." It was also the world in which J. Reuben Clark grew up and came of age.

The proud and accomplished boy could hardly have escaped its influence. He was still a teenager when he began speaking expansively of the mission of the Anglo-Saxon race, and at Columbia University he came under the tutelage of John W. Burgess, the foremost evangelist of that mission. According to Burgess, Anglo-Saxons had been fitted by God to the task of world leadership and were duty-bound to accomplish it. If Reuben missed the message here, there were plenty of chances to hear it later. Roosevelt, Beveridge, Lodge, Root, Hay, Knox, Bacon, Adee, Lansing, Anderson, and many others about the halls of the State Department were avid disciples of the Anglo-Saxon idea.

The Huntington Wilsons were rather more than disciples. They pushed their Anglo-Saxonism to the logical extreme of eugenics. The eugenics—or race betterment—movement rested on a simple premise: that improved human beings, like improved bulldogs or race-horses, could be produced through selective breeding. William Graham Sumner and the social Darwinists had been saying as much all along, of course; but the eugenics people did not want to wait around for the slow purification wrought by the natural selection process—they wanted racial betterment immediately. In order to secure it, Lucy James Wilson wrote a book on the subject, promoted research, and funded eugenics lectures at three hundred universities. When she was traveling abroad, her eugenicist-physician, Dr. Lewellys Barker, transmitted odd messages to her through her attorney, Reuben Clark. One of them read simply: "PRIMUS." "It need not be signed," explained the doctor, "as she will know the source of the cable and its meaning" (Lewellys F. Barker to JRC, 8 June 1914, Box 346).

It is impossible to say how much, if any, of this Reuben took seriously. But in his conversation, especially with the Huntington Wilsons, he displayed the same racial conceits and phobias that a preoccupation with eugenics could impart. Thus, he too fretted over the "yellow peril" and the infestation of the Slavs. Many of his diplomatic analyses were based on the assumed proclivities of this or that race, and his view of the world war was nothing short of a eugenicist's nightmare. This was the dark side of Anglo-Saxonism; a later generation would regard it as unfortunate.

And yet, the forces of the twentieth century were inevitably at work on Reuben too. He performed legal work for the Japanese and grudgingly came to respect them. His contempt for Latin Americans began to soften when he defended the one-time Zelayist outcast, Julián Iriás, and decided that the man had been woefully misrepresented. But the real turnabout came in Mexico, where Reuben discovered in the racially mixed Mexican people unimagined virtues. His fascination with the Aztecs and their civilization represented an attempt to find some sort of eugenic explanation for the discovery.

In the late 1920s, when Reuben came out against interventionism, he also turned a corner on the racial question. Every people before God was different, he concluded, but not necessarily superior or inferior to any other. What the Mexicans may have lacked in technological skills they more than made up in the quality of their human relations. And, just as it would not do for one country to go around telling the others how to live, so there should be no "master race" imposing its values on the rest of humanity. Reuben was coming very close to accepting the brotherhood of man.

This insight gave him a new view of America. He no longer spoke of the United States as that other great Anglo-Saxon nation; indeed, he seemed to become disillusioned with the Anglo-Saxon ideal. "We are now completely subservient to British aims and interests," he complained to his friend Herbert Hoover in 1942. "We are in a sad state." America, rather, became for him that place on the earth where all mankind had learned to live and work together.

> America, multi-raced and multi-nationed, is by tradition, by geography, by citizenry, by natural sympathy, and by material interest, the great neutral of the earth. God has so designed it. Drawn from all races, creeds, and nations, our sympathies run to every oppressed people. . . . Directed in right channels, this great body of feeling for the one side or the other will ripen into sympathy and love for all our misguided and misled fellowmen who suffer in any cause, and this sympathy and love will run out to all humanity in its woe, thus weakly shadowing the infinite compassion of the Master. [. . . *Conference of The Church of Jesus Christ of Latter-day Saints . . . with . . . Report of . . . Discourses* (hereinafter referred to as *Conference Report*), October 1939, p. 15.]

Needless to say, such an insight gave an added dimension to Reuben's view of isolationism—and to the divinely inspired nature of the American government.

3. JRC to Joseph Nelson, 20 February 1914, Box 7; P. E. Corbett, *The Settlement of Canadian-American Disputes* (New Haven, Conn.: Yale University Press, 1937), p. 197.

4. JRC, Memorandum for Mr. Hoyt, 1 February 1910, Box 3.

5. Corbett, *Canadian-American Disputes,* pp. 63–64.

6. JRC to R. W. Young, 2 March 1914, Box 7; Fred K. Nielsen, *American and British Claims Arbitration* (Washington, D.C.: Government Printing Office, 1926), pp. 6–9.

7. *American Journal of International Law* 7 (July 1913):576.

8. JRC, Memorandum for William Phillips, 13 May 1914, Box 77. This suggestion was not made until after the neutral commissioner had been chosen and the work of the commission was nearly completed, but it illustrates the difficulties with which the selection process was fraught.

9. JRC, Memorandum on the personnel of the claims commission, Box 7; JRC to Philander C. Knox, 15 January 1913, Box 7.

10. JRC to John Bassett Moore, 23 January 1913, Box 345.

11. JRC, Memorandum on Claims Commission, Box 7.

12. JRC to Philander C. Knox, 14 February 1914, Box 7.

13. JRC, Confidential memorandum to Huntington Wilson, 1913, Box 346.

14. Ibid. Reuben was replaced as solicitor by Joseph Wingate Folk, former governor of Missouri, who had no particular interest or experience in international law. His selection

Notes

was a commentary, perhaps, on the long-term effect of Huntington Wilson's reforms. One day Reuben happened to drop in at the solicitor's office for old time's sake. He found the office staff assembled together and his former assistant solicitor, Frederick Van Dyne, addressing a birthday toast to Governor Folk. Van Dyne, whose back was to Reuben, proclaimed that in the few short months he had been in office Folk had proven himself to be "the best Solicitor the State Department ever had." Van Dyne was mortified upon seeing his former boss and he apologized profusely. For Reuben the incident seemed particularly symbolic.

15. JRC to John Bassett Moore, 23 January 1913, Box 345.

16. JRC to Heber J. May, 14 December 1912, Box 7.

17. *American Journal of International Law* 7 (July 1913):578.

18. Nielsen, *Claims Arbitration,* p. 17.

19. *American Journal of International Law* 7 (July 1913):577-78.

20. Nielsen, *Claims Arbitration,* p. 17.

21. A splendid photo of the commission can be found in the Clark Papers, Box 470.

22. Corbett, *Canadian-American Disputes,* p. 37.

23. *American and British Claims Arbitration. Award in the Matter of Yukon Lumber* (n.p., n.d.).

24. Corbett, *Canadian-American Disputes,* p. 30; *American and British Claims Arbitration. Award in the Matter of William Hardman* (n.p., n.d.).

25. *American Journal of International Law* 7 (October 1913):687-88.

26. The entire address was reprinted as "Jurisdiction of the American-British Claims Commission," ibid., pp. 687-706.

27. JRC to Preston D. Richards, 10 December 1913, Box 345.

28. The speaker was E. L. Newcombe, assistant agent for Great Britain. The anecdote was recorded by Rowena Miller, 30 August 1946, RM.

29. Nielsen, *Claims Arbitration,* pp. 25, 31.

30. JRC to Enoch H. Crowder, 27 September 1920, RM.

31. Nielsen, *Claims Arbitration,* pp. 26, 30-31.

32. Robert Lansing to JRC, 20 June 1913, Box 7.

33. JRC to Joseph Nelson, 20 February 1914, Box 7.

34. JRC to Preston D. Richards, 14 February 1914, Box 7.

35. Ibid.

36. JRC to Joseph Nelson, 20 February 1914, Box 7.

37. JRC to Philander C. Knox, 14 February 1914, Box 7.

38. Preston D. Richards to JRC, 26 February 1914, Box 7.

39. JRC to James E. Talmage, 4 March 1914, Box 7.

40. Ibid.; JRC, Memorandum of 25 February 1914, Box 7.

41. JRC to Joseph Nelson, 20 February 1914, Box 7.

42. JRC to James E. Talmage, 4 March 1914, Box 7.

43. JRC to Joseph Nelson, 24 February 1914, Box 7.

44. Preston D. Richards to JRC, 14 March 1914, Box 7. Nevertheless, Reuben Clark and William King went on to become good friends. Reuben was never close to Senator Smoot; after King was elected to the Senate from Utah, it was to him rather than to Smoot that Reuben was likely to go for an occasional political favor. Reuben once told a friend that Bill King was the only Democrat for whom he had ever voted.

45. JRC to James E. Talmage, 4 March 1914, Box 7.

46. *Advocate of Peace* 76 (April 1914):76-77.

47. JRC to Enoch H. Crowder, 27 September 1920, RM; Nielsen, *Claims Arbitration,* pp. 24-26.

48. JRC to Harry B. Armes, 25 March 1914, Box 343.

49. JRC to James E. Talmage, 4 March 1914, Box 7.

50. JRC to George Savage, 27 April 1914, Box 329.

51. Nielsen, *Claims Arbitration,* p. 34.

52. JRC, Memoir of 14 January 1949, Box 2.

53. JRC, Memorandum for William Phillips, 13 May 1914, Box 77.

54. Diary of J. Reuben Clark, Sr., 23 May 1914.

55. JRC, Untitled memorandum, Box 7.

56. Memorandum on claims commission, Box 7.

57. Arthur P. McKinstry to JRC, 26 June 1914, Box 7.

58. William Jennings Bryan to JRC, 24 June 1914, Box 7.

59. JRC to Arthur P. McKinstry, 7 July 1914, Box 7; JRC to George Savage, 20 July 1914, Box 329.

60. Memorandum on Madame de Prévost's Charges, Box 6.

61. Ibid.

62. JRC to Philander C. Knox, 11 July 1914, Box 7.

63. Reuben had in fact been offered money while solicitor, in connection with his work on the Alsop claim. The claimants, Madame de Prévost among them, had wanted to give him an honorarium because so much of the work had been done on his own time. Both Reuben and Secretary Knox, however, had rejected the offer as unseemly. Reuben's connection with the Hobson estate began only after he had severed all connection with the State Department, and it is difficult to see how he could have been open to charges of wrongdoing on that account. As for Young, he first became involved with the Alsop claim as secretary to Solicitor Clark during the original negotiations. After the official U.S. case was prepared in 1910, Young was the one delegated to deliver it to London and to answer any questions that might arise. Like Reuben, he entered the employ of the claimants only after he had left the State Department. The $30,797.92 he received from the Alsop award was his payment for legal services rendered to the estate of George Hobson.

64. JRC, Memorandum on personnel of claims commission, Box 7.

65. After the war broke out, Bryan reduced the claims commission to a skeleton crew of loyal Democrats. Reuben continued to storm and fume about the secretary of state, referring to him sarcastically as "the great commonest" and "my great and good friend and well-wisher." Reuben eventually forgave most partisan foes, but the name of William Jennings Bryan would never conjure up for him anything but the specter of blatant political favoritism.

66. Walter Millis, *The Road to War: America, 1914-17* (New York: Houghton Mifflin, 1935), pp. 27-32.

67. Barbara Tuchman, *The Guns of August* (New York: Macmillan, 1962), p. 122.

Chapter Fifteen   THE HORDES OF SATAN

1. William Howard Taft to JRC, 10 June 1912, Box 7.

2. JRC, Speech at Wasatch Stake Seminary, Heber City, 10 May 1952, RM.

3. JRC to J. Reuben Clark, Sr., 14 February 1917, Box 331.

4. David Alexander Lockmiller, *Enoch H. Crowder: Soldier, Lawyer, and Statesman* (Columbia: University of Missouri Press, 1955), pp. 24-85, 133-78.

Notes

5. Hugh Gibson, *A Journal from Our Legation in Belgium* (New York: Doubleday, 1917), pp. 156–58.

6. Marchand, *American Peace Movement,* p. 166.

7. JRC to Theodore Marburg, 18 December 1914, Box 343.

8. James Brown Scott to JRC, 14 June 1915, Box 346.

9. JRC to Theodore Marburg, 18 December 1914, Box 343.

10. "Paragraphs on Preparedness," speech prepared for Philander C. Knox, 6 March 1916, Box 88.

11. JRC to Theodore Marburg, 3 March 1917, Box 343.

12. Tuchman, *Guns of August,* pp. 191–93.

13. JRC to Oscar C. Bass, 14 November 1914, Box 8.

14. JRC to Arthur D. Call, 2 December 1915, Box 343.

15. JRC to C. J. B. Hurst, 4 August 1914, Box 8.

16. JRC to C. J. B. Hurst, 10 January 1915, Box 346.

17. JRC, Memorandum for L. Wolff & Company, 4 March 1915, Box 79.

18. JRC to C. J. B. Hurst, 20 January 1915, Box 346.

19. JRC, Memorandum for J. P. Morgan & Company, 9 September 1915, Box 79.

20. JRC, Editorial for John E. Semmes, Jr., 17 August 1915, Box 79.

According to the international rules, neutrals might lawfully trade noncontraband – that is, nonmilitary – goods with both belligerents, subject only to reasonable inspection. As for contraband, these goods were legally subject to forfeiture if apprehended in a legitimate blockade. In order to qualify as legitimate, a blockade had to be close to the enemy's coastline and it had to be substantially effective: neutrals could not be hailed at random on the high seas. That these rules were hardly observable even in classical situations was attested by the entry of the United States into the War of 1812 as an outraged neutral. In any event, modern technology rendered them hopelessly obsolete. In view of the Germans' long-range artillery, the British blockade of Flanders necessarily had to move out to sea, where it became a law unto itself. But neither was it possible for German submarines to comply with the law of visit and search, which required them to fire a warning, board the merchant vessel in question, inspect cargo and papers, and escort contraband cargoes to a neutral prize court. Belligerent merchantmen flew whatever flags seemed handy, and an easily mounted deck gun could dispatch the hardiest submarine with a single shot.

Secretary of State Bryan, who claimed no particular sophistication in international law, saw this situation for what it was: impossible. He therefore allowed both Britain *and* Germany to violate the rules and assumed that neutrals like the United States would proceed at their own risk. He could not understand the lopsided judgment of international lawyers like Reuben Clark who seemed to overlook the British violations but not the German. When President Wilson delivered a near ultimatum to Germany after the sinking of the *Lusitania,* Bryan, showing unprecedented ministerial courage, resigned in protest. Robert Lansing, who had replaced John Bassett Moore as counselor, succeeded Bryan as secretary. Unlike his predecessor, Lansing was an international lawyer, and he judged the relative violations exactly as Reuben Clark was doing: diplomatic reprisals for the British, "strict accountability" for the Germans. This policy left the German High Command with only two choices: obey the law and lose out to the British on the high seas, or ignore the law and risk war with the United States. Not surprisingly, they chose the latter.

21. *Salt Lake Herald-Republican,* 4 June 1915.

22. JRC to Oscar C. Bass, 14 November 1914, Box 8.

23. JRC to John Clark, 25 January 1915, Box 24.

24. Untitled draft memorandum, 1918, Box 90.

25. JRC to John Clark, 25 January 1915, Box 24.

26. Millis, *Road to War,* pp. 345–47.

27. JRC to Lucy Wilson, 12 July 1915, Box 346.

28. JRC, Work Diary, 28 September 1914 to 9 October 1914, Box 528.

29. Speech prepared for Philander C. Knox, 17 October 1914, Box 88.

30. Draft Speech for Philander C. Knox, 18 June 1915, Box 88.

31. JRC to Luacine, n.d., Box 331.

32. JRC to Fred M. Dearing, 8 January 1923, Box 343.

33. JRC to Preston D. Richards, 26 March 1918, Box 345.

34. Interview with Louise Clark Bennion, Marianne Clark Sharp, and J. Reuben Clark III.

35. *National Cyclopaedia of Biography,* Current Series, A:455.

36. JRC, Memorandum for General Crowder on the Selective Service Regulations, 26 June 1917, Box 95.

37. JRC, Work Diary, 28 April 1917, Box 528.

38. Newton D. Baker to Thomas W. Gregory, 1 May 1917, Box 26.

39. Thomas W. Gregory to JRC, 21 May 1917, Box 26; JRC to Thomas W. Gregory, 23 May 1917, Box 26; JRC, Work Diary, 26 May 1917, Box 528.

40. JRC to Preston D. Richards, 21 April 1917, Box 345.

41. JRC to Luacine, 21 July 1918, Box 331.

42. JRC, Review of Work of Attorney General's Office, 9 March 1918, Box 93.

43. Oscar Theodore Barck, Jr., and Nelson Manfred Blake, *Since 1900: A History of the United States in Our Times* (New York: Macmillan, 1974), pp. 167–68; Gilbert C. Fite and Norman A. Graebner, *Recent United States History* (New York: Ronald Press, 1972), pp. 115–18; John A. Garraty, *The American Nation: A History of the United States* (New York: Harper & Row, 1971), p. 783.

44. JRC, Statement for Director of Publicity, Box 93.

45. A fascinating collection of World War I propaganda posters is housed in the Hoover Institute, Stanford University.

46. Alfred H. Kelley and Winifred A. Harbison, *The American Constitution: Its Origins and Development,* 4th ed. (New York: W. W. Norton, 1970), pp. 663–74.

47. JRC to H. C. Frick, 6 May 1918, Box 88.

48. Ibid.

49. *National Cyclopaedia of Biography,* Permanent Series, 27:201.

50. JRC, Memorandum for Attorney General, 16 July 1917, Box 93.

51. JRC, Memorandum for Attorney General, February 1918, Box 93.

52. JRC, Memorandum for Attorney General, 30 July 1917, Box 93.

53. JRC, Memorandum for Attorney General, 27 July 1917, Box 93.

54. *National Cyclopaedia of Biography,* Permanent Series, 27:201.

55. JRC, Memorandum for Attorney General, 26 February 1918, Box 93.

56. JRC (with Warren F. Martin), "American Policy Relative to Alien Enemy Property," 1926, Box 113. This memorandum was published as Senate Document No. 181, 69th Congress, 2d Session.

57. Ibid.; see also JRC (with Warren F. Martin), "Power to Confiscate Ex-Enemy Property in Time of Peace," 1926, Box 113.

58. JRC to Lucy Wilson, 12 July 1918, Box 346.

59. *Congressional Record,* 65th Congress, 1st Session, p. 4274 (26 June 1917).

60. Memoranda on each of these topics are found in Box 93 of the Clark Papers.

Notes

61. *Congressional Record,* 65th Congress, 1st Session, p. 5367 (21 July 1917).

62. Kelley and Harbison, *The American Constitution,* pp. 664-65, 669-70.

63. JRC, Memorandum for Attorney General, 30 August 1917, Box 93.

64. JRC, Memorandum for Attorney General, 6 November 1917, Box 93.

65. Barck and Blake, *Since 1900,* p. 162.

66. JRC, Draft Article for Philander C. Knox, 1918, Box 90.

67. Ibid.

68. Thomas W. Gregory to Newton D. Baker, 13 September 1920, Locked Case 3, Book IV.

69. JRC to Committee on Admissions, Cosmos Club, 27 December 1921, Box 8.

70. *Emergency Legislation,* "Summary Memorandum," Box 94. *Emergency Legislation* was published by the Government Printing Office in 1918.

71. JRC, Draft of Speech for Enoch H. Crowder, Box 95.

72. Kelley and Harbison, *The American Constitution,* p. 671.

73. JRC, Memorandum for Philander C. Knox on War Powers, 17 May 1918, Box 88.

74. Kelley and Harbison, *The American Constitution,* p. 672.

75. Garraty, *The American Nation,* pp. 786-88.

76. JRC to Marianne Clark, 18 June 1918, Box 332.

77. JRC to John Clark, 6 October 1917, Box 330.

78. JRC to Luacine, 26 July 1918, Box 331. See also Enoch H. Crowder to Thomas W. Gregory, 28 February 1918, Locked Case 3, Book I; Thomas W. Gregory to Enoch H. Crowder, 2 March 1918, Locked Case 3, Book IV; JRC to Thomas W. Gregory, 5 July 1918, Box 26.

79. JRC to Enoch H. Crowder, 15 May 1919, Box 343.

80. JRC to Enoch H. Crowder, 27 September 1920, Box 343.

81. Diary of J. Reuben Clark, Sr., 23 September 1918. The promotion to lieutenant colonel never materialized, however. Such were Crowder's relations with Congress that virtually none of his promotions could win approval.

82. Anecdote related to Rowena Miller, RM.

83. Robert C. Davis to JRC, 31 October 1922, Locked Case 3, Book I; JRC to Assistant Adjutant, 13 November 1922, Box 26.

84. JRC to Messrs. Faust and Wilson, 13 November 1922, Box 26.

Chapter Sixteen   BITTER-ENDER

1. Alan Cranston, *The Killing of the Peace* (New York: Viking, 1945), pp. 18-19; Denna Frank Fleming, *The United States and the League of Nations, 1918-20* (New York: G. P. Putnam's Sons, 1932), pp. 20-21.

2. Garraty, *The American Nation,* pp. 788-89.

3. Fleming, *League of Nations,* pp. 8-9, 12; Ralph A. Stone, *The Irreconcilables: The Fight against the League of Nations* (Lexington: University of Kentucky Press, 1970), p. 15.

4. Fleming, *League of Nations,* pp. 4-5, 23, 30-35.

5. *Congressional Record,* 65th Congress, 2d Session, pp. 11485-88 (28 October 1918).

6. Stone, *Irreconcilables,* pp. 26-27.

7. Ibid., p. 29.

8. Cranston, *Killing of the Peace,* pp. 5, 10-11, 45.

9. Stone, *Irreconcilables,* pp. 90-92.

10.   Cranston, *Killing of the Peace*, pp. 43–45; Fleming, *League of Nations*, pp. 72–76.

11.   Stone, *Irreconcilables*, pp. 179–80.

12.   Ibid., pp. 41–43.

13.   Ibid., pp. 180–82. See pp. 183–88 for biographical sketches of all the irreconcilables, including those not mentioned here.

14.   *Congressional Record*, 65th Congress, 3d Session, pp. 603–4 (18 December 1918).

15.   "I had a profound respect, and indeed almost a filial love for Mr. Knox," Reuben wrote after the senator's death. "In the later years of his life I was perhaps as close to him as any person of all his acquaintances and relations" (JRC to John Bassett Moore, 7 December 1938, Box 345).

16.   "The [Knox] home has for me many memories that make of it a shrine," Reuben later recalled (JRC to J. R. Tindle, 14 June 1922, Box 22. See also JRC to Rebie Knox Tindle, 21 June 1922, Box 27).

17.   "The Spirit and Purpose of American Diplomacy," Box 88. This speech is quoted on pp. 223.

18.   *Salt Lake Tribune*, 9 November 1930. This anecdote was related to Rowena Miller, RM.

19.   JRC, "International Cooperation to Prevent War," August 1916, Box 90.

20.   *Salt Lake Tribune*, 26 February 1917.

21.   "International Cooperation."

22.   Cranston, *Killing of the Peace*, pp. 40–42; Fleming, *League of Nations*, pp. 55–62, 67–68.

23.   Bailey, *Diplomatic History*, p. 608.

24.   Cranston, *Killing of the Peace*, pp. 58–60; Fleming, *League of Nations*, pp. 111–15.

25.   Cranston, *Killing of the Peace*, p. 52.

26.   Stone, *Irreconcilables*, pp. 58–64.

27.   Fleming, *League of Nations*, pp. 136–40.

28.   On December 5, just before Reuben's discharge from the army, the senator had written to him for counsel on a resolution dealing with the League. From that point forward the advice never slackened (Philander C. Knox to JRC, 5 December 1918, Box 22).

29.   Draft Letter for Knox, n.d., Box 88.

30.   *New York Times*, 27 February 1919.

31.   *Congressional Record*, 65th Congress, 3d Session, p. 605 (18 December 1918).

32.   JRC, Work Diary, 17 February 1919, Box 528.

33.   JRC, "America's Interest at the Peace Table," June 1917, Box 90.

34.   JRC to Philander C. Knox, 18 February 1919, Box 88.

35.   Reuben's draft of this speech is found in Box 88.

36.   Cranston, *Killing of the Peace*, pp. 31, 73.

37.   *New York Sun*, 2 March 1919.

38.   *Congressional Record*, 65th Congress, 3d Session, pp. 4687–94 (1 March 1919).

39.   *New York Sun*, 2 March 1919.

40.   *New York Times*, 11 March 1919.

41.   Cranston, *Killing of the Peace*, pp. 78–82; Stone, *Irreconcilables*, pp. 64–70.

42.   Cranston, *Killing of the Peace*, pp. 73–78, 83; Fleming, *League of Nations*, pp. 153–59. Knox himself told Reuben during a meeting at Valley Forge that he had personally authored the round robin (JRC, Confidential Memorandum, 28 September 1920, Box 22).

43.   Cranston, *Killing of the Peace*, pp. 90–91, 95–97.

44. Fleming, *League of Nations,* pp. 189–90, 199–204.

45. Stone, *Irreconcilables,* pp. 77–99.

46. Ibid., pp. 110–13. This resolution was apparently drawn up by Reuben. See Box 88.

47. Draft of speech for Knox, June 1919, Box 88. See also Memorandum for Knox on Article 21, May 1919, Box 88.

48. *Congressional Record,* 65th Congress, 3d Session, p. 23 (3 December 1918).

49. *Congressional Record,* 66th Congress, 1st Session, pp. 1216–22 (17 June 1919). This speech was reprinted in its entirety by the Government Printing Office, Washington, D.C.

50. Philander C. Knox to JRC, n.d., Box 88.

51. Interview with Louise Clark Bennion, Marianne Clark Sharp, and J. Reuben Clark III.

52. JRC to Preston D. Richards, 16 July 1919, Box 345.

53. Stone, *Irreconcilables,* p. 89.

54. JRC, Work Diary, 16 July 1919 and 17 July 1919, Box 528.

55. JRC to Philander C. Knox, 18 May 1921, Box 99.

56. JRC, Memorandum for Knox, 17 November 1919, Box 89.

57. Contrary to what Knox later said on the floor of the Senate, Reuben undertook this study entirely on his own initiative (JRC to James E. Hewes, 3 August 1957, RM).

58. J. Reuben Clark, Jr., *Data on German Peace Treaty,* 66th Congress, 1st Session, Senate Document No. 86 (Washington, D.C.: Government Printing Office, 1919), p. 16.

59. Cranston, *Killing of the Peace,* pp. 145–46.

60. Stone, *Irreconcilables,* pp. 123–26.

61. JRC to Philander C. Knox, 6 August 1919, Box 89.

62. *Congressional Record,* 66th Congress, 1st Session, pp. 4493–4501 (29 August 1919).

63. Ibid.

64. James E. Hewes to JRC, 17 July 1957, RM.

65. Cranston, *Killing of the Peace,* pp. 162–63.

66. *Salt Lake Herald,* 27 August 1919.

67. *Salt Lake Tribune,* 9 November 1930.

68. *Salt Lake Herald,* 1 September 1919; James B. Allen, "Personal Faith and Public Policy: Some Timely Observations on the League of Nations Controversy in Utah," *BYU Studies* 14 (Autumn 1973):81–85, 92, 94.

69. *Salt Lake Herald,* 27 August 1919; *Salt Lake Tribune,* 9 November 1930.

70. *Congressional Record,* 66th Congress, 1st Session, p. 4493 (29 August 1919).

71. *Salt Lake Herald,* 30 August 1919.

72. *Salt Lake Tribune,* 3 September 1919.

73. *Salt Lake Herald,* 3 September 1919.

74. Ibid., 2 September 1919.

75. Ibid., 4 September 1919.

76. Ibid.

77. *Salt Lake Tribune,* 3 September 1919.

78. See Scrapbooks in Clark Papers, Volume I.

79. Stone, *Irreconcilables,* p. 128.

80. Fleming, *League of Nations,* pp. 337–46.

81. Cranston, *Killing of the Peace,* pp. 176–77; Stone, *Irreconcilables,* pp. 114, 139.

82. JRC to Preston D. Richards, 1 October 1919, Box 345.

83.   JRC to Philander C. Knox, 3 October 1919, Box 22; Philander C. Knox to JRC, 8 October 1919, Box 22.

84.   JRC to Philander C. Knox, 10 October 1919, Box 22.

85.   Cranston, *Killing of the Peace,* pp. 207–9; Stone, *Irreconcilables,* pp. 139–41.

86.   JRC to Philander C. Knox, 17 November 1919, Box 89.

87.   Stone, *Irreconcilables,* pp. 143–45.

Chapter Seventeen   THE WASHINGTON CONFERENCE

1.   JRC to Preston D. Richards, 25 November 1919, Box 345.

2.   JRC, Speech to the AIC, 26 November 1919, Box 47.

3.   Stone, *Irreconcilables,* pp. 147–55.

4.   Ibid., pp. 155–70.

5.   Reuben proposed a draft resolution to this effect in a letter on October 23, 1919. The senator formally introduced the resolution on November 6, 1919 (*Congressional Record,* 66th Congress, 1st Session, pp. 8000–8001).

6.   *Congressional Record,* 66th Congress, 2d Session, p. 544 (13 December 1919).

7.   Ibid., pp. 960–61 (20 December 1919). See also JRC to Philander C. Knox, 3 April 1920, Box 89.

8.   *Congressional Record,* 66th Congress, 2d Session, p. 5481 (9 April 1920).

9.   Ibid., p. 6329 (30 April 1920).

10.   JRC to Philander C. Knox, 23 April 1920, Box 89.

11.   *Boston Evening Transcript,* 5 May 1920.

12.   JRC to Philander C. Knox, 5 May 1920, Box 89.

13.   Warren F. Martin to JRC, 5 May 1920, Box 89.

14.   *Congressional Record,* 66th Congress, 2d Session, pp. 6556–66 (5 May 1920).

15.   Ibid.

16.   *New York Sun,* 6 May 1920. See also *New York Times,* 6 May 1920.

17.   *New York Sun,* 6 May 1920.

18.   *Congressional Record,* 66th Congress, 2d Session, pp. 7747–48 (27 May 1920).

19.   JRC to F. P. Gallagher, 23 January 1920, Box 8.

20.   JRC to Philander C. Knox, 29 April 1920, Box 22.

21.   William C. Dennis to JRC, 5 May 1920, Box 343.

22.   Stone, *Irreconcilables,* pp. 171–72.

23.   JRC to Philander C. Knox, 14 June 1920, Box 22.

24.   Reed Smoot to JRC, 21 September 1920, Box 24; JRC to Stephen Abbot, 2 January 1920, Box 24.

25.   See speech outlines, Box 47.

26.   "General Analysis of the Covenant," speech delivered at Provo, Utah, on 18 October 1920, Box 47.

27.   Diary of J. Reuben Clark, Sr., 4 and 5 November 1920.

28.   JRC to Philander C. Knox, 6 December 1920, Box 22.

29.   JRC to John Bassett Moore, 18 March 1921, Box 345.

30.   *Congressional Record,* 67th Congress, 1st Session, p. 596 (22 April 1921).

31.   Philander C. Knox to JRC, 7 April 1921, Box 89.

Notes

32. *Congressional Record,* 67th Congress, Special Session, pp. 748, 752, 783 (28 and 29 April 1921).

33. Ibid., pp. 787–94 (29 April 1921).

34. Ibid., p. 865 (30 April 1921).

35. *Congressional Record,* 67th Congress, 1st Session, p. 3526 (11 July 1921).

36. Fred M. Dearing to JRC, 6 June 1921, Box 24.

37. JRC to Fred M. Dearing, 25 August 1921, Box 26.

38. JRC to John Bassett Moore, 1 July 1921, Box 24.

39. Memorandum for Dearing on the Versailles Treaty, Box 24.

40. Thomas H. Buckley, *The United States and the Washington Conference* (Knoxville: University of Tennessee Press, 1970), p. 33.

41. Ibid., pp. 20–30.

42. Fred M. Dearing to JRC, 16 July 1921, Box 26.

43. Fred M. Dearing to JRC, 17 July 1921, Box 26.

44. Charles Evans Hughes to JRC, 20 July 1921, Box 26.

45. Daniel J. Danelski and Joseph S. Tulchin, eds. *The Autobiographical Notes of Charles Evans Hughes* (Cambridge, Mass.: Harvard University Press, 1971), pp. xii–xiii, 200.

46. JRC to Willard Straight, 19 August 1916, Box 13.

47. JRC to Philander C. Knox, 5 August 1921, Box 26.

48. Ibid.

49. Ibid.

50. Ibid.

51. Ibid.

52. JRC, "Preliminary Suggestions," 29 July 1921, Box 107.

53. Ibid.

54. Fred M. Dearing to JRC, 2 September 1921, Box 26.

55. Ibid.

56. AIC to JRC, 23 March 1925, Box 8; JRC to AIC, 23 March 1925, Box 8.

57. Senate Resolution 445, 63d Congress, 2d Session. Reuben's draft of this resolution is found in Box 88 of the Clark Papers. See also JRC to Philander C. Knox, 29 September 1920, Box 88; *Washington Star,* 21 August 1914; *Washington Post,* 22 August 1914.

58. JRC, "Draft of Proposed Treaty between England, U.S., and Japan," 29 November 1914, Box 11.

59. "Preliminary Suggestions."

60. Fred M. Dearing to JRC, 20 August 1921, Box 26; JRC to Fred M. Dearing, 25 August 1921, Box 26.

61. Diary of Chandler P. Anderson, 1 November 1921, 17 December 1921, Anderson Papers, Library of Congress, Washington, D.C.

62. JRC to Fred M. Dearing, 25 August 1921, Box 26.

63. Charles Evans Hughes to JRC, 1 September 1921, Locked Case 3, Book I.

64. JRC, Work Diary, 3 September 1921.

65. Charles Evans Hughes to JRC, 15 September 1921, Locked Case 3, Book I.

66. Fred M. Dearing to JRC, 20 August 1921, Box 26.

67. JRC, "Some Basic Elements of the Far Eastern Problem," 21 September 1921, Box 107.

68. Huntington-Wilson, *Memoirs,* pp. 145–50.

69. "Some Basic Elements of the Far Eastern Problem."

70. "Some Elements of the Problem of Limitation of Armament," 30 September 1921, Box 107.

71. Fred M. Dearing to JRC, 20 August 1921, Box 26.

72. "Some Elements of the Problem of Limitation of Armament."

73. Ibid.

74. See Miscellaneous memoranda, Box 107.

75. See Instructions to delegates, Box 107.

76. Buckley, *Washington Conference,* pp. 64–68.

77. Ibid., pp. 68–74.

78. Charles N. Spinks, "The Termination of the Anglo-Japanese Alliance," *Pacific Historical Review* 6 (December 1937):332–33.

79. See List of conference sessions, Box 107.

80. JRC to Preston D. Richards, 25 November 1921, Box 26.

81. Buckley, *Washington Conference,* pp. 104–56.

82. Ibid., pp. 138, 172–84.

83. Diary of Theodore Roosevelt, Jr., 7 January 1927, Roosevelt Papers, Library of Congress, Washington, D.C.

84. Alexander DeConde, *A History of American Foreign Policy,* 2d ed. (New York: Charles Scribner's Sons, 1971), p. 502.

85. JRC to Charles Evans Hughes, 14 February 1922, Box 26.

86. Charles Evans Hughes to JRC, February 1921, Box 26.

87. Isaac Don Levine, *Mitchell: Pioneer of Air Power* (New York: Duell, Sloan & Pearce, 1943), pp. 287–90.

88. JRC to Philander C. Knox, 5 August 1921, Box 26.

Chapter Eighteen THE COURT FIGHT

1. Manley O. Hudson, *The World Court, 1921–34* (Boston: World Peace Foundation, 1934), p. 4.

2. Denna Frank Fleming, *The United States and World Organization, 1920–33* (New York: AMS Press, 1966), pp. 236–39, 241–42.

3. Cranston, *Killing of the Peace,* p. 141.

4. Interview with Louise Clark Bennion, Marianne Clark Sharp, and J. Reuben Clark III; Fred M. Dearing to JRC, 12 October 1921, Box 343.

5. Fred M. Dearing to JRC, 12 October 1921, Box 343. See also chapter sixteen, note 15.

6. Fleming, *World Organization,* pp. 60–78, 219–36.

7. Ibid., pp. 241–42.

8. Denna Frank Fleming, *The United States and the World Court* (Garden City, N.J.: Doubleday, 1945), p. 40.

9. John Chalmers Vinson, *William E. Borah and the Outlawry of War* (Athens: University of Georgia Press, 1957), p. 89.

10. Fred M. Dearing to JRC, 12 October 1921, Box 343.

11. Philander C. Knox to George Harvey, 4 December 1920, Locked Case 3, Book I.

12. JRC to William E. Borah, 28 February 1923, Box 25.

13. JRC, "America's Part in the World Court Movement," 2 December 1920, Box 25.

14. William E. Borah to JRC, 1 March 1923, Box 25.

15. *New York Times,* 20 March 1923.

16. JRC to Warren G. Harding, 27 February 1923, Locked Case 3, Book III.

17. Warren G. Harding to JRC, 27 February 1923, Locked Case 3, Book III.

18. Robert H. Ferrell, *Peace in Their Time: The Origins of the Kellogg-Briand Pact* (New Haven, Conn.: Yale University Press, 1952), p. 30.

19. JRC to James E. Hewes, 3 August 1957, RM. See also Reuben's notes on Knox's plan in Box 23 of the Clark Papers.

20. See, for example, the March 1, 1919, speech authored by Reuben for Senator Knox (*Congressional Record,* 65th Congress, 3d Session, p. 4693).

21. Memorandum on Outlawry of War, 1923, Box 47. See also "Criticism of Plan to Outlaw War," 17 January 1922, Box 47.

22. See Material on New York Outlawry Committee in Box 345.

23. Ferrell, *Peace in Their Time,* p. 33.

24. Salmon O. Levinson to JRC, 9 May 1923, Box 35.

25. Memorandum on Permanent Court of International Justice, 28 May 1923, Box 25.

26. Salmon O. Levinson to JRC, 28 June 1923, Box 25.

27. "Rough Draft of International Court System," 30 September 1910, Box 61.

28. "Outline Suggestion on the Establishment of Courts," 15 June 1923, Box 47.

29. JRC to Warren G. Harding, 15 June 1923, Locked Case 3, Book III.

30. Warren G. Harding to JRC, 20 June 1923, Locked Case 3, Book III.

31. DeConde, *American Foreign Policy,* pp. 503, 506.

32. Fleming, *World Court,* p. 49.

33. Fred M. Dearing to JRC, 20 November 1922, Box 343.

34. "Pacific Settlement of International Disputes," 20 July 1923, Box 47.

35. In the memorandum for Senator New, Reuben really took outlawry to task. A treaty outlawing war would only handicap the "righteous" nations, he said, never the "criminal." Moreover, there was the problem of punishing criminal nations and deterring their future misdeeds. "In such cases," said Reuben, "war is a necessary factor in human progress." Finally, there was the old difficulty of protecting nationals and their property "wherever they are." "Their defense may require the instant use, or threat, of force," Reuben concluded ("Criticism of Plan to Outlaw War," 17 January 1922, Box 47).

36. *Unity,* 25 October 1923.

37. Salmon O. Levinson to JRC, 6 October 1923, Box 25.

38. *Christian Science Monitor,* 15 October 1923.

39. *Advocate of Peace* 5 (December 1923):427–33; *Deseret News,* 29 December 1933.

40. *Unity,* 27 December 1923.

41. John A. Widtsoe to JRC, 21 October 1923, Box 25.

42. JRC to Fred M. Dearing, 26 February 1925, Box 343.

43. Analysis of the World Court Statute, February 1925, Box 92.

44. Talk on World Court, 16 February 1925, Box 92.

45. JRC to Fred M. Dearing, 26 February 1925, Box 343.

46. JRC to Salmon O. Levinson, 4 April 1925. The memorandum was entitled "Some Elements of an American Foreign Policy," Box 48.

47. Fleming, *World Organization,* pp. 243–48.

48. Fleming, *World Court,* pp. 58–60.

49. *Washington Post,* 15 January 1926.

50. Fleming, *World Court,* pp. 65, 68–80.

51. Ibid., pp. 80–81.

52. "Some Elements of an American Foreign Policy."

Chapter Nineteen   THE BEST BOLTS

1. JRC to Luacine, 14 July 1913, Box 329.

2. Jessup, *Elihu Root,* 1:449.

3. JRC to Hugh Gibson, 24 April 1913, Box 8.

4. Arthur S. Link and William B. Catton, *American Epoch: A History of the United States since the 1890s,* 3d ed. (New York: Alfred A. Knopf, 1966), pp. 21–28.

5. Carr Morrow to JRC, 10 April 1913, Box 8.

6. Correspondence dealing with Reuben's Washington and New York practices may be found in Boxes 8 to 25. Documents are filed separately in Boxes 79 to 92.

7. Ibid.

8. JRC to Angel Caligaris, 10 February 1919, Box 9.

9. JRC to Arthur M. Thompson, 21 November 1918, Box 9.

10. Arthur M. Thompson to JRC, 23 November 1918, Box 9.

11. Link and Catton, *American Epoch,* pp. 159–61.

12. Memorandum on Rights of Japanese Subjects under the California Alien Land Act and the Treaty of 1911, 1 August 1913, Box 79.

13. Preston D. Richards to JRC, 21 March 1927, RM.

14. Munro, *Intervention,* pp. 409–10.

15. Ibid.

16. Ibid.

17. JRC to Robert Lansing, 10 June 1916, Box 12.

18. Memorandum of 25 September 1916, Box 12. A similar discovery was made years later by Latin American historians. José Santos Zelaya, once thought to be a worthless political incendiary, has come forth in modern scholarship as patriotic, democratic, and progressive, accomplishing more than virtually any contemporary to bring his country into the twentieth century. Zelaya's real crime, it seems, was opposing the United States.

19. Munro, *Intervention,* p. 413.

20. Julián Iriás to JRC, 28 May 1916, Box 12.

21. See p. 97 for a discussion of Reuben's dealings with Haiti as solicitor.

22. JRC to H. R. Kunhardt, 4 November 1921, Box 11.

23. Correspondence and documents on Reuben's work for the Cuban Legation, Boxes 14 and 81.

24. Correspondence and documents on Kate Soler case, Boxes 14 to 16.

25. Miscellaneous Cuban newspaper clippings, Box 14.

26. Correspondence and documents on Kate Soler case, Boxes 14 to 16.

27. Correspondence and documents on Tlahualilo, Boxes 17 and 18.

28. JRC to Severo Mallet-Prevost, 12 June 1914, Box 17.

29. JRC to Severo Mallet-Prevost, 16 September 1916, Box 17.

30. H. A. Vernet to JRC, 1 July 1922, Box 18.

31. Herbert Croly, *Willard Straight* (New York: Macmillan, 1924), pp. 197–285.

32. JRC to Preston D. Richards, 18 November 1915, Box 345.

33.   Ibid.

34.   Carl P. Parrini, *Heir to Empire: United States Economic Diplomacy, 1916–23* (Pittsburgh: University of Pittsburgh Press, 1969), pp. 8, 79.

35.   Letter of Frank A. Vanderlip to Stockholders and to the United States, 27 November 1915, Box 21.

36.   JRC to Preston D. Richards, 4 December 1915, Box 345.

37.   Announcement of opening of New York office, 31 December 1915, Box 9.

38.   Harry N. Scheiber, "World War I as Entrepreneurial Opportunity: Willard Straight and the American International Corporation," *Political Science Quarterly* 84 (September 1969):486.

39.   Preliminary Reports of the President, from Annual Report to AIC Stockholders, 1916, Box 21.

40.   Correspondence and documents regarding the AIC are found in Boxes 19 to 21 and 83 to 87. See also Scheiber, "World War I as Entrepreneurial Opportunity," p. 505.

41.   JRC to Willard Straight, 24 November 1915, Box 13.

42.   JRC to Luacine, 3 August 1916, Box 330.

43.   JRC to Luacine, 14 August 1916, Box 330.

44.   Newton D. Baker to Thomas W. Gregory, 1 May 1917, Box 26; Thomas W. Gregory to JRC, 21 May 1917, Box 26; JRC to Thomas W. Gregory, 23 May 1917, Box 26.

45.   JRC to Luacine, 3 July 1917, Box 331.

46.   Report of the President, AIC, 3 April 1918, Box 21.

47.   Croly, *Willard Straight*, p. 536.

48.   Reports to Stockholders, AIC, 1918, 1919, Box 21.

49.   Report of President to Stockholders at Annual Meeting, AIC, 7 April 1920, Box 21.

50.   Reports to Stockholders, Box 21.

51.   Charles A. Stone to JRC, 5 July 1922, RM.

52.   JRC to Luacine, 13 January 1921, Box 333.

53.   *Who's Who in America, 1930–31,* p. 2116.

54.   Ibid., p. 410.

55.   Luacine to JRC, 17 May 1923, Box 333.

56.   Matthew Brush to JRC, 28 June 1921, Box 18.

57.   JRC to Fred M. Dearing, 25 April 1924, Box 343.

58.   JRC to Preston D. Richards, 18 November 1915, Box 345.

59.   Preston D. Richards to JRC, February 1918, Box 345; JRC to Albert E. Bowen, 9 December 1921, Box 343; Albert E. Bowen to JRC, 19 December 1921, Box 343. Bowen was another of those Utah lawyers with high ambitions. He went to the University of Chicago law school, where he met Preston Richards, and then returned to the West. When he made inquiries through his mother-in-law, Susa Young Gates, about the possibility of breaking into New York law, Reuben Clark, who at the time was riding high with the AIC, replied that New York was no place for a boy from Deseret. Like Preston Richards, Bowen became a friend for life.

60.   JRC to George Savage, 10 December 1913, Box 329.

61.   Diary of J. Reuben Clark, Sr., 6 January 1914.

62.   Correspondence and documents dealing with the Grantsville farm are found in Boxes 329 to 332 and 443 to 452b.

63.   Donald DeLashmutt to JRC, 20 July 1921, Box 10; JRC to Donald DeLashmutt, 3 August 1921, Box 10.

64. JRC to Matthew Brush, 2 July 1921, Box 18.

65. Correspondence concerning various business dealings between Reuben and his brothers can be found in Boxes 329 to 332.

66. Frank Clark to JRC, 10 November 1921, Box 332; JRC to Frank Clark, 29 November 1921, Box 332.

67. Luacine to JRC, 6 August 1914, Box 330.

68. JRC to Fred M. Dearing, 1 July 1921, Box 343.

69. JRC to Edwin Clark, 27 November 1922, Box 330.

70. AIC to JRC, 23 March 1925, Box 18; JRC to AIC, 23 March 1925, Box 18.

71. JRC to Joseph L. Cannon, 24 April 1913, Box 9.

72. JRC to Fred M. Dearing, 1 July 1921, Box 343.

73. JRC to Huntington Wilson, 26 February 1925, Box 346.

74. JRC to Fred M. Dearing, 23 August 1926, Box 343.

75. Soon afterward, Preston Richards also left Salt Lake and settled in Los Angeles, leaving Albert Bowen in command of Clark & Richards. Bowen carried on the practice faithfully until 1937, when he strolled innocently into an LDS general conference one day and heard his name announced from the pulpit as that of the newest apostle of the church.

Chapter Twenty FAMILY LIFE

1. JRC to James Brown Scott, 23 April 1912, Box 346.

2. Luacine to JRC, 23 July 1906, Box 328.

3. Luacine to JRC, 24 September 1906, Box 328.

4. Luacine to JRC, 20 February 1909, Box 329.

5. Various engraved invitations and calling cards are contained in Box 476 of the Clark Papers.

6. Luacine to JRC, 20 October 1906, Box 328.

7. Luacine to JRC, 29 June 1908, Box 328.

8. Luacine to JRC, 3 July 1908, Box 328. Reuben's academic career was short-lived; he taught for only a year. Dr. Scott secured the appointment for him and may well have secured its termination.

9. Luacine to JRC, 11 October 1908, Box 328.

10. Luacine to JRC, 2 January 1909, Box 329.

11. Luacine to JRC, 30 April 1909, Box 329.

12. Mary Clark to JRC, 29 November 1909, Box 329.

13. JRC to Luacine, 19 July 1913, Box 330.

14. Diary of Wilbur J. Carr, 17 April 1927.

15. John Clark to JRC, 19 August 1920, Box 332.

16. Marianne Clark to JRC, 18 November 1920, Box 333.

17. *New York Times,* 28 January 1922.

18. Luacine to JRC, 14 August 1916, Box 330.

19. *Deseret News,* 14 February 1920.

20. J. Reuben Clark III to JRC, 28 February 1928, Box 335.

21. Luacine's Autobiography, p. 12.

22. JRC to Luacine, 4 December 1920, Box 332.

23. Luacine to JRC, 15 May 1923, Box 333.

24. JRC to Fred M. Dearing, 23 April 1925, Box 343.
25. Luacine to JRC, 9 May 1923, Box 333.

Chapter Twenty-one SON, BROTHER, AND FRIEND

1. Interview with Louise Clark Bennion, Marianne Clark Sharp, and J. Reuben Clark III.
2. J. Reuben Clark, Sr., to JRC, 6 January 1909, Box 329.
3. J. Reuben Clark, Sr., to JRC, 24 February 1910, Box 329.
4. Mary Clark to JRC, 24 October 1909, Box 329.
5. JRC, Work Diary, 26 May 1919, 6 June 1919, Box 528.
6. Interview with Louise Clark Bennion, Marianne Clark Sharp, and J. Reuben Clark III.
7. Diary of J. Reuben Clark, Sr., 10 January 1911.
8. Ibid., 6 January 1914.
9. Edwin Clark to JRC, 28 July 1915, Box 330.
10. JRC to Edwin Clark, 27 November 1922, Box 330.
11. Frank Clark to JRC, 25 July 1909, Box 329.
12. Frank Clark to JRC, 15 September 1910, Box 329.
13. Frank Clark to JRC, 30 March 1923, Box 332.
14. JRC to Frank Clark, 4 April 1923, Box 332.
15. Diary of J. Reuben Clark, Sr., 23 August 1928.
16. John Clark to JRC, 12 December 1916, Box 331.
17. JRC to Luacine, 14 July 1912, Box 330.
18. JRC to Samuel Clark, 17 May 1915, Box 329.
19. Samuel Clark to JRC, 7 June 1915, Box 329.
20. JRC to Samuel Clark, 22 January 1917, Box 331.
21. John Clark to JRC, 4 November 1917, Box 331.
22. John Clark to JRC, 25 August 1918, Box 331.
23. John Clark to JRC, 7 April 1918, Box 331.
24. Gordon Clark to JRC, 25 October 1916, Box 331.
25. Luacine to JRC, 15 August 1917, Box 331.
26. Esther Clark to JRC, 27 December 1917, Box 331.
27. Luacine to JRC, 8 August 1914, Box 330.
28. Esther Clark to JRC, 10 October 1914, Box 330.
29. JRC to John Jensen, 27 April 1921, Box 333.
30. Esther Clark to JRC, 13 December 1921, Box 333.
31. JRC to Luacine, 17 July 1914, Box 330.
32. JRC to Tim Savage, 20 August 1917, Box 331.
33. Fred M. Dearing to JRC, 23 April 1921, Box 343.
34. Huntington Wilson to JRC, 17 May 1913, Box 346.
35. Harold Nicolson, *Dwight Morrow* (New York: Harcourt, Brace, 1935), pp. 390–91.
36. Interview with Louise Clark Bennion, Marianne Clark Sharp, and J. Reuben Clark III.
37. JRC, Work Diary, 28 May 1917, Box 528.
38. Matthew Brush to JRC, 28 June 1921, Box 18.
39. Scholes and Scholes, *Foreign Policies,* p. 15.
40. Huntington-Wilson, *Memoirs,* p. 111.

41. Butt, *Taft and Roosevelt,* 2:770–71.

42. Huntington Wilson to JRC, 15 September 1913, Box 346.

43. For a discussion of Reuben's views on race in general, see chapter fourteen, note 2.

44. JRC to Ransford Miller, 16 October 1915, Box 346.

45. JRC to Huntington Wilson, 2 August 1915, Box 346.

46. JRC to Huntington Wilson, 12 May 1915, Box 346.

47. JRC to Lucy James Wilson, 29 May 1915, Box 346.

48. JRC to Huntington Wilson, 26 April 1915, Box 346.

49. JRC to Lucy James Wilson, 29 January 1915, Box 346.

50. JRC to Lucy James Wilson, 9 February 1915, Box 346.

51. JRC to Lucy James Wilson, 29 May 1915, Box 346.

52. JRC to Huntington Wilson, 5 July 1915, Box 346.

53. Huntington Wilson to JRC, 20 May 1917, Box 346.

54. JRC to Huntington Wilson, 12 May 1915, Box 346; JRC to Fred M. Dearing, 23 March 1921, Box 343.

55. JRC to Huntington Wilson, 12 February 1916, Box 346.

56. See, for example, JRC to Newton D. Baker, 12 March 1917, Box 26.

57. Huntington-Wilson, *Memoirs,* p. 324.

58. Ibid., p. 356.

59. Huntington Wilson to JRC, 17 May 1928, Box 346.

Chapter Twenty-two   THE PERILS OF POLITICS

1. Luacine to JRC, 15 August 1906, Box 328.

2. John Bassett Moore to JRC, 7 July 1921, Box 24.

3. William Franklin Sands to JRC, 6 August 1923, Box 8.

4. Luacine to JRC, 18 September 1926, Box 334.

5. JRC to Frank Clark, 18 January 1923, Box 332.

6. Anecdote related to Rowena Miller, RM.

7. *Improvement Era* 36 (September 1933):674.

8. Memorandum of Conversation, 5 September 1931, Box 131.

9. Susa Young Gates to JRC, 17 November 1921, Box 31.

10. JRC, "General Analysis of the Covenant," speech delivered at Provo, Utah, 18 October 1921, Box 47.

11. Ibid.

12. Unfinished draft of speech, "League to Enforce Peace," 1915, Box 90.

13. Draft of speech for Philander C. Knox, 17 October 1914, Box 88.

14. JRC to Reed Smoot, 29 February 1924, Box 346.

15. JRC to Philander C. Knox, 7 May 1920, Box 22.

16. JRC to Philander C. Knox, 20 March 1920, Box 22.

17. JRC to Philander C. Knox, 9 June 1920, Box 22.

18. JRC to John Bassett Moore, 1 July 1921, Box 24.

19. JRC to Philander C. Knox, 29 April 1920, Box 22.

20. Ibid.

21. JRC to Philander C. Knox, 9 June 1920, Box 22.

22. Preston D. Richards to JRC, 9 September 1920, Box 345.

23. Preston D. Richards to Philander C. Knox, 21 March 1921, Box 345.

24. Preston D. Richards to JRC, 18 April 1921, Box 345.

25. Preston D. Richards to JRC, 15 November 1921, Box 345.

26. Ibid.; Preston D. Richards to JRC, 3 December 1921, Box 345.

27. Susa Young Gates to JRC, 13 December 1921, Box 31.

28. JRC to Susa Young Gates, 17 November 1921, Box 31.

29. Preston D. Richards to JRC, 15 May 1922, Box 31.

30. Preston D. Richards to JRC, 1 June 1922, Box 31.

31. Preston D. Richards to JRC, 25 February 1922, Box 31.

32. *Salt Lake Tribune,* 14 July 1922, 16 August 1928; Brad E. Hainsworth, "Utah State Elections, 1916–24" (Ph.D. diss., University of Utah, 1968), pp. 148–53, 165.

33. Dan E. Jones, "Utah Politics, 1926–32" (Ph.D. diss., University of Utah, 1968), pp. 42–44.

34. Draft of "Announcement of Candidacy for U.S. Senate," 3 June 1922, RM.

35. *Salt Lake Tribune,* 14 June 1922.

36. Ibid.

37. JRC to R. Cottrell, 7 July 1922, Box 31.

38. Draft of "Announcement of Candidacy for U.S. Senate."

39. JRC to Fred M. Dearing, 30 August 1922, Box 343.

40. Ibid.

41. *Salt Lake Tribune,* 15 July 1922.

42. F. W. Fishburn to JRC, 19 July 1922, Box 31.

43. N. E. Iverson to JRC, 20 July 1922, Box 31.

44. A. F. Doremus to JRC, 28 July 1922, Box 31.

45. *Deseret Evening News,* 10 June 1922; Hainsworth, "Utah State Elections," p. 152.

46. JRC to Fred M. Dearing, 13 October 1922, Box 343.

47. Recollection of JRC, RM.

48. N. E. Iverson to JRC, 20 July 1933, Box 31.

49. Preston D. Richards to JRC, 21 March 1927, Box 345.

50. JRC to Fred M. Dearing, 30 August 1922, Box 343.

51. S. J. Quinney to JRC, 15 March 1928, Box 31.

52. *New York World,* 10 April 1928; *New York World* to Albert E. Bowen, 9 April 1928, Box 31.

53. JRC to Albert E. Bowen, 17 March 1928, Box 31.

54. JRC to Scott A. Dahlquist, 24 February 1928, Box 31.

55. Luacine to JRC, 22 March 1928, Box 335.

56. JRC to John A. Widtsoe, 24 February 1928, Box 31.

57. Albert E. Bowen to JRC, 18 April 1928, Box 31.

58. S. J. Quinney to JRC, 6 June 1928, Box 31.

59. Ed Hatch to JRC, 14 June 1928, Box 31.

60. Luacine to JRC, 19 April 1927, Box 334.

61. Ibid.

62. C. L. Funk to Albert E. Bowen, 28 June 1928, Box 31.

63. Jones, "Utah Politics," pp. 44–45.

64. JRC, Memorandum of Conversation, 4 October 1929, Box 31.
65. *Salt Lake Times,* 10 August 1928.
66. Political Itinerary, 1928, Box 32.
67. Hainsworth, "Utah State Elections," p. 157.
68. Ibid., p. 160.
69. Jones, "Utah Politics," p. 56.
70. *Salt Lake Tribune,* 17 August 1928.
71. Diary of J. Reuben Clark, Sr., 19 August 1928.
72. *Salt Lake Tribune,* 17 August 1928.
73. JRC to Carl R. Marcusen, 10 October 1928, Box 31.
74. Mrs. Albert Johnson to JRC, 9 October 1930, Box 39.
75. *Deseret News,* 17 August 1928; *Salt Lake Tribune,* 17 August 1928.
76. Carl R. Marcusen to JRC, 7 September 1928, Box 31.
77. Reuben's comments were published in a paper entitled "The Citizen: A Thinking Paper for Thinking People," Clark Scrapbooks, Volume I.
78. JRC to Carl Marcusen, 1 October 1928, Box 31.
79. JRC to Harold P. Fabian, 10 October 1928, Box 31.
80. Frank B. Kellogg to Carl R. Marcusen, 10 October 1928, Box 31.
81. JRC to Harold P. Fabian, 29 October 1928, Box 31.
82. JRC to Carl R. Marcusen, 10 October 1928, Box 31.
83. JRC to Harold P. Fabian, 29 October 1928, Box 31.
84. Oscar W. Carlson to JRC, 30 October 1928, Box 31.
85. JRC to Harold P. Fabian, 29 October 1928, Box 31.
86. Jones, "Utah Politics," p. 84.
87. Ibid., pp. 91–92.
88. Albert E. Bowen to JRC, 30 October 1928, Box 31.
89. Oscar W. Carlson to JRC, 30 October 1928, Box 31.
90. JRC to Oscar W. Carlson, 31 October 1928, Box 31.
91. *Salt Lake Tribune,* 4 November 1928.
92. Jones, "Utah Politics," p. 112.
93. JRC to Harold P. Fabian, 13 November 1928, Box 31.
94. John A. Widtsoe to JRC, 20 July 1922, Locked Case 3, Book II.

Chapter Twenty-three   STRANGER IN BABYLON

1. JRC, Memorandum entitled "Knowledge and Belief," n.d., Box 90.
2. Memorandum of conversation with Mathonihah Thomas, 4 February 1914, Box 90.
3. Handwritten notes from small memo book, Box 61.
4. Luacine to JRC, 21 September 1906, Box 328; Luacine to JRC, 3 October 1906, Box 328.
5. Reuben was ordained a seventy by his father at the age of eighteen. (Diary of J. Reuben Clark, Sr., 30 March 1890). The term refers to an office in the Mormon church priesthood stemming from the seventy ministers called by Christ in the New Testament.
6. JRC to James E. Talmage, 24 November 1912, Box 346.
7. Luacine to JRC, 26 May 1923, Box 333.
8. Luacine to JRC, 3 October 1906, Box 328.

Notes

9. Confidential memorandum concerning William Jennings Bryan, n.d., Box 346.
10. Untitled memorandum, 1917, Box 90.
11. Anecdote related to Rowena Miller, RM.
12. Confidential memorandum concerning William Jennings Bryan.
13. Luacine to JRC, 9 July 1906, Box 328.
14. Interview with Louise Clark Bennion, Marianne Clark Sharp, and J. Reuben Clark III.
15. Recollection of JRC, RM.
16. Interview with Louise Clark Bennion, Marianne Clark Sharp, and J. Reuben Clark III.
17. JRC to William C. Dennis, 30 June 1910, Box 343.
18. Luacine to JRC, 5 September 1920, Box 332.
19. Interview with Luacine Clark Fox, 23 August 1977.
20. J. Reuben Clark, Sr., to JRC, 16 October 1907, Box 328.
21. Samuel Clark to JRC, 25 April 1909, Box 329.
22. Handwritten notes from small memo book, Box 61.
23. Ibid.
24. Ibid.
25. Ibid.
26. Diary of J. Reuben Clark, Sr., 8 September 1914.
27. Luacine to JRC, 19 July 1908, Box 328.
28. Preston D. Richards to JRC, 21 March 1927, Box 345.
29. Luacine to JRC, 15 August 1918, Box 332.
30. JRC to Philander C. Knox, 18 May 1916, Box 22.
31. Memorandum of Matters Handled while Solicitor.
32. JRC to Preston D. Richards, 21 March 1915, Box 345.
33. Preston D. Richards to JRC, 21 March 1927, Box 345.
34. JRC to Preston D. Richards, 3 March 1913, Box 345.
35. *Salt Lake Tribune,* 9 November 1930.
36. J. Reuben Clark, Sr., to JRC, 30 April 1914, Box 330.
37. Milton H. Ross to JRC, 20 May 1914, Box 8; JRC to Milton H. Ross, 22 May 1914, Box 8.
38. J. Reuben Clark, Sr., to JRC, 10 November 1906, Box 328.
39. JRC to John A. Widtsoe, 20 August 1929, Box 33.
40. JRC to Frank Clark, 2 September 1920, Box 332.
41. Luacine to JRC, 9 April 1923, Box 333.
42. JRC, "Biographical Blank," 24 August 1951, Box 373.
43. Ibid.
44. Drafts of these speeches can be found in Box 48.
45. *Deseret News,* 31 October 1925.
46. Ninety-sixth Annual Conference of The Church of Jesus Christ of Latter-day Saints, 1926, Clark Scrapbooks, Volume I.
47. Interview with Louise Clark Bennion, Marianne Clark Sharp, and J. Reuben Clark III.
48. JRC to Ivor Sharp, n.d., Box 335.
49. JRC to Frank Clark, 9 November 1936, Box 337.
50. JRC to Mrs. Harold M. Stephens, n.d., RM.
51. Waldo M. Anderson to Rowena Miller, 31 January 1961, RM.

Chapter Twenty-four   IN THE WAKE OF THE WHIRLWIND

1. Robert E. Olds to JRC, 24 April 1926, Box 33.

2. A. H. Feller, *The Mexican Claims Commissions, 1923–34: A Study in the Law and Procedure of International Tribunals* (New York: Macmillan, 1935), pp. 2–7, 57, 63.

3. Noble Warrum to Reed Smoot, 30 June 1926, Box 33.

4. Ibid.

5. Charles Evans Hughes to JRC, 24 May 1924, Locked Case 3, Book I.

6. JRC to Charles Evans Hughes, 24 May 1924, Locked Case 3, Book I.

7. JRC to Robert E. Olds, 27 May 1926, Box 33; JRC to Noble Warrum, 7 September 1926, Box 33; JRC to Secretary of State, 7 August 1926, Box 33.

8. For the Press, Department of State, 17 June 1926, Box 33.

9. William Hard to JRC, 19 June 1926, Box 33.

10. Outline of Claims, n.d., Box 33; Atkin, *Revolution!,* p. 169; Gibbon, *Mexico under Carranza,* p. 261.

11. Feller, *Mexican Claims Commissions,* p. 33.

12. Clarence C. Clendenen, *The United States and Pancho Villa: A Study in Unconventional Diplomacy* (Ithaca, N.Y.: Cornell University Press, 1961), pp. 313–14.

13. Feller, *Mexican Claims Commissions,* pp. 63–64, 168–69.

14. *New York Times,* 27 April 1926.

15. Feller, *Mexican Claims Commissions,* p. 44.

16. Ibid., pp. 56–57, 60.

17. JRC to Robert E. Olds, 31 August 1926, Box 117.

18. JRC to Henry W. Anderson, 5 July 1926, Box 33.

19. JRC to Robert E. Olds, 31 August 1926, Box 117.

20. JRC to Secretary of State, 21 August 1926, Box 33; Clement L. Bouvé to JRC, 7 November 1926, Box 33.

21. Clement L. Bouvé to JRC, 25 January 1927, Box 33.

22. Interview with Louise Clark Bennion, Marianne Clark Sharp, and J. Reuben Clark III.

23. JRC, Work Diary, 23 July 1926, Box 530.

24. JRC to Robert E. Olds, 31 August 1926, Box 117.

25. JRC to Vernon Romney, 10 July 1926, Box 33.

26. *Who's Who in America, 1930–31,* pp. 1658–59.

27. Fred K. Nielsen to JRC, 6 June 1924, Box 7.

28. Clement L. Bouvé to JRC, 18 August 1928, Box 33.

29. JRC to Henry W. Anderson, 1 September 1926, Box 33; *Who's Who in America, 1930–31,* p. 349.

30. · Clement L. Bouvé to JRC, 1 September 1926, Locked Case 3, Book I.

31. Clement L. Bouvé to JRC, 19 February 1927, Box 33.

32. Bartholemeus Landheer, ed., *The Netherlands* (Berkeley: University of California Press, 1943), pp. 82, 144–45.

33. Fred K. Nielsen to JRC, 26 October 1926, Box 33.

34. Clement L. Bouvé to JRC, 7 November 1926, Box 33.

35. Feller, *Mexican Claims Commissions,* p. 292.

36. Ibid., pp. 293–95.

37. Clement L. Bouvé to JRC, 7 November 1926, Box 33.

38. Clement L. Bouvé to JRC, 27 December 1926, Box 33.
39. Ibid.
40. Clement L. Bouvé to JRC, 12 January 1927, Box 33.
41. Clement L. Bouvé to JRC, 27 December 1926, Box 33.
42. JRC to Clement L. Bouvé, 11 January 1927, Box 33.
43. Clement L. Bouvé, 12 January 1927, Box 33.
44. Ibid.; Clement L. Bouvé to JRC, 29 January 1927, Box 33.
45. JRC to Clement L. Bouvé, 19 January 1927, Box 33.
46. Clement L. Bouvé to JRC, 25 January 1927, Box 33.
47. Ibid.
48. Ibid.
49. JRC to Clement Bouvé, 2 February 1927, Box 33.
50. Clement L. Bouvé to JRC, 29 January 1927, Box 33.
51. Ibid.
52. Ibid.
53. Ibid.
54. JRC to Clement L. Bouvé, 2 February 1927, Box 33.
55. Material regarding John W. DeKay can be found in Boxes 118 and 121A.
56. Ibid.
57. Clement L. Bouvé to JRC, 1 July 1927, Box 33; JRC to Clement L. Bouvé, 13 June 1927, Box 33.
58. JRC to Clement L. Bouvé, 25 January 1927, Box 33.
59. Ibid.
60. Clement L. Bouvé to JRC, 29 January 1927, Box 33.
61. Clement L. Bouvé to JRC, 21 June 1927, Box 33.
62. Clement L. Bouvé to JRC, 22 June 1927, Box 33.
63. Clement L. Bouvé to JRC, 21 June 1927, Box 33.
64. Clement L. Bouvé to JRC, 11 July 1927, Box 33.
65. Clement L. Bouvé to JRC, 1 July 1927, Box 33.
66. Fred K. Nielsen to JRC, 5 July 1927, Box 33.
67. Clement L. Bouvé to JRC, 1 July 1927, Box 33.
68. JRC to Clement L. Bouvé, 25 June 1927, Box 33.
69. See Unidentified newspaper accounts, Box 121A.
70. JRC to Clement L. Bouvé, 25 June 1927, Box 33.
71. Clement L. Bouvé, Memorandum of Conversation with Mr. Olds, 9 July 1927, Box 33.
72. See Reuben's reply, 13 July 1927, Box 33.
73. JRC, Memorandum of Conversation, 3 August 1927, Locked Case 3, Book I.
74. Ibid.
75. JRC, "Biographical Blank," 24 August 1951, Box 373.
76. Feller, *Mexican Claims Commissions,* p. 58.
77. Ibid., p. 44.
78. Clement L. Bouvé to JRC, 30 September 1927, Box 33.
79. JRC, "Memorandum on the Current Petroleum Controversy with Mexico," 21 September 1927, Box 119.

653

80. Feller, *Mexican Claims Commissions,* pp. 60, 68.

81. See Untitled memorandum, Box 33.

Chapter Twenty-five WITH MORROW IN MEXICO

1. Cline, *The United States and Mexico,* pp. 168–69.

2. John W. F. Dulles, *Yesterday in Mexico: A Chronicle of the Revolution, 1919–36* (Austin: University of Texas Press, 1961), pp. 158–72.

3. Ibid., pp. 316–21.

4. L. Ethan Ellis, *Frank B. Kellogg and American Foreign Relations, 1925–29* (New Brunswick, N.J.: Rutgers University Press, 1961), p. 38; Robert Freeman Smith, *The United States and Revolutionary Nationalism in Mexico, 1916–32* (Chicago: University of Chicago Press, 1972), p. 237.

5. Dulles, *Yesterday in Mexico,* pp. 322–23; Ellis, *Frank B. Kellogg,* pp. 24–25.

6. Ellis, *Frank B. Kellogg,* p. 46.

7. Edgar Turlington, *Mexico and Her Foreign Creditors* (New York: Columbia University Press, 1930), p. 312.

8. Ellis, *Frank B. Kellogg,* pp. 47, 56; Stanley R. Ross, "Dwight W. Morrow, Ambassador to Mexico," *The Americas* 14 (January 1958):276.

9. Ellis, *Frank B. Kellogg,* p. 44.

10. JRC to L. Ethan Ellis, 3 January 1957, RM.

11. Ellis, *Frank B. Kellogg,* p. 47; JRC to Robert E. Olds, 23 September 1927, Box 109; JRC to L. Ethan Ellis, 3 January 1957, RM.

12. JRC to Robert E. Olds, 23 September 1927, Box 109.

13. JRC to L. Ethan Ellis, 3 January 1957, RM.

14. Reuben's research concerning the Mexican oil laws was summarized in a 145-page "Memorandum on the Current Petroleum Controversy with Mexico," 21 September 1927, Box 109.

15. *New York Times,* 21 September 1927.

16. JRC to Preston D. Richards, 18 November 1915, Box 345.

17. Interview with Louise Clark Bennion, Marianne Clark Sharp, and J. Reuben Clark III. For similar anecdotes, see Nicolson, *Dwight Morrow,* pp. 49, 153, 154, 162, 174, 399.

18. Nicolson, *Dwight Morrow,* pp. 85, 310.

19. Ibid., pp. 260–66.

20. JRC, "Use of Armed Force in the Collection of Foreign Obligations," 30 September 1924, Box 122.

21. Dwight Morrow, "Who Buys Foreign Bonds?" *Foreign Affairs* 5 (January 1927):219–32.

22. JRC to Dwight W. Morrow, 25 January 1927, Box 124; Smith, *Revolutionary Nationalism,* p. 252.

23. Nicolson, *Dwight Morrow,* p. 289.

24. Elizabeth C. Morrow, *The Mexican Years* (New York: Spiral Press, 1953), p. 4.

25. Ellis, *Frank B. Kellogg,* p. 48.

26. Memorandum on the Agrarian Controversy, Box 124.

27. JRC to Dwight W. Morrow, 26 September 1927, Box 128. Reuben alludes here to a dimension of the oil controversy that was rarely discussed publicly. Overlying the dispute between the United States and Mexico was the larger struggle of international politics—in which oil was rapidly becoming a prime weapon. All the European powers, especially England and Germany, were watching the events in Mexico with eager interest.

Notes

28. JRC to L. Ethan Ellis, 3 January 1957, RM.
29. Frank B. Kellogg to JRC, 3 October 1927, Box 128.
30. *New York Times,* 7 October 1927.
31. JRC to Elizabeth C. Morrow, 28 May 1933, RM.
32. Will Rogers, Address delivered in Beverly Hills, n.d., RM.
33. *Deseret News,* 18 October 1927; *Salt Lake Tribune,* 18 October 1927.
34. Letter of Constance Morrow Morgan to author, 30 November 1976.
35. Ibid.
36. Morrow, *The Mexican Years,* p. 9.
37. Letter of Constance Morrow Morgan to author, 30 November 1976.
38. Anne Morrow Lindbergh, *Bring Me a Unicorn: Diaries and Letters of Anne Morrow Lindbergh, 1922-28* (New York: Harcourt, Brace, Jovanovich, 1971), p. 86.
39. *New York Times,* 22 October 1927.
40. Lindbergh, *Bring Me a Unicorn,* p. 89.
41. Josephus Daniels, *Shirt-Sleeve Diplomat* (Chapel Hill: University of North Carolina Press, 1947), p. 25.
42. Drew Pearson and R. S. Allen, *Washington Merry-Go-Round* (New York: Horace Liveright, 1931), pp. 281–82.
43. Nicolson, *Dwight Morrow,* p. 322.
44. *Excelsior,* 4 October 1930; Pearson and Allen, *Washington Merry-Go-Round,* p. 282.
45. Dulles, *Yesterday in Mexico,* p. 324–25.
46. Ross, "Dwight Morrow, Ambassador," p. 279; Stanley R. Ross, "Dwight Morrow and the Mexican Revolution," *Hispanic American Historical Review* 38 (November 1958):509.
47. Mary Margaret McBride, *The Story of Dwight W. Morrow* (New York: Farrar and Rinehart, 1930), pp. 129–30; Nicolson, *Dwight Morrow,* pp. 322–23. As cited in the latter source, when asked to explain his passion for informality Morrow would tell the following story, as repeated later by Reuben:

> Mr. Morrow stated that during the World War he was connected with the Allied shipping board, an organization which functioned in London, and which controlled the Allied shipping of the world.... One morning after they had had during the previous day a particularly disagreeable time with the representative of one of the European powers, a young English subordinate officer broke in upon his chief and began a series of expressions regarding this trouble. As the young man began to talk he became more interested in his theme and more interested in himself and he finally worked himself up into a fit of rage wherein he said: "If this thing cannot be changed I will resign."
>
> His old commanding officer looked at him with a quizzical smile which brought the young man slowly to attention, and then said:
>
> "Young man, you have forgotten Rule Six."
>
> The young man came to full attention, and conjured his mind for a recollection of Rule Six. Finding no recollection, he said to his superior officer:
>
> "And what is Rule Six, sir?"
>
> The officer again with a quizzical smile, said:
>
> "Do not take yourself so umpty-ump seriously."
>
> The subordinate straightened himself up further and said: "And what are the other rules, sir?"
>
> "Oh," said the officer, "there are no other rules."

48. T. R. Fehrenbach, *Fire and Blood: A History of Mexico* (New York: Macmillan, 1973), pp. 568–69.

49. JRC to L. Ethan Ellis, 3 January 1957, RM; Pearson and Allen, *Washington Merry-Go-Round,* p. 282.

50. JRC, Speech at Grantsville, Utah, 5 May 1950, RM.

51. JRC to Clement L. Bouvé, 4 November 1950, Box 33.

52. *New York Times,* 13 May 1928.

53. Ibid.

54. Letter of Constance Morrow Morgan to author, 30 November 1976.

55. JRC to L. Ethan Ellis, 3 January 1957, RM.

56. See Reuben's handwritten notes of conversations with Morrow, Box 124.

57. Dwight W. Morrow to Frank B. Kellogg, 8 November 1927, Box 128.

58. JRC, Speech at Grantsville, Utah, 5 May 1950, RM.

59. *FRUS,* 1927, 3:196.

60. Nicolson, *Dwight Morrow,* p. 334.

61. Ross, "Dwight Morrow and the Mexican Revolution," pp. 518–19.

62. *Salt Lake Tribune,* 18 October 1927.

63. JRC, "Agrarian Legislation," Box 124.

64. Ellis, *Frank B. Kellogg,* p. 56; Ross, "Dwight Morrow and the Mexican Revolution," pp. 519–21; See also "Confidential Memorandum for Mr. Olds," Box 124.

65. Untitled memorandum, Box 124.

66. Letter of Constance Morrow Morgan to author, 30 November 1976.

67. Box 124.

68. JRC to Dwight W. Morrow, 9 December 1927, Box 128.

69. JRC, Speech at Grantsville, Utah, 5 May 1950, RM.

70. JRC to Dwight W. Morrow, 9 December 1927, Box 128.

71. Dulles, *Yesterday in Mexico,* pp. 327–28.

72. JRC to Dwight W. Morrow, 9 December 1927, Box 128.

73. JRC to Clement L. Bouvé, 30 December 1927, Box 33.

74. See the complimentary memberships extended by the club to the Clarks, Box 335.

75. Luacine to J. Reuben Clark III, 4 January 1928, Box 335.

76. J. Reuben Clark, Jr., "The Oil Settlement with Mexico," *Foreign Affairs* 6 (July 1928):610–11. This article was republished in 1936 as a booklet entitled *The Petroleum Controversy in Mexico.* See also "The Petroleum Memorandum," Box 127.

77. Untitled memorandum, 19 September 1929, Box 131.

78. Memorandum for Morrow, 3 February 1928, Box 124.

79. Dulles, *Yesterday in Mexico,* p. 328.

80. JRC to L. Ethan Ellis, 3 January 1957, RM.

81. Ross, "Dwight Morrow and the Mexican Revolution," pp. 512–13.

82. Ellis, *Frank B. Kellogg,* pp. 53–54.

83. Clark, "The Oil Settlement with Mexico," pp. 612–14.

84. Morrow, *The Mexican Years,* p. 54.

85. JRC, "The Petroleum Controversy," Box 127.

86. JRC to Albert E. Bowen, 30 March 1928, Box 31.

87. See, for example, *Washington Post,* 2 April 1928.

Notes

88. *Deseret News,* 6 April 1928; *Salt Lake Tribune,* 6 April 1928.
89. Ellis, *Frank B. Kellogg,* pp. 54–55.
90. Ibid.
91. See Scrapbooks in Clark Papers, Volume I.
92. Robert E. Olds to JRC, 18 June 1928, Box 128.
93. *New York Times,* 13 May 1928.
94. This article is cited in note 76 above.
95. JRC, Speech at Grantsville, Utah, 5 May 1950, RM.
96. JRC to L. Ethan Ellis, 3 January 1957, RM.
97. Rowena Miller to Richard Vetterli, 13 February 1959, RM.

Chapter Twenty-six UNDERSECRETARY

1. JRC to Albert E. Bowen, 30 March 1928, Box 31.
2. JRC to Dwight W. Morrow, 1 September 1928, Box 34.
3. John Bassett Moore to JRC, 30 August 1928, Box 345.
4. Chandler Anderson to JRC, 6 September 1928, Box 34.
5. Enoch H. Crowder to JRC, 23 August 1928, Locked Case 3, Book IV.
6. I. Paredes to JRC, 21 August 1928, Box 34.
7. Reeve Schley to JRC, 25 August 1928, Box 34.
8. Ellis, *Frank B. Kellogg,* pp. 6–7.
9. Ibid., pp. 7–8.
10. Frank B. Kellogg to Dwight W. Morrow, 7 April 1928, Locked Case 3, Book I.
11. Pearson and Allen, *Washington Merry-Go-Round,* pp. 140–43.
12. JRC to Albert E. Bowen, 30 March 1928, Box 31. It is not definitely known why Reuben refused Kellogg's first request. At the time, however, he was involved with the Mexican claims commission and with his law practice in Utah. As he made clear to both Olds and Bouvé at the time, he was not anxious to return to the East on a permanent basis.
13. JRC to Dwight W. Morrow, 10 September 1928, Locked Case 3, Book I.
14. Pearson and Allen, *Washington Merry-Go-Round,* pp. 137–39.
15. Ibid., pp. 151, 154–56, 157–58.
16. Ibid., pp. 151–53.
17. JRC, Work Diary, 22 October 1928, Box 530.
18. See references to each of these matters in Reuben's work diary for the undersecretary period, Box 530.
19. Pearson and Allen, *Washington Merry-Go-Round,* pp. 30–42.
20. Clement L. Bouvé to JRC, 18 August 1928, Box 129.
21. Ibid.
22. Ibid.
23. Due to this "ill feeling" he discovered, the memoranda of his May interview with the oil attorneys had not been placed in the department files.
24. David C. Bailey, *¡Viva Cristo Rey! The Cristero Rebellion and the Church-State Conflict in Mexico* (Austin: University of Texas Press, 1974), pp. 1–75.
25. Ibid.
26. Ibid., pp. 76–110.

27. Ibid., p. 61.

28. JRC, Work Diary, 30 September 1928, Box 530.

29. Bailey, *¡Viva Cristo Rey!,* p. 61.

30. Ibid., pp. 195–97.

31. Ibid., pp. 217–20.

32. JRC, Work Diary, 27 September 1928, Box 530.

33. Ibid.

34. Ibid., 11 November 1928. The account of this meeting was dictated by Arthur Bliss Lane.

35. Ferrell, *Peace in Their Time,* pp. 228–29.

36. Gene A. Sessions, "The Clark Memorandum Myth," *The Americas* 34 (July 1977):45.

37. JRC, Work Diary, 25 September 1928, Box 530.

38. Robert H. Ferrell, "Repudiation of a Repudiation," *Journal of American History* 51 (March 1965):669.

39. *FRUS,* 1928, 1:573.

40. JRC, Work Diary, 25 September 1928, Box 530.

41. Ibid.

42. JRC, Work Diary, 19 October 1928, Box 530.

43. Memorandum and Correspondence Relating to Telephone Service with Spain and Austria, Box 133.

44. JRC, Work Diary, 25 October 1928, Box 530.

45. See references to these matters in Reuben's work diary, plus memoranda and correspondence in Boxes 133 and 134.

46. Ferrell, "Repudiation," p. 669; Sessions, "Clark Memorandum Myth," p. 46.

47. JRC, Work Diary, 24 November 1928, Box 530.

48. *Congressional Record,* 70th Congress, 2d Session, pp. 25–26 (4 December 1928).

49. JRC, Work Diary, 5 December 1928, Box 530.

50. J. Reuben Clark, Jr., *Memorandum on the Monroe Doctrine* (Washington, D.C.: Government Printing Office, 1930), p. xix.

51. Ibid., pp. xxiii–xxiv.

52. Sessions, "Clark Memorandum Myth," p. 48.

53. Clark, *Memorandum,* pp. xxiv–xxv.

54. Ibid., p. xxv.

55. See pp. 94–98.

56. See pp. 98–108, 189–90.

57. Samuel Flagg Bemis, *The Latin-American Policy of the United States: An Historical Perspective* (New York: Harcourt, Brace & Co., 1943), pp. 211–13.

58. JRC, "Use of Armed Force in the Collection of Foreign Obligations," 30 September 1924, Box 122.

59. See references to the Barco affair in Reuben's work diary for the undersecretary period, Box 530.

60. Ferrell, "Repudiation," pp. 671–72.

61. An alternative view of Hoover's attitude toward the Clark Memorandum is offered in Sessions, "The Clark Memorandum Myth."

62. Ferrell, "Repudiation," pp. 672–73.

63. Department of State Circular, 28 February 1929, DS 710.11/1306a.

64. Ferrell, "Repudiation," p. 672.

65. The following editorial opinions are representative: *Detroit Free Press,* 10 March 1930 ("a monument of erudition"); *Outlook and Independent,* 26 March 1930 ("a great advance in theory"); *Los Angeles Evening Express,* 1 April 1930 ("a return to first principles"); *Washington Daily News,* 8 October 1930 ("a true and accurate statement"); *New York Sun,* 11 September 1931 ("an excellent short definition of what the Monroe Doctrine is *not*").

66. JRC to Tyler Dennett, 21 March 1930, Box 34.

67. See references to each of these matters in Reuben's work diary, Box 530.

68. Ibid., 15 November 1928.

69. Ibid., 16 November 1928.

70. Ibid., 24 November 1928.

71. Ibid., 29 January 1928.

72. Ibid., 18 February 1928.

73. Reuben recorded this warning from Morrow in his work diary, Box 530.

74. JRC to Calvin Coolidge, 6 March 1929, Locked Case 3, Book III.

75. Wilfrid Hardy Callcott, *Liberalism in Mexico* (Stanford, Calif.: Stanford University Press, 1931), pp. 376–78.

76. Untitled memorandum, 30 March 1951, Box 34.

77. Ibid.; Lee H. Burke, "J. Reuben Clark, Jr.: Under Secretary of State," *BYU Studies* 13 (Spring 1973):402–3.

78. Bailey, *¡Viva Cristo Rey!,* p. 245.

79. Burke, "J. Reuben Clark," pp. 402–3.

80. Lyle C. Wilson, UP correspondent, Unidentified newspaper clipping, 3 May 1929, Clark Scrapbooks, Volume I.

81. Pearson and Allen, *Washington Merry-Go-Round,* p. 110; JRC, Work Diary, Box 530.

82. JRC, Work Diary, Box 530.

83. Pearson and Allen, *Washington Merry-Go-Round*, pp. 104–5, 109–10, 115.

84. Albert E. Bowen to JRC, 15 March 1929, Box 31; JRC to Frank Clark, 20 May 1929, Box 334; *Boston Evening Transcript,* 13 May 1929.

85. Unidentified press account, 12 May 1929, Clark Scrapbooks, Volume I.

86. Bailey, *¡Viva Cristo Rey!,* p. 253.

87. Ibid., p. 238.

88. Ibid., p. 253.

89. Ibid., p. 254.

90. Ibid., p. 255.

91. Ibid., p. 258.

92. Ibid., p. 263.

93. Ibid., pp. 266–67.

94. JRC, Memoir of 1 September 1953, RM.

95. *Salt Lake Telegram,* 8 June 1929.

96. Bailey, *¡Viva Cristo Rey!,* p. 274.

97. Ibid., p. 277.

98. Ibid., pp. 277–78.

99. Ibid., pp. 278–79.

100. *Salt Lake Tribune,* 29 June 1929.

101. *Deseret News,* 2 July 1929.

659

Chapter Twenty-seven   KING FOR A DAY

1. JRC to J. H. Anderson, 15 February 1930, Box 35.
2. Arthur H. Springer to JRC, 21 August 1928, Box 34.
3. JRC to Elizabeth C. Morrow, 28 May 1933, RM.
4. Morrow, *The Mexican Years,* p. 258.
5. Luacine's Autobiography, p. 14.
6. "The Petroleum Memorandum," Box 126.
7. Dwight W. Morrow to Ramón DeNegri, 19 May 1929, Box 127.
8. "The Petroleum Memorandum," Box 127.
9. Ellis, *Frank B. Kellogg,* pp. 479–80.
10. Nicolson, *Dwight Morrow,* pp. 383–85.
11. JRC to Clement L. Bouvé, 16 December 1929, Box 130.
12. Morrow, *The Mexican Years,* p. 129.
13. JRC to Walter Lippmann, 28 January 1930, Box 36.
14. "The Petroleum Memorandum," Box 127.
15. Ibid.
16. Ibid.
17. Ibid.
18. Memorandum of Conversation, 5 September 1930, Box 131.
19. Nicolson, *Dwight Morrow,* p. 382.
20. Anecdote related by JRC to Mark E. Petersen, RM.
21. Pearson and Allen, *Washington Merry-Go-Round,* p. 283.
22. Morrow, *The Mexican Years,* p. 255.
23. Diary of Wilbur J. Carr, 11 November 1932.
24. JRC to Susa Young Gates, n.d., Box 37.
25. JRC to Walter Lippmann, 28 January 1930, Box 36.
26. JRC to Ira C. Bennett, n.d., Box 35.
27. Clement L. Bouvé to JRC, 27 February 1930, Box 35.
28. Ibid.; JRC to Clement L. Bouvé, 31 March 1930, Box 35. There was one other voice of opposition to Reuben Clark's appointment. Madame de Prévost had never given up in her quest for revenge over the Alsop award. She testified against Reuben on the occasion of every confirmation hearing thereafter. It was a standing joke around the State Department.
29. Will Rogers, Address delivered in Beverly Hills, n.d., RM. It was no secret that Herbert Hoover, the internationalist, and Reuben Clark, the isolationist, did not get along on questions of foreign policy. According to Drew Pearson, Morrow simply hauled both of them into line. He had prodigious influence.
30. JRC to Susa Young Gates, n.d., Box 37.
31. Interview with Luacine Clark Fox.
32. Ibid.
33. Nicolson, *Dwight Morrow,* p. 381.
34. JRC to Harold Walker, 28 August 1930, Box 130.
35. Dwight W. Morrow to JRC, 29 September 1930, RM.
36. Ibid.
37. Pearson and Allen, *Washington Merry-Go-Round,* p. 159.
38. Interview with Luacine Clark Fox.

39. Ibid.

40. Reuben denied the rumor vehemently, but there was a certain plausibility—and some indirect evidence—in support of it. At least one other millionaire was reported to have made the same offer. Mexico, it must be remembered, was regarded as *the* danger spot for the United States.

41. *Salt Lake Tribune,* 4 October 1930.

42. Marshall Morgan to JRC, 4 October 1930, Box 36.

43. Arthur Bliss Lane to JRC, 20 October 1930, Box 42.

44. *Ogden Examiner,* 4 November 1930.

45. Interview with Luacine Clark Fox.

46. *Fortune* 4 (July 1931):105; *Louisville Times,* 2 March 1931.

47. *Christian Science Monitor,* 4 October 1930.

48. *New York Times,* 4 October 1930.

49. *Boston Transcript,* 6 October 1930.

50. JRC to Lennie Savage Ritter, 23 October 1930, Box 36.

51. JRC, Memorandum of 10 April 1945, RM.

52. JRC to Hal L. Mangum, 15 November 1932, Box 42.

53. JRC to Lennie Savage Ritter, 23 October 1930, Box 36.

54. *Salt Lake Tribune,* 9 November 1930.

55. Interview with Luacine Clark Fox.

Chapter Twenty-eight   AMBASSADOR

1. Lindbergh, *Bring Me a Unicorn,* pp. 89–90.

2. Register of the Department of State, 1 January 1932, p. 190.

3. Ibid., pp. 56, 171, 235, 241.

4. JRC to Wilbur J. Carr, 11 November 1931, Box 31.

5. Interview with J. Reuben Clark III.

6. Interview with Luacine Clark Fox.

7. Ibid.

8. Luacine's Autobiography, p. 15.

9. *Excelsior,* 29 November 1930; *El Universal,* 29 November 1930. A fascinating motion picture recording of this ceremony still exists in the possession of the Clark family.

10. Remarks delivered at presentation of credentials, Box 35.

11. *Conference Report,* October 1930, p. 98; copy in Box 49.

12. Diary of Luacine Savage Clark, Locked Case 4.

13. Unidentified typed statement, Box 44. See also AP and UP releases, 28 November 1930 and 29 November 1930, RM.

14. *Baltimore Evening Sun,* 29 November 1930.

15. Interview with J. Reuben Clark III.

16. *El Paso Times,* 7 December 1930.

17. Graham Greene, *Another Mexico* (New York: Viking Press, 1939), pp. 68–70.

18. See "Chronology Covering Renewal of Claims Conventions," n.d., Box 137.

19. L. M. Lawson, "Confidential Memorandum on the Boundary," Box 128.

20. Joseph P. Cotton to JRC, 19 February 1930, Locked Case 3, Book I.

21. JRC, Memorandum of 18 May 1949, RM.

22. Interview with J. Reuben Clark III.

23. Ibid.

24. Ibid.

25. *Conference Report,* October 1930, p. 98; copy in Box 49.

26. Untitled handwritten manuscript, n.d., Box 142.

27. *Christian Science Monitor,* 1 September 1931.

28. Ibid.

29. Address before Press Congress of the World, 11 August 1931, Box 49.

30. Interview with Luacine Clark Fox.

31. Ibid.

32. Ibid.

33. JRC, Memorandum of 18 May 1949, RM.

34. JRC, Speech at Grantsville, Utah, 5 May 1950, RM.

35. Interview with J. Reuben Clark III.

36. "Chronology Covering Renewal of Claims Conventions."

37. JRC to Walter Lippmann, 7 January 1931, Box 38.

38. JRC to Ira Bennett, 7 January 1931, Box 37.

39. John J. Burke to JRC, 3 February 1931, Box 37.

40. JRC to John J. Burke, 19 February 1931, Box 37.

41. Memorandum of conversation, 9 January 1932, Box 140.

42. Unless otherwise noted, all of the information in section vi is derived from the personal recollections of Luacine Clark Fox.

43. Greene, *Another Mexico,* pp. 68–70.

44. Feller, *Mexican Claims Conventions,* pp. 58–63, 68–69.

45. "Why call the Mexican laws wholly unjust because a foreigner cannot interpret them to his liking?" Reuben once asked an American reporter (*Christian Science Monitor,* 1 September 1931).

46. Bailey, *¡Viva Cristo Rey!,* pp. 295–97.

47. JRC to John J. Burke, May 1932, Box 37.

48. Bailey, *¡Viva Cristo Rey!,* pp. 294–95.

49. JRC, Memorandum of 17 May 1949, RM.

50. Ibid.

51. Ibid.

52. Bailey, *¡Viva Cristo Rey!,* pp. 295–96.

53. Nicolson, *Dwight Morrow,* pp. 390–91.

54. Bailey, *¡Viva Cristo Rey!,* p. 298.

55. Ibid., pp. 296–97.

56. Reuben purchased such a souvenir for each of his children while in Mexico.

57. Memorandum of Telephone Conversation, 25 August 1932, Box 138.

58. Diary of Luacine Savage Clark, 16 September 1932, Locked Case 4.

59. "River Rectification," 7 January 1933, Box 138.

60. Ibid.

61. Ibid.

62. Ibid.

63. *New York Times,* 2 February 1933.

64. L. M. Lawson to JRC, 1935, Box 352.

65. Michael Hogg to E. M. House, 9 January 1933, Box 350.

66. JRC to Hal L. Mangum, 15 November 1932, Box 42; JRC to Raymond Dickson, 26 January 1933, Box 350; JRC to William H. King, 9 January 1933, Box 350.

67. *Excelsior,* 15 February 1933.

68. *El Universal,* 11 February 1933.

69. Arthur Bliss Lane to Secretary of State, 20 February 1933, Box 49.

70. JRC, "Speech at Banquet before Leaving Mexico," 10 February 1933, Box 49.

71. *El Universal,* 15 February 1933; *Excelsior,* 15 February 1933.

72. Herbert Hoover to JRC, 25 February 1933, Locked Case 3, Book IV.

73. *Deseret News,* 21 March 1933.

74. *Excelsior,* 9 November 1932.

Epilogue BETWEEN EAST AND WEST

1. Interview with Rowena Miller, 5 January 1978.

2. JRC to Cordell Hull, n.d., Box 349.

3. Interview with J. Reuben Clark III.

4. The definitive work on Reuben's association with the Foreign Bondholders Protective Council is Gene A. Sessions, "Prophesying upon the Bones: J. Reuben Clark, the Foreign Bondholders, and the Great Depression" (Ph.D. diss., Florida State University, 1974).

5. David H. Yarn, "Biographical Sketch of J. Reuben Clark, Jr.," *BYU Studies* 13 (Spring 1973):241.

6. Copies of each of these addresses can be found in the Special Collections Department, Harold B. Lee Library, Brigham Young University.

7. JRC, "Let Us Have Peace," 14 November 1947, Box 264.

8. JRC, "Public Loans to Foreign Countries," 20 November 1945, Box 233.

9. JRC, Unpublished manuscript; Ezra Taft Benson to J. Reuben Clark III, 10 April 1979, in possession of author.

10. Quoted in *Dialogue: A Journal of Mormon Thought* 2 (Winter 1967):89.

11. JRC, "The Awesome Task of Peace," *Improvement Era* 48 (October 1945):71.

12. "Let Us Have Peace."

13. J. Reuben Clark, Jr., *Stand Fast by Our Constitution* (Salt Lake City: Deseret Book, 1962).

14. JRC, "The Constitution," April 1957, Box 166.

15. Personal recollection of Belle Spafford.

16. JRC to Cordell Hull, n.d., Box 349.

17. Memorandum on American Delegation to Montevideo Conference, Box 143.

18. Montevideo Conference Diary, 6 December 1933, Box 144; Samuel Guy Inman, *Inter-American Conferences, 1826–1954: History and Problems* (Washington, D.C.: Latin American Institute, 1965), p. 155.

19. Ernest Gruening, *Many Battles: The Autobiography of Ernest Gruening* (New York: Liveright, 1973), pp. 159–60.

20. Interview with J. Reuben Clark III.

21. Gruening, *Many Battles,* p. 162.

22. Montevideo Conference Diary, 16 November 1933, 18 November 1933, 21 November 1933, Box 144.

23. Ibid., 18 November 1933.

24. Inman, *Inter-American Conferences,* pp. 146–47.

25. Montevideo Conference Diary, 9 December 1933, 11 December 1933, 14 December 1933, 15 December 1933, 17 December 1933, 18 December 1933, Box 144.

26. Inman, *Inter-American Conferences,* p. 156.

27. Gruening, *Many Battles,* pp. 166–67.

28. Ibid., p. 167; Cordell Hull, *The Memoirs of Cordell Hull,* 2 vols. (New York: Macmillan, 1948), 1:334.

29. Gruening, *Many Battles,* pp. 167–68.

30. *Report of the Delegates of the United States of America to the Seventh International Conference of American States* (Washington, D.C.: Government Printing Office, 1934), p. 20.

31. *FRUS,* 1933, 4:194.

32. Sessions, "Prophesying upon the Bones," pp. 1–60.

33. Ibid., p. 76.

34. Ibid., pp. 70–74.

35. Ibid., pp. 101–73.

36. Ibid., p. 174.

37. Ibid., pp. 174–92.

38. JRC, Memorandum entitled "The Problem," 18 July 1934, Box 347.

39. Sessions, "Prophesying upon the Bones," pp. 123–24.

40. Interview with J. Reuben Clark III.

41. Interview with Louise Clark Bennion, Marianne Clark Sharp, and J. Reuben Clark III.

42. *The World Court: Hearing before the Committee on Foreign Relations, United States Senate,* 73d Congress, 2d Session, 16 May 1934 (Washington, D.C.: Government Printing Office, 1934).

43. JRC to Hiram Johnson, 18 January 1935, Box 352.

44. Unless otherwise noted, the information in section vii is taken from standard reference sources.

45. Montevideo Conference Diary, 24 November 1933, Box 144.

46. Ibid., 23 November 1933.

47. Ibid., 6 December 1933.

48. Fred M. Dearing to JRC, 21 February 1943, Box 369.

49. JRC to Salmon O. Levinson, 19 June 1934, Box 351.

50. See, for example, JRC to Herbert Hoover, 15 January 1943, Box 344.

51. Dulles, *Yesterday in Mexico,* pp. 676–77.

52. Unidentified newspaper clipping, Box 33.

53. John W. DeKay to JRC, 18 July 1935, Box 33.

54. John W. DeKay, "Declaration for the Founding of Intellectus et Labor," n.d., Box 33.

55. JRC to Henry E. DeKay, 19 December 1938, Box 33.

56. Nothing set Reuben apart from other conservatives more clearly than his attitude toward the right of revolution. The issue had always been central to United States foreign policy. The American Revolution was the first of the great republican upheavals of modern time, to be followed by the French Revolution in 1789 and a series of European revolutions in 1830 and 1848. Throughout the nineteenth century Americans proudly regarded themselves as harbingers of revolution, welcoming into the United States such republican firebrands as Thaddeus Kosciusko of Poland. Understandably, they were viewed with consid-

erable alarm by monarchical Europe, much in the same way that Soviet Russia would be viewed in the 1920s and 1930s.

But by the end of the century, the word *revolution* had come to have a different ring to American ears. The revolutionary turmoil then festering in Russia and Mexico was not the simple cry for freedom that America had once sounded, but a call for the redistribution of wealth. Indeed, the Marxist revolutionaries of Lenin's generation claimed to have eclipsed the American revolutionaries of Washington's—to have wrested the course of history away from republican liberalism. For this, among other reasons, the United States turned rigidly conservative.

At the turn of the century, American foreign policy was completely in the hands of a property-owning elite which regarded revolution with special horror. J. Reuben Clark was one of the few State Department functionaries, high or low, who was not a part of this silk-stocking aristocracy, and he was one of the few who had retained the older, more optimistic view of revolution. When Reuben heard the word *revolution,* he still thought of George Washington.

During the course of Reuben's career, the question of revolution was constantly being thrust upon him. It came up first in 1908, with the Pouren case. It followed again and again with every brushfire revolt in Latin America, with every thrust of intervention, with every case of imperiled American interests abroad. And always, it seemed, Reuben's attitude was at odds with those around him. In one heated memorandum he indignantly asked: "What becomes of Washington?" ("Suggestive Points on the Mexican Revolution"). This would be one of the central questions of his career.

Nor were colleagues in the State Department the only sources of opposition to Reuben's view. In May of 1912 he attended the Ninth International Red Cross Conference in Washington, where representatives of thirty-one nations gathered to discuss—though they did not know it at the time—the great cataclysm which was then almost upon the world. They also discussed an extremely unsettling proposal by J. Reuben Clark. Reuben wondered, almost idly, why the Red Cross helped only one side—the "legitimate" side—in a civil disturbance. He accordingly proposed that the organization abandon this partiality and extend its humanitarian assistance to everyone. He saw the issue in terms of simple common sense. There had been battles in the Mexican Revolution, he pointed out, where the wounded had lain in the blistering sun for days after the fighting and finally died of exposure. He seemed to miss the revolutionary implications of his idea.

But others did not miss them. Seated across the table from him in the special committee called to consider the proposal were delegates of four powers which would soon be torn by war and wracked by revolution themselves: General von Pfuel of Germany, General Michel of France, General Ferraro di Cavallerleone of Italy, and—most ironically of all—General Nicolas Yermoloff of Russia. All of them roundly opposed the suggestion of the upstart Yankee civilian. Intoned General Yermoloff:

> As delegate of the Imperial Government, I consider and declare that the Imperial Government could not in any case or in any form be a contracting party or even a discussing party to any agreement or resolution on this subject, and I deem that this subject, in view of its grave political character, cannot even be made the subject matter of discussion in an exclusively humanitarian and pacific conference. I consider furthermore that the Red Cross Societies can have no duty to fulfill with insurrectionary or revolutionary bands, which cannot be considered by the laws of my country otherwise than as criminal. [Translation of Meeting of the Committee Charged with Examining the Report of Mr. Clark, 10 May 1912, Box 68.]

Yermoloff might have been more excited than the other delegates, but he was no more implacable. None would support Reuben's proposal—or even formally discuss it.

Reuben, however, was not discouraged. In fact, he was soon preparing a new assault. As chairman of the American preparatory committee for the Third Hague Conference, he was in a position to advance his view of revolution in a far higher sphere than the International Red Cross. In his report to the president he asked:

> Is the United States prepared to take the position that the existing status quo of the world shall be permanently maintained? . . . Is the United States prepared to say that there shall be no further evolution in the monarchic governments of the world? Would they support a treaty which guaranteed the perpetuation of the absolute monarchy of Russia? . . . Is the United States prepared to say what form of government shall exist in every other country in the world? Is it prepared to say that no people shall rise up and throw off a despotic power, or correct intolerable evils, by force of arms? [Memorandum for American Preparatory Committee for Third Hague Conference, September 1913, Box 76.]

One likely reason that the problems of the Mexican Revolution were dumped in Reuben's lap was that he did not seem to fear them as others did. As far as he was concerned, Madero—or Orozco for that matter—had as much right to seek popular favor as Díaz did. Reuben did not personally like any of the Mexican revolutionaries, but he accorded them all equal place under the doctrine of America's own Declaration of Independence. This was the ground on which he defended Huerta. In "Suggestive Points on the Mexican Revolution," he pointed out that the recent Chinese and Portuguese revolutions were just as bloody and just as morally questionable as Huerta's and that neither all the Chinese nor all the Portuguese had wanted a republic. The key word, once again, was *republic*. Reuben was still thinking in terms of the American experience.

By 1925 Reuben's diplomat friends had nearly succeeded in changing his mind about revolution. But then he went to Mexico, got to know Calles, and saw firsthand the accomplishments of the Mexican Revolution. His eventual blessing on that event was but a reassertion of his old faith that democracy would somehow prevail. It was a faith that he could still apply to the most reprobate of revolutionaries—even Stalin. One day, Undersecretary of State Clark had "quite a talk" with the as-yet-unrecognized representatives of Stalin's brave new Russia:

> They complained rather bitterly that they were misunderstood. I explained to them that I had much sympathy with people who were misunderstood, having belonged to such a people who were supposed to be something far different from what they were. I told them I was not frightened of their communism, that the people to which I belonged had at one time set up a number of new colonies, some of which had proved to be very prosperous. . . . I considered that the Russian people had a perfect right to have any sort of government they wished; that the kind of government which they had was their business and not mine; that I would regard it as most improper and unfriendly for my government to send propagandists to Russia to persuade the Russian people that theirs was a bad form of government, and that ours should be adopted instead thereof. [JRC, Work Diary, 18 January 1929, Box 530.]

The same went for Hitler's Germany. Reuben Clark was not, as once charged, a Nazi sympathizer any more than was that other Morrow affiliate, Charles Lindbergh. What he said about Hitler during the isolationist debates of the 1930s was what he had said about Russia earlier: that the German form of government, revolutionary though it may be, was nobody's business but Germany's. As long as Hitler and Stalin behaved themselves internationally, Reuben had no quarrel with either of them. In point of fact, neither one behaved; on those grounds Reuben wound up opposing them both.

Reuben's belief in revolution was sorely tried by the twentieth century and, as the menace of Russian communism reached its cold war zenith, perhaps was finally overthrown.

But he held onto it longer than most contemporaries. For him the revolutionary message of the American Founding Fathers was still relevant long after his country's worldwide commitment to the status quo.

57.   Sessions, "Prophesying upon the Bones," p. 76.
58.   "Difficulties in Unlimited Compulsory Arbitration," Box 62.
59.   Interview with Rowena Miller.

BIBLIOGRAPHIC ESSAY

General Sources

The informational cornerstone of this study is the collection known as "The Clarkana Papers of Joshua Reuben Clark, Jr.," housed at the Harold B. Lee Library, Brigham Young University, Provo, Utah. The "Clarkana" name was first used to designate a portion of the collected writings and later the collection as a whole. The Clarkana Papers span the years 1873 to 1961 and contain approximately 140,000 individual items. This massive collection is divided into two major categories: The Education, Law, and Government Service Period, and The Church Service Period. Clark's correspondence, speeches, articles, documents, and remarks are preserved in some 500 boxes, divided into the two categories mentioned above. These papers contain a wealth of information on Clark's governmental and diplomatic service. Also included are materials concerning significant world and national issues with which Reuben was involved. The Clarkana Papers also contain correspondence with some of the most noteworthy personalities of the age.

Another invaluable source is the Rowena Miller Collection, also located at the Harold B. Lee Library. This collection contains documents and other material collected by Rowena Miller, Reuben Clark's personal secretary for many years. This collection, along with an interview with Rowena Miller herself, adds significantly to the detail of the work as a whole.

Hundreds of details and insights were gained through interviews with the Clark children: Louise Clark Bennion, Marianne Clark Sharp, J. Reuben Clark III, and Luacine Clark Fox. These have contributed to the overall tone and have been extremely helpful. The Diary of Joshua Reuben Clark, Sr., and the handwritten autobiographical account of Luacine Savage Clark also provided further useful information.

Two published sources concerning Clark's early life and his career in government service are recommended for further reading: David H. Yarn, Jr., *Young Reuben: The Early Life of J. Reuben Clark, Jr.* (Provo, Utah: Brigham Young University Press, 1973), and, for information on Clark's public career, Ray C. Hillam, ed., *J. Reuben Clark, Jr.: Diplomat and Statesman* (Provo, Utah: Brigham Young University Press, 1973). These essays were originally published in the Spring 1973 issue of *BYU Studies* and are highly recommended.

Several good secondary sources on the general history and diplomacy of J. Reuben Clark's time are: Thomas A. Bailey, *A Diplomatic History of the American People* (Englewood Cliffs, N.J.: Prentice-Hall, 1970); Oscar T. Barck and Nelson M. Blake, *Since 1900: A History of the United States in Our Times* (New York: Macmillan, 1974); Ruhl Bartlett, *Policy and Power: Two Centuries of American Foreign Relations* (New York: Hill and Wang, 1963); Alexander DeConde, *A History of American Foreign Policy,* 2d ed. (New York: Charles Scribner's Sons, 1971); Gilbert C. Fite and Norman A. Graebner, *Recent United States History* (New York: Ronald Press, 1972); John A. Garraty, *The American Nation: A History of the United States* (New York: Harper and Row, 1971); R. W. Leopold, *The Growth of American Foreign Policy: A History* (New York: Knopf, 1962); and Arthur S. Link and William B. Catton, *American Epoch: A History of the United States since the 1890s,* 3d ed. (New York: Alfred A. Knopf, 1966). Another source on the foreign service is Martin B. Hickman's "The American Diplomat: The Search for Identity," in *Problems in American Foreign Policy,* 2d ed., ed. Martin B. Hickman (Beverly Hills, Calif.: Glencoe Press, 1975), pp. 170–79.

For more complete insights into the personalities and events with which Reuben was associated, the following collections of papers were consulted at the Manuscript Division of the Library of Congress, Washington, D.C.: Adee Family, Chandler Anderson, Breckinridge Family, Wilbur J. Carr, Henry P. Fletcher, Robert Frazer, G. H. Hackworth, Charles Evans Hughes, Cordell Hull, Nelson T. Johnson, Philander C. Knox, Robert T. Lansing, Frederick K. Nielsen, Theodore Roosevelt, Jr., Elihu Root, Francis B. Sayre, William H. Taft, Leonard Wood, and Lester H. Woolsey. Extensive diplomatic files in the National Archives in Washington, D.C., also provided a wealth of information. Many of the more important diplomatic dispatches were gathered yearly and published by the Government Printing Office in Washington, D.C., in *Papers Relating to the Foreign Relations of the United States (FRUS).*

Secondary sources consulted for biographical and other resource data include *Congressional Record; Dictionary of American Biography,* published in successive years by Scribner, New York; Helen Delper, ed., *Encyclopedia of Latin America* (New York: McGraw-Hill, 1974); *National Cyclopedia of American Biography,* published in successive years by J. T. White & Co., New York; and the *Who's Who in America* series, published yearly by Who's Who, Inc., Chicago. Also helpful is the *Historical Dictionary* series, published by The Scarecrow Press, Metuchen, N.J.

A great deal of material was gained from numerous newspapers and journals, including *Advocate of Peace, Baltimore Evening Sun, Boston Evening Transcript, Christian Science Monitor, Commentary, Deseret Evening News, El Paso Times, El Universal, Excelsior, Fortune, Louisville Times, Nation, New York Sun, New York Times, Outlook, Salt Lake Herald-Republican, Salt Lake Times, Salt Lake Tribune, Unity, Washington Post,* and *Washington Star.*

Prologue   BETWEEN WEST AND EAST

A great majority of the material for the prologue comes from family correspondence and reminiscences, especially from the Diary of Joshua Reuben Clark, Sr., from an autobiographical account in manuscript form left by Reuben's brother John, and from various items in the family papers. In addition to these, several other sources are helpful: Bryant S. Hinckley, "President J. Reuben Clark, Jr.," *Improvement Era* 36 (1933):643–46; Marianne Clark Sharp, "Born to Greatness: The Story of President J. Reuben Clark, Jr.," *Children's Friend* 53 (1954):360–62; and J. Reuben Clark, Jr., "What I Read as a Boy," *Children's Friend* 42 (1943):99. David Yarn's *Young Reuben,* mentioned above, deals in greater detail with many of the episodes and incidents of Reuben's early life and should be consulted.

Part I   APPRENTICESHIP

Some of the most valuable resources on the Columbia experience are Reuben Clark's own reminiscences and exchanges preserved in subsequent correspondence with old law school friends. For more specific information on the university itself, see Fon W. Boardman, "After Class," in *A History of Columbia College on Morningside* (New York: Columbia University Press, 1954); Horace Coon, *Columbia, Colossus on the Hudson* (New York: E. P. Dutton, 1947); and Wesley First, ed., *University on the Heights* (New York: Doubleday, 1969). An important source in terms of establishing the setting during Reuben Clark's years at Columbia is Edwin E. Slosson, *Great American Universities* (New York: Macmillan, 1910). Gordon Hoxie et al., *A History of the Faculty of Political Science, Columbia University* (New York: Columbia University Press, 1955), deals specifically with the prestigious faculty of the political science department, which did so much to shape the university as well as the law school; and Francis M. Burdick, "The School of Law," in *A History of Columbia University, 1754–1904* (New York: Columbia University Press, 1904), deals with the law school itself. Burdick served as the faculty advisor of the law review while Reuben Clark served on the editorial board. For a view of the law school as experienced by one of its faculty, see Alpheus Thomas Mason, *Harlan Fiske Stone: Pillar of the Law* (New York: Viking Press, 1956). The school as experienced by one of its more prestigious students can be viewed in Kenneth S. Davis's *FDR: The Beckoning of Destiny, 1882–1928* (New York: G. P. Putnam's Sons, 1971). Two professors at Columbia contributed extensively to Reuben Clark's life and career: James Brown Scott, who will be treated in a subsequent section, and John Bassett Moore. Richard Megargee's "The Diplomacy of John Bassett Moore: Realism in American Foreign Policy" (Ph.D. diss., Northwestern University, 1963), emphasizes the realistic aspects of Moore's politics and diplomacy.

An excellent source to begin the study of American diplomacy at the turn of the century is Barbara Tuchman, *The Proud Tower: A Portrait of the World before the War, 1890–1914* (New York: Macmillan, 1967), which places the changes occurring in American diplomacy in their world diplomatic context. Julius W. Pratt, *Challenge and Rejection: The United States and World Leadership, 1900–1921* (New York: Macmillan, 1967), approaches the same subject from a more scholarly point of view. Both Howard K. Beale, *Theodore Roosevelt and the Rise of America to World Power* (Baltimore: Johns-Hopkins Press, 1956), and Raymond A. Esthus, *Theodore Roosevelt and the International Rivalries* (Waltham, Mass.: Ginn-Blaisdell, 1970), relate the new diplomacy in America to the personality and character of Theodore Roosevelt. Esthus's work in particular demonstrates the pressures under which Roosevelt worked as he hammered out the American diplomatic style for which he would become so famous in succeeding years.

Important as Roosevelt was to the workings of American diplomacy at the turn of the century, an even more important participant insofar as the State Department was concerned was Elihu Root. The classic biography and standard source on Root remains Philip C. Jessup, *Elihu Root,* 2 vols. (New York: Dodd, Mead & Co., 1938). However, it may be supplemented by Charles Toth, "Elihu Root," in *An Uncertain Tradition: American Secretaries of State in the Twentieth Century,* ed. Norman A. Graebner (New York: McGraw-Hill, 1961), pp. 40–58, and James Brown Scott, "Elihu Root," in *The American Secretaries of State and Their Diplomacy,* ed. Samuel Flagg Bemis, 10 vols. (New York: Pageant Book, 1958), 9:193–282, both of which are much shorter versions. James Brown Scott was an especially close friend of Root's, and the portrait he presents of his mentor is not a particularly critical one. Richard W. Leopold's *Elihu Root and the Conservative Tradition* (Boston: Little, Brown & Co., 1954) is more analytical than either Toth's or Scott's work and offers some useful insights concerning the intellectual underpinnings behind Root's diplomacy. Jack Davis, "The Latin American Policy of Elihu Root" (Ph.D. diss., University of Utah, 1956), is useful as well for a greater understanding of Root's diplomacy, especially regarding his policies in Latin America.

In addition to the secretary himself, there were a number of functionaries in the Department of State whose reminiscences are of some value to this study. Some of these are contained in private papers, as mentioned above. Helpful biographical works include Katherine Crane, *Mr. Carr of State: Forty-seven Years in the Department of State* (New York: St. Martin's Press, 1960), and Galpin Perrin, ed. *Hugh Gibson, 1885–1954: Extracts from Letters and Anecdotes from His Friends* (New York: Belgian American Educational Foundation, 1956). The latter consists of biographical reminiscences by and about Hugh Gibson, who was a leading member of the Mockahi Society and a lifetime friend of Reuben Clark. James Brown Scott, "Robert Bacon," in *The American Secretaries of State and Their Diplomacy,* ed. Samuel Flagg Bemis, 10 vols. (New York: Pageant Book, 1958), 9:285–299, gives some alternative insights into the workings of the State Department insofar as it concerns the character and qualifications of Robert Bacon, who was in no wise qualified to hold the important position that he did. Both Joseph Grew, *Turbulent Era: A Diplomatic Record of Forty Years, 1904–45,* 2 vols. (Boston: Houghton Mifflin, 1952), and William Phillips, *Ventures in Diplomacy* (North Beverly, Mass.: Private Printing, 1952), offer lucid accounts of two men who spent most of their time in the field. Grew, in fact, spent almost all of his time there until the 1920s, when he became undersecretary of state. William Phillips served as an assistant secretary for a short period of time under Theodore Roosevelt. More important than either of these, however, is Benjamin T. Harrison, "Chandler Anderson and American Foreign Relations (1896–1928)" (Ph.D. diss., University of California at Los Angeles, 1969). Anderson succeeded Henry Hoyt as counselor in the State Department and worked quite closely with Reuben Clark in a number of different capacities. The most important reminiscences in both the Root and Knox state departments come from Francis M. Huntington-Wilson, *Memoirs of an Ex-Diplomat* (Boston: B. Humphries, 1945). Huntington Wilson was an insightful observer of as well as a day-to-day participant in the life of the State Department; he held positions of great authority under Knox but had little power under Root. His explicit and detailed memoirs provide a vivid and often critical account of what life was like in the Root State Department. Still, it is doubtless slanted toward Huntington Wilson's own point of view, accenting his tendency to see himself as a more important figure than he actually was. For a more balanced and objective account of Huntington Wilson's role, see Richard J. Eppinga, "Aristocrat, Nationalist, Diplomat: The Life and Career of Huntington Wilson" (Ph.D. diss., Michigan State University, 1972).

A scholarly analysis of the State Department and its functions is developed in George F. Kennan's *American Diplomacy, 1900–1950* (Chicago:

University of Chicago Press, 1951), which presents a warm, nostalgic view of the state departments of Elihu Root and Philander Knox. For an opposing view of early twentieth-century American diplomacy, see Lloyd C. Gardner, "American Foreign Policy, 1900-1921: A Second Look at the Realist Critique of American Diplomacy," in *Towards a New Past: Dissenting Essays in American History,* ed. Barton J. Bernstein (New York: Pantheon Books, 1968), pp. 202-31. Graham Stuart, *The Department of State: A History of Its Organization, Procedure, and Personnel* (New York: Macmillan, 1949), and Graham Stuart, *American Diplomatic and Consular Practice* (New York: D. Appleton-Century, 1936), are standard works on the organization and functions of the State Department. These should be supplemented by Gaillard Hunt, *The Department of State of the United States: Its History and Functions* (New Haven, Conn.: Yale University Press, 1914), and Frederick Van Dyne, *Our Foreign Service: The "ABC" of American Diplomacy* (Rochester, N.Y.: The Lawyers Cooperative Publishing Co., 1909), which were written closer to the events discussed in this study. The latter is especially valuable, as Van Dyne was assistant solicitor under Reuben Clark and provides valuable information about the inner workings of the solicitor's office. Some of the broader currents of change in the State Department during the early years of the twentieth century are discussed in two doctoral dissertations: Robert D. Schulzinger, "The Making of the Diplomatic Mind: The Training, Outlook, and Style of United States Foreign Service Officers, 1906-68" (Ph.D. diss., Yale University, 1971), and Donald J. Murphy, "Professors, Publicists, and Pan Americanism, 1905-17: A Study in the Origins of the Use of 'Experts' in Shaping American Foreign Policy" (Ph.D. diss., University of Wisconsin, 1970).

The only source that places Reuben Clark in the State Department setting is George Parkinson, "How a Utah Boy Won His Way," *Improvement Era* 17 (1914):556-64, which provides a very brief outline of his activities there.

Most of the information about the solicitor's office is contained in materials that Reuben Clark himself collected and annotated while he was solicitor. Many of these materials were used for political or administrative purposes within the State Department itself. Other information comes from Frederick Van Dyne's work, listed above. However, for two of the larger cases discussed—the Pouren case and the Alsop claim—more specific background materials are available. For information on the Pouren case, see Satya Deva Bedi, *Extradition in International Law and Practice* (Buffalo, N.Y.: Dennis & Co., 1966), which discusses the legal background of extradition. Alfreds Bilmanis's *A History of Latvia* (Westport, Conn.: Greenwood Press, 1970) and the anonymous piece, "The Revolution in the Baltic Provinces of Russia," *The Socialist Library,* Extra Volume No. I

(London: Independent Labour Party, n.d.), discuss the larger Latvian problem of which the Pouren case was a part. Sidney S. Harcave, *First Blood: The Russian Revolution of 1905* (New York: Macmillan, 1964), places the Latvian problem in the context of the Revolution of 1905; and Maruta Karklis et al., *The Latvians in America, 1640–1973* (Dobbs Ferry, N.Y.: Oceana Publications, 1974), discusses the experience of the Latvians in the United States. Most of the day-to-day accounts of the Pouren trial and proceedings are carried in the *New York Times.*

The most important sources on the Alsop claim are Reuben Clark's own case and countercase: J. Reuben Clark, Jr., *The Alsop Claim. The Case of the United States of America* (Washington, D.C.: Government Printing Office, 1910), and J. Reuben Clark, Jr., *The Alsop Claim. The Counter-Case of the United States of America* (Washington, D.C.: Government Printing Office, 1910). However, the setting of the Alsop case is treated in William R. Sherman, *The Diplomatic and Commercial Relations of the United States and Chile, 1820–1914* (Boston: R. G. Badger, 1926). As for the extremely difficult and technical problem of distributing the award, see J. Reuben Clark, Jr., "Legal Aspects Regarding the Ownership and Distribution of Awards," *American Journal of International Law* 7 (1913):382–420. On the Orinoco Steamship case, see William C. Dennis, "The Orinoco Steamship Company Case before the Hague Tribunal," *American Journal of International Law* 5 (1911):35–64.

A point of departure for the study of the Taft administration is Paolo E. Coletta, *The Presidency of William Howard Taft* (Lawrence: University Press of Kansas, 1973). Walter V. and Marie V. Scholes's *The Foreign Policies of the Taft Administration* (Columbia: University of Missouri Press, 1970) is the standard work which deals with Philander Knox as secretary of state and with his foreign policies. A shorter work considerably more biased against Knox is Walter V. Scholes's "Philander Knox," in *An Uncertain Tradition: American Secretaries of State in the Twentieth Century,* ed. Norman A. Graebner (New York: McGraw-Hill, 1961), pp. 59–78. Also valuable is Herbert F. Wright, "Philander Knox," in *The American Secretaries of State and Their Diplomacy,* ed. Samuel Flagg Bemis, 10 vols. (New York: Pageant Book, 1958), 9:303–37, which is somewhat more lengthy. For a revisionist view which takes a much kinder look at Knox and his foreign policies, see Paige Elliott Mulhollan, "Philander Knox and Dollar Diplomacy, 1900–1913" (Ph.D. diss., University of Texas, 1966). In spite of the often-impressive arguments in Mulhollan's study, the prevailing viewpoint is in concurrence with Walter Scholes. There are also some valuable reminiscences to be found in Henry M. Hoyt, *Dry Points: Studies in Black and White* (New York: F. Shay, 1921). Hoyt was the first counselor of the State Department to be appointed by Philander Knox.

Bibliographic Essay

The question of professionalism did not begin with Huntington Wilson. For evidence of professionalism before Huntington Wilson's time, Donald M. Dozer, "Secretary of State Elihu Root and Consular Reorganization," *Mississippi Valley Historical Review* 29 (1942):339–50, should be consulted. A broader discussion of professionalism in the State Department is offered by W. F. Ilchman, *Professional Diplomacy in the United States, 1779–1939* (Boston: Houghton Mifflin, 1952). Robert Rossow, "The Professionalization of the New Diplomacy," *World Politics* 14 (1962):561–75, should also be consulted.

The standard work on dollar diplomacy is still Dana G. Munro, *Intervention and Dollar Diplomacy in the Caribbean, 1900–1921* (Princeton, N.J.: Princeton University Press, 1964). Some additional insights of interest are furnished by Charles A. Beard in collaboration with G. H. E. Smith, *The Idea of National Interest: An Analytical Study in American Foreign Policy* (New York: Macmillan, 1934). A particular kind of insight may be gained by examining the personal role of Thomas Dawson in Latin America. For this purpose, Joseph Glenn Kist, "The Role of Thomas C. Dawson in United States–Latin American Diplomatic Relations, 1897–1912" (Ph.D. diss., Loyola University, 1971), is recommended. Several works deal with dollar diplomacy in the Far East. The Japanese problem is treated broadly in Payson Treat, *Japan and the United States, 1853–1921* (Stanford, Calif.: Stanford University Press, 1928), and more superficially yet with considerable insight in Thomas A. Bailey, *Theodore Roosevelt and the Japanese-American Conflict* (Gloucester: Peter Smith, 1964). The Chinese problem as it existed at the time of Philander Knox is examined in John G. Reid, *The Manchu Abdication and the Powers, 1908–12: An Episode in Pre-war Diplomacy* (Westport, Conn.: Greenwood Press, 1973). Meribeth Cameron, "American Recognition Policy toward the Republic of China, 1912–13," *Pacific Historical Review* 2 (1933):214–30, treats the specific problem of recognizing the Chinese republic.

The study of dollar diplomacy in Latin America should begin with J. Fred Rippy, "The Initiation of the Customs Receivership in the Dominican Republic," *Hispanic American Historical Review* 17 (1937):419–57, which discusses the enormous influence of the Dominican Republic on the subsequent evolution of dollar diplomacy under Taft. Diplomatic relations with Venezuela are treated in P. F. Fenton, "Diplomatic Relations of the United States and Venezuela, 1880–1915," *Hispanic American Historical Review* 8 (1928):330–56; with Colombia, in E. Taylor Parks, *Colombia and the United States, 1765–1934* (Durham, N.C.: Duke University Press, 1935); and with Panama, in G. A. Mellander, *The United States in Panamanian Politics: The Intriguing Formative Years* (Danville, Ill.: Interstate Printers & Publishers, 1971). Cuba, which was also very important in the formulation of dollar diplomacy, is discussed broadly in Allan R. Millett, *The Politics of Intervention: The Military Occupation of Cuba, 1906–9* (Columbus: Ohio State University Press, 1968), and more specifically in Robert F. Smith, "Cuba: Laboratory for Dollar Diplomacy, 1898–1917," *Historian* 28 (1966):586–609. The latter work brings out the relationship between events in Cuba and the elaboration of dollar diplomacy.

The centerpiece of dollar diplomacy in Latin America is still the Nicaraguan experience, study of which begins with Harold N. Denny, *Dollars for Bullets: The Story of American Rule in Nicaragua* (New York: The Dial Press, 1929), an early but still quite solid work. The generally negative assessment of the American presence in Nicaragua is continued in John R. McDevitt, "American-Nicaraguan Relations from 1909 to 1916" (Ph.D. diss., Georgetown University, 1954); Dana G. Munro, "Dollar Diplomacy in Nicaragua, 1909–19," *Hispanic American Historical Review* 38 (1958):209–34; and Anna I. Powell, "Relations between the United States and Nicaragua, 1898–1916," *Hispanic American Historical Review* 8 (1928):43–64. However, a contrasting viewpoint may be found in the Mulhollan dissertation mentioned above. Mulhollan also brings out some interesting parallels between the revolution and intervention in Nicaragua and the revolution and intervention a year later in Honduras. For some interesting eyewitness observations of the Nicaraguan intervention, see Lowell J. Thomas, *Old Gimlet Eye: The Adventures of Smedley D. Butler as Told to Lowell Thomas* (New York: Farr & Rinehart, 1933). Information on the Nicaraguan Mixed Claims Commission, which Reuben Clark was instrumental in establishing, is contained in Otto Schoenrich, "The Nicaraguan Mixed Claims Commission," *American Journal of International Law* 19 (1915):858–69. As for the parallels between the Nicaraguan experience of the 1910s and 1920s and the Vietnam experience of later years, see John H. Tierney, Jr., "U.S. Intervention in Nicaragua, 1927–33: Lessons for Today," *Orbis* 14 (1971):1012–28.

Part II WHIRLWIND

A general study of the Mexican Revolution should begin with Henry Bamford Parkes's *A History of Mexico* (Boston: Houghton Mifflin, 1960). Considered a standard work on the history of Mexico, it deals with the revolution itself and its place in the larger historical context. Several other sources on the revolution are recommended: Ronald Atkin, *Revolution!: Mexico, 1910–20* (New York: John Day Co., 1970), and William W. Johnson, *Heroic Mexico: The Violent Emergence of a Modern Nation* (Garden City, N.Y.: Doubleday, 1968), tend to be popularistic works but are quite well researched and very lucidly written, demonstrating not only the main facts of the revolution but something of its inner spirit and dynamics as well. For a contemporary account which contains a wealth of information of an almost primary character, John Reed, *Insurgent Mexico* (New York: D. Appleton & Co., 1914), is recommended. Lowell L. Blaisdell in his *The Desert Revolution: Baja California, 1911* (Madison: University of Wisconsin Press, 1962) deals with the revolution in Baja California, which in some respects is separate from the main Madero revolution in northern Mexico. However, the activities in Baja probably had as great an impact as did Madero on relations between the United States and Mexico during the period of the revolution.

The greatest single resource for an understanding and comprehension of how American policy addressed itself to the problems in Mexico is to be found in the Clark papers themselves, especially in the various drafts of Reuben Clark's State Department memoranda prepared for the president. It is in these memoranda that the picture of the Taft dilemma emerges most clearly, as well as our understanding of Reuben's role in that dilemma. General treatments of the relationship between the United States and Mexico are given in James M. Callahan, *American Foreign Policy in Mexican Relations* (New York: Cooper Square Publishers, 1967); Howard F. Cline, *The United States and Mexico* (Cambridge: Harvard University Press, 1963); and Daniel James, *Mexico and the Americans* (New York: Praeger, 1963). For a Mexican view of these same relations, see Daniel Cosio Villegas, *The United States Versus Porfirio Díaz* (Lincoln: University of Nebraska Press, 1963). Peter Calvert, *The Mexican Revolution, 1910–14: The Diplomacy of Anglo-American Conflict* (London: Cambridge University Press, 1968), deals with the same general material but in a broader context. Calvert brings in the complicating relationship of the United States and Great Britain as related to Mexico and the revolution, and also raises some very interesting points about British-American rivalry in this context. A good short treatment of American policy toward the Mexican Revolution is found in Walter Scholes's study of foreign policies of the Taft administration, mentioned in Part I. The standard work on this question has become P. Edward Haley, *Revolution and Intervention: The Diplomacy of Taft and Wilson with Mexico, 1910–17* (Cambridge: Massachusetts Institute of Technology Press, 1970), which approaches the issues with a great deal of scholarly attention and care. Some of the specific problems regarding the United States, Mexico, and the revolution are discussed in Edward J. Berbusse, "Neutrality–Diplomacy of the United States and Mexico, 1910–11," *The Americas* 12 (1956):265–83, which deals with the formulation of neutrality and the ambiguities it poses. For a broader discussion of the problem of neutrality and foreign wars, see Charles G. Fenwick, *The Neutrality Laws of the United States* (Washington, D.C.: Carnegie Endowment for International Peace, 1954). Roy Emerson Curtis, "The Law of Hostile Military

677

Expeditions as Applied by the United States," *American Journal of International Law* 8 (1914):1–37, 224–55, helps to untangle the complex skein of the international law of neutrality. Frederick S. Dunn, *The Neutrality Laws of the United States* (New York: Columbia University Press, 1933), offers a broad historical discussion of the problem of protecting Americans in Mexico, with much of the material antedating the Mexican Revolution. Frederick C. Turner, "Anti-Americanism in Mexico, 1910–13," *Hispanic American Historical Review* 47 (1967):502–18, sets forth the context of the virulent anti-Americanism within which the revolution erupted. Finally, Archie Butt, *Taft and Roosevelt: The Intimate Letters of Archie Butt, Military Aide,* 2 vols. (Garden City, N.Y.: Doubleday, Doran & Co., 1930), is recommended for glimpses of Taft's reactions to the Mexican Revolution.

The departure point for the study of the Mormons in Mexico is Michael C. Meyer's *Mexican Rebel: Pascual Orozco and the Mexican Revolution, 1910–15* (Lincoln: University of Nebraska Press, 1967). In this work Meyer argues that there was a great deal less wanton destruction and blatant hostility on the part of Orozco and his lieutenants than is generally portrayed in traditional historical accounts. For the experience of the Mormons themselves, see Thomas C. Romney, *The Mormon Colonies in Mexico* (Salt Lake City: Deseret Book Co., 1938), and Karl E. Young, *Ordeal in Mexico: Tales of Danger and Hardship Collected from Mormon Colonists* (Salt Lake City: Deseret Book, 1968), both of which give graphic accounts of the Mormon travail in northern Mexico. Carmon B. Hardy, "Cultural 'Encystment' as a Cause of the Mormon Exodus from Mexico in 1912," *Pacific Historical Review* 34 (1965):439–54, attempts to explain what happened to the Mormons in terms of their exclusiveness and cultural isolation from Mexican affairs. The events in Mexico are connected to the larger response of the LDS church itself in B. H. Roberts, *A Comprehensive History of the Church of Jesus Christ of Latter-day Saints,* 6 vols. (Provo, Utah: Brigham Young University Press, 1965), and are connected to Reed Smoot in Washington in the Diary of Reed Smoot (Harold B. Lee Library, Brigham Young University). Albert Fall played a crucial role in the political use of the Mormon experience in Mexico; for information regarding his involvement, David D. Joyce, "Senator Albert B. Fall and the United States Relations with Mexico, 1912–21," *International Review of History and Political Science* 6 (1969):53–76, and David Stratton, "The Memoirs of Albert B. Fall," *Southwestern Studies* 4(1966):3–62, are recommended. Both William H. Harbaugh, *The Life and Times of Theodore Roosevelt* (New York: Oxford University Press, 1975), and Elting E. Morison, ed., *The Letters of Theodore Roosevelt,* 8 vols. (Cambridge, Mass.: Harvard University Press, 1954), deal with Theodore Roosevelt's political response to the events in Mexico. There is very little written by way of secondary literature concerning the other victims of the Mexican Revolution, such as those who were killed in the fighting in Douglas, Arizona, and El Paso, Texas. However, the *New York Times* features lengthy and well-documented accounts of these battles and of the damage done to American citizens.

Cole Blaiser, "The United States and Madero," *Journal of Latin American Studies* 4 (1972):207–31, gives a short but adequate introduction to the whole relationship between the United States and Madero. Henry Lane Wilson's role in the event is portrayed in Henry Lane Wilson, *Diplomatic Episodes in Mexico, Belgium, and Chile* (Garden City, N.Y.: Doubleday, 1927). Then, for a spirited opposing view, consult Daniel James's work, *Mexico and the Americans,* cited above. A more balanced account is offered by Lowell L. Blaisdell, "Henry Lane Wilson and the Overthrow of Madero," *Southwest Social Science Quarterly* 43 (1962):126–35. Kenneth J. Grieb, *The United States and Huerta* (Lincoln: University of Nebraska Press, 1969), discusses the question of the recognition of Huerta.

For information on the occupation of Veracruz, see Robert E. Quirk, *An Affair of Honor: Woodrow Wilson and the Occupation of Veracruz* (Lexington: University of Kentucky Press, 1962). A good source to consult regarding the Columbus raid and Pershing's expedition across the border into Mexico is Clarence E. Clendenen, *The United States and Pancho Villa: A Study in Unconventional Diplomacy* (Ithaca, N.Y.: Cornell University Press, 1961). And for an account of how these events impinged directly on Mormon settlers in northern Mexico, see Thomas Romney as mentioned above.

Part III　ARMAGEDDON AND AFTER

There are three sources which provide important introductions to the study of the legal settlement movement. Recommended are Wallace M. McClure, *World Legal Order: Possible Contributions by the People of the United States* (Chapel Hill: University of North Carolina Press, 1960); John Bassett Moore, *History and Digest of International Arbitrations to Which the United States Has Been a Party,* 6 vols. (Washington, D.C.: Government Printing Office, 1898); and especially C. Roland Marchand, *The American Peace Movement and Social Reform, 1898–1918* (Princeton, N.J.: Princeton University Press, 1972), for an excellent general survey of the movement. A discussion of the Hague conferences may be found in James Brown Scott, *The Hague Peace Conferences of 1899 and 1907,* 2 vols. (Baltimore: The Johns Hopkins Press, 1909). Scott, as a participant in the 1907 Hague conference, gives important eyewitness accounts of many of its events. His thought was important to the development of the legal settlement movement in the United States, and he is responsible for a large number of publications. The essence of his thought is contained in James Brown Scott,

"The Legal Nature of International Law," *American Journal of International Law* 1 (1907):831–66; James Brown Scott, "Judicial Proceedings as a Substitute for War or International Self-Redress" (Maryland Peace Society, February 1910), Clark Papers, Box 314; and James Brown Scott, *The American Society for Judicial Settlement of International Disputes—Its Scope and Work* (Baltimore: The American Society for Judicial Settlement of International Disputes, 1910). For an early view of the development of the world court movement, see James Brown Scott, *The Status of the International Court of Justice* (New York: Oxford University Press, 1916). George A. Finch, "James Brown Scott, 1866–1943," *American Journal of International Law* 38 (1944):183–217, provides a summary of the career of James Brown Scott.

A good introduction to the subject of British-American relations is given by Bradford Perkins in his *The Great Rapprochement: England and the United States, 1895–1914* (New York: Atheneum, 1968). Perkins draws specific applications from events discussed in British-American rapprochement to the greater context of the world war. For a look at the more narrow subject of settling disputes involving Canada and the United States, both Percy E. Corbett, *The Settlement of Canadian-American Disputes* (New Haven, Conn.: Yale University Press, 1937), and Charles C. Tansill, *Canadian American Relations, 1895–1911* (New Haven, Conn.: Yale University Press, 1943), are recommended. The American-British claims arbitration is treated in Fred K. Nielsen, *American and British Claims Arbitration* (Washington, D.C.: Government Printing Office, 1926). After the war, Nielsen became the American agent of this claims arbitration. See J. Reuben Clark, Jr., "Jurisdiction of American-British Claims Commission," *American Journal of International Law* 7 (1913):687–706, for the discussion of jurisdiction that Reuben wrote during his tenure on the commission. The Atlantic fisheries arbitration is treated in Edwin M. Borchard, "The North Atlantic Coast Fisheries Arbitration," *Columbia Law Review* 11 (1911):1–23, and Robert Lansing, "The North Atlantic Coast Fisheries Arbitration," *American Journal of International Law* 5 (1911):1–31. Lansing was a counsel for the American team during the arbitration. See John B. Campbell, "Taft, Roosevelt, and the Arbitration Treaties of 1911," *Journal of American History* 42 (1966):279–98, for a discussion of the ill-fated arbitration treaties of 1911.

An excellent introduction to World War I and its nature is given in the highly readable and interesting account by Barbara Tuchman, *The Guns of August* (New York: Macmillan, 1962). The single best source for the American perspective on the war is the massive biography of Woodrow Wilson by Arthur Link, *Wilson,* 5 vols. to date (Princeton, N.J.: Princeton University Press, 1947–65). The specific events leading to America's involvement in the war have been exhaustively and repeatedly analyzed in

Bibliographic Essay

Walter Millis, *The Road to War: America 1914–17* (New York: Houghton Mifflin, 1935); Thomas A. Bailey, *Woodrow Wilson and the Great Betrayal* (New York: Macmillan Co., 1945); Daniel M. Smith, *The Great Departure: The United States and World War I, 1914–20* (New York: J. Wiley, 1965); and John Milton Cooper, Jr., *The Vanity of Power: American Isolationism and the First World War, 1914–17* (Westport, Conn.: Greenwood Publishing Corp., 1969). All these works are rather critical of Woodrow Wilson and the American point of view. Robert Lansing's role is emphasized in Daniel M. Smith, *Robert Lansing and American Neutrality, 1914–17* (Berkeley: University of California Press, 1958), and Joseph V. Fuller, "The Genesis of the Munitions Traffic," *Journal of Modern History* 6 (1934):280–93, treats the impact that the munitions traffic had upon the events of the war. There are several studies of Allied propaganda and its impact upon the American mind. David L. Larson, "Objectivity, Propaganda, and the Puritan Ethic," in *The Puritan Ethic in United States Foreign Policy*, ed. David L. Larson (Princeton, N.J.: D. Van Nostrand Co., 1966), pp. 3–24, contains a brief introduction to the subject, and an example of that kind of propaganda is provided by Hugh Gibson, *A Journal from Our Legation in Belgium* (New York: Doubleday, 1917). Gibson was attached to the American legation in Brussels at the time. Probably the best general discussion of the United States at war is given in Frederick Palmer, *Newton D. Baker: America at War*, 2 vols. (New York: Dodd, Mead & Co., 1931). A discussion of the opponents of the war and what happened to them in subsequent years may be found in Horace C. Peterson and Gilbert C. Fite, *Opponents of War, 1917–18* (Madison: University of Wisconsin Press, 1957). The Creel Committee is discussed in George Creel, *How We Advertised America: The First Telling of the Amazing Story of the Committee on Public Information that Carried the Gospel of Americanism to Every Corner of the Globe* (New York: Harper & Bros., 1920), and James R. Mock and Cedric Larson, *Words that Won the War: The Story of the Committee on Public Information, 1917–19* (Princeton, N.J.: Princeton University Press, 1939). The political aspects of the war are outlined in Seward W. Livermore, *Politics Is Adjourned: Woodrow Wilson and the War Congress, 1916–18* (Middletown, Conn.: Wesleyan University Press, 1966), and David A. Lockmiller, *Enoch H. Crowder: Soldier, Lawyer, and Statesman* (Columbia: University of Missouri Press, 1955).

The League fight is put in its general setting by Selig Adler, *The Isolationist Impulse: Its Twentieth-Century Reaction* (London: Abelard-Schuman, Ltd., 1957); and for a discussion of the League to Enforce Peace, which was the antecedent organization of the League of Nations in the United States, Ruhl Bartlett, *The League to Enforce Peace* (Chapel Hill: University

681

of North Carolina Press, 1944), is recommended. The fight over the League itself is detailed in several works: Denna F. Fleming, *The United States and the League of Nations, 1918-20* (New York: G. P. Putnam's Sons, 1932); Thomas A. Bailey, *Woodrow Wilson and the Lost Peace* (New York: Macmillan, 1944); and Alan Cranston, *The Killing of the Peace* (New York: Viking, 1945). The irreconcilables and their role in the controversy are discussed in Ralph A. Stone, *The Irreconcilables: The Fight against the League of Nations* (Lexington: University of Kentucky Press, 1970). Also important is James E. Hewes, Jr., "Henry Cabot Lodge and the League of Nations," *Proceedings, American Philosophical Society* 114 (1970):245-55, which considers Lodge and his pivotal role in the Senate. Dexter Perkins, "The Department of State and American Public Opinion," in *The Diplomats, 1919-39,* ed. Gordon A. Craig and F. Gilbert (Princeton, N.J.: Princeton University Press, 1953), pp. 282-308, provides insights concerning the influence of American public opinion on the events surrounding the League fight. Some of the constitutional considerations of joining the League are outlined in Alfred H. Kelly and Winifred A. Harbison, *The American Constitution: Its Origins and Development,* 4th ed. (New York: W. W. Norton, 1970). The continuing influence of isolationism in the United States after the League fight is treated in Denna F. Fleming, *The United States and World Organization, 1920-33* (New York: AMS Press, 1966); but it should be compared with William A. Williams, "The Legend of Isolationism in the 1920s," *Science & Society* 17 (1954):1-20, and with Justus D. Doeneke, "Isolationists of the 1930s and 1940s: A Historiographical Essay" (paper read at the Southeastern Regional Meeting of the Society for Historians of American Foreign Relations, 24 February 1973), for a historiographical discussion on isolationism. For a view of the League fight in Utah, an excellent source is James B. Allen, "Personal Faith and Public Policy: Some Timely Observations on the League of Nations Controversy in Utah," *BYU Studies* 14 (1973):77-98.

The Washington arms conference is placed in the broader context of Republican foreign policy in Selig Adler, *The Uncertain Giant, 1921-41: American Foreign Policy between the Wars* (New York: Macmillan, 1965) and also in L. Ethan Ellis, *Republican Foreign Policy, 1921-33* (New Brunswick, N.J.: Rutgers University Press, 1968). For information on the conference itself, see both Thomas H. Buckley, *The United States and the Washington Conference, 1921-22* (Knoxville: University of Tennessee Press, 1970), and John Chalmers Vinson, *The Parchment Peace: The United States Senate and the Washington Conference, 1921-22* (Athens: University of Georgia Press, 1955). The centerpiece of the conference, the Anglo-Japanese alliance, is discussed in Charles N. Spinks, "The Termination of the Anglo-Japanese Alliance," *Pacific Historical Review* 6 (1937):321-40. Two good biographies of Charles Evans Hughes are recommended: Merlo J. Pusey, *Charles Evans Hughes,* 2 vols. (New York: Macmillan, 1951), and Dexter Perkins, *Charles Evans Hughes and American Democratic Statesmanship* (Boston: Little, Brown, 1956). Hughes's own biographical notes are published in Daniel J. Danelski and Joseph S. Tulchin, eds. *The Autobiographical Notes of Charles Evans Hughes* (Cambridge, Mass.: Harvard University Press, 1971). A footnote to the Washington arms conference is Isaac D. Levine, *Mitchell: Pioneer of Air Power* (New York: Duell, Sloan & Pierce, 1943). Captain Billy Mitchell believed that the ships themselves were of secondary importance to the growing significance of air power in the Pacific field of operations in any conceivable war between the United States and Japan.

The World Court question in the 1920s is dealt with in Manley O. Hudson, *The World Court, 1921–34* (Boston: World Peace Foundation, 1934), and Denna F. Fleming, *The United States and the World Court* (Garden City, N.Y.: Doubleday, 1945). For information on the Kellogg-Briand Pact and its relationship to the Court fight, see both Robert H. Ferrell, *Peace in Their Time: The Origins of the Kellogg-Briand Pact* (New Haven, Conn.: Yale University Press, 1952), and John C. Vinson, *William E. Borah and the Outlawry of War* (Athens: University of Georgia Press, 1957).

Part IV   INTERLUDE

Sources for Part IV are found almost entirely in the private papers of the Clark family and in the Clarkana Papers, which give valuable information on relationships within the Clark family and between Reuben and his friends. The memoirs of Huntington Wilson, mentioned earlier, should also be consulted for aspects of the friendship between Huntington Wilson and Reuben in the later years, particularly Huntington Wilson's attempts to reenter the State Department in 1928. Interviews with the Clark family provided important insights and information for this section, as did interviews with associates such as Rowena Miller. Seldom does Reuben's private practice touch upon issues of such concern that secondary sources are available for background insights. For information on the Japanese land legislation problem in 1913, see Thomas A. Bailey, "California, Japan, and the Alien Land Legislation of 1913," *Pacific Historical Review* 1 (1932):36–59. For a discussion of the reorientation of American economic priorities in the new world market caused, to a great degree, by the war, there are several good sources available: Carl P. Parrini, *Heir to Empire: United States Economic Diplomacy (1916–23)* (Pittsburgh: University of Pittsburgh Press, 1969), and Harry N. Scheiber, "World War I as Entrepreneurial Opportunity: Willard Straight and the American International Corporation," *Political Science Quarterly* 84 (1969):486–511, are recommended. An excellent biography of Willard Straight may be found in Herbert Croly, *Willard Straight* (New York: Macmillan, 1924).

683

Standard sources for Utah's political, economic, and religious history are Richard D. Poll et al., *Utah's History* (Provo, Utah: Brigham Young University Press, 1978); Leonard J. Arrington and Davis Bitton, *The Mormon Experience* (New York: Alfred A. Knopf, 1979); and James B. Allen and Glen M. Leonard, *The Story of the Latter-day Saints* (Salt Lake City: Deseret Book Co., 1976). Thomas O'Dea, *The Mormons* (Chicago: University of Chicago Press, 1957), may also be of interest. Jan Shipps has written an interesting and thoughtful but necessarily brief article dealing with politics in the beginning of the twentieth century in "Utah Comes of Age Politically: A Study of the State's Politics in the Early Years of the Twentieth Century," *Utah Historical Quarterly* 35 (1967):91–111. Also valuable and to the point are two doctoral dissertations dealing with Utah politics in a later period: Dan E. Jones, "Utah Politics, 1926–32" (Ph.D. diss., University of Utah, 1968), and Brad E. Hainsworth, "Utah State Elections, 1916–24" (Ph.D. diss., University of Utah, 1968). Almost all of the information on the political machine known as the Sevens and on the election of 1928 comes out of these two dissertations.

Ron Walker of the Utah Historical Society is currently researching a biography of Heber J. Grant, which will detail the impact of Grant on the Mormon church and its development.

There are several works dealing with the shift in Mormonism in the early twentieth century. Thomas Alexander is currently working on this problem in a study for the sesquicentennial history of the LDS church. Leonard Arrington, "Mormonism: Views from Within and Without," *BYU Studies* 14 (1974):140–54, and Jan Shipps, "From Satyr to Saint: American Attitudes toward the Mormons, 1860–1960" (paper presented at the Chicago meeting of the Organization of American Historians, April 1973), should also be consulted. Kenneth L. Cannon II, "Beyond the Manifesto: Polygamous Cohabitation among LDS General Authorities after 1890," *Utah Historical Quarterly* 46 (1978):24–36, discusses an issue particularly difficult for Reuben Clark. The Fall 1977 issue of the *Utah Historical Quarterly* deals with the career and politics of Reed Smoot and should be consulted for more information. As a side note, M. Paul Holsinger, "Philander Knox and the Crusade against Mormonism, 1904–7," *Western Pennsylvania Historical Magazine* 52 (1969):47–55, demonstrates that during the Smoot controversy in the Senate one of the Utah politician's staunch supporters was Philander Knox. This fact was to have considerable significance later on when Knox became Reuben Clark's mentor and confidant.

Part V   GOOD NEIGHBOR

The Good Neighbor policy signaled a change of direction in the foreign policy of the United States toward Latin America in the middle of the

1920s, and Reuben Clark was once again pulled into the Mexican situation through the Mexican claims commission. For a picture of the broader U.S.–Latin American situation during this time, see Samuel Flagg Bemis, *The Latin American Policy of the United States: An Historical Perspective* (New York: Harcourt, Brace & Co., 1943), and Bryce Wood, *The Making of the Good Neighbor Policy* (New York: Columbia University Press, 1961), both of which deal with the historical antecedents of the Good Neighbor policy. But David Green, *The Containment of Latin America: A History of the Myths and Realities of the Good Neighbor Policy* (Chicago: Quadrangle Books, 1971), takes a modern and somewhat different view of the evolution of good-neighborism for Latin America.

Almost the entire source material for background on the U.S.-Mexico Claims Commission is contained in A. H. Feller, *The Mexican Claims Commissions, 1923–34: A Study in the Law and the Procedure of International Tribunals* (New York: Macmillan, 1935), an exhaustive case-by-case analysis of the law and procedure of the Mexican claims commission and its activities. Jackson H. Ralston, *The Law and Procedure of International Tribunals* (New York: Garland, 1973), is also useful for understanding how such tribunals operated, not only in the case of the U.S.-Mexico Claims Commission but also in that of the American-British Claims Commission discussed earlier. For information regarding the Santa Ysabel case, which did so much to destroy the effectiveness of the Mexican claims commission, see the Clendenen study on the United States and Pancho Villa mentioned in Part II.

The most concise single work on the Mexican oil controversy and its settlement is contained in J. Reuben Clark, Jr., "The Oil Settlement with Mexico," *Foreign Affairs* 6 (1928):600–614, which summarizes the work done on this matter by Clark and Morrow. Longer summaries and compendia of the legal and technical problems of the oil settlement are contained in the Clark papers. A sense of contrast between the methods of Sheffield and Dwight Morrow is elucidated quite well by James J. Horn, "Diplomacy by Ultimatum: Ambassador Sheffield and Mexican-American Relations, 1924–27" (Ph.D. diss., State University of New York, Buffalo, 1969). Americans voiced a great deal of concern about the Mexican Revolution and its implications for American policy in the 1920s, and both J. Fred Rippy et al., *American Policies Abroad: Mexico* (Chicago: University of Chicago Press, 1928), and Wilfrid H. Callcott, *Liberalism in Mexico* (Stanford, Calif.: Stanford University Press, 1931), deal with this psychological and emotional background. Wallace Thompson, "Wanted–A Mexican Policy," *The Atlantic Monthly,* March 1927, pp. 381–91, issues the call for a Mexican policy for the United States in dealing with the revolutionary turmoil there. Historical summaries of the intense nationalism generated by the Mexican Revolution in the 1920s are given in John W. F. Dulles, *Yesterday in Mexico: A Chronicle of the Revolution, 1919–36* (Austin: University of Texas Press, 1961); Robert F. Smith, *The United States and Revolutionary Nationalism in Mexico, 1916–32* (Chicago: University of Chicago Press, 1972); and T. R. Fehrenbach, *Fire and Blood: A History of Mexico* (New York: Macmillan, 1973). The oil controversy is placed in its broader international context in Ludwell Denny, *We Fight for Oil* (New York: A. H. Knopf, 1928), which emphasizes the rivalry of the great powers over Mexican oil. The Mexican debt problem, which was entangled with oil and land difficulties, is outlined in Edgar Turlington's *Mexico and Her Foreign Creditors* (New York: Columbia University Press, 1930). There is no single source that focuses upon the land expropriation problem, but land is mentioned prominently in the Freeman work listed above.

An early biography of Dwight Morrow by Mary M. McBride, *The Story of Dwight W. Morrow* (New York: Farrar and Rinehart, 1930), is essentially replaced by the much more sophisticated work by Harold Nicholson, *Dwight Morrow* (New York: Harcourt, Brace, 1935). The latter biography, heavily imbued with neo-Freudian analysis, was almost utterly rejected by Reuben Clark and to some extent by Mrs. Morrow after its publication. A current biography of Morrow by Richard Meltzer is in progress at the University of New Mexico. The Nicholson biography should be supplemented by two articles: Stanley R. Ross, "Dwight W. Morrow, Ambassador to Mexico," *The Americas* 14 (1958):273–89, and Stanley R. Ross, "Dwight Morrow and the Mexican Revolution," *Hispanic-American Historical Review* 38 (1958):482–505. Reminiscences by members of the Morrow family are included in Anne Morrow Lindbergh's beautifully written *Bring Me a Unicorn: Diaries and Letters of Anne Morrow Lindbergh, 1922–28* (New York: Harcourt, Brace, Jovanovich, 1971), and Elizabeth Cutter Morrow's *The Mexican Years: Leaves from the Diary of Elizabeth Cutter Morrow* (New York: Spiral Press, 1953).

One of the best introductions to Reuben Clark's tenure as undersecretary of state is the standard biography of Frank Kellogg by L. Ethan Ellis, *Frank B. Kellogg and American Foreign Relations, 1925–29* (New Brunswick, N.J.: Rutgers University Press, 1961). There are, however, two good doctoral dissertations which deal with aspects of Kellogg's career and foreign policy: Charles G. Cleaver, "Frank Kellogg: Attitudes and Assumptions Influencing His Foreign Policy Decisions" (Ph.D. diss., University of Minnesota, 1956), and Jeanne C. Traphagen, "The Inter-American Policy of Frank B. Kellogg" (Ph.D. diss., University of Minnesota, 1956). One event that hung over Kellogg's career at the State Department was the Nicaraguan intervention, which is discussed in Henry L. Stimson, *American Policy in Nicaragua* (New York: C. Scribner's Sons, 1927). Stim-

son was special negotiator and troubleshooter in Nicaragua during a crucial part of the affair. J. Reuben Clark as undersecretary of state is introduced in Lee H. Burke, "J. Reuben Clark, Jr., Under Secretary of State,"
BYU Studies 13 (1973):396–404—a brief article, yet one with some interesting comments on the day-to-day life and affairs in the State Department
at that time. The status of foreign relations during 1928 is discussed in
Charles P. Howland, *Survey of American Foreign Relations, 1928* (New
Haven, Conn.: Yale University Press, 1928), and T. C. Lay, *The Foreign
Service of the United States* (New York: Prentice Hall, 1928), both of which
contain a wealth of information about how American foreign relations operated during the period of Clark's undersecretaryship. Some interesting as-
sessments of personalities involved in the State Department and in American diplomacy are offered in Drew Pearson and R. S. Allen, *Washington
Merry-Go-Round* (New York: Horace Liveright, 1931), and Drew Pearson
and R. S. Allen, *The Mirrors of 1932* (New York, 1931). Both are popular,
journalistic works, but Pearson's direct connection with the events gives
them a considerable amount of value. Also valuable are Hugh Wilson's
memoirs, *Diplomat between Wars* (New York: Longmans, Green & Co.,
1941), and Joseph Grew's *Turbulent Era,* referred to in Part I. Grew was
undersecretary of state at the time that Hugh Wilson was prominent in the
State Department.

The Clark Memorandum is discussed in virtually every treatment of
American foreign policy, particularly those focusing on the 1920s. To these
general discussions should be added Robert H. Ferrell, "Repudiation of a
Repudiation," *Journal of American History* 51 (1965):669–73, which sug-
gests the extent to which the Clark Memorandum was repudiated by the
Roosevelt administration. Another very insightful article by Gene A. Sessions, "The Clark Memorandum Myth," *The Americas* 34 (1977):40–58, argues that the Clark Memorandum not only was repudiated in succeeding
years but was never accepted in his own time as official administrative policy. For information on the church-state controversy in Mexico, which
came to a head during Clark's tenure as undersecretary, see David C. Bailey, *¡Viva Cristo Rey! The Cristero Rebellion and the Church-State Conflict in
Mexico* (Austin: University of Texas Press, 1974), which is the standard
work in this area. Supplemental to it are L. Ethan Ellis's article, "Dwight
Morrow and the Church-State Controversy in Mexico," *Hispanic American
Historical Review* 38 (1958):482–505, and Mollie C. Davis's "American Religious and Religiose Reaction to Mexico's Church-State Conflict,
1926–27: Background to the Morrow Mission," *Journal of Church and State*
13 (1971):79–96.

Study of Clark as ambassador is best begun with the recent biography
of Herbert Hoover by David Burner, *Herbert Hoover: A Public Life* (New

York: Alfred A. Knopf, 1979), and with Herbert Hoover's *Memoirs* (New York: Macmillan, 1951–52). The foreign policy of Hoover and Stimson is discussed in a general manner by Robert H. Ferrell in *American Diplomacy in the Great Depression: Hoover-Stimson Foreign Policy, 1929–33* (New Haven, Conn.: Yale University Press, 1957), while Alexander DeConde, *Herbert Hoover's Latin American Policy* (Stanford, Calif.: Stanford University Press, 1951), deals with the Hoover-Stimson Latin American Policy specifically. Two of the largest and most consequential problems that Reuben Clark faced as ambassador were the church-state controversy, detailed above, and the Rio Grande boundary controversy, which was to some degree settled before Reuben left office. For information on the river controversy several sources are recommended: Thomas M. Davies, "The Rio Grande Treaty of 1933," *New Mexico Historical Review* 40 (1965):277–92; Sheldon B. Liss, *A Century of Disagreement: The Chamizal Conflict, 1864–1964* (Washington, D.C.: University Press of Washington, D.C., 1965); and Jerry E. Mueller, *Restless River: International Law and the Behavior of the Rio Grande* (El Paso: Texas Western Press, 1975). Probably the most valuable source on the river problem in the earlier years is Charles A. Timm, *The International Boundary Commission: United States and Mexico* (Austin: University of Texas Press, 1941).

Of the people with whom Reuben served at the American embassy in Mexico City at least one left memoirs behind: John M. Cabot, *Toward Our Common Destiny: Speeches and Interviews on Latin American Problems* (Medford, Mass.: Fletcher School of Law and Diplomacy, 1955). In addition, a good biography of Arthur Bliss Lane is Vladimir Petrov's *A Study in Diplomacy: The Story of Arthur Bliss Lane* (Chicago: H. Regnery Co., 1971), although it makes little mention of Lane's earlier Mexican experience. Graham Green, in *Another Mexico* (New York: Viking Press, 1939), provides some very interesting background and insight on Mexico City through the eyes of a sophisticated traveler, and Elizabeth Morrow leaves some delightful impressions of Casa Mañana in Elizabeth Cutter Morrow, *Casa Mañana* (Croton Falls, N.Y.: The Spiral Press, 1932). As an epilogue to Reuben's experience as ambassador in Mexico, E. David Cronon, *Josephus Daniels in Mexico* (Madison: University of Wisconsin Press, 1960), is recommended. Cronon's work is the standard treatment of Daniels's experience in Mexico; this should be consulted along with Daniels's own memoirs: Josephus Daniels, *Shirt-Sleeve Diplomat* (Chapel Hill: University of North Carolina Press, 1947).

Epilogue   BETWEEN EAST AND WEST

The standard sources to consult on the Montevideo conference are Samuel G. Inman, *Inter-American Conferences, 1826–1954: History and Prob-*

lems (Washington, D.C.: Latin American Institute, 1965), and *Report of the Delegates of the United States to the Seventh International Conference of American States* (Washington, D.C.: Government Printing Office, 1934). However, most of the insights into behind-the-scenes affairs of the conference are found in such sources as Cordell Hull, *The Memoirs of Cordell Hull* (New York: Macmillan Co., 1948); Spruille Braden, *Diplomats and Demagogues: The Memoirs of Spruille Braden* (New Rochelle, N.Y.: Arlington House, 1971); and Ernest H. Gruening, *Many Battles: The Autobiography of Ernest Gruening* (New York: Liveright, 1973). Gruening's memoirs are especially helpful by virtue of his active and influential role in the conference and its outcome.

Virtually the only source on the Foreign Bondholders Protective Council is Gene A. Sessions, "Prophesying upon the Bones: J. Reuben Clark, the Foreign Bondholders, and the Great Depression" (Ph.D. diss., Florida State University, 1974). There is, however, a tremendously large amount of material on this council in the Clarkana Papers, since Reuben was associated with the council in one capacity or another for almost ten years; and boxes of materials and reports may be found there. A good exposition of Reuben Clark's constitutionalism is given in J. Reuben Clark, Jr., *Stand Fast by Our Constitution* (Salt Lake City: Deseret Book, 1962), which was written in the last years of his life. And, finally, Robert W. Tucker, *A New Isolationism: Threat or Promise?* (New York: Universe Books, 1972), brings the isolationism of the 1930s and 1940s up to the present day and discusses it in terms of the resurgence of isolationism after Vietnam.

INDEX

Adee, Alvey, 58, 59, 434
Agrarian dispute in Mexico. *See* Mexico
Agua Prieta, 142; access to Douglas, Arizona, 143; battle of, 144–45; effects of battle at, 145–46
Aguirre, Steven, 545, 601
Alabama claims, 222, 235, 236, 622n. *See also* Claims
Alien Enemy Act, 263
Allied Powers: desire revenge more than peace, 281; and J. P. Morgan & Co., 254; JRC moves behind cause of, 254–55; and reparations, 281, 286. *See also* Versailles, Treaty of
Alsace-Lorraine, 281
Alsop claim: distribution of, 615n; history of, 65–69, 75–76; results, 77, 227, 228, 247–48, 342; settlement, 76–77. *See also* Claims
Alte, Viscount d', 522
American-British Pecuniary Claims Commission: American agency of, 237; Chandler Anderson justice on, 233, 342, 343; contrasted to United States-Mexico Mixed Claims Commission, 455; first session of, 239–42; JRC helps to organize, 227, 235; JRC's ideas about and experiences with, 248–50, 254; JRC serves as general counsel to, 234; and the Lea affair, 246–47; second session of, 242–45; third session of, 245–246; tribunal established, 236–38. *See also* Arbitrations
American Civil War, 209, 410
American Institute of International Law, 599
American International Corporation (AIC): JRC's affiliation with, 355–60, 362, 364, 382, 383, 385–86, 412; operations of, 355–60; origins of, 355
American Journal of International Law, 32, 50

American Peace Society (APS): JRC resigns from, 253; members of, attend Lake Mohonk conference, 29; organization of, 222; prints JRC article in *Advocate of Peace,* 331
American Society for Judicial Settlement of International Disputes (ASJSID), 226, 233
American Society of International Law (ASIL): founding of, 30, 221, 223; James Brown Scott's association with, 49; JRC allows membership to lapse, 252; JRC's presentation at 1909 annual meeting of, 56
Anderson, Chandler, 59–60, 223, 503; American agent in Atlantic fisheries disputes, 82; American commissioner, American-British Claims Commission tribunal, 233, 236–37, 240; associate legal advisor to Washington arms conference, 315; at founding of ASIL, 221; at Lake Mohonk conference of 1905, 29; special counsel in State Department, 57–58, 342; writes essay on World Court movement, 325
Anderson, Henry, 456, 457, 460
Anglo-Japanese Alliance: alternatives to, proposed, 318; and arms race, 309; four-power treaty officially abrogates, 319
Arango, Doroteo. *See* Villa, Pancho
Arbitrations organizations: American-British Claims Commission, 227, 233, 234, 235, 236–38, 342, 343; consultative claims commission set up by Madero, 156;
Hague Court, 29, 222, 224, 226, 229, 322, 325, 328, 470, 508; International Prize Court, 81, 225, 228; Nicaraguan-American Claims Commission, 227–28; United States-Mexico Mixed Claims Commission, 365, 451, 454, 456, 458–75, 501, 508, 523, 538, 552, 563, 573

691

Index